Successful
Writing
at Work

Successful
Writing
at Work

Sixth Edition

Philip C. Kolin
University of Southern Mississippi

Houghton Mifflin Company   Boston   New York

To Kristin, Eric, Theresa, and Evan
Julie and Loretta
and
MARY

Senior Sponsoring Editor: Dean Johnson
Editorial Associate: Bruce Cantley
Project Editor: Tracy Patruno
Senior Manufacturing Coordinator: Priscilla J. Bailey
Senior Marketing Manager: Nancy Lyman

Cover design: Sarah Melhado Bishins
Cover image: Jeffrey Pelo, © Stock Illustration Source, Inc.

Printed in the U.S.A.

Library of Congress Catalog Card Number: 00-133893

ISBN: 0-618-04023-4

6789-DOC-04 03 02

Contents

Preface

Successful Writing at Work is a comprehensive introductory text for use in technical, business, professional, and occupational writing courses. As in the first five editions, the approach in this sixth edition remains practical, emphasizing that communication skills are essential for career advancement and that writing (often as part of a team) is a vital part of almost every job. The sixth edition, however, even more strongly emphasizes the importance and application of the most significant communication technologies—such as the Internet, computer graphics, e-mail, and teleconferencing—to writing successfully for and in the world of work. Moreover, the sixth edition stresses that occupational writing today is frequently directed to an international audience at work in a global marketplace.

Even more than previous editions, too, this sixth edition emphasizes throughout the importance and variety of visuals in workplace communications. Illustrating what it teaches, the sixth edition highlights the graphic options available for business communications and documents through the use of real-world examples the way visuals work in conjunction with text.

The sixth edition continues to stress that writing is a problem-solving activity that helps workers meet the needs of their employers, co-workers, customers, clients, and vendors. But with this edition's special emphasis on the most current communication technologies, students are shown how to become better problem solvers, and hence better writers, by understanding and using the vastly changing Internet. In light of these expanding communication resources, *Successful Writing at Work* presents multiple situations and problems that students as business and technical writers will have to address and asks them to consider the rhetorical and technical options available for solving these problems.

As in earlier editions, the sixth edition continues to provide students with detailed guidelines for writing and designing clear, well-organized, and readable documents. This edition contains a wide range of examples (many of them annotated and visually varied) drawn from such diverse sources as Web sites, e-mail, student papers and reports, letters and memos, proposals, graphic packages, instructions, minutes, summaries, and magazine and journal articles. These examples—all focusing directly on practical issues in the world of work—reveal writers as successful problem solvers.

Consistent with this overall view of writing as workplace problem-solving, the sixth edition expands its coverage of writing as a process. Students will find helpful and concise explanations of the *hows* as well as the *whys* of writing for the world of work. Accordingly, *Successful Writing at Work* helps students develop the critical skills of brainstorming, researching (through print and on-line sources), drafting, revising, editing, formatting, and proofreading various business and technical documents—correspondence, instructions, summaries, reports, Web sites, and so forth. It also helps them understand why the mastery of such skills is essential to career advancement.

The sixth edition continues to emphasize audience analysis, with greater attention to the writer's obligation to make ethical decisions to meet the readers' needs and fulfill commitments to them as well as to employers. Moreover, given the revolution in information technology, the concept of audience inevitably extends to readers worldwide, whether as co-workers, employers, clients, or representatives of various agencies and organizations. E-mail, letters, Web sites, instructions, proposals, and short and long reports are all considered from the points of view of the intended audience(s)—that is, from the vantage point of employers, human resource managers, co-workers, vendors, and customers, again with greater emphasis on the needs of non-native speakers of English, both in this country and abroad.

To engage students fully in job-related writing, *Successful Writing at Work* treats them as professionals seeking advancement at different phases of a business career. For example, they are addressed as employees who must learn to collaborate as part of a writing team in Chapter 3; as customer relations representatives addressing the needs of employers and customers with specific requests, problems, and complaints in Chapter 6; as job candidates preparing a variety of documents related to a job search in Chapter 7; as assistants who are asked to summarize a document or a report for a superior in Chapter 10; as Web site designers in Chapter 11; as competitive businesspeople writing a persuasive proposal to win a contract in Chapter 14; as a senior training specialist preparing a long report in Chapter 16; and as teleconferencing experts making a sales presentation in Chapter 17.

The organization of the sixth edition reflects even more helpfully the student's own progress in researching and writing for the world of work. The text moves logically and smoothly from consideration of basic concepts in writing (audience, tone, message, purpose, ethical obligations) in Chapter 1 to the overall process of writing (brainstorming, researching, drafting, revising, editing, formatting, proofreading) in Chapter 2. Chapter 3 is devoted to the dynamics of collaborative writing and the procedures groups must go through to resolve conflicts and to produce successful documents, thus increasing the document's chances of approval by corporate officials and customers. These three chapters form the foundation on which students can further develop and apply their writing skills. From these introductory chapters, the sixth edition moves sequentially from relatively short and simple assignments (e-mail, faxes, memos, letters) in Chapters 4 through 7 to longer and more complex business writing (instructions, proposals, reports, presentation outlines) in Chapters 13 through 17. Chapters 8 through 12 provide students with necessary information on doing research, summarizing, and designing visuals.

As in the previous five editions, this edition is rich in practical applications, equally useful to readers who have no job experience and to those with years of experience in one or several fields. The needs of nontraditional students are most directly addressed in Chapter 7 on job searching. Another strong feature of the sixth edition is a series of additional case studies showing how writers have used varied resources and rhetorical strategies to solve problems in the business world. An abundance of exercises, including many new ones, at the end of each chapter gives students opportunities to practice a variety of writing skills: analyzing the weakness and strengths of diverse documents, generating ideas, researching topics, organizing information, drafting, revising, editing and formatting documents, incorporating visuals, designing documents, and working as part of a collaborative writing team.

New Material in the Sixth Edition

The sixth edition has been improved and greatly expanded to make it a more effective tool for the instructor and a more comprehensive and contemporary resource for the student. Throughout the text, new guidelines, examples, figures, case studies, and exercises make the discussion of occupational writing more useful and current. Much updated information has been added about Internet and other on-line resources in business and technical writing. The following features are new to the sixth edition:

- New, expanded, updated, and even more accessible TECH NOTES help students better understand the ways in which computers, the Internet, and other communication technologies can help them with their work. More than seventy-five TECH NOTES offer advice on applying recent technology (for example, how to send an attachment with e-mail; how to use color; where to go to learn about electronic note taking; or why a digital camera is a valuable tool) while others elaborate on a topic mentioned in the chapter. Many TECH NOTES include relevant Web sites for students to find further information.
- Greatly expanded material in Chapter 1 on ethical issues in business and technical writing emphasizes the importance of ethics in the writing process, explains how to revise unethical (misleading, exaggerated) writing, and offers possible solutions for addressing ethical dilemmas, especially those involving the use of a computer. A new figure, "The Ten Commandments of Computer Ethics," is a helpful addition to the sixth edition. The discussion of ethics is not limited to Chapter 1 but continues in other chapters—on e-mail (Netiquette), letters, visuals, instructions, summaries, reports—with specific guidelines about ethical communication as it pertains to each type of document and to the varied audiences for such documents.
- There is additional practical advice in Chapter 3 on the dynamics of team writing, including several collaboration models. A new case on writing in a laboratory setting further helps students to become better readers/editors/writers/employees.
- An updated Chapter 4 explains and illustrates more fully memos, faxes, and e-mail, some of the most frequently written correspondence in the world of work. The chapter also revises discussion of the technology and the protocols students need to understand to produce these documents professionally and concisely. E-mail guidelines receive greater attention.
- New examples and guidelines on respecting the cultural traditions and communication needs of a global audience have been added to Chapters 5, 7, and 16.
- Greater in-depth coverage of sexist language and ways to avoid it in correspondence and reports appear throughout the sixth edition.
- Fully revised and reformatted examples in Chapter 6 introduce students to the types of problems they are likely to face as writers in the workplace and guide them toward using the most effective rhetorical strategies in their letters.
- A thoroughly revised and updated Chapter 7 on job application letters and résumés contains even more advice about the variety of resources available to job seekers. Sensitive to the needs of individuals reentering the workplace or

changing careers, this chapter devotes greater space to their situation. Additional new formats and rhetorical strategies for electronic job searches and on-line résumés provide new valuable information to this much-used chapter.

- A completely revised and thoroughly updated Chapter 8, on finding and using information resources, introduces students to the most important research tools. New sections on the strategies and tools of research followed by specific steps students need to take in doing research open the chapter. The sections are followed by fully revised coverage of on-line catalogs, databases, and reference works, both on-line and in print. The second half of the chapter, devoted exclusively to the Internet, offers the latest discussion (and illustrations) of types of Internet searches, search engines, and Web browsers. A new section on precautions when using the Web gives students much-needed instruction in this critical area. New illustrations of Web sites, menus, and hyperlinked texts offer students a thorough but not overwhelmingly technical introduction to the Internet.

- Updated coverage, based on the fifth edition of the *MLA Handbook* and the most recent APA guidelines, in Chapter 9 on how to document Internet, on-line, and print sources supplies students with clear citation guidelines and plentiful examples. New sections on plagiarism and on precautions in verifying constantly changing Web sites are also especially useful. An updated, better formatted research paper on telecommuting illustrates how to incorporate and to document information from electronic sources and Internet sites.

- New examples of abstracts and summaries in Chapter 10 draw upon and highlight the most current communication technologies to teach students how to summarize carefully. Information on preparing and writing minutes and executive summaries is new to the chapter as well.

- A much expanded Chapter 11 introduces students to the ABCs of document design, including page layout, levels of headings, type and font size, and offers specific guidelines on mistakes to avoid as they plan and print their work. A before-and-after example of a document illustrates graphically the importance of design in the communication process. New to this chapter is an extended section on creating a Web site, giving students basic instruction on researching the Web community, creating hyperlinks, coordinating verbal and visual elements, and writing appropriate texts.

- A completely revised and redesigned Chapter 12 on visuals, including the addition of four-color illustrations, emphasizes computer-generated graphics. New examples throughout stress the importance of document design to reinforce the concepts in Chapter 11. Updated examples of tables, graphs, charts, photographs, and clip art focus on central business-related issues. New sections on finding, using, and documenting visuals from the Internet and the importance of PowerPoint provide guidelines on these essential topics.

- A fully revised and reformatted Chapter 13 on writing instructions includes new examples (many with computer applications) throughout. Further emphasizing the vital interplay between text and graphics, this chapter concludes with a new model set of complete instructions on setting up and running a laser printer.

- New and updated examples of RFPs and proposals in Chapter 14 reinforce the importance of persuasive writing, careful documentation, and the use and placement of visuals.
- A new model report in Chapter 16, on multinational employees and meeting their needs in the U.S. workplace, further stresses that cultural considerations play a major role in business communications.
- Revised and new material in Chapter 17 on oral presentations at work offers concise and practical advice on analyzing audiences, using appropriate visuals (including a new section on PowerPoint), writing a clear outline, and avoiding pitfalls of public speaking. An updated presentation outline on telecommuting concludes the chapter.
- An expanded "Writer's Brief Guide to Paragraphs, Sentences, and Words" concisely explains and illustrates the most significant and recurrent problems of punctuation, usage, mechanics, and style relevant to writing for the world of work. This section is a condensed but not watered-down handbook, useful to the instructor who wants a standard but not intrusive guide for students and for students who need a quick but effective review.

A brief overview of the sixth edition will show how these new materials have been integrated.

An Overview of Part I

Part I deals with the overall writing process. Chapter 1, setting the stage for all occupational writing, identifies the basic concepts of audience analysis, purpose, message, style, tone, and ethics, and relates these concepts to on-the-job writing.

Chapters 2 and 3 continue this important unit on the basic elements of effective writing. Chapter 2, on the writing process at work, introduces students to prewriting strategies, drafting, revising, and editing their written work. Chapter 3 emphasizes the importance of collaborative writing in the world of work and gives students valuable guidelines for being productive, cooperative members of a writing team. This chapter also explores some of the major problems writers face when working together and suggests positive, effective strategies for dealing with problems and resolving them. Three case studies reinforce these points.

An Overview of Part II

Part II concentrates on business correspondence. Chapter 4 offers abundant examples of and guidelines for writing memos, faxes, and e-mail. Chapter 5 introduces the nuts and bolts of letter writing and focuses on selecting the appropriate format, language, tone, and content. Chapter 6 examines the rhetorical strategies for producing a variety of business correspondence—inquiry, complaint, adjustment, and sales letters—with additional material on organizational strategies for good-news or bad-news letters, and an expanded discussion of writing for international readers.

Chapter 7, covering the job search, takes students through the process of preparing a placement file, writing, scanning, and sending a résumé and organizing it by skill area and/or chronology, and sending it via the Internet as well as through more conventional means, locating appropriate openings, writing a letter of application, anticipating interviewers' questions, and accepting or declining a job offer. For greater teaching flexibility, instructors will find six application letters and six résumés from applicants with varying degrees of experience—helpful models for new and veteran job seekers alike.

An Overview of Part III

Part III, on gathering and summarizing information, occupies a key position in the sixth edition. It helps students acquire the techniques they need to be skilled researchers and accurate writers. Chapter 8 takes students on a guided tour of a computerized library, shows them how to locate, use, coordinate, and evaluate a variety of research tools from the on-line catalog to a variety of databases and reference works on-line and in print. The chapter also provides a full introduction to the Internet—its usefulness, organization, search engines, and prominent Web sites in various disciplines. Chapter 9 is devoted to documentation and is based on the most recent methods advocated by the MLA and APA style guides. Detailed guidelines show students how to document a variety of print and electronic sources, including Web sites, e-mail, listservs, and discussion groups. A completely revised and updated student research paper, "The Advantages of Telecommuting in the Information Age," illustrates how to quote and document print, electronic, and Internet sources. In Chapter 10 students learn how to write clear and concise summaries and abstracts by seeing how a police officer summarizes an article on virtual reality and law enforcement for a superior, prepare minutes for a meeting, and write executive summaries for decision makers.

An Overview of Part IV

In Part IV students have the opportunity to apply the skills they learned in Part III to more complex writing assignments. The section focuses on key business and technical writing documents—instructions, proposals, and reports. Chapters 11 and 12 form a unit on the related topics of designing documents and creating visuals. A much expanded and updated Chapter 11 stresses the significance of document design and gives students practical advice and pertinent examples for making their work more reader-friendly and visually appealing; the chapter also contains detailed guidelines, with several models, for preparing Web sites. Chapter 12 supplies practical advice on using, designing, and writing about visuals, with emphasis on including visuals in instructions and reports; the chapter discusses and illustrates a variety of visuals, especially from the Web, along with the necessary precautions that students need to take. The chapter concludes with a greatly expanded and updated section on computer graphics.

A completely rewritten Chapter 13 covers writing accurate instructions in depth and selecting the most appropriate language and visuals. Chapter 14 explores three common types of proposals: an internal proposal for an employer, a sales proposal (solicited and unsolicited) for customers, and a research proposal for an instructor. Chapter 15 outlines the principles common to all short reports and then discusses specific types, with detailed coverage of test and laboratory reports and a thorough discussion of audience. Finally, students are cautioned about the legal implications of what they write and are shown how to avoid some legal pitfalls.

To make it easily accessible to students, Chapter 16, on long reports, has been revised for this edition to emphasize the *process* of writing such a report. Students are encouraged to see a long report as the culmination of all their work in the course or on a major project at work. The individual parts of such a report are discussed and illustrated in detail, with a fully documented and illustrated model report from a training specialist to her boss on the importance of multinational workers in the U.S. workforce. This paper, together with the Chapter 9 report on telecommuting and the long report on AIDS and health care workers in the Instructor's Guide, give instructors three complete, documented research papers from which to teach the long report.

Chapter 17, which stresses the importance of audience analysis in presentations at work, offers commonsense advice for preparing briefings and conferences and on generating, organizing, and delivering formal presentations; this chapter includes a new speech outline on the benefits of teleconferencing.

Acknowledgements

In a very real sense, the sixth edition has profited from a collaboration of various reviewers with the author. I am, therefore, honored to thank the following reviewers who have helped me improve the sixth edition significantly:

Laura N. Black, Southern Wesleyan University (SC)
Molly Breeden
John A. DeSando, Franklin University (OH)
Patricia A. Doherty, Boston University (MA)
Lynette L. Emanuel, Wisconsin Indianhead Technical College
Marlene A. Hess, Davenport College (MI)
Ann Jahnke, Fox Valley Technical College (WI)
David Neiman
Keith Peterson, Brigham Young University—Hawaii
Sheila Reiter, Doane College (NE)
Christine Uber Grosse, Thunderbird—The American Graduate School of International Management (AZ)
James A. Von Schilling, Northampton Community College (PA)

I am also deeply grateful to the following individuals at the University of Southern Mississippi for their help as I prepared the sixth edition. From the Department of English I thank Cole Bennett, Beverly Ciko, Marilyn Ford, Christina Hunter, Deana Holifield, Christopher L. Reese, Terri Ruckel, and Michael Salda; Cliff Burgess (Department of Computer Science); Mary Lux and Holly Bishop (Department of Medical Technology); Jeni Halimun (Department of Mathematics); Lisa Williams (Health and Recreation); and, with a continuing debt of gratitude, Liam Kennedy, the Government Documents Librarian at Cook Library.

Several individuals from business and industry also gave me valuable assistance, for which I am thankful. They include Joycelyn Woolfolk at the Federal Reserve Bank in Atlanta; Sally Eddy at Georgia Pacific; John Krumpos at Gulf Paper Company; Hilary J. Englert at Rice's Potato Chips; Don McCarthy, an independent computer programmer; and Russell Dukette at Petro Automotive Group. To Janice Fisk of Baxter Healthcare I owe a special debt of gratitude for assisting me in innumerable ways as I prepared the sixth edition.

I am also especially grateful to Father Michael Tracey for his counsel and his contributions to Chapter 11 on document design, especially on Web sites.

My thanks go to my editors at Houghton Mifflin for their assistance, encouragement, and friendship—Dean Johnson, Bruce Cantley, Charline Lake, and Tracy Patruno, and to Nancy Benjamin at Books By Design.

Finally, I thank my family—Sister Carmelita Stinn, Ed Lundin, Margie and Al Parish, Eric, Theresa, Evan, and Kristin—for their encouragement, patience, and love.

P. C. K.

To the Student

This book is based on the belief that writing substantially influences your career. Effective writing can help you obtain a job, perform your duties more successfully, and earn promotions for your efforts. Guidelines and examples found in this book emphasize the progress you can make in your career as you acquire effective writing skills. Specifically, *Successful Writing at Work*

- explains the writing process and shows you how planning, drafting, revising, and editing can help you to produce a variety of essential job-related communications.
- describes the function and format of these job-related communications.
- teaches you how to supply an audience with the information it needs to make decisions and solve problems.
- introduces you to various research tools, including the Internet.
- prepares you to write a variety of business documents, from simple e-mail messages to longer, more complex proposals and reports and even Web sites.

The sixth edition is organized to coincide with your own progress in writing. Part I gives you solid, useful background information to be a successful writer in the world of work. Chapter 1 introduces you to key ideas, strategies, and requirements for writing on the job and stresses ethical requirements. Chapter 2 explains and illustrates the process of writing. Chapter 3 explains the advantages and techniques of collaborative writing and the pitfalls to avoid.

Part II, Correspondence, discusses the basics you should know in order to write these major on-the-job documents and so advance in your career. Chapter 4 focuses exclusively on memos and electronic correspondence—faxes and e-mail. Chapter 5 surveys some essential information on style, format, and organization of business letters. Chapter 6 turns to the strategies to be used with specific types of correspondence you will write for your employer and customers. Chapter 7 focuses on how to write a letter of application and to prepare several kinds of résumés, including bullet and electronic (or Internet) résumés.

Part III is devoted to helping you gather and summarize information. On your job you will be expected to know how to use a variety of research tools (including the Internet) and strategies. Chapter 8 describes how to find, retrieve, and use research materials, with an emphasis on the Internet and database resources. Chapter 9 is devoted to documenting the information you gather, particularly from on-line sources, and Chapter 10 covers summarizing what you find and know.

Part IV concentrates on effective ways to record your findings in instructions, proposals, and reports. This part helpfully begins with two chapters on designing documents and using visuals. Chapter 11 will teach you how to design documents, including Web sites, in order to help and persuade your readers. The way your document looks can be as important as the way it is written. Visuals and graphics are components in all the types of documents discussed in the other Part IV chapters—instructions (Chapter 13), proposals (Chapter 14), short reports (Chapter 15), long reports (Chapter 16), and oral reports or business presentations (Chapter 17).

Finally, this new edition stresses throughout that you will be writing for a global audience and that many of your readers may be non-native speakers of English. Pay special attention to the long report in Chapter 16 on how the workplace is changing and expanding.

Finally, A Writer's Brief Guide will assist you in the mechanics of writing paragraphs, composing sentences, and improving your word choice and spelling.

Backgrounds

Getting Started: Writing and Your Career

What skills have you learned in school or on the job this year? Perhaps you have learned techniques of health care in order to become a nurse, respiratory therapist, or dental hygienist. Maybe you have received training in law enforcement to prepare yourself for work with a crime-detection unit or a traffic-control department. Possibly you have studied or worked in industrial technology, agriculture, computer science, hotel and restaurant management, or forestry. Or maybe you have improved certain skills that will make you a better marketing specialist, salesperson, office manager, computer programmer, or accountant. Whatever your area of accomplishment, the practical know-how you have acquired is crucial for your career.

Writing—An Essential Job Skill

To ensure a successful career, you will also need to write clearly about the facts, procedures, and problems of your job. Writing is a part of every job. In fact, your first contact with a potential employer is through your letter of application, which determines a company's first impression of you. And the higher you advance in an organization, the more writing you will do. Promotions are often based on a person's writing skills.

The Associated Press reported in a recent survey that "most American businesses say workers need to improve their writing . . . skills." The same report cited a survey of 402 companies that identified writing as "the most valued skill of employees." Still, the employers polled in that survey indicated that 80 percent of their employees need to improve their writing skills. Clearly, writing is an essential skill important to everyone in business—employers and employees alike. Figure 1.1 is an e-mail from the manager of a company offering an incentive to employees to improve their writing skills on the job.

FIGURE 1.1   An employer's view of the importance of writing.

Subject: **New company benefit**
Date: 5/10/2001 8:45 AM Eastern Standard Time
From: rpinkerton@greer.com (Rowe Pinkerton)
To: All Employees

I am pleased to announce a new company benefit approved by the Board
at its meeting last week. In its continuing effort to improve writing in the
workplace, Greer, Inc. will give tuition reimbursement to any employee for
taking a course in business, technical, or occupational writing, starting
this fall.

Three Requirements:
To qualify, employees must do the following:

(1) Submit a two-page proposal on how such a course will improve the
employee's job performance here at Greer.

(2) Take the class at one of the approved colleges or universities in the
Cleveland area listed on the attachment to this e-mail.

(3) Provide proof (through a transcript or final grade report) that he or she
has successfully completed the course.

To apply, submit your proposal to Dawn Wagner-Lawlor in Human Resources
(dwlawlor@greer.com) at least one month before you intend to enroll in the
course.

Here's to productive writing!

As Rowe Pinkerton, the author of that e-mail, realizes, among the most cost-effective skills you can offer a prospective employer is your writing ability. Businesses pay a premium price for good writing. According to Don Bagin (*Communication Briefings* [May 1995]: 3), most people need an hour or more to write a typical business letter. If an employer is paying someone $30,000 a year, one letter costs $14 of that employee's time; for someone who earns $50,000 a year, the cost of the average letter jumps to $24.

Offices and other workplaces contain numerous reminders of the importance of writing—printers, PCs, disks, monitors, scanners, keyboards, mouses, modems, fax machines. Why? Writing keeps business moving. It allows individuals working for a company to communicate with one another and with the customers and clients they must serve if the company is to stay in business. Clearly today's most ambitious communication tool is the Internet, the all-purpose information superhighway. Almost every type of written communication can be found on the Internet—e-mail, letters, memos, summaries, instructions, questionnaires, proposals, reports, and much, much more. This book will show you, step by step, how to write those and other job-related communications easily and well.

TECH NOTE

Know Your Computer at Work
A large part of your responsibilities in the workplace will involve writing electronically. To enhance your value as an employee, become knowledgeable about your company's computer system. That includes being familiar with its computer support services, how to report computer problems, the software packages your employer uses, and the location of user manuals. In addition, try to stay informed about new and updated versions of business software packages as they become available. With such knowledge you will increase your opportunities for success.

Chapter 1 presents some basic information about writing and offers some questions you can ask yourself to make the writing process easier and the results more effective. It also describes the basic functions of on-the-job writing and introduces you to one of the most important requirements in the business world—writing ethically.

Four Keys to Effective Writing

Effective writing on the job is carefully planned, thoroughly researched, and clearly presented. Whether you send a routine e-mail to a co-worker or a special report to the president of the company, your writing will be more effective if you ask yourself four questions.

1. *Who* will read what I write? (Identify your *audience*.)
2. *Why* should they read what I write? (Establish your *purpose*.)
3. *What* do I have to say to them? (Formulate your *message*.)
4. *How* can I best communicate? (Select your *style* and *tone*.)

The questions *who? why? what?* and *how?* do not function independently; they are all related. You write (1) for a specific audience (2) with a clearly defined purpose in mind (3) about a topic your readers need to understand (4) in language appropriate for the occasion. Once you answer the first question, you are off to a good start toward answering the other three. Now let us examine each of the four questions in detail.

Identifying Your Audience

Knowing *who* makes up your audience is one of your most important responsibilities as a writer. In fact, it is important to analyze your audience throughout the composing process.

Look for a minute at the American Heart Association posters reproduced in Figures 1.2, 1.3, and 1.4. The main purpose of all three posters is the same: to discourage people from smoking. The essential message in each poster—smoking is dangerous to your health—is also the same. But note how the different details—words, photographs, situations—have been selected to appeal to three different audiences.

The poster in Figure 1.2 emphasizes smoking problems that are especially troublesome to teenagers: red eyes, bad breath, discolored teeth, and unattractive hair. The smiling teen pictured without a cigarette appears to have avoided those prob-

FIGURE 1.2   No-smoking poster aimed at teenagers.

© Reprinted with permission of the American Heart Association.

FIGURE 1.3   No-smoking poster directed at pregnant women.

© Reprinted with permission of the American Heart Association.

lems. The message at the top of the poster plays on two meanings of the word *heart:* (1) smoking can cause heart disease, and (2) smoking can be a deterrent to romance. Teenagers are particularly sensitive to the second meaning.

The poster in Figure 1.3 is aimed at an audience of pregnant women and appropriately shows a woman with a lit cigarette. The words at the top and bottom of the poster appeal to a mother's sense of responsibility as the reason to stop smoking, a reason to which pregnant women would be most likely to respond.

Figure 1.4 is directed toward fathers and appropriately shows a small child seated on his father's lap. The situation depicted appeals to a father's wish for his child's happiness. The words in the poster warn that a father who smokes may die prematurely and make his child's life unhappy.

The copywriters for the American Heart Association have chosen appropriate details—words, pictures, captions, and so on—to convince each audience not to smoke. With their careful choices, they successfully answered the question "How can we best communicate with each audience?" As an indication of their skill, note that details relevant for one audience (teenagers, for example) could not be used as effectively for another audience (such as fathers).

FIGURE 1.4   No-smoking poster appealing to fathers.

© Reprinted with permission of the American Heart Association.

The three posters illustrate some fundamental points you need to keep in mind when identifying your audience.

- Members of each audience differ in backgrounds, experiences, needs, and opinions.
- How you picture your audience will determine what you say to them.
- Viewing something from the audience's perspective will help you to select the most relevant details for that audience.

Some Questions to Ask About Your Audience

You can form a fairly accurate picture of your audience by asking yourself some questions *before* you write. For each audience for whom you write, consider the following questions.

1. Who is my audience? What individual(s) will most likely be reading my work?

If you are writing for individuals at work:

- What is my reader's job title?

- What is my reader's relationship to me? Co-worker? Immediate supervisor? Vice president?
- What kind of job experience, education, and interests does my reader have?

If you are writing for clients or consumers (a very large, sometimes fragmented audience):

- How can I find out about their interest in my product or service?
- How much will this audience know about my company? About me?

2. **How many people will make up my audience?**

- Will just one individual read what I write (the nurse on the next shift, the production manager) or will many people read it (all the consumers of a product manufactured by my company)?
- Will my boss want to see my work (say, a letter to a consumer in response to a complaint) to approve it?
- Will my letter bear someone else's name, not mine?
- Will I be sending my message to a large group of people sharing a similar interest in my topic, such as a Usenet or chat-room group on the Internet?
- Will I potentially be communicating with people all around the globe via the Internet?

3. **How well does my audience understand English?**

- Are all my readers native speakers of English?
- Will some of my readers have lesser command of English and require extra sensitivity on my part to their needs as non-native speakers of English? (See pp. 173–176 for guidelines about communication with this audience.)

4. **How much does my audience already know about my writing topic?**

- Will my audience know as much as I do about the particular problem or issue, or will they need to be briefed or updated?
- Does my audience know little or nothing about the message I am sending them?
- Are my readers familiar with, and do they expect me to use, technical terms and descriptions, or will I have to provide easy-to-understand comparisons and nontechnical summaries?
- Will I need to include detailed visuals or sketches, or will a photograph or simple drawing be enough?

5. **What is my audience's reason for reading my work?**

- Is reading my communication part of their routine duties, or are they looking for information to solve a problem or make a decision?
- Will they want my writing to describe benefits that another writer or company cannot offer—that is, am I trying to persuade them to buy a product or a service?
- Will my readers expect complete details, or will a short summary of the main points be enough for their purpose?

- Are they reading my work to take some action affecting a co-worker, a client, or a community official?
- Are they reading something I write because they must (a legal notification, for instance), or are they looking at it just as a courtesy?
- What will my boss want from me—information alone, some analysis and conclusions drawn from the information, or a specific set of recommendations?

6. **What are my audience's expectations about my written work?**

- Do they want an e-mail or will they expect a formal letter?
- Will they expect me to follow a certain format and organization?
- Are they looking for a one-page memo or for a comprehensive ten-to-fifteen-page report?
- Should I use a formal tone or a more relaxed and conversational style?

7. **What is my audience's attitude toward me and my work?**

- Will I be writing to a group of disgruntled and angry customers or vendors about a very sensitive issue—a product recall, a refusal of credit, or a shipment delay?
- Will I have to be sympathetic while at the same time give firm reasons for my company's (or my) decision?
- Will my readers—customers whose business I want to attract—be skeptical?
- Will I need to overcome my readers' indifference by arousing their interest and encouraging a response?
- Will my audience be eager and friendly, happy to read what I write?
- Will my readers feel guilty that they have not answered an earlier message of mine, not paid a bill now overdue, or not kept a promise or commitment?

8. **What do I want my audience to do after reading my work?**

- Do I want my reader to purchase something from me or my company?
- Do I expect my reader to approve my plan or to send me additional materials or information?
- Do I simply want my reader to get my message and not respond at all?
- Do I expect my reader to get my message, acknowledge it, save it for future reference, or review it and e-mail it to another individual or office?
- Does my reader have to take immediate action, or does he or she have several days or weeks to respond?
- Do I want my reader to share my message on the Internet?

As your answers to these questions will show, you may have to communicate with many different audiences on your job. If you work for a large organization that has numerous departments, you may have to write to such diverse readers as accountants, office managers, personnel directors, engineers, public relations specialists, marketing specialists, computer programmers, and individuals who install, operate, and maintain equipment. In addition, you will need to communicate effectively with customers about your company's products and services. Each group of readers will have different expectations and requirements; you need to understand those audience differences if you want to supply relevant information.

The advertisement in Figure 1.5 (p. 12) concisely illustrates how the writer for a manufacturer of heavy-duty equipment identified the priorities of five different audiences and selected appropriate information to communicate with each one.

Audience	Information to Communicate
Owner or principal executive	The writer appropriately stresses financial benefits: the machine is a "money-maker" and is compatible with other equipment so additional equipment purchases are unnecessary.
Production engineer	The writer emphasizes "state-of-the-art" transmissions, productivity, upkeep.
Operator	The writer focuses on how easy it is to run the machine—the pressurized cab keeps out environmental problems that interfere with a job.
Maintenance worker	Since this reader is concerned primarily about such things as "lube points" and "test ports," not costs or operations, the writer correctly selects appropriate information about making the worker's job easier and safer.
Production supervisor	The writer emphasizes the speed and efficiency the machine offers, thus zeroing in on this reader's needs and interests.

The lesson of this ad is clear: Give each reader the details he or she needs to accomplish a given job. Sometimes you are not able to identify all the members of your potential audience. In such cases, just assume that you have a general audience and keep your message as simple as possible—nontechnical and straightforward.

Establishing Your Purpose

By knowing *why* you are writing, you will communicate better and find writing itself to be an easier process. The reader's needs and your goal in communicating will help you to formulate your purpose. It will guide you in determining exactly what you can and must say. With your purpose clearly identified, you are on the right track.

Make sure you follow the most important rule in occupational writing: **Get to the point right away.** At the start of your message, state your goal clearly. Don't feel as if you have to entertain or impress your reader. Don't worry about the way your words sound. It is more helpful to work on your ideas.

I want new employees to know how to log on to the computer.

Think over what you have written. Rewrite your purpose statement until it states precisely why you are writing and what you want your readers to do or to know.

I want to teach new employees the security code for logging on to the company computer.

Since your purpose controls the amount and order of information you include, state it clearly at the beginning of every e-mail, memo, letter, and report. Such an overview will help the reader to follow and act on your communication.

FIGURE 1.5   An advertisement aimed at the needs of five different audiences.

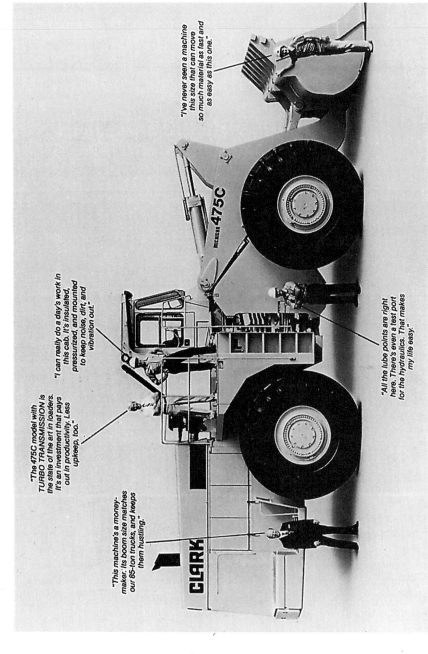

Courtesy of the Clark Company. Reprinted with permission.

> This e-mail will acquaint new employees with the security measures they must take when logging on to the company computer.

> This report will give you a detailed account of my progress to date on completing my research this semester.

In the opening purpose statement that follows, note how the author clearly informs the reader as to what the report will and will not cover.

> As you requested at last week's organizational meeting, I have conducted a study of our use of the Internet to advertise our services. This report describes, but does not evaluate, our current practices.

The following preface to a pamphlet on architectural casework details contains a model statement of purpose suited to a particular audience.

> This publication has been prepared by the Architectural Woodwork Institute to provide a source book of conventional details and uniform detail terminology. For this purpose a series of casework detail drawings, . . . representative of the best industry-wide practice, has been prepared and is presented here. By supplying both architect and woodwork manufacturer with a common authoritative reference, this work will enable architects and woodworkers to communicate in a common technical language. . . . Besides serving as a basic reference for architects and architectural drafters, this guide will be an effective educational tool for the beginning drafter-architect-in-training. It should also be a valuable aid to the project manager in coordinating the work of many drafters on large projects.[1]

After reading that preface, readers have a clear sense of why they should use the source book and what to do with the material they find in it.

Formulating Your Message

Your message is the sum of *what* facts, responses, and recommendations you put into writing. A message includes the scope and details of your communication.

- The *details* are those key points you think readers need to know to perform their jobs.
- *Scope* refers to how much information you give readers about those key details.

Some messages will consist of one or two sentences: "Do not touch; wet paint." "Order #756 was sent this afternoon by Federal Express. It should arrive at your office on March 21." At the other extreme, messages may extend over twenty or thirty pages. Messages may carry good news or bad news. They may deal with routine matters, or they may handle changes in policy, special situations, or problems.

Keep in mind that you will adapt your message to fit your audience. For technical audiences, such as engineers or technicians, you may have to supply a complete report with every detail noted or contained in an appendix. For other readers—busy executives, for example—you would be wrong to include such technical details. A short discussion or summary of the financial or managerial significance of the details is what this group of readers prefers.

---

[1]Reprinted by permission of Architectural Woodwork Institute.

Consider the message of the following excerpt from a section entitled "Technology in the Grocery Store" included in a consumer handbook. The message provides factual information and a brief explanation of how a grocery store clerk scans an item, informing consumers about how and why they may have to wait longer in line. It also tells readers that the process, which looks so simple, is far more intricate than they imagine.

Bar Code Readers

Every time you check out at the grocery store, many of your purchases are scanned to record the price. The scanner uses a laser beam to read the bar codes, those zebra-striped lines imprinted on packages or canned goods. These codes are fed into the store's computer, which provides the price to go with the product code. The product and its price are then recorded on your receipt.

Scanning an item requires more skill than you might think. To make sure that the scanner accurately reads the bar codes, the clerk has to take into account the following four conditions:

Speed: The clerk has to know how fast to pass the item across the scanner, which is geared to a particular speed. If he or she moves the item too slowly, the bars will look too long or too wide and the computer will reject the item. If the item is moved too fast, the scanner cannot identify the code.

Angle: The clerk needs to know precisely at what angle to pull the item across the scanner. If the angle is wrong there will be insufficient reflection of the laser beam back to the scanner and so it will not be able to read the code. Since it is best for the item to reflect as much of the laser as possible, the clerk should try to hold the code at right angles to the laser.

Distance: Moving the item too close to the scanner is as unproductive as holding it too far away. Either way the code can be out of focus for the scanner reader. Holding the item about 3–4 inches away is best; holding it out more than 8–9 inches ensures that the scanner will not read the code.

Rotation: The code needs to be facing the scanner so that the lines can be read properly.

780669 297140

Direction in
which clerk
moves product

If your clerk makes a mistake in any one of these calibrations, your wait in line is sure to be longer.

This bar code message is appropriate for a general audience of consumers, who are given neither more nor less information than they need or desire. Other audiences, however, would need different messages and different details. Individuals responsible for entering data into the computer or doing inventory control would need more detailed instructions on how to program the supermarket's computer to make sure it automatically tells the point-of-sale (POS) terminal what price and product match each bar code.

The product technicians responsible for affixing the bar codes at the manufacturer's plant would require still more detailed and technical information. For example, they would need to be very familiar with the Uniform Product Code (UPC), which specifies bar codes worldwide. They would also have to know about the UPC binary code formulas and how they work—that is, the number of lines, width of spacing, and the framework to indicate to the scanner when to start reading the code and when to stop. Such formulas, technical details, and functions of photoelectric scanners certainly would be inappropriate for consumers or store cashiers.

Selecting Your Style and Tone

Style

Style is *how* something is written rather than what is written. Style helps to determine how well you communicate with an audience, how well your readers understand and receive your message. It involves the choices you make about

- the construction of your paragraphs
- the length and patterns of your sentences
- your choice of words

You will have to adapt your style to take into account different messages, different purposes, and different audiences. Your words, for example, will certainly vary with your audience. If all your readers are specialists in your field, you may safely use the technical language and symbols of your profession. Your audience will be familiar with such terminology and will expect you to use it. Nonspecialists, however, will be confused and annoyed if you write to them in the same way. The average consumer, for example, will not know what a *potentiometer* is; by writing "volume control on a radio," you will be using words that the general public can understand.

Tone

Tone in writing, like tone of voice, expresses your attitude toward a topic and toward your audience. In general, your tone can range from formal and impersonal (a scientific report) to informal and personal (e-mail to a friend or a how-to article for consumers).

Tone, like style, is indicated in part by the words you choose. For example, saying that someone is "interested in details" conveys a more positive tone than saying the person is a "nitpicker." The word *economical* is more positive than *stingy* or *cheap*.

The tone of your writing is especially important in occupational writing, because it reflects the image you project to your readers and thus determines how they will respond to you, your work, and your company. Depending on your tone, you can appear sincere and intelligent or angry and uninformed. Of course, in all your written work, you need to sound professional and knowledgeable about the topic and genuinely interested in your readers' opinions and problems. The wrong tone in a letter or a proposal might cost you a customer.

A Description of Heparin for Two Different Audiences

To better understand the effects of style and tone on writing, read the following two excerpts. In both, the message is basically the same, but because the audiences differ, so do the style and the tone. The two pieces are descriptions of *heparin,* a drug used to prevent blood clots.

Technical/Scientific Style and Tone
The first description of heparin appears in a reference work for physicians and other health care providers and is written in a highly technical style with an impersonal tone.

HEPARIN SODIUM INJECTION, USP
STERILE SOLUTION
Description: Heparin Sodium Injection, USP is a sterile solution of heparin sodium derived from bovine lung tissue, standardized for anticoagulant activity.

Each ml of the 1,000 and 5,000 USP units per ml preparations contains: heparin sodium 1,000 or 5,000 USP units; 9 mg sodium chloride; 9.45 mg benzyl alcohol added as preservative. Each ml of the 10,000 USP units per ml preparations contains: heparin sodium 10,000 units; 9.45 mg benzyl alcohol added as preservative.

When necessary, the pH of Heparin Sodium Injection, USP was adjusted with hydrochloric acid and/or sodium hydroxide. The pH range is 5.0–7.5.
Clinical pharmacology: Heparin inhibits reactions that lead to the clotting of blood and the formation of fibrin clots both *in vitro* and *in vivo.* Heparin acts at multiple sites in the normal coagulation system. Small amounts of heparin in combination with antithrombin III (heparin cofactor) can inhibit thrombosis by inactivating activated Factor X and inhibiting the conversion of prothrombin to thrombin.
Dosage and administration: Heparin sodium is not effective by oral administration and should be given by intermittent intravenous injection, intravenous infusion, or deep subcutaneous (intrafrat, i.e., above the iliac crest or abdominal fat layer) injection. **The intramuscular route of administration should be avoided because of the frequent occurrence of hematoma at the injection site.**[2]

The writer made the appropriate stylistic choices for the audience, the purpose, and the message. Physicians and other health care providers reading the description will understand and need the technical vocabulary the writer uses; this audience will also require the sophisticated and lengthy explanations in order to prescribe and/or administer heparin correctly. The author's authoritative, impersonal tone is coldly clinical, which, of course, is also correct because the purpose is to convey the accurate, complete scientific facts about this drug, not the writer's or reader's opinions or beliefs. The author sounds both knowledgeable and appropriately objective.

Nontechnical Style and Tone

The following description of heparin, on the other hand, is written in a nontechnical style and with an informal, caring tone. This description is similar to those found on information cards given to patients about the drugs they are receiving in a hospital.

> Your doctor has prescribed for you a drug called *heparin*. This drug will prevent any new blood clots from forming in your body. Since heparin cannot be absorbed from your stomach or intestines, you will not receive it in a capsule or tablet. Instead, it will be given into a vein or the fatty tissue of your abdomen. After several days, when the danger of clotting is past, your dosage of heparin will be gradually reduced. Then another medication you can take by mouth will be started.

The writer of this description also made the appropriate choices for the readers and their needs. Familiar words rather than technical ones are suitable for nonspecialists such as patients. Note also that this audience does not need elaborate descriptions of the origin and composition of the drug. The tone is both personal and straightforward because the purpose is to win the patient's confidence and to explain the essential functions of the drug, a simpler message than the one for professionals.

The trend today in occupational writing is to make letters, reports, and proposals more natural and personal and less impersonal, formal, or stuffy. But adopting a personal tone does not mean you should address the reader in a chummy or disrespectful way. Quite the contrary, a business letter or report needs to be personal and professional at the same time.

Characteristics of Job-Related Writing

Job-related writing characteristically serves six basic functions: (1) to provide practical information, (2) to give facts rather than impressions, (3) to provide visuals to clarify and condense information, (4) to give accurate measurements, (5) to state responsibilities precisely, and (6) to persuade and offer recommendations. These six functions tell you what kind of writing you will produce after you successfully answer the *who? why? what?* and *how?*

Providing Practical Information

On-the-job writing requires a practical here's-what-you-need-to-do-or-to-know approach. One such practical approach is *action oriented*. You instruct the reader to do something—assemble a ceiling fan, test for bacteria, perform an audit, create an

Internet Web site. Another practical approach of job-related writing is knowledge oriented: to have someone understand something—why a procedure was changed, what caused a problem or solved it, how much progress occurred on a job site, why a new piece of equipment should be purchased. Examples of knowledge-oriented practical writing are a letter from a manufacturer to customers to explain a product recall and an e-mail to employees about changes in their group health insurance.

The following description of Energy Efficiency Ratio combines both the action-oriented and knowledge-oriented approaches of practical writing.

> Whether you are buying window air-conditioning units or a central air-conditioning system, consider the performance factors and efficiency of the various units on the market. Before you buy, determine the Energy Efficiency Ratio (EER) of the units under consideration. The EER is found by dividing the BTUs (units of heat) that the unit removes from the area to be cooled by the watts (amount of electricity) the unit consumes. The result is usually a number between 5 and 12. The higher the number, the more efficiently the unit will use electricity.
>
> You'll note that EER will vary considerably from unit to unit of a given manufacturer, and from brand to brand. As efficiency is increased, you may find the purchase price is higher; however, operating costs will be lower. Remember, a good rule to follow is to choose the equipment with the highest EER. That way you'll get efficient equipment and enjoy operating economy.[3]

Giving Facts, Not Impressions

Occupational writing is concerned largely with those things that can be seen, heard, felt, tasted, or smelled. The writer uses *concrete language* and specific details. The emphasis is on facts rather than on the writer's feelings or guesses.

The following discussion by a group of scientists about the sources of oil spills and their impact on the environment is an example of writing with objectivity. It describes events and causes without anger or tears. Imagine how much emotion could have been packed into this paragraph by the residents of the coastal states who have watched such spills come ashore.

> The most critical impact results from the escapement of oil into the ecosystem, both crude oil and refined fuel oils, the latter coming from sources such as marine traffic. Major oil spills occur as a result of accidents such as blowout, pipeline breakage, etc. Technological advances coupled with stringent regulations have helped to reduce the chances of such major spills; however, there is a chronic low-level discharge of oil associated with normal drilling and production operations. Waste oils discharged through the river systems and practices associated with tanker transports dump more significant quantities of oils into the ocean, compared to what is introduced by the offshore oil industry. All of this contributes to the chronic low-level discharge of oil into world oceans. The long-range cumulative effect of these discharges is possibly the most significant threat to the ecosystem.[4]

Providing Visuals to Clarify and Condense Information

Visuals are indispensable partners of words in conveying information to your readers. On-the-job writing makes frequent use of visuals such as tables, charts, photo-

---

[3]Reprinted by permission of New Orleans Public Services, Inc.

[4]*The Offshore Ecology Investigation,* Galveston: Gulf Universities Research Consortium.

graphs, flow charts, diagrams, and drawings to clarify and condense information. Thanks to various software packages, you can easily create and insert visuals into your writing. The use of visuals—including computer visuals—is discussed in detail in Chapters 12 and 13.

Visuals play an important role in the workplace. Note how the drawing in Figure 1.6 from the National Safety Council's booklet "Working Safely with Your Computer" can help computer users better understand and follow the accompanying written guidelines. A visual like this, reproduced in an employee handbook or displayed as a poster, can significantly reduce stress and increase productivity.

Visuals are extremely useful in making detailed relationships clear to readers. A great deal of information about the growth and diversity of commercial TV stations is condensed into Table 1.1. Consider how many words a writer would need to supply the data contained in the table. Note, too, how easily the numbers can be read when they are arranged in columns. The figures would be far more difficult to decipher if they were printed like this: Commercial TV stations in operation: 1978, Total 727, VHF 516, UHF 211; 1979, Total 732, VHF 516, UHF 216; and so forth.

In addition to the visuals already mentioned, the following graphic devices (created quickly with the help of a computer) in your letters, reports, and Web sites will make your writing easier for your audience to read and follow:

- headings, such as **Four Keys to Effective Writing** or **Characteristics of Job-Related Writing**
- subheadings to divide major sections into parts, such as "Providing Practical Information" or "Giving Facts, Not Impressions"
- numbers within a paragraph, or even a line, such as (1) this, (2) this, and (3) also this
- different types of s p a c i n g
- CAPITALIZATION
- *italics* (easily made by a word processing command or indicated in typed copy by <u>underscoring</u>)
- **boldface** (darker print for emphasis)
- *Scripting* (simulating handwriting)
- icons (visual markers such as ➞)
- HYPERTEXT (the use of color, shading, or boldface to mark words or icons that indicate links on the Internet)
- Asterisks * to * separate * items * or to note key items *
- Lists with "bullets" (symbols like the square before each entry in this list)

Keep in mind that graphic devices must be used carefully and with moderation. They should never be used just for decoration or to dress up a letter or report. Used properly, they can help you

- to organize, arrange, and emphasize your ideas
- to make your work easier to read and to recall
- to preview and summarize your ideas, for example, headings
- to list related items to help readers distinguish, follow, compare, and recall them—as this bulleted list does

FIGURE 1.6   Use of a visual to convey information.

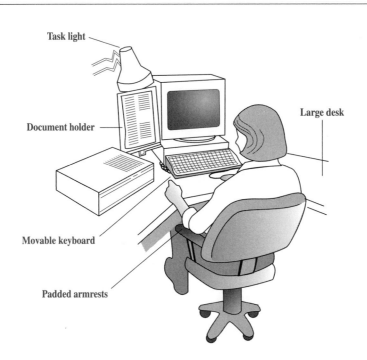

Your working area

❑ Having a **desk** or other place to work that's big enough, and of the right size and height, is of first importance.

❑ **Keyboard** should be movable, non-glossy, and tilted slightly forward. Put a notebook under the back edge if it doesn't have built-in height adjustment pegs.

❑ **Padded wrist rests** for anyone who types a good deal. Or, use a chair with padded armrests. If the desk has a movable keyboard tray, adjust the height so that wrists are straight and forearms are parallel to the floor when fingers are on the keys.

❑ **Desk** large enough to hold computer monitor and keyboard, telephone, desk set, and all other needed accessories. It also should provide space for writing and doing other work comfortably.

❑ **Task light** adjustable so it can shine on a book or note pad without casting an annoying reflection on the screen.

❑ **Document holder** movable, upright, tilted, and at the same height as the video screen for easy reading.

❑ **Video monitors** at least four feet apart.

❑ **Muted desk top surface** doesn't reflect light into operator's eyes.

❑ **Screen** positioned so it won't reflect light from windows or overhead lights; also so operator won't be distracted by persons walking by.

TABLE 1.1   Commercial TV Stations in Operation, 1978–1999

Year	Total	VHF	UHF
1978	727	516	211
1979	732	516	216
1980	746	517	229
1981	752	519	233
1982	772	524	248
1983	802	526	276
1984	870	536	334
1985	904	539	365
1986	922	541	381
1987	982	547	435
1988	1,017	541	476
1989	1,092	544	548
1990	1,115	563	552
1991	1,128	556	572
1992	1,144	557	587
1993	1,151	556	595
1994	1,157	559	598
1995	1,181	559	622
1996	1,174	554	620
1997	1,197	639	558
1998	1,210	560	650
1999	1,229	561	668

Supplied by the Federal Communications Commission.

Giving Accurate Measurements

Much of your work will depend on measurements—acres, bytes, calories, centimeters, degrees, dollars and cents, grams, percentages, pounds, square feet, units. Numbers are clear and convincing. An architect depends on specifications to accomplish a job; a nurse must record precise dosages of medications; a sales representative keeps track of the number of customer visits; and an electronics technologist has to monitor antenna patterns and systems.

The following discussion of mixing colored cement for a basement floor would be useless to readers if it did not supply accurate quantities.

The inclusion of permanent color in a basement floor is a good selling point. One way of doing this is by incorporating commercially pure mineral pigments in a topping mixture placed to a 1-inch depth over a normal base slab. The topping mix should range in volume between 1 part portland cement, 1 1/4 parts sand, and 1 1/4 parts gravel or crushed stone and 1 part portland cement, 2 parts sand, and 2 parts gravel or crushed stone. Maximum size gravel or crushed stone should be 3/8 inch.

Mix cement and pigment before aggregate and water are added and be very thorough to secure uniform dispersion and the full color value of the pigment. The proportion varies from 5 to 10 percent of pigment by weight of cement, depending on the shade desired. If carbon black is used as a pigment to obtain grays or black, a proportion of from 1/2 to 1 percent will be adequate. Manufacturers' instructions should be followed closely; care in cleanliness, placing, and finishing are also essential. Colored topping mixes are available from some suppliers of ready mixed concrete.[5]

Stating Responsibilities Precisely

Job-related writing, because it is directed to a specific audience, must make absolutely clear what it expects of, or can do for, that audience. Misunderstandings waste time and cost money. Directions on order forms, for example, should indicate how and where information is to be listed and how it is to be routed and acted on. The following three directions are taken from different business-related communications, showing readers how to perform different tasks and/or explaining why.

Include agency code numbers in the upper-right corner.

Items 1 through 16 of this form should be completed by the injured employee or by someone acting on his or her behalf, whenever an injury is sustained in the performance of duty. The term *injury* includes occupational disease caused by the employment. The form should be given to the employee's official superior within 48 hours following the injury. The official superior is that individual having responsible supervision over the employee.

What is a **credit report?** A credit report is a record of how you've paid bills with credit grantors such as stores and banks. Credit grantors use credit reports to determine whether or not you will be extended credit. The report identifies you by information such as your name and address, credit accounts, and payment history. Your credit report also includes public record data, such as bankruptcies, court judgments, and tax liens. A list of those who have recently requested a copy of your credit report is also included. A credit report does not contain information on arrest records, specific purchases, or medical records.[6]

Other kinds of job-related writing deal with the writer's responsibilities rather than the reader's, for example, "Tomorrow I will meet with the district sales manager to discuss (1) July's sales, (2) the possibility of expanding our Madison home market, and (3) next fall's production schedule. I will e-mail a short report of our discussion by August 5, 2000." In a letter of application for a job, writers should conclude by asking for an interview and clearly inform a prospective employer when they are available for an interview, for example, weekday mornings, only during the afternoon, or any time after February 15.

Persuading and Offering Recommendations

Much writing in the business world is directed to employers, customers, and clients to persuade them to (a) buy a product or service or (b) adopt a plan of action. To be persuasive, you will need to get your readers' attention, communicate clearly so they understand your message, and make sure they remember it. Your very first job-related writing will likely be a persuasive letter of application to obtain a job inter-

---

[5]Reprinted by permission from *Concrete Construction Magazine,* World of Concrete Center, 426 South Westgate, Addison, Illinois 60101.

[6]Reprinted by permission of Associated Credit Bureaus, Inc.

view with a potential employer, whom you will have to get to recall and select your application from among the hundreds he or she receives. Once on the job, you may be required to write persuasive e-mails, letters, reports, proposals, or even Web sites.

In much job-related writing, you will have to convince readers that you (and your company) can save them time and money, increase efficiency, reduce risks, and improve their image. At the same time, you may have to show readers why you are better able than your competitors to deliver on those promises.

Effective persuasive writing involves using all the skills you will learn about audience analysis, tone, organization, research, and the overall process of drafting, revising, and editing your work. Writing persuasive letters, proposals, and reports requires that you have a clear sense of your audience's needs, priorities, preferences, and even dislikes. You will have to conduct research, provide logical arguments, supply concrete examples or appropriate data, and, especially important, identify the most relevant information for your particular audience.

Notice how the advertisement in Figure 1.7 offers a persuasively bulleted list of reasons—based on cost, time, safety, efficiency, and convenience—to convince correctional officials that they should use General Medical's services rather than those of a hospital or clinic.

Much job-centered writing also requires you to be highly persuasive when you make a recommendation to your employer. In many of your memos, letters, reports,

FIGURE 1.7 An advertisement using arguments based on cost, time, efficiency, safety, and convenience to persuade a potential customer to use a service.

General Medical Services Corp.

A subsidiary of

Federal Medical Industries, Inc. O.T.C.
950 S.W. 12th Avenue, 2nd Floor Suite, Pompano, Florida 33069
(305) 942-1111   FL WATS: 1-800-654-8282

GENERAL MEDICAL WILL STOP THE UNNECESSARY TRANSPORTING OF YOUR INMATES.

- We'll bring our X-ray services to your facility, 7 days a week, 24 hours a day.
  We can reduce your X-ray costs by a minimum of 28%.
  X-ray cost includes radiologist's interpretation and written report.
  Same day service with immediate results telephoned to your facility.
- Save correctional officers' time, thereby saving your facility money.
- Avoid chance of prisoner's escape and possible danger to the public.
- Avoid long waits in overcrowded hospitals.
- Reduce your insurance liabilities.
- Other Services Available: Ultrasound, Two Dimensional Echocardiogram, C.T. Scan, EKG, Blood Lab and Holter Monitor.

General Medical Is Your On-Site Medical Problem Solver

and e-mail you will have to evaluate various options and products for your employer. Your reader will expect you to offer clear-cut, logical, convincing reasons for your choice. The reader will want to know why and how you arrived at your conclusions.

The following summary states why it is better for a company to lease a truck than to purchase one. Note the persuasive tone and logical presentation of information the writer uses.

> After studying the pros and cons of buying or leasing a company truck, I recommend that we lease it for the following five reasons.
>
> 1. We will not have to expend any of our funds for a down payment, which is being waived.
> 2. Our monthly payments for leasing the vehicle will be at least $150 less than the payments we would have to make if we purchased the truck on a three-year contract.
> 3. All major and minor maintenance (up to 36,000 miles) is included as part of our monthly leasing payment.
> 4. Insurance (theft and damage) is also part of our monthly leasing payment.
> 5. We have the option of trading in the truck every 16 months for a newer model or trading up every 12 months.

Ethical Writing in the Workplace

On-the-job writing involves much more than conveying facts about products, equipment, costs, and the day-to-day operations of a business. Your writing also has to be ethical. Writing ethically means doing what is right and fair and being honest and just with your employer, co-workers, and customers. Your reputation and character plus your employer's corporate image will depend on your following an ethical course of action. Note how proud the Southern Company and its employees are of their ethical commitments to the environment, the community, and the country in the excerpt from a consumer publication on p. 25.

Many of the most significant bywords in the world of business reflect an ethical commitment to honesty and fairness: *accountability, public trust, equal opportunity employer, good faith effort, truth in lending, fair play, honest advertising, full disclosure, high professional standards, community involvement, social responsibility.*

Unethical business dealings, on the other hand, are stigmatized in *cover-ups, shady deals, spin doctors, foul play, misrepresentations, price gouging, bias,* and *unfair advantage.* Those are the activities that keep Better Business Bureaus active and make customers angry.

Ethical Requirements on the Job

In the workplace, you will be expected to meet the highest ethical standards by fulfilling the following requirements.

- Supplying honest and up-to-date information about yourself in your résumé and job applications. The résumé (see pp. 240–266) is one key place where most people must make ethical decisions about candor and honesty.

- Maintaining accurate and current records at work. Remember: "If it isn't written, it didn't happen."
- Complying with all local, state, and federal regulations, especially those ensuring a safe, healthy work environment, products, and/or service.
- Adhering to your profession's code or standard of ethics. (For example, certified internal auditors promise to be fair and impartial in all their audits).
- Following your company's policies and procedures.
- Honoring guarantees and warranties and meeting customer needs impartially.
- Cooperating fully and honestly with any collaborative team of which you are a member.
- Respecting all copyright obligations and privileges.

Our Environmental Responsibility

Southern Company is entering the 21st Century not only as a leader in the energy market, but also a leader in protecting the environment. We believe our environmental initiatives and our strong compliance record will give us a competitive advantage.

The Southern Company's environmental policy spells out each company's commitment to protecting the environment. The first and foremost goal is to meet or exceed all regulatory requirements for domestic and international operations. To do that, we're using a combination of the best technologies and voluntary pollution-prevention programs. We also set aggressive environmental goals and make sure employees are aware of their individual environmental responsibilities. We are good citizens wherever we serve.

As an affiliate of Southern Company, Mississippi Power's environmental issues are business issues. In addition to regulatory obligations, our employees carry out a most active grassroots environmental program. It's this employee involvement and strong environmental commitment that gives our commitment life and promises future generations a healthy environment.

For example, one employee's concern that motor oil is properly discarded led to the founding of a countrywide annual household hazardous waste collection program. Thousands of tons of waste have been collected, including jars of DDT, mercury, paint, batteries, pesticides and other poisons.

Scores of employees participate in island, beach, and river cleanups throughout Mississippi Power's 23-county service area. More than 30 employees compiled "The Wolf River Environmental Monitoring Program."

This report is the first-ever historical, biological assessment completed on the Wolf River by scientists and engineers. Employees volunteered countless hours to compile the statistical data. Today, Mississippi Power employees continue to support the Wolf River Project by producing note cards, photographs, and slides as an educational and community awareness project.

Our commitment to the environment goes beyond our business. By sponsoring a variety of programs, we're helping to teach the public, students, and teachers about environmental responsibility.

Following those eight guidelines may not be only an ethical requirement; it could also be a legal one. Legal obligations and ethical considerations often merge. For example, doing personal (or outside consulting) work on company time, padding expense accounts, using company equipment for personal use, or accepting a bribe is unethical and illegal. It would also be neglectful and unethical to allow an unsafe product to stay on the market just to spare your company the expense and embarrassment of a product recall. It would be wrong, legally and ethically, to e-mail information about your employer's pending patent plans to the Internet world.

Computer ethics, especially when using the Internet, are essential in the world of work. It would be grossly unethical to erase a computer program intentionally, violate a software licensing agreement, or misrepresent (by fabrication or exaggeration) the scope of a database. Follow the Ten Commandments of Computer Ethics prepared by the Computer Ethics Institute and listed in Figure 1.8.

FIGURE 1.8   The Ten Commandments of Computer Ethics.

1. Thou shalt not use a computer to harm other people.

2. Thou shalt not interfere with other people's computer work.

3. Thou shalt not snoop around in other people's computer files.

4. Thou shalt not use a computer to steal.

5. Thou shalt not use a computer to bear false witness.

6. Thou shalt not copy or use proprietary software for which you have not paid.

7. Thou shalt not use other people's computer resources without authorization or proper compensation.

8. Thou shalt not appropriate other people's intellectual output.

9. Thou shalt think about the social consequences of the program you are writing or the system you are designing.

10. Thou shalt always use a computer in ways that insure consideration and respect for your fellow humans.

Computer Ethics Institute, London.

Writing for the world of multinational corporations places additional ethical demands on you as a writer. You have to make sure you respect the ethics of the foreign countries where your firm does business. Some behavior regarded as normal or routine in the United States might be seen as highly unethical elsewhere. And you should be on your ethical guard not to take advantage of a host country, such as allowing or encouraging poor environmental control because regulatory and inspection procedures are not as strict or using pesticides or conducting experiments outlawed in the United States.

Some Guidelines to Help You Reach Ethical Decisions

The workplace presents all sorts of conflicts that will require you to make decisions and to justify your reasons for those decisions. Expect to be involved in conflicts over who is right and who is wrong, what is best for the company and what is not, and whether a service or product should be changed and why. You will be asked to take a stand. Here are a few guidelines that will help you to comply with the ethical requirements of your job.

1. Follow your conscience and "to thine own self be true." Do what you know is right. You cannot authorize something that you believe is wrong, dangerous, unfair, contradictory, or incomplete. But don't be hasty. Leave plenty of room for diplomacy and for careful questioning. Recall the story of Chicken Little, who always cried that the sky was falling. Don't blow a small matter out of proportion, but similarly don't overlook something serious just because there is no history of a problem.

2. Be suspicious of convenient (and false) appeals that go against your beliefs. Watch out for these red flags that anyone places in the way of your conscience: "No one will ever know." "It's ok to cut corners every once in a while." "We got away with it last time." "Don't rock the boat." "No one's looking." "As long as the company makes money, who cares?" Those excuses are traps you must avoid.

3. Maintain good faith in meeting your obligations to your employer, your co-workers, your customers, and your community. Examine their reasons for reading your information (see pp. 9–10) and consider how and in what contexts they will use it. It is unethical to lie, exaggerate, or even dodge an issue. Keeping information from a co-worker who needs it, using a password belonging to someone else, omitting a fact, justifying unnecessary expenses—all are unethical acts, just as cheating on an examination or plagiarizing are unethical in your schoolwork.

4. Take responsibility for your actions. Saying "I do not know" when you do know can constitute a serious ethical violation. Keep your records up-to-date and accurate. Sign and date your work. Never backdate a document to delete information or to fix an error that you committed. Such action constitutes a cover-up and a serious breach of ethics. Also, do not use someone's password, which is equivalent to his or her electronic signature. If you make a mistake, the other person would be held responsible. Be familiar with contracts and what is expected of you in terms of documentation and notification. Not testing a set of instructions thoroughly, for example, might endanger readers thousands of miles away.

5. Weigh all sides before you commit to a conclusion. Research what you write and communicate orally. Rely on hard evidence: documentation, testimony, valid precedents. Do your homework by studying code books and agency handbooks; confer with a customer or a co-worker when you are in doubt about a major issue. Your employer will expect you to know company protocols and specifications about the procedures, methods, and materials of your job. Your company's lawyers or engineers have scrutinized those protocols, or standard operating procedures (SOPS), to make sure the documents are accurate and comply with the appropriate state and federal regulations.

6. Anticipate the consequences of your decisions. You may think a particular course of action is right at the time, but don't overlook the possibility that your decision may create a bigger problem in the future. For example, you hear that a co-worker is involved in wrongdoing; you report it to your boss, and a reprimand is placed in that worker's file. Later you learn that what was reported to you was malicious gossip or only a small part of a much larger but very ethical picture. Give people the benefit of the doubt until you have sufficient facts to the contrary. Giving incomplete information on an incident report may temporarily protect you but may falsely incriminate someone else or unfairly increase your company's liability insurance rates.

Ethical Dilemmas

Sometimes in the workplace you will face situations where there is no clear-cut right or wrong choice, even with regard to the six ethical categories described above. You may be involved in an ethical dilemma, or conflict, regarding a decision by your employer, a customer, or a co-worker, or even something you said or did earlier.

Here are a few scenarios, similar to ones in which you may find yourself, that are gray areas, ethically speaking, along with some possible solutions.

- You see an opening for a job in your area but the employer wants someone with a minimum of two years of field experience. You have just completed an internship and had one summer's (12 weeks) experience in the field, which together total almost 7 months. Should you apply for the job describing yourself as "experienced"?

  Yes, but honestly state the type and the extent of your field experience and the conditions under which you obtained it.

- You work for a company that usually assigns commissions to the salesperson for whom a customer asks. One afternoon a customer visits your store and asks for a salesperson whose name he cannot remember but from whose description you realize is an employee who happens to have the day off. You assist the customer all afternoon, making several long distance calls to locate a particular model and even arrange to have that item shipped overnight to your store so the customer can pick it up in the morning. When it comes time to ring up the sale, should you list your employee number for credit (and the commission) or the off-duty employee's?

  You probably should defer crediting the sale to either number until you speak to the absent employee and suggest a compromise—splitting the commission.

- A piece of computer equipment, scheduled for delivery to your customer the next day, arrives with a damaged part. You decide to replace it at your store before the customer receives it. Should you inform the customer?

  Yes, but assure the customer that the equipment is still under the same warranty and that the replacement part is new and also under the same warranty. If the customer protests, agree to let him or her use the computer until a new unit arrives.

As these brief scenarios suggest, sometimes you have to make concessions and compromises to be ethical in the world of work.

Writing Ethically

Your writing as well as your behavior must be ethical. Words, like actions, have implications and consequences. If you slant your words to conceal the truth or gain an unfair advantage, you are not being ethical. False advertising is false writing. In your written work, strive to be careful and straightforward, reporting events and figures honestly and without bias or omissions. Be fair, reliable, and accurate.

As we saw earlier in this chapter, you have to respect your audience, taking their needs and reactions into account. If you lie, exaggerate, or minimize, an audience's distrust can come back to haunt you in the form of lost business.

Unethical writing is usually guilty of one or more of the following faults, which can conveniently be listed as the three *M*s: misquotation, misrepresentation, and manipulation. Here are seven examples:

1. Plagiarism is stealing someone else's words (work) and claiming it as your own. At work, plagiarism is unethically claiming a co-worker's ideas, input, or report as your contribution. In a research report or paper, you are guilty of plagiarism if you use another person's words (or even a rough paraphrase) without documenting the source. Do not think that by changing a few words here and there you are not plagiarizing. Copying someone else's software is also an act of plagiarism. Give proper credit to your source, whether in print, in person (through an interview), or on-line.

2. Selective misquoting deliberately omits damaging or unflattering comments to paint a better (but untruthful) picture of you or your company. By picking and choosing words from a quotation, you unethically misrepresent what the speaker or writer originally intended.

> **Full Quotation:** I've enjoyed at times our firm's association with Technology, Inc., although I was troubled by the uneven quality of their service. At times, it was excellent while at others it was far less so.
>
> **Selective Misquotation:** I've enjoyed . . . our firm's association with Technology, Inc. The quality of their service was . . . excellent.

The dots, called *ellipses,* unethically suggest that only extraneous or unimportant details were omitted.

3. Arbitrary embellishment of numbers unethically misrepresents, by increasing or decreasing percentages or other numbers, statistical or other information. It is unethical to stretch the differences between competing plans or proposals to gain an unfair advantage or to express accurate figures in an inaccurate way.

> **Embellishment:** An overwhelming majority of residents voted for the new plan.
> **Ethical:** The new plan was passed by a vote of 53 to 49.
>
> **Embellishment:** Our competitor's sales volume increased by only 10 percent in the preceding year while ours doubled.
> **Ethical:** Our competitor controls 90 percent of the market, yet we increased our share of that market from 5 percent to 10 percent last year.

4. Manipulation of data or context, closely related to #3, is the misrepresentation of events, usually to "put a good face" on a bad situation. The writer here unethically uses slanted language and intentionally misleading euphemisms to misinterpret events for readers.

> Manipulation: Looking ahead to 2002, the United Funds Group is exceptionally optimistic about its long-term prospects in an expanding global market. We are happy to report steady to moderate activity in an expanding sales environment last year. The United Funds Group seeks to build on sustaining investment opportunities beneficial to all subscribers.
>
> Ethical: Looking ahead to 2002, the United Funds Group is optimistic about its long-term prospects in an expanding global market. Though the market suffered from inflation this year, the United Funds Group hopes to recoup its losses in the year ahead.

The writer minimizes the negative effects of inflation by calling it "an expanding sales environment."

5. Using fictitious benefits to promote a product or service seemingly promises customers advantages but delivers none.

> False Benefit: Our bottled water is naturally hydrogenated from clear underground springs.
>
> Truth: All water is hydrogenated because it contains hydrogen.

6. Unfairly characterizing (by exaggerating or minimizing) hiring or firing conditions is unethical.

> Unethical: One of the benefits of working for Spelco is the double pay you earn for overtime.
>
> Truth: Overtime is assigned on the basis of seniority.

> Unethical: Our corporate restructuring will create a more efficient and streamlined company, benefiting management and workers alike.
>
> Truth: Downsizing has led to 150 layoffs.

Companies faced with laying off employees want to protect their corporate image and maintain their stockholders' good faith, so they often "put the best face" on such an action.

7. Misrepresenting through distorting or slanted visuals is one of the most common types of unethical communication. Making a product look bigger, better, or more professional is all too easy with graphics software packages. Other examples of unethical uses of visuals are making warning or caution statements (see p. 465) the same size and type font as ingredients or directions and enlarging advertising hype (Double Your Money Back) while reducing major points to small print.

Ethical writing is clear, accurate, fair, and honest. These are among the most important goals of any work communication. Because ethics are such an important topic in writing for the workplace, they will be stressed throughout this book. See, for example, pp. 138–140 and 580–581.

✓ Revision Checklist

At the end of each chapter is a checklist you should review before you submit the final copy of your work, either to your instructor or to your boss. The checklists include the types of research, planning, drafting, editing, and revising you should do to ensure the success of your work. Regard each checklist as a summary of the main ideas in the chapter as well as a handy guide to quality control. You may find it helpful to check each box as you verify that you have performed the necessary revision/review. Effective writers are also careful editors.

- ❑ Identified my audience—their background, knowledge of English, reason for reading my work, and likely response to my work and me.
- ❑ Made it clear what I want my audience to do after reading my work.
- ❑ Tailored my message to my audience's needs and background, giving them neither too little nor too much information.
- ❑ Pushed to the main point right away; did not waste my reader's time.
- ❑ Selected the most appropriate language, technical level, tone, and level of formality.
- ❑ Did not waste my audience's time with unsupported generalizations or opinions; instead gave them accurate measurements, facts, and carefully researched material.
- ❑ Used appropriate visuals to make my work easier for my audience to follow.
- ❑ Used persuasive reasons and data to convince my reader to accept my plan or work.
- ❑ Ensured that my writing is ethical—accurate, fair, honest, a true reflection of the situation or condition I am explaining or describing.
- ❑ Followed the Ten Commandments of Computer Ethics.
- ❑ Gave full and complete credit to any sources I used, including resource people.
- ❑ Avoided plagiarism and unfair or dishonest use of copyrighted materials, both written and visual, including all electronic media.

Exercises

1. What is your chosen career? Make a list of the types of writing you think you will do, or have already been assigned, on the job.

2. Make a list of the kinds of writing you have done in a history or English class or for a laboratory or shop course.

3. Compare your lists for Exercises 1 and 2. How do the two types of writing differ?

4. Write a memo (see pp. 118–121 for format) addressed to a prospective supervisor to introduce yourself. Your memo should have four headings **education**—including goals and accomplishments; **job information**—where you have worked and your responsibilities; **community service**—volunteer work, church work, youth groups; and **writing experience**—your strengths and what you would like to see improved.

5. Write a memo in response to Rowe Pinkerton's e-mail in Figure 1.1. Explain how you will use the skills you learn in the company reimbursed writing course on your job.

6. Bring to class a set of printed instructions, a memo, a sales letter, or a brochure. Comment on how well the printed material answers the following questions.
   a. Who is the audience?
   b. Why was the material written?
   c. What is the message?
   d. Are the style and tone appropriate for the audience, the purpose, and the message? Why?
   e. Discuss the use of color in the document. How does color (or the lack of it) affect an audience's response to the message?

7. Cut out a newspaper ad that contains a drawing or photograph. Bring it to class together with a paragraph of your own (75–100 words) describing how the message of the ad is directed to a particular audience and commenting on why the illustration was selected for that audience.

8. Pick one of the following topics and write two descriptions of it. In the first description, use technical vocabulary. In the second, use language suitable for the general public.
   a. spark plug
   b. blood pressure cuff
   c. carburetor
   d. computer chip
   e. camera
   f. legal contract
   g. electric sander
   h. cyberspace
   i. muscle
   j. protein
   k. compact disc player
   l. e-mail
   m. bread
   n. money
   o. color scanner
   p. soap
   q. calculator
   r. Nintendo game
   s. AIDS
   t. thermostat
   u. trees
   v. food processor
   w. earthquake
   x. recycling

9. Redo Exercise 8 as a collaborative writing project.

10. Select one article from a daily newspaper and one article from either a professional journal in your major field or one of the following journals: *Advertising Age, American Journal of Nursing, Business Marketing, Business Week, Computer, Computer Design, Construction Equipment, Criminal Justice Review, Food Service Marketing, Journal of Forestry, Journal of Soil and Water Conservation, National Safety News, Nutrition Action, Office Machines, Park Maintenance, Sci-*

entific American. State how the two articles you selected differ in terms of audience, purpose, message, style, and tone.

11. Assume that you work for Appliance Rentals, Inc., a company that rents TVs, microwave ovens, stereo components, and the like. Write a persuasive letter to the members of a campus organization or civic club urging them to rent an appropriate appliance or appliances. Include details in your letter that might have special relevance to members of this specific organization.

12. Evaluate how well the advertisement on p. 34 illustrates the technique of occupational writing described in this chapter. Specifically comment on what analysis of the ad reveals about the copywriter's analysis of the intended audience. Pay attention to advertising copy (words), the images of people and equipment (visuals), and the situation depicted. Also explain how the ad illustrates the six functions of on-the-job writing.

13. Read the article on pages 35–36 and identify its audience (technical or general), purpose, message, style, and tone.

14. The following statements contain embellishments, selected misquotations, false benefits, and other types of unethical tactics. Revise each statement to eliminate the unethical aspects.
    a. Storm damage done to water filtration plant #3 was minimal. While we had to shut down temporarily, service resumed to meet residents' needs.
    b. All customers qualify for the maximum discount available.
    c. The service contract . . . on the whole . . . applied to upgrades.
    d. We followed the protocols precisely with test results yielding further opportunities for experimentation.
    e. All our costs were within fair-use guidelines.
    f. Customers' complaints have been held to a minimum.
    g. All the lots we are selling offer easy access to the lake.

15. A co-worker tells you that he has no plans to return to his job after he takes his annual two-week vacation. You know that your department cannot meet its deadline short-handed and that your company will need at least two or three weeks to recruit and hire a qualified replacement. You also know that it is your company's policy not to give paid vacations to employees who do not agree to work for at least three months following a vacation. What should you do? What points would you make in a confidential, ethical memo to your boss? What points would you make to your co-worker?

16. Your company is regulated and inspected by the Environmental Protection Agency. In ninety days, the EPA will relax a particular regulation about dumping industrial waste. Your company's management is considering cutting costs by relaxing the standard now, before the new, easier regulation is in place. You know that the EPA inspector probably will not return before the ninety-day period elapses. What do you recommend to management?

Courtesy of Trans-Lux Corporation, Norwalk, Conn. Reprinted with permission.

Microwaves

Much of the world around us is in motion. A wave-like motion. Some waves are big like tidal waves and some are small like the almost unseen footprints of a waterspider on a quiet pond. Other waves can't be seen at all, such as an idling truck sending out vibrations our bodies can feel. Among these are electromagnetic waves. They range from very low frequency sound waves to very high frequency X-rays, gamma rays, and even cosmic rays.

Energy behaves differently as its frequency changes. The start of audible sound—somewhere around 20 cycles per second—covers a segment at the low end of the electromagnetic spectrum. Household electricity operates at 60 hertz (cycles per second). At a somewhat higher frequency we have radio, ranging from shortwave and marine beacons, through the familiar AM broadcast band that lies between 500 and 1600 kilohertz, then to citizen's band, FM, television, and up to the higher frequency police and aviation bands.

Even higher up the scale lies visible light with its array of colors best seen when light is scattered by raindrops to create a rainbow.

Lying between radio waves and visible light is the microwave region—from roughly one gigahertz (a billion cycles per second) up to 3000 gigahertz. In this region the electromagnetic energy behaves in special ways.

Microwaves travel in straight lines, so they can be aimed in a given direction. They can be *reflected* by dense objects so that they send back echoes—this is the basis for radar. They can be *absorbed*, with their energy being converted into heat—the principle behind microwave ovens. Or they can pass *through* some substances that are transparent to the energy—this enables food to be cooked on a paper plate in a microwave oven.

Microwaves for Radar

World War II provided the impetus to harness microwave energy as a means of detecting enemy planes. Early radars were mounted on the Cliffs of Dover to bounce their microwave signals off Nazi bombers that threatened England. The word *radar* itself is an acronym for *RAdio Detection And Ranging*.

Radars grew more sophisticated. Special-purpose systems were developed to detect airplanes, to scan the horizon for enemy ships, to paint finely detailed electronic pictures of harbors to guide ships, and to measure the speeds of targets. These were installed on land and aboard warships. Radar—especially shipboard radar—was surely one of the most significant technological achievements to tip the scales toward an Allied victory in World War II.

Today, few mariners can recall what it was like before radar. It is such an important aid that it was embraced universally as soon as hostilities ended. Now, virtually every commercial vessel in the world has one, and most larger vessels have two radars: one for use on the open sea and one, operating at a higher frequency, to "paint" a more finely detailed picture, for use near shore.

Microwaves are also beamed across the skies to fix the positions of aircraft in flight, obviously an essential aid to controlling the movement of aircraft from city to city across the nation. These radars have also been linked to computers to tell air traffic controllers the altitude of planes in the area and to label them on their screens.

A new kind of radar, phased array, is now being used to search the skies thousands of miles out over the Atlantic and Pacific oceans. Although these advanced radars use microwave energy just as ordinary radars do, they do not depend upon a rotating antenna. Instead, a fixed antenna array, comprising thousands of elements like those of a fly's eye, looks everywhere. It has been said that these radars roll their eyes instead of turning their heads.

High-Speed Cooking

During World War II Raytheon had been selected to work with M.I.T. and British scientists to accelerate the production of magnetrons, the electron tubes that generate microwave energy, in order to speed up the production of radars. While testing some new, higher-powered tubes in a laboratory at Raytheon's Waltham, Massachusetts, plant, Percy L. Spencer and several of his staff engineers observed an interesting phenomenon. If you placed your hand in a beam of microwave energy, your hand would grow pleasantly warm. It was not like putting your hand in a heated oven that might sear the skin. The warmth was deep-heating and uniform.

Spencer and his engineers sent out for some popcorn and some food, then piped the energy into a metal wastebasket. The microwave oven was born.

From these discoveries, some 35 years ago, a new industry was born. In millions of homes around the world, meals are prepared in minutes using microwave ovens. In many processing industries, microwaves are being used to perform difficult heating or drying jobs. Even printing presses use microwaves to speed the drying of ink on paper.

In hospitals, doctors' offices, and athletic training rooms, that deep heat that Percy Spencer noticed is now used in diathermy equipment to ease the discomfort of muscle aches and pains.

Telephones Without Cable

The third characteristic of microwaves—that they pass undistorted through the air—makes them good messengers to carry telephone conversations as well as live television signals—without telephone poles or cables—across town or across the country. The microwave signals are beamed via satellite or by dish reflectors mounted atop buildings and mountaintop towers.

Microwaves take their name from the Greek *mikro* meaning very small. While the waves themselves may be very small, they play an important role in our world today: in defense; in communications; in air, sea, and highway safety; in industrial processing; and in cooking. At Raytheon the applications expand every day.

Reprinted by permission of *Raytheon Magazine*.

The Writing Process at Work

In Chapter 1 you learned about the different functions of writing for the world of work and also explored some basic concepts all writers must master. To be a successful writer, you need to

- identify your audience's needs
- determine your purpose in writing to that audience
- make sure your message meets your audience's needs and your established purpose
- use the most appropriate style and tone for your message
- format your work to clearly reflect your message for your audience

Just as significant to your success is knowing how effective writers actually create their work for their audiences. This chapter will give you some practical information about the strategies and techniques careful writers use when they work. These procedures are a vital part of what is known as the *writing process.* This process involves such matters as how writers gather information, how they transform their ideas into written form, and how they organize and revise what they have written to make it suitable for their audiences.

What Writing Is and Is Not

As you begin your study of writing for the world of work, it might be helpful to identify some notions about what writing is and what it is not.

What Writing Is Not

- **Writing is not something mysterious done according to a magical formula known only to a few.** Even if you have not done much writing before, you can learn to write effectively.
- **Writing is not simply a hit or miss affair, left up to chance.** Successful writing requires hard work and thoughtful effort. It is not done well by simply going

through an ordered set of steps as if you were painting by number. You cannot sit down for fifteen minutes and expect to write the perfect memo, letter, or short report straight through. Writing does not proceed in some predictable way, in which introductions are always written first and conclusions last.

- **Just because you put something on paper or on a computer screen does not mean it is permanent and unchangeable.** Writing means rewriting, revising, rethinking. The better a piece of writing is, the more the writer has reworked it.

What Writing Is

- Writing is a fluid process; it is dynamic, not static. It enables you to discover and evaluate your thoughts.
- A piece of writing changes as your thoughts and information change and as your view of the material changes.
- Writing takes time. Some people think that revising and polishing are too time consuming. But poor writing actually takes more time and costs more money in the end. It can lead to misunderstandings, lost sales, product recalls, and even damage to your and your company's reputations.
- Writing means making a number of judgment calls.
- Writing grows sometimes in bits and pieces and sometimes in great spurts. It needs many revisions; an early draft is never a final copy.

Researching

Before you start to compose any e-mail, memo, letter, or report, you'll need to do some research. Depending on the size of your assignment, your research can be simple or elaborate. Yet whatever the size of the job, research is crucial to obtain the right information for your audience. They expect the information you give them to be factually correct and intellectually significant. The world of work is based on conveying information—the logical presentation and sensible interpretation of facts. You will have to do research to obtain that kind of information.

Don't ever think you are wasting time by not starting to write your report or letter immediately. Actually, you will waste time and risk doing a poor job if you do not find out as much as possible about your topic (and your audience's interest in it).

First, find out as much as you can about the nature of your assignment and your readers:

- audience (expert? technicians? general? routed to other departments?)
- audience's purpose
- kinds of information audience needs and why
- format (e-mail? memo? letter? report?)
- scope (limited—one page? extensive—twenty pages?)

Next, determine the exact kind of research you must do to gather and interpret the information your audience needs. Your research can include

- interviewing people inside and outside your company
- doing fieldwork or performing lab studies

- preparing for conferences to ask the right questions
- collaborating with colleagues in person or by e-mail
- distributing a questionnaire and conducting a survey
- surfing the Net
- searching abstracts, indexes, and other references on the Web or in print (see Chapter 8)
- belonging to a chat room
- reading current periodicals, reports, and other documents
- evaluating reports, products, and services
- getting briefings from sales or technical staff
- contacting customers

TECH NOTE

Research: Sources and Strategies

A vital part of your research will be searching efficiently and thoroughly through thousands of databases for key articles, reports, and other reference works—encyclopedias, handbooks, abstracts—on-line. The resources of the Internet are limitless. You can easily access databases, reference works, and the Net itself. Computerized information retrieval will give you the most current data about the stock market, technological advances, and world events. See Chapter 8.

You can also do research among company records—e-mail and memos from your boss and co-workers, previous communications with customers, and company ads, brochures, newsletters, reports, catalogs, and budgets. By becoming familiar with the history of a specific problem or with a particular customer, you will be better able to document and assess your topic. Such in-house research will give you the necessary edge to succeed. You can also call up previously prepared documents (boilerplates) to insert into your document later.

As you do your research, take notes at your terminal and copy them into new files for use when you outline and draft. You can also transfer quotations, graphs, and other visuals, statistical data, and ideas and opinions from your notes into a file for later use in writing your document. During your research, create a Works Cited file, listing all the sources you consulted, and then include it in the final version of your document.

Research is not confined to the beginning of the writing process; it goes on throughout. As you start to tackle your subject, take a little extra time during this formative period to think about the information you have gathered so you can most effectively adapt it for your audience.

Case Study: The Writing Process

Office manager Melissa Hill asked Gordon Reynolds to recommend ways to improve office efficiency and customer relations. In preparing his report, Reynolds knew he had to do some research. To make a recommendation, he needed to find out information about different kinds of communication technologies. He used search engines to guide him to relevant materials in print and on-line. As he read articles in various business journals and magazines and home pages on the Web, he learned about the various laser printers on the market.

As he studied the literature about printers and their vendors, he realized that several offered strong benefits for his company in the areas of concern to his boss. He visited a few dealers in his city and, after seeing some demonstrations, was convinced that purchasing a laser printer was feasible and economically wise. The results of all his research were reflected in his final report.

Planning

At this stage in the writing process, your goal is to get something—anything—down on paper or on your computer screen. For most writers, many of whom are fearful of writer's block, getting started is the hardest part of the job. But you will feel more comfortable and confident once you begin to see your ideas before your eyes. It is always easier to clarify and criticize something you can see.

TECH NOTE

Generating Text
Plan your document by creating either an outline or a brainstormed list. Don't jump right into the drafting stage, however tempting a blank computer screen (or sheet of paper) might be. A computer can help you to generate items for your outline or list. You might even use one of the software packages designed to generate and organize information so you can identify ideas quickly. You can then add, delete, rearrange, combine, expand, and organize points into categories and subcategories. Be sure to save your outline or brainstormed list in a file that you can call up when you begin drafting your document.

Getting started is also easier if you have researched your topic, because you have something to say and to build on. Each part of the process relates to and supports the next. Careful research prepares you to begin writing.

Still, getting started is not easy. You can take advantage of a number of widely used strategies that can help you to develop, organize, and tailor the right information for your audience. Use any one of the following techniques, alone or in combination.

1. Clustering. In the middle of a sheet of paper, write the word or phrase that best describes your topic, then start writing other words or phrases that come to mind. As you write, circle each word or phrase and connect it to the word from which it sprang. Note the clustered grouping in Figure 2.1. The writer used this strategy to get started on a report encouraging a manager to switch to **flex time,** a system in which employees may work on a flexible time schedule within certain limits. Although the resulting diagram is an incomplete picture of the final report, it does give the writer a rough sense of some of the major divisions of the topic and where they may belong in the report.

2. Brainstorming. At the top of a sheet of paper or your computer screen, describe your topic in a word or phrase and then list any information you know or found out about that topic—in any order and as quickly as you can. Brainstorming is like thinking aloud except that you are recording your thoughts.

- Don't stop to delete, rearrange, or rewrite anything, and don't dwell on any one item.
- Don't worry about spelling, punctuation, grammar, or whether you are using words and phrases instead of complete sentences.
- Keep the ideas flowing. The result may well be an odd assortment of details, comments, and opinions.
- After ten to fifteen minutes, stop and take a short break. When you come back to your list, you will no doubt want to make some changes. Some of your points will be irrelevant, so strike them.
- Expect to add some ideas or combine or rearrange others as you start to develop them in more detail. Your list is not final by any means: you have just begun to mine the raw ore.

Figure 2.2 (p. 43) shows Gordon Reynolds's initial brainstormed list. After he began to revise it, he realized that some items were not relevant for his audience (6, 8, and 13) and that others were pertinent but needed to be adapted for his reader (5). He also recognized that some items were repetitious (1, 2, and 11). Further investigation revealed that his company could purchase a color laser printer for far less than his initial high guess (17). As Reynolds continued to work on his list, other important points came to mind that were not part of his original brainstorming.

3. Outlining. For most writers, outlining is the easiest and most comfortable way to begin planning their report or letter. Outlines can go through stages, so don't worry if your first attempt is brief and messy. It does not have to be formal (with roman and arabic numerals), complete, or pretty. It is intended for no one's eyes but yours. Use your preliminary outline as a quick way to sketch in some ideas, a convenient container into which you can put information. You might simply jot down a few major points and identify a few subpoints.

FIGURE 2.1   Clustering on the topic of flex time.

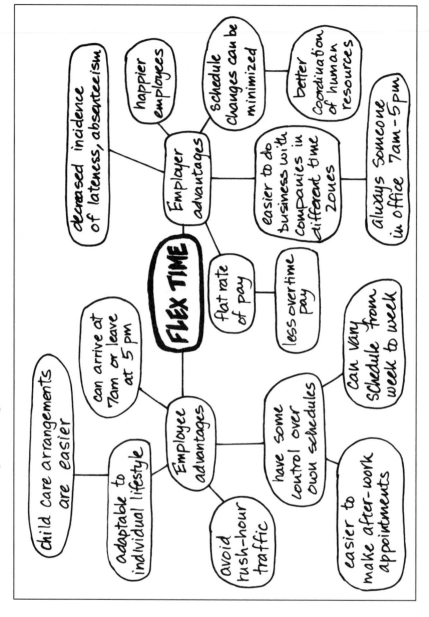

FIGURE 2.2   Gordon Reynolds's initial, unrevised brainstormed list.

1. color laser printers work better

2. color laser printers faster and quieter

3. would blend into office better

4. greatly enhanced print quality and graphics capability

5. more font options

6. takes up same space as old laser

7. would use variety of paper stocks

8. laser optics-real contribution to technology

9. compatible with new software

10. help get the most out of our inhouse documents

11. color laser printers reliable and energy efficient

12. can print envelopes, labels

13. stock is doing better on Wall Street

14. would be easy to change over

15. would drastically reduce our cost for color copying

16. would help us do our work better

17. top-of-the-line can be bought for a little over $1600

As you continue to work on your outline, you will discover key relationships about major points and supporting ideas and different ways to develop them. You will also be able to delete and add details. If you have done your research, you should find that with each successive outline you are coming closer and closer to the next stage—drafting.

As with a brainstormed list, leave your outline to cool for a while. When you return, you can juggle points and add or delete others.

Case Study: Outline

Note that Gordon Reynolds organized his revised brainstormed list into an outline (Figure 2.3). There is no one right way to get started. If you are not sure which way works best for you, experiment with a few techniques, as Reynolds did.

Drafting

If you have done your planning carefully, you will find it easier to start your first draft. When you draft, you convert the words and phrases from your outlines, brainstormed lists, or clustered groups into paragraphs. Think of your earlier jottings as the material out of which the basic building blocks (paragraphs) of your drafts will come. During drafting, as elsewhere in the writing process, you will see some overlap as you look back over your lists or outlines to create your draft(s).

Keep in mind that drafting is still preliminary to the creation of your final copy. Don't expect to wind up with a polished, complete version of your paper after working on only one draft. In most cases, you will have to work through many drafts, but each draft should be less rough and more acceptable than the preceding one.

Function of Drafting

The purpose of drafting is to get your main points down in the most logical order for your readers. The most common reader complaint is that key information is hard to find. Effective drafting means making big decisions about (1) what you say and (2) where you say it. Accordingly, during drafting you need to pay special attention to the content and organization of your work.

Key Questions to Ask as You Draft

As you work on your drafts, ask yourself the following questions about your content and organization.

- Is this the best way to start?
- Am I giving my readers too much or too little information?
- Is my information too technical for my audience?
- Does this point belong where I have it, or would it more logically follow or precede something else?
- Is this point necessary and relevant?

FIGURE 2.3   Gordon Reynolds's early outline after revising his brainstormed list.

I. Convenience

    A. One cable hookup like any other printer

    B. Easy to install and operate

    C. Can be configured easily through our operating system

    D. Can handle the output for the entire office

    E. Excellent print and color quality

    F. Uses variety of paper stocks

    G. Less noise

II. Time/Efficiency

    A. Fast – 15 to 21 pages per minute

    B. Can print envelopes, labels

    C. Greater graphics capability – 75 scalable true type fonts

    D. 50,000-page monthly duty cycle means less maintenance

III. Money

    A. Save on service calls

    B. Can handle the workload of the entire office

    C. Save cost of color copies by making our own

    D. Will be compatible with future upgrades of the office PCs

- Am I repeating myself?
- Have I contradicted myself?
- Have I ended appropriately for my audience?

To answer those questions successfully, you may have to continue researching your topic and reexamining your audience's needs. But in the process new and even better ideas will come to you, and ideas that you once thought were essential may in time appear unworkable or unnecessary.

TECH NOTE

Drafting on Your Computer

When you draft your document, try to get some writing on the monitor quickly. A word processing program keeps pace with the speed of your thought process and allows you to concentrate on your writing rather than on the more technical aspects of creating a document. Do not stop to check spelling or punctuation; you can return to those tasks later. If you run into a snag on any draft, do not lose momentum by stopping to fix it. Simply flag items to which you want to return or about which you need more information.

You can also insert notes to yourself to supply information, qualification, or even documentation, reminding you that your draft is a document in the making.

Be prepared to create, expand, delete, move, save, and retrieve different drafts or even portions of one or more of your drafts. That way you can go back to see which version (of a draft) you like best or what might be salvaged from one version and incorporated into another. For that reason, it is best to use the save command after every page or at regular intervals of every two to three minutes. When you save drafts (or revisions), your file names should always clearly reflect their contents (e.g., Draft 1, Works Cited).

Print a draft as often as you like to see what it looks like; that way, you will get a sense of work being done. Drafting at your terminal gives you maximum flexibility and reduces the risk of mistakes and omissions. During drafting some writers will go back and forth between hard copy and the text on the screen.

Guidelines for Successful Drafting

Following are some suggestions to help your drafting go more smoothly and efficiently.

- Select a comfortable place to write. Use a pen, typewriter, PC, or laptop computer—whatever gives you the most satisfying feeling about creating. Take another look at Figure 1.6 to see proper posture.
- In an early draft, write the easiest part first, regardless of where in the paper it may finally end up. Some writers feel more comfortable drafting the body (or middle) of their work first.
- As you work on a later draft, write straight through. Do not worry about spelling, punctuation, or the way a word or sentence sounds. Save those concerns for later stages.
- Allow enough time between drafts so you can evaluate your work with fresh eyes and a clear mind.
- Get frequent outside opinions. Show, e-mail, or fax a draft to a fellow student, a co-worker, or maybe an employer for comment. A new pair of eyes will see things you missed.
- Start considering what visuals might enhance the quality of your work and where they might best be positioned.

Case Study: Drafting

Figure 2.4 shows one of the several drafts Gordon Reynolds prepared. Because he wisely recognized that his outline was not final, he continued to work on it during the drafting stage. Note that he has added an introduction and a conclusion, which were not part of his outline (Figure 2.3). Those parts are necessary to the report if Reynolds is to convince Melissa Hill to purchase a laser printer. Even so, Reynolds recognized that his draft was still not ready for his boss to see, so he showed it to a co-worker for suggestions.

From discussions with his co-worker and after further work on his draft, Reynolds realized that he had placed one of the most important considerations for his audience (savings) last. In his final version, shown in Figure 2.5 (pp. 50–51), he moved that section to the beginning of his memo because he realized that Melissa Hill would be most concerned about costs. Reynolds thus paid attention to his audience's priorities and needs.

He also added headings and bulleted lists to help his reader find information. The design of his earlier draft in Figure 2.4 did not assist his readers in finding information quickly or reflect a convincing organizational plan.

Revising

Revision is an essential stage in the writing process. It requires more than giving your work one more quick glance. Do not be tempted to skip the revision stage just because you have written the required number of words or sections or because you think you have put in too much time already. Revision is done *after* you produce a draft that you think conveys the appropriate message for your audience. The quality of your letter or report depends on the revisions you make now.

FIGURE 2.4   Intermediate draft of Gordon Reynolds's report.

To: Melissa Hill, Office Manager
From: Gordon Reynolds
Date: September 4, 2000
Subject: Improving Efficiency

As you requested, I have been researching what to do about improving office efficiency and customer relations. The most beneficial and immediate solution I have found so far is to replace our old laser printers with a new color laser printer. More and more businesses today have color printers, and these printers are fast becoming a part of many companies' information technology systems. With the advances in printer technology in the past few years, it makes good sense to replace our Tech World printers with one Baxter Color Laser Jet GTP. Today, color laser printers are faster, quieter, and more efficient than ever.

A color laser printer is easy to set up and operates just like our old printers and can be configured through our operating system. Among the models of color laser printers I have seen, most are about the same size as one of our old printers. It should be easy, too, for our staff to learn to operate the new color laser printer. Because a color laser printer would be faster and quieter, one could easily handle the output of our entire office. Furthermore, the print and color quality and the fact that it uses a variety of paper would make it just that much more convenient. From several demonstrations I have seen, I am truly impressed.

A color laser printer is fast and efficient, printing 21 color pages a minute with a high-quality resolution of 1200 dpi for monochrome and color. It operates with little or no noise. A color laser printer is also more versatile because it can print on different types of paper and even envelopes. It would be so much easier for the large mailings we routinely have just before the holidays.

Continued

FIGURE 2.4   (Continued)

Page 2

With 75 scalable type fonts, we can produce top-quality color documents in-house, saving us the trouble of finding an outside contractor to provide color copies. And finally, with a 50,000-page monthly duty cycle, a color laser printer would be low-maintenance.

The greatest benefit to our company is the money a laser printer will save. Generally speaking, a laser printer runs about $1200 to $1300, depending on the model. The Baxter Color Laser Jet GTP can be purchased direct from USA Computers for $1239 plus shipping and handling, not much more than a 400-MHz desktop computer. Because a color laser printer can go longer without maintenance, we can save on service calls. Also, USA Computers offers a two-year warranty. A new color laser printer will also be compatible with future upgrades of our PCs, should we decide to do so.

Allow Enough Time to Revise

Like planning or drafting, revision is not done well in one big push. It evolves over a period of time. Because revision is so important, allow yourself enough time to do it carefully.

- Avoid drafting and revising in one sitting. If possible, wait at least a day before you start to revise. (In the busy work world, waiting a couple of hours may suffice.)
- Ask a co-worker or friend familiar with your topic to comment on your work, as Gordon Reynolds did.
- Plan to read your revised work more than once.

Revision Is Rethinking

When you revise, you resee, rethink, and reconsider your entire document. You ask questions about the major issues of content, organization, and tone. Revision involves going back and repeating earlier steps in the writing process. You can also get help reseeing from colleagues through a collaborative effort (see Chapter 3).

When effective writers revise their work, they go through their drafts several times to check for content, organization, and tone. Note the extent of changes Gordon Reynolds made between his draft in Figure 2.4 and the final, revised copy of his memo in Figure 2.5.

FIGURE 2.5   Final copy of Gordon Reynolds's report.

To: Melissa Hill, Office Manager
From: Gordon Reynolds
Date: September 4, 2000
Subject: Purchasing a New Color Laser Printer

As you requested, I have investigated some ways to improve our office efficiency and customer relations. The best solution I have found is to replace our two TechWorld laser printers with a new-generation color laser printer. With advances in printer technology in the past few years (I enclose a copy of a review article "Share and Share A Lot" from *Computer World Magazine* [June 2000]: 121-29), it makes good business sense to replace our outmoded laser printers with a **Baxter Color Laser Jet GTP**. Color printers are economical, more efficient and will significantly improve the design of our documents.

Cost
The greatest benefit of a color laser printer is the money it will save us. We can purchase it from USA Computers for $1239 plus shipping and handling, totalling $1312. Purchasing one would allow us to recoup that cost easily in just a month or two because we would

- have less maintenance, saving at least $200 per month in service calls
- receive a two-year warranty with guarenteed overnight service, which should decrease down time
- save an additional $50 to $100 each month by not having to go outside the office for color copies
- be able to trade in old laser printers for $275 each
- can be used for all in-house documents, reports, and monthly newsletters, saving us the trouble and expense of using an outside contractor for color copying

Continued

FIGURE 2.5 (Continued)

Page 2

Efficiency
A color laser printer would be easy to set up and is compatible with our current computer system. Other key features include

- prints twice as fast as our laser printers and built-in auto duplex capability
- expanded paper capacity (500 sheets)
- enhanced memory to manage multiple jobs easily, accepting and printing them in the order sent
- ability to print 21 high-resolution color pages per minute with little or no noise
- ability to handle the output of our entire office, including our large quarterly mailings

Quality
The **Baxter Color Laser Jet** prints high-quality documents because it

- has 1200 dpi with monochrome and color resolution
- exhibits same color density on the 1000th copy as on the first; solid ink sticks ensure no toner spills
- produces near-photographic-quality graphics
- functions with different paper stocks and types (ledger or letterhead)
- can print envelopes, labels
- offers 75 scalable type fonts

I recommend that we purchase a **Baxter Color Laser Jet GTP** from USA Computers. It will unquestionably save us money, improve office efficiency, and help us to project a much more professional corporate image in brilliant color.

TECH NOTE

Revising On-Line

Revising on-line, you can expect to add, delete, qualify, and rearrange words, sentences, and paragraphs, or even transform the appearance of your material. Experimenting with a number of different versions of your work is at the heart of the revision process. Just remember to save what you have done each time.

At the revision stage, too, insert visuals exactly where you want them and format your document to include headings, different fonts, and other design elements (see Chapter 11).

Various software packages allow you to split your monitor screen into two or four parts (windows) to view different versions of a text or several pages of the text simultaneously. Or you can view one page while working on another. Moreover, you can go to the print mode and enter "print preview" to see each page layout. That way you can judge if your document falls under or exceeds the page limits your boss or instructor has set for you. From the broader perspective of your overall document, you will be able to make global revisions, rather than just line changes.

Revision means asking again the questions you have already asked and answered during the planning and drafting stages. In the process you will discover gaps to fill, points to change, and errors to correct in your draft. Revision gives you a second (or third or fourth) chance to get things right for your audience and to clarify your purpose in writing to them.

Don't Forget Your Audience

As you revise your draft to make it better, ask the same questions about your audience that we studied in Chapter 1 (pp. 8–10). Once more you will inspect your draft to make sure that it meets your audience's priorities. Your audience's reason for reading your work will determine the three big issues you should be concerned with when you revise: content, organization, and tone.

Key Questions to Ask as You Revise

Content

1. Is it accurate? Are my facts (figures, names, dates, costs, references, statistics) correct?
2. Is it relevant for my audience and purpose? Have I included information that is unnecessary, too technical, not appropriate? Does every detail belong in this communication with my readers?
3. Have I included sufficient information for my readers' purpose? Have I given enough evidence to explain things adequately and to persuade my readers? (Too

little information will make readers skeptical about what you are describing or proposing, so they may question your conclusions.) Have I left anything out? Do I need to clarify or explain more for my readers' purpose?

Organization

1. Is the arrangement of my information clear and straightforward? Is it easy to follow?
2. Have I clearly identified my main points and shown my readers why those points are important?
3. Is everything proportionate to my purpose and my readers' needs, or have I spent too much (or too little) effort on one section? Do I repeat myself? What can be cut?
4. Is everything in the right, most effective order? Do I need to regroup sections or paragraphs of my document? Should anything be switched or moved closer to the beginning or the end of my document?
5. Have I grouped related items in the same part of my report or letter, or have I scattered details that really need to appear together in one paragraph or section?
6. Is my work logical? Do my conclusions follow from the evidence I present? Are my recommendations valid and based on the conclusions I draw?

Tone

1. How do I sound to my readers—professional and sincere, or arrogant and unreliable? What attitude do my words or expressions convey?
2. How will my readers think I perceive them? Will they know I believe they are honest and intelligent, or have I used words and details that seem to question their judgments, professionalism, or intelligence?

Case Study: The Revision Process

Mary Fonseca, an employee at Seacoast Labs, was asked by her supervisor to prepare a short report for the general public on the lab's most recent experiments. One of her later drafts begins with the paragraphs in Figure 2.6.

As Fonseca worked on her ideas and thought about her audience's needs, she realized that the opening section of her draft presented some problems that she would need to resolve. As she started to revise, she asked herself questions like those above about the content, order, and tone of her work. Answering these questions in turn led her to make a number of major changes that often occur at the revision stage.

Putting Ideas in Order

Fonseca knew that her first paragraph lacked focus. It was not carefully organized, jumping back and forth between drag on a ship and drag on an airplane. Consequently, she decided to delete information about planes, especially since Seacoast

FIGURE 2.6   Opening paragraphs of Mary Fonseca's draft.

> Drag is an important concept in the world of science and technology. It has many implications. Drag occurs when a ship moves through the water and eddies build up. Ships on the high seas have to fight the eddies, which results in drag. In the same way, an airplane has to fight the winds at various altitudes at which it flies; these winds are very forceful, moving at many knots per hour. All these forces of nature are around us. Sometimes we can feel them, too. We get tired walking against a strong wind. The eddies around a ship are the same thing. These eddies form various barriers around the ship's hull. They come from a combination of different molecules around the ship's hull and exert quite a force. Both types of molecules pull against the ship. This is where the eddies come in.
>
> Scientists at Seacoast Labs are concerned about drag. Dr. Karen Runnels, who joined Seacoast about three years ago, is the chief investigator. She and her team of highly qualified experts have constructed some fascinating multilevel water tunnels. These tunnels should be useful to ship owners. Drag wastes a ship's fuel.

Labs did not work in that area. She also decided that the information on the effect of drag on a ship was so important that it deserved a separate paragraph. So she removed the details on that topic from the long first paragraph and started to develop them separately. In the process, she discovered that her explanation of molecules, eddies, and drag was unclear; it needed to be reorganized and made more reader friendly.

Often additional ideas come to you even as you revise your work. As Fonseca continued reading about the topic, she came across an interesting analogy that she felt was appropriate for her audience, so she included it. Working on that explanation, she had to decide how to organize her information. After some deliberation, she decided to follow a cause-and-effect pattern—drag is the cause and the effect is how it slows a ship.

Fonseca was then left with the job of finding an opening for her short report. She wanted to start with something that would both introduce the topic and encourage her layperson audience to continue reading.

Buried in the original paragraph from her last draft was an idea she found worth developing—that we cannot always *see* the forces of nature, but we can *feel* them. So rather than beginning with a wooden statement about the scientific concept of drag (which did not have to be scientifically defined for her general audience), Fonseca revised her draft to start with the simple but visual example about an individual walking against the wind. Through continued revisions she created two useful, carefully organized paragraphs out of the one long opening paragraph of her last draft.

Keeping Readers in Mind

Throughout the revision process Fonseca kept her readers' needs in mind. Working on her original second paragraph, she realized that it said very little about the lab's experiments with drag. In fact, what she had initially written might even confuse readers about how and why the tunnels were useful. Once Fonseca put herself in her readers' place, however, she asked the exact question that helped her to develop the paragraph: "What specifically is Seacoast Labs doing to reduce drag?"

Generating a precise starting sentence from that question made all the difference. Focusing now on the lab's "ways to reduce drag on ships," Fonseca chose specific examples about experiments at Seacoast. Instead of interesting but unnecessary information (such as that Dr. Runnels has been at the lab for three years), Fonseca sought concrete illustrations and explained their significance to her audience. She also determined that the last sentence in her original second paragraph did not belong in the new revised paragraph on experiments. The cost of drag was much more appropriately placed in her new opening paragraph.

Choosing the Right Format/Design for the Message

Concerned about the design of her revised document, Fonseca recognized that though it was better written than her draft, it looked no different. Her page appeared crowded and uninviting and offered no signposts to direct her readers. Accordingly, she added two headings and double-spaced the text. The result was a much more professional-looking document.

Fonseca's final revision is shown in Figure 2.7. Through revising, she transformed two poorly organized and incomplete paragraphs into three carefully separated yet logically connected paragraphs.

Editing

Editing means getting the final copy ready for your audience. This last stage in the writing process might be compared to detailing an automobile—the preparation a dealer goes through to ready a new car for prospective buyers. Editing is done only after you are completely satisfied that you have made all the big decisions about content and organization—that you have said what you wanted to, where and how you intended, for your audience.

When you edit, you will check your work for

- sentences
- word choices
- punctuation
- spelling
- grammar and usage

FIGURE 2.7   A revision of Mary Fonseca's draft in Figure 2.6.

What is drag?

We cannot see or hear many of the forces around us, but we can certainly detect their presence. Walking or running into a strong wind, for example, requires a great deal of effort and often quickly leaves us feeling tired. When a ship sails through the water, it also experiences these opposing sources known as **drag**. Overcoming drag causes a ship to reduce its energy efficiency, which leads to higher fuel costs.

How drag works

It is not easy for a ship to fight drag. As the ship moves through the water, it drags the water molecules around its hull at the same rate the ship is moving. Because of the cohesive force of those molecules, other water molecules immediately outside the ship's path get pulled into its way. All the molecules become tangled rather than simply sliding past each other. The result is an eddy, or small circling burst of water around the ship's hull, which intensifies the drag. Dr. Charles Hester, a noted engineer, explains it using an analogy: "When you put a spoon in honey and pull it out, half the honey comes out with the spoon. That's what is happening to ships. The ship is moving and at the same time dragging the ocean with it."

At Seacoast Labs, scientists are working to find ways to reduce drag on ships. Dr. Karen Runnels, the principal investigator, and a team of researchers have constructed water tunnels to simulate the movement of ships at sea. The drag a ship encounters is measured from the tiny air bubbles emitted in the water tunnel. Dr. Runnels's team has also developed the use of polymers, or long carbon chain molecules, to reduce drag. The polymers act like a slimy coating for the ship's hull to help it glide through the water more easily. When asbestos fibers were added to the polymer solutions, the investigators measured a 90 percent reduction in drag. The team has also experimented with an external pump attached to the hull of a ship, which pushes the water away from a ship's path.

As with revising, don't skip or rush through the editing process, thinking that once your ideas are down, your work is done. Your style, punctuation, spelling, and grammar matter a great deal to your readers. If your work is hard to read or contains mistakes in spelling or punctuation, your readers will think that your ideas, your research, and your organization are also faulty.

The following sections will help you understand what to look for when you edit your sentences and words. The appendix, "A Writer's Brief Guide to Paragraphs, Sentences, and Words" (pp. 671–687), contains helpful suggestions on correct spelling and punctuation. You can also benefit from various style guides and computer software programs such as spell-checkers.

TECH NOTE

On-Line Editing

Numerous software programs make editing on-line efficient and easy. These programs flag errors in spelling, punctuation, usage, word choice, and sentence length (readability). Use your spell-checker to identify and correct misspelled words. If there are several words that you frequently misspell, add them to your on-line dictionary. It will be worth the time and effort. Also, include in your dictionary any proper names, brand names, technical terms, or concepts that you use often.

Other programs will, by using the search command, help you eliminate wordiness by deleting excessive words (for example, *due to the fact that*) or by highlighting overused or misused words and suggesting alternatives.

When you edit on-line, be careful that you do not focus only on the lines you can see on the screen and neglect the larger organization of your document. Scroll or print out the text to check for editing problems throughout the document or to observe how a change in one place affects (contradicts, duplicates, weakens) something earlier or later.

When you finish editing, always make a back-up and a hard copy. Your document could be lost because of a power surge, hard disk crash, or problems retrieving the file at a later date.

Editing Guidelines for Writing Lean and Clear Sentences

Here are three of the most frequent complaints readers voice about poorly edited writing in the world of work:

- The sentences are too long. I could not follow the writer's meaning.
- The sentences are too complex. I could not understand what the writer meant the first time I read the work; I had to reread it several times.

- The sentences are unclear. Even after I reread them, I am not sure I understood the writer's message.

Wordy, unclear sentences frustrate readers and waste their time. Writing clear, readable sentences is not always easy. It takes effort, but the time you spend editing will pay off in rich dividends for you and your readers.

If you follow the nine guidelines below during the editing phase of your work, you will be better able to write easy-to-read—lean and clear—sentences. As you study these guidelines, keep in mind that readability depends on

- the length of your sentences
- the order in which you list information
- the way in which you signal the relationships among your sentences

1. Avoid Needlessly Complex or Lengthy Sentences

How long should a sentence be? Most readers have very little trouble with sentences ranging from eight to fifteen words. On the other hand, readers find sentences over twenty words much more difficult. As a general rule keep your sentences under eighteen words. The longer your sentence is, the more difficult it will be to understand.

Do not pile one clause on another. Instead, edit one overly long sentence into two or even three more manageable ones.

> **Too long:** The planning committee decided that the awards banquet should be held on May 15 at 6:30, since the other two dates (May 7 and May 22) suggested by the hospitality committee conflict with local sports events, even though one of those events could be changed to fit our needs.
>
> **Edited for easier reading:** The planning committee has decided to hold the awards banquet on May 15 at 6:30. The other dates suggested by the hospitality committee—May 7 and May 22—conflict with two local sports events. Although the date of one of those sports events could be changed, the planning committee still believes that May 15 is our best choice.

2. Combine Short, Choppy Sentences

Don't shorten long, complex sentences only to turn them into choppy, simplistic ones. A memo or letter written exclusively in short, staccato sentences sounds immature and makes for boring reading.

Effective editing blends short sentences with longer ones to achieve variety and to reflect logical relationships. For example, a sentence containing a subordinate clause followed by an independent clause may signal a cause-to-effect relationship to readers. A sentence with a series of parallel independent clauses points to the equality of the ideas spelled out in those clauses. A short sentence at the end of a paragraph can emphatically summarize a main idea.

When you find yourself looking at a series of short, blunt sentences, as in the following example, combine them where possible and use connective words similar to those italicized in the edited version.

TECH NOTE

Computers as Writing Tools

The computer will help you increase your writing productivity, improve your writing skills, and design more professional-looking documents. But it will not do your writing and thinking for you. Keep the following points in mind:

- A software package may help you organize your ideas, but *you* must first do research to discover what ideas are relevant and convincing for your audience.
- The computer enables you to produce more writing, but, again, *you* are the one who must select the right words with appropriate tone and put them into readable sentences and logically organized paragraphs.
- A computer cannot tell you what points will please or alienate your audience. *You* must decide what must be changed, modified, retained, or moved, and why and how.
- A software program can tell you your sentences are too long, but changing every one into a short (ten-word) statement will make your work choppy and less pleasing to read.
- Finally, never be lulled into thinking that a clear, professionally printed document will hide or make up for incorrect grammar, irrelevant content, or poor organization.

Your computer is an efficient writing tool, not a substitute writer for you.

Choppy: Medical transcriptionists have many responsibilities. Their responsibilities are important. They must be familiar with medical terminology. They must listen to dictation. Sometimes physicians talk very fast. Then the transcriptionist must be quick to transcribe what is heard. Words could be missed. Transcriptionists must also prepare final reports. This will take a great deal of time and concentration. These reports are copied and stored properly for reference.

Edited: Medical transcriptionists have many important responsibilities. *These* include transcribing physicians' orders using correct medical terminology. *When* physicians talk rapidly, transcriptionists have to keyboard accurately *so* that no words are omitted. *Among the most demanding* of their duties are preparing final transcriptions *and then* making and storing those copies properly for future reference.

3. Edit Sentences to Tell Who Does What to Whom or What

The clearest sentence pattern in English is the subject-verb-object (s-v-o) pattern.

     S   V   O

Sue mowed the grass.

     S   V   O

Our Web site contains a link to key training software programs.

Readers find this pattern easiest to understand because it provides direct and specific information about the action. Hard-to-read sentences obscure or scramble information about the subject, the verb, or the object. Unedited sentences bury the subject in prepositional phrases (see the appendix, p. 674) in the middle or the end of the sentence, smother the verb in phrases, or allow an object to act like a subject.

Not all clear sentences, however, follow the subject-verb-object pattern. You might use a subordinate clause in addition to the subject, verb, and object in the independent clause.

To edit your sentences to tell readers clearly what's going on, follow these steps.

a. Identify the subject—the person, place, or concept that controls the main action. (Avoid using vague words such as *factors, conditions, processes,* or *elements* for subjects.)
b. Select an action-packed verb that shows what the subject does.
c. Specify the object that is acted upon by the real subject through the verb.

In the following unedited sentences, subjects are hidden in the middle rather than being placed in the most crucial subject position.

Unclear: An assessment of the market helped our company design its new food blender. (The main action is *designing.* Who did it?)
  Edited: Our company designed its new food blender by assessing the market.

Unclear: The control of the ceiling limits of glycidyl ethers on the part of the employers for the optimum safety of workers in the workplace is necessary. (Who is responsible for taking action? What action must they take? For whom is such action taken?)
  Edited: For the workers' safety, employers must control the ceiling limits of glycidyl ethers.

4. Arrange Information Logically Within Sentences

The order in which you list information in a sentence can help or hinder a reader in understanding your message. You cannot list details in random order. Edit your sentences to make sure readers receive information in the most logical, helpful sequence. The content of the sentence will help you choose the best pattern: chronological, cause to effect, action to reaction, and the like.

Not Logical: They shut off the computer once they finish with their program.
    Edited: Once they finish their program, they shut off the computer. (Since finishing the program precedes shutting the computer off, give readers the information in that order.)

5. Use Strong, Active Verbs Rather Than Verb Phrases with Verbs Disguised as Nouns

In trying to sound important, many bureaucratic writers avoid using simple, graphic verbs. Instead, these writers add a suffix *(-ation, -ance, -ment, -ence)* to a direct verb *(determine)* to make a noun *(determination)* and then couple the new noun with *make, provide,* or *work* to produce a weak verb phrase (for example, *provide maintenance of* instead of *maintain, work in cooperation with* instead of *cooperate).* Such verb phrases imprison the active verb inside a noun format and slow a reader down.

Note how the edited versions below rewrite weak verb phrases.

Weak: The officer made an assessment of the damages the storm had caused.
Strong: The officer assessed the damage the storm had caused.

Weak: The city provided the employment of two work crews to assist the strengthening of the dam.
Strong: The city employed two work crews to strengthen the dam.

6. Avoid Piling Modifiers in Front of a Noun

It can be hard for readers to grasp your message when you string a series of modifiers in front of a noun. Modifiers are subordinate units (see the appendix, pp. 671–687) that clarify and qualify a noun. Putting too many of them in the reader's path to the noun will confuse the reader, who cannot decipher how one modifier relates to another modifier or to the noun. To avoid that problem, edit the sentence to place some of the modifiers in prepositional phrases after or before the nouns they modify.

Crowded: The ordinance contract number vehicle identification plate had to be checked against inventory numbers.
Readable: The ordinance contract number on the vehicle identification plate had to be checked against the inventory numbers.

Crowded: The vibration noise control heat pump condenser quieter can make your customer happier.
Readable: The quieter on the condenser for the heat pump will make your customer happier by controlling noise and vibrations.

7. Replace a Wordy Phrase or Clause with a One- or Two-Word Synonym

Wordy: The college has parking zones for different areas for people living on campus as well as for those who do not live on campus and who commute to school.
Edited: The college has different parking zones for resident and commuter students. (Twenty words of the original sentence—everything after "areas for"—have been reduced to four words: "resident and commuter students.")

8. Combine Sentences Beginning with the Same Subject or Ending with an Object That Becomes the Subject of the Next Sentence

Wordy: I asked the inspector if she were going to visit the plant this afternoon. I also asked her if she would come alone.
Edited: I asked the inspector if she were going to visit the plant alone this afternoon.

Wordy: Homeowners want to buy low-maintenance bushes. These low-maintenance bushes include the ever-popular holly and boxwood varieties. These bushes are also inexpensive.

Edited: Homeowners want to buy such low-maintenance and inexpensive bushes as holly and boxwood. (This revision combines three sentences into one, condenses twenty-four words into fourteen, and joins three related thoughts.)

9. Avoid Unnecessary That/Which Clauses

That/which clauses using some form of the verb *to be (is, are, were, was)* are infamous for adding words but not meaning to your sentences. They are popular with bureaucratic writers, who like to draw out an idea beyond the number of words needed. Edit them by eliminating *that/which* clauses or using an adjective to represent the clause.

Wordy: The pain medication that was prescribed by the doctor was very helpful to her father.

Edited: The pain medication prescribed by the doctor helped her father. (Note how the editing reduces "was helpful to" to "helped" to further save words and time.)

Wordy: The organizational plan that was approved last week contains a number of points, all of which are considered to be especially important for new employees.

Edited: The organizational plan approved last week contains important points for new employees.

Editing Guidelines for Cutting Out Unnecessary Words

Too many people in business and industry think the more words, the better. Nothing could be more self-defeating. Your readers are busy; unnecessary words slow them down. Make every word work. A word that gives no meaning just takes up space. Cut out any words you can from your sentences. If the sentence still makes sense and reads correctly, you have eliminated wordiness.

The phrases on the left should be replaced with the precise words on the right.

Wordy	Concisely Edited
at a slow rate	slowly
at an early date	early
at the point where	where
at this point in time	now
be in agreement with	agree
bring to a conclusion	conclude, end
bring together	combine, join
by means of	with
come to terms with	agree, accept
due to the fact that	because
express an opinion that	believe
feel quite certain about	believe
for the length of time that	while
for the period of	for
for the purpose of	to

Wordy	Concisely Edited
in an effort to	to
in such a manner that	so
in the area / case / field of	in
in the event that	if
in the neighborhood of	approximately
look something like	resemble
serve the function of	function as
show a tendency to	tend
take into consideration	consider
take under advisement	consider
take place in such a manner	occur
with reference to	regarding, about
with the result that	so

Another kind of wordiness comes from using redundant expressions. Being redundant means that you say the same thing a second time, in different words. "Fellow colleague," "component parts," "corrosive acid," and "free gift" are phrases that contain this kind of double speech; a fellow *is* a colleague, a component *is* a part, acid *is* corrosive, and a gift *is* free. Redundant expressions are uneconomical and are often clichés. The suggested changes on the right are preferable to the redundant phrases on the left.

Redundant	Concise
absolutely essential	essential
advance reservations	reservations
basic necessities	necessities, needs
close proximity	proximity, nearness
each and every	each, every, all
end result	result
eradicate completely	eradicate
exposed opening	opening
fair and just	fair
final conclusions/final outcome	conclusions/outcome
first and foremost	first
full and complete	full, complete
grand total	total
null and void	void
passing fad	fad
personal opinion	opinion
prerecorded	recorded
over and done with	over
tried and true	tried, proven

Watch for repetitious words, phrases, or clauses within a sentence. Sometimes one sentence or one part of a sentence needlessly duplicates another.

Redundant: The post office hires part-time help, especially around the holidays, to handle the large amounts of mail at Christmas time.

Edited: The post office often hires part-time help to handle the large amounts of mail at Christmas time. ("Especially around the holidays" means the same thing as "at Christmas time.")

Redundant: The fermenting activity of yeast is due to an enzyme called zymase. This enzyme produces chemical changes in yeast.

Edited: The fermenting activity of yeast is due to an enzyme called zymase. (The second sentence says vaguely what the first sentence says precisely; delete it.)

Redundant: To provide more room for employees' cars, the security department is studying ways to expand the employees' parking lot.

Edited: The security department is studying ways to expand the employees' parking lot. (Since the first phrase says nothing that the reader does not know from the independent clause, cut it.)

Adding a prepositional phrase can sometimes contribute to redundancy. The italicized words below are redundant because of the unnecessary qualification they impose on the word they modify. Be on the lookout for the italicized phrases and delete them.

audible *to the ear*	hard *to the touch*
bitter *in taste*	honest *in character*
fly *through the air*	light *in weight*
orange *in color*	soft *in texture*
rectangular *in shape*	tall *in height*
second *in sequence*	twenty *in number*
short *in duration*	visible *to the eye*

Certain combinations of verbs and adverbs are also redundant. Again, the italicized words below should be deleted.

advance *forward*	lift *up*
burn *up*	merge *together*
cancel *out*	open *up*
circle *around*	plan *ahead*
commute *back and forth*	prove *conclusively*
combine *together*	refer *back*
continue *on*	repeat *again*
drop *down*	reply *back*
funnel *through*	revert *back*
join *together*	write *down*

Figure 2.8 shows an e-mail that Trudy Wallace wants to send to her boss about installing cellular phones in the company cars. Wallace attempted to get her ideas down

FIGURE 2.8   Wordy, unedited e-mail.

Subject: **Installing cellular phones**
Date: 5/15/2001 2:45PM Eastern Standard Time
From: twallace@transtech.org (Trudy Wallace)
To: lchadwick@transtech.org (Lee Chadwick)

Due to the amount of time our sales force spends traveling the roads each
day, it strikes me as beneficial to look into the distinct possibility of installing
cellular car phones in our company cars. Such an installation would benefit
our sales force in a variety of multiple ways. The sales force could increase
their efficiency and morale with the installation of these car phones. With the
aid of a cellular phone we could bring together our customers and our sales
force a lot easier. Rather than wasting an amount of time in the neighborhood
of 40 to 50 minutes each day tracking down phones on the road, our
salespeople could have a shortened period of time to respond using their
cellular phones in their cars. The response rate of returning a call could be
markedly reduced and dropped down. Moreover, by having cellular phones
in their cars salespeople would minimize the problems of returning calls to
people and then finding out they are out and then having to call them back. It
is difficult to catch people this way. Cellular phones would increase both the
convenience and the ease by which we operate our business. I think it would
be absolutely essential to the ongoing operation of our company's business
today to respond fully and completely to the possibility such a proposal
affords us. It would therefore appear safe to conclude that with reference
to the issue of cellular phones that every means at our disposal should be
brought to bear on including such phones in our company cars.

without worrying about finding the most concise and precise words. Her unedited
work is bloated with unnecessary words, expendable phrases, and repetitious ideas.

After careful editing, Wallace was able to streamline her e-mail to Lee Chadwick and eliminate the wordiness. Note how, in Figure 2.9, she pruned wordy
expressions and combined sentences to cut out duplication. The revised version is
only 102 words, as opposed to 266 words in the draft. Not only has Wallace shortened her message, she has made it easier to read.

Editing Guidelines to Eliminate Sexist Language

Editing involves far more than just making sure your sentences are readable and free
from wordiness. It also reflects your professional style—how you see and characterize the world of work and the individuals in it, not to mention how you want

FIGURE 2.9   The e-mail in Figure 2.8 edited for conciseness.

Subject:	**Installing cellular phones**
Date:	5/15/2001 3:15 PM Eastern Standard Time
From:	twallace@transtech.org (Trudy Wallace)
To:	lchadwick@transtech.org (Lee Chadwick)

Because our salespeople spend so much time on the road, I think we should install cellular phones to increase employee efficiency and improve morale. Cellular phones would help our salespeople communicate with their clients a lot easier and faster. They would not waste 40 to 50 minutes each day looking for phones to call clients. And they would save even more time by not having to play phone tag.

I think installing cellular phones is a wise investment, and so with your approval, I will obtain more information from suppliers to prepare a formal proposal to request bids.

your readers to see you. Your words should reflect a high degree of ethics and honesty, free from bias and offense. Prejudice has no place in business and technical writing or in any other type of writing or speaking.

Sexist language offers a distorted view of our society and discriminates in favor of one sex at the expense of another, usually women. Accordingly, you should avoid sexist language for a variety of reasons:

- You will offend and demean female readers by depriving them of their equal rights.
- You run the risk of readers branding you as sexist and biased.
- You decrease the effectiveness and persuasiveness of any points you are trying to make.
- You will cost your company business.

To avoid sounding prejudiced, eliminate sexist terms and attitudes as you edit your work. Escape displaying gender bias by using inclusive language for women and men alike.

Sexist language unfairly assigns responsibilities, jobs, or titles to individuals on the basis of sex. It is often based on sexist stereotypes that depict men as superior to women. For example, calling politicians *city fathers* or *favorite sons* follows the stereotypical picture of seeing politicians as male. Such phrases discriminate against women who do or could hold public office at all levels of government. Not all bosses are male, either.

Sexist language also prejudiciously labels some professions as masculine and others as feminine. For example, sexist phrases assume engineers, physicians, and pilots are male (*he, his,* and *him* are often linked with these professions in sexist descriptions) while social workers, nurses, and secretaries are female (*she, her*), although members of both sexes work in those professions. Sexist language also wrongly points out gender identities when such roles do not seem to follow biased expectations—*lady lawyer, male nurse, female surgeon,* or *female astronaut.* Such offensive distinctions reflect prejudiced attitudes that you should eliminate from your writing. Using those phrases is just as sexist as saying, "There's a girl in our office who is as good at troubleshooting as a man."

Always prune the following sexist phrases: *every man for himself, gal Friday, little woman, lady of the house, masterpieces, the best man for the job, the weaker sex, woman's work, working wives,* and *young man on the way up.* Sexist terms will not only offend but also exclude many of the members of the audience you want to reach.

Ways to Avoid Sexist Language

1. Replace Sexist Words with Neutral Ones
Neutral words do *not* refer to a specific sex; they are genderless. The sexist words on the left in the following list can be replaced by the neutral nonsexist substitutes on the right.

Sexist	Neutral
actress	actor
alderman; assemblyman	representative
authoress	writer, author
businessman	businessperson
cameraman	photographer
chairman	chair, chairperson
congressman	representative
craftsman	skilled worker
divorcée	divorced person
fireman	firefighter
foreman	supervisor
freshman week	orientation week
housewife	homemaker
janitress	cleaning person
landlord, landlady	owner
maiden name	family name
mailman/postman	mail carrier
man-hours	work-hours
mankind	humanity, human beings
manmade	synthetic, artificial
manpower	strength, power
man to man	candidly
men	human beings, people
modern man	modern society
policeman	police officer

Sexist	Neutral
repairman	repair person
salesman	salesperson, clerk
spokesman	spokesperson
stewardess	flight attendant
woman's intuition	intuition
workman	worker

2. Watch Masculine Pronouns

Avoid using the masculine pronouns *(he, his, him)* when referring to a group that includes both men and women.

> *Every worker must submit his travel expenses by Monday.*

Workers may include women as well as men, and to assume that all workers are men is misleading and unfair to women. You can edit such sexist language in several ways.

a. Make the subject of your sentence plural and thus neutral.

> *Workers must submit their travel expenses by Monday.*

b. Replace the pronoun *his* with *the* or *a* or drop it altogether.

> *Every employee is to submit a work activity report by Monday.*
> *Every worker must submit travel expenses by Monday.*

c. Use *his or her* instead of *his.*

> *Every worker must submit his or her travel expenses by Monday.*

d. Reword the sentence using the passive voice.

> *All travel expenses must be submitted by Monday.*

Moreover, in some contexts exclusive use of the masculine pronoun might invite a lawsuit. For example, you would be violating federal employment laws prohibiting discrimination on the basis of sex if you wrote the following in a help-wanted advertisement for your company.

> *Each applicant must submit his transcript with his application. He must also supply three letters of recommendation from individuals familiar with his work.*

The language of that ad implies that only men can apply for the position.

3. Eliminate Sexist Salutations

Never use the following salutations when you are unsure of who your readers are:

- Dear Sir
- Gentlemen
- Dear Madam

Any woman in the audience will surely be offended by the first two greetings above and may also be unhappy with the pompous and obsolete *madam.* It is usually best to write to a specific individual, but if you cannot do that, direct your letter to a particular department or office: *Dear Warranty Department* or *Dear Selection Committee.*

Be careful, too, about using the titles *Miss, Mr.,* and *Mrs.* Sexist distinctions are unjust and insulting. It would be preferable to write *Dear Ms. McCarty* rather than *Dear Miss or Mrs. McCarty.* A woman's marital status should not be an issue. Try to find out if the person prefers *Ms.* to another courtesy title (e.g., Editor Hawkins, Supervisor Jones). If you are in doubt, write *Dear Barbara Hawkins.* Review p. 156 about the acceptable salutations in your letters.

4. Never Single Out a Person's Physical Appearance

> *The manager is a tall blonde who received her training at Mason Technical Institute.*

Such sexist physical references negatively draw attention to a woman's gender. Sexist writers would not describe a male manager that way.

✓ Revision Checklist

- ❑ Investigated the research, drafting, revising, and editing benefits available through home or work computer.
- ❑ Researched my topic carefully to obtain enough information to answer all my readers' questions. Used such appropriate means as library research, on-line data search, interviews, questionnaires, personal observations, or a combination of methods.
- ❑ Before writing, determined how much and what kind of information are needed to complete writing task.
- ❑ Spent enough time planning—brainstorming, outlining, clustering, or a combination of those techniques. Produced enough substantial material from which to shape a draft.
- ❑ Prepared enough drafts to decide on major points in message to readers. Made major changes and deletions if necessary in drafts.
- ❑ Revised drafts carefully to successfully answer reader questions about content, organization, and tone.
- ❑ Made time to edit work so that style is clear and concise and sentences are readable and varied. Checked words to make sure they are spelled correctly and appropriate for audience.
- ❑ Eliminated sexist language.

Exercises

1. Below is a writer's initial brainstormed list on stress in the workplace. Revise the brainstormed list, eliminating repetition and combining related items.

   leads to absenteeism
   high costs for compensation for stress-related illnesses

proper nutrition
numerous stress reduction techniques
good idea to conduct interviews to find out levels, causes, and extent of stress
    in the workplace
low morale caused by stress
higher insurance claims for employees' physical ailments
myth to see stress leading to greater productivity
various tapes used to teach relaxation
environmental factors—too hot? too cold?
teamwork intensifies stress
counseling
work overload
setting priorities
wellness campaign
savings per employee add up to $4,800 per year
skills to relax
learning to get along with co-workers
need for privacy
interpersonal communication
employee's need for clear policies on transfers, promotion
stress management workshops very successful in California
physical activity to relieve stress
affects management
breathing exercises

2. Prepare a suitable outline from your revised list in Exercise 1 for a report to a decision maker on the problems of stress in the workplace and the necessity of creating a stress management program.

3. From the revised brainstormed list in Exercise 1, write a short memo to a decision maker about how the problems of stress negatively affect workplace production.

4. Write a short report (2–3 pages) to the manager of the small company you work for to convince him or her to establish a system of flex time. Prepare an outline based on the clustered items in Figure 2.1 (p. 42). Add, delete, or rearrange anything in this clustered grouping to complete your outline. Submit your final outline along with your report to your instructor.

5. Compare the draft of Gordon Reynolds's report in Figure 2.4 (pp. 48–49) with the final copy of his report in Figure 2.5 (pp. 50–51). What kinds of changes did he make? Were they appropriate and effective for his audience and purpose? Why or why not?

6. Assume you have been asked to write a short report (similar to Gordon Reynolds's in Figure 2.5) to a decision maker (the manager of a business you work for or have worked for; the director of your campus union, library, or security force; a city official) about one of the following topics.
   a. computer software

    b. Internet resources
    c. security lighting
    d. food service
    e. insurance plans
    f. public transportation
    g. sporting events/activities
    h. training programs
    i. morale
    j. hiring more part-time student workers

Do some research and planning about one of those topics and the audience for whom it is intended by answering the following questions.

- What is my precise purpose in writing to my audience?
- What do I know about the topic?
- What information will my audience expect me to know?
- Where can I obtain relevant information about my topic to meet my audience's needs?

7. Using one or more of the planning strategies discussed in this chapter (clustering, brainstorming, outlining), generate a group of ideas for the topic you chose in Exercise 6. Work on your planning activities for about 15–20 minutes or until you have about 10–15 items. At this stage do not worry about how appropriate the ideas are or even if some of them overlap. Just get some thoughts down on paper.

8. Go through the list you prepared in Exercise 7 and eliminate any entries that are inappropriate for your topic or audience or that overlap. Try to see how many of them you might expand or rearrange into categories or subcategories. Then create an outline similar to the one in Figure 2.3 (p. 45).

9. Using your outline in Exercise 8, prepare some drafts of your memo report. Submit at least two drafts to your instructor.

10. Revise your drafts as much as necessary to create the final copy of your report.

11. In a few paragraphs, explain to your instructor the changes you made between your early drafts and your revised drafts. Explain why you made them. Concentrate on major changes—adding and moving paragraphs—as well as matters of style, tone, and even format.

12. In another memo—addressed to your instructor—describe any problems that bothered you at various phases of working on your report. Also point out what planning, drafting, and revising strategies worked especially well for you.

13. The following paragraphs are wordy and full of awkward, hard-to-read sentences. Edit these paragraphs to make them more readable by using clear and concise words and sentences.
    a. It has been verified conclusively by this writer that our institution must of necessity install more bicycle holding racks for the convenience of students,

faculty, and staff. These parking modules should be fastened securely to walls outside strategic locations on the campus. They could be positioned there by work crews or even by the security forces who vigilantly patrol the campus grounds. There are many students in particular who would value the installation of these racks. Their bicycles could be stationed there by them, and they would know that safety measures have been taken to ensure that none of their bicycles would be apprehended or confiscated illegally. Besides the precaution factor, these racks would afford users maximized convenience in utilizing their means of transportation when they have academic business to conduct, whether at the learning resource center or in the instructional facilities.

b. On the basis of preliminary investigations, it would seem reasonable to hypothesize that among the situational factors predisposing the Smith family toward showing pronounced psychological identification with the San Francisco Giants is the fact that the Smiths make their domicile in the San Francisco area. In the absence of contrariwise considerations, the Smiths' attitudinal preferences would in this respect interface with earlier behavioral studies. These studies, within acceptable parameters, correlate the fan's domicile with athletic allegiance. Yet it would be counterproductive to establish domicility as the sole determining factor for the Smiths' preference. Certain sociometric studies of the Smiths disclose a factor of atypicality which enters into an analysis of their determinations. One of these factors is that a younger Smith sibling is a participant in the athletic organization in question.

14. Following are very early drafts of memos that businesspeople have sent to their bosses or fellow workers. Revise and edit each draft, referring to the revising and editing checklists. Turn in your revision and the final, reader-ready copy. As you revise, keep in mind that you may have to delete and add information, rearrange the order of information, and make the tone suitable for the reader. As you edit, make sure your sentences are clear and concise and your words well chosen.

a. DATE: April 29, 2002
   TO: All workers
   FROM: B.J. Blackwell
   RE: Parking

The parking violations around here have gotten very very bad. And the administration is provoked and wants some action taken. I don't blame them. I have been late for meetings several times in the last month because inconsiderate folks from other divisions have parked their cars in our zone. That just is not fair, and so I must not be the only one who is upset. No wonder the management finds things so bad they have asked me to prepare this memo.

A big part of the problem it seems to me is that employees just cannot read signs. They park in the wrong zones. They also park in visitors' spots. The penalties are going to be stiff. The administration, or so I was led to believe, is thinking of fining any employee who does not obey the parking policies. I know for a fact that I saw someone from the research department pull right into a visitor parking area last week just because it was 8:55 and he did not want to be late for work. That gives our business a bad name. People will not want to do business with us if they cannot even find a parking spot in the area that the company has reserved for them.

Ms. Watson has laid the law down to me about all this and told me to let each and every one of you know that things have to improve. One of the other big problems around here is that some employees have even parked their cars in loading zones, and security had to track them down to move.

As part of the administration's new policy, each employee is going to be issued a company parking policy and will have to come in and sign for it verifying that he received it. I think things really have gotten out of hand and that some drastic action has to be taken. We will all have to shape up around here.

b. DATE: April 21, 2003
    TO: Betty Jones, Director
    FROM: Tom Cranford
    RE: Vacation request for vacation from June 12–24

I have been a highly productive employee and so I do not think that it is out of line for me to make this request. I have put in overtime and even done others' work in the department while they were away. So, I think that it is fair and just, and I can see no reason why I should not be allowed to take my vacation during the last two weeks of June.

Let me explain some of the reasons. I could have others watch my desk and do the work. I have helped them out, too, and they know it. I have been remarkably dependable. I have been readily accessible whenever their vacations have come around, and so I know it can be done.

I fully realize that this is the busiest time of the year for our company and that vacations are not usually granted during this season. But I do have personal reasons which I think should be honored/respected. Peak business times are major. I understand this, and I do hope an exception will be made in my case. After all, I do have the on-the-job training that other companies would reward. Thanks very much.

c. DATE: February 21, 2000
    TO: All Employees
    FROM: George Holmes
    RE: Travel

Every company has its policies regarding travel and vouchers. Ours strike me as important and fairly straightforward. Yet for the life of me I cannot fathom why they are being ignored. It is in everyone's best interest. When you travel, you are on company time, company business. Respect that, won't you. Explain your purpose, keep your receipts, document your visits, keep track of meals.

If you see more than one client per day, it should not be too hard or too much to ask you to keep a log of each, separate, individual visit. After all, our business does depend on these people, and we will never know your true contributions on company trips unless you inform us (please!) of whom you see, where, why, and how much it costs you. That way we can keep our books straight and know that everything is going according to company policy.

Please review the appropriate pages (I think they are pages 23–25) about travel procedures. Thanks. If you have questions, give me a call, but check your procedures book or with your office/section manager, first. That will save everyone more time. Good luck.

15. Find a piece of writing—e-mail, memo, letter, brochure, or short report—that you believe was not carefully drafted or revised. In a short memo or e-mail, point out to your instructor what is wrong with the piece of writing—for example, not logically organized, inappropriate tone, incomplete or too technical information. Attach a copy of the poor example to your e-mail or memo.

16. Revise the piece of poor writing you analyzed in Exercise 15. Submit your improved version to your instructor.

Collaborative Writing and Meetings at Work

In the workplace you will not always have to write alone, isolated from co-workers or managers. Much of your business writing time may be spent working as part of a team. You will prepare a document with other employees or managers who will collaborate or, at the very least, review your work and help improve it.

Collaborative writing occurs when a group of individuals—as few as two to as many as seven or more—

- combine their efforts to prepare a single document
- share authorship
- work together for the common good, maybe even the survival, of your department, company, or agency

The trend in business is toward increased collaboration. One survey estimates that in the world of work 90 percent of all businesspeople spend some time writing as part of a collaborative team. Simply put, then, collaborative writing is one very real way you can expect to communicate in the world of work.

Teamwork Is Crucial to Business Success

Communication and quality experts emphasize that the success of a business depends on how well people interact as a team. Working as part of a writing team is an essential responsibility in a technical world in which each employee is connected to co-workers and managers via computer modems and customers are connected to almost every company through the worldwide marketplace of the Internet. Collaboration is networking, and collaborative writing is, therefore, a vital part of the global network in which individuals depend on each other's expertise, experience, and viewpoints to benefit their company and customers.

The heart of collaboration is being a team player, a highly valued skill in the workplace. Being a collaborative, or team, player means you

- interact successfully on an interpersonal level
- talk to people to get information
- provide feedback
- give and take constructive criticism
- raise important and relevant questions
- get assistance from resource experts in other departments and fields
- put the good of your company above your ego.

Collaboration helps get writing done more easily and more efficiently.

This chapter introduces you to successful ways to collaborate with co-workers in your office as well as people with whom you'll do business around the globe. In this chapter you'll receive practical advice on how to write in and for a group and how to solve communication problems within a group setting. It takes much work and skillful negotiation to be a member of an effective collaborative writing group, but it is worth the effort.

Collaboration takes place in preparing many types of writing, from brochures to technical manuals, from proposals to long reports. Collaboration can be done in a variety of ways—face to face, one on one, over the telephone, and via e-mail and the Internet. Several companies market software packages, called *groupware*, that facilitate collaborative writing efforts through electronic conferencing (see Figure 3.9).

Advantages of Collaborative (Group) Writing

Collaborative writing teams benefit both employers and employees. Specific advantages of collaboration include the following:

1. It builds on collective talents. Because no one individual has all the answers, a writing team profits from the diverse expertise and talents of individual members. A group of writers and researchers together can do a much more thorough job than can one writer working without the advantage of outside help or commentary. One team member may have strengths in statistical research, another in writing, and a third in document design and graphics.

2. It provides productive feedback. A company profits by pooling the professional resources of its work force, getting the benefit of diverse viewpoints, insightful criticism, and immediate feedback, as Lee Booker, lab supervisor at Keeton Pharmaceuticals, points out in Figure 3.1. Members can offer helpful critiques of each other's suggestions, drafts, and revisions. Constructive discussion clarifies issues, sorts out appropriate from inappropriate solutions, and leads to better, more persuasive recommendations for a customer or an employer. Thanks to collective planning and decision making, the group can identify and solve major problems and survey more opinions than an individual writer could.

3. It increases productivity and can save time. When a group has planned its strategies carefully, collaboration actually cuts down on the number of meetings and

FIGURE 3.1   The advantages of collaboration in the workplace: A manager's view.

————————————— MEMO —————————————

Collaborative writing is essential to the success and morale of the Environmental Testing Lab I work in at Keeton Pharmaceuticals. I supervise four microbiologists, each of whom is responsible for testing a specific area of our plant. We routinely test the environment in production areas throughout the plant by sampling the air, water, and surfaces (e.g., belts, floors, vents). When we find unacceptable ranges of bacteria, we have to investigate and report our findings to management and ultimately to the FDA. The report that emerges is the collaborative effort of microbiologists, production personnel, and management.

The protocols for such collaboration are as follows. When an unacceptable limit is found, the microbiologist for that area first interviews the production supervisor as well as line personnel to find potential causes of contamination. From such interviews the microbiologist can obtain honest, objective feedback about what happened. Then the microbiologist prepares a memo report in collaboration with the other three microbiologists, who offer helpful and diplomatic suggestions on how such unacceptable ranges could be eliminated or reduced. This collective brainstorming helps our lab not to overlook key information, strengthens professional communication, and improves team spirit.

After drafting the memo, the microbiologist for that area of the specific plant sends it to me as the Lab Supervisor and to my boss, the Quality Lab Section Manager, for our response. We confer with the microbiologist and production personnel, as necessary, and make any revisions to ensure that the report follows all company guidelines.

Continued

FIGURE 3.1   (Continued)

Page 2

The report is then forwarded to the Quality Control Manager and finally to the plant manager for their approval and signatures. Finally, the report is placed in the plant repository — the Document Center — where it is subject to periodical FDA inspections.

The collaborative efforts of production personnel, microbiologists, and management guarantee that the report will be a model of clear, precise, and ethical writing. In the last three years, management has frequently commended the labs and production for our helpful spirit of cooperation.

Lee Booker
Lab Supervisor
Keeton Pharmaceuticals

conferences, saving the company and employees valuable time. Also, with group checks and balances, the likelihood of wasting resources on false leads and irrelevant issues is reduced.

4. It ensures overall writing effectiveness. The more people involved in developing a document, the greater its chances for thoroughness and cohesion. Guided by shared principles of style, a collaborative team can better guarantee the uniformity and consistency of a piece of writing than can two or three individuals each writing a different section of a document. Effective collaboration can uncover inconsistencies in organization, format, and style.

5. It offers psychological benefits. Collaboration contributes significantly to employee confidence and morale, which Booker emphatically points out in Figure 3.1. By sharing information and offering suggestions, members feel that they are helping others while simultaneously fulfilling themselves. Furthermore, working as part of a team relieves individuals of some job-related stress. Knowing that he or she is not carrying sole responsibility for planning, drafting, and writing a document lightens the pressure and may be an incentive to work more effectively. A division of labor makes deadlines less fearsome, too.

6. It contributes to customer service and satisfaction. Collaborative writing teams can assess and describe a product effectively by pooling their knowledge. Their collective judgment of an audience's needs, including those of a government agency such as the FDA in Figure 3.1, helps their company better meet those needs. Moreover, a collaborative team is much more likely—through discussions, interactions, even disagreements—to anticipate a customer's requests or complaints and thereby respond to or resolve them. A collaborative environment fosters greater opportunities for originality. In the give-and-take of discussion, groups are challenged to move beyond ordinary methods to construct more creative, compelling presentations that may ultimately lead to greater sales.

Collaborative Writing and the Writing Process

The writing process described in Chapter 2 also applies to collaborative writing. Groups use the same strategies and confront the same problems individual writers do. Writing teams brainstorm, plan, research, draft, revise, and edit. Like the individual writer, too, a team moves through the writing process only by identifying its audience, following a common purpose, defining the problem, and deciding on the best ways to solve that problem.

Effective collaborative writing merges with individual writing at times. That is, although collaboration involves group interaction, it also allows for independent time so individual members can perform tasks on their own that will contribute to the team's success.

Below is a brief rundown of how groups move through the writing process.

1. Groups must plan before they can write. The planning phase includes brainstorming on the group scale with each member contributing to the overall discussion. Members should be encouraged to express ideas freely and without fear of criticism at an early planning session. Groups will perform outlining and looping at this stage as well. (Review pp. 41–44.) During planning, the group, like the individual writer, should identify its audience and determine the audience's purpose in reading the document. In this early phase, the group must also establish the ground rules by which it will operate, including making individual assignments, establishing schedules, and selecting a facilitator.

2. Groups do research. Researching entails more than chitchat or a casual pooling of undocumented opinions. It requires searching, interviewing, and reading. Some tasks may be undertaken by individuals working alone to prepare for the next group session. Each member may be assigned to research one part of a subject, and all will be expected to contribute to the overall research process.

Never hoard information; always share for the benefit of the group. As a team member, you may even be called on to distribute copies of documents you retrieved from the Internet or other sources or to report on an interview you conducted.

3. Groups prepare drafts. While it is possible for a group to draft a document together, requiring everyone to sit down together and write word for word is not always feasible or justifiable. Individuals are more likely to draft sections of a document on their own and then present their work for group discussion and revision.

4. Groups revise and edit. These phases of the writing process can benefit from group interaction by collectively spotting and resolving problems—omissions, difficulties in organization (a section out of order), length, inconsistencies in content, and so on. Discussion also helps groups agree on final style and document design,

TECH NOTE

In-House Research

As part of your research, you may have to e-mail someone in another department or division of your company for information to incorporate into your report. Many documents include boilerplates, or specific contractual statements, that you can pick up directly from another company document without having to create, revise, or edit new text. With the help of scanners, you can also obtain research graphics from other company divisions to include in your work. Finally, don't forget to check your company's Web page for other sources of information. Many large corporations maintain e-mail addresses exclusively for frequently asked questions (FAQs), both in-house and outside the company.

provided one individual's personal preferences do not override everyone else's or accepted rules of usage. It often makes sense to appoint someone who has more writing ability to give the group document a final editing for style.

Each stage of the writing process just outlined can be modified to account for group activities. Flexibility is as important to a group of writers as it is to an individual writer.

A Case Study in Collaborative Editing

Figure 3.2 contains an e-mail written by Tara Edwards Barber, the Documentation Manager of CText, Inc., a large firm in Ann Arbor, Michigan, that develops software for the publishing industry. In it, Barber describes the writing process followed by her team of collaborative writers. Communicated over the Internet, Barber's observations—based on many years of experience in corporate writing—shed light on the practical, day-to-day process of group writing and editing. Group harmony means documents are completed successfully and on time.

Study Barber's approach: She effectively works *with* and *not against* her staff. She manages the collaborative effort without being heavy-handed or squelching individual creativity. Her strategy is a good one to follow.

Guidelines for Successful Group Writing

The success of a team-written document depends on (1) the cooperation of team members, (2) the information the team gathers, and (3) the ability of the team to adapt that information to meet the audience's needs and the employer's goals. Making sure a team functions smoothly and productively benefits a company. In fact,

FIGURE 3.2   Collaborative editing: Advice from a pro.

Subject:	**Collaborative Writing/Editing**
Date:	7 Mar 1996 13:35:15–0600
From:	tara.barber@ctext.com
Newsgroups:	bit.listserv.techwr-1

I would like to describe some ways to edit constructively to help new writers improve.

I agree that the more you make collaborative, the better results you will get. Here's how we do it in my department. Although all my writers are experienced, they come from such different backgrounds that some of the ways I have coordinated editing activities are similar to how I would interact with new writers. It's my job to make sure all the pieces fit.

When I first took this job, there were several documentation styles being used for the company's manuals. But the department at that time was very small and so the senior writer and I sat down and prepared a cohesive and consistent style manual. We experienced some tension, but by compromising, we were able to iron out our differences. We developed a style guide and a set of manual conventions that gave new writers precise and helpful guidelines and procedures to follow from the start. The new manual helped us to eliminate glaring editing problems. That way we do not worry about inconsistencies in spelling, capitalization, formats, headings, or reference documentation.

But the department has grown since that time, and on at least two occasions all of us have sat down as a department to reassess the style guide and manual. By doing this, we are able to get input from everyone and to allow for new ideas. When a problem arises now, we are comfortable addressing it as a group.

In addition to the usual subject-matter expert reviews, all of us review each other's materials. This review helps us remain familiar with each other's projects and homogenizes our writing styles, which keeps our documentation consistent. It's also a great way to get a good "clean-eyes edit." And, happily, a writer will offer an original idea about how to approach a problem that eliminates a potential editing dilemma. We all win.

Continued

FIGURE 3.2   (Continued)

In my role as documentation manager, I try to edit early and late, but not in the middle. Our materials usually go through several edits before they're printable (usually due to the changes in software). I try to look over early material in the form of outlines and first drafts, to make sure everything looks on track and follows our house style and procedures. I always edit final drafts because I am responsible for the output of my department. But I try not to do too much in the middle unless there is a problem. Peer review works well during this intermediate phase, and I don't want to step on individual creativity.

If I have to make comments, I make them at various levels. And here I'm not talking about catching grammar mistakes, spelling errors, typos, mis-numberings, etc. Instead,
a) I point out problems, or sections that seem confusing, but let the writer suggest fixes.
b) I make suggestions and provide examples–more than one if I can.
c) I actively work with the writer to develop ways around a problem. Sometimes this means coming up with a whole new way of approaching the documentation, which is then addressed at our next style meeting. Sometimes it also works to get the rest of the department involved in a brainstorming session.
d) If nothing else works, I play the heavy manager and say "do it this way because I say so." I try to avoid this, however, if I possibly can.

Working as a constructive team, we rarely have editing problems that we can't solve, and everyone is happy with the comments and the final product. And our customers find the documents usable and valuable. You can't really ask for more than that.

Tara Barber
Documentation Manager
CText, Inc.

Reprinted with the permission of Tara Barber.

many firms hire consultants to assist them in forming the most compatible and creative groups possible.

Following the ten guidelines below will increase your chances of success when you write in a group.

1. Know the individuals in your group. Establish rapport with your team. If you do not know them, introduce yourself before you start working on a document. Even if you know them, assure them that you are looking forward to working with them. Learn as much as you can about their schedules, backgrounds, special competencies, experiences within your organization, and even their pet peeves. By being concerned and friendly, you create an environment that enhances productivity.

2. Do not regard one person on the team as more important than another. Favoritism leads to hard feelings and decreases the group's productivity. Instead, adopt the attitude that the group succeeds or fails as a whole. Think collectively. Everyone's input is necessary to group effort and success. When individuals regard themselves as the most important or indispensable member of the team, group harmony is jeopardized. A unified team accomplishes more than a collection of disgruntled individuals.

3. Set up a preliminary meeting to establish guidelines. Unless members share the same vision and objectives, they may work at cross-purposes and head in different directions. The group should discuss the objectives, audience, scope, format, and importance of the document at an introductory meeting. It is helpful at the first meeting to identify and discuss any directions and/or directives from management and to set up priorities. Such a preliminary meeting is crucial to the success of all subsequent meetings. Each member should take the opportunity to ask questions or share comments and concerns before research and drafting begin.

4. Agree on the group's organization. Here are some questions to consider.

- Is the group to appoint a leader? If so, how is that person to be chosen?
- Will the leader be the most experienced or skilled writer? The member who has been with the company longest?
- What are the leader's responsibilities?
- Will the leader have the authority to settle disputes, break deadlocks, or make final decisions?

An effective group leader must be skillful at initiating discussions, encouraging team members, compromising for the sake of consensus, and generally presiding over meetings. The leader is the group's moderator.

The group must also consider how to communicate with management and decide whether its work should be shared with individuals outside the group (such as co-workers from another department). As Lee Booker points out in Figure 3.1, management also plays a role in giving feedback. Members will also have to decide how and how often to communicate between meetings. For example, since one member's work might affect another's, it will be important to be able to notify other team members expeditiously. Finally, the group must decide whether it will appoint a recorder to distribute minutes or documents from meetings.

5. Identify each member's responsibilities, but allow for individual talents and skills. Members should be aware of one another's strengths—in document design, graphics, software, marketing, editing. Don't underestimate or overestimate the time necessary for each member's (or the entire group's) tasks. Individuals should feel comfortable with their assigned duties, whether gathering data, drafting a section, editing, verifying documentation, and so on. Because some jobs are more demanding and may take longer than others, one member may need extra time or help from an outside expert (statistician, engineer). Make sure members have opportunities to voice difficulties and to request help.

6. Establish the times, places, and length of group meetings. The group must decide on a calendar of scheduled meetings and ensure that each member has a copy. When making its schedule, the group should consider likely conflicts and other obligations members may have (forthcoming business trips, conventions). Various software programs can help the group to write collaboratively (see p. 102). It's a good idea for the leader to be available between meetings if members have questions.

7. Follow an agreed-on timetable, but leave room for flexibility. The group should estimate a realistic time necessary to complete the various stages of their work—when drafts are due or when editing must be concluded, for example. A project schedule based on that estimate should then be prepared. Everyone in the group must be aware of the short- and long-range deadlines. The group's timetable, with major **milestones** (dates when key parts are to be completed) boldfaced or highlighted, should be sent to each member. Either collectively or through its leader or recorder, the group should also build some failsafe time into the schedule. **Remember: Projects always take longer than initially planned.** Prepare for a possible delay at any one stage—say, research is not completed because materials are not available, or someone fails to complete a task because of illness or a transfer. The group may have to submit progress reports (see pp. 587–593) to its members as well as to management.

8. Provide clear and precise feedback to members. Feedback is the most essential ingredient in group dynamics; it should be relevant, intelligent, and timely. (Review the benefits of the collaborative efforts outlined in Figures 3.1 and 3.2.) Don't come to a meeting without having done your homework. Also, you are not doing yourself or the group a favor by simply responding "OK" or "Looks good" on a draft. Skimming helps no one. Be precise and helpful. Nothing frustrates a writer more than having a reader offer superficial concluding comments—for example, "needs improvement," "lacks focus," "does not flow." Supply specific reasons why you find something wrong, incomplete, or misleading. Then be ready to offer detailed advice on where and how to fix the shortcoming. If something is effective, state why you think so, but be honest. Holding back valid criticism is unethical and hurts group effort.

9. Be an active listener. Good listeners are active participants in a group discussion, not passive observers. Listen to what members say and resist the temptation to interrupt. Develop what some communication consultants call a "third ear," listening to the meanings and feelings behind a person's words as well as to the words themselves. Try to identify the themes of a discussion. By following the ideas of an argument, you'll understand the big picture, as Lee Booker points out in Figure 3.1. But don't tune out the technical details. You need to hear the smaller elements as well as the larger framework of a dialogue to write effectively with and for the group.

10. Use a standard reference guide for matters of style, documentation, and format. Establishing guidelines about word processing programs, style, documentation, format, graphics, and so forth makes the group's task easier. Many large companies have policy or style manuals that their teams must use, as Tara Barber notes in Figure 3.2. If such a document is not available, your group should select a manual or other reference work to which members should adhere, such as the APA (American Psychological Association) guide or *The Chicago Manual of Style.*

Sources of Conflict in Group Dynamics and How to Solve Them

The success of collaborative writing depends on how well the team interacts. Discussion and criticism are essential to discover ideas, results, and solutions. Members must build on one another's strengths and eliminate or downplay weaknesses. Inevitably, members have different perspectives or viewpoints out of which conflicts will arise.

"Conflict" in the sense of conflicting opinions—a healthy give-and-take—can be positive if it alerts the group to problems (inconsistencies, redundancies, incompleteness) and provides ways to resolve them. A conflict can even help the group generate and refine ideas, thus leading to a better organized and written document.

Establishing Group Rules

When conflict translates into ego-tripping and personal attacks, however, nothing productive emerges. Everyone in the group must agree beforehand on three ironclad working policies of group dynamics: (1) individuals must seek and adhere to group consensus, (2) compromise may be advisable, even necessary, to meet a deadline, and (3) if the group decides to accept compromise, the group leader's final decision on resolving conflicts must be accepted.

Following are some common problems in group dynamics, with suggestions on how to avoid or solve them.

Common Problems; Practical Solutions

1. **Resisting constructive criticism.** No one likes to be criticized, yet criticism can be vital to the group effort. Collaboration requires being open to suggestions. But when an individual responds to criticism with anger and threatens to disrupt a meeting or lead the group away from its main goals, serious miscommunication results. Some individuals insist on "their way or no way" and so want to force everything through their very narrow, limiting perspective. They can become hostile to any change or revision, no matter how small.

Solution: When emotions become too heated, the group leader may wisely move the discussion to another section of the document or to another issue and allow some cooling-off time. Negotiation is an essential skill.

TECH NOTE

Good and Poor Negotiators

A *good* negotiator

- Is assertive
- Is diplomatic
- Keeps details of negotiations confidential
- Remembers that everything has a price and clearly defines the exchange rate for any concession to be offered
- Works for incentives that appeal to the opponent
- Does not "dumb down" his or her behavior for the benefit of the opponent
- Abandons persuasion when talks reach the negotiation point
- Enables the opponent to save face

A *poor* negotiator

- Has a negative attitude
- Is argumentative
- Dismisses his or her own statements with self-deprecating laughs
- Criticizes freely
- Is rude
- Whines
- Attempts to buy off the opposition by conceding a point without defining what is expected in return
- Expresses statements of fact as if they were questions by raising the voice at the end of sentences
- Discusses personal issues
- Presses for an admission of error
- Fails to allow the opponent to save face

Reprinted from the March 1999 issue of *Occupational Hazards* magazine. Copyright © 1999 by Penton Media Inc. Used by permission.

2. Failing to give constructive criticism. Just as it is counterproductive to reject criticism, it is also tiresome to saturate a meeting with nothing but negatives. You will block communication if you start criticizing with words such as "Why don't you try," "What you need is," "Don't you realize that," or "If you don't. . . ."

Solutions: When you criticize an idea, link your reaction to the team's overall goals. Diplomatically remind the individual of those goals and point to ways in which revision (criticism) furthers them. Identify a specific section in the document, explain the problem, and offer a helpful revision. Stressing that "we are all in this together" may defuse some anger. Never attack an individual. Mutual respect is everyone's right and obligation. Take a "let's work on this together" attitude rather than disrupt group harmony. Be objective, constructive, and cooperative.

3. Refusing to participate. This is a lethal problem in group dynamics. Withholding your opinions hurts the group efforts; identify what you believe are major problems and give the group a chance to consider them.

Solutions: When one individual in the group cannot, or will not, take a stand, the leader may be forced to say, "Even though you have not expressed your preference, we need you to make a choice anyway." If you don't feel sure of yourself or your points, talk to another member of the group before a meeting to "test" your ideas or to see if he or she reacts the same way.

4. Interrupting with incessant questions. Some people interrupt a meeting so many times with questions that all group work stops. Sometimes the individual questioner is simply trying to exercise control by asking irrelevant questions.

Solutions: When that happens, a group leader can turn the tables on the person by remarking, "We appreciate your interest, but would you try an experiment, please, and attempt to answer your own questions." If the person claims not to know, the leader might then say, "If you can't come up with an answer now, why don't you think about it for a while and then get back to us." If that tactic fails, the leader may have to confront the disrupter privately after the meeting.

5. Inflating small details out of proportion. Some individuals waste valuable discussion and revision time by dwelling on relatively insignificant points—the choice of a single word, an optional comma—and overlook larger problems in content and organization. Nitpickers can derail the group.

Solution: If there is consensus about a matter, leave it alone and turn to more important issues. Bring the group back to the big picture.

6. Dominating a meeting. Developing interpersonal skills means sharing and responding, not taking over. Sometimes a group member is so aggressive and focused on individual achievement that he or she seems to occupy the floor every minute.

Solutions: A couple of intervention strategies can work when one person monopolizes a discussion. The leader may say, "We've been hearing from primarily one or two people; now we need to hear from the rest of the group." The leader may even have to take the person aside to remind him or her of the others' right to speak. Some groups operate democratically with the "one-minute rule." Each member has one minute to voice objections, suggest revisions, report on progress, and so on, and does not get the floor again until everyone else has had a chance to speak.

7. Being too deferential to avoid conflict. This problem is the opposite of that described in #1. You will not help your group by being a "yes person" simply to appease a strong-willed member of the group. Saying that an idea or a plan is excellent when you know that it is flawed and contradictory will only increase your team's workload. Being too deferential is as counterproductive as being too aggressive.

Solution: Feel free to express your opinions politely; if tempers begin to flare, call in the group leader or seek the opinions of others on the team.

8. Not finishing on time or submitting an incomplete document. Meeting deadlines is the group's most important obligation to one another and to the company. Deadlines exist for various stages of a document as well as for the most important deadline of all—the date when final work must be submitted to the boss or to the customer. When some members are not involved in the planning stages or when they skip meetings, deadlines are invariably missed. If you miss a meeting, get briefed by an individual who was there. Repeated absences seriously violate group work. A deadline can also be jeopardized when a member does not clearly understand his or her assignment and therefore risks duplicating or delaying what someone else in the group has been asked to do.

Solution: The group leader can institute networking through e-mail to announce meetings, keep members updated, or provide for ongoing communication and questions. (See Figure 3.10 on pp. 105–107.)

TECH NOTE

Two Valuable Institute Seminars

Two seminars might be especially of value to the nonparticipating team player. Both are taught by institutes and are available in most large cities.

- **Interpersonal Communication Skills.** This program offers easy-to-use communication techniques that will help you be more effective and productive immediately and permanently. It is designed to help you discover how to speak up and be heard and get your ideas accepted more often. It is offered by Fred Pryor Seminars, 2000 Shawnee Mission Pkwy., Shawnee Mission, KS 66205; 1-800-488-0928.
- **Hotwire Your Thinking.** This seminar helps you break out of a rut and to generate new ideas, solve problems, and make better decisions. It teaches you to overcome the mental roadblocks put in place by years of traditional thinking and problem-solving techniques. It is offered by Skillpath Seminars, 6900 Squibb Road, Mission, KS 66201-2768; 1-800-873-7545.

Models for Collaboration

There are as many types of collaborative writing activities and methods as there are companies. Writers interact with other writers, editors, and outside specialists in a variety of ways. The process can range from relatively simple phone calls or e-mail to a much more extensive network of checks and balances, revisions and refinements.

The scope, size, and complexity of your document as well as your company's organization will determine what type of (and how much) collaboration is necessary. A shorter assignment (say, a memo) will not require the same type of group structure and participation as would a policy handbook, a technical proposal, or a long report. At some large companies, for example, a staff of professional editors (such as Tara Barber's team in Figure 3.2) revises the final draft prepared by a departmental team. The more important and more complex a document is, the more extensive collaboration will be.

The following sections describe five possible models for collaboration that are used in the world of work.

Cooperative Model

The cooperative collaborative model is one of the simplest and most expedient ways to write in the business world. An individual writer is given an assignment and then goes through the writing process (see Chapter 2) to complete it. Along the way, he or she may show a draft to a peer to get feedback or to a supervisor for a critique. That is what Randy Taylor did in Figure 3.3. He showed a draft of a letter to a potential client to his boss, Felicia Krumpholtz, who made changes in content, wording, and format and then sent it back to Taylor. Following his boss's suggestions, Taylor then created the revised letter in Figure 3.4.

If Taylor had sent his first draft, the customer would hardly have been impressed with the company's professionalism and might have reconsidered placing an order. Following Krumpholtz's revisions, though, Taylor made his letter much more effective. Careful writers always benefit from constructive criticism. Even though Felicia Krumpholtz helped Randy Taylor improve his work, strictly speaking it was not a case of group writing. Although the two interacted, they did not share the final responsibility for creating the letter.

Preparing a longer, more detailed piece of work, a writer may interview technical experts and lawyers, write an early draft and show it to co-workers to gather their opinions, and then submit the document to a mid-level supervisor who may further revise it, as described in Figure 3.1.

Sequential Model

In the sequential model, each individual in a group is assigned a specific, nonoverlapping responsibility—from brainstorming to revising—for a section of a proposal, report, or other document. There is a clear-cut, rigid division of labor. If four people are on the team, each will be responsible for his or her part of the document. For example, one employee may write the introduction, another the body of the report, another the conclusions, and the fourth, the group's recommendation.

Team members may discuss their individual progress and even choose a coordinator to oversee the progress of their work. They may even exchange their work for group review and commentary. When each team member finishes his or her section, the coordinator then assembles the individual parts to form the report.

FIGURE 3.3   A draft of Randy Taylor's letter edited by his supervisor Felicia Krumpholtz.

servitron

4083 Randolph Street
Houston, TX 77016
(713) 555-6761

November 18, 2002

Terry Tatum
Manager
Consolodated Industries
Houston, TX *add zip code*

Dear ~~Sir,~~ *Terry Tatum:*

Thank you for asking
~~I am taking the opportunity of answering your request~~ for a price list of Servitron
products. Servitron has been in business in the Houston area for more than ~~twenty-~~
22 ~~two~~ years and we offer unparalleled equipment and service to ~~any customer.~~
Using a Servitron product will give you both efficiency and economy.   *Consolidated*
can   *boldface*   *Industries*
boldface
Whatever Servitron model you choose carries with it a full one-year warranty on all
parts and labor. After the expiration date of your warranty you ~~should~~ purchase our
service contract for $75,000 a year.   *might*
boldface

~~Here are the models Servitron offers~~

Zephyr   81072 $459.95
Colt   86085 $629.95
Meteor   88096 $769.95

Depending on your needs, one of these models should be right for you.

If I might be of further assistance to you, please call on me. I am also enclosing a
brochure giving you more information, including specifications, on those Servitron
products.

~~Truly,~~ *Sincerely yours,*   *add phone number*   *reverse*
and e-mail   *the order*
of these
Servitron — *leave 4 spaces*   *two*
Randy Taylor *sign your name*   *sentences*
Sales Associate

www.servitron.com

FIGURE 3.4   The edited, final copy of Figure 3.3.

servitron

4083 Randolph Street
Houston, TX 77016
(713) 555-6761

November 18, 2002

Terry Tatum
Manager
Consolidated Industries
Houston, TX 77005-0096

Dear Terry Tatum:

Thank you for asking for a price list of Servitron products. Servitron has been in business in the Houston area for more than 22 years and we can offer unparalleled equipment and service to Consolidated Industries. Using a Servitron product will give you both **efficiency** and **economy**.

Depending on your needs, one of these models should be right for you.

Model Name	Number	Price
Zephyr	81072	$459.95
Colt	86085	$629.95
Meteor	88096	$769.95

Whatever Servitron model you choose carries with it a full **one-year warranty** on all parts and labor. After the expiration date of your warranty you might purchase our service contract for $75.00 a year.

I am also enclosing a brochure giving you more information, including specifications, on those Servitron products. If I might be of further assistance to you, please call me at (713) 555-6761 or e-mail me at rtaylor@servitron.com.

Sincerely yours,

SERVITRON

Randy Taylor

Randy Taylor
Sales Associate

www.servitron.com

Functional Model

The division of labor in the functional collaborative model is assigned not according to parts of a document but by skill or job function of the members. For example, a four-person team may be organized as follows:

- The **leader** schedules and conducts meetings, assists team members, issues progress reports to management, solves problems by proposing alternatives, and generally coordinates everyone's efforts to keep the project on schedule.
- The **researcher** collects data, conducts interviews, searches the literature, administers tests, classifies the information, and then prepares notes on the work.
- The **designated writer/editor,** who receives the researcher's notes, prepares outlines and drafts and circulates them for corrections and revisions.
- The **graphics expert** obtains and prepares all visuals, specifying why, how, and where visuals should be placed, and might even suggest that visuals replace certain sections of text; the graphics expert may also be responsible for the design (layout) of the document.

This organizational scheme fosters much more group interaction than does the sequential model.

Figure 3.5 illustrates the workings of a functional model. It describes the behind-the-scenes joint effort that went into Joycelyn Woolfolk's proposal for her boss to authorize a new journal, which would incorporate a newsletter her office currently prepares. A publications coordinator for a large, regional health maintenance organization (HMO), Woolfolk supervises a small staff and reports directly to the public affairs manager, who in turn is responsible to the vice president of the regional office.

As you will see from Woolfolk's scenario, she assigned specific duties to the members of her team. Then, based on their initial research and documentation, she drafted a document for her staff and her boss to read. As Woolfolk's functional approach shows, collaboration can move up and down the chain of command, with participation at all levels.

Woolfolk's plan is a common one in business. Often, individual employees will pull together information from their separate functional areas (such as finance, marketing, sales, and transportation), and someone else will put that information into a draft that others read and revise until the document is ready to send to the boss. By the time the boss reviews the document, it has been edited and revised many times and by many individuals.

Integrated Model

In the integrated model, all members of the team are engaged in planning, researching, and revising. Each shares the responsibility of producing the document. Members participate in every stage of the document's creation and design, and the group goes back to each stage as often as needed. This model offers intense group interaction. Even though individual writers on the team may be asked to draft different sections of the document, all share in revising and editing that document. Depending on

FIGURE 3.5   Joycelyn Woolfolk's account of how one proposal originated and was collaboratively prepared following a functional model.

The idea to start a regional magazine was first expressed in passing by our vice president, who is interested in getting more and higher-level visibility for our regional office. Several other regional offices in our company put out fairly attractive magazines, and one office in particular has earned a lot of good publicity.

The public affairs manager (my boss) and I quickly picked up on the vice president's hint and began to formulate ways to investigate the need for such a publication and ways to substantiate our recommendation. For several weeks the public affairs manager and I had a number of conversations addressing specific points, such as the kind of documentation our proposal would need, what our resources for researching the question were, what our capabilities would be for producing such a publication, and so on. We were guided by the twofold goal of getting the vice president's approval and, ideally, meeting a genuine market need.

After discussions with my boss, I met with members of my staff to ask them to do the following tasks:

1. review existing HMO publications and report on whether there was already a regional magazine for the Northwest
2. develop, administer, and analyze a readership survey for current subscribers to our newsletter, which would potentially be incorporated into the new magazine
3. formulate general design concepts for the magazine in print and on-line, that we can implement without increasing staff, while still producing the quality magazine the vice president wants
4. prepare a budget for projected costs
5. consult with experts on our staff (actuaries, physicians, nurses) about topics of interest
6. confer with our Web expert about on-line possibilities and problems

Continued

FIGURE 3.5   (Continued)

I requested e-mails and other written documentation from my staff members about most of these tasks, and then I used that information to draft the proposal that eventually would go to the vice president, and perhaps even to the president's office. And I communicated with my staff often, through e-mail and personal meetings.

I revised my draft several times and had my staff look over each draft for feedback and proofreading. Based on their comments, I made further revisions and did careful editing. My boss reviewed my proposal, revising and editing it in minor ways innumerable times. Ultimately, the proposal will go out as a memo from me to my boss, who will then send it under her name to the vice president.

The copy of my proposal may be further revised in response to the vice president's comments when she gets it. She may use some portion or all of it in another report from her to the president, or she may write her own proposal to the president supporting her argument with the specifics from my proposal. The vice president will word the proposal to fit the expressed values and mission of our regional office as well as provide information that addresses budgetary and policy concerns for which her readers (our company president and board members) have final responsibility.

This is how a proposal started and where it will eventually end.

the scope of the document and company policy, the group may also go outside the team to solicit reviews and evaluations from experts.

Evolution of a Collaboratively Written Document

Figures 3.6, 3.7, and 3.8 show the evolution of a memo that follows an integrated model of collaboration. This memo informed employees that their company was enhancing a recycling program. Alice Schuster, the vice president of Fenton Industries, an appliance manufacturing company, asked two employees in the human resources department—Abigail Chappel and Manuel Garcia—to prepare a memo ("a few paragraphs" is how Schuster put it) to be sent to all Fenton employees.

Schuster had an initial conference with Chappel and Garcia, at which she stressed that their memo had to convey Fenton's renewed commitment to conservation and that, as part of that commitment, the employees had to intensify their recycling efforts. Chappel and Garcia thus shared the responsibility of convincing co-workers of the importance of recycling and educating them about practicing it.

Chappel and Garcia also had the difficult job of writing for several audiences simultaneously—the boss, whose name would not appear on the memo, other managers at Fenton, and the Fenton work force itself.

First Draft

Figure 3.6 is the first draft that Chappel and Garcia collaborated on and then presented to the manager of the human resources department—Wells McCraw—for his comments and revisions. As you can see from McCraw's remarks, written in ink, he was not especially pleased with their first attempt and asked them to make a number of revisions. As a careful reader (conscious of the memo's audience), McCraw found Chappel and Garcia's paragraphs to be rambling and repetitious— the writers were unable to stick to the point. Specifically, he pointed out that they included too much information in one paragraph and not enough in others.

As a good editor, McCraw also directed their attention to factual mistakes, irrelevant and even contradictory comments, and essential information they had omitted. Finally, McCraw offered some advice on using visual devices (see Chapter 1, pp. 18–19) to make their information more accessible to readers.

Subsequent Draft

Figure 3.7 shows the next stage in the collaboration. In this version of the memo, prepared through several revisions over a two-day period, the authors incorporated McCraw's suggestions as well as several changes of their own. It was this revision that they submitted to Vice President Schuster, who also made some comments on the memo. Schuster's suggestions—all valid—show how different readers can help writing teams meet their objectives.

Note that in the process of revising their memo Chappel and Garcia had to make major changes from the first draft in Figure 3.6 through several versions to the document in Figure 3.7. Those changes—shortening and expanding paragraphs, adding and deleting information, and refocusing their approach to meet the needs of their audience—are the revisions a collaborative writing team, like an individual writer, would expect to make.

Final Copy

With Schuster's input and continuing to revise the memo on their own, Chappel and Garcia submitted the final, revised memo found in Figure 3.8 to the vice president a few days later. This final copy received Schuster's approval and was then routed to the Fenton staff.

FIGURE 3.6   Early draft of the Chappel and Garcia collaborative memo, with revisions suggested by Wells McCraw.

FENTON INDUSTRIES

TO: All Employees
FROM: Abigail Chappel; Manuel Garcia
RE: Improving Our Recycling Program
DATE: February 10, 2002

This ¶ is too long Too many topics — costs, protecting the environment keep it short — say what we are doing and why

An in-house study has shown that Fenton sends approximately 26,000 pounds of paper to the landfill. The landfill charge for this runs about $2,240, which we could save by recycling. <u>Fenton Industries is conscious of our responsibility to save and protect the environment</u>. Accordingly, starting March 1 we will begin a more intensive paper recycling program. Our program, like many others nationwide, will use the latest degradable technology to safeguard the air, trees, and water in our community. It has been estimated that of the 250 million tons of solid waste, three quarters of goes to landfills. These landfills across the country are becoming dangerously overcrowded. Such a practice wastes our natural resources and endangers our air and drinking water. For example, it takes 10 trees to make 1 ton of paper, or roughly the amount of paper Fenton uses in four weeks. If we could recycle that amount of paper, we could save those trees. Recycling old paper into new paper involves less energy than making paper from new trees. Moreover, waste sent to landfills can, once broken down, leach, seep into our water supply, and contaminate it. The dangers are great.

start off with this key idea

word "it" left out

Check your facts; I think it is closer to 16–17

Delete - not relevant to our purpose

Add the fact about our saving trees in this ¶

No cap

By enhancing our recycling, we will not be sending so much to the Springfield Landfill and so help alleviate a dangerous condition there. We will keep it from overflowing. Fenton will also be contributing to transforming waste products into valuable reusable materials. Recycling paper in our own office shows that we are concerned about the environmental clutter. By having an improved paper recycling program, we will establish our company's reputation as an environmentally conscious industry and enhance our company's image.

Delete- makes us look bad

Start ¶ with this point

Fenton is primarily concerned with recycling paper. The 200 old phone books that otherwise would be tossed away can get our recycling program off to a good start.

When? How? Implications for saving costs?

Give some examples

We encourage you to start thinking about the additional kinds of paper around your office/workspace that needs to be earmarked for recycling. When you start to think about it, you will see how much paper we as a company use.

Continued

FIGURE 3.6   (Continued)

Page 2

↑ not into your wastebaskets

Starting the last week of February, paper bins will be placed by each office door inside the outer wall. These bins will be green—not unsightly and blending with our decor. Separate your waste paper (white, colored, and computer) and put it into these bins. You do not need to remove paper clips and staples, but you must remove rubber bands, tape, and sticky labels. They will be emptied each day by the clean-up crew. There will also be large bins at the north end of the hallway for you to deposit larger paper products. The crucial point is that you use these specially marked bins rather than your wastebasket to deposit paper.

Delete - repetitious

¶ lacks effective "call to action"

Fenton Industries will deeply appreciate your cooperation and efforts. Thanks for yout cooperation.

This memo needs more work
— add at least one ¶ on how recycling will save us money
— make directions clearer and easier to follow;
*   try using numbered steps*
— end on a more upbeat note; tell employees about the benefits
*   coming to them for recycling — i.e., a bonus/our contribution to*
*   their favorite charity*

Thanks to an integrated model of collaboration and careful critiques by McCraw and Schuster, Chappel and Garcia successfully revised their work. Effective team effort and shared responsibility were at the heart of Chappel and Garcia's assignment.

Co-writing Model

According to the co-writing model, everyone on the team actually drafts the document together, word for word. Each person may work at a different computer terminal, but all their efforts are focused on the same section of the document at the same time. This model offers the highest degree of collaboration and might be compared to a committee, in which everyone has a direct say (or hand) in every phase of the document.

While co-writing may work for a relatively short document such as a memo, it is rarely used in business because it is neither cost-effective nor practical. Co-writing collaboration is extremely labor intensive, because it ties up all members of the team to draft the document.

FIGURE 3.7   Revision of the Chappel and Garcia memo with changes suggested by Vice President Schuster.

FENTON INDUSTRIES

TO: All Employees
FROM: Abigail Chappel; Manuel Garcia
RE: Improving Our Recycling Program
DATE: February 10, 2002

To save money and protect our environment, Fenton Industries will begin a more intensive waste paper recycling program on March 1. Recycling continues to be an environmental necessity. It has been estimated that three quarters of the 250 million tons of solid waste dumped annually in America could be recycled. Our program will still use the latest recycling technology to safeguard trees, air, and water.
— say strengthen or continue

¶ needs more information This new program will ~~establish~~ Fenton's reputation as an environmentally conscious company. Fenton now uses one ton of paper every four weeks. This represents 17 trees that can be saved just by recycling our paper waste. Recycling also means we will send less waste to the landfill, alleviating problems of overfill and reducing the potential for contamination of the water supply. Waste sent to large landfills can leach and seep into water systems. By recycling paper, Fenton will also reduce the risk of long-term environmental pollution.
Add that we no longer use styrofoam and that our suppliers use only biodegradable products

Indicate how much we save Recycling saves us money. Right now Fenton pays $180 per month to dump 2,000 pounds (one ton) of paper waste at the landfill. However, scrap paper is worth $100 per ton. Recycling will generate $100 each month in new revenue while eliminating the $180 dumping expense.

This sentence more logically goes in ¶ 3 Ultimately, the success of our project depends on renewed awareness of the variety of office paper suitable for recycling. Paper products that can be recycled include newspapers, scrap paper, computer printouts, letters, envelopes (without windows), shipping cartons, old phone books, and uncoated paper cups.
Put in itemized bulleted list to stand out better

Do not start new ¶ here; keep as part of previous ¶ Recycling 200 or so old phonebooks each year alone will save 22 cubic yards of landfill space (or close to $100) and will generate $25 in scrap paper income for our company. The old 2001 phone books, which will be replaced by new 2002 ones on March 1, will give us an excellent opportunity to intensify our recycling.

Continued

FIGURE 3.7   (Continued)

Page 2

Here are some easy-to-follow directions to make our recycling efforts even more effective:

Boldface these words 1. Starting the last week in February, <u>paper bins will be placed inside each office door</u>. Put all waste paper into these bins, which will be emptied by maintenance.
2. Place <u>larger paper products</u>–such as cartons or phone books–in the <u>green</u> bigger paper bins at the end of each main corridor.
3. Put white, colored, computer printout, and newspapers into seperate marked bins. Remove all rubber bands, tape, and sticky notes.

Thanks for your cooperation. To show our appreciation for your help, 50 percent of all proceeds from the recycled paper will go toward employee bonuses and the other 50 percent will be given to the office's favorite charity. The benefits of our new recycling program will more than outweigh the inconvenience it may cause.]

Add another sentence to this ¶ on how a safer environment will benefit our company and the employees, too

Collaborating On-Line

Collaborating on-line takes writers into a different communication environment. Individuals in the world of work are meeting much more frequently in cyberspace to get a job done. E-mail is an important factor in aiding collaboration (see Chapter 4 for more about e-mail.)

Thanks to e-mail, employees communicate more and better with each other and with their customers and management. E-mail allows individuals to send more messages more quickly and more efficiently than any other form of communication. Using e-mail, employees can speed the flow of collaborative information, especially using software designed to enhance teamwork in business.

Going far beyond the potential of basic e-mail, Lotus Notes (Figure 3.9) is an example of software that can be linked with the programs and databases already in use by the organization, allowing it to customize employees' collaborative tasks, scheduling, and networks easily and seamlessly. E-mail will not completely eliminate the need for a group to meet in person to discuss thorny issues, to clarify subtleties, or to build group harmony. But face-to-face communications, though essential, are frequently supplemented with on-line collaboration.

Advantages of Collaborating On-Line

Collaborating via e-mail offers significant advantages to employers and workers. As you develop your on-line communication skills, here are some of the benefits you can count on.

FIGURE 3.8   Final copy of the memo prepared by Chappel and Garcia using an integrated model of collaboration.

FENTON ¦NDUSTRIES

TO: All Employees
FROM: Abigail Chappel; Manuel Garcia
RE: Improving Our Recycling Program
DATE: February 10, 2002

To save additional money and to protect the environment, Fenton will begin a more intensive waste paper recycling program on March 1. For the new program to succeed, we need to increase our paper recycling efforts. Recycling continues to be an environmental necessity. It had been estimated that three quarters of the 250 million tons of solid waste dumped annually in America is still not being recycled. Our program will continue to rely on the latest recycling technology to safeguard trees, air, and water.

Recycling has already saved us money. Right now Fenton pays $180 per month to dump 2,000 pounds (one ton) of paper waste at the landfill, compared to $360.00 last year. However, scrap paper is worth $100 per ton. Increased recycling will generate $100 each month in revenue while eliminating the $180 dumping expense.

This new, more intensive program will also strengthen Fenton's reputation as an environmentally conscious company. Three years ago, we stopped using styrofoam products and asked suppliers to use biodegradable materials for all our shipping containers. Our efforts have proved successful, but Fenton still uses one ton of paper every four weeks. This paper represents 17 trees that can be saved just by recycling our paper waste. We need to send even less waste to the landfill, alleviating problems of overfill and reducing the potential for contamination of the water supply. Waste sent to large landfills can leach and seep into water systems.

Ultimately, the success of this project depends on our being aware of the variety of office paper suitable for recycling. An expanded list of paper products that can be recycled include:

- newspapers
- letters
- envelopes (without cellophane windows)
- phone books
- uncoated paper cups

- scrap paper
- computer printouts
- junk mail (only black print on white paper)
- shipping cartons

Continued

FIGURE 3.8   (Continued)

Page 2

The old 2001 phone books, which will be replaced by new 2002 ones on March 1, will give us an excellent opportunity to launch our intensified recycling program.

Here are some easy-to-follow directions to make our recycling efforts even more effective:

1. Starting the last week in February, put all waste paper into the **paper bins** that will be placed **inside each office door.** These bins will be emptied by maintenance.
2. Place **larger paper products**–such as bulky cartons–in the **green** bigger paper bins at the end of the main corridor.
3. Remove all rubber bands, tape, and sticky notes and put white, colored, computer printout, and newspapers into separate marked bins.

Thanks for your cooperation. To show our appreciation for your increased efforts, 50 percent of all proceeds from the recycled paper will go into an annual employee bonus fund and the other 50 percent will be given to the office's favorite charity. The benefits of our new recycling program will more than outweigh the inconvenience it may cause. A safer environment—and a more cost-effective way to run our company—benefits us all.

1. Eliminating time barriers. Communicating by e-mail, team members do not have to worry about tight schedules, conflicts, delays, and so on. Members can send and receive messages and commentary via e-mail at any time from anywhere. Employers and employees can take advantage of a handless clock.

2. Removing geographic limitations. With e-mail, a team member does not have to be physically present in order to contribute to group work. Team members can be in different cities from all over the globe, which benefits international firms that want to involve employees from overseas offices in decision-making processes.

3. Increasing the amount and quality of feedback. E-mail allows participants to exchange ideas with individuals from around the globe and to learn about the latest research quickly. Collaborating on-line also inspires individuals to analyze and solve problems more quickly. E-mail can thereby increase the level and even the objectivity of feedback in collaboration.

4. Generating more information through on-line exchanges. Many writers are willing to take more chances via e-mail than they would be in person, encouraging some writers to risk innovative suggestions and proposals they might fear to voice in face-to-face meetings. By reading and responding to drafts and revisions at times

TECH NOTE

Software That Helps You Write Collaboratively

Office software programs such as Microsoft Office, Corel Office Suites, and Lotus Notes offer an efficient way to collaborate. The programs are easy to use and speed up the process of collaborative writing. For example, Corel WordPerfect has a feature called "Workflow" (Lotus calls the feature "Work in Progress") that enables co-workers, authors, and editors to collaborate on a project by editing it in the same way they would edit any other document.

Reviewing a document is as easy as pulling down the File menu, pointing to Document, and clicking on Review.

- Most programs keep track of all document revisions by labeling each revision and keeping it separate from the original document.
- Each contributor can color-code his or her suggested revisions/additions by using the program's highlighting tool, which operates in much the same way as a transparent highlighting pen. Networking groups may predetermine the colors used by different contributors.
- Corel WordPerfect, like most office software packages, allows the author to have more than one document open at the same time in multiple windows and to arrange them easily on the screen simply by clicking the mouse.
- As the author(s) and the reviewers edit the document, they can save all the different versions as either temporary or permanent versions. However, the original remains unchanged until the author(s) accepts or rejects the edited selections.

most convenient for them, team members are given more time to offer more carefully considered responses.

5. Allowing team members to work on a project with less pressure. Collaborating via e-mail can make criticism easier to take and to give without the intimidating presence of an especially difficult colleague. Moreover, on-line collaboration lessens the likelihood of interruptions, miscommunications, or unpleasant confrontations.

6. Broadening the range of participation in the collaborative process. E-mail encourages the most flexible and extensive kinds of group organization possible. Supervisors within a writer's department and from related areas as well as customers and vendors or suppliers can join in the discussion and revision to improve the quality and service a company provides.

7. Lowering the cost of communicating in the world of work. The expense a company incurs to put several workers on-line to draft and revise documents is far less than if employees from different branches had to meet in person to perform the same writing tasks. An employer is also able to take advantage of more economical e-mail rates, compared to phone or fax charges.

FIGURE 3.9   An advertisement for Lotus Notes® emphasizing groupware.

It Is Easy To Get Started With
Notes

Notes gives you your choice of functionality.

Lotus Notes provides you with three licensing options for building a unified groupware infrastructure: Lotus Notes Mail, Lotus Notes Desktop, and Lotus Notes.

Lotus Notes Mail.

Notes Mail is a state-of-the-art, client/server messaging system. Notes Mail includes the cc:Mail user interface, OLE 2.0 support, platform independent viewers, collapsible sections, the InterNotes Web Navigator, task management, document libraries, personal journal, phone messages, and unparalleled mobile user support.

Lotus Notes Desktop.

Lotus Notes Desktop is a run-time Notes client with the ability to run any Notes application. Notes Desktop enables you to extend your most strategic applications to everyone in your workgroup. Includes Notes Mail functionality and sample application templates. Notes Desktop is an affordable solution ideal for Notes users who need to access customized applications.

Lotus Notes.

Lotus Notes gives you the full-function power to create custom applications for improving the quality of everyday business processes. Includes an application development environment, system administration capabilities, and Notes Mail functionality.

Build your Notes system as you build your business.

Start with the core capabilities of Lotus Notes and build strategic business process applications for your workgroup. Tailor your application development, database and messaging capabilities as your needs change and your workgroup expands. There's a rapidly-growing industry of value-added software products and services based on Lotus Notes. Choose from hundreds of off-the-shelf applications or work with one of the 11,000 Lotus Business Partners to customize an application appropriate for your company.

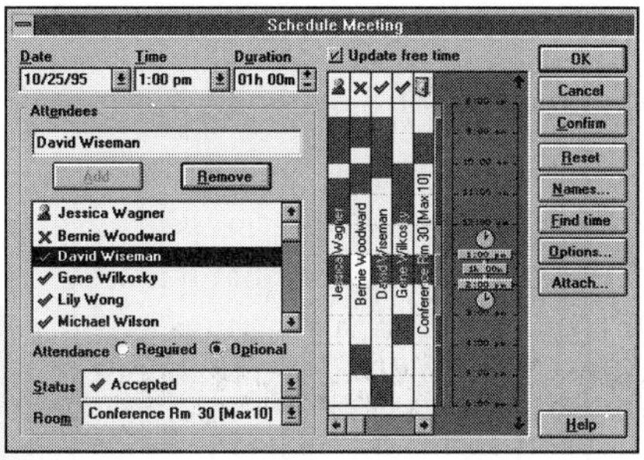

GROUP SCHEDULING IS EASY WITH LOTUS ORGANIZER AND NOTES

Lotus Organizer® uses existing Notes and cc:Mail directories to set up group meetings and address meeting notices. There is no faster or easier way to manage your workload, stay in touch with business contracts, and schedule meetings, than with Lotus Organizer and Notes.

The Collaborative Dynamics of E-Mail Technology

E-mail is widely used in the business world, and its impact is sure to grow. But it is not just for short exchanges. E-mail plays a vital role in allowing individuals to write and edit all types of documents—letters, memos, reports, proposals. Like a conference call or a videoconference (see Chapter 17), e-mail helps a group to share information and responses and to communicate with one another about them.

Using E-Mail to Write Collaboratively

E-mail technology is central to groupware, allowing for a variety of types of collaboration. Here are just two of the most likely ways a group can create and edit a document using e-mail. The first method which is essentially the sequential model of collaboration (see p. 89) using e-mail technology, is as follows:

1. Each member of the writing team drafts his or her assigned section of a document on a computer.
2. Then each writer e-mails that section to everyone else in the group for review and comments. (To send an e-mail attachment, see p. 130.)
3. All the individuals in the group then receive and react to each writer's draft and e-mail their comments—corrections, suggestions for revisions, additions, whatever—back to the individual contributors.
4. Each writer revises his or her draft based on the group's comments and sends the revised draft to the team leader or coordinator.
5. The team coordinator receives all the revised drafts and puts them together in one file, making sure that all changes are accurate and appropriate and that the style and format of the assembled final document are consistent.

A second method of e-mail collaboration is as follows:

1. Each member of the writing team actually revises the document he or she receives and then sends the revised document on to the leader or coordinator rather than back to the original writer.
2. The coordinator selects from among the revisions which ones to include in the final draft and which ones to leave out.

It is essential for the team leader to link revisions with the individuals who made them. Current technology allows for the identification of multiple versions by multiple authors of the same document so the leader will know which group member made a particular change.

Case Study: Collaborating via E-Mail

The following series of e-mail exchanges in Figure 3.10 were sent among a team trying collaboratively to write a single document, a report on expanding a hospital parking facility. In these exchanges you will see the dynamics of collaboration through e-mail. As you read the participants' comments, identify each person's concerns and how other team members react to them. Who is leading this collaborative effort? Whose ideas most influence the final report? Who raises an ethical issue and what is it? In broad terms, how will the revised document differ from the first draft?

FIGURE 3.10   Four on-line collaborative writers revise a report via e-mail.

Subject: **Report on Expanded Hospital Parking**
Date: Wed. 10 April 2003 16:55:00EST
From: Nicole_Goings@citymed.org
To: Ramon_Calderez@citymed.org, Alex_Latriere@citymed.org,
                    Loretta_Bartel@citymed.org

Now that we have a pretty clear outline and a first draft of the report before us, I think we all need to try to flesh it out. Thanks for reviewing the attached document to see how it hangs together. My initial reaction is that the draft needs reorganization and more attention to detail.

Subject: **Report on Expanded Hospital Parking**
Date: Wed. 10 April 2003 18:01:00EST
From: Ramon_Calderez@citymed.org
To: Nicole_Goings@citymed.org, Alex_Latriere@citymed.org,
                    Loretta_Bartel@citymed.org

Thanks for the draft. Our opening is not very strong or convincing. There is too little sense of the overall reason for the hospital investing $3.2 million in expanded parking facilities. I have rewritten the opening, as you will see, and tried to link the currently inadequate parking facilities (a detriment) to the overall growth of patient care (our strong suit). Then I tried to emphasize how responsive Bloomington Memorial has been to the needs of visitors and the patients they have come to see.

Let me know what you all think.

Subject: **Report on Expanded Hospital Parking**
Date: Thurs. 11 April 2003 8:23:00EST
From: Loretta_Bartel@citymed.org
To: Nicole_Goings@citymed.org, Alex_Latriere@citymed.org,
                    Ramon_Calderez@citymed.org

I agree with Ramon and think the revised introduction will work much better, but aren't we being too dramatic and not very pro-Bloomington Memorial by using the last sentence of his in the second paragraph—"new parking facilities will prevent visitors from walking long, bone-soaking distances in the rain"—and so I cut it and used a different closing sentence.

Subject: **Report on Expanded Hospital Parking**
Date: Thurs. 11 April 2003 8:54:00EST
From: Alex_Latriere@citymed.org
To: Nicole_Goings@citymed.org, Ramon_Calderez@citymed.org,
                    Loretta_Bartel@citymed.org

Loretta's change is o.k., but I want to point out two much more important revisions we need to make. One, it is unfair to say we are adding 500 new parking spaces. The exact number is 417. I am more comfortable with saying "more than 400" or just giving the exact number. Two, we should add another paragraph under the section now labeled "Increased Traffic Flow" and devote it entirely to Wentworth Avenue becoming a one-way street.

I inserted one or two points at the end of that section that I think would make a coherent paragraph.

Continued

FIGURE 3.10   (Continued)

Subject: **Report on Expanded Hospital Parking**
Date: Thurs. 11 April 2003 11:08:00EST
From: Nicole_Goings@citymed.org
To: Alex_Latriere@citymed.org, Ramon_Calderez@citymed.org,
                 Loretta_Bartel@citymed.org

Alex, all right, bravo—I hear you have taken your ideas to draft a new paragraph on Wentworth
and have also done some slight editing to make the transition to this topic a little smoother. What
do the rest of you think?

Subject: **Report on Expanded Hospital Parking**
Date: Thurs. 11 April 2003 13:45:00EST
From: Loretta_Bartel@citymed.org
To: Nicole_Goings@citymed.org, Ramon_Calderez@citymed.org,
                 AlexLatriere@citymed.org

Alex's suggestion and Nicole's additional paragraph work very well together.

Subject: **Report on Expanded Hospital Parking**
Date: Thurs. 11 April 2003 14:23:00EST
From: Ramon_Calderez@citymed.org
To: Nicole_Goings@citymed.org, Alex_Latriere@citymed.org,
                 Loretta_Bartel@citymed.org

Yes, a good job. The more I looked at the section on "Entry Points" the more I was troubled by
including the topic of handicap access under this heading. Given the fact that the new parking
facility will also involve widening the entrance to the ER, thus making 11 additional handicap spots
available, is, in my mind, worthy of a separate section in the report. Accordingly, I think we should
take handicap access out of the "Entry Points" section and create a new, even if small, section on
"Handicap Access."

Subject: **Report on Expanded Hospital Parking**
Date: Thurs. 11 April 2003 17:17:00EST
From: Loretta_Bartel@citymed.org
To: Ramon_Calderez@citymed.org, Nicole_Goings@citymed.org,
                 Alex_Latriere@citymed.org

We should emphasize the new technology behind this facility, but since the report is going to the
board of directors and to other general readers, we need to cut back on the technical descriptions.

Eliminate—or at least tone down—the details on stress points, pre-cast concrete, and the low slope
vehicular access ramps. Still include some information about the safety and engineering benefits,
but since we are also making the architect's site plans available, couldn't we tighten and shorten
this section. I have tried to take some things out. Have I taken out too much? Not enough? Let me
hear from you!

Continued

FIGURE 3.10   (Continued)

Subject: **Report on Expanded Hospital Parking**
Date: Fri. 12 April 2003 9:49:00EST
From: Nicole_Goings@citymed.org
To: Loretta_Bartel@citymed.org, Ramon_Calderez@citymed.org,
                      Alex_Latriere@citymed.org

Thanks and more thanks, Loretta. I spoke with Lee Bukowski, the hospital architect, last evening about your changes. You are on target and so I have let your revisions stand. BUT...I do think we need to retain some information about the access ramps and covered areas surrounding them.

Subject: **Report on Expanded Hospital Parking**
Date: Mon. 15 April 2003 10:23:00EST
From: Ramon Calderez@citymed.org
To: Loretta_Bartel@citymed.org, Nicole_Goings@citymed.org,
                      Alex_Latriere@citymed.org

We must have a visual about the hospital's efforts. I e-mailed the archives earlier this morning and they found the photograph of an aerial view of the hospital's original parking lot in 1971. Let's incorporate that somewhere in the introduction and then use the artist's drawing of what the new parking lot will look like to begin the section "Expanded Parking Facilities Planned." I have scanned (and now attach) both documents to give you an idea of what I have in mind.

Subject: **Report on Expanded Hospital Parking**
Date: Mon. 15 April 2003 14:04:00EST
From: Nicole_Goings@citymed.org
To: Ramon_Calderez@citymed.org, Alex_Latriere@citymed.org,
                      Loretta_Bartel@citymed.org

Ramon, you deserve a pat on the back. Yes, the visuals definitely work.

I think we have done a good job in revising and editing the report. I want to give it to Christine Murphrey tomorrow for her approval before it goes to the Board.

Let me know before 4:30 today if you have any further suggestions or revisions.

Thanks for all your help. I'm going to acknowledge each of you for your excellent work in my cover letter to Director Murphrey.

Meetings

One of the most frequent ways to collaborate is through meetings, which can be small group discussions (like chat rooms on the Net) or large, formal conferences. Whether it is regularly scheduled (a weekly staff meeting) or a special, unscheduled one, a meeting requires teamwork. Collective energy and goodwill will bear much fruit. Though videoconferencing is used frequently in the workplace, that technology will never take the place of face-to-face meetings. The guidelines on collaborative writing (pp. 80–85) also apply to group interactions at meetings. Basically, you need to know how to plan a meeting, create an agenda, and prepare minutes.

Planning a Meeting

You will have to schedule a time, place, and a date and then notify the people who are to attend. Lotus Organizer® (see Figure 3.9) contains a Calendar option to help you reach the people who need to attend the meeting. If someone on your team cannot attend and you cannot reschedule the meeting, try to get that person's input through e-mail.

TECH NOTE

Scheduling with Lotus Organizer®

Lotus Organizer® (see Figure 3.9) automatically schedules meetings for those listed in your group directory. It will notify the group of the date, time, and place; automatically set up an appointment in their calendars; and alert you about any conflicts. The program also provides an alarm to remind group members 10 minutes, 30 minutes, or even a day or two in advance of the meeting. Other options you can choose include specifying whether the meeting is confidential or if visitors have been invited. Such a program eliminates the need for phone calls or e-mail messages and speeds up the process of group communication.

To prepare for the meeting, jot down the main ideas you (and your group) must cover. Collect any data (test results, reports, client communications, statistics) the group will discuss. If you are using graphics such as PowerPoint (see pp. 494–496), make sure you prepare them ahead of time. Careful planning leads to a careful agenda. Have copies of any documents you plan to discuss available for the group to review.

Creating an Agenda

Out of your planning will come your *agenda,* or the topics to be covered at the meeting. An agenda is a one-, sometimes two-page outline of the main, pertinent points. The agenda should list only those items that your group, based on its work and interaction, regards as most crucial. Try to prioritize your action items so the most important ones come first. An agenda might also include short reports or presentations for which one or two members of your group are responsible. Always distribute the agenda ahead of time (at least a day or two) through a software program such as Lotus Notes or e-mail, so your team will be prepared and better able to contribute.

Writing the Minutes

The *minutes* are a summary of what happened at the meeting. Distribute copies of the minutes to the team members to help them recall what happened at the meeting and to help them prepare for the next one. Copies of minutes are kept on file—they are the official record of the group's deliberations and are regarded as legal documents. Accordingly, minutes must be clear, accurate, and impartial. (Keep the minutes free from your own opinions of how well or poorly the meeting went; for example, "Ms. Saunders customarily offered the right solutions" and "Once more Hicks got off the topic" are not appropriate comments.) Because the person chairing a meeting cannot take minutes and preside at the same time, another member of the group designated as the secretary should prepare the minutes. Minutes are distributed usually within twenty-four to forty-eight hours after the meeting has adjourned.

Minutes of a meeting should include the following information:

- date, time, and place of meeting
- name of the group holding the meeting and why
- name of the person chairing the meeting
- names of those present and those absent
- the approval or amendment of the minutes of the previous meeting
- for each major point—the action items—indicate what was done:
  - who said what
  - what was discussed/suggested/proposed
  - what was decided and the vote, including absentions
  - what was continued (tabled) for a subsequent study, report, or meeting
  - time of next meeting
  - time the meeting officially concluded

To be effective, minutes must be concise and to the point. Here are a few guidelines to help you.

- Make sure of your facts; spell all names, products, tests correctly.
- Concentrate on the major facts surrounding action items. Save the reader's time and your own by condensing lengthy discussions, debates, and reports given at the meeting.
- Do not report verbatim what everyone said; readers will be more interested in what the group did.
- List each motion (or item voted on) exactly as it is worded and in its final form.
- Avoid words that interpret (negatively or positively) what the group or anyone in the group did or did not do.

Figure 3.11 shows how these parts fit together.

FIGURE 3.11   Minutes from a business meeting.

Minutes for Environmental Safety Committee (ESC) meeting on February 3, 2001, in Room 203 of Lab Annex Building at 1:10 p.m. E.S.T.

Members Present:

Thomas Baldanza, Grace Corlee (**President**), Virginia Downey, Victor Johnson, Roberta Koos, Kent Leviche (**Secretary**), Ralph Nowicki, Barbara Poe-Smith, Williard Ralston, Morgan Tachiashi, Asah Rashid, and Carlos Zandrillia

Members Absent:

Paul Gordon (sick leave); Marty Wagner

Old Business:

The minutes from the previous meeting on January 5, 2001, were approved as read.

Reports:

(1) Morgan Tachiashi reported on the progress the Site Inspection Committee was making in getting the plant ready for the March 29 visit of the State Board of Examiners. All preparations are on schedule.

(2) The proposal to study the use of biometric identification in place of employee ID badges was nearly complete, according to Asah Rashid, Chair of the Proposal Committee, and will be presented at next month's meeting for approval.

New Business:

(1) Virginia Downey and Ralph Nowicki expressed concern about a computer virus that may strike the plant—Monkey. Disguised as a familiar e-mail, the virus is contained in an attachment that destroys files. A motion was made by Barbara Poe-Smith, seconded by Virginia Downey, that management upgrade its antivirus protection software. Objecting to this expense, Williard Ralston thought the current software was sufficient. The vote carried by 9 to 3.

Continued

FIGURE 3.11   (Continued)

(2) Thomas Baldanza believed that cross-training should be accelerated, especially in safety areas, to meet the target date of August 8, which the ESC had set in December of 2000. Agreeing, Roberta Koos stressed that, without cross-training, some departments would be vulnerable to safety violations. Victor Johnson, on the other hand, found that such cross-training could not feasibly be accomplished in the original time frame since several departments could not spare employees to participate. He moved that the target date motion be amended and pushed to November 15. The vote to amend was defeated 10–2.

Calling attention to the importance of the target date, Grace Corlee will ask Zandria Dickens, Plant Training Coordinator, to come to the next ESC meeting to discuss the current status of the training program and to offer suggestions for its speedy implementation.

(3) Kent Leviche calculated computer downtime in the plant during the month of January–4 outages totaling 7.5 lost working hours—and asked the ESC to address this problem. After discussion, the ESC unanimously agreed to appoint a subcommittee to investigate the outages and determine solutions. Roberta Koos and Thomas Baldanza will chair the subcommittee and present a survey report at next month's meeting.

(4) Personnel in the Environmental Testing Lab were commended for their extra effort in ensuring that their department maintained the highest professional standards during the month of January. A letter of commendation was sent to Emily Lu, the Lab Supervisor, and her staff.

(5) Grace Corlee adjourned the meeting at 3:41 p.m.

Next Meeting:

The next meeting of the ESC will be on March 6 at 1:00 p.m. in Room 203 of the Lab Annex Building.

✓ Revision Checklist

- ❑ Tried to be a team player by putting the success of my group over the needs of my own ego.
- ❑ Followed necessary steps of the writing process to take advantage of team effort and feedback.
- ❑ Attended all group meetings and understood responsibilities of the group and my own obligations.
- ❑ Finished research, planning, and drafting expected of me.
- ❑ Conducted necessary interviews and conferences to gather and verify information.
- ❑ Shared my research, ideas, and suggestions for revision through constructive criticism.
- ❑ Participated honestly and politely in discussions with colleagues.
- ❑ Treated members of my team with respect and courtesy.
- ❑ Was open to criticism and suggestions for change.
- ❑ Read colleagues' work and gave specific and helpful criticism and suggestions.
- ❑ Kept matters in proper perspective by not being a nitpicker and by not interrupting with extraneous points or unnecessary questions.
- ❑ Sought help when appropriate from relevant subject matter experts and from co-workers.
- ❑ Secured responses and approval from management.
- ❑ Took advantage of e-mail to disseminate information, to communicate with my collaborative team, and to keep my own research current.
- ❑ E-mailed messages in clear, diplomatic, and correct sentences.
- ❑ Attached pertinent documents in e-mail to collaborative team.
- ❑ Answered e-mail questions and responded to requests promptly.
- ❑ Used groupware available to me.
- ❑ Prepared agenda for meetings clearly and distributed ahead of time.
- ❑ Wrote minutes that objectively reported what happened.

Exercises

1. Assume you belong to a three- or four-person editing team that functions the way Tara Barber's does in Figure 3.2. Each member of your team should bring in four copies of a paper done for this course or another one. Exchange copies with the other members of your team so that each team member has everyone else's papers to review and revise. For each paper you receive, comment on the style, organization, tone, and discussion of ideas as Wells McCraw did in Figure 3.6.

2. With members of your collaborative team (selected by your teacher or self-appointed) select four different brands of the same leading product (such as a software package, a Web browser, a CD player, a microwave, a DVD player, a power tool, or other item). Each member of your team should select one of the brands and prepare a two-page memo report (see pp. 118–126), evaluating it for your instructor according to the following criteria:

   - convenience
   - performance
   - technical capabilities/capacities
   - appearance
   - adaptability
   - price
   - weaknesses/strengths compared with competitors' models

   Each team member should then submit a draft to the other members of the team to review. At a subsequent group meeting, the group should evaluate the four brands based on the team's drafts and then together prepare one final recommendation report for your instructor.

3. Your company is planning to construct a new office, and you, together with other employees from your company, have been asked to serve on a committee to make sure that plans for the new building adhere precisely to the Americans with Disabilities Act, passed in 1993. According to that act, it is against the law to discriminate against anyone with disabilities that limit "major life activities"—walking, seeing, speaking, working.

   The law is expressly designed to remove architectural and physical barriers and to make sure that plans are modified to accommodate those protected by the law (for example, wider hallways to accommodate individuals in wheelchairs). Other considerations include choosing appropriate nonstick floor surfaces (reducing the danger of slipping), placing water fountains low enough for use by individuals in wheelchairs, and installing doors that require minimal pressure to open and close.

   After studying the plans for the new building, you and your team members find several problem areas. Prepare a group-written report advising management of the problems and what must be done to correct them to comply with the law. Divide your written work according to areas that need alteration—doors, floors, water fountains, restroom facilities. Each team member should bring in his or her section, which the group will edit and revise. The group should then prepare the final report for management.

4. A new president will be coming to your college in the next month, and you and five other students have been asked to serve on a committee that will submit a report about campus safety problems and what should be done to solve them. You and your team must establish priorities and propose guidelines that you want the new administration to put into practice. After two very heated meetings, you realize that what you and two other students have considered solutions, the

other half of your committee regards as the problems. Here is a rundown of the leading conflicts dividing your committee:

- **Speed bumps.** Half the committee likes the way they slow traffic down on campus, but the other half says they are a menace because they jar car CD players.
- **Sound pollution.** Half your team wants Campus Security to enforce a noise policy preventing students from playing loud music while driving on campus, but the other half insists that would violate students' rights.
- **Van and sport utility vehicle parking.** Half the committee demands that vans and sport utility vehicles park in specially designated places because they block the view of traffic for any vehicle parked next to them; the other members protest that people who drive these vehicles will be singled out for less desirable parking places on campus

Clearly your committee has reached a deadlock and will be unproductive as long as those conflicts go unresolved. Based on the above scenario, do the following:

a. Have each student on the committee write (or e-mail, if available) the other five students suggesting a specific plan on how to proceed—how the group can resolve their conflicts. Prepare your e-mail message and send it to the other five committee members and to your instructor. What's your plan to get the committee moving toward writing the report to the incoming president?

b. Assume that you have been asked to convince the other half of the committee to accept your half's views on the three areas of speed bumps, noise control, and parking. Send the three opposition students a memo or e-mail persuading them to your way of thinking. Keep in mind that your message must assure them that you respect their point of view.

c. Assume that the committee members reach a compromise after seeing your plan put forth in (a). Collaboratively draft a three-page report to the new president.

d. Collaboratively draft a letter to the editor of your student newspaper defending your recommendations to the student body and explaining how the group resolved its difficulty. This is a public statement that the group felt it was important to write; you will have to choose your words carefully to win campuswide support.

5. You work for a hospital laboratory, and your lab manager, under pressure from management to save money, insists that you and the three other med-techs switch to a different brand of vacuum blood drawing tubes. You and your colleagues much prefer the brand of tubes you have been using for years. Moreover, the price difference between the two brands is small. As a group project, prepare a memo to the business manager of the hospital explaining why the switch is unnecessary, unwise, and unpopular. Then prepare another collaboratively written memo to your lab manager. Be sensitive to each reader's needs as you diplomatically explain the group's position.

Correspondence

Writing Memos, Faxes, and E-Mail

Memos, faxes, and e-mail are the types of writing you can expect to prepare most frequently on the job. These three forms of business correspondence are quick, easy, and effective ways for a company to communicate internally as well as externally. You will find yourself preparing one or more of these types of writing each day to co-workers in your department, to colleagues in other departments and divisions of your company, and to decision makers at all levels. You can expect to send memos and e-mail to co-workers anywhere in the world.

What Memos, Faxes, and E-Mail Have in Common

1. Each of these three forms of writing is streamlined for the busy world of work. Memos are far less formal in tone than letters; e-mail can be even more informal than a memo. Memos, faxes, and e-mail also require you to follow different formats than you do for letters. As you will see, these formats are designed to expedite communication between you and your readers. E-mail, faxes, and memos can be composed and sent to various sites from your PC.

2. Memos, faxes, and e-mail give busy readers information fast. Each type of document should be clear, direct, and narrowly focused. Memos, faxes, and e-mail are *not* designed for long messages but for shorter ones (usually a page or two). While these messages can be about any topic in the world of work, most often they focus on the day-to-day activities and operations at your company—sales and product information, policy and schedule changes, progress reports, orders, personnel decisions, and so on.

3. Even though memos, faxes, and e-mail are routine, they still demand a great deal of your thought and time. Each is a vital piece of documentation that requires your best written work. While some individuals believe we are moving toward a paperless office, a company will still want to see a paper or electronic trail documenting what has been done when and by whom. Your success as an employee can depend as much on your preparing a readable and effective memo, fax, or e-mail as it will on your technical expertise.

Memos

Memorandum, from which the term *memo* comes, is a Latin word for "something to be remembered." The Latin meaning points to the memo's chief function: to record information of immediate importance and interest in the busy world of work. **Memos** are in-house correspondence sent up and down the corporate ladder—from managers to employees and from employees to managers. They are also sent to and from co-workers. Memos allow a business or an agency to communicate with itself in its day-to-day operations. They can be handwritten, faxed, or sent through e-mail.

Functions of Memos

Memos have a variety of functions, including

- announcing a company policy or plan
- making a request
- explaining a procedure or giving instructions
- clarifying or summarizing an issue
- alerting readers to a problem
- confirming the outcome of a conversation
- reminding readers about a meeting, policy, or procedure
- providing documentation necessary for business
- offering suggestions or recommendations

Memos are valuable written records used for a variety of purposes. They are used for short reports; see Chapter 15 for examples of field trip or progress reports in memo format. Many internal proposals (pp. 556–560) also are written as memos.

Memo Format

Memos vary in format. Some companies use standard, printed forms (Figure 4.1), while others have their names (letterhead) printed on their memos, as in Figure 4.2. Memos can be printed on 8½" × 11" sheets of paper or on half-sheets. The smaller option is useful for shorter communications to encourage the writer to be concise and to conserve paper. You can also make a memo by including the necessary parts in an e-mail.

As you can see from looking at Figures 4.1 through 4.4, memos look different from letters. They are more streamlined and less formal. Because they are sent to individuals within your company, memos do not need the formalities necessary in business letters, such as an inside address, salutation, complimentary close, or signature line, as discussed in Chapter 5. (See pp. 154–162.)

Basically, the memo consists of two parts: the identifying information at the top and the message itself. The identifying information includes these easily recognized parts: the **To, From, Date,** and **Subject** lines.

```
TO:       Aileen Kelly, Chief Computer Analyst
FROM:     Stacy Kaufman, Operator, Level II
DATE:     January 31, 2001
SUBJECT: Progress report on the fall schedule
```

FIGURE 4.1   Standard memo format without letterhead.

MEMO

TO: All RNs
FROM: Margaret Wojak, Director of Nurses *M. W.*
DATE: August 16, 2001
SUBJECT: RN Identity Patches

Effective September 1, 2001, all RNs will be asked to wear an identity patch in addition to any other means of identification (name or badge). You should sew your patch on the upper right arm of lab coats or uniforms so that staff and patients can easily identify you as an RN.

You may obtain an authorized Memorial Hospital identity patch for two dollars at the Health Uniform Shop directly across the street from the hospital on Ames Street.

Please write me at my e-mail address, mwojak@memorial.com, or call me at Extension 310 if you have any questions.

On the **To** line, write the name and job title of the individual(s) who will receive your memo or a copy of it. If your memo is going to more than one reader, make sure you list your readers in the order of their status in your company or agency, as Mike Gonzalez does in Figure 4.3 (the vice president's name appears before the public relations director's). If you are on a first-name basis with the reader, use just his or her first name. Otherwise, include the reader's first and last names.

In some companies memos are sent to everyone whose name is on a distribution list. For example, your name might be on the list for receiving all company information on a given project or weekly reports from certain departments. Your name may appear on a number of lists, and some of your memos may be distributed to several people. Don't send copies of your memos (or your e-mail for that matter) to individuals who don't need them, however. You will only increase the paper inflation or electronic traffic in your company.

On the **From** line, write your name (first name only if your reader refers to you by it) and your job title (unless it is unnecessary for your reader). Some writers handwrite their initials after their typed name to verify that the message comes from them.

FIGURE 4.2   Printed memo on letterhead stationery.

Greenwood Corp.

56 North Jones • Canton, Ohio 45307-0299

phone (216) 555-4232   fax (216) 555-1172

TO: Lucy Valdez
FROM: Roger Blackmore *RB*
DATE: November 23, 2001
SUBJECT: Review of Successful Web Site Seminar

I attended the "How to Build a Successful Web Site" seminar on November 20 and learned the "rules and tools" we will need to redesign our own site.

Here is a review of the major topics covered by the director, Jackie Lowery.

1. Keep your Web site content-based—hit your target audience.
2. Visualize and "map out" your site's ad links.
3. Design your Web site to look the way you envision it—make it aesthetically pleasing.
4. Make your site easy to navigate.
5. Maintain your page outline; make changes when necessary.
6. Create hot links and image maps to usher users from page to page.
7. Complete your site with sound and animation.

Could we meet in the next day or two to discuss re-creating our own Web site in light of these guidelines? I would like your suggestions to proceed with this project. Thanks.

email rblack@gwc.com

On the **Subject** line, write the purpose of your memo. The subject line serves as the title of your memo. Be precise so readers can file your memo correctly. Vague subject lines such as "New Policy," "Operating Difficulties," or "Shareware" do not identify your message precisely and may suggest that your message is not carefully restricted or developed. "Shareware," for example, does not tell readers if your memo will discuss new equipment, corporate arrangements, or vendors; offer additional or fewer benefits; or warn employees about abusing the system.

On the **Date** line, do not simply name the day of the week—Friday. Give the full calendar date—June 8, 2001.

TECH NOTE

Using a Template

A template is a predesigned word processing form created by either a company (Microsoft or Corel for example) or a user (such as you or your boss) as a basis for all subsequent similar documents in order to save time. A memo template is a predesigned form you can use every time you send a memo. You simply open the template and fill in the blanks. Below is an example of a memo template. The document heading (in the example below, "Memorandum," "TO," "FROM," "DATE," and "RE") always remains the same, and the date is inserted automatically. The only entries you must add are the reader, the subject, and—of course—the body of the memo.

Memorandum

TO:
FROM: Linda Cowan
DATE: October 2, 2002
RE: (Enter subject here.)

****

(Body of text goes here.)

Memo Protocol and Company Politics

Memos are important tools for any company or agency. They reflect a company's politics, policies, and organization. Memos are sent down the administrative ladder from presidents, vice presidents, managers, and so on, to employees, and memos are sent up the ladder, too, from employees to their supervisors. Workers also send memos to one another. Figures 4.1 and 4.4 illustrate memos sent from the top down; Figure 4.2 contains a memo from one worker to another; and Figure 4.3 shows a memo sent from an employee to management.

FIGURE 4.3   A memo that uses headings to highlight organization.

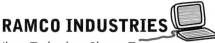

RAMCO INDUSTRIES

Where Technology Shapes Tomorrow
ramco@gem.com   http://www.Ramcogem.com

TO: Rachel Mohler, Vice President
                    Harrison Snowden, Public Relations
FROM: Mike Gonzalez
SUBJECT: Ways to Increase Ramco's Community Involvement
DATE: March 2, 2001

At our planning session in early February, our division managers stressed the need to generate favorable publicity for our new Ramco plant in Mayfield. Knowing that such publicity will highlight Ramco's visibility in Mayfield, I think the company's image might be enhanced in the following ways:

CREATE A SCHOLARSHIP FUND
Ramco would receive favorable publicity by creating a scholarship at Mayfield Community College for any student interested in a career in technology. A one-year scholarship at Mayfield Community College would cost $4,800. The scholarship could be awarded by a committee composed of Ramco executives and staff. Such a scholarship would emphasize Ramco's support for technical education at a local college.

OFFER FACTORY TOURS
Guided tours of the Mayfield facility would introduce the community to Ramco's innovative technology. The tours might be organized for community and civic groups. Individuals would see the care we take in production and equipment choice and the speed with which we ship our products. Of special interest to visitors would be Ramco's use of industrial robots alongside Ramco employees. Since these tours would be scheduled well in advance, they should not conflict with our production schedules.

PROVIDE GUEST SPEAKERS
Many of our employees would be excellent guest speakers at social and educational meetings in Mayfield. Possible topics include the technological advances Ramco has made in designing and engineering and how these advances help consumers.

Thanks for giving me your comments as soon as possible. If we are going to put one or more of the suggestions into practice before the plant opens, we'll need to act before the end of the month.

FIGURE 4.4   Memo with a clear introduction, discussion, and conclusion.

MEMORANDUM

Dearborne Equipment Company

To: Machine Shop Employees
From: Janet Hempstead, Shop Supervisor *JH*
Date: September 27, 2000
Subject: Cleaning Brake Machines

Introduction During the past two weeks I have received several reports that the brake machines are not being cleaned properly after each use. Through this memo I want to emphasize and explain the importance of keeping these machines clean for the safety of all employees.

When the brake machines are used, the cutter chops off small particles of metal from brake drums. These particles settle on the machines and create a potentially hazardous situation for anyone working on or near the machines. If the machines are not cleaned routinely before being used again, these metal particles could easily fly into an individual's face when the brake drum is spinning.

Discussion **To prevent accidents like this from happening, please make sure you vacuum the brake machines after each use.**

You will find two vacuum cleaners for this purpose in the shop—one of them is located in work area 1-A and the other, a reserve model, is in the storage area. Vacuuming brake machines is quick and easy: it should take no more than a few seconds. This is a small amount of time to make the shop safer for all of us.

Conclusion Thanks for your cooperation. If you have any questions, please call me at Extension 324 or come by my office.

204 South Mill St., South Orange, NJ 02341-3420 (609) 555-9848 JHEMP@dearco.com

Most companies have their own memo protocol—accepted ways in which in-house communications are formatted, organized, written, and routed. In fact, some companies offer protocol seminars on how employees are to prepare in-house communications. In the corporate world, protocol determines where your memo will go. For example, it would be presumptuous to send copies of all your memos to the vice president. You would offend your immediate supervisor, who would think that you are trying to avoid going through proper channels.

Conversely, a vice president may want a certain memo to be distributed to the staff by another, lower administrator to ensure that the staff is being informed but that responses are sent not back up to the vice president but through a lower administrative channel. Familiarize yourself early in your employment with how your company wants memos (or even e-mail) to be directed.

You may be asked to write a memo for the vice president or supervisor to sign, as were Lee Booker in Figure 3.1 and Jocelyn Woolfolk in Figure 3.4. Your writing skills may, therefore, need to include the ability to write in another person's voice to some degree. Moreover, as you learned in Chapter 3, collaborative writing—of memos, reports, and so on—is common in the world of work.

Memo Style and Tone

The style and tone of your memos will be controlled by your audience within your company or agency. Writing to a co-worker whom you know well, you can adopt a casual, conversational tone. You want to be seen as friendly and cooperative. In fact, to do otherwise would make you look self-important, stuffy, or hard to work with. Consider the friendly tone appropriate for one colleague writing to another in Roger Blackmore's memo to Lucy Valdez in Figure 4.2.

When writing a memo to a manager, though, you want to use a more formal tone than when communicating with a co-worker or peer. Your boss will expect you to show a more respectful, even official, posture. Here are two ways of expressing the same message, the first more suitable when writing to a co-worker and the second more appropriate for a memo to the boss.

Co-worker: I think we should go ahead with Marisol's plan for reorganization. It seems like a safe option to me, and I don't think we can lose.

Boss: I think that we should adopt the organizational plan developed by Marisol Vega. Her recommendations are carefully researched and persuasively answer all the questions our office has about the plan.

Finally, keep in mind that your employer and co-workers deserve the same clear and concise writing and attention to the "you attitude" (that is, the attitude that your readers and their needs are important; see pp. 162–167) as your customers do. Memos require the same care and follow the same rules of effective writing as letters do.

Strategies for Organizing a Memo

Organize your memos so readers can find information quickly and act on it promptly. For longer, more complex communications, such as the memos in Figures 4.2 through 4.4, your message might be divided into three parts: (1) introduction, (2) discussion, and (3) conclusion.

Introduction

In the introduction of your memo, do the following:

- Tell readers clearly about the problem, procedure, question, or policy that prompted you to write.
- Link the first sentence of your memo to the subject line.
- Explain briefly any background information the reader needs to know.
- Be specific about what you are going to accomplish in your memo.

Note, for example, the ways in which the writers of Figures 4.2 and 4.3 tell readers why a list of items is provided and why recommendations are included. Do not hesitate to come right out and say: "This memo explains new e-mail security procedures" or "This memo summarizes the action taken at the site near Evansville to reduce air pollution."

Discussion

In the discussion section (the body) of your memo, help readers in these ways:

- State why a problem or procedure is important, who will be affected by it, and what caused it and why.
- Indicate why changes are necessary.
- Give precise dates, times, locations, and costs.

See how Janet Hempstead's memo in Figure 4.4 carefully describes an existing problem and explains the proper procedure for cleaning the brake machine.

Conclusion

In your conclusion, state specifically how you want the reader to respond to your memo. To get readers to act appropriately, you can do one or more of the following in your conclusion:

- Ask readers to call you if they have any questions.
- Request a reply—in writing, over the telephone, via e-mail, or in person—by a specific date.
- Provide a list of recommendations that the readers are to accept, revise, or reject.

Organizational Markers

Throughout your memo use the following organizational markers, where appropriate.

- **Headings** organize your work and make information easy for readers to follow, as in Figure 4.3. Headings will emerge from your brainstorming session.
- **Numbered** or **bulleted lists** help readers see comparisons and contrasts readily and thereby comprehend your ideas more quickly, as in Figure 4.2.
- **Underlining** or **boldfacing** emphasize key points (see Figure 4.4). Do not overuse this technique; draw attention only to main points and those that contain summaries or draw conclusions.

Organizational markers are not limited to memos; you will find them in e-mail, letters, and reports as well. (See Chapter 11.)

Faxes

Even though you may use e-mail extensively, fax (facsimile) machines are still widespread in the world of work. Most businesses and home offices have fax machines, as stand-alone units or as part of a printer. A fax machine can send copies of letters, memos, reports, graphs, blueprints, and artwork over ordinary phone lines. You can send graphics that resemble actual photos. Faxes are especially effective if you have to make a few changes in a detailed document (for example, a contract or a boilerplate) and do not want to rekey the entire work. Simply indicating your changes on a copy of the document and then faxing it will save you and your reader time. You will reduce costs if you send faxes at times when phone rates are lower—evenings and weekends. Some fax machines are programmed to offer **broadcasting,** allowing a business to send the same fax to numerous customers in a relatively short time.

When you send a fax, be sure to include a fax cover sheet (Figure 4.5). A cover sheet indicates the persons sending and receiving the fax, their addresses, phone and fax numbers, and the total number of pages being faxed. This last information is essential so the recipient will know when the transmission is complete and can alert the sender of any interruption in transmission.

Be aware that, unless the recipient has her or his own secured fax machine, your confidentiality is not easily protected when communicating by fax. If your fax is sent to a machine available to the entire office staff, anyone can read it.

Fax Guidelines

When you send a fax, observe the following guidelines.

1. As a courtesy, e-mail your reader ahead of time to let him or her know you are sending a fax.
2. Because the type size of a document is reduced in transmission, print your fax message in a larger point size (12 or 14).
3. Avoid writing any comments in the margins or at the very top or bottom of a fax. Your notes might be cut off or blurred in transmission.
4. Make sure the document you are faxing is clear, but always include your phone and fax numbers in case the recipient needs to verify your message or has questions about it.
5. Be careful about sending anything longer than three to four pages. You can tie up the recipient's phone line. Call before you fax to see whether the recipient will allow you to fax a longer document or would prefer that you send it another way.
6. While it may be permissible to send a fax to a company after business hours, do not risk sending one after hours to a customer's home unless he or she has agreed or requested it.

TECH NOTE

E-Mail and Your Faxes

You can use your computer as a fax machine. You simply need a modem, which converts information from the way your computer handles it to the way the telephone lines handle it; nearly all computers now come with modems already installed. To send a fax, you tell the computer to print your document, and then, instead of choosing the printer normally connected to your computer, you choose FAX.

Also, you can have an Internet-based company, such as jfax.com (*http://www.jfax.com*) or eFax.com (*http://www.efax.com*), direct faxes to your electronic mailbox (e-mail). Because the services are Internet-based, you do not need to purchase a special computer program, and you can access your account from anywhere.

To receive a fax:

- You get a personal fax number without having to add a phone line or even a fax machine.
- Faxes received at your fax number are converted into e-mail messages, which are sent directly to your e-mail in-box.
- You can read, save, print, answer, and even forward the messages to a third party. Printed messages look like regular faxes.

To send a fax:

- Simply compose an e-mail message with the destination fax phone number and send it as you normally send e-mail.
- The service converts your e-mail into a message that is received at the destination fax phone number as a fax.
- A confirmation of fax transmission is sent to you within minutes.

These services include the ability to do broadcast faxing.

E-Mail

What Is E-Mail?

E-mail, or electronic mail, is one of the most popular basic features of the Internet. E-mail has become an essential communication tool and is found almost everywhere. Millions of consumers, perhaps billions by the year 2005, use e-mail to communicate with businesses each day. Everyone who has computer access to an Internet service provider can send and receive e-mail. E-mail is also available through Web TV. As with a fax, the recipient of e-mail does not need to be present to receive the message. But there are major differences between the two media.

FIGURE 4.5   A fax cover sheet.

Westwood Communications Inc.
4277 Old Trail Road
El Paso, TX 79968
www.westwood.com

FAX COVER SHEET

Date: _May 16, 2001_____

PLEASE DELIVER THE FOLLOWING PAGE(S) TO:

NAME: _Deborah Shapiro_____

COMPANY/DEPARTMENT: _Marketing Department_____

FAX NUMBER: _(502) 555-8449_____

THIS FAX IS BEING SENT BY:

NAME/DEPARTMENT: _Malcolm T. Belleau, Design Dept._____

NUMBER OF PAGES: __3__INCLUDING COVER SHEET

TIME SENT: _10:30_ AM _X__ PM ____

IF YOU DO NOT RECEIVE ALL PAGES CLEARLY,
PLEASE CALL (915) 555-3200

TECH NOTE

Fax vs. Phone

As long as a fax phone line is open, a fax will be transmitted in a matter of seconds. A fax may not be as fast as e-mail. Of course, e-mail is delivered more slowly if the traffic on the Internet is heavy or if a server is down.

With e-mail you send and receive messages through your PC, which is linked via a phone line and a modem to a worldwide communication network. Functioning like an electronic mailbox, your computer can receive and store messages until you are ready to open them. You can then read the messages on your screen, make hard (printed) copies if necessary (see Figures 4.6 through 4.9), forward them, file messages on disk for future reference, or delete them.

You can communicate quickly and efficiently with hundreds of people in your office, co-workers at branch offices, or employees and customers across the country or around the world. For example, you can e-mail the president of the United States at *president@whitehouse.gov* or the CEO of IBM at *ceo@ibm.com*.

Advantages of E-Mail

E-mail is fundamentally different from paper-based communications. It has many advantages over conventional "snail mail," as the U.S. Postal Service is sometimes called. Among them, e-mail is

1. Quick. E-mail can usually reach its destination within seconds, if there is not a Net slowdown. You don't have to wait for postal or overnight deliveries. E-mail can expedite immensely any domestic or international communication.

2. Convenient. You can send e-mail anytime and know that it will be delivered even if the receiver is away from his or her computer. When the individual returns, your message will be waiting. Consequently, you don't have to worry about being in a different time zone from your recipient's, repeatedly exchanging phone messages, or hearing busy signals when sending a fax. Moreover, you can send your e-mail via a laptop computer when you are away from your office—sitting in a hotel lobby, riding in a car, or even flying in an airplane.

3. Cost-effective. E-mail does not require stamps, envelopes, or even paper (assuming you don't need a hard copy for your records). It is also cheaper than long-distance telephone calls or faxes. Because Internet access fees are usually on a fixed monthly basis and the dial-up usually is a local number, it costs no more to send a message around the world than it does across town.

4. Efficient. Sending and receiving e-mail makes it easier to conduct business than by communicating through conventional channels. Recipients can read and reply at their convenience (when there is a window in a hectic business day). They can ask questions or provide clarifications immediately. Even when they are busy, they can e-mail you that your message was received and they will answer it later.

   5. Conducive to collaborative writing. E-mail enables many individuals to "talk" with each other simultaneously. With a click of your "Reply to All" button, you can e-mail everyone on your team who received a particular message. You might send the same message by e-mail to a variety of individuals or a variety of messages to just one or two people. They can read, comment on, incorporate, and revise your document and then send the revised version back to you or to everyone else in the group. (Review the collaborative e-mail exchange on pp. 105–107). Correspondingly, you can reply to messages from a team member and, with his or her permission, share your comments with the group. You can also incorporate changes from a team member's e-mail message directly into your draft. See page 104 for additional uses of e-mail in collaborative writing.

Business Applications of E-Mail

E-mail is the most informal type of business correspondence, far more so than a printed memo or letter. (As we'll see in Chapter 5, e-mail should never be sent in place

---

TECH NOTE

Sending an E-Mail Attachment
Your e-mail program will tell you whether an attachment has been sent, but be aware that attachments may arrive in an unusable or partly usable form. You and your sender need to use the same or compatible software to open and manipulate each other's documents, especially if the files contain graphics, databases, or spreadsheets. Even simple word processing documents may arrive mangled if the sender and the receiver use different operating systems or incompatible programs.

- Attach a test document and ask your reader to send you one in return. If this experiment fails with a word processing document, launch your word processor and save the document again, this time as a text file.
- Although some formatting may be lost (italics, boldface, indentations), text files can be read by most word processing programs.
- Consult the Help files of your software for information about attaching and translating various kinds of files.
- Consider adding translation software to your computer system, to let you cross platforms (DOS, Windows, Macintosh, Unix) or programs.

of a formal letter.) Basically, e-mail is informal and casual. Yet this informality is an asset. E-mail is used extensively within organizations and their various branches—from one individual to another and from one department to another—and between and among businesses as well.

Think of e-mail as a polite, informative telephone conversation—friendly, to the point, but always accessible. E-mail allows individuals to conduct business professionally with a minimum of wasted time. E-mail is easy and immediate.

The number of messages that can be sent over e-mail is limitless. You can send pictures, spreadsheets, even soundbites and video clips via on-line transmissions, but realize that downloading such documents takes time.

Figures 4.6 through 4.9 are examples of effectively written e-mail. Notice that e-mail can be cordial without being unprofessional.

Using an E-Mail Address

With most software you will find a **header** at the top of each e-mail that contains the sender's address. Everyone on the Net has an e-mail address at the top of each piece of e-mail. An e-mail address contains three parts: the e-mail user's name, the name of the host computer the person uses, and finally the zone for the type of organization or institution to which the host belongs. This last part of the e-mail address is called the **Internet domain** for the computer system through which mail flows. For example, *dkehler@mail.sdsu.edu* refers to Dorothy Kehler's mailbox, located at San Diego State University, an educational institution (note the zone suffix *edu*).

The address *lpolowski@aol.com* refers to Leslie Polowski's mailbox on America Online, a commercial provider. E-mail addresses are usually listed in lowercase letters and contain no spaces, as in *josh_reynolds@trans.gov,* which means Josh Reynolds's e-mail address is at the Department of Transportation, a government agency.

Be careful not to omit any part of an e-mail address and to punctuate it completely and accurately. Even a small error will affect whether the intended recipient receives your message.

In addition to your e-mail address you will also want to include your fax and voice mail numbers. Together these addresses constitute your signature file, as in the following example.

>>>>Marvin Cooper/Senior Sales Rep/RTS Technologies<<<<
Voice: (708) 555-1970   FAX: (708) 555-1980
mcooper@rts.com

Guidelines for Using E-Mail

Using e-mail technology does not mean you can forget about preparing and organizing your messages carefully with your reader's needs in mind. The following guidelines will help you write effective e-mail.

FIGURE 4.6   An example of interoffice e-mail.

Subject: **Status of Hinson-Davis Order**
Date: Tuesday, 24 July 2001 11:38:35-0400
From: peter_zacharias@craftworks.com
To: marge_parish@craftworks.com

At last the Hinson-Davis Company received its order, and they are very
pleased with our service. In fact, Victor Arana, their district manager, made
a point of calling me first thing this morning to say the order came in at
8:00 a.m. and by 8:15 it was operable on their docks.

Things could not have gone smoother. Congrats to all. In my last update (20
July) to you, we had anticipated some delays, but luckily we avoided them.

I am going to send Arana a thank-you letter today to keep up the goodwill.

TECH NOTE

Using an E-Mail Address Book
The most convenient place to store names and addresses for easy retrieval is
an e-mail address book. Address books are available in most software
office packages and are now fully integrated with Web browsers and e-mail
programs. Internet-based e-mail services, such as HotMail and Yahoo!, also
provide address books and calendars to access Internet directory services.
The benefits of an address book are many.

- Address books allow you to store phone numbers and e-mail and
  Web page addresses.
- If you need to know someone's address or phone number, a variety
  of Internet-based directories will locate the information for you.
  From those services you can create mailing lists.
- By printing all or part of your address book, you have a hard copy
  to take with you.
- Most address books allow you to import and export from other address
  books so you can combine information from several address books.

FIGURE 4.7   An example of an ongoing e-mail.

Subject: **Status of Hinson-Davis Order**
Date: Tuesday 24 July 2001 11:55:26-0400
From: peter_zacharias@craftworks.com
To: lee_thornton@craftworks.com

Lee, you did a great job expediting Hinson's order this a.m. Getting the order there by 7:38 took a lot of hard work, and I appreciate your effort.

Hinson's previous order was three days late because it had to be specially designed at the factory. I am glad we could deliver the order exactly according to the specs.

I received a warm phone call this a.m. from Mr. Hinson himself thanking us.

It might be wise to pay him a visit next week when you circle back to Dayton while he still recalls our (and your) good work. Who knows— Hinson might place yet another order with us.

Format

1. **Make your e-mail easy to read.**

   - Do not send e-mail in all capital letters. It's harder to read and looks as if you are shouting at your readers. It also looks unprofessional printed in hard copy.
   - Watch the length of your paragraphs. Keep them to three or four lines and double space between them. A screen filled up with long, unbroken paragraphs is intimidating for readers.
   - Keep line length under sixty characters. The average computer screen is only eighty characters wide, and pushing every line to the edge of the screen makes reading difficult; it can also cause annoying line breaks on the recipient's end.

2. **Make your e-mail easy to process.**

   - Include all parts of your message—correct address, subject line, date, and so on.
   - Put the most important part of your message first. Because your readers receive vast amounts of e-mail, they may look only at the first few lines you write.

FIGURE 4.8   E-mail sent to a distribution list of co-workers.

Subject: **Collaboration on annual report**
Date: 5 Feb 2002 13:18:33-0400
From: melinda_bell@netech.com
To: allen_cranston@netech.com; peter_maxwell@netech.com;
          margaret_habermas@netech.com
X-VMS-To: IN% "allen_cranston@netech.com; peter_maxwell@netech.com;
          margaret_habermas@netech.com"
From: NAME: Melinda Bell
          FAX: (603) 555-2162
          Voice: (603) 555-1505

FUNC:
TEL: <BELL, MELINDA AT NORTHEAST TECHNOLOGIES COM>
To: IN% "allen_cranston@netech.com; peter_maxwell@netech.com;
          margaret_habermas@netech.com"

To follow up on our conversation yesterday regarding working together on this year's annual report, I'm glad our schedules are flexible. I've checked our calendars and we are all available next Tuesday the 12th at 10:30 a.m. Let's meet in Conference Room 410.

Don't forget we have to first draft a two- to three-page overview that explains Northeast's strategic goals and objectives for fiscal year 2003. Not an easy assignment, but we can do it, gang.

It would be a big help if Allen would bring copies of the reports for the last three years. Would Peter call Ms. Jhandez for a copy of the speech she gave last month to the Powell Chamber of Commerce? BTW, if memory serves me correctly, she did a first-rate job summarizing Northeast's accomplishments for 2001. We will certainly want to quote some of her remarks. Margaret, TIA for doing stats on the last quarter's outlays for us before Tuesday.

FIGURE 4.9   An e-mail response to a customer.

Subject: **Internet addresses for upgrades, etc.**
Date: 10 Sept. 2001 09:10:13-0400
From: waller@bnet.tcb.com
To: luceyc@lance.netdoor.com

Hello Lucy,

Thanks for your e-mail asking about how to obtain print drivers and other components and software. To find out about the availability of drivers, upgrades, bios, specs, fixes, and csd's (corrective service disks) via the Internet, check out the following addresses:

> http://www.pc.bnet.com
> ftp://ps.omaha.bnet.com
> ftp://software.jensen.bnet.com

These addresses will be able to tell you about what we have in stock and how we can get it to you asap.

You might also be interested in the following address for feedback, FAQ's, and tips. Visit us at

> news://msnews.gen.com/bnet.public internet mail

I hope these leads help. If you run into any trouble, please e-mail me. I'm at the keyboard all day today until 7:00 p.m. CST.

Cheers,

Larry Waller

- Use a concise (three or four words), direct subject line. Avoid vague one-word subjects such as "Conference" or "Software"; instead say "Conference is set" or "Advantages of new software." A one-word subject line like "Bill" would leave your reader wondering if your e-mail is about a person, an unpaid account, or a notice just sent.
- Where appropriate, divide your message into an introduction, a body, and a conclusion.
- Don't send anything lengthy. It clogs up the company network system and slows down the delivery of important messages and documents.

"Netiquette"

1. **Identify your audience.**

   - Send your e-mail to the right address (is it an individual or a group?).
   - Verify if your reader wants unsolicited mail.
   - Learn all you can about your reader to allow you to
     - shape the tone of your mail to your reader's needs
     - judge how much information the reader needs.

2. **Guide your audience in its response to your e-mail.**

   - Tell them what you want them to do (verify information, send data, respond in writing).
   - Reply the same day to responses, if possible. Let the respondents know you received their replies and when you will respond if you can't do so immediately.
   - Respond to replies with diplomacy and all necessary information, not just a one- or two-word reply tacked on to their message.

3. **Be courteous to your e-mail readers.**

   - Don't send the same message over and over (just as you would not send hard copies or faxes of the same information).
   - Never e-mail an advertisement unless the recipient has requested that you do so. People do not like "spam," or unsolicited e-mail. A short signature file with a message is the acceptable way of letting people know your talent.
   - Check your e-mail every day.
   - Respect the cultural traditions of non-native speakers of English when you e-mail your audience. See pages 172–182.
   - Delete any long list of previous messages that may appear when you reply to a message. After you have used the Reply method of response once, choose the New Message option to avoid sending old news again and again.

Style

1. **Don't be a sloppy writer. Follow all the rules of proper spelling, punctuation, and correct word choice.**

- Use your e-mail spell checker.
- Verify all proper names and product names.
- Proofread before you press the Send key.

2. **Keep your message concise.**

- Cut out wordy phrases. See how many words you can eliminate without distorting the sense of your message.
- Don't turn your e-mail into a telegram. "Report immediately: need for meeting" makes you sound discourteous and demanding.
- Send only the information needed to answer a reader's questions or concerns.
- Exclude any details, comments, and descriptions not essential to your message, for example, reporting on another totally different situation or circumstance.

3. **Avoid unfamiliar abbreviations** and catchwords or phrases no one outside your office would know. Table 4.1 lists some abbreviations commonly used in e-mail. (Remember that such abbreviations will likely not be understood by non-native speakers of English.) The writer in Figure 4.8 uses some of them.

4. **Do not use slang or jargon** unless it is appropriate for the context and your audience.

TABLE 4.1   Some Commonly Used E-Mail Abbreviations

Abbreviation	Meaning
AFK	Away from keyboard
BAK	Back at keyboard
BRB	Be right back
BTW	By the way
FWIW	For what it's worth
FYI	For your information
IMHO	In my humble opinion
IOW	In other words
LOL	Laughing out loud
OTOH	On the other hand
TIA	Thanks in advance
WB	Welcome back
WRT	With respect to
WTG	Way to go

5. End your message politely.

- Make sure you have addressed all the reader's questions.
- Let readers know you appreciate or welcome their help.

Confidentiality and Ethics

1. Never use e-mail for confidential messages.

- The Internet is not secure; messages can be intercepted and read by someone other than the intended recipient.
- Send nothing through e-mail that you would not want to see posted on your company bulletin board.

TECH NOTE

E-Mail Security

As more and more people send e-mail messages and use the Internet to acquire information and products, privacy protection is increasingly important. You don't want your name and e-mail address sold to unprofessional mailing lists or your messages intercepted. If you make financial transactions over the Internet, you certainly don't want your checking account or credit card numbers stolen. Finally, many people want some kind of assurance concerning the integrity of Internet businesses. The following types of protection are available.

- Most e-mail servers protect their subscribers' privacy. Make sure the server provides a legally binding statement concerning your personal information and whether it will distribute your information to marketing companies.
- Your account should be protected by a simple password that you determine. No one can access your account without this password.
- More sophisticated programs involving the use of "virtual IDs" and "digital IDs" allow you to prove your identity in electronic transactions with an electronic identity card. Such IDs, which involve a complicated series of codes, are issued through independent certifying authorities. Different classes of IDs provide different levels of security. With the use of a virtual or digital ID, you can be sure that your financial transactions on the Internet are made even more secure.
- Privacy seal programs offer businesses and consumers a way to trust that an Internet business is engaged in ethical on-line practices. Seals of approval are awarded to businesses that carry a privacy policy that clearly tells consumers what information is being collected and how it will be used. These programs are especially important, for example, to alert parents that material is suitable for their children.

FIGURE 4.10   A flaming e-mail.

> Subject: **Upgrades**
> Date: 3/6/2002 09:59:15-0400
> From: sammy@trinet.rad.com
> To: smith@eagle.com
>
> Hey guys and gals,
>
> Are you awake out there? I have been trying for over three blooming hours to get someone—ANYONE!!!!!—at your place to get back to me asap about the upgrades. But no luck. WTG. What will it take? A note from Bill Gates himself at Microsoft, your arch competitor, to let you know we are going to jump ship?
>
> Once more, I STRESS that your sales team—Rob T., Janet S., and Tim A.—have not given the upgrades we were promised. I don't like to say you lied, but what else would you call it, huh?
>
> To put it bluntly, you obviously don't want to stay in business. If you fold, we won't cry.
>
> TTFN
>
> Sammy

2. **Observe all the legal requirements of using e-mail.**

- Do not forward a co-worker's or boss's e-mail unless they approve.
  - Never forward (report) something that is copyrighted without first securing permission from the copyright holder(s).
  - When you attach a document, clearly inform readers what can and cannot be copied.
- Do not refer readers to another document and ask them to copy it without the writer's permission.
- Do not change the wording of a message that you are expected simply to read and then forward.
- Always tell people if you plan to publish something they will send you, and get their express permission to do so.
- Avoid *flaming*, that is, using strong, angry language that mocks, attacks, or insults your reader, as in Figure 4.10.

Flaming
  – hurts your image and that of your company
  – can lead to charges of libel against you and your employer
  – can be grounds for your dismissal

3. Avoid unprofessional behavior.

  ▪ Do not use company e-mail for personal business.
  ▪ Never attack your company, your boss, co-workers, the competition, or customers. Your message could be read and stored to be used against you later.
  ▪ Do not spread gossip. You never know who will read (and reveal) your message.

E-Mail versus Other Types of Business Communications

Table 4.2 compares and contrasts the function, scope, and format of e-mail with memos and letters. Note that e-mails are brief, informal, and to-the-point messages that might be likened to the workhorses of business. They should never take the place of far more formal and official documents such as letters, the subject of the next three chapters, or reports, covered in Chapters 15 and 16.

TABLE 4.2   The Uses of E-Mail versus Memos or Letters

	E-Mail	Memo	Letter
Brief messages	X	X	
Informal	X	X	
Formal			X
Legal record		X	X
Relaxed tone	X	X	
Confidential material		X	X
Multiple pages			X
Reports		X	X
In-house messages	X	X	
Proofreading	X	X	X

✓ Revision Checklist

Memos
  ❑ Used appropriate and consistent format.
  ❑ Announced purpose of memo early and clearly.
  ❑ Organized memo according to reader's need for information, with main ideas up front, supplied clear conclusion.

❑ Made style and tone of memo suitable for audience.
❑ Included bullets, lists, underscoring where necessary to reflect logic and organization of memo and for ease of reading.
❑ Refrained from overloading reader with unnecessary details.

Faxes
❑ Verified reader's fax number.
❑ Sent cover sheet with number of pages faxed and phone number to call in the event of transmission trouble.
❑ Enlarged font to minimize reduction of type in transmission.
❑ Excluded anything confidential or sensitive if reader's fax machine is not secure.
❑ Sent fax through e-mail program.
❑ Promptly returned any calls regarding transmission difficulties with fax.

E-Mail
❑ Avoided sending unsolicited mail.
❑ Sent to reader's correct address.
❑ Formatted e-mail with acceptable margins and spacing.
❑ Observed Netiquette, especially by avoiding flaming.
❑ Wrote a message rather than returning sender's message with a short reply.
❑ Kept paragraphs short but used full—not telegraphic—sentences.
❑ Avoided unfamiliar abbreviations or terms that would cause reader trouble.
❑ Received permission to repeat or incorporate another person's e-mail.
❑ Observed all legal obligations in using e-mail.
❑ Safeguarded employer's confidentiality and security by excluding sensitive or privileged information.
❑ Included enough information for reader's purpose.
❑ Honored reader by observing proper courtesy.
❑ Began with friendly greeting; ended politely.

Exercises

1. Write a memo to your boss saying that you will be out of town two days next week and three days the following week for **one** of the following reasons: (a) to inspect some land your firm is thinking of buying, (b) to investigate some claims, (c) to look at some new office space for a branch your firm is thinking of opening in a city five hundred miles away, (d) to attend a conference sponsored by a professional society, or (e) to pay calls on customers. In your memo, be specific about dates, places, times, and reasons.

2. Write a memo to two or three of your co-workers on the same subject you chose for Exercise 1.

3. Send a memo to your public relations department informing it that you are completing a degree or work for a certificate. Indicate how the information could be useful for your firm's publicity campaign.

4. Write a memo to the payroll department notifying it that there is a mistake in your last paycheck. Explain exactly what the error is and give precise figures.

5. You are the manager of a local art museum. Write a memo to the Chamber of Commerce in which you put the following information into proper memo format.

   Old hours: Mon.–Fri. 9–5; closed Sat. except during July and August, when you are open 9–12
   New hours: Mon.–Th. 8:30–4:30; Fri.–Sat. 9–9
   Old rates: Adults $3.00; senior citizens $1.00; children under 12 free
   New rates: Adults $4.50; senior citizens $1.00; children under 12 free but must be accompanied by an adult
   Added features: Paintings by Thora Horne, local artist; sculpture from West Indies in display area all summer; guided tours available for parties of six or more; lounge areas will offer patrons sandwiches and soft drinks during May, June, July, and August

6. Select some change (in policy, schedule, or personnel assignment) you encountered in a job you held in the last two or three years and write an appropriate memo describing that change. Write the memo from the perspective of your former employer explaining the change to employees.

7. How would any of the memos in Exercises 1–6 have to be rewritten to make it suitable as an e-mail message? Rewrite one of them as an e-mail.

8. Bring five or six examples of company e-mail to class. As a group evaluate them for style, tone, and layout.

9. Send a fax to a company or an organization requesting information about the products or services it offers. Include an appropriate cover sheet.

10. Write an e-mail to a business that provides daily or weekly information to interested customers and submit its response along with your e-mail request to your instructor. Choose one of the following:
    a. an airline: an up-to-date schedule along a certain route and information about any bonus-mile or discount programs
    b. a catalog order company: information about any weekly specials for Net users
    c. a stock brokerage firm: free quotes or research about a particular stock
    d. a resort: special rates for a given week

11. Write an e-mail with one of the following messages, observing the guidelines discussed in this chapter.
    a. You have just made a big sale and you want to inform your boss.
    b. You have just lost a big sale and you have to inform your boss.

   c. Tell a co-worker about a union meeting.

   d. Notify a company to cancel your subscription to one of its publications because you find it to be dated and no longer useful in your profession.

   e. Request help from a listserv (see Tech Note on pp. 260–261) about research for a major report you are preparing for your employer.

   f. Advise your district manager to discontinue marketing one of the company's products because of poor customer acceptance.

   g. Send a short article (about two hundred words) to your company newsletter about some accomplishment your office, department, or section achieved in the last month.

   h. Write to a friend studying finance at a German university about the biggest financial news in your town or neighborhood in the last month.

12. Rewrite the following e-mail to make it more suitable.

Hi––

This new territory is a pain. Lots of stops; no sales. Ughhhh. People out here resistant to change. Could get hit by a boulder and still no change. Giant companies ought to be up on charges. Will sub. reports asap as long as you care rec.

The long and short of it is that market is down. No news=bad news.

13. As a collaborative venture, join with three or four classmates to prepare one or more of the e-mail messages for Exercise 11. Send each other drafts of your messages for revision. Submit the final copy of the group's effort.

14. Assume you have received permission to repost in an e-mail all or part of the article on microwaves (pp. 35–36) or virtual reality and law enforcement. Prepare an e-mail message to a listserv or Usenet group (p. 371) containing part of the article you have chosen.

15. Send your instructor an e-mail message about the project you are now working on for class, outlining your progress and describing any difficulties you are having.

16. You have just missed work or a class meeting. E-mail your employer or your instructor explaining the reason and telling how you intend to make up the work.

CHAPTER 5

Letter Writing: Some Basics

Letters are among the most important kind of writing you will do on your job. Although you may receive helpful criticism as you prepare your letters (as Randy Taylor did in Figure 3.3), more often than not you'll be solely responsible for them. Your signature on your letter tells readers that you are accountable for everything in it. Because letters are so important to your career, Chapters 5, 6, and 7 are devoted exclusively to effective letter writing. This chapter introduces the entire process and provides some guidelines, problem-solving techniques, definitions, and revision strategies common to all letter writing.

The Importance of Letters

Even in this age of electronic communication, letters are still vital. In terms of materials and time, the average business letter can cost between $12 and $14 to compose, keyboard, proofread, transmit, store, and retrieve. Even with the speed of telecommunications, companies need qualified employees to research, draft, revise, edit, proofread, and transmit letters. Many businesses offer employee seminars on how to write clear and appropriate letters, a skill that can lead to promotions and raises.

Why are letters so important? They are both a personal and a professional means of communication and occupy an essential place in the business world for the following reasons.

1. **Letters represent your company's public image and your competence.** Effectively written letters can create goodwill; poorly written letters can anger customers and cost your company business.
2. **Letters are more personal than a report, yet more formal than memos or e-mail.** There are occasions when a memo or an e-mail message would be inappropriately casual.
3. **Letters are more permanent than e-mail.** They provide documented hard copy that cannot be deleted.

4. **Letters constitute an official legal record of an agreement.** They state, modify, or respond to a commitment and become part of a company's records. When sent to a customer, a signed letter constitutes a legally binding contract. Be extra careful about what you put in a letter about prices, warranties, guarantees, equipment specifications, delivery dates, or other promises. Your reader can hold you and your company to such written commitments. Double-check your facts.

5. **Letters follow up on telephone calls and other types of oral communications.** They provide documentation and official clarification of oral agreements and prevent misunderstandings about what was said or agreed upon and by whom.

6. **Letters provide a wide range of corporate information.** They give instructions; announce or amend policies; describe changes in a product, service, or procedure; or report events or the results of a study or test.

7. **Letters can prompt action.** They can help a company collect money from overdue accounts, alter a city ordinance, institute a policy, call a meeting, or waive a requirement.

8. **Letters sell.** They can promote a product, a service, an idea, even the writer's own skills.

9. **Letters are efficient for targeted mass mailings.** It is easier for a company to buy a mailing list of addresses than it is to obtain sometimes difficult-to-find e-mail addresses.

Letters accomplish those goals by following certain conventions, or customary practices, which include the ways readers expect letters to look and to sound. Effective letters (1) announce their purpose clearly, (2) follow an appropriate format, (3) address the reader courteously, and (4) use more formal language.

This chapter will show you how to incorporate those conventions into the drafts, revisions, and final versions of your letters.

The Process of Writing a Letter

Though far shorter than a proposal, report, or manual, a one- or two-page business letter still requires planning and research. All the techniques of the writing process discussed in Chapter 2 apply to letters as well. An effective letter may require several drafts, revisions, and edits before the final copy is satisfactory. Any letter you just dash off is unlikely to portray you and your company in the best light.

Analyze Your Audience

Before you even start to draft your letter, you need to ask and successfully answer five sets of questions.

1. Who is my audience? Do I know them or are they strangers? Are they familiar with my company and its products or services, or is everything I am writing about new to them?

2. Will my audience be favorably disposed to what I am going to say, or will they be disappointed or angry about my news?

3. What kinds of information will my audience expect me to supply—schedules, costs, model numbers, descriptions, measurements, copies of reports?
4. How will my audience use the information I am sending?
5. What impression do I want my letter to make on readers? Do I want to sound courteous and friendly? Informed and efficient? Firm and decisive?

Do Necessary Research

Once you have a strong sense of your audience's needs, you are in a better position to know what to research, the next stage in the process of creating successful letters. Your research could be as simple as refreshing your memory about one of your company's products or services, looking through your company's files to study previous correspondence with the customer, conferring with a co-worker about the client's special needs, or seeing whether your client has a Web site on the Internet.

Draft and Revise

Armed with information about your audience and their purpose, get your thoughts down first by drafting and then revising and editing to arrive at the appropriate language and tone. Many writers wrongly believe that the hardest part of writing a letter is putting their ideas into the right language. In truth, the hardest part of writing a letter is knowing what must be said to whom, why, and where in the letter. Once you have successfully resolved those points, you can focus more intently on language during the later revising and editing stages. Pages 167–171 offer guidelines for making the language of your letters clear, concise, and contemporary.

Preparing Letters

The first thing a reader will notice about your letter is how it looks—the way the words and paragraphs are arranged on the page. Your audience will be influenced by the way your letter looks even before they read its contents. A neat, professional-looking letter implies to the reader that the work, service, or skill that you promise to deliver will be done in the same way. Handwritten insertions or changes to fix errors all look shabby and immediately detract from your message. Word processors, of course, help you produce professional-looking letters with ease.

Printing Your Letter

The way a letter is printed significantly affects the visual impression it makes. Avoid crowded or lopsided letters by taking a few minutes to estimate the length of your message before you print it. Don't key in a brief letter at the top of the page and then leave the lower three-fourths of the page blank. Readers will feel as if you left them hanging. Plan to start a shorter letter near the center of the page. Also avoid cramming a long letter onto one page; use a second sheet. A letter that is squeezed onto one page deprives readers of necessary and eye-pleasing white space.

Guidelines on Printing Your Letter

Here are a few general hints on printing your letters.

- **Leave generous margins of approximately 1 inch all around your type area.** Set 1-inch margins as the default on your PC. Leave more white space at the top than at the bottom, and watch the right margin in particular, since it is easy to exceed that limit. Shorter letters may require wider margins than longer letters, but don't exceed a margin of 1 inch on the right side.
- **Use a letter-quality laser printer.** Letters from a dot matrix printer generally do not look as crisp, fresh, or professional as those printed on a laser printer.
- **Always use a fresh toner cartridge for your printer.** A fuzzy, faint, or messy script hurts your chances of convincing your reader.
- **Choose a type font that is inviting to the eye.** Crowding too many letters on a line makes your letter harder to read. You will not win any points from your readers if your letter looks cramped. Avoid script or other fancy type fonts.
- **Use high-quality paper.** Twenty-pound bond paper says your message is important and substantial; thin, lightweight paper signals that your message is flimsy.

Proofreading Your Letter

Proofread everything that has your name on it, even if you did not keyboard it. You cannot blame a keyboarder for spelling mistakes or other blunders. As the writer, you are responsible for the final product. Proofread your letter for errors of fact, miscalculations, and misrepresentations; contradictions between what you say in your letter and what is stated on a Web site or other company document are unethical. Pay special attention to the accuracy of prices, dates, and serial numbers.

Typographical errors can be costly and embarrassing. If you want to tell a steady customer, "The order will be hard to fill," but you keyboard, "The order will be hard to bill," confusion will result. Poor keyboarding and proofreading can also lead to omitted letters ("the ill arrived" for "the bill arrived"), transpositions ("het" for "the," "nad" for "and"), or omitted words ("the market value of the was high").

TECH NOTE

Use Your Spell-Checker with Care
Don't rely too heavily on your spell-check program. Mistakes can still creep in. A spell-check will not differentiate between *their* and *there*, *its* and *it's*, or *effect* and *affect*; the wrong word spelled correctly is still the wrong word. After you have run a spell-checker, you still need to proofread your letter carefully to make sure each correction was made (none overlooked) before you print a final copy.

Proofreading Methods

You can't be too careful when you proofread. Proofreading is reading in slow motion. Here are seven ways to proofread effectively.

1. Read your letter word for word from the bottom to the top.

2. Read your letter from start to finish aloud. Pronounce each word carefully to make yourself more aware of typographical errors or omitted words. Look at every letter of every word. Don't skim.

3. Place your finger under each word as you silently read the letter.

4. Double-check the spelling of all names. Errors here are sure to cause problems. Also watch for inconsistencies (*Phillip* in one place, *Philip* in another; *Anderson* for *Andersen*).

5. Have a friend read the letter. Four eyes are better than two.

6. Have your friend read aloud a hard copy of your letter while you follow the copy on your computer screen.

7. Never proofread when you are tired, and avoid proofreading large amounts of material at one sitting.

Letter Formats

Letter format refers to the way in which you type or print a letter—where you indent and where you place certain kinds of information. A number of letter formats exist. Two of the most frequently used business letter formats are the full-block format and the semiblock format. Gaining popularity is the Administrative Management Society (AMS) simplified style. Before you choose a letter format, find out whether your employer has a preference.

Full-Block Format

In the full-block format all information is flush against the left margin, with spaces between paragraphs. Figure 5.1 shows a full-block letter on letterhead stationery (specially printed giving a company's name and logo, business and World Wide Web addresses, fax and telephone numbers, and sometimes the names of executives). If you don't use letterhead, place the company's address directly above the date.

Semiblock Format

The semiblock style (Figure 5.2) positions the writer's address (if it is not imprinted on a letterhead), date, complimentary close, and the signature to the right side of the letter. The date aligns with the complimentary close, and notations of any enclosures with the letter are flush left below the signature. Paragraphs in the semiblock style can be indented or not.

TECH NOTE

Formatting Letters Using Software Programs

Word processing programs such as Microsoft Word and Corel WordPerfect make letter writing easier by providing templates that automatically set up the paragraphs, the spacing, even the current date for you.

You can define the overall "look" of the letter, which means that the program will select a type face and size that fits a general description, like "traditional," "formal," or "contemporary." For example, when you choose a contemporary look for your letter, the typeface is what you might find in an upbeat, faddish magazine; the traditional choice features characters that look more like basic typewriter letters.

When you select a look for your letter, you are not selecting the letter's formatting style. You must further specify whether you want to use full-block, semiblock, simplified, or indented-paragraph format. After you have selected a look and a format, just enter the appropriate addresses and then type the letter. In fact, you need to type the addresses only once, because the software's address file saves the information for future use.

Some of the many features available for preparing letters include:

- **Sample letterheads,** as well as your own if you have them saved on the computer, can be customized and printed on your letter. You can even design your own using the word processing program's graphics program (see pp. 430–434).

- **Access to graphics and watermarks.** A watermark is any graphic, logo, letterhead, or image that is enlarged, usually to fill most of the page but printed only very lightly and behind the text that is typed on the page. Watermarks give the appearance of expensive stationery. Images of any kind can be sized, cropped, and otherwise manipulated to fit your needs. (See Figures 5.7 and 5.8.)

- **Addresses.** You can enter and later retrieve one or thousands of addresses using the program's address book. That means not only that you do not need to type addresses more than once, but that you could print thousands of letters at one time, if necessary.

- **Numerous sample greetings and closings,** usually defined by the style categories, such as "formal" or "informal."

As useful as these programs are, never let the computer dictate your correspondence. Follow the principles of clear and concise writing outlined in this chapter; no computer can match your personal voice and style.

FIGURE 5.1   Full-block letter format.

NIRA

Nevada Insurance Research Agency
7500 South Maplewood Drive, Las Vegas, Nevada 89152-0026
(702) 555-9876 NIRA@troll.org http://www.NIRA.org

April 4, 2002

Ms. Molly Georgopolous, C.P.A.
Business Manager
Meyers, Inc.
3400 South Madison Rd.
Reno, NV 89554-3212

Dear Ms. Georgopolous:

As I promised in our telephone conversation this afternoon, I am enclosing a study of the Nevada financial responsibility law. I hope that it will help you prepare your report.

All printing lined up against the left-hand margin

I wish to emphasize again that probably 95 percent of all individuals who are involved in an accident do obtain reimbursement for hospital and doctor bills and for damages to their automobiles. If individuals have insurance, they can receive reimbursement from their own carrier. If they do not have insurance and the other driver is uninsured and judged to be at fault, the State Bureau of Motor Vehicles will revoke that party's driver's license and license plates until all costs for injuries and damages are paid.

Please call me again if I can help you.

Sincerely yours,

Carmen Tredeau

Carmen Tredeau, President

CT/IMB

Encl.

Bradley Fuller, CPCU	Carmen Tredeau, CPCU	Theodore Kendrick	Iping Li, CPCU	Dora Salinas-Diego, CPCU
Chairperson	President	Vice President	Vice President	Vice President
		Public Affairs	Research	Actuary

FIGURE 5.2   Semiblock letter format.

Writer's address and date are indented. { 7239 East Daphne Parkway
Mobile, AL 36608-1012

January 31, 2001

Mr. Travis Boykin, Manager
Scandia Gifts
703 Hardy St.
Hattiesburg, MS 39401-4633

Dear Mr. Boykin:

I would appreciate knowing if you currently stock the Crescent pattern of model 5678 and how much you charge per model number. I would also like to know if you have special prices per box order.

The name of your store is listed in the Annual Catalog as the closest distributor of Copenhagen products in my area. Would you please give me directions to your shop from Mobile and the hours you are open?

I look forward to hearing from you.

Complimentary close and writer's names are indented. { Sincerely yours,

Arthur T. McCormack (signature)

Arthur T. McCormack

Simplified Format

Like the full-block format, the simplified letter begins every line at the left margin, including any numbered items such as those in Figure 5.3. But unlike the block format, the simplified style omits the salutation and the complimentary close. A subject line (without using the word *subject*) in all capital letters appears three spaces down from the inside address. The first paragraph of the letter follows three line spaces after the subject line. The writer's name and title are typed in capital letters on the same line four lines after the last paragraph of the letter.

Indented Paragraph Format

A fourth format is identical to the semiblock except each paragraph is indented five spaces (see Figure 5.12). Although this format is far less popular today than it once was, it offers some visual benefits, as you'll see on page 181.

Continuing Pages

To indicate subsequent pages if your letter runs beyond one page, use one of the following three conventions. Note the use of the recipient's name.

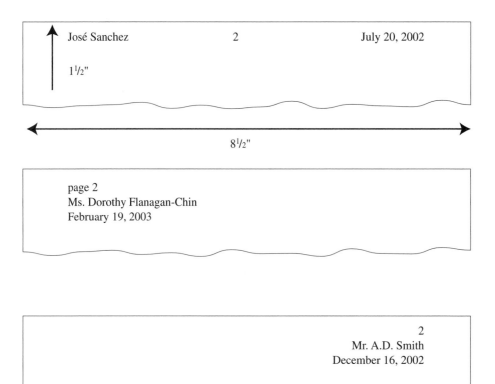

FIGURE 5.3   AMS simplified letter format.

Office Property Management Associates
2400 South Lincoln Highway
Livingston, NJ 07040-9990
(201) 555-3740   E-mail OPMA@troll.com

May 8, 2002

Mr. W. T. Albritton
Albritton and Sharp Accounting Services
Suite 400
Suburban Office Complex
Livingston, NJ 07038-2389

IMPROVED SERVICES AT SUBURBAN OFFICE COMPLEX

At our April meeting, Office Property Management Associates
discussed a number of requests you and other tenants made about the
Suburban Office Complex. I am happy to inform you that the following
improvements in services will go into effect at the complex within 45
days.

1. Effective June 6, you will have an on-site manager, Judy Fiorelli, who
   will be happy to answer any questions you may have about the
   complex and help you solve any problems.
2. The parking lot on the southwest side will be resurfaced during the
   week of June 13–20. During that time, would you and your staff
   please park your vehicles in the north or east lot.
3. A new outdoor security system will be installed June 21. Work on this
   system should not inconvenience you.

I welcome your comments on these changes or suggestions for
additional ones. Please feel free to call or write me.

Gladys T. Mullins-Osborne

GLADYS T. MULLINS-OSBORNE, VICE PRESIDENT

tc

Parts of a Letter

A letter contains many parts, each of which contributes to your overall message. The parts and their placement in your letter form the basic conventions of effective letter writing. Readers look for certain information in key places. It is your responsibility as a letter writer to meet your reader's expectations and, in doing so, to create a favorable impression.

In the following sections, those parts of a letter marked with an asterisk should appear in every letter you write. Figure 5.4 is a sample letter containing all the parts discussed below. Note where each part is placed in the letter.

*Date Line

Where you place the month, day, and year depends on the format you are using. In the full-block or the simplified style, the date line is flush with the left margin. The semiblock style places the date at the center point, centered under a company letterhead, or flush with the right margin. The date line appears two lines below the writer's address or the letterhead.

Spell out the name of the month in full—"September" or "March" rather than "Sept." or "Mar." The date line is usually keyboarded this way: November 12, 2003. Many international firms prefer to date correspondence with the day first, followed by month and year (12 November 2003), with no commas separating the day, month, and year.

*Inside Address

The inside address, the same address on the envelope, is always placed against the left margin, two lines below the date line. It contains the name, title (if any), company, street address, city, state, and ZIP code of the person to whom you are writing. Single-space the inside address and do not use any punctuation at the ends of the lines.

> Dr. Mary Petro
> Director of Research
> Midwest Laboratories
> 1700 Oak Drive
> Rapid City, SD 56213-3406

Always try to write to a specific person rather than just "Sales Manager" or "President." To find out the person's name, check previous correspondence, e-mail lists, the company's or individual's Web site or call the company. Abbreviate courtesy titles (Mr., Dr., Ms.); however, do not abbreviate military titles (Captain, Sergeant), academic ranks (Professor, Assistant Professor), religious designations (Reverend, Father, Sister), or civic or political titles (Senator, Councilperson). When writing to an elected official, use an honorific (Honorable) and her or his exact title.

> The Honorable Barbara Karnes-Bolton
> Representative, 10th Congressional District
>
> The Honorable J. T. Hwang
> Mayor of Freemont

FIGURE 5.4   A sample letter, full-block format, with all parts labeled.

Madison and Moore, Inc.
Professional Architects

7900 South Manheim Road
Crystal Springs, NE 71003-0092
Phone 402-555-2300   E-mail mmpro@aol.com   http://www.MMI.com

Letterhead

Date line   December 12, 2002

Inside address
Ms. Paula Jordan
Systems Consultant
Broadacres Development Corp.
12 East River Street
Detroit, MI 48001-0422

Salutation   Dear Ms. Jordan:

Subject line   SUBJECT: Request for alternative duplex plans, No. 32134

Body of letter

Thank you for your letter of December 6, 2002. I have discussed your request with the officials in our planning department and have learned that the design modules we used are no longer available.

In searching through my files, however, I have come across the enclosed catalog from a California firm that might be helpful to you. This firm, California Concepts, offers plans very similar to the ones you are interested in, as you can tell from the design I checked on page 23 of their catalog.

I hope this will help you and I wish you every success in your project.

Complimentary close   Sincerely yours,

Company name   MADISON AND MOORE, INC.

Signature   *William Newhouse*

Writer's name and title   William Newhouse
Office Manager

Keyboarder's identification   WN/kpl

Enclosure   Encl.: Catalog
Copy to   cc: Planning Department

Do not add the initials M.D., Ph.D., or D.P.H. after a name if you use Dr. as a title. Use either *Janice Howell, M.D.,* or *Dr. Janice Howell.* When writing to a woman, use *Ms.* unless she expressly has asked to be called *Mrs.* or *Miss.*

The last line of the inside address contains the city, state, and ZIP code. Table 5.1 lists the official U.S. Postal Service abbreviations—two capital letters without periods—for the states and territories and the accepted abbreviations for Canadian provinces.

Salutation

The salutation is the greeting part of your letter. Begin with *Dear,* a convention showing respect for your reader, and then follow with a courtesy title, the reader's last name, and a colon (Dear Mr. Brown:). **Never use a comma for a formal letter.** However, if you are on a first-name basis with your reader and using his or her last name would be awkward, by all means write "Dear Bill" or "Dear Sue."

Sometimes you may not be sure of the sex of the reader. There are women named Stacy, Robin, and Lee, and men named Leslie, Kim, and Kelly. If you aren't certain, you can use the reader's full name: "Dear Terry Banks." If you know the person's title, you might write "Dear Credit Manager Banks." Or you might use the simplified letter format (see Figure 5.3), which omits the salutation altogether.

Never use the sexist "Dear Sir," "Gentlemen," or "Dear Madam," and avoid the stilted "Ladies and Gentlemen or "Dear Sir/Madam." (For a discussion of sexist language and how to avoid it, see pp. 65–69.)

If you are writing to a large group of readers, you might use the occupational designation—"Dear Pilot," "Dear Homeowners." When writing to a company, use the company name—"Dear Apple," "Dear Saperstein Textiles."

Also avoid salutations such as "Hello," "Greetings" (which sounds as if it came from a draft board or is a holiday message), and "Good Morning" (it may be late afternoon when your reader opens your letter). And never begin your letter "To whom it may concern," which is trite and rudely impersonal.

Subject Line

The subject line can provide a concise summary of your topic (like a title for your letter) or it can list account numbers, order notations, or referral numbers so the reader can at once check the files and see the status of your account or policy. In both the full-block and the semiblock formats, the subject line, preceded by the word SUBJECT in capital letters, is double-spaced below the salutation, flush with the left margin.

Dear Ms. Salazar:

SUBJECT: Repair of model 7342

Alternatively, it can be moved to the right side of the letter, on the same line as the salutation.

Dear Ms. Salazar: SUBJECT: Repair of model 7342

Review page 152 and Figure 5.3 for style and placement of the subject line in the simplified style letter.

TABLE 5.1   U.S. Postal Service Abbreviations and Canadian Province Abbreviations

U.S. State/ Territory	Abbreviation	U.S. State/ Territory	Abbreviation
Alabama	AL	Montana	MT
Alaska	AK	Nebraska	NE
American Samoa	AS	Nevada	NV
Arizona	AZ	New Hampshire	NH
Arkansas	AR	New Jersey	NJ
California	CA	New Mexico	NM
Colorado	CO	New York	NY
Connecticut	CT	North Carolina	NC
Delaware	DE	North Dakota	ND
District of Columbia	DC	Ohio	OH
Florida	FL	Oklahoma	OK
Georgia	GA	Oregon	OR
Guam	GU	Pennsylvania	PA
Hawaii	HI	Puerto Rico	PR
Idaho	ID	Rhode Island	RI
Illinois	IL	South Carolina	SC
Indiana	IN	South Dakota	SD
Iowa	IA	Tennessee	TN
Kansas	KS	Texas	TX
Kentucky	KY	Utah	UT
Louisiana	LA	Vermont	VT
Maine	ME	Virginia	VA
Maryland	MD	Virgin Islands	VI
Massachusetts	MA	Washington	WA
Michigan	MI	West Virginia	WV
Minnesota	MN	Wisconsin	WI
Mississippi	MS	Wyoming	WY
Missouri	MO		

Canadian Province	Abbreviation	Canadian Province	Abbreviation
Alberta	AB	Nova Scotia	NS
British Columbia	BC	Nunavat	NT
Labrador	LB	Ontario	ON
Manitoba	MB	Prince Edward Island	PE
New Brunswick	NB	Quebec	PQ
Newfoundland	NF	Saskatchewan	SK
Northwest Territories	NT	Yukon Territory	YT

*Body of the Letter

The body of the letter contains your message. Some of your letters will be only a few lines long, while others may extend to three or more paragraphs. Keep your sentences short and try to hold your paragraphs to under six or seven lines. **Always double-space between paragraphs.** Your letters will look more inviting and professional when your paragraphs are balanced in length and not crowded onto the page.

In organizing the body of your letter, follow this plan:

- In your first paragraph tell readers why you are writing and why your letter is important to them. Depending on your message, begin with your most persuasive point. Also let your readers know, at the start, that you value your relationship with them. Be concerned and courteous.
- Put the most significant point of each paragraph first to make it easier for the reader to find. Never bury important ideas in the middle or end of your paragraph.
- In a second (or subsequent) paragraph, develop your message with factual support. Consider using lists to break your message up and to help readers recall details or groups of items. (See the correspondence in Figure 5.3.) Readers may benefit from your using headings, too. Also, where appropriate, boldface key words or sentences, but don't overdo the visual effects.
- In your last paragraph, bring readers to a true sense of conclusion. Tell them what you have done for them, what they should do for you, what will happen next, when they will hear from you again, or any combination of those messages. Don't leave readers hanging. Above all, encourage readers to continue their association with you and your company.

Complimentary Close

Except in a letter using AMS simplified style (which omits the complimentary close), the complimentary close always appears two spaces below the body of the letter, flush with the left margin in the full-block format and at the center point, aligned with the date, for the semiblock format. Capitalize only the first letter of the complimentary close and follow the entire close with a comma.

For most business correspondence, use one of these standard closes:

Sincerely,

Respectfully,

Sincerely yours,

Yours sincerely,

If you and your reader know each other well, you might try

Cordially,

Warmest regards,

Best wishes,

Regards,

But avoid flowery closes such as

> Forever yours,
>
> Devotedly yours,
>
> Faithfully yours,
>
> Admiringly yours,

Those belong in a romance novel, not a business letter.

*Signature

Print your name four line spaces below the complimentary close (or in the AMS simplified style four line spaces below the last line of the body), either on the left side (full-block or AMS simplified format) or at the center point (semiblock format). Allow four spaces so that your signature will not look squeezed in. Always sign your name in ink. An unsigned letter indicates carelessness or, worse, indifference toward your reader.

If you are a woman, you have the option of indicating how you want your letters addressed. You can sign your letter "Julie Macklin," which signals to the recipient to address you as Ms. Julie Macklin. If you prefer, you can sign your letter "(Mrs.) Julie Macklin." Married women should always sign their own name, never "(Mrs.) Harold Macklin."

Some firms prefer using their company name along with the employee's name in the signature section. If so, type the company name in capital letters two line spaces below the complimentary close and then sign your name. Add your title underneath your typed name. Here is an example:

Sincerely yours,

THE FINELLI COMPANY

Robert Stravopoulos

Robert Stravopoulos
Cover Coordinator

Reference Initials

When a letter is keyboarded for you by someone else, your initials and the keyboarder's initials are placed two spaces below your typed name. Your initials appear in capital letters, followed by the keyboarder's initials in lower-case letters. The notation WBT/vgh or WBT:vgh, for example, means that Winnie B. Thompson's letter was keyboarded by Victor G. Higgins. Do not list any initials if you keyboarded your own letter.

Enclosure(s) Line

The enclosure line is placed two line spaces beneath the reference initials (or your name if you keyed your own letter). This line informs the reader that additional materials (such as brochures, diagrams, forms, contract(s), a proposal) accompany your letter.

Enclosure

Enclosures (2)

Encl.: 2000 Sales Report

Copy Line

The abbreviation *cc:* informs your reader that a copy of your letter has been sent to other readers.

cc: Service Dept.

cc: Janice Algood
    Ivor Vas

Letters are copied and sent to third parties for a variety of reasons: (a) to document a paper trail and (b) to indicate to other readers who else is being sent a copy. Professional courtesy dictates that you tell the reader if others will receive a copy of your letter.

Addressing an Envelope

When sending a letter, use a standard $9\frac{1}{2}$" $\times$ $4\frac{1}{8}$" white envelope. Because most mail is sorted by high-speed electronic scanning equipment, the U.S. Postal Service has strict regulations concerning envelope size. In particular, avoid odd-shaped envelopes and small, invitation-size ones.

Figure 5.5 shows a properly prepared envelope. The recipient's address should be single-spaced and centered on the envelope. The postal service recommends using all capitals and no punctuation on the envelope. Always use a ZIP code, even if a letter is being mailed to someone in your city.

FIGURE 5.5   A properly addressed envelope.

THOMAS ADDINGTON
45 SIMMONS ROAD APT 2B   *Return Address*
MEDVALE VT 05402-1521

Outside Address   MS PATRICIA BARNES
GENERAL MANAGER
COURTESY MOTORS
1700 LAKEWOOD STREET
BOSTON MA 02127-3106

TECH NOTE

Finding ZIP Codes

The U.S. Postal Service's Web site—*http://www.usps.gov*—can help you locate your reader's ZIP code. Just enter a street address, city, and state, and the ZIP code will automatically appear. This service is also available through most Internet search engines. For example, Yahoo's home page—*http://www.yahoo.com*—lists "Yellow Pages" and "White Pages," where you can get ZIP codes and country codes.

Sometimes special mailing directions are also required. In such cases, one of the following designations is added to the envelope.

- **Attention.** When an attention line is necessary, always put it first, as in Figure 5.6. The attention line is particularly helpful when you have been dealing regularly with one section, department, or individual in a large company, such as the credit officer, parts warehouse, or statistics office.
- **Hold for Arrival.** Individuals may be away on business or on vacation, and you want the letter to reach them on their return.
- **Personal** or **Confidential.** No one but the person named should read the letter.
- **Please Forward.** Note that the U.S. Postal Service forwards mail for only six months.

Place all special instructions, except the attention line, at the top left, two line spaces below the return address.

FIGURE 5.6   An envelope with attention line and special instructions.

```
KATHY  KOOPERMAN
769  EAST 45TH STREET
BALTIMORE  MD 21224-6025


HOLD FOR ARRIVAL

                            ATTENTION  MS  FAYE GLADSTONE
                            THE  PLACEMENT  OFFICE
                            EAST  CENTRAL  COMMUNITY  COLLEGE
                            BALTIMORE  MD  21228-0710
```

Making a Good Impression on Your Reader

You have just learned about formatting and printing your letters. Now we will turn to the content of your letter—what you say and how you say it. Writing letters means communicating to influence your readers, not to alienate or antagonize them. Keep in mind that writers of effective letters are like successful diplomats in that they represent both their company and themselves. You want readers to see you as courteous, credible, and professional.

First put yourself in the reader's position. What kinds of letters do you like to receive? You would at once rule out letters that are vague, impersonal, sarcastic, pushy, or condescending. You want letters addressed to you to be polite, businesslike, and considerate. If you have questions, you want them answered honestly, courteously, and fully. You do not want someone to waste your time with a long, puffy letter when a few sentences would suffice.

What do you as a writer have to do to send such effective letters? Adopt the **you attitude;** in other words, signal to readers that they and their needs are of utmost importance. Incorporating the "you attitude" means you should be able to answer "Yes" to each of these two questions:

1. Will my readers receive a positive image of me?
2. Have I chosen words that convey both my respect for the readers and my concern for their questions and comments?

The first question deals with your overall view of readers. Do your letters paint them as clever or stupid, practical managers or spendthrifts? The second question deals with specific language and tone conveying your view of the reader. Words can burn or soothe. Choose them carefully. As you revise your letters, you will become more aware of and concerned about the ways a reader will respond to you and your message.

Figures 5.7 and 5.8 contain two versions of the same letter. Which one would you rather receive? Why? Note the use of a watermark in both figures.

Achieving the "You Attitude": Four Guidelines

As you draft and revise your work, pay special attention to the following four guidelines for making a good impression on your reader.

1. Never forget that your reader is a real person. Avoid writing cold, impersonal letters that sound as if they were form letters or voice mail instructions. Let the readers know that you are writing to them as individuals. Neglecting this rule, a large clinic sent its customers this statement: "Your bill is overdue. If you pay it by the 15th of this month, no one except the computer will know that it was late." Similarly, the letter below violates every rule of personal and personable communications.

> It has come to our attention that policy number 342q-765r has been delinquent in payment and is in arrears for the sum of $302.35. To keep the policy in force for the duration of its life, a minimum payment of $50.00 must reach this office by the last day of the month. Failure to submit payment will result in the cancellation of the aforementioned policy.

FIGURE 5.7   A letter lacking the "you attitude."

Brown County • Office of the Tax Assessor

County Building, Room 200, Ventura, Missouri 56780-0101

March 5, 2001

Mr. Ted Ladner
451 West Hawthorne Lane
Morris, MO 64507-3005

Dear Mr. Ladner:

You have written to the wrong office here at the County Building. There
is no way we can attempt to verify the kinds of details you are demanding
from Brown County.

Simply put, by carefully examining the 2000 tax bill you said you
received, you should have realized that it is the Tax Collector's Office, not
the Tax Assessor's, that will have to handle the problem you claim exists.

In short, call or write the Tax Collector of Brown County.

Thank you!

Tracey Kowalski

Tracey Kowalski

712-555-3000 • http://www.browncounty.gov

FIGURE 5.8   A you-centered revision of Figure 5.7.

Brown County • Office of the Tax Assessor

County Building, Room 200, Ventura, Missouri 56780-0101

March 5, 2001

Mr. Ted Ladner
451 West Hawthorne Lane
Morris, MO 64507-3005

Dear Mr. Ladner:

Thank you for writing about the difficulties you encountered with your
2000 tax bill. I wish I could help you, but it is the Tax Collector's Office
that issues your annual property tax bill. Our office does not prepare
individual homeowners' bills.

If you will kindly direct your questions to Paulette Sutton at the Brown
County Tax Collector's Office, County Building, Room 100, Ventura,
Missouri 56780-0100, I am sure that she will be able to assist you.
Should you wish to call her, the number is 458-3455, extension 212.

Respectfully,

Tracey Kowalski

Tracey Kowalski

712-555-3000 • http://www.browncounty.gov

That example displays no sense of one human being writing to another, of a customer with a name, personal history, or specific needs. The letter uses cold and stilted language ("delinquent in payment," "in arrears for," "aforementioned policy"). Revised, this letter contains the necessary personal (and human) touch.

> We have not yet received your payment for your insurance policy (#342q-765r). By sending us your check for $50.00 within the next two weeks, you will keep your policy in force and can continue to enjoy the financial benefits and emotional security it offers you.

The benefits to an individual reader are stressed, and the reader is addressed directly as a valued customer.

Don't be afraid of using "you" in your letters. Readers will feel more friendly toward you and your message. (Of course, no amount of "you's" will help if they appear in a condescending context, such as the letter in Figure 5.7.) In fact, you might even use the reader's name or the name of his or her company in your letter to create goodwill and to show your sincerity.

2. Keep the reader in the forefront of your letter. Make sure the reader's needs control the tone, message, and organization of your letter—the essence of the "you attitude." No one likes people who talk about themselves all the time. What is true about conversation is equally true of letters. Stress the "you," not the "I" or the "we." Again, try to find out about your readers. Here is a paragraph from a letter that forgets about the reader.

Draft

```
I think that our rug shampooer is the best on the market.
Our firm has invested a lot of time and money to ensure that
it is the most economical and efficient shampooer available
today. We have found that our customers are very satisfied
with the results of our machine. We have sold thousands of
these shampooers, and we are proud of our accomplishment.
We hope that we can sell you one of our fantastic machines.
```

The draft talks the reader into boredom by spending all its time on the machine, the company, and the sales success. Readers are interested in how *they* can benefit from the machine, not in how much profit the company makes from selling it.

To win the readers' confidence, the writer needs to show how and why they will find the product useful, economical, and worthwhile at home or at work. Here is a reader-centered revision.

Revision

```
Our rug shampooer would make cleaning your Happy Rest Motel
rooms easier for you. It is equipped with a heavy-duty motor
that will handle your 200 rooms with ease. Moreover, that
motor will give frequently used areas, such as the lobby or
hallways, a fresh and clean look you want for your motel.
```

Note how in the revision the writer shifted attention away from bragging about how "we have sold thousands" to the specific benefits the reader will gain by purchasing the product.

3. Be courteous and tactful. However serious the problem or the degree of your anger at the time, refrain from turning your letter into a punch through the mail. Don't inflame your letter or e-mail readers. Capture the reader's goodwill, and your rewards will be greater. The following words can create a bad taste in the reader's mouth.

it's defective	unprofessional (job, attitude, etc.)
I demand	your failure
I insist	you contend
we reject	you allege
that's no excuse for	you should have known
totally unacceptable	your outlandish claim

Use words that emphasize the "you attitude," and avoid offensive language. Compare the following discourteous sentences with the courteous revisions.

Discourteous	Courteous Revision
We must discontinue your service unless payment is received by the date shown.	Please send us your payment by November 4 so your service will not be interrupted.
Your claim that our product was defective on delivery is outlandish.	We are sorry to learn that you were dissatisfied with the condition of our product when it reached you.
The rotten coil you installed caused all my trouble.	The trouble may be caused by a malfunctioning coil.
You are sorely mistaken about the contract.	We are sorry to learn about the difficulty you experienced over the service terms in our contract.
The new printer you sold me is third-rate and you charged first-rate prices.	Since the printer is still under warranty, I hope you can make the repairs easily and quickly.
Obviously your company is wrong. I wonder if all the people at Acme are as inept as you.	I would appreciate receiving a more detailed explanation from your home office about this matter.
Needless to say, you have misread your warranty agreement.	Clause 17 in your warranty agreement does not cover the problem you have called to our attention.
It goes without saying that your suggestion is not worth considering.	It was thoughtful of you to send me your suggestion, but unfortunately we cannot implement it right now.

The last two discourteous examples begin with phrases that frequently set readers on edge. Avoid using *needless to say* or *it goes without saying*—they can quickly set up a hostile barrier between you and your reader.

4. Be neither boastful nor meek. Two strategies—one based on pride and the other on humility—often lead inexperienced letter writers into trouble. On the one hand, they believe that a forceful statement will make a good impression on the reader. On the other hand, they assume that a cautious and humble approach will be the least offensive way to earn the reader's respect. Both paths are wrong.

Aggressive letters, filled with boasts, rarely appeal to readers. Letters should radiate confidence without sounding as if the writer had written a letter of self-recommendation. Letters should let the facts speak directly and pleasantly for themselves. Compare the following boastful sentences with their graceful revisions.

Boastful	Graceful Revision
You will find me the most diplomatic employee you ever hired.	Much of my previous work has been in answering and adjusting customer complaints.
The Sun and Sea unqualifyingly promises the nicest rooms on the Coast.	Each room at the Sun and Sea has a refrigerator and microwave.
I have performed that procedure so many times I can do it in my sleep.	I have performed all kinds of IV therapy as part of standard care.
The Debit Card offers you incomparable customer convenience.	The Debit Card gives you a 30 percent discount on a safe-deposit box.

At the other extreme, some writers stress only their own inadequacy. Their attitude as projected in their letters is "I am the most unworthy person who ever lived, and I would be eternally grateful if you even let my letter sit on your desk, let alone open it." Readers will dismiss such writers as pitiful, unqualified weaklings. Note how the meek sentences on the left are rewritten more positively on the right.

Meek	Positive Revision
I know that you have a busy schedule and do not always have time to respond, but I would be appreciative if you could send me your brochure on how to apply Brakelite.	Please send me your brochure on how to apply Brakelite.
I will be grateful for whatever employment opportunities you could kindly give me.	I will welcome the opportunity to discuss my qualifications with you.

Using the Most Effective Language in Your Letters

How you say something in a letter is just as crucial to your success as *what* you say. An effective letter requires you to pay attention, especially during the revision stage, to your words and their tone. Three simple suggestions can help. Your letters should be (1) **clear,** (2) **concise,** and (3) **contemporary.** Regard these principles of letter writing as the three C's.

1. Be clear. Clarity is the most important element in a business letter. If your message cannot be understood easily, you have wasted your reader's time and money. Plan what you are going to say—jot down some questions you want answered or some answers to questions asked of you. Doing that will actually save you time. Review pages 45–47 in Chapter 2.

Choose precise details appropriate for your audience. In choosing exact words, answer the reader's five fundamental questions—*who? what? why? where? when?* and *how?* Supply concrete words, facts, details, numbers. In the following examples the vague sentences on the left will puzzle a reader because necessary details are missing. In the revisions on the right, exact words have replaced unclear ones.

Vague	Clear Revision
Please send me some copies of your recent brochure I can use at work.	Please send me 4 copies of your brochure on the new salt substitute to share with my fellow dietitians.
You can expect an appraisal in the next few weeks.	You will receive an estimate on the installation of a new 50,000-BTU air conditioning unit no later than July 12.
One of our New York stores carries that product.	Our store at 856 East Fifth Avenue sells the entire line of Texworld gloves.
The fee for that service is nominal.	The fee for caulking the five windows on the first floor will be $50.00.

2. Be concise. "Get to the point" is a necessity in the business world. A concise letter is easy to read and to act on. As you draft and then revise your letter, ask yourself these two questions: (1) What is the main message I want to tell my reader? (2) Does every sentence and paragraph stick to the main point? **The secret to efficient correspondence is to get to the main point immediately and politely,** as in the following examples.

Your order will be delivered by October 26, as you requested.

I am happy to confirm the figures we discussed via e-mail last Wednesday.

Please accept our apologies for the damaged Movak shipped to you last week.

Here is the report you asked our accountant to prepare with new figures on the Manchester store.

Many letter writers get off to a deadly slow start by repeating, often word for word, the contents of the letter to which they are responding.

First Draft
I have your letter of March 23 before me in which you ask if our office knows of any all-electric duplexes for rent less than five years old and that would be appropriate for senior citizens. You also ask if these duplexes are close to shopping and medical facilities.

Revised
Thank you for your letter of March 23. Our office does rent all-electric duplexes suitable for senior citizens. We have two units, each renting for $375 a month, that are four blocks from the Ortega Clinic and two blocks from the Edgewater Mall.

Another way to write a concise letter is to include only material that is absolutely relevant. For example, in a letter complaining about inadequate or faulty telephone service, mentioning color preferences for cellular telephones would be inappropriate. In a request for information on transferring credits from one college to another, do not ask about intramural sports.

Finally, make sure that your letter is not wordy (review the pertinent sections in Chapter 2, pp. 62–65). Revise your letters before they are printed to make them shorter and more useful.

3. Be contemporary. Being contemporary does not mean you should use slang expressions ("I had a tire ripped off"; "That rejection was a bummer") or informal language that is inappropriate ("Doing business with Bindex is a hassle"). Nor should you go to the other extreme and become stiff and formal. Sound friendly and natural. Write to your reader as if you were carrying on a professional conversation with him or her. A business letter should be upbeat, simple, and to the point. It needs to be readable and believable, not old-fashioned and flowery.

Often individuals are afraid to write naturally because they fear they will not sound important. They resort to using phrases that remind them (and the reader) of "legalese"—language that smells of contracts, deeds, and starched collars. In the following list, the words and phrases on the left are musty expressions that have crept into letters for years; the ones on the right are contemporary equivalents.

Musty	Contemporary Revision
aforementioned	previously mentioned
as per your request	as you requested
at this present writing	now
I am in receipt of	I have
attached herewith	enclosed
at your earliest possible convenience	soon
we beg to advise	we believe, we think
I am cognizant of	I know
endeavor	try
forthwith	at once
henceforth	after this
hereafter, heretofore, hereby	(drop these three "h's" entirely)
immediate future	soon
in lieu of	instead of
kindly advise	let us know
pursuant	concerning
please be advised that	I am happy (or sorry) to tell you that
please find enclosed	I am enclosing
pending your reply	until I hear from you
per our conversation	when we spoke
we regret to inform you that	we are sorry that
remittance	payment
rest assured that	you can be sure that
your letter arrived and I have same	I have your letter
thanking you in advance	thank you
under separate cover	I'm also sending you
the wherewithal	the way
this writer	I
yours of recent date	your recent letter
your communication	your phone call, your fax, your e-mail

Figure 5.9 is a letter in stilted language written by Brendan T. Mundell to Patricia Lipinski, an executive whose firm has been overcharged for airplane tickets. Mundell's letter overflows with flowery, old-fashioned expressions. The effect is that Mundell's message—offering an apology, a credit, and a promise to correct the situation—is long-winded and pompous. It even sounds insincere. Note how the revision in Figure 5.10, free of such stilted expressions, is shorter, clearer, and far more personable.

FIGURE 5.9   A letter written in stilted, old-fashioned language.

NORTHERN AIRWAYS

July 12, 2002

Ms. Patricia Lipinski
Vice President
Lindsay Electronics
4500 South Mahoney Drive
Buffalo, NY 14214-4514

Dear Ms. Lipinski:

Please be advised that I am in receipt of yours of July 6th. I would like to take this opportunity to say that we are cognizant of our commitment to good corporate customers like Lindsay and extend our deepest regret and disappointment for the problems your firm has experienced with Northern.

Payment is due your firm, and I hasten to rectify the situation with regard to our error. Forthwith we are adjusting your account #7530, crediting it with the $706.82 you were surcharged erroneously. Moreover, inasmuch as Lindsay is a valuable customer of our services, we are also enhancing your Travel-Pass account with another 3,000 miles.

I would also like to bring to your attention that in an endeavor to correct such billing errors in the immediate future, I have routed copies of your communication to the manager of the billing department, A. T. Padua. I am confident he will take necessary action at his earliest possible convenience to ascertain the situation and make the necessary adjustments in our procedures.

Once again, I want to take the liberty to assure you that Lindsay Electronics is one of our most valued clients. Rest assured that we will take every step imaginable not to jeopardize our long-standing relationship with you. I hope that all the aforementioned problems have now been satisfactorily resolved. Thanking you, I am

Faithfully yours,

Brendan T. Mundell

Brendan T. Mundell
General Manager

3000 Airline Highway Tyler, ME 04462-3000 (207) 555-6300 E-MAIL: norair@abc.com
Fly over to our Web site at www.norair.com

FIGURE 5.10   A revised version of the stilted letter in Figure 5.9.

NORTHERN AIRWAYS

July 12, 2002

Ms. Patricia Lipinski
Vice President
Lindsay Electronics
4500 South Mahoney Drive
Buffalo, NY 14214-4514

Dear Ms. Lipinski:

Thank you for your letter of July 6. I am sorry to learn about the billing problems your employees encountered while traveling on Northern earlier this month. We care very much when we have inconvenienced a good customer like Lindsay Electronics. Please accept my apology.

Lindsay is unquestionably entitled to compensation for our billing error. I am crediting your account #7530 with $706.82, the amount you were overcharged. Furthermore, in appreciation of Lindsay's business, I am also crediting your Travel-Pass account with a bonus 3,000 miles.

To help us avoid similar incidents, I have sent a copy of your letter to the manager of our billing department, A. T. Padua. I know he will want to learn about Lindsay's experience and will use your comments constructively in an effort to revise our billing procedures.

As a Frequent Flyer account member, Lindsay is one of our most important customers, and we will continue to work hard to deserve your support. Please call me if I can help you in the future.

Sincerely yours,

Brendan T. Mundell

Brendan T. Mundell
General Manager

3000 Airline Highway Tyler, ME 04462-3000 (207) 555-6300 E-MAIL: norair@abc.com
Fly over to our Web site at www.norair.com

Writing for International Readers

Electronic communications have made the world so compact that, in effect, we live and work in a global village. Companies today depend on international trade to stay in business. Many U.S. businesses are multinational corporations with sales branches, plants, and customers throughout the world. In fact, many businesses in the United States are themselves branches of international firms.

Each year a larger share of the U.S. gross national product (GNP) depends on foreign markets. Some American firms estimate that as much as 70 percent of their business is done outside the United States. Every country is affected by every other country, connected by vast interlinked communication networks like the Internet.

As a result, don't presume that you will be writing only to native American English speakers. As part of your job, you will very likely write to readers for whom English is not their first (or native) language; these individuals constitute a large and important audience of **non-native speakers of English,** and writing for them requires you to broaden your sense of audience analysis. Such an audience might reside in a foreign country or in the United States.

Expect your international readers to have varying degrees of proficiency in English. Some readers will have an excellent command of American (or British) English; others will have only basic literacy in English. But do not necessarily conclude that all your international contacts are non-native speakers of English. Many readers in Singapore, Malaysia, and India, for example, have English as their first language. They simply speak a dialect different from American Standard English. Keep in mind, too, that your reader may not speak any English at all but will rely on an English grammar book and a foreign language dictionary to translate your work. Your audience may be a customer, a co-worker, or a specialist in your field who needs written information from you to get a job done right.

You can expect to write a variety of documents to and for these readers— e-mail, reports, ads, Web sites, product descriptions, proposals, even operating instructions. If you find the set of directions accompanying your computer or a software package confusing, imagine how much more intimidating such a document would be to a non-native speaker of English.

You cannot write too clearly or too carefully for these readers. Because so much technical and scientific literature is written in English, your work must be clearly understood by non-native readers for them to translate it into their native language and share your message with fellow specialists.

Your company will profit from having its documents written clearly for all its readers—both customers and employees. In fact, the easier and more understandable your written communications are for international readers, the better your chances of doing business with them. Successful collaboration with non-native speakers of English in your company's work force will also depend on clear and unambiguous explanations, descriptions, and procedures. Companies frequently offer seminars to educate their employees to be sensitive to an audience's multicultural and multilingual background. Study Terri Ruckel's long report (pp. 629–644) to see how advantageous such training programs are to both the firms and their employees and clients who are non-native speakers of English.

Being sensitive to your reader's cultural heritage is vital in business today. The three books below will give you some important background information on this rich and complex topic.

Alfons Trompenaars and Charles Hampden-Turner, *Riding the Waves of Culture: Understanding Cultural Diversity in Global Business* (New York: McGraw-Hill, 1997)

David A. Victor, *International Business Communication* (Reading, MA: Addison Wesley Longman, 1992)

Philip R. Harris and Robert T. Moran, *Managing Cultural Differences: Leadership Strategies for a New World of Business* (Houston: Gulf Publishing, 1996)

Guidelines for Communicating with International Readers

To communicate with customers and co-workers who are non-native speakers of English, you will have to write "international English," a language that is easily understood in a world that international trade has condensed to a single global marketplace. It would be impossible to give you information about how best to communicate with every audience; there are at least 100 major languages representing diverse ethnic and cultural communities around the globe. You must keep in mind two crucial points:

1. You need to be aware of cultural differences between you and your reader.
2. The conventions of writing—the words, sentences, even the type of information you offer—can and do change from one culture to another.

The following eight guidelines will help you communicate more successfully with an international audience and significantly reduce the chances of their misunderstanding you.

1. **Use common, easily understood vocabulary.** Write basic, simplified English. Choose words that are widely understood as opposed to those that are not used or understood by many speakers. Consult a helpful dictionary of basic English such as *The New York Times Everyday Dictionary,* edited by Thomas M. Paikeday (New York Times Books, 1982). Avoid low-frequency words by substituting simpler synonyms; for example, use *stop,* not *refrain; prevent,* not *forestall; discharge,* not *exude; happy,* not *exultant.*

2. **Avoid ambiguity.** Words that have double meanings force non-native readers to wonder which one you mean. For example, "We fired the engine" would baffle your readers if they were not aware of the multiple meanings of *fire.* Unfamiliar with the context in which *fire* means "start up," a non-native speaker of English might think you're referring to "setting on fire or inflaming," which is not what you intend. Such interpretation is likely because most bilingual dictionaries would list those two meanings. Or because *fire* also means "dismiss" or "let go," a non-native speaker of English might even suspect the engine was replaced by another model. Be especially careful of using synonyms just to vary your word choice. For example, do not write *quick* in one sentence and then, referring to the same action, describe it as *rapid.* Your reader may assume you have two different things in mind instead of just one.

3. Be careful about technical vocabulary. While a reader who is a non-native speaker may be more familiar with technical terms than with other English words, make sure the technical word or phrase you include is widely known and not just a word or meaning used only at your plant or office. If you write something about a *trackball* and your audience does not know that this object has replaced a *mouse*, your point will be missed. Also steer clear of technical terms in fields other than the one with which your reader is familiar.

4. Avoid idiomatic expressions. Idioms are the most difficult part of a language for an audience of non-native speakers to master. As with the example of *fire*, the following colorful idiomatic expressions will confuse and may even startle a non-native reader:

I'm all ears	sleep on it
throw cold water on it	burn the midnight oil
hit the nail on the head	land in hot water
easy come, easy go	you bet your life
get a handle on it	cut off your nose to spite your face

The meanings of those and similar phrases are not literal but figurative, a reflection of our culture, not necessarily your reader's. A non-native speaker of English will approach such phrases as combinations of the separate meanings of the individual words, not as a collective unit of meaning. By using idioms, you risk confusing or offending your audience.

Imagine the horror a non-native speaker of English—a potential customer in Asia or Africa, for example—might experience if you wrote about a sale concluded at a branch office this way: "Last week we made a killing in our office." Omit the idiomatic expression and substitute a clear, unambiguous translation easily understood in international English. "We made a big sale last week." Or in place of "You hit the nail on the head," write "You have clearly understood what must be done." For "Sleep on it," you might say, "Please take a week or two to make your decision."

5. Delete sports and gambling metaphors. These metaphors, which are often rooted in American popular culture, do not translate word for word for non-native speakers and so again can interfere with your communication with your readers. In all likelihood, your audience has no equivalent in its culture for American sporting games and events. Here are a few examples to avoid:

out in left field	a ballpark figure
struck out	fumbled the ball
go out for a long pass	the bases are loaded
drop the ball	out of bounds
down for the count	made a pass
top of the ninth	beat the odds
long shot	

Use a basic English dictionary and your common sense to find nonfigurative translations for those and similar expressions.

6. Watch units of measure. Adapt your references to units of measurement, money, and time to your reader's culture. Do not fall into the cultural trap of assuming that your reader measures distances in miles and feet (instead of kilometers and meters), buys gallons of gasoline (instead of liters), and spends dollars (rather than pesos, marks, rupees, or yen). Just as not everyone in the world uses 110/220 wiring, keep in mind that not everyone sees the world marketplace solely in terms of the U.S. economy. Adapt your message to the reader's practices.

Be aware of seasonal differences, too. While New York is in the middle of the winter, Australia and Chile are enjoying summer. Be respectful of your readers' cultural (and physical) environment. Thanksgiving is celebrated in the United States in November, but in Canada the holiday is the second Monday in October; elsewhere around the world it may not be a holiday at all.

7. Avoid culture-bound descriptions of place and space. For example, when you tell a reader in Hong Kong about the Sunbelt or a potential client in Africa about the Big Easy, will he or she know what you mean? When you write from California to a non-native speaker in India about the eastern seaboard, meaning the East Coast of the United States, the directional reference may not mean the same thing to your audience as it does to you.

8. Keep your sentences simple and easy to understand. Short, direct sentences will cause a reader whose native language is not English the least amount of trouble. World languages, especially those in Asia, divide information into sentence units far differently from the way English does. A good rule of thumb is that the shorter and less complicated your sentences, the easier they will be for a reader to process. Long (more than fifteen words) and complex (multiclause) sentences can be so difficult for readers to unravel that they may skip over them or guess at your message. Always try to avoid the passive voice; it is one of the most difficult sentence patterns for a non-native speaker to comprehend. Stick to the common subject-verb-object pattern as often as possible.

Respecting the Cultural Traditions of International Readers

Using simple words and concise sentences certainly will help you to write more effectively and clearly to an international audience. But to avoid even greater troubles, you also must be concerned with respecting the cultural traditions, customs, and preferences of your readers—how they dress, walk, eat, and interact at formal and informal meetings. Cultures differ widely in the way they send and receive information. What is acceptable in one culture may be offensive in another.

For example, in Japan you would impress a potential client by bowing rather than shaking hands. But you must learn the protocol involved in bowing—who bows first, for how long, and how deeply. Similarly, Japanese businesspeople are more accustomed to negotiating side by side, unlike U.S. businesspeople, who prefer to sit face to face.

Respecting Your Reader's Nationality and Ethnic/Racial Heritage

Do not risk offending any of your readers, whether they are native speakers of English or not, with language that demeans or stereotypes their nationality or ethnic and racial background. Here are some precautions to take into account.

1. Respect your reader's nationality. Always spell your reader's name and country properly, which may mean adding diacritical marks (such as accent marks) not used in English.

2. Honor your reader's place in the world economy. Phrases like "third-world country," "emerging nation," "undeveloped/unprivileged area" are derogatory. Using such phrases signals that you regard your reader's country as inferior. Use the name of your reader's country instead. Saying that someone lives in the Far East implies that the United States, Canada, or Europe is the center of culture, the hub of the business community. It would be better to simply say "East Asia." Never use the word "Oriental," which is insulting.

3. Avoid insulting stereotypes. Expressions such as "oil-rich Arabs," "time-relaxed Latinos," and "aggressive foreigners" unfairly characterize particular groups. Similarly, prune from your communications any stereotypical phrase that insults one group or singles it out for praise at the expense of another—"Mexican standoff," "Russian roulette," "Chinaman's change," "Irish wake," "Dutch treat," "Indian giver." The word *Indian* refers to someone from India; use *Native American* to refer to the indigenous people of North America.

4. Be visually sensitive to your reader's culture. Colors, for example, carry much cultural symbolism. Do not offend your audience by using colors in a context that would be offensive. Green and orange have a strong political context in Ireland. In China white does not symbolize purity and weddings but mourning and funerals. Similarly, in India if a married woman wears all white, she is inviting widowhood. Several years ago, Air Canada opened new routes to East Asia and painted their planes black. But because black represents bad luck in that region of the world, Air Canada had to repaint its planes. A signature or a note written in red would signify anger to an Indonesian reader. And a Saudi audience would be highly offended to see individuals in short-sleeve shirts or bathing suits in any sales literature sent to them. Respecting the cultural practices of your readers can have far more impact on them than touting the price and quality of your product or service.

Here are some culturally conditioned elements of interpersonal communication you may need to adjust when writing to readers whose culture is different from yours:

- what your status is in relationship to the reader
- how you address the reader in your salutation
- the beginning and the conclusion of your letter
- the type and amount of information you give
- the overall tone you use
- the format and design of your document

Internet Guides to a Country's Culture

Nearly all countries in the world maintain some kind of World Wide Web presence, which can give you invaluable information. Once you locate the Web site of your reader's country (often prepared by its Division of Tourism), you can click your way to a deeper knowledge of and respect for your reader's customs. For example, the official site provided by the Egyptian Tourist Authority and Ministry of

Tourism (*http://www.touregypt.net/*) contains information about that country's geography, language, religion, education, government, and economy. A map and other statistical information are also part of the Web site.

Travel bureaus, businesses, and major search engines on the Internet (for example, Yahoo! and Excite) also maintain Web sites dedicated to specific cultures and people. For example, Lonely Planet (*http://www.lonelyplanet.com/*) publishes hundreds of books and articles on global travel and produces a popular television show of world travel. Lonely Planet provides useful, free, and current advice on the culture, customs, attractions, history, weather, and necessities of travel for all areas of the world. You can find everything from weather to up-to-the-minute news about labor strikes plus ways (chat-room access, e-mail addresses, listservs) to contact experienced travelers to ask about language and customs. (Lonely Planet Online also provides **eKno,** a free communications kit for business travelers that includes e-mail and voice messaging services.)

Columbus Publishing's World Travel Guide Online (*http://www.wtgonline.com/navigate/world.asp*) claims to be "the most comprehensive and objective guide to the traveler's world, and [one that] has been designed to answer all the questions you will ever need to ask with speed, confidence and authority." This Internet version of the best-selling *World Travel Guide* contains information about every country in the world, from Afghanistan to Zimbabwe.

The following sources will help you to understand proper communication etiquette for crossing cultural boundaries.

General Information and Travel Search Sites

- *http://www.search-ti-all.com/* presents an easy set of links for finding government offices, embassies, company information, and contact information for individuals.
- *http://city.net/destinations/* by Excite lets you choose the continent or city of your choice, then links you to a variety of country-specific Web sites, including those dedicated to business and ethnic information. For example, from the Côte d'Ivoire (Ivory Coast), Africa section, *http://www.sas.upenn.edu/African_Studies/Country_Specific/Cote.html/* includes a link to the Africa Business Network site (*http://www.ifc.org/abn/index.htm*).
- *http://www.travel.yahoo.com* by Yahoo! offers similar information.

On-Line Chat Groups

Chat groups make it possible for you to ask questions directly to seasoned travelers or to citizens of the country in question.

- *http://www.about.com* takes you to About.com, where you can choose to chat with expert guides concerning hundreds of human-interest topics.
- *http://www.talkaway.com* provides an "exchange of ideas on practically everything" through on-line group discussions.

U.S. Government Guides to World Cultures

- *http://www.odcilgov/cia/publications/factbook/index.html,* the on-line version of the widely consulted and authoritative *CIA World Factbook,* contains maps, statistical, contact, and cultural information for every country in the world, as well as describing current U.S. relations with each country.

- *http://www.cweb2.loc.gov/frd/cs/cshome.html* is the on-line version of the *Country Studies* handbooks from the Library of Congress.
- *http://www.lib.umich.edu/libhome/Documents.center.foreign.html* is a site organized by the University of Michigan that includes links to background, cultural, and travel information.

Case Study: Writing to a Client from a Different Culture

Let's assume that you have to write a sales letter to an Asian business executive. You will have to employ a very different strategy in writing to an Asian executive as opposed to an American executive. For an American reader, the best strategy would be to take a direct approach—fast, hard-hitting, to the point, and stressing your product's strengths versus the opposition's weaknesses. A sales letter to an American reader would be polite but direct.

But such a strategy would be counterproductive in a sales letter to an Asian reader. Business in East Asia is associated with religion and friendship and is wrapped up in a great many social courtesies. The Asian way of doing business, including writing and receiving letters, is far more subtle, indirect, and complimentary than in the United States. The American style of directness and forcefulness would be perceived as rude or unfair in, say, Japan, China, Malaysia, or Korea. A hard-sell letter to an Asian reader would be a sign of arrogance, and arrogance suggests inequality for the reader.

Courtesy for an Asian reader would be of paramount importance, more persuasive than a thorough description of a product or service. A sales letter to an Asian reader, therefore, should establish a friendship, a relationship in which trust is established first and business details are dealt with later. It is standard in Japanese companies, for example, to have executives meet three or four times just to socialize before they begin business negotiations.

Two Versions of a Sales Letter

To better understand the differences between communicating with a U.S. reader and an Asian one, study the two versions of the sales letter in Figures 5.11 and 5.12. The letters, written by Susan DiFusco for Starbrook Electronics, sell the same product, but Figure 5.11 is addressed to a U.S. executive, while Figure 5.12 adapts the same message for a businessperson in Seoul. The two letters differ not only in content but also in the way each is printed.

Format

The full-block style of the letter to the American reader signals a no-nonsense, all-business approach. Everything is lined up in neat, orderly fashion. For the Korean reader, however, DiFusco wisely chose the more varied pattern of indenting her paragraphs. For Asian readers the visual effect suggests a much more relaxed and friendly, yet respectful communication. Note the different typefaces, too.

Opening

Pay special attention to how the American letter in Figure 5.11 starts off politely but much more directly, an opening the Korean reader would regard as blunt and

FIGURE 5.11   Sales letter to a native English speaker in an American firm.

Starbrook Electronics
Perry, TX 75432-3456
phone (713) 555-2121 E-mail starbrook.com
http://www.starbrook.org

December 5, 2002

Mr. Ellis Fanner
Administrator
Morgan General Hospital
300 Oakland Drive
Morgan, OR 97342-0091

Dear Mr. Fanner:

How many times have the physicians who work at Morgan General asked
when you would be getting MRI (magnetic resonance imaging) equipment?
Having the latest, state-of-the-art imaging equipment is important to
maintain your reputation as a leading health care provider in the Morgan
River Valley.

As the world leader in designing and manufacturing MRI equipment,
Starbrook can offer you the latest technology available. This diagnostic
technology will save your patients time and improve the care you give them.
With the MRI capability of our Imaging 500, Morgan General can deliver
more accurate and timely diagnoses. Within two hours you can determine
whether a patient has had a stroke rather than having to wait a day or longer
with more conventional X-ray or scanner technology.

Thanks to our Imaging 500 model, Morgan General can also improve
diagnoses for orthopedic and cardiac problems. Our Imaging 500 delivers
much more extensive internal imaging than any other of our competitors'
equipment.

By obtaining the Imaging 500, Morgan General will surpass all other health
care providers in the Morgan River Valley. No other hospital within a
hundred-mile radius has one. By acting now, you, too, will receive
Starbrook's unsurpassed guarantee of service and clarity. You are
guaranteed one year's free maintenance by our team of experts.

Continued

FIGURE 5.11   (Continued)

Mr. Ellis Fanner   December 5, 2002   2

And we will even give you free upgrades to make sure your Imaging 500 continues to be state of the art. Since software updates change so often and so radically, no other MRI vendor dares make such an offer. We deliver what we promise. Ask any of our recent satisfied customers—Tennessee General, Grantsville Uptown Clinic, or Nevada Statewide HMO.

We are hosting a demonstration for hospital administrators on the 4th of January in Portland and would like to see you there. Don't hesitate to call me to arrange for your free showing.

Sincerely yours,

Susan DiFusco
Assistant Manager

---

discourteous. The sales letter written to the Korean audience (Figure 5.12) starts not with business talk but with a compliment to the reader and his company, praising them for trustworthiness and wishing them much prosperity in the future. The successful writer addressing a Korean administrator would not get to the bottom line right away but would use the introductory paragraph to show respect for the company and the reader—the equivalent of Japanese business executives socializing before any mention of business is made.

The Body
Compare the second and third paragraphs of the letters in Figures 5.11 and 5.12. While the letter to the American reader launches an aggressive campaign to get the reader's business, the letter to the Korean reader avoids the hard sell of American business tactics. Susan DiFusco knew that for her Korean reader she must not promote too strenuously. The more she boasted about Starbrook's work, the less likely it was that she would make a sale. She recognized from discussions with other Asian businesspeople over the years that she had to supply key information—such as the application and the advantages of her product—without overwhelming or pressuring her audience. Yet DiFusco subtly reassures Mr. Kim that her company is honorable and worthy to be recommended to his friends.

View of Competitors
Observe, too, how the letter to the American executive (Figure 5.11) undermines the competition by stating how much better Starbrook's offer is. For most Asian

FIGURE 5.12   Sales letter to a non-native speaker of English in a foreign firm.

Starbrook Electronics
Perry, TX 75432-3456
phone (713) 555-2121 E-mail starbrook.com
http://www.starbrook.org

December 5, 2002

Mr. Kim Sun-Lim
Administrator, Tangki Hospital
210-214 Jenji Road
Seoul, Korea

Dear Mr. Kim:

In your beautiful language I say "Gyuihauie bunyanggwa hangbokul kiwonhamnida" on behalf of my firm Starbrook Electronics. I am honored to introduce myself to you through this letter.

Please let us know how we might be of service to you. One of the ways we may be able to serve you is by informing you about our new Imaging 500 MRI (magnetic resonance imaging) equipment. This new model can offer you and your patients many advantages. It is far better than conventional X-ray or even scanner models. Your physicians can offer quicker diagnoses for patients with strokes, heart attacks, or orthopedic injuries. MRI pictures will give you clearer and deeper pictures than any X-ray can.

It would be an honor to provide Tangki Hospital with one of our Imaging 500s. If you select the Imaging 500, we will be happy to give you all maintenance and software updates free for one year. Such service will provide the best in health care for the many people who come to you for help. Our firm is well known for its quality service.

Kindly let me know if I might send you information about the Imaging 500. It would be a privilege to meet you and to give you and your staff a demonstration of our Imaging 500.

Respectfully,

Susan DiFusco
Assistant Manager

readers, it would be considered impolite to claim that your product is better than another company's or that your firm is currently doing business with other firms in the reader's country. Asian audiences prefer to avoid anything that hints of impoliteness or assertiveness.

Conclusion

Finally, contrast the conclusions of the two letters. In the letter to an American audience, DiFusco strongly urges her potential customer to get in touch with her. Such a call to action is customary in a sales letter to an American firm. But in her concluding paragraph to Mr. Kim, DiFusco adopts a more reserved and personal tone. Her use of such appropriate phrases as "kindly let me know" and "it would be a privilege" expresses the friendly sentiments of respect and esteem that would especially appeal to her reader. Note, too, that DiFusco has chosen a complimentary close ("Respectfully") much more in keeping with Mr. Kim's cultural sensitivities than the "Sincerely yours," which was suitable for the letter in Figure 5.11.

As these two letters show, writers must know and respect their culture. In addressing an audience of non-native speakers of English, a writer must consider the readers' communication patterns, use protocols, and cultural (or subcultural) traditions. The same guidelines apply whether you are writing to non-native speakers abroad or in this country. Your message and vocabulary should always be clear, understandable, and appropriate for the intended audience.

✓ Revision Checklist

Audience Analysis and Research

❑ Made sure reader's name and job title are right.
❑ Found out something about my audience—interests and background, well informed or unfamiliar with topic, former clients or new ones.
❑ Determined whether audience will be friendly, hostile, or neutral about my message.
❑ Did sufficient research—in print and through on-line sources—to give audience what they need.
❑ Acknowledged previous correspondence.
❑ Spent sufficient time drafting and revising letter before printing final copy.

Content/Organization

❑ Clearly understood my purpose in writing to reader(s).
❑ Put most important point first in my letter.
❑ Started each paragraph with the central idea of that paragraph.

❑ Answered all the reader's questions and concerns.

❑ Omitted anything offensive, irrelevant, or repetitious.

❑ Used numbers, bullets, and/or boldfacing to make it easier for reader to find and remember main ideas.

❑ Stated clearly what I want reader to do.

❑ Used last paragraph to summarize and encourage reader to continue cordial relations with me and my company.

Style: Words, Tone, Sentences, Paragraphs

❑ Emphasized the "you attitude" by seeing things from reader's perspective.

❑ Was not too casual or colloquial.

❑ Chose words that are clear, precise, and friendly.

❑ Cut anything sounding flowery or stuffy, especially legalese.

❑ Ensured that my sentences are readable, clear, and not too long (less than fifteen to twenty words).

❑ Wrote paragraphs that are easy to read and that flow together.

Writing to Non-Native Speakers of English

❑ Did appropriate research about reader's culture, both in print and through on-line sources, especially accepted ways of communicating.

❑ Adopted a respectful, not condescending, tone.

❑ Avoided anything offensive to my reader, especially references to politics, religion, or cultural taboos.

❑ Used language that my reader would understand.

❑ Tested my sentences for length and active voice.

❑ Made sure nothing in my letter might be misinterpreted by my reader.

❑ Selected the right format, salutation, and complimentary close for my reader.

❑ Chose colors culturally appropriate for the context of my message.

Format/Appearance

❑ Followed one letter format (full-block, semiblock, simplified) consistently.

❑ Left wide-enough margins to make my letter look attractive and well proportioned.

❑ Included all the necessary parts of a letter.

❑ Made sure that my letter looks neat and professional—toner cartridge was fresh and type font is not crowded or showy.

❑ Printed my letter on company letterhead or quality bond paper.

❑ Proofread my letter carefully and made sure each correction was made before final copy was printed.

❑ Eliminated any grammatical and spelling errors.

❑ Signed my letter legibly in blue or black ink.

❑ Sent copies to appropriate parties.

❑ Addressed envelopes properly.

Exercises

1. Find two business letters and bring them to class. Be prepared to identify the various parts of a letter discussed in this chapter.

2. Find a form letter that is addressed to "Dear Customer," "Postal Patron," or "Dear Resident" and rewrite it to make it more personal.

3. Correct the following inside addresses:

   a. Dr. Ann Clark, M.D.
   1730 East Jefferson
   Jackson, MI. 46759
   b. To: Tommy Jones
   Secretary to Mrs. Franks
   Donlevey labs
   Cleveland, O. 45362
   c. Debbie Hinkle
   432 Parkway
   N. Y. C. 10054
   d. Mr. Charles Howe, Acme Pro.
   P.O. Box 675
   1234 S. e. Boulevard
   Gainesville, Flor. 32601

   e. Alex Goings, man.
   Pittfield Industries
   Longview, TEXAS 76450
   f. ATTENTION: G. Yancy (Mrs.)
   Police Academy
   1329 Tucker
   N. O., La. 3410-70122
   g. David and Mahenny
   Lawyers
   Dobbs Build.
   L.A. 94756
   h. CONFIDENTIAL
   Jordon Foods, INC.
   Miller Str.
   Lincoln, Neb. 2103

4. Write appropriate inside addresses and salutations to (a) a woman who has not specified her marital status; (b) an officer in the armed forces; (c) a professor at your school; (d) an assistant manager at your local bank; (e) a member of the clergy; (f) your congressperson.

5. Properly address envelopes with the following mailing instructions:

   a. Revised Data
   b. Confidential
   c. Open at Once

   d. Dated Contents
   e. Contract Enclosed
   f. Do Not Open Until 10/2

6. Rewrite the following sentences to make them more personal.

   a. It becomes incumbent upon this office to cancel order #2394.
   b. Management has suggested the curtailment of parking privileges.
   c. ALL USERS OF HYDROPLEX: Desist from ordering replacement valves during the period of Dec. 19–29.
   d. The request for a new catalog has been honored; it will be shipped to same address soon.
   e. Perseverance and attention to detail have made this writer important to company in-house work.
   f. The Director of Nurses hereby notifies staff that a general meeting will be held Monday afternoon at 3:00 P.M. sharp. Attendance is mandatory.
   g. Reports will be filed by appropriate personnel no later than the scheduled plans allow.

7. The following sentences from letters are discourteous, boastful, excessively humble, vague, or lacking the "you attitude." Rewrite them to correct those mistakes.
   a. Something is obviously wrong in your head office. They have once more sent me the wrong model number. Can they ever get things straight?
   b. My instructor wants me to do a term paper on safety regulations at a small factory. Since you are the manager of a small factory, send me all the information I need at once. My grade depends heavily on all this.
   c. It is apparent that you are in business to rip off the public.
   d. I was wondering if you could possibly see your way into sending me the local chapter president's name and address, if you have the time, that is.
   e. I have waited for my confirmation for two weeks now. Do you expect me to wait forever or can I get some action?
   f. Although I have never attempted to catalog books before, and really do not know my way around the library, I would very much like to be considered at some later date convenient to you for a part-time afternoon position.
   g. It goes without saying that we cannot honor your request.
   h. May I take just a moment of your valuable time to point out that our hours for the next three weeks will change and we trust and pray that no one in your agency will be terribly inconvenienced by this.
   i. Your application has been received and will be kept on file for six months. If we are interested in you, we will notify you. If you do not hear from us, please do not write us again. The soaring costs of correspondence and the large number of applicants make the burden of answering pointless letters extremely heavy.
   j. My past performance as a medical technologist has left nothing to be desired.
   k. Credit means a lot to some people. But obviously you do not care about yours. If you did, you would have sent us the $249.95 you rightfully owe us three months ago. What's wrong with you?

8. The following letter, filled with musty expressions and in old-fashioned language (legalese), buries key ideas. Rewrite and reorganize it to make it shorter, clearer, and more reader-centered.

Dear Ms. Granedi:

This is in response to your firm's letter of recent date inquiring about the types of additional services that may be available to business customers of the First National Bank of Bentonville. The question of a possible time frame for the implementation of said services was also raised in the aforementioned letter. Pursuant to these queries, the following answers, this office trusts, will prove helpful.

Please be advised that the Board of Directors at First National Bank has a continuing reputation for servicing the needs of the Bentonville community, especially the business community. For the last fifty years—half of a century—First National Bank has provided the funds necessary for the growth, success, and expansion of many local firms, yours included. This financial support has bestowed many opportunities on a multitude of business owners, residents of Bentonville, and even residents of surrounding local communities.

The Board is at this present writing currently deliberating, with its characteristic caution, over a variety of options suggested to us by our patrons, including your firm. These options, if the Board decides to act upon them, would enhance the business opportunities for financial transactions at First National Bank. Among the two options receiving attention by the Board at this point in time are the creation of a branch office in the rapidly growing north side of Bentonville. This area has many customers who rely on the services of First National Bank. The Board may also place a business loan department in the new branch.

If this office of the First National Bank of Bentonville might be of further helpful assistance, please advise. Remember banking with First National Bank is a community privilege.

Soundly yours,

M. T. Watkins

Public Relations Director

9. Either individually or in a small group, write a business letter to one of the following individuals and submit an appropriate envelope with your letter.
   a. your mayor, asking for an appointment and explaining why you need one
   b. your college president, stressing the need for more parking spaces or for additional computer terminals in a library
   c. the local water department, asking for information about fluoride supplements
   d. an editor of a weekly magazine, asking permission to reprint an article in a school newspaper
   e. the author of an article you have read recently, telling why you agree or disagree with the views presented
   f. a disc jockey at a local radio station, asking for more songs by a certain group
   g. a computer dealer, asking about costs and availability of software packages and explaining your company's special needs

10. Rewrite the following letters, making them appropriate for a reader whose native language is not English. As you revise the letters, pay attention to the words you use as well as the sentence constructions you employ. Be sure to consider the reader's cultural traditions.

a. Dear Chum,

Our stateside boss hit the ceiling earlier today when she learned that our sales quota for this quarter fell precipitously short. Ouch! Were I in her spot, I would have exploded too. Numerous missives to her underlings warned them to get off the dime and on the stick, but they were oblivious to such. These are the breaks in our business, right?

Let's hope that next quarter's sales take a turn for the best. If they are as disastrous, we all may be in hot water. Until then, we will have to watch our p's and q's around here.

Cheers,

b. Dear Mr. Wong,

It's not every day that you have the chance to get in on the ground floor of a deal so good you can actually taste it. But Off-Wall Street Mutual can make the difference in your financial future. Give me a moment to convince you.

By becoming a member of our international investing group, you can just about ensure your success. We know all the ins and outs of long-term investing and can save you a bundle. Our analysts are the hot shots of the business and always look long and hard for the most propitious business deals. The stocks we select with your interests in mind are as safe as a bank and not nearly so costly for you. We can save you money by investing your money. We are penny pinchers with our client's initial investments, but we are King Midas when it comes to transforming those investments into pure gold.

I am enclosing a brochure for you to study, and I really hope you will examine it carefully. You would be foolish to let a deal like Off-Wall Street Mutual pass you by. Go for it.

Hurriedly,

c. Dear Mr. Bafaloukos,

My firm is taking a survey of businesses in your part of the world to see if there is any likelihood of getting you on board our international computer network and so I thought I would drop you a line to see if you might like to take the chance. In today's uncertain world, business events can change overnight and without the proper scoop you could be left out in the cold. We can alleviate that mess.

> Not only do we interface with major exchanges all around the globe but we make sure that we get the facts to you pronto. We do not sit on our hands here at Intertel. Check out the enclosed data sheet on who and how we serve and I have no doubts that you will e-mail or ring us up to find out about joining up.
>
> One last point: can you really risk going out on a limb without first knowing that you have all the facts at your fingertips about worldwide business events? Intertel is there to save you.
>
> Fondly,

11. Interview a student at your school or a co-worker who was born and raised in a foreign country about the proper etiquette in writing a business letter to someone from his or her country. Collaborate with that student to write a letter (for example, a sales letter or a letter asking for information) to an executive from that country.

12. In a letter to your instructor, describe the kinds of adaptations you had to make for the international reader you wrote to in Exercise 11.

13. Assume you work for a large international corporation that has just opened new offices in the following cities:
   a. Dar es Salaam, Tanzania
   b. Istanbul, Turkey
   c. Caracas, Venezuela
   d. Manila, Philippines

   Using the resources mentioned on pages 177–178, write a short report on the main points of letter etiquette your boss will have to observe in communicating with the non-native speaker of English who is the branch manager at one of the four new offices.

14. As a collaborative project, team up with three other students in your class to write separate letters tailored to executives in each of the following cities:
   a. Buenos Aires, Argentina
   b. Tokyo, Japan
   c. Munich, Germany

   Assume you are selling the same product or service to each reader but you will have to adapt your communication to the culture represented by the reader.
   Turn in the three letters and explain to your instructor in an accompanying memo how you met the needs of those diverse cultural audiences in terms of style, tone, level of content, format, and sales tactics. Describe the research tools you used to find out about your reader's particular culture (and communication protocols) and how you benefited from using those sources.

Types of Business Letters

Receiving and answering business correspondence is vital to the success of a company and its employees. Businesses take their letter writing very seriously and employers pay a high price, as we saw in Chapter 1, for employees to write effective letters. Letter writing is a prized skill in the world of work. In fact, the higher up the corporate ladder you climb, the more you will be expected to write letters—and write them well. For that reason, we cannot overemphasize how important it is to your career to be an effective letter writer.

Letters in the Age of the Internet

As we saw in Chapter 5, letters play a significant role in the business world. They continue to be especially important in the changing electronic business culture of the twenty-first century. Letters perform the following functions:

1. **Letters are far more formal and official**—in tone, structure, and sense of authorship—than any other type of business communication. Memos and internal e-mail are the least formal.
2. **Letters offer personal and verifiable (traceable) authorization.** Although electronic signatures are gaining acceptance, a signed letter directly and legally links the writer and his or her organization to the communication with the reader.
3. **Unlike e-mail, letters in many businesses must be routed through channels before they are sent out.** Because they convey how a company looks and what it offers to customers, letters must be approved at a variety of corporate levels. Moreover, they are logged in while e-mail or memos are not. E-mail can be easily deleted; letters are often part of a permanent file.
4. **Although the Web may be a company's foremost avenue of advertisement, the business letter is still one of its most binding forms of communication.** A firm's corporate reputation is on the line when it sends out a letter.

5. **A letter is still the official and expected medium through which important documents and attachments (contracts, specifications, proposals) are sent to readers.** Sending such attachments via e-mail or with a memo lacks the formality a reader deserves.

Writing Effective Letters

One of the biggest mistakes you can make is to think that writing a letter, even a short one, does not require preparation. Don't think you can just sit down for a few minutes at your keyboard and fire off an acceptable, well-crafted letter. Like other types of occupational writing—proposals, reports, instructions—writing an effective letter requires you to follow, though perhaps in abbreviated fashion, the writing process discussed in Chapter 2. That is true whether you print your letter and drop it in a mailbox or you upload it to the Internet via e-mail.

Accordingly, you need to identify your audience and have a clear sense of your purpose and theirs; do appropriate research; select the best strategy for communicating with your audience; and draft, revise, and edit your letter.

Although it is more likely that you will collaborate on longer documents, you still can expect to work with others on certain letters. For instance, you may be asked to confer with specialists in other divisions of your company to answer a complaint about one of your company's products. You may be required to meet with individuals in your company's law or marketing department when drafting a sales letter. Also, there may be times when your boss will ask to edit a letter (see pp. 94–100) before you send it.

Types of Letters

This chapter discusses the common types of business correspondence that you will be expected to write on the job:

1. inquiry letters
2. special request letters
3. sales letters
4. customer relations letters

These four types of letters involve a variety of formats and writing strategies and techniques. Business letters can be classified as **positive, neutral,** or **negative,** depending on their message and the anticipated reactions of your audience. Inquiry and special request letters are examples of neutral letters. They carry neither good nor bad news; they simply inform, responding to routine correspondence. Neutral letters request information about a product or service, place an order, or respond to some action or question. Sales letters promoting a product carry good news, according to the companies that spend millions of dollars a year preparing them. Customer relations letters can be positive (responding favorably to a writer's request or complaint) or negative (refusing a request, saying no to an adjustment, denying credit, seeking payment, critiquing poor performance, or announcing a product recall).

TECH NOTE

Designing Your Letters

Keep in mind that your letters must make a good visual as well as verbal impression on your readers.

- Take advantage of the "print preview" function of your word-processing software to see how your letter will look on the page before you print it. If necessary, readjust margins and add white space. But don't insert too much white space because your letter will look inflated and insincere.
- Never print a letter in all capital letters. Not only will you make it harder to read but your letter will look unprofessional, like an old-fashioned telegram. It also looks like you are shouting.
- Choose a print font that is appropriate for your message and audience. Your readers will find a serif font much more open and inviting than a sans serif one. Among the most cordial serif fonts are Goudy and Palatino, available on many word processing software packages.
- Depending on the length and the details of your letter, use bullets to itemize a series of points, boldface or italic type to emphasize a key point or word, or underscoring and color for highlighting. But use those devices sparingly. Overdoing color, boldfacing, underscoring, and italicizing makes a letter busy looking and conveys an image of you as overanxious, even self-conscious, not professional and self-controlled.

Inquiry Letters

An inquiry letter asks for information about a product, service, publication, or procedure. Businesses frequently exchange such letters. As a customer, you too have occasion to ask in a letter, over e-mail, or through a fax for catalogs, names of stores in your town selling a special line of products, the price, size, and color of a particular object, or delivery arrangements. Businesses are eager to receive such inquiries and will answer them swiftly because they promise a future sale.

You might also fill out a survey on a specific Web site. Such a survey allows a business to send product information to your e-mail or your home address.

Figure 6.1 illustrates a letter of inquiry. Addressed to a real estate office managing a large number of apartment complexes, Michael Ortega's letter follows the three basic rules for an effective inquiry letter by

- stating exactly what information the writer wants
- indicating clearly why the writer must have the information
- specifying when the writer must have the information

FIGURE 6.1   A letter of inquiry.

> **Michael Ortega**
> **403 South Main Street Kingsport, TN 37721-0217**
> **mortega@erols.com**
>
> March 1, 2002
>
> Mr. Fred Stonehill
> Property Manager
> Acme Property Corporation
> Main and Broadway
> Roanoke, VA 24015-1100
>
> Dear Mr. Stonehill:
>
> *States precise request*
>
> Please let me know if you will have any two-bedroom furnished apartments available for rent during the months of June, July, and August. I am willing to pay up to $475 a month plus utilities. My wife, one-year-old son, and I will be moving to Roanoke for the summer so I can take classes at Virginia Western Community College.
>
> *Explains need for information*
>
> If possible, we would like to have an apartment that is within two or three miles of the college. We do not have any pets.
>
> *Specifies exact date when a reply is needed*
>
> I would appreciate hearing from you within the next two weeks. My e-mail address is mortega@erols.com, or you can call me at home (606-555-8957) any evening from 6–10 p.m.
>
> *Offers to confer with reader*
>
> If you have any suitable vacancies, we would be happy to drive to Roanoke to look at them and give you a deposit to hold an apartment. Thanks for your help.
>
> Sincerely yours,
>
> *Michael Ortega*
>
> Michael Ortega

Whenever you request information, be sure to supply appropriate stock and model numbers, pertinent page numbers, or exact descriptions. You might even clip and mail the advertisement describing the product you want. Vague or general letters delay a response to you. Had Michael Ortega written the following letter to Acme, he would not have helped his family move: "Please send me some information on housing in Roanoke. My family and I plan to move there soon." Such a letter does not indicate whether he wants to rent or buy, whether he is interested in a large or small apartment, furnished or unfurnished, where he would like to be located, or the rent he is able to pay.

Similarly, the letter writer who asks a firm to "send me all the information you have on microwave ovens" might receive back a detailed service manual or no information at all instead of what the writer really wanted—the prices of the top-selling models.

Special Request Letters

Special request letters make a special demand, not a routine inquiry. For example, these letters can ask a company for information that you as a student will use in a paper, an individual for a copy of an article or a speech, or an agency for facts that your company needs to prepare a proposal or sell a product. The person or company being asked for help stands to gain no financial reward for supplying the information; the only reward is the goodwill a response creates.

Make your request clear and easy to answer. Supply readers with an addressed, postage-paid envelope, an e-mail address, and fax and telephone numbers in case they have questions. But don't ask a company to fax a long document to you. It is discourteous to ask someone else to pay the fax charges for something you need. If you request information via e-mail, don't expect your reader to tie up computer lines by sending a lengthy attachment.

Saying "please" and "thank you" will help you get the information you want. Also, do not expect your reader to write the paper or proposal for you. Asking for information is quite different from asking readers to organize and write it for you. Follow these seven points when asking for information in a special request letter.

1. State who you are and why you are writing.
2. Indicate clearly your reason for requesting the information.
3. State precisely and succinctly the questions you want answered. List, number, and separate the questions.
4. Specify exactly when you need the information. Allow sufficient time—at least three weeks.
5. Offer to forward a copy of your report, paper, or survey in gratitude for the help you were given.
6. If you want to reprint or publish the materials you ask for, indicate that you will secure whatever permissions are necessary. State that you will keep the information confidential, if that is appropriate.
7. Thank the reader for helping.

Figure 6.2 gives an example of a letter that follows these guidelines.

FIGURE 6.2   A special request letter.

---

234 Springdale Street
Rochester, NY 14618-0422
<u></u>
phone: 716-555-4329
jkawatsu@golf.edu

February 5, 2002

Ms. Victoria Lohrbach-Vitelli
Research Director
Creative Marketing Association
198 Madison Avenue
New York, NY 10016-0092

Dear Ms. Lohrbach-Vitelli:

I am a sophomore at Monroe College in Rochester, and I am preparing a term paper on the topic "Current Internet Marketing Strategies." As part of my research, I am writing an overview of marketing practices for the past eight years. Two of your publications would be of great help to me. Would you please send me the following pamphlets:

1. <u>A History of Internet Marketing</u> (CMA 15)
2. <u>Creative Marketing on the Internet</u> (CMA 27)

I would appreciate receiving these materials by March 10 and will be pleased to send you a copy of my paper in late May. Creative Marketing Association, will, of course, be fully cited in my bibliography.

Thank you for your assistance. I look forward to hearing from you. Should you have any questions or need to speak to me about my request, you can reach me at jkawatsu@golf.edu or at (716) 555-4329.

Sincerely yours,

Julie Kawatsu

Julie Kawatsu

TECH NOTE

Finding a Target Audience

Companies can obtain mass mailing lists of target customers in a variety of ways. Many businesses use a grand opening or special sales event as an opportunity to have potential customers sign up for a free gift: the sign-up list then becomes a marketing list of motivated customers' names, addresses, and phone numbers. Firms use their Web sites not only to advertise but also to solicit information about a target audience—asking Net surfers to answer a brief questionnaire, fill out a form, or sign up for a tour or gift. Once the potential customer clicks on "send," the company has information to include in a directory. Internet directories are also available from which your company can establish a client base.

Direct mail and marketing companies will also, for a fee, supply you and your company with specific demographic data about a presorted target audience, including age, income, occupation, and recent types of purchases. Some of these specialized firms will even supply you with a database of such information on CD-ROM. Always find out where such lists have been generated so you don't duplicate your company's other efforts or send sales messages to individuals who are definitely not part of your target audience.

Sales Letters: Some Preliminary Guidelines

A sales letter is written to persuade the reader to buy a product, try a service, support some cause, or participate in some activity. A sales letter can also serve as a method of introducing yourself to potential customers. No matter what profession you have chosen, knowing how to write a sales letter is an invaluable skill. There will always be times when you have to sell a product, a service, an idea, a point of view, or yourself!

You have undoubtedly received numerous sales letters from military recruiters, large companies, local merchants, charitable organizations, and campus groups. Web sites on the Internet (discussed in Chapter 8) constitute a special type of sales announcement.

Because of the great volume of sales letters in the business world, the ones you write face a lot of competition. To write an effective sales letter that stands out and does its job, you have to do the following:

1. Identify and limit your audience. Determine how many people are in your audience. Sometimes a sales letter is written to just one person (Figure 6.3) or to

FIGURE 6.3   A sales letter soliciting a financial contribution.

**Elmwood Volunteer
Fire Department**
Elmwood, Idaho 87549

To report a fire   **911**
To volunteer   **555-7878**

January 31, 2002

Mr. Alex B. Sutton
1453 North Prentiss Drive
Elmwood, ID 87549

Dear Mr. Sutton:

Do you want to know how to better protect your home from life-threatening fire? Support Elmwood Volunteer Fire Department. The safety and security of our homes depend on the proven ability of your Volunteer Fire Department.

Thanks to your support in the past, the Elmwood VFD purchased a new Powers V-10 pumping engine last year that offers state-of-the-art capabilities in firefighting. Most large city fire departments own this engine to protect their citizens. All of our volunteers have been trained to operate the Powers and have proven themselves many times in the past year. These volunteers work to guard you, and their invaluable service costs you, the taxpayer, nothing.

In 2001 alone the Elmwood volunteer firefighters logged over 1,300 hours in responding to 47 emergency calls, three of them within a few blocks of your home on Prentiss Drive. Insurance adjusters have estimated that without the Elmwood VFD more than 100 lives and more than $20 million in property might have been lost. One of your neighbors, Ms. Sarah Capsky, told the *Elmwood News*: "Our volunteer fire department saved my house, my three kids, and our two dogs. They deserve everyone's respect and gratitude."

To continue to protect you and your home, the Elmwood VFD needs your support. We cannot make it on our tax allocation from the county alone. In fact, tax dollars covered only the down payment for the Powers V-10. The balance of $145,000—nearly $110,000—must come from all of us in Elmwood.

Won't you take a minute to fill out the enclosed, postage-paid pledge card and return it with your donation by February 28? You can authorize a deduction from your checking account or use your credit card. At the end of our pledge drive, I will send you a full financial report. Please help us protect Ms. Capsky's neighbors as if your life depended on it.

Respectfully,

Alice Sano

Alice Sano
Captain, Elmwood VFD

FIGURE 6.4   A sales letter sent to a business reader.

Workwell Software
3700 Stewart Avenue   Chicago IL 60637-2210
Phone: (312) 555-3720   **Fax:** (312) 555-7601   **E-mail:** sales@workwell.com
http://www.workwell.com

October 1, 2001

Dear Office Manager:

Gets reader's attention with a question Do you know how much money your company loses from one of the great dangers in the workplace—repetitive strain injury? Each year employers spend millions of dollars on employee insurance claims and the resulting decreased productivity because of back pains, fatigue, eye strain, and carpal tunnel syndrome.

Emphasizes to the product's appeal **Workwell** can solve your problems with its easy-to-use Exercise Program Software. This program will automatically monitor the time employees spend at their computers and also measure keyboard activity. After each hour (or the specified number of keystrokes), **Workwell** Software will take your employees through a series of exercises that will help prevent carpal tunnel syndrome and strains and give you the assurance that you have taken necessary precautions to reduce a workplace hazard.

Shows specific application of the product **Workwell's Exercise Program Software** will not interfere with busy schedules. Developed by a leading orthopedic surgeon, Dr. Anna Chang, each of the 27 exercises is demonstrated on screen with audio instructions. The entire program takes less than 3 minutes and can be performed at the employee's workstation. The software is available for Windows 98 and above.

You can protect your employees for a fraction of the money you will spend on claims. For $1499.00, you can provide a networked version of this valuable software to all of your employees. And if you place your order within the next week, **Workwell** will supply you with free upgrades for a year.

Ends with a call for action To make sure your employees are at the peak of their efficiency in a safe work environment, please call us at 1-800-555-WELL or contact us at http://www.workwell.com to order your **Workwell Software** today.

Thank you,

Cory Soufas

Cory Soufas
Manager, Sales

hundreds of readers (Figure 6.4). However, Cory Soufas's sales letter in Figure 6.4 could also be addressed personally to individual readers if Workwell Software purchased a targeted audience mailing list.

2. Use reader psychology. Think like your reader and ask yourself: "What are we trying to do for our customer?" Ask that question before you begin writing and you will be using effective reader psychology. The "you attitude" is essential to your sales letter (see Chapter 5). Appeal to your readers' emotions, health, security, comfort, or pocketbooks by focusing on the right issues (for instance, make a point of informing buyers that your product research involves no animal testing).

3. Don't boast or be a bore. Save elaborate explanations about a product for after the sale. Put detailed documentation in instruction booklets and warranties. Further, do not turn your sales letter into a glowing commendation of your company, or yourself.

4. Use words that appeal to the readers' senses. Use concrete, specific words instead of abstract, vague ones. As you draft and revise, find verbs that are colorful, that put the reader in the picture, so to speak. You will have a greater chance of selling readers if they can hear, see, taste, or touch your product in their mind. That way they can visualize themselves buying or using your product or service.

5. Be ethical. Avoid untruths, insincere flattery, exaggerations, false comparisons, and unsupported generalizations. Honesty is the best way to make a sale. If you do your homework about your product or your service, you will be able to give readers the honest, essential evidence they deserve and demand. (You might want to review pp. 24–30 in Chapter 1.)

The Four A's of Sales Letters

Successful sales letters follow a time-honored and workable plan; each sales letter follows what can be called the "four A's":

1. It gets the reader's *attention.*
2. It highlights the product's *appeal.*
3. It shows the customer the product's *application.*
4. It ends with a specific request for *action.*

Those four goals can be achieved in fewer than four or five paragraphs. Look again at Figure 6.4, a one-page letter in which those four parts are labeled. Holding a sales letter down to one page or less will keep the reader's attention. Television commercials and magazine ads provide useful models of the fourfold approach to a customer. The next time you see one of these variations of the sales letter, try to identify the four A's.

Getting the Reader's Attention

Your opening sentence is crucial. That first sentence is bait on a hook. If you lose readers there, you will have lost them forever. A typical television commercial has thirty to sixty seconds to sell viewers; your first sentence has about two to five seconds to catch the readers' attention and prompt them to read on. Keep your opening short, one or two sentences at most. It must show readers how their problems could be solved, their profits increased, or their pleasures enriched. The readers' attitude will be, "What's in this for me?" Tell them right away that you *can* increase their profits or happiness or decrease their problems or troubles.

The following six techniques are a few of the many interest-grabbing ways to begin a sales letter. Adapt these techniques to your product or service.

1. Ask a question. Mention something that readers are vitally concerned about that is also relevant to your product or service. Look, for example, at the opening questions in Figures 6.3 and 6.4. Avoid such general questions as "Are you happy?" or "Would you like to make money?" Use more specific questions with concrete language. An ad for Air Force Reserve Nursing asks nurses, "Are you looking for something 30,000 feet out of the ordinary?" Similarly, a sales letter beginning with "Could you use $100?" zeroes in on one particular desire of the reader. Ask a question that your reader(s) will want to see answered.

2. Use a "how to" statement. This is one of the most frequently used openers in a sales letter. Here are some effective how-to statements: "We can show you how to increase your plant growth up to 91%." "Here is how to save $500 on your next vacation." "This is how to provide nourishing lunches for less than eighty cents a person." Note that the opening sentence of Cory Soufas's sales letter in Figure 6.4 combines both a "how-to" and a question approach.

3. Compliment your reader. Appeal to the reader's ego. But remember that readers are not naive; they will be suspicious of false praise.

4. Offer a gift. Often you can lure readers further into your letter by telling them they can save money or get a second product free or at half price. One realtor tempts customers to see lots for sale with, "Enclosed is a coupon worth $25 in gas after you tour Deer Run Trails Estates."

5. Introduce a comparison. Compare your product or service with conventional or standard products or procedures. For instance, a clothing firm told police officers that if they purchased a particular jacket, they were really getting three coats in one, because the product had a lining for winter and a covering used for greater visibility at night.

6. Announce a change. Link your sales offer to a current event that will directly affect your prospective customer. When the sales tax on cars was about to be increased, an automobile dealer sent sales letters to potential buyers, alerting them to the implications of delaying their purchase: "The sales tax on new cars will jump a WHOPPING 4 percent effective next month. You may not think that 4 percent will mean that much money, but on a new 2001 model that increase could cost you an extra $1200." The sales letter continued: "Couldn't you use that money for something else, say, those extras you've always wanted, like a CD player or an extended warranty?"

Highlighting the Product's Appeal

Once you have aroused your reader's attention, introduce your product or service. Make it so attractive, so necessary, and so profitable that the reader will want to buy or use the product or service. Don't lose the momentum you have gained with your introduction by boring the reader with petty details, flat descriptions, elaborate inventories, or trivial boasts. Appeal to the reader's intellect or emotions (or both) while introducing the product. In Figure 6.4 Workwell Software's mass mailing letter to office managers appeals to their desire for greater employer productivity and improved safety. In Figure 6.3 the captain of a volunteer fire department urges citizens to help pay for a piece of fire equipment that might save their lives and property. Here is an emotional appeal by the Gulf Stream Fruit Company:

> Can you, when you bite into an orange, tell where it was grown? If it tastes better than any you have ever eaten . . . full of rich, golden flavor, brimming with juice, sparkling with sunshine . . . then you know it was grown here in our famous Indian River Valley where we have handpicked it, at the very peak of its flavor, just for your order.[1]

From a leading question, the sales letter moves to a vivid description of the product, the name of the supplier, and the reader's ability to recognize how special both the product and the customer are to the Gulf Stream Fruit Company.

Showing the Customer the Product's Application

In the third part of your sales letter supply evidence of the value of what you are selling. You have to be careful, though, that you do not overwhelm readers with facts, statistics, detailed mechanical descriptions, or elaborate arguments. The emphasis is still on the reader's use of the product and not on the company that manufactures or sells it. Shifting the focus from your company to the prospective customer is essential to any sale.

1. Supply the right evidence. What evidence best convinces readers about a product's or service's appeal?

- **Descriptions** that emphasize state-of-the-art design and construction, efficiency, convenience, usefulness, and economy.
- **Special features** or changes that make your product or service more attractive. A greenhouse manufacturer stressed that in addition to using its structure just for growing plants, customers would also find it a "perfect sun room enclosure for year-round 'outdoor' activities, gardening, or leisure health spa."
- **Testimonials,** or endorsements, from previous customers as well as from specialists. Rather than saying hundreds of people are satisfied with your product, get two or three of those happy customers to allow you to quote them in your letter. In Figure 6.3 Captain Sano persuasively uses Ms. Capsky's endorsement, and Cory Soufas in Figure 6.4 cites "a leading orthopedic surgeon" by name.

---

[1]"Gifts from Gulf Stream," Gulf Stream Fruit Company, Ft. Lauderdale, Fla. Reprinted by permission.

- **Guarantees, warranties, services, or special considerations** that will make your customer's life easier or happier—loaner cars, free home deliveries, ten-day trial period, a year's free Internet access.

2. Do I mention costs? You may be obligated to mention costs in your letter. But postpone them until the reader has been shown how appealing and valuable your product is. Readers will react more favorably to costs after they have seen the reasons why the product or service is useful. Of course, if price is a key selling point, mention it early in the letter.

As a general rule, do not bluntly state the cost. Relate prices, charges, or fees to the benefits provided by the services or products to which they apply. Customers then see how much they are getting for their money. A dealer who installs steel shutters did not tell readers the exact price of the product but indicated that they will save money by buying it: "Virtually maintenance free, your Reel Shutters also offer substantial savings in energy costs by reducing your loss through radiation by as much as 65% . . . and that lowers your utility bills by 35%."

Ending with a Specific Request for Action

The last section of your letter is vital. If the reader ignores your request for action, your letter has been written in vain. Tell readers exactly what you want them to do by when. Make it easy for them to

- send for a brochure
- come into your store
- take a test drive
- participate in a meeting
- fill out a pledge card (as in Figure 6.3)
- respond via the Internet (as in Figure 6.4)
- sign an order blank
- fill out an enclosed stamped envelope

As with price, link the benefits the customers will receive to their responses. "Respond and be rewarded" is the basic message of the last section of your letter. Note that in Figure 6.4 the call to action is made in the last two paragraphs, and urges the reader to act immediately in order to take advantage of the free upgrades and maintenance.

Customer Relations Letters

Much business correspondence deals explicitly with establishing and maintaining friendly working relations. Such correspondence, known as **customer relations letters,** sends readers good news or bad news, acceptances or refusals. Good news tells customers that

- you have the product or service they want at a reasonable price
- you agree with them about a problem they brought to your attention
- you are solving their problem exactly the way they want

- you are approving their loan
- you are grateful to them for their business

Thank-you letters, congratulations letters, and adjustment letters saying "Yes" are examples of good news messages.

Bad news messages inform readers that

- you do not like their work or the equipment they sold you
- you do not have the equipment or service they want or you cannot provide it at the price they want to pay
- you are rejecting a proposal they offered
- you are denying someone further use of a facility
- you cannot refund their purchase price or perform a service again as they requested
- you are raising their rent or not renewing their lease
- you want them to pay what they owe you now

Bad news messages often come to readers through complaint letters, adjustment letters that say "No," and collection letters.

Diplomacy and Reader Psychology

Writing effective customer relations letters requires skill in human relations and reader psychology. Regardless of the news—good or bad—you need to be a diplomatic and persuasive writer. Customer relations letters show how you and your company regard the people with whom you do business. The letters should reveal your sensitivity to their needs. The first lesson to learn is that you cannot look at your letter only from your (the writer's) perspective. You have to see the letter from the reader's perspective and anticipate the reader's needs and reactions. What would be your view of the writer and the writer's company?

The Customers Always Write

As you read this section on customer relation letters, keep in mind the two basic principles captured in the words "the customers always write."

1. Customers will write about how they would like to be or have been treated—to thank, to complain, to request an explanation.
2. Customers have certain rights that you must respect in your correspondence with them. They deserve a prompt and courteous reply, whether or not they are correct. If you refuse their request, they deserve to know why; if they owe you money, you should give them an opportunity to explain and a chance, up to a point, to set up a payment schedule.

Planning Your Customer Relations Letters

Whether you are sending good news or bad, determine what to say and how to say it. Do some preliminary planning. Outline for a few minutes to find your ideas. Your outline does not have to be formal or even neatly written—a few scribbles sometimes will be enough to get you started. By outlining, you will save (not lose) time, because you can identify your main points, exclude unnecessary or unimportant ones, and avoid the risk of forgetting something essential.

Fortified by your outline, you will feel more confident as you draft your letter. In the process of drafting and revising that letter, consider whether your reader will bristle at or accept the words you use. Your choice of words will determine the success or failure of your letter. You might want to review the discussions on tone and the "you attitude" (pp. 162–167).

Being Direct or Indirect

Your message, tone, and knowledge of your reader are essential ingredients in a successful customer relations letter. But success also involves knowing where and how to start, and, especially, where to present your main point. Not every customer relations letter starts by giving the reader the writer's main point, judgment, conclusion, or reaction. *Where you place your main idea is determined by the type of letter you are writing.* Good news messages require one tactic; bad news, another.

Good News Message

If you are writing a good news letter, use the direct approach. Start your letter with the welcome, pleasant news that the reader wants to hear. Don't postpone the opportunity to put your reader in the right frame of mind. Then provide any relevant supporting details, explanations, or commentary. Being direct is advantageous when you have good news to convey.

Bad News Message

If you have bad news to report, do *not* open your letter with it. Be indirect. Prepare your reader for the bad news; keep the tension level down. If you throw the bad news at your reader right away, you jeopardize the goodwill you want to create and sustain. Consider how you would react to a letter that begins, "We regret to inform you that . . . ," "Your order cannot be filled," or "Your application for a loan has been denied." Having been denied, disappointed, or even offended in the first sentence or paragraph, the reader is not likely to give you his or her attentive cooperation thereafter.

Notice how A. J. Griffin's bad news letter in Figure 6.5 (p. 204) curtly starts off with the bad news of a rent increase. Receiving such a letter, the owner of Flowers by Dan certainly could not be blamed for looking for a new place of business. Or if he did pay the increase, Griffin's letter would hardly ensure that Mr. Sobol would remain a happy tenant. Griffin was too direct when he should have been diplomatically indirect. He did not consider his reader's reaction; all he was concerned about was delivering his message.

Compare the curt version of Griffin's letter in Figure 6.5 with his revised message in Figure 6.6 (p. 205). In the revised version, Griffin begins tactfully with pleasant, positive words designed to put his reader in a good frame of mind about the management of River Road Mall. Then Griffin gives some background information that the owner of Flowers by Dan can relate to. A businessperson himself, Mr. Sobol doubtless has experienced some recent increases in his own costs. Griffin makes one

FIGURE 6.5   An ineffective bad news letter.

**River Road
Mall**

December 1, 2000

Mr. Daniel Sobol
Flowers by Dan
Lower Level
River Road Mall

Dear Mr. Sobol:

This is to inform you of a rent increase. Starting next month your new rent will be $2500.00, resulting in a 15 percent increase.

Please make sure your January rent check includes this increase.

Sincerely yours,

A. J. Griffin
Manager

300 First Street
Canton, Ohio 44701
(216) 555-6700
ajg@rrdmall.com

FIGURE 6.6   A diplomatic revision of the bad news letter in Figure 6.5.

**River Road
Mall**

December 1, 2000

Mr. Daniel Sobol
Flowers by Dan
Lower Level
River Road Mall

Dear Mr. Sobol:

It has been a pleasure to have you as a tenant at the Mall
for the past two years, and we look forward to serving
you in the future.

Over the last two years we have experienced a dramatic
increase in costs at River Road Mall for security,
maintenance, landscaping, pest control, utilities,
insurance, and taxes. Last year we absorbed those
increases and so did not have to raise your rent.
Unfortunately, we find we cannot do it again for 2001,
and so regretfully we must increase your rent by 15
percent, to $2,500, effective January 1, 2001.

Although we do not like to raise rents, we also know
that you do not want us to compromise on the quality of
service that you and your customers expect and deserve
from River Road Mall.

Please let us know how we can assist you in the future.
We wish you a very successful and profitable 2001. If
you have any questions, please call or visit my office.

Cordially,

A. J. Griffin

A. J. Griffin
Manager

300 First Street
Canton, Ohio 44701
(216) 555-6700
ajg@rrdmall.com

more attempt to encourage Sobol to recall his good feelings about the Mall—last year they did not raise rents—before introducing the bad news of a rent increase.

Even after giving the bad news, Griffin softens the blow by saying that the Mall knows it is bad news. Griffin's tactic here is to defuse some of the anger that Sobol will inevitably feel. Griffin then ends on a positive, upbeat note: a prosperous future for Flowers by Dan.

Follow-Up Letters

A follow-up letter is sent by a company after a sale to thank the customer for buying a product or using a service and to encourage the customer to buy more products and services in the future. A follow-up letter is a combination thank-you note and sales letter. The letter in Figure 6.7 is sent to customers soon after they have purchased an appliance and offers them the option of a continued maintenance policy. The letter in Figure 6.8 shows how an income tax preparation service attempts to obtain repeat business. Both letters

1. begin with a brief and sincere expression of gratitude
2. discuss the benefits (advantages) already known to the customer and then transfer the company's dedication to the customer from the product or service to a new or continuing sales area
3. end with a specific request for future business

Occasionally, a follow-up letter is sent to a good customer who, for some reason, has stopped doing business with the company. Such a follow-up letter should try to find out why the customer has stopped doing business and to persuade that customer to resume business dealings. Study the letter in Figure 6.9, in which Jim Margolis first politely inquires whether Mr. Janeck has experienced a problem and then urges him to come back to the store.

Complaint Letters

Each of us, either as consumers or businesspeople, at some time has been frustrated by a defective product, inadequate service, or incorrect billing. Usually our first response is to write a letter dripping with juicy insults. But a hate letter, like the flaming e-mail in Figure 4.10, rarely gets results and can in fact hurt the writer and create an unfavorable image of his or her company. A complaint letter is a delicate one to write.

Establishing the Right Tone

A complaint letter is written for more reasons than just blowing off steam. You want some specific action taken. By adopting the right tone, you increase your chances of getting what you want. Do not call the reader names, hurl insults, or refuse to do business with the company again. Register your complaint courteously and tolerantly. Companies want to be fair to you to keep you as a satisfied customer and to correct defective products so other customers will not be inconvenienced. The "you attitude" is especially important here to maintain the reader's goodwill.

FIGURE 6.7   A follow-up letter to sell a maintenance agreement.

Dynamic Appliance Company

100 Walden Parkway
Denver, Colorado 80203-4296
(303) 555-9681
http://www.dac.com

August 9, 2001

Mr. John H. Abbott
3715 Mayview Drive
Cottage Grove, MN 53261-1852

Dear Mr. Abbott:

We are delighted that you have purchased a Dynamic appliance. To help ensure your satisfaction, this appliance is backed by a Dynamic warranty. At the same time, we realize that you bought the appliance to serve you not just for the period covered by the warranty but for many years to come. That's why purchasing a Dynamic Maintenance Agreement now is one of the wisest investments you can make.

A Dynamic Maintenance Agreement provides savings benefits many cost-conscious customers want and look for today. It helps extend the life of your appliance through an annual, on-request maintenance check-up. And if you need service, it gives you as many service calls as necessary for repairs due to normal use—at no extra charge.

All this coverage is now available at a special introductory price of $55 a year. This price includes the warranty coverage you have remaining.

Please act now by visiting our Web site to sign up for your Dynamic Maintenance Agreement.

Sincerely,

Carole Morrow

Carole Morrow
Sales Representative

FIGURE 6.8   A follow-up letter to encourage repeat business.

Taylor Tax Service
Highway 10
North Jennings, TX 78326
phone (888) 555-9681 e-mail taylor@aol.com
http://www.taylor.com

December 3, 2001

Ms. Laurie Pavlovich
345 Jefferson St.
Jennings, TX 78326

Dear Ms. Pavlovich:

Thank you for using our services in February of this year. We were pleased to help you prepare your 2000 federal and state income tax returns. Our goal is to save you every tax dollar to which you are entitled. If you ever have questions about your return, we are open all year long to help you.

We are looking forward to serving you again next year. Several new federal tax laws, which go into effect January 1, will change the types of deductions you can declare. These changes might appreciably increase your refund. Our consultants know the new laws and are ready to apply them to your return.

Another important tax matter influencing your 2001 returns will be any losses you may have suffered because of the hailstorms and tornadoes that hit our area three months ago. Our consultants are specially trained to assist you in filing proper damage claims with your federal and state returns.

To make using our services even easier, we can help you file your tax return electronically, to speed up any refund you are entitled to. Please call us at (888) 555-9681 or e-mail us at taylor@aol.com as soon as you have received all your forms in order to set up an appointment. We are waiting to serve you seven days a week from 9:00 a.m. to 9:00 p.m.

Sincerely yours,

TAYLOR TAX SERVICE

J. P. Sanchez

J. P. Sanchez
Manager

FIGURE 6.9   A follow-up letter to maintain customer goodwill.

BROADWAY CLEANERS

April 6, 2001

Mr. Edward Janeck
34 Brompton Lane, Apt. 13
Baltimore, MD 21227-0102

Dear Mr. Janeck:

Thank you for allowing us to take care of your cleaning needs for more than three years now. It has been our pleasure to see you in the store each week and to clean your shirts, slacks, and coats to your satisfaction. Since you have not come in during the last month, we are concerned that in some way we may have disappointed you. We hope not, because you are a valuable customer whose goodwill we do not want to lose.

If there is something wrong, please tell us about it. We welcome any suggestions on how we can serve you better. Our goal is to have a spotless reputation in the eyes of our customers.

The next time you need your garments cleaned, won't you please bring them to us, along with the enclosed coupon worth $10 on your next bill? We look forward to seeing you again—soon.

Cordially,

Jim Margolis

Jim Margolis, Manager

Encl. coupon

**Broadway at Davis Drive   Baltimore, Maryland 21228-6210
(443) 555-1962 broadclean@aol.com**

An effective complaint letter can be written by an individual consumer or by a company. Figure 6.10 shows Michael Trigg's complaint about a defective fishing reel; Figure 6.11 expresses a restaurant's dissatisfaction with an industrial dishwasher.

TECH NOTE

Help in Registering Complaints

Several organizations can assist you when you have a problem with a particular company or agency. These organizations will give you valuable advice on how to proceed with your complaint.

- The Better Business Bureau: *http://www.bbb.org/complaints/file.html*
- U.S. Chamber of Commerce: *http://www.uschamber.org*
- International Chamber of Commerce—World Business Organization: *http://www.iccwbo.org*

Writing an Effective Complaint Letter

To increase your chances of receiving a speedy settlement, follow these five steps in writing your letter of complaint.

1. Begin with a detailed description of the product or service. Give the appropriate model and serial numbers, size, quantity, and color. Specify check and invoice numbers. Indicate when and where (specific address) you purchased it and also the remaining warranty. If you are returning the product to the company, note how you are sending it—U.S. mail, UPS, through a sales representative, or the like. If you are complaining about a service, give the name of the company, the date of the service, the personnel providing it, and their exact duties.

2. State exactly what is wrong with the product or service. Precise information will enable the reader to understand and act on your complaint.

- How many times did the machine work before it stopped?
- What parts were malfunctioning?
- What parts of a job were not done or were done poorly?
- When did all this happen?

Stating that "the brake shoes were defective" tells very little about how long they were on your car, how effectively they may have been installed, or what condition they were in when they ceased functioning safely. Reach some conclusion, even if you qualify your remarks with words like "apparently," "possibly," or "seemingly" when you describe the difficulty.

FIGURE 6.10   A complaint letter from a consumer.

17 Westwood Drive

Magnolia, MA 02171

mtrigg@roof.com

September 15, 2001

Mr. Ralph Montoya
Customer Relations Department
Smith Sports Equipment
P.O. Box 1014
Tulsa, OK 74109-1014

Dear Mr. Montoya:

On August 31, 2001, I purchased a Smith reel, model 191, at the Uni-Mart Store on Marsh Avenue in Magnolia. The reel sold for $54.95 plus tax. The reel is not working effectively, and I am returning it to you under separate cover by first-class mail.

I had made no more than five casts with the reel when it began to malfunction. The button that releases the spool and allows the line to cast will not spring back into position after casting. In addition, the gears make a grinding noise when I try to retrieve the line. Because of these problems, I was unable to continue my participation in the Gloucester Fishing Tournament last week.

I am requesting that a new reel be sent to me free of charge in place of the defective one I returned. I would also like to know what was wrong with the defective reel.

I would appreciate your processing my claim within the next two weeks.

Sincerely yours,

Michael Trigg
Michael Trigg

FIGURE 6.11   A complaint letter faxed from a business.

The Loft Cameron and Dale, Sunnyside, California 91793-4116   213-555-7500

June 8, 2001

Priscilla Dubrow
Customer Relations Department
Superflex Products
San Diego, CA 93141-0808

Dear Ms. Dubrow:

On September 15, 2000, we purchased a Superflex industrial dishwasher, model 3203876, at the Hillcrest store at 3400 Broadway Drive in Sunnyside, for $5,000. In the last three weeks, our restaurant has had repeated problems with this machine. Three more months of warranty remain on the unit.

The machine does not complete a full cycle; it stops before the final rinsing and thus leaves the dishes dirty. It appears that the cycle regulators are not working properly because they refuse to shift into the next necessary gear. Attempts to repair the machine by the Hillcrest crew on June 3, 10, and 16 have been unsuccessful.

The Loft has been greatly inconvenienced. Our kitchen team has been forced to sort, clean, and sanitize utensils, dishes, pans and pots by hand, resulting in additional overtime. Moreover, our expenses for proper detergents have increased.

We want your main office to send another repair crew at once to fix this machine. If your crew is unable to do this, we want a discount worth the amount of the warranty life on this model to be applied to the purchase of a new Superflex dishwasher. This amount would come to $1,000, or 20 percent of the original purchase price.

So that our business is not further disrupted, we would appreciate your resolving this problem within the next week.

Sincerely yours,

Emily Rashon

Emily Rashon
Manager

▲ **Browse our menu, which changes daily, at www.theloft.com**

---

3. Briefly describe the inconvenience you have experienced. Show that your problems were directly caused by the defective product or service. To build your case, give precise details about the time and money you lost. Don't just say you had "numerous difficulties." If you purchased a calculator and it broke down during a mathematics examination, say so (but do not blame the calculator company if you failed the course). Did you have to pay a mechanic to fix your car when it was stalled on the road? Did you have to take time away from your other responsibilities to clean up a mess made by a leaky new washing machine? Did you have to buy a new printer or recording machine?

4. Indicate precisely what you want done. Do not simply write that you "want something done," that "adequate measures must be taken," or that "the situation should be corrected." State that you want

- your purchase price refunded
- your model repaired or replaced
- a completely new repair crew provided
- an apology from the company for discourteous treatment

If you are asking for damages, state your request in dollars and cents and include copies of bills documenting your expenses related to the problem. Perhaps you had to rent a car, were forced to pay a janitorial service to clean up, or had to rent equipment at a higher rate because the company did not make its deliveries as promised.

5. Ask for prompt handling of your claim. Ask that an answer be provided to any question you may have (such as finding out where calls came from that you were billed for but did not make). And ask that your claim be handled as quickly as possible. You might even specify a reasonable time by which you want to hear from the writer or need the problem fixed. Note the last paragraph in Figure 6.11.

Adjustment Letters

Adjustment letters respond to complaint letters by telling customers dissatisfied with a product or service how their claim will be settled. Adjustment letters should reconcile the differences that exist between a customer and a firm and restore the customer's confidence in that firm.

The Importance of Complaint Letters to a Business

Rather than ignoring or quarreling with complaint letters, most companies view answering them as good for business. By writing to complain about a product or service, the customer alerts your company to a problem that can be remedied to avoid similar complaints in the future. Customers who have taken the time to write obviously want and deserve a reply. If you do not answer the customer's letter politely, you may lose a lot of business—not just the customer's business, but also that of his or her friends, family, and associates, who will all have been told about your discourtesy.

How to (and Not to) Write an Adjustment Letter
An effective adjustment letter requires diplomacy. Be prompt, courteous, and decisive; do not brush the complaint aside in hopes that it will be forgotten. Investigate the complaint quickly and determine its validity by checking previous correspondence, warranty statements, guarantees, and your firm's policies on merchandise and service. In some cases you may even have to send returned damaged merchandise to your company's laboratory to determine who is at fault.

A noncommittal letter signals to the customer that you have failed to investigate the claim or are stalling for time. Do not resort to vague statements like the following:

- We will do what we can to solve your problems as soon as possible.
- A company policy prohibits our returning your purchase price in full.
- Your request, while legitimate, will take time to process.
- We will act on your request with your best interest in mind.
- While we cannot now determine the extent of an adjustment, we will be back in touch with you.

Customers want to be told that they are right; if they cannot get what they request, they will demand to know why, in the most explicit terms. When you comply with a request, a begrudging tone will destroy the goodwill that your refund or replacement would have created. At the other extreme, do not overdo an apology by agreeing that the company is "completely at fault," that "such shoddy merchandise is inexcusable." An expression of regret need not jeopardize all future business. If you make your company look too bad, you risk losing the customer permanently.

Adjustment Letters That Tell the Customer "Yes"
If investigation reveals the customer's complaint to be valid, write a letter saying, in effect, "Yes, you are right; we will give you what you asked for." It is easy to write if you remember a few useful suggestions. As with a good news message, start with the favorable news the customer wants to hear; that will put him or her in a positive frame of mind to read the rest of your letter. Let the customer know that you sincerely agree with him or her—don't sound as if you are reluctantly honoring the request. For example, if your airline lost or misplaced luggage, apologize before you offer a settlement.

The two examples of adjustment letters saying "Yes" show you how to write this kind of correspondence. The first example, Figure 6.12, says "Yes" to Michael Trigg's letter in Figure 6.10. You might want to reread the Trigg complaint letter to see what problems Ralph Montoya faced when he had to write to Mr. Trigg. The second example of an adjustment letter that says "Yes" is in Figure 6.13. It responds to a customer who has complained about an incorrect billing.

Writing a "Yes" Letter
The following four steps will help you write a "Yes" adjustment letter.

1. Admit immediately that the customer's complaint is justified and apologize.
Briefly state that you are sorry and thank the customer for writing to inform you.

FIGURE 6.12   An adjustment letter saying "Yes."

Smith Sports Equipment
P.O. Box 1014   Tulsa, Oklahoma 74109-1014
(918) 555-0164 ▪ www.smithsport.com

September 21, 2001

Mr. Michael Trigg
17 Westwood Drive
Magnolia, MA 02171

Dear Mr. Trigg:

Thank you for alerting us in your letter of September 15 to the problems you had with one of our model 191 spincast reels. I am sorry for the inconvenience the reel caused you. A new Smith reel is on its way to you.

We have examined your reel and found the problem. It seems that a retaining pin on the button spring was improperly installed by one of our new soldering machines on the assembly line. We have thoroughly inspected, repaired, and cleaned the soldering machine to eliminate the problem.

Since we began making quality reels in 1955, we have taken pride in helping our customers who use a Smith reel. We hope that your new Smith reel brings you years of pleasure and many good catches, especially next year at the Gloucester Fishing Tournament.

Thank you for your business. Please let me know if I can assist you again.

Respectfully,

SMITH SPORTS EQUIPMENT

Ralph Montoya

Ralph Montoya, Manager
Customer Relations Department

FIGURE 6.13   An adjustment letter saying "Yes."

Brunelli Motors

Route 3A, Giddings, Kansas 62034-8100 (913) 555-1521

October 5, 2000

Ms. Kathryn Brumfield
34 East Main
Giddings, KS 62034-1123

Dear Ms. Brumfield:

We appreciate your notifying us, in your letter of September 30, about the problem you experienced regarding warranty coverage on your new Phantom Hawk GT. The bills sent to you were incorrect, and I have cancelled them. Please accept my apologies. You should not have been charged for a shroud or for repairs to the damaged fan and hose, since all those parts, and labor on them, are covered by warranty.

The problem was the result of an error in the way the charges were listed. Our firm has begun using new software to give customers better service, and the mechanic apparently entered the wrong code for your account. I have instructed our mechanics to double-check code numbers before submitting them to the Billing Department. We hope that this policy will help us serve you and our other customers more efficiently.

We value you as a customer of Brunelli Motors. When you are ready for another Phantom, I hope that you will once again visit our dealership.

Sincerely yours,

Susan Chee-Saafir

Susan Chee-Saafir
Service Manager

Experience virtual reality: Drive a new Phantom
at **http://www.brunelli.com**

2. State precisely what you are going to do to correct the problem. Let the customer know that you will

- cancel a bill
- repair a damaged camera
- repaint a room
- enclose a free pass
- provide a complimentary dinner
- give the customer credit toward another purchase
- upgrade software

Do not postpone the good news the customer wants to hear. The rest of your letter will be much more appreciated and convincing if the customer is told the good news right away. In Figure 6.12 Michael Trigg is told that he will receive a new reel; in Figure 6.13 Kathryn Brumfield learns she will not be charged for parts or service.

3. Tell customers exactly what happened. They deserve an explanation for the inconvenience they suffered. Note that the explanations in Figures 6.12 and 6.13 give only the essential details; they do not bother the reader with side issues or petty remarks about who was to blame. Assure customers that the mishap is not typical of your company's operations. While your comments should not shift the blame, your letter should center on the unusual reason or circumstance for the difficulty. Avoid promising, however, that the problem will never recur. Not only is such a guarantee unnecessary, but keeping it may be beyond your control.

4. End on a friendly—and positive—note. Do not remind customers of the trouble they have gone through. Leave them with a good feeling about your company. Say that you are looking forward to seeing them again, that you will gladly work with them on any future orders, or that you can always be reached for questions.

Adjustment Letters That Tell the Customer "No"
Writing to tell customers "No" is obviously more difficult than agreeing with them. You are faced with the sensitive task of conveying bad news, while at the same time convincing the reader that your position is fair, logical, and consistent.

What Not to Say
Do not accuse or argue. Avoid remarks that blame, scold, or remind customers of a wrongdoing. Remarks like these are likely to cost you business:

- You obviously did not read the instruction manual.
- Our records show that you purchased the set after the policy went into effect.
- The company policy plainly states that such refunds are not allowed.
- You were negligent in running the machine.
- You claim that our word processor was poorly constructed.
- You must be mistaken about the merchandise.

- As any intelligent person could tell, the switch had to be "off."
- Your complaint is unjustified.

How to Say "No" Diplomatically

The following five suggestions will help you say "No" diplomatically. Practical applications of these suggestions can be found in Figures 6.14 and 6.15. Contrast the refusal of Michael Trigg's complaint in Figure 6.14 with the favorable response to it in Figure 6.12.

1. Thank customers for writing. Make a friendly start by putting them in a good frame of mind. The letter writers in Figures 6.14 and 6.15 thank the customers for bringing the matter to their attention. As with other bad news letters, never begin with a refusal. You need time to calm and convince customers. Telling them "No" ("We regret to inform you") in the first sentence or two will negatively color their reactions to the rest of the letter. Also, never begin letters with "I was surprised to learn that you found our product defective (or our service inefficient)" or "We have been in business for years, and nothing like this has ever happened." Such openings put customers on the defensive. Use the indirect approach discussed on pages 203–206.

2. State the problem so the customer realizes that you understand the complaint. You thereby prove that you are not trying to misrepresent or distort what the customer has told you.

3. Explain what happened with the product or service before you give the customer a decision. Provide a factual explanation to show the customer that he or she is being treated fairly. Rather than focusing on the customer's misunderstanding the instructions or failure to observe details of a service contract, state the proper ways of handling a piece of equipment. For instance, instead of writing "By reading the instructions on the side of the paint can, you would have avoided the streaking condition that you claim resulted," tell the customer that "Hi-Gloss Paint requires two applications, four hours apart, for a clear and smooth finish." That way you remind the customer of the right way of applying the paint without pointing an accusing finger. Note how the explanations in Figures 6.14 and 6.15 emphasize the right way of using the product.

4. Give your decision without hedging. Do not say, "Perhaps some type of restitution could be made later" or "Further proof would have been helpful." Indecision will infuriate customers who believe that they have already presented a sound, convincing case. Never apologize for your decision. Avoid using the words *reject, claim,* or *grant. Reject* is harsh and impersonal. *Claim* implies your distrust of the customer's complaint. *Grant* signals that you have it in your power to respond favorably but decline to do so. Instead, use words that reconcile.

5. Leave the door open for better and continued business. Whenever possible, help customers solve their problem by offering to send them a new product or part and quote the full sales price. Note how the second-to-last paragraph in Figure 6.14 and the last paragraph in 6.15 do that diplomatically.

FIGURE 6.14   An adjustment letter saying "No."

Smith Sports Equipment
P.O. Box 1014   Tulsa, Oklahoma 74109-1014
(918) 555-0164 ▪ www.smithsport.com

September 21, 2001

Mr. Michael Trigg
17 Westwood Drive
Magnolia, MA 02171

Dear Mr. Trigg:

Thank you for writing to us on September 15 about the trouble you experienced with our model 191 spincast reel. We are sorry to hear about the difficulties you had with the release button and gears.

We have examined your reel and found the trouble. It seems that a retaining pin in the button spring was pushed into the side of the reel casing, thereby making the gears inoperable. The retaining pin is a vital yet delicate part of your reel. In order to function properly, it has to be pushed gently. Since the pin was not used in this way, we are not able to refund your purchase price.

We will be pleased, however, to repair your reel for $29.98 and return it to you for hours of fishing pleasure. Please let us know your decision.

I look forward to hearing from you.

Respectfully,

SMITH SPORTS EQUIPMENT

Ralph Montoya

Ralph Montoya, Manager
Customer Relations Department

FIGURE 6.15   Another adjustment letter saying "No."

4300 Marshall Drive
Salt Lake City, Utah 84113-1521
(801) 555-6028
www.healthair.com

August 19, 2002

Ms. Denise Southby, Director
Bradley General Hospital
Bradley, IL 60610-4615

Dear Ms. Southby:

Thank you for your letter of August 10 explaining the problems you have
encountered with our Puritan MAII ventilator. We were sorry to learn that you
were unable to get the high-volume PAO_2 alarm circuit to work.

Our ventilator is a high-volume, low-frequency machine that can deliver up to
40 ml of water pressure. The ventilator runs with a center of gravity attachment
on the right side of the diode. The trouble you had with the high oxygen alarm
system is due to an overload on your piped-in oxygen. Our laboratory inspection of the ventilator you returned indicated that the high-pressure system had
blown a vital adaptor in the machine. Our company cannot be responsible for
any overload caused by an oxygen system. We cannot, therefore, send you a
replacement ventilator free of charge. Your ventilator is being returned to you by
National Express.

We would, however, be pleased to send you another model of the adaptor,
which would be more compatible with your system, as soon as we receive your
order. The price of the adaptor is $600, and our factory representative will be
happy to install it for you at no charge. Please let me know your decision.

Sincerely yours,

R. P. Gifford

R. P. Gifford
Customer Service Department

Refusal-of-Credit Letters

A special set of bad news letters deals with a company refusing credit to an individual or another company. Writing such a letter requires a great deal of sensitivity. You want to be clear and firm about your decision; at the same time, you do not want to alienate the reader and risk losing his or her business in the future.

How to Say "No"

1. Begin on a positive—not a negative—note. Find something to thank the reader about; make the bad news easier to take. Compliment the reader's company or previous good credit achievements (if known); certainly express gratitude to the individual for wanting to do business with your company.

2. In a second paragraph provide a clear-cut explanation of why you must refuse the request for credit, but base your explanation on facts, not personal shortcomings or liabilities. Appropriate reasons to cite for a refusal of credit include

- a lack of business experience or prior credit
- the individual or company's being "overextended" and needing more time to pay off existing obligations
- current unfavorable or unstable financial conditions
- an order that is too large to process without some prepayment
- a lack of equipment or personnel for the company to do the business for which they are seeking credit

3. End on a positive note, too. Encourage the reader to reapply when business conditions have improved or when the reader's firm is in a better financial position. Make an attempt to keep the reader as a potential customer, eager to try you again. Figure 6.16 (p. 222) illustrates an effective letter that denies credit, following the organizational plan just discussed.

Writing About Credit to a Non-Native Speaker of English

Writing a letter denying credit to a non-native speaker of English requires double tact. As you saw in Chapter 5, you have to consider the cultural expectations of such an audience and use easily understood international English. Compare the inappropriate refusal letter in Figure 6.17 (p. 223) with the far more diplomatic and more acceptably worded letter in Figure 6.18 (p. 224). The letter in Figure 6.17 is rude, uses words a non-native speaker of English may not understand ("expedited," "herewith"), and does not encourage future business dealings with Consolidated Plastics.

The diplomatic letter in Figure 6.18 follows the guidelines for effective communication with non-native speakers and adheres to the suggestions for denying credit. In Figure 6.18 Emma Corson compliments her reader and his firm, expresses an interest in doing business with Mendson SA, and helps her reader to understand how Consolidated's credit policy might even help Mendson in the future.

FIGURE 6.16   An effective letter refusing credit.

WEST COAST CREDIT INC.

4800 Ridge Road
Los Angeles, CA 91666
Phone (714) 555-3500
FAX (714) 555-4323
www.wccredit.com

October 19, 2002

Mr. Otto L. King
Sunshine Interiors
8235 Mimosa Highway
Vinedale, CA 92004

Dear Mr. King:

Begins on a positive note

We appreciate your interest in wanting to do business with West Coast Credit. It is always gratifying to see a store like yours open in an expanding community like Vinedale.

Denies credit but explains why

In reviewing your credit application, we checked into the business history and credit references you supplied. We also called your local credit bureau. While we found nothing negative in your credit history, we did determine that for a business of your size you have already reached a maximum level of indebtedness. For that reason, we believe that this would not be the best time to extend your credit line.

Encourages reader to reapply

We would, however, encourage you to visit our Web site and fill out the credit survey. This site is periodically reviewed and can give you up-to-date information on credit availability. In the meantime, we wish you every success in your new business.

Cordially,

B. Rimes-Assante

B. Rimes-Assante
Manager

FIGURE 6.17   An inappropriate letter refusing credit to a non-native speaker of English.

CONSOLIDATED PLASTICS

May 25, 2001

Mr. Jan Buwalda
Mendson SA
Hoofdstraat 23
Dokkum, The Netherlands 1324 XK

Dear Mr. Buwalda:

I have received herewith your request and news about your company.
Thanks.

Regarding that request to open a credit account with us, it just cannot be
done. I don't know how things are expedited in your country, but in America
giving credit to a first-time foreign customer is just not standard business
practice. As you will understand, your credit rating could be unacceptable as
far as we are concerned. You will be expected to pay in cash for your first
transaction with us. We'll evaluate the situation thereafter.

Let me know how you anticipate proceeding.

Sincerely,

Emma Corson

Emma Corson
Accounts Executive

999 Industrial Blvd., Bambrake, NH 03243
Phone (603) 555-7000 ▪ FAX (603) 555-4321 ▪ conplastics@compuserv.com
www.conplastics.com

FIGURE 6.18   A diplomatic revision of Figure 6.17, a letter refusing credit to a non-native speaker of English.

CONSOLIDATED PLASTICS

May 25, 2001

Mr. Jan Buwalda
Mendson SA
Hoofdstraat 23
Dokkum, The Netherlands 1324 XK

Dear Mr. Buwalda:

Thank you very much for your letter inquiring about opening a credit account with our firm. It is always a pleasure to hear from potential customers in Holland. I was most interested to learn about Mendson's diverse activities.

We understand and share your company's wish to have an American supplier to work with you. Having Mendson as a customer would be beneficial for Consolidated Plastics, too. Working with you would allow us to enter a new market.

However, I am sorry that we cannot open any new account on credit. If you would kindly send us your check for the first month's supplies you need, we would rush your shipment to you. This will establish an account with us, and you can charge your second month's supplies on that account.

Please write or e-mail me if you have any questions. I look forward to serving you and Mendson in the future.

Cordially,

Emma Corson
Accounts Executive

999 Industrial Blvd., Bambrake, NH 03243
Phone (603) 555-7000 ▪ FAX (603) 555-4321 ▪ conplastics@compuserv.com
www.conplastics.com

✓ Revision Checklist

❑ Planned what I am going to say to my readers. Did necessary home-work and double-checking to answer any questions. Proved to my readers that I am knowledgeable about my topic.

❑ Used an appropriate (and consistent) format and page layout for my letters.

❑ Followed acceptable company protocol in format, organization, style, and tone of my letters.

❑ Adapted style and length of my message for my readers.

❑ Organized and, if necessary, highlighted information in my letters in the most effective way for my message and for my readers.

❑ Emphasized the "you attitude" with my readers, whether employer, customer/client, or co-worker.

❑ Conveyed impression of being courteous, professional, and easy to work with.

❑ Used clear and concise language appropriate for my reader.

❑ Began my correspondence with reader-effective strategies. If reporting good news, told the reader right away. If reporting bad news, was diplo-matically indirect and considerate of my reader's reactions.

❑ Followed the four A's of effective sales letters. Identified and convinced my target audience.

❑ Wrote complaint letters in a calm and courteous tone. Informed the reader what is wrong, why it is wrong, and how the problem should be solved.

❑ Wrote adjustment letters that say "Yes" sincerely and to the point. Made those that say "No" fair. Acknowledged reader's point of view and provided clear explanation for my refusal.

❑ Ensured correspondence was timely. Was prompt and reasonable in answering all my correspondence—both from people in my company and from customers.

❑ Took special care to meet the needs of non-native speakers of English in both tone and message.

Exercises

1. Write a letter of inquiry to a utility company, a safety or health care agency, or a company in your town and ask for a brochure describing its services to the community. Be specific about your reasons for requesting the information.

2. In which course(s) are you or will you be writing a paper or report? Write to an agency or company that could supply you with helpful information and request

its aid. Indicate why you are writing, precisely what information you need, and why you need it. Offer to share your paper or report with the company.

3. Examine an ad in a magazine or a TV commercial and then write a one-page assessment in which you identify the four parts of its sales message.

4. Choose one of the following and write a sales letter addressed to an appropriate audience on why they should
   a. major in the same subject you did
   b. live in your neighborhood
   c. be happy taking a vacation where you did last year
   d. dine at a particular restaurant
   e. shop at a store you have worked for
   f. have their cars repaired at a specific garage
   g. give their real estate business to a particular agency
   h. visit your Web site

5. Find at least two sales letters you, your family, or your firm has received, and in an e-mail or a memo to your instructor or employer evaluate how well they follow the four parts of a sales letter discussed in this chapter. Attach a copy of the sales letters to your evaluation. If your e-mail or memo is addressed to your boss, indicate how you would improve your competition's sales letters.

6. As a collaborative project, rewrite the following sales letter to make it more effective. Add any details you think are relevant.

   ```
   Dear Pizza Lovers:

   Allow me to introduce myself. My name is Rudy Moore and I am
   the new manager of Tasty Pizza Parlor in town. The Parlor is
   located at the intersection of North Miller Parkway and
   95th Street. We are open from 10 a.m. to 11 p.m., except on
   the weekends, when we are open later.

   I think you will be as happy as I am to learn that Tasty's
   will now offer free delivery to an extended service area. As
   a result, you can get your Tasty Pizza hot when you want it.

   Please see your weekly newspapers for our ad. We also are
   offering customers a coupon. It is a real deal for you.

   I know you will enjoy Tasty's and I hope to see you. I am
   always interested in hearing from you about our service and
   our fine product. We want to take your order soon. Please
   come in.
   ```

7. Send a follow-up letter to one of the following individuals:
   a. a customer who informs you that she will no longer do business with your firm because your prices are too high
   b. a family of four who stayed at your motel for two weeks last summer
   c. a wedding party that used your catering services last month
   d. a customer who exchanged a coat for the purchase price

  e. a customer who purchased a used car from you and who has not been happy with warranty service

  f. a company that bought software from you nine months ago, alerting them to improvements in the software

8. Write a bad news letter based on an experience at your workplace—rejecting an applicant for a job, a warranty claim, or a request for funding. If you have already written such a letter, rewrite it by applying the principles you learned in this chapter.

9. Write a bad news letter to an appropriate reader about one of the following:

  a. Your company has to discontinue Saturday deliveries because of rising labor and fuel costs.

  b. You are the manager of an insurance company writing to tell one of your customers that, because of reckless driving, his or her rates are going to increase.

  c. You have to refuse to send a bonus gift to a customer who sent in an order after the expiration date for qualifying for the gift.

  d. You have discontinued a model that a business customer wants to reorder.

  e. You have to notify residents of a community that a bus route is being discontinued.

  f. You represent the water department and have to tell residents of a community that they cannot water their lawns for the next month because of a serious water shortage in your town.

  g. You cannot send customers a catalog—which your company used to send free of charge—unless they first send $10 for the cost of that catalog.

  h. You cannot repair a particular piece of equipment because the customer still owes your company for three previous service visits.

10. Write a good news letter about the opposite of one of the situations listed in Exercise 9.

11. You just found out that a business that applied for credit has missed its last mortgage payment. You have to refuse credit to this local firm, which has been in business successfully for eight years. Write a refusal letter without jeopardizing future business dealings.

12. Write a complaint letter about one of the following:

  a. an error in your utility, telephone, or credit card bill

  b. discourteous service you received on an airplane or bus

  c. a frozen food product of poor quality

  d. a shipment that arrived late and damaged

  e. an insurance payment to you that is $100 less than it should be

  f. a public television station's policy of not showing a particular series

  g. junk mail or spam that you are receiving

  h. equipment that arrives with missing parts

  i. misleading representation by a salesperson

  j. incorrect information given at a Web site

13. Write the complaint letter to which the adjustment letter in Figure 6.13 responds.

14. Write the complaint letter to which the adjustment letter in Figure 6.15 responds.

15. Rewrite the following complaint letter to make it more precise and less emotional.

```
Dear Sir:

We recently purchased a machine from your Albany store and
paid a great deal of money for it. This machine, according
to your Web site, is supposedly the best model in your line
and has caused us nothing but trouble each time we use it.
Really, can't you do any better with your technology?

We expect you to stand by your products. The warranties you
give with them should make you accountable for shoddy work-
manship. Let us know at once what you intend to do about our
problem. If you cannot or are unwilling to correct the sit-
uation, we will take our business elsewhere, and then you
will be sorry.

Sincerely yours,
```

16. Write an adjustment letter saying "Yes" to the manager of The Loft, whose letter is in Figure 6.11.

17. Write an adjustment letter saying "No" to the customer who received the "Yes" adjustment letter included in Figure 6.13.

18. Rewrite the following ineffective adjustment letter saying "Yes."

```
Dear Mr. Smith:

We are extremely sorry to learn that you found the suit you
purchased from us unsatisfactory. The problem obviously
stems from the fact that you selected it from the rack
marked "Factory Seconds." In all honesty, we have had a lot
of problems because of this rack. I guess we should know
better than to try to feature inferior merchandise along
with the name-brand clothing that we sell. But we originally
thought that our customers would accept poorer quality mer-
chandise if it saved them some money. That was our mistake.

Please accept our apologies. If you will bring your "Fac-
tory Second" suit to us, we will see what we can do about
honoring your request.

Sincerely yours,
```

19. Rewrite the following ineffective adjustment letter saying "No."

```
Dear Customer:

Our company is unwilling to give you a new toaster or to
refund your purchase price. After examining the toaster you
```

sent to us, we found that the fault was not ours, as you insist, but yours.

Let me explain. Our toaster is made to take a lot of punishment. But being dropped on the floor or poked inside with a knife, as you probably did, exceeds all decent treatment. You must be careful if you expect your appliances to last. Your negligence in this case is so bad that the toaster could not be repaired.

In the future, consider using your appliances according to the guidelines set down in warranty books. That's why they are written.

Since you are now in the market for a new toaster, let me suggest that you purchase our new heavy-duty model, number 67342, called the Counter-Whiz. I am taking the liberty of sending you some information about this model. I do hope you at least go to see one at your local appliance center.

Sincerely,

20. You are the manager of a computer software company, and one of your salespeople has just sold a large order to a new customer whose business you have tried to obtain for years. Unfortunately, the salesperson made a mistake writing out the invoice, undercharging the customer $229. At that price, your company would not break even and so you must write a letter explaining the problem so the customer will not assume all future business dealings with your firm will be offered at such "below market" rates. Decide whether you should ask for the $229 or just "write it off" in the interest of keeping a valuable new customer.
   a. Write a letter to the new customer, asking for the $229 and explaining the problem while still projecting an image of your company as accurate, professional, and very competitive.
   b. Write a letter to the new customer, not asking for the $229 but explaining the mistake and emphasizing that your company is both competitive and professional.
   c. Write a letter to your boss explaining why you wrote letter a.
   d. Write a letter to your boss explaining why you wrote letter b.
   e. Write a letter to the salesperson who made the mistake, asking him or her to take appropriate action with regard to the new customer.

CHAPTER 7

How to Get a Job: Résumés, Letters, Applications, and Interviews

Obtaining a job today involves a lot of hard work. Before your name is added to a company's payroll, you will have to do more than simply walk into the human resources office and fill out an application form. Furthermore, finding the *right* job takes time. And finding the right person to fill that job also takes time for the employer.

Steps the Employer Takes to Hire

From the employer's viewpoint, the stages in the search for a valuable employee include the following:

1. deciding what duties and responsibilities go with the job and determining the qualifications the future employee should possess
2. advertising the job on their Web site, in newspapers, and in professional publications
3. reading and evaluating résumés and letters of application
4. having candidates complete application forms
5. requesting further proof of the candidates' skills (letters of recommendation, transcripts)
6. interviewing selected candidates
7. offering the job to the best-qualified individual

Sometimes those steps are interchangeable, especially steps 4 and 5, but generally speaking, employers go through a long and detailed process to select employees. Step 3, for example, is among the most important for employers (and the most crucial for job candidates). At that stage employers often classify job seekers into one of three groups: those they definitely want to interview; those they may want to interview; and those in whom they have no interest.

Steps to Follow to Get Hired

As a job seeker you will have to know how and when to give the employer the kinds of information the seven steps require. You will also have to follow a certain schedule in your search for a job. The following eight procedures will be required of you:

1. analyzing your strengths and restricting your job search
2. preparing a dossier (placement file)
3. looking in the right places for a job
4. preparing a résumé
5. writing a letter of application
6. filling out a job application
7. going to an interview
8. accepting or declining a job

Your timetable should match that of your prospective employer.

Chapter 7 shows you how to begin your job search and how to prepare appropriate letters that are a part of your job search. You will need to write a letter of application, letters requesting others to write recommendations for you, letters thanking employers for interviews, and letters accepting or declining a job offer. In addition to discussing each of those kinds of letters, this chapter shows you how to assemble the supporting data—dossiers, résumés—that employers request. You will also find some practical advice on how to handle yourself at interviews.

The eight steps of your job search are arranged in this chapter in the order in which you are most likely to proceed when you start looking for a job. By reading about these stages in sequence, you will have the benefit of going through a dry run of the employment process itself.

Analyzing Your Strengths and Restricting Your Job Search

Two "Fatal Assumptions"

Individuals who advise students about how to get a job have isolated two "fatal assumptions" that many job seekers make. If you assume either of the following statements to be true, chances are that you will *not* be very successful in your job search.

1. I should remain loose (vague) about what I want so I will be free to respond to any opportunity.
2. The employer has the upper hand in the whole process.

The first "fatal assumption" will disqualify you for any position for which your major has prepared you. Your first responsibility is to identify your professional qualifications. Employers want to hire individuals with highly developed technical skills and training. Your education and experience should help you to identify and emphasize your marketable skills.

The second "fatal assumption"—assuming that the employer controls the entire job-search process—is equally misleading. To a large extent, *you* can determine whether you are a serious contender for a job by the letters and résumés you write and the self-image you present. Even in today's highly competitive job market, you can secure a suitable job if you keep in mind that the basic purpose of all job correspondence is to sell yourself. Letters and résumés are sales tools to earn you an interview and eventually a job. Be confident and convincing. Believe in yourself and your abilities. Employers almost always have a shortage of good, qualified employees.

Finding the Right Job—Some Tips

Here are some pointers on finding the right job.

1. Make an inventory of your most significant accomplishments in your major and/or on the job. What are your greatest strengths—writing and speaking, working with people in small groups, organizing and problem solving, speaking a second language, developing software, performing accounting audits?

2. Decide which specialty within your chosen career appeals to you most. If you are in a nursing program, do you want to work in a large teaching hospital, for a home health or hospice agency, or in a physician's office? What kinds of patients do you prefer to care for—geriatric, pediatric, psychiatric?

3. What are the most rewarding prospects of a job in your profession? What most interests you about a position—travel, international contacts, on-the-job training, helping people, being creative?

4. Avoid applying for positions for which you are either overqualified or underqualified. If a position requires ten years of related work experience and you are just starting out, you will only waste the employer's time and your own by applying. However, if a job requires a certificate or license and you are in the process of obtaining one, go ahead and apply.

5. Take advantage of career counseling available at your school, through your state employment agency, and from numerous guides and books. One important career guide is *What Color Is Your Parachute? A Practical Manual for Job Hunters and Career Changers,* by Richard Bolles. *Parachute* has been read by more than 6 million people and will give you sound advice on how to identify your most marketable strengths, package your credentials, and prioritize your job goals. You might also want to consult *Electronic Job Search Revolution: How to Win with the New Technology That's Reshaping Today's Job Market,* by Joyce Lain Kennedy and Thomas J. Morrow, and *What Do I Do Now? Making Sense of Today's Changing Workplace,* by Shena Crane.

6. Check with federal, state, and local employment offices. The U.S. government is one of the biggest employers in the country. During 1999–2000, for instance, the most active career site on the Web was operated by the U.S. government, with 1.4 million new hires. Consult the following Web sites for listings of government jobs:

- U.S. Office of Personnel Management (*http://usajobs.opm.gov*)
- Federal Government Employment Opportunities (*http://iccweb.com.federal/*)

- Federal Jobs.Net (*http://federaljobs.net/*)
- HRS Federal Job Search (*http://www.hrsjobs.com/*)

Also check America's Job Bank (*http://www.ajb.dni.us*) and *Federal Jobs Digest* (*http://www.jobsfed.com*), a privately published sourcebook that lists more than 40,000 civil service jobs each month. If you are a veteran, consider checking with the Department of Veterans Affairs on campus or with an office in your town about specific programs and job opportunities. Finally, visit a Civil Service Commission office, a Federal Job Information Center (*http:www.jobsfed.com*), and your state and local employment offices. All those agencies maintain current files of positions and offer some counseling free of charge.

Changing Careers: Some Guidelines for Success

Because of downsizing, reorganization, and mergers, even experienced professionals may be forced to find jobs after being laid off. Other individuals, such as Patrice Cooper Bolger, whose résumé is shown in Figure 7.7, are reentering the job market after years of absence. Still others are seeking a more fulfilling career. A laid-off engineer found a satisfying new position as a private investigator and an insurance salesperson forced to take an early retirement went to work for a hospital as a patient accounts manager. If you are forced to make a career change, follow these guidelines as well as the ones on pages 237–240.

1. Identify those activities that brought you success (raises, promotions, recognitions) in your old career or job and relate them to what you can do for a new employer. Doubtless you have skills in working with people and delegating authority, submitting and managing a budget, advising and evaluating personnel, working closely with vendors and customers, and keeping a schedule. Being a team player and an effective communicator are also invaluable assets to any employer (as we saw in Chapter 3).

2. Don't panic! You don't have to start over from scratch. Translate your experiences and achievements in step 1 into marketable skills you can use on a new job or in a new career. Show the continuity of your achievements.

3. Seek out-placement counseling, if available, from your former employer; if it is not available, identify placement counselors through such agencies as your state employment agency and the Career Planning and Adult Development Network.

4. Investigate job retraining programs available through federal, state, and local agencies listed above.

5. Look at current issues of *Business Week, Occupational Outlook Quarterly, Fortune,* and the *Wall Street Journal* to find out about trends and job opportunities in new or related areas. Read the *Occupational Outlook Handbook (http://stats.bls. gov/oco-home.htm).*

Preparing a Dossier

The job placement office or career center at your school will assist you by providing counseling, notifying you of available, relevant jobs, and arranging on-campus interviews. The job placement office may also help you establish your **dossier,** sometimes referred to as your placement file.

Your *dossier,* French for "bundle of documents," is your personal file stored at the placement office. It contains information about you that substantiates and supplements the facts listed on your résumé and letter of application. Basically your dossier contains

- solicited letters of recommendation
- unsolicited letters that awarded you a scholarship, praised your work on the job, or honored you for community service
- your résumé, including job experiences
- your academic transcript(s)

Be selective about unsolicited letters; you do not want to crowd your dossier with less important items that will compete for attention with your academic recommendations. You may ask that your dossier be sent to an employer, or employers may request it themselves if you have listed the placement office address on your résumé.

Whom You Should Ask for Letters of Recommendation

The most important part of your dossier consists of your letters of recommendation. They can sell you or sink your chances, so select them carefully. Ask the following individuals to write letters describing your work qualifications and habits:

- your current or previous employer (even for a summer job)
- two or three of your professors who know and like your work, have graded your papers, or have supervised you in fieldwork or laboratory activities
- superiors who evaluated your work in the military
- community leaders or officials with whom you have worked on civic projects

Recommendations from such individuals will be regarded as more objective—and more relevant—than a letter from your clergy or a neighbor. Of course, if you are asked specifically for a character reference, by all means ask a member of the clergy.

Always Ask for Permission

Ask permission before you list an individual as a reference. You could jeopardize your chances for a job if a prospective employer called someone whom you named but did not ask to be a reference and that person responds that he or she did not even know you were looking for a job or, worse yet, reveals that you did not have the courtesy to ask to use his or her name.

When you ask for permission in a letter or in person, stress how much a strong letter of support means to you and find out whether the individual is willing to write such a letter for your dossier. Generalized or weak letters may hurt your chances in your job search, so be specific in your requests. Tell your references what kind of jobs you are applying for and keep them up-to-date about your educational and occupational achievements, as Robert Jackson does in Figure 7.1.

Should You Ask Your Current Boss?

Asking your boss to recommend you for another job can be tricky. Be cautious. If your current employer knows that your education is preparing you for another

FIGURE 7.1   Request for a letter of recommendation.

5432 South Kenneth Avenue
Chicago, IL 60651

March 30, 2002

Mr. Sonny Butler, Manager
Empire Supermarket
4000 West 79th Street
Chicago, IL 60652-4300

Dear Mr. Butler:

I was employed at your store from September 2000 through August 2001. During my employment, I worked part time as a stock clerk and relief cashier, and during the summer months I was a full-time employee in the produce department, helping to fill in while Bill Dirksen and Vivian Rogers were away on their vacations.

I enjoyed my work at Empire, and I learned a great deal about ordering stock, arranging merchandise, and assisting customers.

This May I will receive my A.A. degree from Moraine Valley Community College in retail merchandising. I have already begun preparing for my job search for a position in retail sales. Would you be willing to write a letter of recommendation for me in which you mention what you regard as my greatest strengths as one of your employees? Having your endorsement would be a great help to me.

To assist you, I can send you a letter of recommendation form from the Placement Office at Moraine Valley. Your letter would become part of my permanent placement file.

I look forward to hearing from you. I thought you might like to see the enclosed résumé, which shows what I have been doing since I left Empire.

Sincerely yours,

Robert B. Jackson

Robert B. Jackson

Encl.: Résumé

TECH NOTE

Electronic Résumés and Files at Placement Centers

Many college and university placement offices offer students the opportunity to file electronic dossiers and to access job information electronically. For example, the placement office at the University of South Alabama not only prepares and sends out dossiers, it also posts employment announcements on the USA Career Services electronic network. Professional staff members "develop and maintain contacts with industrial, business, governmental, and public service employers to enhance career prospects for students."

Boston's Emerson College has an on-line career resource library, as does Middlebury Community College in Vermont. Middlebury provides its students with an on-line recruiting and job database. Students can access a broad range of recruiting contacts, job postings, and interview information twenty-four hours a day. Become familiar with the services your school placement office provides.

profession, or if you are a student working at a part-time job, you should obtain a letter of recommendation to include in your dossier. However, if you are employed and are looking for professional advancement or a better salary elsewhere, you may not want your current employer to know that you are searching for another job.

You have the right to ask a prospective employer to respect your confidentiality (for instance, not to call you at work) until you become a leading candidate. At that point you may be happy to have your current employer consulted for a reference. On the other hand, if you are not on particularly good terms with your current employer and want to find another, more suitable position, inform the prospective employer as honestly and professionally as you can with the least damage to yourself. Use your best judgment depending on the circumstances of your search.

Should You See Your Letters?

You have a legal right to determine whether you want to see your letters. If you have read them, the fact is noted on the dossier. Some employers believe that if the candidates see what is written about them, the references may be less frank and may withhold critical information. If you waive your right to see the letters written about you, you must sign an appropriate form, a copy of which is then given to the individual recommending you. Remember, though, that some individuals may refuse to write a letter that they know you will see; they may prefer absolute confidentiality. Before you make any decision about seeing your letters, get the advice of your instructors and placement counselors.

When Should You Establish Your Dossier?

Do not wait until you begin applying for jobs to compile your dossier. Placement offices recommend that candidates set up their dossiers at least three to six months before they begin looking for jobs. With that lead time, you can be sure that your letters of recommendation are on file and that you have benefited from the placement office's services. In advising you, the placement counselor will ask you to complete a confidential questionnaire about your geographic preferences, salary expectations, and the types of positions for which you are qualified. With that information on hand, the placement office will be better prepared to notify you of appropriate openings.

Some placement offices charge a small fee for their services, while others provide their services free of charge.

Looking in the Right Places for a Job

One way to search for a job is simply to send out a batch of letters to companies you want to work for. But how do you know what jobs, if any, those companies have available, what qualifications they are looking for, and what application procedures and deadlines they want you to follow? You can avoid uncertainties by knowing where to look for a job and knowing what a specific job entails. Such information will make your search easier and, in all likelihood, more successful. Consult the following resources for a wealth of job-related information.

1. The Internet. Many prospective employers rely on the efficiency of the Internet to find new employees. Information about a variety of employment opportunities—as many as a million—exists in cyberspace. The Net gives employers a vehicle for finding and recruiting qualified applicants in many fields—technical, sales, marketing, legal, and more. Companies can post job openings and describe precisely what they are looking for in far more detail than in a classified ad.

You can learn about jobs on the Net in several ways. If you have a particular company in mind, you can call up its Web site to see whether position openings are posted there. Or using a search engine like Yahoo!, you can investigate such large categories as "Employment Opportunities" or "Jobs" and follow leads through various Web sites. You can also check into the many on-line job services that list positions and sometimes give advice as well. The largest of those on-line services are

- America's Employers (*http://www.americasemployer.com*)
- Yahoo! Careers (*http://www.classified.yahoo.com*)
- College Grad Job Hunter (*http://www.collegegrad.com*)
- Employment Guide's Career Web (*http://www.cweb.com*)
- Job Database (*http://www.zdnet.com/ce/jobs/jobs/*)
- Job Trak (*http://www.jobtrak.com*)
- Job Web (*http://www.JobWeb.org/*)
- Headhunters (*http://www.headhunter.net*)
- Online Career Center (*http://www.occ.com/*)
- Nation Job Network (*http://www.nationjob.com/*)
- People Network, Inc. (*http://www.peoplenetwork.com/*)

Similar services are devoted to specific types of jobs or employers. Once you see a position advertised, you can e-mail your letter of application and résumé directly to the prospective employer's Web site.

2. Newspapers. Look at local newspapers as well as large city papers with a wide circulation, such as the *New York Times,* the *Chicago Tribune,* the *Los Angeles Times,* the *New Orleans Times-Picayune,* and the *Cleveland Plain Dealer.* The Sunday editions usually advertise positions available all over the country. The *National Business Employment Weekly,* published by the *Wall Street Journal,* lists jobs in many different areas, including technical and managerial positions. You can access job listings found in many large newspapers through CareerPath.com (*http://www.careerpath.com*).

Make sure you check every possibly relevant category (for example, "Computer Programmers" as well as "Programmers").

3. Professional and trade journals and associations in your major. Identify the most respected periodicals in your field and search their ads. The *American Journal of Nursing,* for example, carries notices of openings arranged by geographic location in each of its monthly issues, and each issue of *Food Technology* features a section called "Professional Placement," listing jobs all over the country. Consult the *Encyclopedia of Associations* for a list of journals and newsletters in your profession. Many journals are also available on-line.

Professional associations (American Microbiologists Association, for example) often offer lower rates for student memberships. Being a member of such an organization not only will give you information about jobs in your field, it will look good on your résumé.

4. Your college placement office. Counselors keep an up-to-date file of available positions and can also tell you when a firm's recruiter will be on campus to conduct interviews. They can also help you locate summer and part-time work, both on and off campus. Most important, they can give you sound advice on your job search.

5. Personal contacts. Let your professors, friends, neighbors, relatives, and even your clergy know you are looking for a job. They may hear of something and can notify you. Better yet, they may recommend you for the position—with a phone call, a visit to their own company's human resources department, or a letter. This sort of networking definitely pays off; referrals are among the most successful ways to land a job. John D. Erdlen and Donald H. Sweet, experts on the job search, cite the following as a primary rule of job hunting: "Don't do anything yourself you can get someone with influence to do for you."

6. The human resources department of a company or agency you would like to work for. Often you will be able to fill out an application even if there is no current opening. But do not call employers asking about openings: a visit shows a more serious interest. Also, the human resources officers are more likely to remember you if a job does develop. New openings often arise unexpectedly in business and industry and a visit may have put you in the right place at the right time.

FIGURE 7.2   A description of one résumé database service.

Employers Benefit from ACM Résumé Database

The ACM Résumé Database is composed of résumés of ACM members—high-caliber, information-technology professionals who can bring expertise to your company. All résumés are up-to-date and can be searched according to criteria you provide, in a short period of time and at low rates. Single searches as well as annual subscriptions to the database can be requested from the database administrator, Resume-Link, at 614-529-0429. ACM Institutional members get a 10% discount off the cost of the search.

And for ACM members! Our database also is now searchable for internships and co-op positions, as well as for full-time and consultant placements. Use this free career development service and submit your résumé online at **http://www.Resume-Link.com/**.

7. Your local Chamber of Commerce. Although not a placement center, the Chamber of Commerce can give you the names and addresses of employers likely to hire individuals with your qualifications, as well as information about those companies to use in a letter of application or at an interview. Many companies planning to relocate or expand notify a Chamber of Commerce to assess the potential labor force.

8. A résumé database service. A number of on-line services will put your résumé in a database and make it available to prospective employers, who scan the database regularly to find suitable job candidates. The Tech Note on pages 260–261 lists the addresses of some of the more popular databases. Figure 7.2 describes a résumé database service offered by one professional organization—the Association for Computing Machinery (ACM)—for its members. Check to see if a professional society to which you belong (or might join) offers a similar service.

9. A video résumé. In some parts of the country, job hunters can make twenty-second "video résumés" that are aired on local television stations. In a video résumé, the job seeker must make a sales pitch quickly and effectively, emphasizing the one or two strengths—such as the sales dollars generated or the ability to speak several languages—that will prompt a potential employer to call the station for the candidate's phone number. Inquire at your local state employment service about whether any local stations offer this public service.

10. Recruiters at a professional employment agency. Some agencies list two kinds of jobs—those that are found for the applicant free of charge (because the employer pays the fee) and those for which the applicant pays a stiff fee—usually a percentage of your first year's salary. If you do use an agency, be sure to ask who pays the fee for the service. Because employment agencies often find out about jobs through channels already available to you, exhaust all the services listed here before you rely on an agency.

Preparing a Résumé

The résumé, sometimes called a **data sheet** or **curriculum vitae,** may be the most important document you prepare in your job search. It deserves your attention.

TECH NOTE

How Employers Sort Through Résumés
Employers may receive hundreds of résumés for one position and spend as little as thirty seconds on each. Keep in mind that employers process résumés at three levels of scrutiny.

 First level: the elimination phase. Employers scan résumés to make the first cut, deciding very quickly (thirty to sixty seconds) whose résumé is worth further attention.

 Second level: the "let's take-a-second-look" phase. Employers may take two to three minutes to see who might be worth further consideration.

 Third level: the interview list. At this stage employers read the job seekers' letters of application to determine whom they will interview.

What Is a Résumé?

A résumé is a factual and concise summary of your qualifications. It is not your life history or your emotional autobiography, nor is it a transcript of your college work. A résumé highlights your proven accomplishments and abilities. It is a record of results, showing a prospective employer that you have what it takes (in education and experience) to do the job.

 The résumé is a short (preferably one-page, never longer than two) outline accompanying your letter of application. Write your résumé before your job search gets underway and certainly before preparing any letters of application. Never send a résumé alone, but do bring one with you to an interview. And you should certainly have copies available for recruiters if you schedule campus interviews.

What Employers Like to See in a Résumé

Prospective employers will judge you and your work by your résumé, their first view of you and your qualifications. They like to see the following five characteristics in an applicant's résumé:

- **Attractive.** The document is pleasing to the eye with appropriate spacing, typeface, and use of boldface; it shows you have a sense of proportion and document design and that you are neat.
- **Carefully organized.** The orderly arrangement of information is easy to follow, logical, and consistent; it shows you have the ability to process information and to summarize. Employers prize analytical thinking.
- **Accurate.** Grammar, spelling, dates, names, titles, programs, systems are correct; it shows you can communicate effectively.
- **Current information.** All information is up-to-date and documented, with no gaps or sketchy areas, and demonstrates your computer literacy and ethics.
- **Relevance.** The information is appropriate for the job level and the employer and shows you have the necessary education and experience. Your résumé also indicates that you can be an effective team player, a vital asset.

Your goal is to prepare a résumé that shows the employer you possess the sought-after job skills. A résumé that is unattractive, hard to follow, poorly written, filled with typos and other errors, and not relevant for the prospective employer's needs will not make the first cut.

The Process of Writing Your Résumé

As with other types of writing, preparing your résumé requires that you work through a process. You cannot produce a polished résumé in an hour. But having a clear idea about the type of job you want and your qualifications for it should get you off to a good start.

It might be to your advantage to prepare several versions of your résumé and then adapt each one you send out to the specific job skills a prospective employer is looking for. Following the process below will help you prepare any résumé.

Getting Started—Ask Key Questions

Begin with the prewriting strategies discussed in Chapter 2 to identify your strengths and achievements. Ask yourself important questions about what you are most proud of from your school work and jobs you have held.

1. What classes did you excel in?
2. What papers or reports earned you your highest grades?
3. What computer skills have you mastered—languages, software knowledge, navigating and developing Net resources? Knowledge of e-commerce?
4. On the job, what technical skills have you acquired?
5. Do you work well with people? What skills do you possess as a member of a team? Can you organize complicated tasks or solve problems quickly?
6. Have you won any awards or scholarships or received a raise, bonus, or promotion?
7. Do you have any skills or activities that would show your professional or occupational talents and ability?

Write down everything you think is a skill or achievement—jobs (full- or part-time, summer), school (course work, workshops, labs, extracurricular activities, sports), the military, community work. Circle or underline awards or honors as well as major responsibilities. Don't be worried if you produce a lengthy list of seemingly unrelated activities. From this brainstormed list (or clustered grouping) you will have a working inventory of accomplishments from which you can begin to pull pertinent material.

Scrutinize Your Accomplishments

The next step is to be highly critical of your working inventory. Cross off any repetitions, eliminate unimportant or irrelevant items, try to sort items into related categories, and add whatever information you think is valuable.

As you criticize and supplement your list, examine your accomplishments the way a prospective employer might. The chief questions an employer will ask about you are

- What can this person do for our company?
- How does this person compare with other job applicants?

Employers are results oriented; they read résumés looking for clear proof of your marketable skills. You have to convince your reader (or group of readers—résumés often circulate among a hiring committee) that you have succeeded in the past and will do so in the future.

Pay special attention to your four or five most significant, job-worthy strengths and work especially hard on listing them concisely. While not everything you have done relates directly to a particular job, indicate how your achievements could be relevant to the employer's overall needs. For example, handling money responsibly or supervising staff in a grocery store points to your ability to perform the same duties in another business context.

Use Selling Clauses

The next step in preparing a winning résumé is to translate the items in your list of accomplishments into appropriate résumé entries. There is a big difference between résumés and other types of work-related documents. Résumés generally are written in short sentences (clauses really) that omit the subject "I." Instead of complete sentences, résumés use action-packed *selling clauses* that convince prospective employers that you are the right person for the job. Use the action verbs listed in Table 7.1.

How Much Should You Include in a Résumé?

How much should you include in your résumé? Both experienced candidates and recent graduates with limited experience ask that question. The dangers involve including too much or putting in too little.

How Long Should My Résumé Be?

Some employment counselors advise candidates to prepare no more than a one-page résumé. However, depending on your education and job experience, you may want to include a second page. On-line résumés (pp. 257–263) can exceed one page. A good rule of thumb is that if you have more than one degree beyond high school

TABLE 7.1   Action Verbs to Use in Your Résumé

accommodated	coordinated	increased	reduced
achieved	created	informed	researched
administered	customized	initiated	scheduled
analyzed	dealt in	installed	searched
arranged	determined	instituted	selected
assembled	developed	instructed	served
assisted	directed	interacted with	settled
attended	drafted	maintained	sold
awarded	earned	managed	solved
built	established	monitored	supervised
calculated	estimated	navigated	taught
coached	evaluated	negotiated	tracked
collected	expedited	operated	trained
communicated	figured	organized	tutored
compiled	guided	oversaw	updated
completed	handled	performed	verified
composed	headed	planned	weighed
computed	implemented	prepared	worked
conducted	improved	reconciled	wrote

and if you have held more than two full-time professional jobs, you may need a two-page résumé. You might want to experiment with preparing a two-page chronological résumé, as Anna Cassetti has done (Figure 7.3), or a one-page bullet résumé (explained on pp. 252–254), like Donald Kitto-Klein's (see Figure 7.8).

Balancing Education and Experience
If you have years of experience, don't flood your prospective employer with too many details. You cannot possibly include every detail of your job(s) for the last ten or twenty years.

- Emphasize only those skills and positions most likely to earn you the job.
- Eliminate your earliest jobs that do not relate to your present employment search.
- Combine and condense skills acquired over many years and through many jobs.

Figure 7.3 shows the résumé of Anna Cassetti, who had years of job experience before she returned to school. Take a look, too, at Patrice Cooper Bolger's résumé (see Figure 7.7) and Donald Kitto-Klein's (Figure 7.8). Those individuals also have a great deal of experience to offer prospective employers.

Many job candidates who have spent most of their lives in school are faced with the other extreme: not having much job experience to put down. The worst thing to do is to write "None" for experience. Any part-time, summer, or other seasonal jobs, as well as volunteer work done at school for a library or science laboratory, shows a prospective employer that you are responsible and knowledgeable about the obligations of being an employee. So, too, do internships and community work. Figure 7.4

FIGURE 7.3   Résumé from an individual with ten years' job experience.

ANNA C. CASSETTI

6457 Blackstone Avenue   MacMurray Real Estate
Fort Worth, TX 76321-6733   1700 Ross Boulevard
(817) 555-5657   Haltom City, TX 77320-1700
acassetti@netdor.com   (817) 555-7211

CAREER OBJECTIVE
Full-time sales position with large real estate office in the Phoenix or
Tucson areas with opportunities to use proven skills in real estate
appraisal and tax counseling.

EXPERIENCE

2001–present *MacMurray Real Estate, Haltom City, Texas*
Real estate agent. Excelled in small suburban office (four
salespersons plus broker) with limited listings; **sold individually
over three million dollars in residential property**; appraised both
residential and commercial listings.

1995–2000 *Dallman Federal Savings and Loan, Inc., Fort Worth, Texas*
Chief Teller. Responsible for supervising, training, and coordinating
activities of six full-time and two part-time tellers. Promoted to
Chief Teller, March 1997, with bonus.

1995 *H&R Block, Westover Hills, Texas*
(Sept.-Dec.) Tax Consultant. Prepared personal and business returns.

1992–1994 *Cruckshank's Hardware Store, Fort Worth, Texas.* Salesperson.

1988–1992 *U.S. Navy*
Honorably discharged with rank of Petty Officer, Third Class.
Served as stores manager.

EDUCATION

1994–2000 *Texas Christian University, Fort Worth, Texas*
Awarded B.S. degree in Real Estate Management. Completed thirty-
three hours in business and real estate courses with a concentration
in finance, appraising, and property management. Also took twelve
hours in computer science and Web designing. Wrote reports on
appraisal procedures as part of supervised training program.

Continued

FIGURE 7.3   (Continued)

Cassetti 2

1994   *H&R Block, Westover Hills, Texas*
(Sept.-Dec.) Earned diploma in Basic Income Tax Preparation after completing
                  intensive ten-week course.

1989–1991   *U.S. Naval Base, San Diego, California*
                  Attended U.S. Navy's Supply Management School.
                  Applied principles of stores management at Newport Naval Base.

SKILLS AND ACTIVITIES
Texas Realtor's License: 756a2737
Chair, Financial Committee, Grace Presbyterian Church, Fort Worth.
Advised teenagers in Junior Achievement about business practices
and management.

REFERENCES
References available upon request.

---

shows a résumé from Anthony Jones, a student with very little job experience; Figure 7.5 shows one from María Lopez, a student with only a few years of experience.

What Should You Exclude from a Résumé?

Knowing what to exclude from a résumé is as important as knowing what to include. Here are some details best left out of your résumé:

- salary demands or expectations
- preferences for work schedules, days off, or overtime
- comments about fringe benefits
- travel restrictions
- reasons for leaving your last job
- your photograph (unless you are applying for a modeling or acting job)
- comments about your family, spouse, or children
- height, weight, hair, or eye color
- personal information, hobbies, interests (unless relevant to the job you are seeking, in which case put under Education or Skills and Activities)
- any disabilities

Save questions and statements of preference for your interview. The résumé should be written appropriately to get you that interview.

Parts of a Résumé

Name, Address, Phone
Center this information at the top of the page. Capitalize all the letters of your name (do not use a nickname) to make it stand out, but do not capitalize every letter

FIGURE 7.4   Résumé from a student with little job experience.

ANTHONY H. JONES
73 Allenwood Boulevard
Santa Rosa, California 95401-1074
(707) 555-6390
E-mail: *ajones@plat.com*

CAREER OBJECTIVE

Full-time position as a layout artist with a commercial publishing house using my knowledge of state-of-the-art design technology.

EDUCATION

2000–2002 Santa Rosa Junior College, A.S. degree to be awarded in May 2002
Dean's List in 2001, GPA 3.45
Major: Commercial Graphics Illustration, with specialty in design layout
Related courses included:
Design Principles
Digital Photography
Graphics Programs: Illustrator, Photoshop
Desktop Publishing: QuarkXPress, WordPerfect Suite 8

Apprenticeship, McAdam Publishers
Major projects included:
Assisting layout editors with page composition and importing images
Writing detailed reports on digital photography, designs, and artwork used in *Living in Sonoma County* and *Real Estate in Sonoma County* magazines.
1997–2000 Santa Rosa High School
Electives included drawing, photography, and computer graphics
Created Web site for student magazine, *Thunder*
(*http://www.Thunder.edu*)

EXPERIENCE

1995–2002 Salesperson (part-time), Buchman's Department Store
Duties included assisting customers in sporting goods and appliance departments and coordinating sport shop by displaying merchandise.

SKILLS AND ACTIVITIES

Volunteer; designed 3-fold brochure for the Santa Rosa Humane Society's 2001 fund drive.

REFERENCES

References, college transcripts, and a portfolio of designs and photographs available upon request.

FIGURE 7.5   Résumé from a student with some job experience.

MARÍA H. LOPEZ
1725 Brooke Street
Miami, Florida 32701-2121
(305) 555-3429   **mlopez@eagle.com**

Career Objective   Full-time position assisting dentist in providing dental health care and counseling and performing preventative dental treatments, especially in applying my clinical skills in the practice of pedodontics.

Education
August 2000–   **Miami Dade Community College, Miami, Florida**
May 2002   Will receive A.S. degree in dental hygiene in May. Have completed nine courses in oral pathology, dental materials and specialties, periodontics, and community dental health.

Currently enrolled in clinical dental hygiene program. Experienced with procedures and instruments used with oral prophylaxis techniques. Subject of major project was proper nutrition for preschoolers.

Minor area of interest is psychology (twelve hours completed). Received excellent evaluations in business writing course. GPA is 3.3. Bilingual: Spanish/English.

Plan to take American Dental Assistants' Examination on June 2.

1993–1997   **Miami North High School, Miami, Florida**
Took electives in computers, electronics, and public relations

Work Experience
April 1998–   **St. Francis Hospital, Miami Beach, Florida**
July 2000   Full-time unit clerk on the pediatric floor. Duties included ordering supplies, maintaining records, transcribing orders, and greeting and assisting visitors.

June 1997–   **Murphy Construction Company, Miami, Florida**
April 1998   Secretary-receptionist. Did keyboarding, billing, and mailing in small office (three employees).

Summers   **City of Hialeah, Florida**
1995–1996   Water meter reader.

Continued

FIGURE 7.5   (Continued)

Lopez 2

References   The following individuals have written letters of recommendation for my placement file, available from the Placement Center, Miami-Dade Community College, Medical Center Campus, Miami, FL 33127-2225.

Sister Mary James
Head Nurse
Pediatric Unit
St. Francis Hospital
10003 Collins Avenue
Miami Beach, FL 33141
(305) 555-5113

Professor Mitchell Pelbourne
Department of Dental Hygiene
Miami-Dade Community College
Medical Center Campus
Miami, FL 33127
(305) 555-3872

Tia Gutierrez, D.D.S.
9800 Exchange Avenue
Miami, FL 33167
(305) 555-1039

Mr. Jack Murphy
1203 Francis Street
Miami, FL 33157
(305) 555-6767

of your address. Include your ZIP code, telephone number, and e-mail address, to make it easy for a prospective employer to reach you for an interview. If you have two addresses, it is wise to list both. List all appropriate phone numbers: where you can be reached or where you receive messages during the day and evening or home and work numbers.

Career Objective Statement

One of the first things a prospective employer reads is your career objective statement, also called an **employment objective.** This statement tells the employer the specific type of job you are looking for and in what ways you are qualified to hold it. Such a statement is the result of your focused self-evaluation and will influence everything else you include. To write an effective career objective statement, ask yourself four basic questions:

1. What kind of job do I want?
2. What kind of job am I qualified for?
3. What kinds of capabilities do I possess?
4. What kinds of skills do I want to learn?

As part of your objective, indicate the title of the position you are seeking, the skills you have for that position, and what benefits you can promise the employer.

Formulate your career objective statement precisely. Let a prospective employer know that you have carefully defined goals and skills that will benefit his or her company. Avoid trite or vague goals like "looking for professional advancement" or "want to join a progressive company." Compare the vague objectives on the left with the more precise ones on the right:

Unfocused	Focused
Job in sales to use my aggressive skills in expanding markets.	Regional sales representative using my proven skills in marketing and communication to develop and expand a customer base.
Full-time position as staff nurse.	Full-time position as staff nurse on cardiac step-down unit to offer excellent primary care nursing and patient/family teaching.

Ethically you cannot apply for a position that requires experience or skills you do not possess. On the other hand, do not give the impression that you will take anything. Be careful not to make your objective either too broad or too restricted. If your focus is too broad, the employer won't have a clue as to the particular job you are seeking. If your focus is too restricted, you might not be considered for other related openings available at a company.

Depending on your background and the types of jobs you are qualified for, you might formulate two or three different career or employment objectives to use with different versions of your résumé. If your career objective statement is irrelevant or even slightly off the mark for an employer, you will in all likelihood be excluded from the competition.

Credentials

The order of the next two categories—**education** and **experience**—can vary. Generally, if you have lots of work experience before, during, or after college, list experience first. Years of experience will impress a prospective employer. Note that for Anna Cassetti (Figure 7.3), Patrice Cooper Bolger (Figure 7.7), and Donald Kitto-Klein (Figure 7.8), experience is their best selling point, so they placed that category ahead of education. However, if you are still in school or are a recent graduate short on job experience, list education first, as Anthony Jones (Figure 7.4) did. María Lopez (Figure 7.5) also decided to place her education before her job experience because the job she was applying for required the formal training she received at Miami-Dade Community College.

Education

Begin with your most recent education first, then list everything **significant since high school.** Give the names of the schools and the dates you attended. Don't overlook military schools or major training programs (EMT, court reporter), institutes, workshops, or apprenticeships you have completed. Indicate when you received your latest degree, diploma, or certificate or when you expect to receive it.

Remember, however, that a résumé is not a transcript. Simply listing a series of courses will not set you apart from hundreds of other applicants taking similar courses across the country. Avoid vague titles such as Science 203 or Nursing IV. Instead, concentrate on describing the kinds of skills you learned.

30 hours in planning and development courses specializing in transportation, land use, and community facilities and 12 hours in field methods of gathering, interpreting, and describing survey data in reports.

Completed 28 hours in major courses in business marketing, management, and materials in addition to 12 hours in computer science, including HTML/Web publishing.

Also note any laboratory work, fieldwork, internship, or cooperative educational work. Such extras are important to employers looking for someone with previous practical experience. List your grade point average (GPA) only if it is 3.0 or above and your rank in class only if you are in the top 35 percent. Otherwise, indicate your GPA in just your major or during your last term, if it is above 3.0.

List any academic honors you have won (dean's list, department awards, school honors, scholarships, grants, honorable mentions). Memberships in honor societies in your major and professional associations also demonstrate that you are professionally accomplished and active.

Experience

Your job history is the key category for many employers. It shows them that you have held jobs before and that you are responsible. Here are some guidelines to follow in listing information about your experience.

1. Begin with your most recent position and work backward in reverse chronological order. List the company or agency name, location (city and state), and your title. Do not mention why you left a job.

2. Give the most attention to your most relevant position. If it happens to be your second most recent position, keep the correct order, but devote more space to it. If you have held many jobs, highlight the positions that are most relevant for the job you are seeking now. Your summer job as a lifeguard who knew life-saving techniques may help you in finding a position as a respiratory therapist.

Discuss jobs you held eight or nine years ago *only* if your experiences then are relevant to your current job search. Avoid stringing out five or six temporary, short-term jobs (each under three months). Combine them into one brief statement or omit them. Remember, space is at a premium on your résumé.

If you have been a full-time parent for ten years, indicate the management skills you developed in running a household and any community or civic service, as Patrice Cooper Bolger does in her résumé in Figure 7.7. She skillfully relates her family and community accomplishments to the specific job she seeks.

3. Provide short descriptions of your duties and achievements using your "selling clauses" (pp. 242–243). Don't just say you "worked for a newspaper"—your prospective employer won't know whether you wrote editorials, sold advertising space, or delivered papers. Perhaps you were an assistant to the advertising editor and were responsible for providing and verifying copy. Say so. That is impressive and informative. Rather than saying you were a secretary, indicate that you wrote business letters and contracts, learned various software programs, designed a company Web site, prepared schedules for part-time help in an office of twenty-five people, or assisted the manager in preparing accounts. See how Donald Kitto-

Klein's résumé (Figure 7.8) uses effective selling clauses to describe the skills he has acquired in several positions.

4. In describing your position(s), emphasize any responsibilities that involved handling money; managing other employees; working with customer accounts, services, and programs; or writing letters and reports. Prospective employers are interested in your leadership abilities, financial shrewdness (especially if you saved your company money), tact in dealing with the public, and communication skills. They are also favorably impressed by promotions you may have earned.

5. Never exaggerate or lie about your job duties. It will catch up with you. Don't call yourself an assistant buyer when you were a sales clerk. If you were a clerical assistant to an attorney, don't describe yourself as a paralegal. Do not inflate your role with fancy terminology; a receptionist is not a "communications consultant," nor is a server a "food services manager."

On the other hand, don't assume that your work experience was so routine or so ordinary that it is unimportant and unhelpful in your job search. Show your prospective employer that no matter what you did, you did it well, exceptionally well in fact. If you were a nurse's aide, include some selling clauses about working with patients, carrying out various procedures, and assisting the nursing staff. Emphasize your responsibilities and how you carried them out professionally as part of a health care team.

Personal Information

Federal employment laws prohibit discrimination on the basis of sex, race, national origin, religion, marital status, or disability, and you should not include any such information on your résumé. But if you think that any personal information might help land you the job, then you are free to include it. If you are applying for a position in a day-care center or as a teacher's aide, the fact that you have children may be important to your employer. Under Education or Skills and Activities, you could include such information as:

- second or third languages you speak or write
- extensive travel
- certificates or licenses you hold
- memberships in professional associations
- memberships in community groups (Lions, Red Cross, Elks; list any offices you hold—recorder, secretary, fund drive chairperson)

Do not include a section called Personal or Hobbies and Interests; information of a personal nature can work against you.

References

You can inform readers of your résumé that you will provide references on request or that they may obtain a copy of your dossier (which contains reference letters) from your placement center; or you can list on your résumé the names, titles, e-mail and street addresses, and telephone numbers of no more than three or four individuals, as María Lopez did. Be sure to obtain their permission first. Prospective employers can then write to you, ask for your dossier, or directly write or call your references.

List your references only when they are well known in the community or belong to the same profession in which you are seeking employment—you profit from your association with a recognizable name or title.

In this section of your résumé, you may also indicate that a portfolio of your work is available for review, as Anthony Jones did in Figure 7.4.

Organizing Your Résumé by Chronology or by Function

There are two primary ways to organize your résumé: chronologically or by function or skill area.

Chronologically

The résumés in Figures 7.3 through 7.5 are organized chronologically. Information about the job applicants is listed year by year under two main categories, education and experience. This is the traditional way to organize a résumé. It is straightforward and easy to read, and employers find it acceptable. The chronological sequence works especially well when you can show a clear continuity toward progress in your career through your job(s) and in schoolwork or when you want to apply for a similar job with another company. A chronological résumé is appropriate for students with limited experience who want to emphasize recent educational achievements.

By Function or Skill Area

Depending on your experiences and accomplishments, you might organize your résumé according to function or skill areas. According to this plan, you would *not* list your information chronologically in the categories "Experience" and "Education." Instead, you would sort your achievements and abilities—whether from course work, jobs, extracurricular activities, or technical skills—into two to four key skill areas, such as "Sales," "Public Relations," "Training," "Management," "Research," "Technical Capabilities," "Counseling," "Group Leadership," "Communications," "Network Operations," "Customer Service," "Working with People," "Multicultural Experiences," "Computer Skills," "Problem-Solving Skills."

Under each area you would list three to five points illustrating your achievements in that area. Skills or functional résumés are often called **bullet résumés** because they itemize the candidate's main strengths in bulleted lists. Some employers prefer the bullet résumé because they can skim the candidate's list of qualifications in a few seconds.

The most important goal of a functional résumé is to highlight the strengths or skills in which you believe a prospective employer is most interested. Figure 7.6 shows what Anna Cassetti's chronological résumé (Figure 7.3) might look like if she had organized it according to function; Figure 7.7 shows Patrice Bolger's résumé organized by function. Note that the three functional areas Cassetti selected ("Sales/Financial Management," "Public Relations," and "Business Communication") effectively allow her to capitalize on her diverse experiences.

Who Should Use a Functional Résumé?

The following individuals would probably benefit from organizing their résumés by function instead of by chronology:

FIGURE 7.6   Anna Cassetti's résumé organized by function or skill areas.

ANNA C. CASSETTI

Home
6457 Blackstone Avenue
Fort Worth, TX 76321-6733
(817) 555-5657
acassetti@netdoor.com

Office
MacMurray Real Estate
1700 Ross Boulevard
Haltom City, TX 77320-1700
(817) 555-7211

CAREER OBJECTIVE

Full-time sales position with large real estate office in the Phoenix or Tucson areas with opportunities to use proven skills in real estate appraisal and tax counseling.

SALES/ FINANCIAL MANAGEMENT SKILLS

• Licensed (Texas) real estate appraiser with extensive knowledge of real estate codes, appraisal procedures, and market conditions
• Sold over 3 million dollars of residential property in 2 years
• Served as a tax consultant with special interest in real estate sales
• Performed general banking procedures as chief teller
• Responsible for maintaining, purchasing, and ordering supplies for ship's store in U.S. Navy

PUBLIC RELATIONS SKILLS

• Helped clients select appropriate property for their needs and income
• Counseled commercial and individual clients about taxes
• Supervised, trained, and coordinated the activities of six bank tellers
• Earned bonus for rapport in assisting customers with their banking needs
• Chaired a financial committee at Grace Presbyterian Church, Fort Worth, Texas

BUSINESS COMMUNICATION SKILLS

• Prepared standard real estate appraisals
• Wrote in-depth business reports on appraisal procedures, property management problems, and banking policies affecting real estate transactions
• Achieved proficiency in CorpSheet and other spreadsheet programs
• Conducted small group training and sales sessions

Continued

FIGURE 7.6   (Continued)

Cassetti 2

EDUCATION	B.S. in Real Estate Management, 2000 Texas Christian University, Fort Worth, Texas Advanced course work taken in business, finance, and real estate; minor in data processing
	Diploma, Basic Income Tax Preparation, 1994 H&R Block, Westover Hills, Texas
EMPLOYMENT HISTORY	MacMurray Real Estate, Haltom City, Texas 2001–present: sales agent
	Dallman Federal Savings and Loan, Inc., Fort Worth, Texas 1995–2000; Chief Teller
	H&R Block, Westover Hills, Texas 1994 Sept.–Dec.; consultant, tax preparer
	Cruckshank's Hardware Store, Fort Worth, Texas 1992–1994; salesperson
	U.S. Navy, San Diego, California (last duty station): 1988–1992; stores manager; honorably discharged with rank of Petty Officer, Third Class
REFERENCES	Complete dossier available from the Placement Office, Texas Christian University, Fort Worth, TX 76119-6811

- nontraditional students who have diverse job experiences
- individuals who are changing their profession because of downsizing or seeking new professional opportunities
- individuals who have changed jobs frequently over the last five to ten years
- individuals who are entering the civilian marketplace after retiring from the military

Preparing a Skills Résumé

When you prepare a functional or skills résumé, start with your name, address, telephone number, and career objective, just as in a chronological résumé. To find the best two or three functional areas to include, use the prewriting strategies (especially clustering and brainstorming) discussed in Chapter 2. Think of your skills areas as the common denominators that cross job and educational boundaries—the common threads that link your diverse experiences. Note how Donald Kitto-Klein (Figure 7.8) was able to pull together a series of related, marketable skills from the many different jobs he had held over several years.

FIGURE 7.7   Patrice Cooper Bolger's résumé organized by skill areas.

PATRICE COOPER BOLGER
1215 Lakeview Avenue
Westhampton, MI 46532
616-555-4772   pcbolger@aol.com

EMPLOYMENT OBJECTIVE   **Seek full-time position as public affairs officer in health care, educational, or charitable facility**

SKILLS, RESPONSIBILITIES, EXPERIENCES

Organizational Communication
- **Delivered** 20 presentations to neighborhood and civic groups on educational and civic issues
- **Recorded** minutes and helped formulate agenda as president for large, local PTA for last $6^{1}/_{2}$ years
- **Possess** excellent software skills in PeopleSoft and Microsoft Word
- **Updated** and **maintained** computerized mailing lists for Teens in Trouble and Foster Parents' Association

Money Management
- **Spearheaded 3 major fundraising drives** (total of $178,000 collected)
- **Prepared and implemented large family budget** (3 children, 8 foster children) for 15 years
- **Served as financial secretary**, Broad Street United Methodist Church for 4 years
- **Awarded "Volunteer of the Year"** (2000) by Michigan Foster Child Placement Agency for Budget Planning

Administration
- **Organized** volunteers for American Kidney Fund (last 5 years)
- **Established** and **oversaw** neighborhood carpool (17 drivers; more than 50 children) for 7 years
- **Coordinated** after-school tutoring program for Teens in Trouble; president since 1990

EDUCATION   A.A. Metropolitan Community College, 1994
B.S. Mid-Michigan College, expected 2002, major: public administration; minor: psychology. GPA 3.40

WORK EXPERIENCE   Secretary, 1983–1993 (full and part-time):
Merrymount Plastics; Foley and Wasson;
Westhampton Health Dept.; G & K Electric

REFERENCES   Available upon request

FIGURE 7.8   Functional résumé by a candidate who has held a variety of jobs.

DONALD KITTO-KLEIN
kitto@gar.com

56 South Ardmore Way
Petersburg, NY 15438
(716) 555-9032

Garland.Com
Grand Banks, NY 15532
(716) 555-4800, Ext. 5398

Objective

Seek supervisory position in Computer Maintenance and Service Department to provide excellent service to staff and clients.

Computer Languages

C, C+, C++, Java, Unix

Computer Programs

Microsoft Word, Quark Xpress, Lotus Notes

Systems Experience

MACHINES: IBM, RS60000, Macintosh, Sun
NETWORKS: Novell, Banyan; set up Internet sites

Computer Maintenance/ Service Skills

• Serviced PCs and workstations on a regular basis for $3\frac{1}{2}$ years
• Worked extensively on spreadsheets/database software
• Modified software billing program
• Coordinated maintenance/service activities

People Skills

• Supervised Computer Servicing with three technicians
• Worked closely with computer manufacturers and suppliers to minimize hardware down time
• Elected to employee benefits committee
• Promoted to first-shift Computer Services Manager

Communication Skills

• Collaboratively wrote safety manual for power company road crews
• Taught in-house training sessions on computer maintenance, networking, data security
• Devised routing systems to expedite work orders and follow-ups
• Coordinated small group meetings in systems analysis

Employment

Garland.Com Team Leader, Maintenance, 1998–present
Business Graphics and Computers Store, Salesperson, 1994–1998
U.S. Army, Specialist, 4/E 1989–1996

Education

B.S., Grand Valley Technical Institute, 1997
U.S. Army schools in computer programs, 1991–1995

References

Available on request.

After you discover and suitably revise the information to be included in your categories, briefly list your educational and work experiences, as Anna Cassetti (Figure 7.6), Patrice Cooper Bolger (Figure 7.7), and Donald Kitto-Klein (Figure 7.8) do.

Advantages of a Functional Résumé
A functional résumé has a number of advantages for some job seekers.

- It can offer a productive way to fill in gaps in education or employment, since a job seeker is not tied to a strict chronological account. If you were laid off, left school for several years, or moved around, you do not have to worry about accounting for the gaps in time.

    Note Patrice Cooper Bolger's profitable use of a functional résumé format in Figure 7.7. She was out of school for more than ten years because of family commitments, yet she uses the experiences she acquired during those years to her advantage in her résumé organized by "Skills, Responsibilities, Experiences." She successfully translates her many accomplishments in managing a home and working on charitable and community projects into marketable skills of great interest to a prospective employer, and no gap of ten years interrupts a work experience list.

- Because a functional résumé clearly emphasizes general skills acquired over long periods of time, individuals who have had many different types of jobs in diverse fields may prefer this format over a chronological résumé, as Donald Kitto-Klein does in Figure 7.8.

- Unlike a chronological résumé, a functional résumé does not force the job seeker to emphasize his or her most recent experience or educational achievement at the expense of more pertinent earlier accomplishments.

You might want to prepare two different versions of your résumé—one functional and one chronological—to see which sells your talents better. Don't hesitate to seek the advice of your instructor or placement counselor about which one works best for you.

The On-Line Résumé

With many jobs being advertised on-line, prospective employers want applications sent to their Web addresses. Consequently, job seekers can expect to apply for at least some positions on-line and will have to send their résumés by disk, e-mail, or other Internet channels. This is the way to secure the widest possible exposure to attract prospective employers. Numerous résumé databases services will post your résumé. Consider registering with one or more of the listservs found in the Tech Note on pages 260–261.

An on-line résumé contains essentially the same information found in the various types of résumés already discussed. Figure 7.9 is an on-line version of Anthony Jones's résumé (Figure 7.4). While the information is the same, the design is different. An on-line résumé is scannable so a prospective employer can read and possibly file it in the company's database. The more matches, or "hits," the employer finds between appropriate keywords on your résumé and the descriptors for the job

FIGURE 7.9   An On-Line Résumé.

≡ **RESUME OF ANTHONY H. JONES** ≡

Location: http://www.plat.com/users/ajones/resume.html

ANTHONY H. JONES
73 Allenwood Boulevard
Santa Rosa, California 95401-1074
(707) 555-6390
ajones@plat.com

OBJECTIVE
A position as layout and design editor with commercial publisher.

EDUCATION
Santa Rosa Junior College, A.S. degree to be awarded in May 2002.
Commercial Graphics Illustration major. Digital photography minor.
GPA 3.45

COMPUTER SKILLS
Excellent working knowledge of computer graphics: Illustrator,
Photoshop, QuarkXPress, WordPerfect Suite 8

EXPERIENCE
McAdam Publishers, 8 Parkway Heights, Santa Rosa, CA 94211:
Intern in layout and design department. Preparing page composition,
importing visuals, manipulating images.

Buchman's Department Store: Greenview Mall, Santa Rosa;
Salesperson; display merchandise coordinator.

Santa Rosa Humane Society: Volunteer; designing brochures and
other artwork for successful fund drive.

Thunder: Student magazine. Responsible for creating Web page,
major artwork, proofreading.

REFERENCES
Career Center, Santa Rosa Junior College;
ahjones1@santarosa.career.edu/~dossier

TECH NOTE

Developing Your Own Web Site for Your Job Search

The Internet is transforming the job search process. In addition to sending your résumé by e-mail, you can create your own Web site with your résumé, samples of your work, a cover letter, and perhaps scanned copies of awards you have received. Multimedia options allow you to add voice and pictures as well.

If you include your Web page address in your correspondence, prospective employers will be able to look at your qualifications quickly. Because your e-mail address will appear on your Web page, requests for additional information can be directed to you immediately.

Other advantages of having a résumé linked to your Web page are these.

- Prospective employers looking for computer-literate employees are impressed by résumés that include a Web URL.
- You can change and revise your résumé quickly and at no expense. Printed résumés can be expensive, and revisions only increase the cost.
- Remember that "job spam" does not make a favorable impression. Do not send unsolicited electronic résumés or Web pages to prospective employers. Apply for the job *before* you click the send button. Also, be prepared to send a hard copy of your résumé as well as an electronic copy.

The Internet is full of user-friendly places to find simple-to-use instructions for building a Web page; for instance, Web Letter's Guide to Publishing a Web Page (*http://www.writething.com/weblet1.html*) and Creating a Web Page: Do It Yourself (*http://www.cesa3.k12.wi.us/web-course.html*). See Chapter 11 for specific advice on designing a Web site.

---

opening, the greater your chances of being hired. On-line résumés can take many different formats. Note how Angela Burgess's résumé in Figure 7.10 differs from Anthony Jones's on-line version (Figure 7.9).

Using an On-Line Résumé

To compete successfully for jobs on-line, you will have to adapt the conventional résumé format for transmission as a hypertext document. Follow the nine guidelines below to prepare an effective on-line résumé; as you read these guidelines, refer to Figures 7.9 and 7.10.

1. **Format your résumé properly and consistently—as an ASCII text file—to be received and read around the globe.** That means preparing a document in plain text. Always follow the directions given by the résumé database service or the prospective employer.

TECH NOTE

Résumé Database Services

Don't worry if you cannot format your résumé in ASCII text. You might want to take advantage of one of the résumé database services that prepare and post on-line résumés in the proper format for a small fee. Not only will such a service format your résumé, it will classify your résumé according to your area(s) of expertise, making it easy for employers to find you. Below are the addresses of some of the most popular database and job listing services.

General Listings

These large services post job opportunities in a variety of fields and with many types of employers.

- **Riley Guide** (describes over fifty major job sites such as America's Job Bank, CareerPath, and JOBTRAK): *http://www.dbm.com/jobguide/multiple.html*
- **e span** (provides a job database, résumé service, and employer listings): *http://www.joboptions.com/esp/plsql/espan_enter.espan_home*
- **Online Career Center** (provides a searchable job database and online résumé services): *http://www.occ.com/*
- **The Best Résumés on the Net:** *http://tbrnet.com*
- **Résumé Net:** *http://www.resumenet.com*
- **At On-Line Résumés:** *http://ol-resume.com*
- **Virtual Résumé:** *http://virtualresume.com*

Specialized Services

- **Advertising and public relations**   American Academy of Advertising: *http://www.advertising.utexas.edu/AAA/*
- **Arts and arts administration**   ArtsEdge: *http://www.artsedge.kennedy-center.org/artsedge.html*
- **Agriculture**   *http://www.careers.eharvest.com*
- **Architecture jobs**   American Institute of Architects: *http://www.e-architect.com/career/jobs.htm*
- **Business**   BizWeb: *http://www.bizweb.com/*; *http://www.columbia.edu/cu/business/career/links/*
- **Accounting and finance**   *http://www.accountingjobs.com/*
- **Marketing**   *http://www.marketingjobs.com/jsearch.html*
- **Criminal justice**   *http://www.corrections.com/student*
- **Education**   Academic Employment Network: *http://www.academploy.com/*
- **Engineering and computer science**   Comrise Technology: *http://www.comrise.com/empl7.html*; Careers in Computer Science: *http://www.cs.oswego.edu/./careers.html*

- **Health care**
    Hospital Web: *http://neuro-www.mgh.harvard.edu/ hospitalweb.shtml*
    Medical/Health Care Job Openings (listings from hospitals and medical centers nationwide, primarily in the Midwest, maintained by NationJob): *http://www.nationjob.com/medical*
    MedSearch America (hundreds of current listings nationwide, including many entry-level positions): *http://www.medsearch.com/*
    Nurses World: *http://www.nursesworld.com/resume.htm*
- **Journalism**   H-Rhetor Job Guide: *http://www.h-net.msu.edu/ ~rhetor/jobguide2/*
- **Sports**   Online Sports Career Center: *http://www.onlinesports.com/pages/careercenter.html*

2. Make your résumé readable, functional, and easy to scroll. Use plenty of white space. If you are sending it as an e-mail, put no more than 65 characters on a line. Reading a résumé on a screen is different from seeing it on a printed page. Use a sans serif font (see pp. 440–445) and a type size of 10 to 14 points.

3. Do not use italics, bullets, underlining, boldfacing, fancy scripts, or logos. Such features interfere with the transmission of your résumé, garbling it when a prospective employer clicks on it. To emphasize, use full caps or an asterisk (*) or a plus sign (+) at the beginning of a line.

4. Test your formatting by sending your résumé to a friend's e-mail address.

5. Start with your on-line address to make it easy for employers to reach you. If you use a résumé database service, you could begin with that location and list your e-mail address as well. Angela Burgess gives readers both locations in her on-line résumé in Figure 7.10. For the subject line, list the prospective employer's job referral number (if any) or the position you are applying for.

6. Use hyperlinks at the top of the résumé to connect to key categories. Angela Burgess's hyperlinks are OBJECTIVE, HIGHLIGHTS, EMPLOYMENT HISTORY, HONORS, EDUCATION, COMMUNITY SERVICE, and REFERENCES. Highlighting those categories as headers makes it easy for a prospective employer to jump to the résumé section he or she deems most important. Keep in mind a prospective employer may be scrolling as many as 200 or 300 résumés a day to compile a short list of candidates to interview.

7. Use keywords as hyperlinks. The electronic résumé emphasizes nouns, whereas conventional résumés (see Figures 7.6 and 7.7) use strong verbs. Nouns function as the keywords by which a résumé is scanned by Web search engines and organized in a database; they reflect your specialized skills and experience. Prospective employers search the Web by keywords to find what they want to see in the job seeker's experience,

FIGURE 7.10   An on-line résumé.

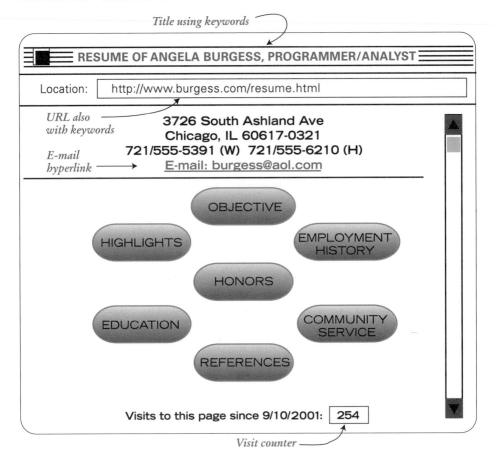

Title using keywords

═══ **RESUME OF ANGELA BURGESS, PROGRAMMER/ANALYST** ═══

Location: http://www.burgess.com/resume.html

URL also with keywords

E-mail hyperlink →

**3726 South Ashland Ave
Chicago, IL 60617-0321
721/555-5391 (W) 721/555-6210 (H)
E-mail: burgess@aol.com**

OBJECTIVE

HIGHLIGHTS

EMPLOYMENT HISTORY

HONORS

EDUCATION

COMMUNITY SERVICE

REFERENCES

Visits to this page since 9/10/2001:   254

Visit counter

Continued

education, or activities. Repeat several times in your résumé the two or three key nouns that most accurately reflect your accomplishments, as Angela Burgess (Figure 7.10) and Anthony Jones (Figure 7.9) do. In the following list, the on-line keywords on the right replace the action verbs from conventional résumés on the left.

Conventional Descriptions	On-Line Keywords
edited company newsletter	newsletter editor
wrote technical report	technical writer
performed laboratory tests	laboratory technologist
responsible for managing accounts	accounts manager
won two awards	award winner
solved software problems	software specialist

Don't be afraid of using shop talk (or jargon) for your keywords. An employer searching for a specialist will expect the résumé writer to be aware of current terminology, especially in computer programming or networking.

FIGURE 7.10   (Continued)

RESUME OF ANGELA BURGESS, PROGRAMMER/ANALYST

Location: http://www.burgess.com/resume.html

OBJECTIVE
To find position as a Programmer/Analyst to demonstrate my extensive and innovative skills in Programming Techniques, Languages, Networking, Internet Navigation, Desktop Publishing, Team Management, and Technical/Business Writing.

HIGHLIGHTS
- Highly experienced programmer/analyst
- Knowledgeable about state-of-the-art software and hardware
- Excellent communication skills
- Programmer consultant for many team projects
- Goal-directed, self-motivated

EMPLOYMENT HISTORY
2000–present   Programmer Analyst
Conrad Industries
Palatine, IL 60312

Programmer of variety of developmental languages; chief consultant for document design; policy creator/navigator of Internet Website (conradind@com); technical report writer; Programmer/Manager of new Manufacturing Execution System; developer of UNIX scripts

1997–2000   Computer Specialist
Computer Systems, Inc.
Chicago, IL 60638

Member of programming staff; assistant manager of service-delivery system for improved customer service

Visits to this page since 9/10/2001: 254

Continued

8. **Keep your on-line résumé to two or at the most three screens.** Avoid inflating your accomplishments with unnecessary details or boasts. Consider, too, that a prospective employer may have little time and patience to scroll down two or three screens to find information quickly. Moreover, downloading and printing multiple pages makes the employer's job harder and does not help your chances.

9. **Send a hard copy of your résumé and a cover letter to a prospective employer.** Simply posting your résumé on-line is not enough. When you send your hard-copy résumé, do not fold it. Put it, along with your cover letter, in a large envelope to make it easier for an employer to scan and file.

The Appearance of Your Résumé

The appearance of your résumé is as important as its content. If your résumé looks professional, employers will predict that the work you do for them will be done the same way. A résumé can make that good first impression for you; a poorly prepared one ensures that you will not get a second chance.

There are a variety of ways you can prepare your résumé.

FIGURE 7.10   (Continued)

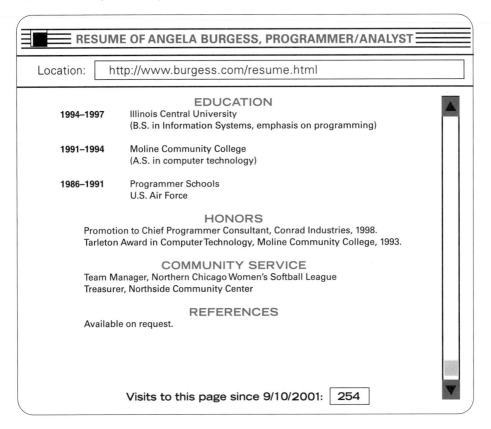

- You can put it on computer disk, as Anthony Jones and María Lopez did in Figures 7.4 and 7.5.
- You can use desktop publishing software, as Patrice Cooper Bolger and Donald Kitto-Klein did in Figures 7.7 and 7.8.
- You can have a printer typeset your résumé, as Anna Cassetti did (Figure 7.3 and 7.6).
- You can prepare it electronically, as Anthony Jones and Angela Burgess did in Figures 7.9 and 7.10.

Keep in mind that if an outside service typesets your résumé, there is no way you can tailor it. You cannot add, delete, or emphasize information as your job search progresses without having the résumé redone.

Regardless of the method you use, follow these guidelines:

1. Spacing. Avoid the twin dangers of crowding too much information on the page or of leaving huge, highly conspicuous chunks of white space at the bottom and sides. A crowded résumé suggests that you cannot summarize; too much blank space points to a lack of achievements. Leave plenty of white space between categories to emphasize certain points and to make reading your résumé easier. Study

TECH NOTE

Privacy and On-Line Résumés: Some Precautions

The Internet is a public medium. Keep in mind that your current employer can access your electronic résumé as easily as any prospective employer can. Moreover, there is some information in your job application materials that you should not make available to anyone other than a prospective employer.

If you are considering putting your résumé on-line either with a service or on your own Web site, you may want to take these precautions to protect your privacy.

- Many résumé posting services guarantee that your personal information will not be disclosed on the Internet. Resurom, for example, gives every job candidate a personal identification number and makes only that number and an abstract of your qualifications available to interested employers. You must approve the release of your full résumé. (Resurom will also create a professional résumé for you and provide periodical updates.)
- Limit the information available on your Web page to an abstract of your qualifications; then e-mail copies of your résumé only to prospective employers that meet your own criteria.
- If you do not want to give out your home address, use a P.O. box number and have voice mail to receive messages.

the sample résumés in this chapter again. Print a number of versions of your résumé to experiment with spacing.

2. Type. With your PC, take advantage of different type sizes and use boldface or italics to separate and highlight information. Help employers spot your achievements by using clearly divided sections with headings in boldface type. Don't make the print size so small that it is difficult for a prospective employer to read. Stay as close to 10-point type as possible. Be careful that you do not overuse visual effects. You can also justify your margins (that is, make the right side of your résumé line up just as the left side does).

3. Proofreading. Make sure your résumé is letter-perfect. Prospective employers will be looking for accuracy (a spelling mistake can be ruinous) and consistency. Double-check the spelling of any words or names about which you are unsure. Ask two or three people to check your document for you, too. Because you will be supplying many prospective employers with your résumé, a single error is multiplied by the number of times you send it out or the number of people who see it.

4. Paper. Print your résumé on good quality $8\frac{1}{2}$" × 11" white or off-white bond paper (at least 20-pound stock). In fact, recruiters in one study preferred white to colored paper. Never use flimsy computer paper with perforated strips. Do not print your résumé on a dot matrix printer; for best results, use a laser printer with dark type.

TECH NOTE

Visits Counter

Each Web site contains a "visits counter," which records the number of times Web users have visited a particular site, functioning much as caller ID does on a telephone line. A visits counter is especially helpful for job seekers because it alerts them to the amount of traffic—and potential interest—their résumé is generating. The way to increase the number of visits your Web site receives is to include key words and phrases as hyperlinks so prospective employers will be directed to your résumé a maximum number of times. The more visits your on-line résumé receives, the better your chances of getting an interview and eventually a job.

5. Copies. Your prospective employer will expect a professional-looking original of your résumé, so never send a poor copy. Make sure your printer works well. Avoid rushing to the nearest photocopy machine in the library or student union to make copies. You may end up with a résumé peppered with black dots or smudgy streaks.

Writing a Letter of Application

Along with your résumé, you must send your prospective employer a letter of application, one of the most important pieces of correspondence you may ever write. Its goal is to get you an interview and ultimately the job. Letters you write in applying for jobs should be personable, professional, and persuasive—the three P's. Knowing how the letter of application and résumé work together and how they differ can give you a better idea of how to compose your letter.

How Application Letters and Résumés Differ

The résumé is a compilation of facts—a record of dates, your important achievements, names, places, addresses, and jobs. You will have your résumé duplicated, and you will send a copy to each prospective employer. As we saw, you may even prepare two or three different résumés depending on your experiences and the job market.

Your letter of application, however, is much more personal. Because you must write a new, original letter to each prospective employer, you might write (or adapt) many different letters. Photocopied letters of application say that you do not care enough to spend the time and energy to answer the employer's help wanted ad personally.

Each letter of application should be tailored to a specific job. It should respond precisely to the kinds of qualifications the employer seeks. The letter of application is a sales letter that emphasizes and applies the most relevant details (of education, experience, and talents) in your résumé. In short, the résumé contains the raw material that the letter of application transforms into a finished and highly marketable product—you.

Résumé Facts to Exclude from Your Letter of Application

The letter of application should not simply repeat the details listed in your résumé. In fact, the following details are relevant information you list in your résumé and should *not* be restated in the letter.

- personal data, including license or certificate numbers
- specific names of courses in your major
- names and addresses of all your references

Duplicating those details in your letter gives no new information that might persuade prospective employers that you are the individual they are seeking.

Finding Information About Your Prospective Employer

One of the best ways to sell yourself to future employers is to demonstrate that you have some knowledge of their company. Recently, a software firm was looking for a computer analyst and was impressed with one candidate who referred to the company's specific products by name in her letter of application. This individual went to the profitable trouble of reading the company's Web site before applying for the job.

Do a little similar homework; investigate the job and the company. It is to your advantage to find out as much as possible about a prospective employer. Some things you need to find out include whether the company is privately or publicly owned; what its chief products or services are; whether it has subsidiaries or is a subsidiary of a larger company in the United States or overseas; who its chief officers are.

There are many ways to find out about a prospective employer.

1. Check your prospective employer's Web site. Figure 7.11 shows the first screen of the Web site for TRW, a large research and manufacturing company. Note the valuable options a job seeker can explore, including TRW News, Company Profile, and Careers.

2. In addition to consulting a company's Web site, look at the following directories, all of which contain useful information about businesses you may be applying to.

- *Million Dollar Directory* and *Principal International Businesses* are both published by Dun and Bradstreet. They do not have separate Internet addresses. Information on both can be found at the Dun and Bradstreet Web site (*http://www.dbisna.com*).
- *Directory of Corporate Affiliations* does not have its own address either, but you can find information on the Knight Ridder Information, Inc. Web site (*http://www.krinfo.com*).
- *Standard & Poor's Register of Corporations, Directors and Executives* does not have an individual address, but you can find information at the McGraw-Hill

FIGURE 7.11   A company's Web site with information about jobs and company products and services.

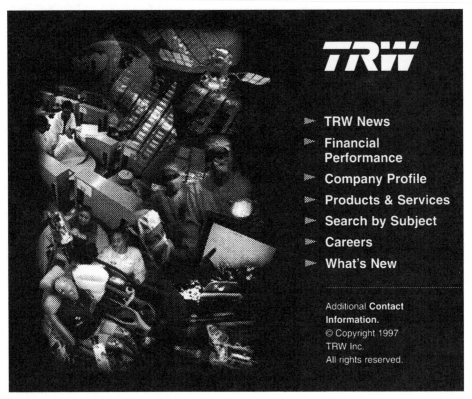

Continued

Web site (S&P is a division of McGraw-Hill) and the Standard & Poor's Compustat page (*http://www.mcgraw-hill.com* and *http://www.compustat.com*).

3. Consult such useful sources and databases as these:

- *The Executive Desk Register of Publicly Held Corporations* provides information on 6,700 U.S. corporations and financial institutions.
- *The Thomas Register of Manufacturers* (*http://thomas-register.com/*) offers background information on 150,000 U.S. companies.
- *Hoover's Handbook On-Line* (*http://www.hoovers.com/*) claims to be "the ultimate source for company information."
- the Annual Directory in the May issue of *Forbes* as well as issues of *Fortune*.

4. Obtain information from companies directly by writing an inquiry letter or e-mail requesting brochures, newsletters, company magazines, and annual reports

FIGURE 7.11   (Continued)

Company Profile

- What is TRW?
- Facts about TRW
- Financial Goal
- Mission and Values Statement
- Industry Segments
  TRW Inc. provides high-technology products and services to the automotive and
  space & defense markets. The financial results of the company's operations are reported
  in two core business segments: Automotive and Space & Defense.
  o **Automotive**
    TRW designs, manufactures, and sells five automotive product lines for cars, trucks,
    buses, and off-highway vehicles **steering and suspension systems**, **engine
    components**, **occupant restraints**, **electrical and electronics**, and fasteners. These
    products are distributed directly to vehicle makers and through independent distributors.
  o **Space & Defense**
    Space & Defense consists of **space & electronic systems** and **systems integration**.
  o **Other Businesses**
- **History**
- **Community Relations**
- **TRW Global Locations**

TRW Home Page   Search   Contacts
Additional Contact Information © Copyright 1996 TRW Inc. All rights reserved.

Continued

several months before you actually apply. Current employees of a company are also an invaluable source of information for you in your job search.

Drafting the Letter of Application

The letter of application can make the difference between getting an interview and being eliminated early from the competition. Keep in mind that employers receive many letters and that you will have to compete for attention. You want your letter to be placed in the "definitely interview" category.

The best application letters are (a) professional, (b) readable, and (c) to the point. Limit your letters to one page. As you prepare your letter, follow these general guidelines:

1. Follow the standard conventions of letter writing discussed in Chapter 5. Print your letter on good-quality, $8\frac{1}{2}$" × 11" paper. Make sure your printer works perfectly; the print should be dark and distinct. Proofread meticulously; a spelling error will harm your chances. Never send a photocopy. Your letter to prospective employers is a reflection of you and what you think of them.

FIGURE 7.11   (Continued)

For more information, contact:

TRW Communications
1900 Richmond Road
Cleveland, Ohio 44124

| TRW Home Page | | Search |

Additional Contact Information © Copyright 1996 TRW Inc. All rights reserved.

2. Make sure your letter looks attractive. Use wide margins and don't crowd your page.

3. Send your letter to a specific person. Never address an application letter "To Whom It May Concern," "Dear Sir or Madam," or "Director of Human Resources." Try to get an individual's name; double-check the company's Web site; if you cannot find the human resources director there, try calling the company's switchboard and then verify the spelling of the person's name and his or her title.

4. Don't forget the "you attitude" discussed on pages 162–167. Approach your qualifications in terms of how and why they are valuable to a particular employer. Convince readers that you will be a valuable addition to their organization. You will need to make appropriate changes in details and emphasis from one letter to another so as to focus on each reader's needs.

Remember that employers are not impressed by vain boasts ("I am the most efficient and effective safety engineer"). One applicant spent so much time on the advantages he would get from the job that he forgot the employer entirely: "I have worked with this kind of equipment before, and this experience will give me the edge in running it. Moreover, I can adjust more quickly to my working environment."

5. Strive for brevity and clarity. Summarize your qualifications convincingly without being long-winded. But don't write telegraphic messages in two or three sentences. Stay away from abbreviations ("nite" for "night," "thru" for "through"). Avoid slang and legalese. (See pp. 167–169.)

6. Don't be tempted to send out your first draft. Remind yourself to be thorough in following the steps of the writing process. A first or even second draft rarely sells your abilities as well as a third, fourth, or even fifth revision does. Write and rewrite your letter of application until you are convinced it presents you in the best possible light. Your job may depend on it.

The discussion that follows will give you some suggestions on how to prepare the various parts of an application letter successfully.

Your Opening Paragraph. The first paragraph of your application letter is your introduction. It must get your reader's attention by answering three questions:

1. Why are you writing?
2. Where or how did you learn of the company or the job?
3. What is your most important qualification for the job?

Begin your letter by stating directly that you are writing to apply for a job. Don't say that you "want to apply for the job"; such an opening raises the question, "Why don't you, then?" And don't waste the employer's time and your space on the page repeating verbatim the words of the advertisement.

Avoid an unconventional or arrogant opening: "Are you looking for a dynamic, young, and talented photographer?" Do not begin with a question; be more positive and professional.

If you learned of the job through a newspaper or journal, make sure you italicize or underscore the title.

> I am applying for the food-service manager position you advertised in the May 10 edition of the *Los Angeles Times* on the Internet.

Since many companies announce positions on the Internet, you need to check the Net to see if their position is listed on-line, as Anthony Jones in Figure 7.12 (p. 272) and Donald Kitto-Klein in Figure 7.13 (p. 273) did. As one job counselor observed, a candidate who can use the Net readily, can probably do many other related tasks as well.

If you learned of the job from a professor, friend, or employee at the firm, state that fact. Take advantage of a personal contact who is confident you are qualified for the position, as María Lopez in Figure 7.14 (p. 275) and Patrice Cooper Bolger in Figure 7.15 (p. 276) do. But first confirm that your contact gives you permission to use his or her name.

The Body of Your Letter

This section of your letter, comprising one or two paragraphs, provides the evidence based on information from your résumé to show you are qualified for the job.

Follow these guidelines for the body of your letter.

1. **Keep your paragraphs short and readable—four or five sentences.** Avoid long, complex sentences. Use the active voice to emphasize yourself as a doer.
2. **Don't begin each sentence with "I."** Vary your sentence structure.
3. **Concentrate on seeing yourself as your employer sees you.** Focus on how your education and experience can meet the employer's needs, as Anthony Jones does by citing Megalith publications as models he followed (Figure 7.12), or as Patrice Cooper Bolger does in framing her public speaking abilities as an asset to the Tanselle Agency (Figure 7.15).
4. **Highlight your qualifications by citing specific accomplishments.** Don't simply state what you have done. Tell your reader exactly how your schoolwork and job experience qualify you to function and advance in the job advertised. Here your homework on the company's history, goals, and structure will pay

FIGURE 7.12   Letter of application from Anthony Jones, a recent graduate with little job experience.

May 23, 2002

Ms. Jocelyn Nogasaki
Human Resources Manager
Megalith Publishing Company
1001 Heathcliff Row
San Francisco, CA 94123-7707

Dear Ms. Nogasaki:

I am applying for the layout editor position advertised on your Web site I accessed on 14 May. Early next month, I will receive an A.S. degree in commercial graphics illustration from Santa Rosa Junior College.

With a special interest in the publishing industry, I have successfully completed more than forty credit hours in courses directly related to layout design, where I acquired experience using QuarkXPress as well as Illustrator and Photoshop. You might like to know that many of the design patterns of Megalith publications were used as models in my graphic communications and digital photography classes.

My studies have also led to practical experience at McAdam Publishers as part of my Santa Rosa apprenticeship program. While working at McAdam, I was responsible for assisting the design department in page composition and importing images. Other related experience I have had includes creating a Web site for and proofreading the student magazine, *Thunder*. As you will note on the enclosed résumé, I have also had experience in displaying merchandise at Buchman's Department Store.

I would appreciate the opportunity to discuss with you my qualifications in commercial graphics. After June 12, I will be available for an interview at any time that is convenient for you.

Sincerely yours,

Anthony H. Jones

Anthony H. Jones
Encl. Résumé

73 Allenwood Boulevard · Santa Rosa, CA 95401-1074
phone: (707) 555-6390 · email: ajones@platt.com

FIGURE 7.13   Letter of application from Donald Kitto-Klein, who has strong work experience.

Donald Kitto-Klein
56 South Ardmore Way
Petersburg, NY 15438
(716) 555-9032   kitto@gar.com

November 4, 2001

Ms. Akki Shibuto
Vice President, Operations
Patterson Corporation
Sun Valley, CA 94356

Dear Ms. Shibuto:

I am applying for the position of Director of Computer Services advertised on your Web site last week. My knowledge of computers and my proven ability to work with people in a large organization such as Patterson's qualify me to be a productive member of your management team.

For the last three years, I have been responsible for all phases of computer maintenance and service at Garland.Com. As a regular part of my duties I have serviced and repaired 15 to 20 PCs a month as well as supervised a mainframe. I have successfully coordinated the activities of my department with Garland's other offices and worked closely with vendors and manufacturers. The training programs and in-house conferences I have conducted repeatedly receive high praise from Garland's management. Because I have worked so effectively with management and staff, I was promoted to repair team leader.

My educational achievements include a degree in computer technology from Grand Valley and certificates from U.S. Army schools in computers. The enclosed résumé will give you information about these and my other accomplishments.

I would like to put my ability to motivate personnel and to manage computer services to work for you and Patterson Corporation. I am available for an interview at your convenience. I look forward to hearing from you.

Sincerely yours,

Donald Kitto-Klein

Donald Kitto-Klein

Encl. Résumé

off. Note how María Lopez uses her knowledge of Dr. Henrady's speciality in pedodontics to her advantage (Figure 7.14).

Education. You might want to spend one paragraph on your educational qualifications and one on your job experience. Perhaps your work or civic and community experiences are so rich that you will spend an entire paragraph on them, as Patrice Cooper Bolger does. At any rate, do not neglect education for experience or vice versa. Refer to your résumé, and do not forget to say that you are including it with your letter.

Recent graduates with little work experience will, of course, spend more time on their education, but even if you have much experience, don't forget to mention your education. Stress your most important educational accomplishments. Employers want to know what skills and expertise your education has given you and how those skills apply to their particular job.

For instance, simply saying that you will graduate with a degree in criminal justice does not explain how you, unlike all the other graduates of all the other criminal justice programs, are best qualified for the job. But when you indicate that in thirty-six hours of course work you have specialized in software security and that you have twelve course hours in business and communications, that says something specific. Rather than just claiming that you are qualified, give the facts to prove it.

If your GPA is relatively high or if you have won an award, mention it. Do not worry about repeating such important information in both your letter and your résumé.

Job Experience. After you discuss your educational qualifications, turn to your job experience. But if your experience is your most valuable and extensive qualification for the job, put it before a discussion of your education. If you are switching careers or are returning to a career after years away from the work force, start the body of your letter with your work experiences. Then mention your specific educational achievements. The best letters show how the two are related. Employers like to see continuity between a candidates's school and job experience.

Provide that link by showing how the jobs you have held have something in common with your major—in terms of responsibility, research, customer relations, community service. Show how your course work in computer science helped you to be a more efficient programmer for your previous employer or how your summer jobs for the local park district reinforced your skills in providing client services. Do not, however, dwell on being a nurse's aide three years ago when you have nearly completed a degree program to be a registered nurse. Busing tables in a restaurant last summer was good experience, but do not let that job overshadow your current work as a management trainee for a large hotel chain.

Your Closing Paragraph. Make your closing paragraph short—about two or three sentences—but be sure it fulfills three important functions.

1. Emphasize once again your major qualifications.
2. Ask for an interview or a phone call.
3. Indicate when you are available for an interview.

FIGURE 7.14   Letter of application from María Lopez, a recent graduate with some job experience.

1725 Brooke Street
Miami, FL 32701-2121
mlopez@eagle.com

May 14, 2002

Dr. Marvin Henrady
Suite 34
Medical/Dental Plaza
839 Causeway Drive
Miami, FL 32706-2468

Dear Dr. Henrady:

Mr. Mitchell Pelbourne, my clinical instructor at Miami-Dade Community College, informs me that you are looking for a dental hygienist to work in your northside office. I am writing to apply for that position. This month I will graduate with an A.S. degree in the dental hygienist program at Miami-Dade Community College, and I will take the American Dental Assistants' Examination in early June.

I have successfully completed all course work and clinical programs in oral hygiene, anatomy, and prophylaxis techniques. During my clinical training, I received intensive practical instruction from a number of local dentists, including Dr. Tia Gutierrez. Since your northside office specializes in pedodontal care, you might find the subject of my major project—proper nutrition for pre-schoolers—especially relevant.

I have also had some related job experience in working with children in a health care setting. For a year and a half, I was employed as a unit clerk on the pediatric unit at St. Francis Hospital, and my experience in greeting patients, transcribing orders, and assisting the nursing staff would be valuable to you in running your office. You will find more detailed information about me and my experience in the enclosed résumé.

I would welcome the opportunity to talk with you about the position and my interest in pedodontics. I am available for an interview any time after 2:30 until June 11. After that date, I could come to your office any time at your convenience.

Sincerely yours,

María H. Lopez

María H. Lopez

Encl. Résumé

FIGURE 7.15   Letter of application from Patrice Cooper Bolger, a recent graduate with community and civic experience.

Patrice Cooper Bolger
1215 Lakeview Avenue
Westhampton, MI 46532
616-555-4772   pcbolger@aol.com

February 10, 2001

Dr. Lindsay Bafaloukos
Tanselle Mental Health Agency
4400 West Gallagher Drive
Tanselle, MI 46932-3106

Dear Dr. Bafaloukos:

At a recent meeting of the County Services Council, a member of your staff, Homer Strickland, informed me that you will be hiring a public affairs coordinator. Because of my extensive experience and commitment to community affairs, I would appreciate your considering me for this opening. I expect to receive my B.S. in Public Administration from Mid-Michigan College next year.

For the last ten years, I have organized community groups with outreach programs similar to Tanselle's. I have held administrative positions in the PTA and the Foster Parents' Association and was president of Teens in Trouble, a volunteer group providing assistance to dysfunctional teens. My responsibilities with Teens have included coordinating our activities with various school programs, scheduling tutorials, and representing the organization before government agencies. I have been commended for my organizational and communication skills. My twenty presentations on foster home care and Teens in Trouble demonstrate that I am an effective speaker, a skill your agency would find valuable.

Because of my work at Mid-Michigan and in Teens and Foster Parents, I have the practical experience in communication and psychology to promote Tanselle's goals. The enclosed résumé provides details of my experience and education.

I would enjoy discussing my work with Teens and the other organizations with you. I am available for an interview any day after 11:00 a.m. Thank you for reaching me at the phone number or e-mail address at the top of this letter.

Sincerely yours,

Patrice Cooper Bolger

Patrice Cooper Bolger

Encl. Résumé

End gracefully and professionally. Don't leave the reader with a single weak, vague sentence: "I would like to have an interview at your convenience." That does nothing to sell you. Say that you would appreciate talking with the employer further to discuss your qualifications. If the employer's office is far from your city, you might ask for a phone call instead. Then mention your chief talent. You might also express your willingness to relocate if the job required it.

After indicating your interest in the job, give the times you are available for an interview and tell specifically where you can be reached. You might even repeat your phone number or e-mail address. If you are going to a professional meeting that the employer might also attend, or if you are visiting the employer's city soon, say so.

The following samples show how *not* to close your letter and why not.

Pushy:	I would like to set up an interview with you. Please phone me to arrange a convenient time. (That's the employer's prerogative, not yours.)
Too Informal:	I do not live far from your office. Let's meet for coffee sometime next week. (Say instead that since you live nearby, you will be available for an interview.)
Too Humble:	I know that you are busy, but I would really like to have an interview. (Say you would like to discuss your qualifications further.)
Introduces New Subject:	I would like to discuss other qualifications you have in mind for the job. (How do you know what the interviewer might have in mind?)

Note that the closing paragraphs in Figures 7.12 through 7.15 avoid those errors.

Filling Out a Job Application

At some point in your job search, you will be asked to complete a prospective employer's application form. A recruiter may hand you a job application form at a campus interview, or you may be e-mailed a form in response to your letter of application. Most often, though, you will be given an application to complete when you are at the employer's office. The job application form, your letter of application, and your résumé are the three key written documents employers use to screen applicants.

Application forms can vary tremendously. But they all ask you to give information about your education, any military service, present and previous employment, references, general state of health, and reasons for wanting to work for the company or agency. Because the topics will overlap with those on your résumé, bring the résumé with you to the employer's office to make sure you don't omit something important. Some forms even require you to attach your résumé. But *under no circumstances* should you attach a résumé to a blank form instead of filling the form out. Employers want their own forms completed by job seekers.

Some forms ask applicants to give reasons for leaving previous jobs and also require them to write a "personal essay" stating why the company should hire them. Both requirements will require tact and thought. If you were fired from a past job, it is not to your advantage to simply state that fact. Indicate further relevant information, such as that your company was downsized and you were laid off, or that your company merged and your department was eliminated. More frequently, though, your reasons for leaving a job will be financial, educational, or geographic. You may have received a better offer, decided to return to school, or relocated.

Going to an Interview

An interview can be challenging, threatening, friendly, or chatty; sometimes it is all of those. By the time you arrive at the interview stage, you are far along in your job search. Basically, there are two kinds of interviews. One is a *screening interview,* to which numerous applicants have been invited so a company can narrow down the candidates. Campus interviews are an example of screening interviews. The other kind of interview is known as a *line interview;* the employer invites only a few select applicants to the company's office for a tour and detailed conversation.

Preparing for an Interview

Interviews can last half an hour or extend to two or three days. Most often, though, an interview will last approximately one hour. It has been estimated that the applicant will do about 80 to 90 percent of the talking. Since you will be asked to speak at length, make the following preparations before your interview.

1. Do your homework about the employer—history, types of products or services provided, number of employees, location of main, branch, and overseas offices, contributions to industry or the community. Consult such relevant sources as those listed on pages 267–268 as well as the company's Web site.
2. Review the technical skills most relevant for the job. You might want to do some focused Web searching, reread sections of a textbook, study some recent journal articles, or talk to a professor or an employee you know from the company.
3. Prepare a brief (one- or two-minute) review of your qualifications to deliver orally should you be asked about yourself.
4. Be able to elaborate on and supplement what is on your résumé. Your interviewer will have a copy on the desk, so you can be sure that its contents will be the subject of many questions. Any extra details or information that bring your résumé up to date ("I received my degree last week"; "I'll get the results of my state board examinations in one week") will be appreciated.

Questions to Expect at an Interview

You can expect questions about your education, job experience, and ambitions. An interviewer will also ask you about courses, schools, technical skills, and job goals.

Through these questions an interviewer attempts to discover your good points as well as your bad ones. A common interviewer strategy is to postpone questions about your bad points until near the end of the interview. Once a relaxed atmosphere has been established, the interviewer thinks that you may be less reluctant to talk about your weaknesses. The following questions are typical of those you can expect from interviewers, with advice on how to answer them.

- Tell us something about yourself. (Here's where the prepared one-minute oral presentation of yourself comes in handy.)
- Why do you want to work for us? (Recall any job goals you have and apply them specifically to the job under discussion.)
- What qualifications do you have for the job? (Mention educational achievements in addition to relevant work experience, especially computer skills.)
- What could you possibly offer us that other candidates do not have? (Say "enthusiasm," being a team player, and problem-solving abilities in addition to educational achievements.)
- Why did you attend this school? (Be honest—location, costs, programs.)
- Why did you major in "X"? (Do not simply say financial benefits; concentrate on both practical and professional benefits. Be able to state career objectives.)
- Why did you get a grade of "C" in a course? (Do not hurt your chances of being hired by saying that you could have done better if you tried; that response shows a lack of motivation most employers find unacceptable. Explain what the trouble was and mention that you corrected it in a course in which you earned a B or an A.)
- What extracurricular activities did you participate in while in high school or college? (Indicate any duties or responsibilities you had—handling money, writing memos, coordinating events; if you were not able to participate in such activities, tell the interviewer that a part-time job, community or church activities, or commuting a long way to school each day prevented your participating. Such answers sound better than saying that you did not like sports, activities, or clubs in school.)
- Did you learn as much as you wanted from your course work? (This is a loaded question. Indicate that you learned a great deal but now look forward to the opportunity to gain more practical skill, to put into practice the principles you have learned; say that you will never be through learning about your major.)
- Why was your summer job important? (Highlight skills you learned, people you helped, employers you pleased.)
- What is your greatest strength? (Being a team player, cooperation, willingness to learn, ability to grasp difficult concepts easily, managing time or money, taking criticism easily, and profiting from criticism are all appropriate answers.)
- What is your greatest shortcoming? (Be honest here and mention it, but then turn to ways in which you are improving. You obviously don't want to say something deadly like, "I can never seem to finish what I start" or "I hate

being criticized." You should neither dwell on your weaknesses nor keep silent about them. Saying "None" to this kind of question is as inadvisable as rattling off a list of faults.)

- How do you handle conflict with a co-worker, boss, customer? (Stress your ability to be courteous and honest and to work toward a productive resolution. State that you avoid language, tone of voice, or gestures that interfere with healthy dialogue.
- Describe your strengths and weaknesses as a communicator. (Point to a report or paper for which you received praise from a teacher or employer and then emphasize your abilities as a speaker or how careful you have been in explaining a product or service to a customer or co-worker. Indicate your willingness to be an even more effective writer and presenter through taking another writing course, participating in a relevant chat room, attending seminars on communicating more clearly.)
- How much did you earn at your last job, and what salary would you expect from us? (Some job counselors wrongly advise interviewees to lie about their past salaries in order to get a larger one from the future employer. But if the prospective employer checks your last salary and finds that you have lied, you lose. It is better to round off your last salary to the nearest thousand.)
- Why did you leave your last job? (Usually you will have educational reasons: "I returned to school full-time" or geographical reasons: "I moved from Jackson to Springfield." *Never attack your previous employer.* That only makes you look bad.)
- Is there anything else you want to discuss? (Here is your opportunity to end the interview with more information about yourself. You might take time to reiterate your strengths, to correct an earlier answer, or to express your desire to work for the company.)

Of course, you will have a chance throughout the interview to ask questions, too. Do not forget important points about the job: responsibilities, opportunities for further training, security, and chances for promotion. You will also want to ask about salary (but do not dwell on it), fringe benefits, schedules, vacations, and bonuses. If you spend time on these subjects, especially during the first part of the interview, you tell the interviewer that you are more interested in the rewards of the job than in the duties and challenges it offers. Do not go to the interview with dollar signs flashing in your eyes.

There are some questions an interviewer may not legally ask you. Questions about your age, marital status, ethnic background, race, or any physical disabilities violate equal opportunity employment laws. Even so, some employers may disguise their interest in those subjects by asking you indirect questions about them. A question such as "Will your husband care if you have to work overtime?" or "How many children do you have?" could probe into your personal life. Confronted with such questions, it is best to answer them positively ("My home life will not interfere with my job," "My family understands that overtime may be required") rather than bristling defensively, "It's none of your business if I have a husband."

Interview Dos and Don'ts

Keep in mind some other interview "dos" and "don'ts."

1. Be on time. If you are unavoidably delayed, telephone to apologize and set up another interview.
2. Go to the interview alone.
3. Dress appropriately for the occasion.
4. Speak slowly and distinctly; do not nervously hurry to finish your sentences, and never interrupt or finish an interviewer's sentences.
5. Do not smoke, even if the interviewer offers you a cigarette. Also refrain from chewing gum, fidgeting, or tapping your foot against the floor or a chair.
6. Maintain eye contact with the interviewer; do not sheepishly stare at the floor or the desk. Body language is equally important. For instance, don't fold your arms—that's a signal indicating you are closed to the interviewer's suggestions and comments.
7. One last point: When the interview is over, thank the interviewer for considering you for the job.

The Follow-up Letter

Within a week after the interview, it is wise to send a follow-up letter thanking the interviewer for his or her time and interest in you. The letter will keep your name fresh in the interviewer's mind. Do not forget that this individual interviewed other candidates, too—some of them probably on the same day as you.

In your follow-up letter, you can reemphasize your qualifications for the job by showing how they apply to conditions described by the interviewer; you might also ask for further information to show your interest in the job and the employer. You could even refer to a detail, such as a tour or film that was part of the interview. A sample follow-up letter appears in Figure 7.16.

Accepting or Declining a Job Offer

Even if you have verbally agreed to take a job, you still have to respond formally in writing. Your letter will make your acceptance official and will probably be included in your permanent personnel file. Accepting a job is easy. Make the communication with your new employer a model of clarity and diplomacy. Respond to the offer as soon as possible (certainly within two weeks). Often a time limit is specified.

A sample acceptance letter appears in Figure 7.17. In the first sentence tell the employer that you are accepting the job and refer to the date of the letter offering you the position. Indicate when you can begin working. Then mention any pleasant associations from your interview or any specific challenges you are anticipating. That should take no more than a paragraph.

In a second paragraph express your plans to fulfill any further requirements for the job—going to the human resources office, taking a physical examination, having

FIGURE 7.16   A follow-up letter.

2739 EAST STREET
LATROBE, PA 17042-0312
610-555-6377

September 20, 2001

Mr. Jack Fukurai
Manager of Human Resources
Transatlantic Steel Company
1334 Ridge Road N.E.
Pittsburgh, PA 17122-3107

Dear Mr. Fukurai:

I enjoyed talking with you last Wednesday and learning more about
the security officer position available at Transatlantic Steel. It was
especially helpful to take a tour of the plant's north gate section to
see the challenges it presents for the security officer stationed there.

As you noted at my interview, my training in surveillance electronics
has prepared me to operate the sophisticated equipment Transatlantic
has installed at the north gate. I was grateful to Ms. Turner for taking
time to demonstrate the equipment.

I am looking forward to receiving the brochure about Transatlantic's
employee services. Would it also be possible for you to include a copy
of the newsletter that introduces the new security equipment to the
employees.

Thank you for considering me for the position and for the hospitality
you showed me. I look forward to hearing from you. After my visit last
week, I know that Transatlantic Steel would be an excellent place to
work.

Sincerely yours,

Marcia Le Borde

Marcia Le Borde

FIGURE 7.17   Letter accepting a job.

73 Park St.
Evansville, WI 53536-1016
June 29, 2001

Ms. Melinda Haas, Manager
Weise's Department Store
Janesville Mall
Janesville, WI 53545-1014

Dear Ms. Haas:

I am pleased to accept the position of assistant controller that you offered
me in your letter of June 22. Starting on July 18 will be no problem for me.
I look forward to helping Ms. Meyers in the business office. In the next few
months I know that I will learn a great deal about Weise's.

As you requested, I will make an appointment for early next week with the
Human Resources Department to discuss travel policies, salary payment
schedules, and insurance coverage.

I am eager to start working for Weise's.

Cordially,

Kevin Dubinski

Kevin Dubinski

a copy of a certificate or license forwarded, sending a final transcript of your college
work. A final one-sentence paragraph might state that you look forward to starting
your new job.

Refusing a job requires tact. You are obligated to inform an employer why you
are not taking the job. Since the employer has spent time interviewing you, respond
with courtesy and candor. For an example of a refusal letter, see Figure 7.18.

Do not bluntly begin with the refusal. Instead, prepare the reader for bad
news by starting with a complimentary remark about the job, the interview, or the
company. Then move to your refusal and supply an honest but not elaborate
explanation of why you are not taking the job. Many students cite educational
opportunities, work schedules, geographic preference, health reasons, or better,
more relevant professional opportunities. End on a friendly note, because you
may be interested in working for the company in the future and do not want to
arouse any bad feelings.

FIGURE 7.18   Letter refusing a job.

George Alexander

March 8, 2002

Ms. Gail Buckholtz-Adderley
Assistant Editor
The Everett News
Everett, WA 98421-1016

Dear Ms. Buckholtz-Adderley:

I enjoyed meeting you and the staff photographers at my recent interview for the photography position at the *News*. Your plans for the special weekend supplements are exciting, and I know that I would have enjoyed my assignments greatly.

However, because I have decided to continue my education part time at Western Washington University in Bellingham, I have accepted a position with the *Bellingham American*. Not having to commute to Everett will give me more time for my studies and also for my freelance work.

Thank you for your generous offer and for the time you and the staff spent explaining your plans to me. I wish you much success with the supplements.

Sincerely yours,

George Alexander

George Alexander

345 Melba Lane ▪ Bellingham, WA 98225-4912 ▪ galexander@micro.com

✓ Revision Checklist

- ❏ Restricted the types of job(s) for which I am qualified.
- ❏ Prepared a dossier at school placement office, including letters from professors, employers, and community officials.
- ❏ Identified places where relevant jobs are advertised.
- ❏ Notified instructors, friends, relatives, clergy, and individuals who work for the companies I want to join that I am in the job market.
- ❏ Checked with Chamber of Commerce, state employment office, and relevant government agencies.
- ❏ Researched the companies I am interested in—on the Internet, through printed sources, and in interviews with current employees I know.
- ❏ Inventoried my strengths carefully to prepare résumé.
- ❏ Eliminated weak, irrelevant, repetitious, and dated material from inventory.
- ❏ Wrote a focused and persuasive career-objective statement.
- ❏ Determined the most beneficial format of résumé to use—chronological, functional, or both.
- ❏ Prepared an electronic résumé to send on-line if employer so directs.
- ❏ Investigated creating a Web site for my job search–related documents.
- ❏ Made résumé attractive and easy to read with logical and persuasive headings and hyperlinks.
- ❏ Made sure résumé contains neither too much nor too little information.
- ❏ Proofread résumé to ensure everything is correct, consistent, and accurate.
- ❏ Wrote letter of application that shows how my specific skills and background apply to and meet an employer's exact needs.
- ❏ Prepared short oral presentation about myself and my accomplishments for an interview.
- ❏ Sent prospective employer a follow-up letter within a few days after interview to show interest in position.
- ❏ Sent prospective employer a polite acceptance or rejection letter.

Exercises

1. Make a brainstormed list of your marketable job skills. To do that, first concentrate on the specialized kinds of skills you learned in your major or on your job (for example, giving injections, fingerprinting, preparing specialized menus, learning a computer language, creating a Web site). List as many skills as you can think of; then organize them into three or four separate categories that reflect your major abilities.

2. Translate the list of skills from Exercise 1 into a number of "selling clauses" (see pp. 242–243), each introduced with a strong action verb.

3. Using at least four different sources, including the Internet, compile a list of ten employers for whom you would like to work. Get their names, street and e-mail addresses, phone numbers, and the names of the managers or human resources officers. Then select one company and write a profile about it—locations, services, kinds of products or services offered, number of employees, clients served, types of schedules used, and other pertinent facts.

4. Write an e-mail message to your instructor describing the resources you used to find three to four jobs in your area that you could apply for upon graduation.

5. Obtain some personal evaluation forms from your placement office. Write a sample letter to a former or current teacher and employer, asking for a recommendation. Tell the individuals what kinds of jobs you will be looking for and politely mention how a strong letter would help you in your job search. Make sure you bring them up-to-date about your educational progress and any employment you have had since you worked for them.

6. Which of the following would belong on your résumé? Which would not belong? Why?
    a. student ID number
    b. social security number
    c. the ZIP codes of your references' addresses
    d. a list of all your English courses in college
    e. section numbers of the courses in your major
    f. statement that you are recently divorced
    g. subscriptions to journals in your field
    h. the titles of any stories or poems you published in a high school literary magazine or newspaper
    i. your GPA
    j. foreign languages you studied
    k. years you attended college
    l. the date you were discharged from the service
    m. names of the neighbors you are using as references
    n. your religion
    o. job titles you held
    p. your summer job washing dishes
    q. your telephone number
    r. the reason you changed schools
    s. your current status with the National Guard
    t. the URL of your Web site
    u. your volunteer work for the Red Cross
    v. hours a week you spend reading science fiction
    w. the title of your last term paper in your major
    x. the name of the agency or business where you worked last

7. Indicate what is wrong with the following career objective statements and rewrite them to make them more precise and professional.
   a. Job in a dentist's office.
   b. Position with a safety emphasis.
   c. Desire growth position in a large department store.
   d. Am looking for entry position in health sciences with an emphasis on caring for older people.
   e. Position in sales with fast promotion rate.
   f. Want a job working with semiconductor circuits.
   g. I would like a position in fashion, especially one working with modern fashion.
   h. Desire a good-paying job, hours: 8–4:30, with double pay for overtime. Would like to stay in the Omaha area.
   i. Insurance work.
   j. Working with computers.
   k. Personal secretary.
   l. Job with preschoolers.
   m. Full-time position with hospitality chain.
   n. I want a career in nursing.
   o. Police work, particularly in suburb of large city.
   p. A job that lets me be me.
   q. Desire fun job selling cosmetics.
   r. Any position for a qualified dietitian.
   s. Although I have not made up my mind about which area of forestry I shall go into, I am looking for a job that offers me training and rewards based upon my potential.

8. As part of a team or on your own, revise the following poor résumé to make it more precise and persuasive. Include additional details where necessary and exclude any details that would hurt the job seeker's chances. Also correct any inconsistencies.

RÉSUMÉ OF

Powell T. Harrison
8604 So. Kirkpatrick St.
Ardville, Ohio
345 37 8760
614 234 4587
harrison@gem.com

PERSONAL	Confidential
CAREER OBJECTIVE	Seek good paying position with progressive Sunbelt company.
EDUCATION	
1998–2001	Will receive degree from Central Tech. Institute in Arch. St. Earned high average

```
                    last semester. Took necessary courses for
                    major; interested in systems, plans, and
                    design development.

1994-1998           Attended Ardville High School, Ardville, OH;
                    took all courses required. Served on several
                    student committees.

EXPERIENCE          None, except for numerous part-time jobs and
                    student apprenticeship in the Ardville area.
                    As part of student app. worked with local
                    firm for two months.

HOBBIES             Surfing the Net, playing Nintendo. Member of
                    Junior Achievement.

REFERENCES          Please write for names and addresses.
```

9. Determine what is wrong with the following sentences in a letter of application. Rewrite them to eliminate any mistakes, to focus on the "you attitude," or to make them more precise.
   a. Even though I have very little actual job experience, I can make up for it in enthusiasm.
   b. My qualifications will prove that I am the best person for your job.
   c. I would enjoy working with your other employees.
   d. This e-mail résumé is my application for any job you now have open or expect to fill in the near future.
   e. Next month, my family and I will be moving to Detroit, and I must get a job in the area. Will you have anything open?
   f. If you are interested in me, then I hope that we make some type of arrangements to interview each other soon.
   g. I have not included a résumé since all pertinent information about me is in this letter.
   h. My GPA is only 2.5, but I did make two Bs in my last term.
   i. I hope to take state boards soon.
   j. Your company, or so I have heard through the grapevine, has excellent fringe benefits. That is what I care about most, so I am applying for any position which you may advertise.
   k. I am writing to ask you to kindly consider whether I would be a qualified person for the position you announced in the newspaper.
   l. I have made plans to further my education.
   m. My résumé speaks for itself.
   n. I could not possibly accept a position which required weekend work, and night work is out, too.
   o. In my own estimation, I am a go-getter—an eager beaver, so to speak.
   p. My last employer was dead wrong when he let me go. I think he regrets it now.

q. When you want to arrange an interview time, give me a call. I am home every afternoon after four.

10. Explain why the following letter of application is ineffective. Rewrite it to make it more precise and appropriate.

```
Apartment 32
Jeggler Drive
Talcott, Arizona

Monday

Grandt Corporation
Production Supervisor
Capital City, Arizona

Dear Sir:

I am writing to ask you if your company will consider me
for the position you announced in the newspaper yesterday.
I believe that with my education (I have an associate
degree) and experience (I have worked four years as a
freight supervisor), I could fill your job.

My schoolwork was done at two junior colleges, and I took
more than enough courses in business management and modern
technology. In fact, here is a list of some of my courses:
Supervision, Materials Management, Work Experience in
Management, Business Machines, Safety Tactics,
Introduction to Packaging, Art Design, Modern Business
Principles, and Small Business Management. In addition, I
have worked as a loading dock supervisor for the last two
years, and before that I worked in the military in the
Quartermaster Corps.

Please let me know if you are interested in me. I would
like to have an interview with you at the earliest
possible date, since there are some other firms also
interested in me, too.

Eagerly yours,


George D. Milhous
```

---

11. From the Sunday edition of your local newspaper or from one of the other sources discussed on pages 237–240, find notices for two or three jobs you believe you are qualified to fill and then write a letter of application for one of them.

12. Write a chronologically organized résumé to accompany the letter you wrote for Exercise 11.

13. Write a functional résumé for your application letter in Exercise 11.

14 Prepare an on-line résumé of the résumé in either Exercise 12 or 13.

15. Bring the two résumés you prepared for Exercises 12 and 13 to class to be critiqued by a collaborative writing team. After your résumés are reviewed, revise them.

16. Write an appropriate job application letter to accompany Anna Cassetti's résumés in Figures 7.3 and 7.6.

17. Write a letter to a local business inquiring about summer employment. Indicate that you can work only for one summer and that you will be returning to school by September 1.

Gathering and Summarizing Information

Doing Research: Finding and Using Print, On-Line, and Internet Information Sources

A human resources director asked an applicant during a job interview to name the titles of two or three major journals in the applicant's field. When the applicant could not come up with even one, the applicant's chances for employment at the company became slim. The question was typical, fair, and relevant. The interviewer knew that an applicant's success in the job depends on the quality of information supplied to the employer. Employers expect carefully researched answers; they will not be satisfied with guesses.

The Importance of Research

Research, or the careful investigation of material found in books, periodicals, films, the Internet, and other sources (including resource people), is a vital part of every occupation. Companies expect their employees to be able to research a problem, find information, and reach informed conclusions for any number of assignments, such as writing proposals, reports, and correspondence.

You can conduct research by searching the on-line catalog, going through databases, e-mailing someone in another department for information, or scrolling through a company's Web site. You might engage in research by downloading a section of a reference work or by preparing statistical or marketing surveys. You need to be informed about the latest developments in your field, and you need to be able to communicate your findings accurately and concisely.

Doing research is a practical skill, like swimming, running, or keyboarding. Once learned, it is easy to perform. Knowing how to do research in your field brings lifelong benefits. The information in Chapter 8 can save you from suffering the embarrassment experienced by the job applicant described above.

The Process of Doing Research

Just as there is a process for writing—brainstorming, drafting, revising, editing—there is a process involved in doing research. In research, you go through the steps of finding, assessing, and incorporating information into your written work. Basically, that process includes using the following strategies, which sometimes overlap (especially steps 2, 3, and 4), since doing research is a recursive activity.

1. **Identify a significant topic.** Discovering an important subject is crucial to your success. Restating the obvious—mercury in drinking water is dangerous both to human health and to the ecosystem; computers can save a business time and money—unimaginatively duplicates what is well known without providing new interpretations or solutions. Check with your boss or your instructor to make sure that the subject of your research is both timely and significant. Usually the assignment will involve investigating some problem—its importance, its impact, and how to resolve, reverse, or contain it.

Once you have identified a significant topic, you are well on your way to establishing the **purpose** for your research. Look at the report in Chapter 9 on telecommuting (pp. 374–393) and the report in Chapter 16 on non-native speakers of English in the work force (pp. 629–644) to see how their authors identified and restricted a major subject to research.

2. **Limit the scope of your topic.** Select a topic that you can realistically research in the time you have. For example, you would have trouble writing a restricted report on lasers—certainly an important subject but one that is too broad and complex. You could not research the thousands of books, articles, reports, and Web sites that have been written on every aspect of laser technology for a course or in the busy, deadline-bound world of work. To restrict the scope of your topic, focus on a problem that applies to your audience and their responsibilities. Here are some ways to zero in on a large topic such as lasers:

audience: physicians who use lasers for gallbladder surgery

environment: the risks posed by lasers in security

costs: the price/efficiency of laser printers in office technology

By limiting your topic to a particular audience, space, or time and in a specific context (for example, medical, security, office technology), you would be in a much better position to research it. In the world of work, you may be given a problem to investigate but have to break it down into different parts to research it thoroughly.

3. **Next, identify the location of materials for your research.** Finding the **resources** that will enable you to carry out your research involves more than

quickly surfing the Net or glancing at a few books or periodicals. To do thorough research, you cannot stop with a handful of books or articles picked up on one visit to a library or ten or fifteen minutes on the Web. **Resources** often involve a diversity of media—print, electronic, audiovisual, Internet—located in a variety of places. You may start your research in your college library but then continue it at home or at your office with your computer; or you may have to read company reports on file or join a discussion group on the Internet or your company's intranet. Doing quality research means exploring a range of opinions and not settling for quick, superficial answers. You will have to locate the most pertinent information to prove you have conscientiously investigated your topic.

TECH NOTE

Intranets

To store and share information, diversified companies, government agencies, and large organizations have created **intranets.** As the name suggests, intranets are communication networks modeled after the Internet and use the same tools and procedures—hyperlinks, directories, passwords, and multimedia content. Unlike the Internet, though, an intranet is designed for internal use by the personnel of a particular company or organization. Coordinating the "Web sites" of various groups and departments, Web administrators and editors oversee a company's intranet. From a centralized directory, information is sent to, from, and about various divisions within the company—management, engineering, human resources, sales, public relations. Information can be designated "public" or "private," restricting audience and content.

    4. Know how to use the sources you find. Based on the restricted topic you are researching, you will have to determine what methods and tools you will need to do your research—such as indexes, abstracts, and databases. Determine any special preparations you have to make. You may also have to use special audiovisual equipment or software. If you are conducting an Internet search (see pp. 321–336), you will need to use various search techniques and search engines.

    5. Next, familiarize yourself with the research materials, especially the way they are organized. Look at the **organization** and parts of a work that readily alert readers to the topics it covers. Prefaces and introductions typically spell out an author's or reference work's purpose and scope. Also examine indexes to find out about their coverage. Home pages and hyperlinks on the Internet are equally important in directing you to further, possibly major, information. If you are looking at articles in journals, examine abstracts or summaries and note key terms and subject headings. Pay special attention to endnotes, bibliographies, and works cited lists to find other relevant sources. Additionally, don't neglect dialoguing or collaborating with co-workers and other resource people.

6. Know how to evaluate sources. Doing research means more than just being on a search mission to uncover facts. Don't be a human copying machine, naively repeating everything you read. Be prepared to ask the right kinds of questions to **evaluate** the information you uncover.

- What are the most significant sources I need for my purpose?
- Is this the most recent opinion?
- What other studies have been done?
- Is this information complete?
- Is it biased?
- Does this Web site, article, report, or study raise further questions that I must consider?
- What's missing in this interpretation or in this presentation of data?
- What conclusions must I cite and perhaps modify or adapt for my purpose and my audience?

Never be afraid to question and seek further information. As your research progresses, you will find that the shape and quality of your report or paper will improve. Don't be discouraged if you seem to go down a few blind alleys or dead-end streets; those so-called false leads may in fact result in a better informed and more useful report.

7. Always document where and from whom you received information. If you are using information from a source, including a co-worker or another department in your company, you are obligated to provide **documentation.** This is not a matter of simple courtesy; it is an ethical and legal necessity. See Chapter 9 to find out what and how you must document for each source. Don't think that because so much may have been written on your topic or that because you found your source on the Internet that you can regard any information as "public domain" and hence do not have to give the author full credit. As you do your research, pay attention to and respect any copyright notice that appears in print or over the Internet. Chapter 9 will show you how to document your sources correctly and consistently.

Each of the seven steps above involves a major ingredient of successful research—you will need to establish your **purpose,** restrict your **scope,** identify your **resources,** develop appropriate research **methods,** familiarize yourself with a work's **organization,** subject it to your critical **evaluation,** and provide careful and thorough **documentation.**

Tools and Strategies

Doing research in the so-called Information Age means taking advantage of all the resources of contemporary technology as well as print sources. You need to consult many of the sources of information to do your work at school and on the job.

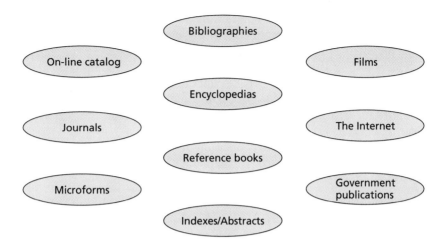

Yet you cannot go from one of those sources to another randomly and without a knowledge of how they relate to and build on each other. Doing that is like viewing your research as a game of hopscotch and jumping from one of the elliptical shapes above to another.

To do effective research, formulate and follow a plan, a strategy. A vital part of that strategy is knowing the function, scope, even the limits of your research sources. Not all of them will yield the same results or give you the same types of information. Instead, view your research as a triangle, with the broadest category of information as the base.

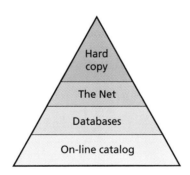

The triangle shape suggests the order you should follow in your search as well as the relationship of the tools you use along the way. Here is the rationale:

1. The foundation of your search should be your school's on-line catalog; it will tell you what is available to you and also direct you to other major sources, including pertinent Web sites.

2. Through your on-line catalog you can use a variety of databases to locate and even receive full texts of relevant periodicals, reports, and some books.

3. While the Internet has been rightfully called "the virtual library" or "the library without walls," it is not necessarily the first place you should go. The Net is vast, but contrary to popular belief, it does not have everything. In fact, it has much misinformation. The on-line catalog and databases are better organized and more focused. Not every journal you need, however, is available on the Net.

4. At the top of the triangle—the conclusion of your research—will be the exact information you need, most likely in hard copy. All the other sources in the triangle should lead you to this point in your research.

The steps up the triangle are not distinct and separate. Expect to repeat the steps and to see them overlap. The main point is that by visualizing your research as a carefully outlined and cohesive process, rather than jumping from one source to another or missing some sources and staying fixed on others, you will better accomplish your purpose.

Using Computerized Searches

Here is some practical advice on running a computer literature search.

1. Prepare for your search. Do not just walk into the library and tell the librarian you are interested in taxes, credit cards, drug enforcement, or another broad topic. Rather than asking for all the information on acid rain, first decide what specific aspect of acid rain you need to research in detail—its effect on crops, its prevention, its danger to the ozone layer, its political effects on neighboring countries, and so on.

2. Conduct a preliminary search. Find out approximately how much is written on the topic. This overview will give you some idea of whether you will be asking for ten entries or a hundred. Take a look at relevant subject headings in FirstSearch (see pp. 309–310) or in a print index for the last two or three years to get a rough estimate.

3. Refine your search. Experiment with the most appropriate key words for carrying out your search. Often you will have to try two or three different key phrases or words or combine or modify them. Keep in mind that you are not limited to subject terms found in print indexes. You can search databases by subject, author, and title. The more precise you make your search with key words, the more effective it will be.

4. Be realistic. Realize that databases do not scan an unlimited period of time. In some cases, databases cover only a specified time.

5. Know the types of resources your library has available. If your library's access to databases in your field is limited, you may need to use another library that subscribes to additional databases and certainly try other sources that include Internet citations.

The Library and the Internet

Recognizing the central importance of your library and the Internet, this chapter is divided into two main parts. The first part concentrates on the research materials and strategies available at a library. The second part, beginning on page 321, is devoted to the Internet. The chapter concludes with suggestions on taking research notes, both bibliographic and informational.

The Library and Its Services

You may think of your library as a single building with a single function. Yet that building is divided into many sections, each offering many services. When you walk into a library, probably the first section you see is the circulation desk—in many ways, the business center of the library. From there you can move to any one of the following parts of the library to use materials. (The page numbers after each area refer to the page numbers of this chapter where you will find a description of the particular information retrieval service and the materials in it.)

- the on-line catalog (pp. 299–303)
- guides to periodicals, indexes, abstracts, and databases (pp. 303–312)
- reference books and other reference sources (pp. 312–316)
- government documents (pp. 317–319)
- the popular press (pp. 319–320)
- audiovisual materials (pp. 320–321)

Keep in mind that every library is different and that your library may combine services or even offer many more.

The On-Line Catalog

The on-line catalog is often the starting place to look for research materials. The on-line catalog is your guide to the library; it will tell you what materials your library owns and where you can find them. It is not restricted to books; but also lists the microform materials, computer software, encyclopedias, periodical indexes, audio recordings, visuals, and the magazines and journals (electronic and print) to which your library subscribes. But while the on-line catalog may list specific journal or magazine titles, it will not give you information about the contents of individual articles. For that kind of information you have to consult abstracts or the periodical itself. On-line catalogs may also include CD-ROM networks and databases such as **FirstSearch** or **CARL UnCover** (see pp. 309–311).

Usually, terminals for an on-line catalog can be found on every floor of a library. If you have an access code, you may also be able to access the on-line catalog from your dorm room, house, or office.

An on-line catalog links users via a computer system to the automated database that contains information about materials in the library. The catalog will offer you commands and on-line help screens. As you search the catalog for the information you need, you will see bibliographic data displayed on the screen. You can print or download the information, saving you time and eliminating errors in transcribing. With access to the database, you can find information about titles, authors, and subject areas as well as other information not available to library patrons only a decade ago, including

- **the status of the book:** noncirculating, reserve, available, or checked out (and due date)
- **call number:** a number that indicates the location and subject matter in the Dewey Decimal or Library of Congress system
- **location of a book or other item** if your college has several libraries or is part of a library consortium (for example, stacks, information center, business library, fine arts library, regional library)
- **type of document:** retrieval of only certain media you specify, like *films* or *dissertations*
- **author's name**
- **title**
- **publishing information**
- **works published or sponsored by a certain organization** (only material released, a specific entity, say, by the American Cancer Society or the National Institute of Technology)

Figure 8.1 is a sample screen from an on-line catalog.

TECH NOTE

The New Experimental Library of Congress Digital Catalog*

The Library of Congress is developing the Experimental Search System (ESS), which will allow you to identify, locate, and access its vast resources on the Web through a point-and-click interface. This new catalog to the Library of Congress's digital library resources will consist of *query pages* and *result pages* (with brief and full displays), and help files that link directly from significant words on those pages. By exploiting powerful hyperlinking and search engines, the ESS will provide new and more innovative ways of searching the traditional on-line catalog. Through the ESS patrons will eventually have access to catalog records for "over 4 million books; 263,000 motion pictures, filmstrips, etc.; 200,000 sound recordings and musical scores; 150,000 maps; 4,300 computer files; and 140,000 photographs." Links will also be provided to more than 2,500 on-line books from sites across the Internet. Users of the ESS will be able to easily access government documents in full texts. The new digital catalog will not replace the current Library of Congress catalog but can be used in conjunction with it.

*Information for this Tech Note comes from "Library of Congress Experimental Search System," http://lcweb21oc.gov/resdev/ess/experime.html, 8 December 1997.

FIGURE 8.1   Internet services available through an on-line catalog.

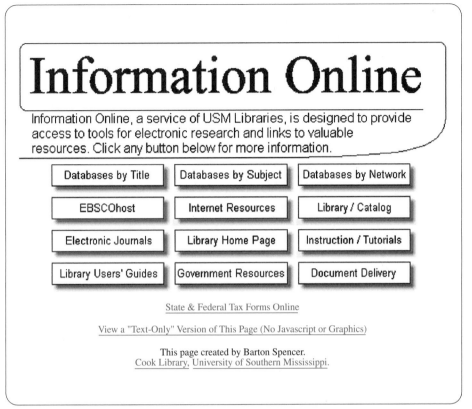

Information Online

Information Online, a service of USM Libraries, is designed to provide access to tools for electronic research and links to valuable resources. Click any button below for more information.

Databases by Title	Databases by Subject	Databases by Network
EBSCOhost	Internet Resources	Library / Catalog
Electronic Journals	Library Home Page	Instruction / Tutorials
Library Users' Guides	Government Resources	Document Delivery

State & Federal Tax Forms Online

View a "Text-Only" Version of This Page (No Javascript or Graphics)

This page created by Barton Spencer.
Cook Library, University of Southern Mississippi.

This page created by Barton Spencer, Cook Library, University of Southern Mississippi. Courtesy of The University of Southern Mississippi libraries.

Ways to Search the On-Line Catalog

Perhaps the most significant advantage of an on-line catalog is that it makes your library search easier, giving you more extensive and helpful access to the library's holdings and other resources, as shown in Figure 8.1, which lists Internet services available through an on-line catalog. You can search a computerized catalog by a variety of methods.

Author/Title Searches. When you enter the author's name, you will see a screen displaying all of the author's work(s). Even if you don't know an author's full name (assuming you know just the surname), the on-line catalog can help. For example, if you know the author's last name is Ponder, and you key in that name, the on-line catalog will display all works by authors named Ponder—whether they are by Anthony, Mary, Trey, or Zack. You then could select which work by which Ponder you needed.

Similarly, if you know only the first part of a title—*The Growth of the Internet* for the full title *The Growth of the Internet and Reasons for Regulation*—you could enter the incomplete title, and the on-line catalog will list all the titles that begin with those five words on the screen; you can then select the one you are searching for.

Subject Searches. If you don't have specific authors or titles in mind, then it is best to do a subject search. By entering two or three words (see "Keyword Searches," below) and pressing the subject option, you can call up books and other relevant materials that contain the key subject terms you are investigating. Start with broad terms that will generate large general categories. Often, looking at the longer lists will give you ideas about focusing your topic; then you can limit the scope of your investigation.

Keyword Searches. You can also search for keywords that appear in the titles of works included in the on-line catalog. If you already know the title of a work or the author's name, you can save time by making those choices and entering the specific keyword you want. You will get exactly what you ask for. If you entered "Bill Gates" as the keyword in an author search, your list would consist only of items written by Bill Gates. The same concept applies to the title search; you get a limited return. Researchers generally prefer the broader scope of materials produced by the subject search because it covers more data.

Narrowing and Expanding Your Search. Thanks to keyword searching on an on-line catalog, you can narrow or expand your topic, as necessary. Suppose you are researching the use of lasers in printing. An on-line catalog subject search finds only documents with *both* words ("lasers" *and* "printing"). To expand your search, you might search for "lasers" *or* "printing" separately. On the other hand, to narrow your search, you can specify exactly what you want *excluded* from your search— "lasers not military." That allows you to narrow the broad topic "lasers" by focusing only on nonmilitary aspects. (See pp. 332–333 for advice on keyword searching.)

Call Numbers. All searches will give you a **call number,** which indicates where the book or document is located in the library.

Web-Based Catalogs

Your library's on-line catalog is much more than a guide to just the materials that are available to you at your school or company. The most recent versions of on-line catalogs are Web based, which gives you more flexibility and options, as Figure 8.1 shows. You can be linked directly to a Web source through an entry in your on-line catalog. Each citation you pull up will include hyperlinks, allowing you to navigate through the entire catalog as well as through relevant Web sites. And through hyperlinks you can obtain full-text resources that you can download and print. You can also e-mail search results from your on-line catalog to your PC or e-mail account.

The Web-based catalogs will be part of a global search network in which you can receive information about all relevant books to your search from libraries anywhere.

Case Study: Women in Business

Let's say you want to find relevant documents in your library on "women in business," a very general topic. Entering those keywords for a subject search, you find a list of pertinent subtopics, one of which is "women-owned business enterprises."

FIGURE 8.2   Browsing the catalog.

1) WOMEN-OWNED BUSINESS ENTERPRISES [7]

2) see related headings for: WOMEN-OWNED BUSINESS ENTERPRISES

3) WOMEN-OWNED BUSINESS ENTERPRISES CASE STUDIES [6]

4) WOMEN-OWNED BUSINESS ENTERPRISES DIRECTORIES [1]

5) WOMEN-OWNED BUSINESS ENTERPRISES GOVERNMENT POLICY UNITED STATES [4]

6) WOMEN-OWNED BUSINESS ENTERPRISES GREAT BRITAIN [1]

7) WOMEN-OWNED BUSINESS ENTERPRISES PERIODICALS [2]

8) WOMEN-OWNED BUSINESS ENTERPRISES LAW AND LEGISLATION UNITED STATES [3]

9) WOMEN-OWNED BUSINESS ENTERPRISES MANAGEMENT [10]

10) WOMEN-OWNED BUSINESS ENTERPRISES MASSACHUSETTS BOSTON [1]

11) WOMEN-OWNED BUSINESS ENTERPRISES UNITED STATES [15]

TOP

Continued

Figure 8.2 shows the subheadings for that narrower topic. Note that among the subtopics are areas for investigation, such as directories and case studies. Choosing to locate information on the second subtopic, "women-owned business enterprises," you would then see your screen fill up with the items that the library holds on that topic. The number of items, of course, will vary from one library to another. Some of the items from one college library are shown in Figure 8.3. Note that the list includes books, periodicals, government documents, microforms, and even a Web site. Also keep in mind that a subject search may give you titles that include a broader discussion but still cover the area of your investigation.

Figure 8.3 illustrates the Web-based on-line catalog. It lists title, author, date, call number, and where the item can be found in the library. But on screen you will also find how many records were found and see that there are cross-references that would allow you to gather further information.

Clicking on one of the items, you then see a full display of bibliographic information—author, title, publisher for each, and availability status—as shown in Figure 8.4 (p. 307).

Guides to Periodicals: Indexes, Abstracts, and Databases

Your research will not be confined exclusively to books. Don't neglect the wealth of information contained in periodicals. A **periodical** is a magazine or journal that is published at established, frequent intervals—weekly, bimonthly (once every two months), quarterly. The word *magazine* refers to periodicals that appeal to a diverse audience and that treat popular themes in nontechnical language, for example, *National Parks,*

FIGURE 8.2   (Continued)

1) WOMEN-OWNED BUSINESS ENTERPRISES UNITED STATES **[15]**

2) WOMEN-OWNED BUSINESS ENTERPRISES UNITED STATES BIBLIOGRAPHY **[3]**

3) WOMEN-OWNED BUSINESS ENTERPRISES UNITED STATES CASE STUDIES **[4]**

4) WOMEN-OWNED BUSINESS ENTERPRISES UNITED STATES DIRECTORIES **[2]**

5) WOMEN-OWNED BUSINESS ENTERPRISES UNITED STATES FINANCE **[3]**

6) WOMEN-OWNED BUSINESS ENTERPRISES UNITED STATES HANDBOOKS MANUALS ETC. **[2]**

7) WOMEN-OWNED BUSINESS ENTERPRISES UNITED STATES MANAGEMENT **[5]**

8) WOMEN-OWNED BUSINESS ENTERPRISES UNITED STATES PERIODICALS **[1]**

9) WOMEN-OWNED BUSINESS ENTERPRISES UNITED STATES STATISTICS **[6]**

10) WOMENS AIR SERVICE PILOTS U S **[1]**

11) WOMENS AIR SERVICE PILOTS U S BIOGRAPHY **[1]**

12) see related headings for: WOMENS APPAREL INDUSTRY

TOP

Used by permission of The University of Southern Mississippi Libraries.

Redbook, and *Time.* The term *journal* characterizes technical or scholarly periodicals, such as the *American Journal of Nursing* and *Chemical Engineering,* whose audiences consult them for professional or scientific information. Some periodicals are published both in print and on-line.

> Brown, Marge, Bruce Brown, and Kathy Yakal. "The Web as a Post Office." *PC Magazine* (5 Oct. 1999): 48–49. 3 illustrations.

Advantages of Using Periodicals

Periodicals have certain advantages over books when it comes to research. Because they take less time to produce than books, periodicals can give you more recent information on a topic. Further, periodicals are not as restricted as books. A book usually discusses a subject from one point of view, but a periodical may contain ten different articles, each conveying a separate topic and each offering a different perspective. That is not to imply that you should ignore books and focus solely on magazines or journals. Use both but be aware of the differences.

Using Indexes and Abstracts

To find appropriate articles in magazines and journals, you need to use indexes. An **index** is a listing by subject, sometimes also by author, of articles that have appeared within a specified period of time. An index tells you what articles have been published

FIGURE 8.3   Results of complex search.

```
┌─────────────────────────────────────────────────────────────────────────────┐
│  CATALOG  RESERVE DESK  INFO. DESK                                            │
│                                                                                │
│   GO BACK    NEW      BACKWARD   FORWARD   JUMP   PRINT    REQUEST  PREFS.  EXIT │
│             SEARCH                                CAPTURE                       │
│                                                                                │
│  Results of completed search                                                   │
│                                                                                │
│  37 records were found. Viewing 1 through 20. There are also cross references. │
│  Use checkboxes ☐ below to mark list items for Print/Capture.                  │
```

#1 ☐   **HD6054.3.M4 1999**   copies: 1 (BROOKSRR)
   VIEW   Entrepreneurs / Krista McLuskey.   at: MAIN
          McLuskey, Krista, 1974-   pubyear: 1999

#2 ☐   **EP 1.102:W 84/998**   copies: 2 (VIEW for detail)
   VIEW   Women-owned directory [microform].   at: MAIN
          United States. Environmental Protection Agency. Office of Small and   pubyear: 1998
          Disadvantaged Business Utilization.

#3 ☐   **URL   http://www.womexs.org**   at: MAIN
   VIEW   Women Executives   pubyear: 1998
          Internet Site Maintained by
          Association of Women Executives

#4 ☐   **HD.451.s**   Periodicals
   VIEW   <u>Minority Women Leaders</u> (1998-   )

#5 ☐   **Y 4.SM 1:105-33**   copies:1 (INFOSERV)
   VIEW   Making the federal government user friendly : hearing before the Subcommittee on   at: MAIN
          Government Programs and Oversight of the Committee on Small Business, House   pubyear: 1998
          of Representatives, One Hundred Fifth Congress, first session, Frederick, MD,
          November 20, 1997.
          United States. Congress. House. Committee on Small Business. Subcommittee on
          Government Programs and Oversight.

#6 ☐   **Y 4.SM 1:105-28**   copies: 1 (INFOSERV)
   VIEW   Women business enterprises : hearing before the Subcommittee on Government   at: MAIN
          Programs and Oversight of the Committee on Small Business, House of   pubyear: 1998
          Representatives, One Hundred Fifth Congress, first session, Washington, DC,
          October 8, 1997.
          United States. Congress. House. Committee on Small Business. Subcommittee on
          Government Programs and Oversight.

Continued

on a subject, where they are published, who wrote them, and whether they contain any special information, such as bibliographies, illustrations, diagrams, or maps.

Some leading specialized indexes are

Applied Science and Technology Index
Business Periodicals Index
Engineering Index
Index to Legal Periodicals

Indexes are invaluable. You could never successfully thumb through all the periodicals in the library to determine which ones contain articles you could use. Furthermore, your library might not subscribe to all the journals and magazines that contain articles related to your subject. The indexes let you know what is available beyond your library's holdings.

FIGURE 8.3   (Continued)

#7 ☐ **VIEW**	**EP 1.102:W 84/998** Women-owned directory [microform]. United States. Environmental Protection Agency. Office of Small and Disadvantaged Business Utilization.	copies: at: pubyear:	2 (VIEW for detail) MAIN 1998
#8 ☐ **VIEW**	**HF5549 .G647 1998** Gender and successful human resource decisions in small businesses / Deborah Cain Good. Good, Deborah Cain, 1958-	copies: at: pubyear:	1 (STACKS) MAIN 1998
#9 ☐ **VIEW**	**HD2344.5.U6 W45 1998** Women entrepreneurs : developing leadership for success / Sandra J. Wells. Wells, Sandra J., 1949-	copies: at: pubyear:	2 (STACKS) MAIN 1998
#10 ☐ **VIEW**	**HD6054.4 U6 B35 1997** Doing it for ourselves : success stories of African-American women in business / Donna Ballard. Ballard, Donna.	copies: at: pubyear:	1 (STACKS) MAIN 1997
#11 ☐ **VIEW**	**EP 1.2:M 66** EPA guidance for utilization of small, minority and women's business enterprises in procurement under assistance agreements [microform]. United States. Environmental Protection Agency. Office of Small and Disadvantaged Business Utilization.	copies: at: pubyear:	2 (VIEW for detail) MAIN 1997
#12 ☐ **VIEW**	**National Foundation for Women Business Owners** www.nfwbo.org database	pubyear:	1989
#13 ☐ **VIEW**	**HF5386 .L8x 1981a** A study of the existence of selected characteristics that may be necessary for entrepreneurial success among black female college students majoring in business / by Millicent G. Lownes. Lownes, Millicent G.	copies: at: pubyear:	1 (STACKS) MAIN 1987
#14 ☐ **VIEW**	**HD2346.G7 G63 1985** Women in charge : the experience of female entrepreneurs / Robert Goffee and Richard Scase. Goffee, Robert.	copies: at: pubyear:	1 (STACKS) MAIN 1985

Used by permission of The University of Southern Mississippi Libraries.

An index may also contain an abstract. An **abstract** is a short summary of the content and scope of a book, article, or report. By condensing information, an abstract can save users hours by letting them know whether the work is relevant to their topic.

Figure 8.5 contains an abstract that appears in *Communication Abstracts* of an article about videophones. In Chapter 10 you will learn how to write an abstract.

Use abstracts with caution—they are not a substitute for the work they summarize. A few sentences highlighting the content of a book or article obviously omit much. When in doubt about what is omitted, read the original work to uncover the details, the rationale, and the dimensions of the whole problem. Never quote from an abstract; always cite material from the original work.

The following titles give you an idea of the many types of abstracts available: *Biological Abstracts, Forestry Abstracts, Oceanic Abstracts, Work Related Abstracts, Metals Abstracts.*

Using Databases

Given the information explosion, it would be difficult, if not impossible, to search manually through individual indexes and abstracts. For that reason you need to

FIGURE 8.4   On-line catalog display of book.

Doing it for ourselves : success stories of African-American women in...

Type of Material: Book
Personal Name: Ballard, Donna.
Main Title: Doing it for ourselves: success stories of African-American women in business / Donna Ballard
Portion of Title: African-American women in business
Published/Created: New York, N.Y.: Berkley Books, c1997.
Description: xx, 150 p.; 22 cm.
ISBN: 0425156133
Notes: Includes interviews with Benita Pierce, Karen Gibbs, Brenda Neal, Margot Lee, Judith Aidoo, Toni Banks and eighteen others. Includes bibliographical references (p. 147-150).
Subjects: Afro-American women executives--United States--Interviews.
LC Classification: HD6054.4.U6 B35 1997

Status: Available

CALL NUMBER: HD6054.4.U6 B35 1997

Used by permission of The University of Southern Mississippi Libraries.

know about databases, which collect many individual indexes or abstracts. A computerized database will let you go through ten years of indexes or abstracts in minutes. Moreover, through a database you will often receive both a bibliographic citation and a brief abstract combined.

Keep in mind, though, that some databases do not go farther back than 1988. You will need to consult a print index or abstract for information published before then.

A **database** is an electronic index service that contains a file of information from which the computer retrieves the key citations (and sometimes abstracts) you need. Thousands of databases have been compiled. In fact, almost every professional discipline has its own database.

You can even research the on-line catalog for databases by subject, as in Figure 8.3. Here are some examples of specific databases in specialized areas: aerospace, *Aerospace Database;* criminal justice, *Criminal Justice Periodical Index;* nursing, *Cumulative Index to Nursing & Allied Health Literature;* chemistry, *Chemistry Abstracts;* business, *Business Periodical Index* and *Trade and Industry Index;* psychology, *Psych Lit;* engineering, *COMPENDEX;* and sports, *Heracles.*

A library subscribes to a particular computerized information retrieval service that has numerous databases stored in its host server computer. Via its computer

FIGURE 8.5   Abstract of a journal article from *Communication Abstracts*.

COMMUNICATION TECHNOLOGY. ELDERLY. HOME HEALTH CARE. TELECOMMUNICATIONS TECHNOLOGY. VIDEOPHONE.

The authors introduced a videophone system of full-color motion pictures, using Integrated Systems for Digital Networks, into home health care services and evaluated its effects. Twenty households including the disabled elderly were enrolled into the project for a three-month period. Communication and social cognition independence after the trial, as examined by means of the Functional Independent Measure, were statistically improved as compared with those before the trial. The videophone also improved activity of daily living (ADL), instrumental ADL, family health, and accessibility to medical consultations. The advantages of a wider application of this telecommunications technology to home health care services are discussed as well.

Source: Communication Abstracts, Volume 19, p. 95, copyright © 1997. Reprinted with permission of Sage Publication, Inc.

terminals, your library is able to dial into those databases. There are thousands of different databases, and while no one retrieval service offers access to all of them, the services do supply their customers with vast amounts of information. Many of the databases correspond to printed indexes (such as the *Business Periodicals Index*), while others are available only through on-line searches, that is, there is no print equivalent for them. Many of them are also available on CD-ROM.

To search a database, first narrow your topic and then find a keyword or phrase (plus suitable alternatives) that best summarizes your topic. For example, you would find it difficult to research such a broad topic as child abuse, artificial intelligence, or virtual reality. You would need to restrict your focus (see p. 224).

Types of Information Available from a Database

Searching an on-line database, you can receive the following types of information.

- **bibliographic citations:** author, title, publication, volume and issue number for journal, publisher, date, page numbers, language in which source is written
- **abstracts**
- **keywords:** identify the subject of an article that you can use to locate similar studies
- **full text of most articles**
- **factual information:** everything from stock quotations to new patents, news of public affairs, product information, names and addresses of company executives

Figure 8.6 contains an entry for an article on electronic commerce listed in the *Applied Science and Technology* database.

FIGURE 8.6   An entry from a database.

Record 1 of 12 - Applied Sci&Technol Abst 1/99-7/99
TI -   TITLE: E-commerce is becoming a way of life
AU - PERSONAL AUTHOR: Zurawski, Laura
SO - SOURCE: Control-Engineering. v. 46 no5 May 1999 p. 48
PY - PUBLICATION YEAR: 1999
PD - PHYSICAL DESCRIPTION: il [illustrated]
IS - ISSN: 0010-8049
LA - LANGUAGE OF DOCUMENT: English
AB - ABSTRACT: The automation and control industry is one of the fastest growing groups offering
       online purchase of products and services. Some of the players in the electronic commerce
       market are detailed, and security issues are discussed.
DE - DESCRIPTORS: Electronic-commerce
DT - DOCUMENT TYPE: Feature-Article

Source: Applied Science & Technology Abstracts.

Some Widely Used Databases

1. EBSCOhost. Surveying thousands of popular magazines, professional journals, reports, and newspapers from all over the world, EBSCOhost provides indexing, abstracting, and in most cases a full text service. Figure 8.7 shows some of the databases you can search using EBSCOhost and the types of information they offer. All databases are continuously updated, and new ones are added regularly.

2. FirstSearch. Among the most popular and widely used databases, FirstSearch is found in many libraries as well as on the Web. As its "Welcome" screen announces, FirstSearch will help you research your topic in "books, articles, theses,

---

TECH NOTE

CD-ROMs

Many reference works—encyclopedias, books, even databases—are available on CD-ROM ("compact disk, read-only memory"). "The storage capacity of a CD-ROM is about 680 megabytes (about 470 times that of a 3.5 diskette and unlike diskettes. CD-ROMs are not tied to the operating system of a specific computer). . . . Any computer can read the data on a CD-ROM" (*Dictionary of Computer and Internet Terms*, 6th ed. [Hauppauge, N.Y.: Barron's, 1998]: p. 77). But CD-ROMs are not closed systems, as they once were. Most encyclopedia-like CDs allow you to click on a link that will (a) use your modem to connect you to the Internet and (b) retrieve any additional, updated information the vendor might provide. Still much in use, CD-ROMs, the experts say, will be replaced by Internet sources.

FIGURE 8.7   Some of the databases offered through EBSCOhost.

[Enter]

☐ **Academic Search Elite**
Provides full text for over 1,230 journals covering the social sciences, humanities, general science, multi-cultural studies, education, and much more. Click here for a complete title list. Click here for more info

☐ **The Serials Directory**
Provides up-to-date and accurate bibliographic information and pricing for over 155,000 U.S. and international periodicals. Click here for more info

☐ **ERIC**
Provides citation and abstract information from over 750 educational journals and related documents from the Educational Resource Information Center and educational symposium report literature dating back to 1967. Click here for more info

☐ **Health Source Plus**
Provides full text for over 255 health periodicals, over 1,065 health pamphlets, and 23 health reference books. Click here for a complete title list. Click here for more info

☐ **MasterFILE Premier**
Provides full text for over 1,810 periodicals covering nearly all subjects including general reference, business, health, and much more. Click here for a complete title list. Click here for more info

☐ **Newspaper Source**
Provides selected full text articles from 143 U.S. and international newspapers. Click here for a complete title list. Click here for more info

☐ **Business Source Elite**
Provides full text for nearly 930 journals covering business, management, economics, finance, banking, accounting, and much more. Click here for a complete title list. Click here for more info

☐ **EBSCO Animals**
Provides in-depth information on a variety of topics relating to animals. The database consists of indexing, abstracts, and full text records describing the nature and habitat of familiar animals. Click here for more info

☐ **MAS FullTEXT Premier**
Provides abstracts and indexing for over 500 general interest and research magazines plus the searchable full text for 210 periodicals and thousands of Magill's Book Reviews. The earliest abstracts begin in 1984 and earliest full text in 1990. Click here for a complete title list. Click here for more info

☐ **Clinical Reference Systems**
Provides over 7,000 reports, in every-day language, describing symptoms, treatments, risks and after-effects of a vast array of medical topics and conditions. Click here for more info

☐ **USP DI Volume II, Advice for the Patient**
Provides patient-oriented drug information in lay language. Monographs are organized into the following sections: Brand Names commonly used in both the United States and Canada, Description, Before Using This Medicine, Proper Use of This Medicine, Precautions, and Side Effects. Click here for more info

EBSCOhost displays copyright EBSCO Publishing, 1999. Display example created March 1999. The EBSCOhost interface may have changed since that date.

films, computer software, and other types of material. . . ." FirstSearch accesses more than eighty-five databases in a variety of subject areas, including business and economics, conferences and proceedings, consumer affairs and people, engineering and technology, general and reference sources, and medicine and health services. Table 8.1 lists some of the databases available on FirstSearch.

3. CARL UnCover. This database indexes more than 20,000 multidisciplinary journals in such areas as business, science, and current events. More than 400 current citations are added each day. You can also access "20 commercial databases and over 420 individual library catalogs that are part of the CARL system." In early 2000, CARL

TABLE 8.1   Some Databases Available on FirstSearch

Database	Contents
AGRICOLA	Materials relating to aspects of agriculture
AIDS/Cancer (new)	AIDS and cancer research
Article 1st	Index of articles from nearly 12,500 journals
Arts and Humanities Search	Index of more than 1,300 arts and humanities journals and selected articles from more than 5,800 social science and science journals
BasicBIOSIS	A wide range of bioscience topics
Business Dateline	Focuses on regional information vital to business from more than 450 sources
Consumer Index	Includes more than 90,000 entries on individual products and 60,000 abstracts of articles about consumer issues
FactSearch	Indexes over 1,000 newspapers, periodicals, newsletters, and government documents dealing with criminal justice and legal issues
MEDLINE	Indexes more than 3,500 journals covering all areas of medicine
Microcomputer Abstracts	Covers popular magazines and professional journals on micro-computing for business, industry, education, and home use
NetFirst (new)	Online Computer Library Center (OCLC) database of Internet
WorldCat	Books and other materials in libraries worldwide

UnCover "contained brief descriptive information for over 8,800,000 articles which have appeared since Fall 1988." It is possible to search CARL UnCover by keyword, topic, author, or through a browse feature that allows you to see the table of contents for any issue of a periodical that is available on-line. As with other searches, CARL UnCover provides full bibliographic citations, and in some cases, summaries of articles.

An especially helpful feature of CARL UnCover is its on-line periodical delivery service. For a fee, you can order an article, a book review, or a letter to the editor from the database and have it faxed or e-mailed to you.

4. WILSONLINE. This database offers subscribers access to the bibliographic information contained in many of the indexes published by the H. W. Wilson Company as well as other sources, thirty-five indexes in all. The indexes hold up to fifteen years of information and are updated twice each week. Some of the indexes included on WILSONLINE are

Applied Science and Technology Index
Biological and Agricultural Index
Book Review Digest
Business Periodicals Index

Index to Legal Periodicals and Books

Publisher's Directory

Wilson Business Abstracts

Like many databases, WILSONLINE is not cumulative; coverage goes back only to 1986. As years pass and more information is added, individual databases will become larger.

5. ProQuest. This database indexes and abstracts more than 6,000 periodicals ranging from *Discover* to *Journal of Paleontology* and offers full-image coverage of over 2,000 of those periodicals. Especially useful is ProQuest's international databases from newspapers and news wires. Some of the databases you will find through ProQuest are

ABI/INFORM Global

Banking Information Source

ProQuest Medical Library

ProQuest Newstand™ International Newspapers

ProQuest Asian Business™

ProQuest European Business™

Case Study: Searching the Databases

Vivian Petros, a sophomore at Grand Central College, wanted to write a long report on some aspect of electronic commerce. Through EBSCOhost Vivian was able to search three databases: Academic Search Elite, Newspaper Source, and Business Source Elite.

First, Vivian had to enter the topic she was interested in and keywords relating to that topic. Her first attempt using only the general phrase "electronic commerce" brought back nearly 22,000 items, including everything from marketing and buying furniture to trading stocks in e-commerce firms. The prospect of looking at 22,000 entries was staggering! Clearly, Vivian had not restricted her topic or found the most useful, practical keywords to limit her search. Giving some more thought to her search, she decided to focus only on those studies dealing with electronic commerce *and* e-cash, a much more carefully focused topic. Her search of the databases was now far more productive, relevant, and brought up sixteen items, as seen in Figure 8.8. The titles appeared in professional journals—*InfoWorld, CommunicationsWeek,* and *American Banker*—and appeared to provide the type of information she would need to write the report for her class. Those marked by a page icon were available in full text, which she could easily download. Her next step was to click on those articles that seemed most crucial to her research to look at a brief abstract, as in Figure 8.9, to see if she needed to find full texts of them in her library's microforms collection (see pp. 320–321).

Reference Books and Other Sources

Reference books include encyclopedias, dictionaries, abstracts, manuals, and almanacs—sources of useful facts and basic information that are housed in a library's ref-

FIGURE 8.8   Researching the EBSCOhost database.

| Keyword Search | Natural Language Search | Advanced Search | Options | Search Tips | More ... |

Searched: *Academic Search Elite; Newspaper Source; Business Source Elite* for **SU electronic commerce AND e-cash**

◀ **(1 to 10) of 16** ▶   Refine Search   Print / E-mail / Save   **View Web Link Results**

Mark	Full Text	Select Result For More Detail
☐	📄	***E-cash*** in the *E*-age.; By: Hurley, Hanna., Telephony, 07/12/99, Vol. 237 Issue 2, p32, 5p, 1 diagram, 2c 📄 Full Page Image
☐		Fear and greed rule in the age of *e-cash*.; By: Newman, Peter C.., MacLean's, 04/05/99, Vol. 112 Issue 14, p50, 1p, 1c
☐		***E-cash*** Holds No Currency In U.S.; By: Steinert-Threlkeld, Tom., Inter@ctive Week, 11/16/98, Vol. 5 Issue 45, p30, 3/4p
☐		***E-cash*** spreads its tentacles.; By: Irvine, Steven., Euromoney, Aug98 Issue 352, p33, 2p, 2c
☐	📄	Holding your breath waiting for *e-cash*? You can exhale now.; By: Tweney, Dylan., InfoWorld, 07/06/98, Vol. 20 Issue 27, p56, 2/5p, 1c
☐		When will ***E-cash*** jingle in your *E*-pocket? (cover story); By: Flohr, Udo. and Rupnik, Jelena., Byte, Jan98, Vol. 23 Issue 1, p85, 1p 1 diagram, 1c
☐	📄	Blockbuster presents ***E-cash*** benefits for all audiences., Chain Store Age, Aug97, Vol. 73 Issue 8, p96, 2p, 2c
☐	📄	***E-commerce*** may not be a huge success yet, but it soon will be.; By: Mason, David., CommunicationsWeek, 04/28/97 Issue 660, p53, 1/2p, 1c
☐	📄	Top Austrian, Norwegian banks to sign up with Digicash.; By: Bloom, Jennifer Kingso., American Banker, 04/24/97, Vol. 162 Issue 78, p17, 2/7p
☐	📄	Mondex *e-cash* coming to the U.S., Automatic I.D. News, Feb97, Vol. 13 Issue 2, p10, 1/8p

◀ **(1 to 10) of 16** ▶   Refine Search   Print / E-mail / Save   **View Web Link Results**

Continued

erence room. Reference books, marked **Ref.** or **R** in an on-line catalog, usually cannot be checked out of the library. When you look for reference books, always make sure that you use the most up-to-date ones. Ask your librarian for help in identifying them. Keep in mind that many reference sources are also on the Internet.

Encyclopedias

The word *encyclopedia* comes from a Greek phrase meaning "general education." A general encyclopedia can get you started in your research by giving you relevant background information, explaining key terms, offering quick summaries, and supplying a list of further readings. Six useful, general encyclopedias are *Collier's Encyclopedia, Encyclopedia Americana, New Encyclopaedia Brittanica* (located on the Internet at *http://www.eb.com*), *Smithsonian Encyclopedia* (*www.si.edu*), *Encyclopedia.com* (*http://www.encyclopedia.com*), and *Funk and Wagnalls Encyclopedia* (*http://www.funkandwagnalls.com*).

Also consult specialized encyclopedias, which include far more technical information. Two helpful specialized encyclopedic references are the *Encyclopedia of Associations,* which gives information (addresses, phone and fax numbers, descriptions of purpose and publications) on over 30,000 groups, and the *Occupational Outlook Handbook,* which provides overviews of the requirements for and responsibilities of

FIGURE 8.8   (Continued)

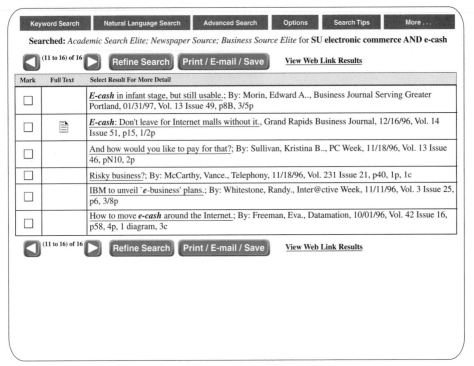

EBSCOhost displays copyright EBSCO Publishing, 1999. Display example created March 1999. The EBSCOhost interface may have changed since that date.

numerous technical and managerial positions. Following is a list of some specialized encyclopedias.

Encyclopedia of Banking and Finance
Encyclopedia of Chemical Technology

TECH NOTE

CD-ROM Encyclopedias

With rare exceptions like the *Encyclopaedia Britannica,* CD-ROM encyclopedias may not always give the full text of entries. Instead, multimedia encyclopedias like *Encarta* (*http://www.iac-on-encarta.com*) and *Grolier's* (*http://www.grolier.com*) provide direct links from the CD-ROM articles to related sites on the Internet. Do not be misled into thinking that by consulting CD-ROM encyclopedias you are receiving full coverage of the topic you are researching.

FIGURE 8.9   Abstract of an article on EBSCOhost database.

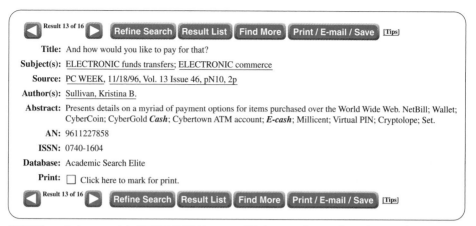

Encyclopedia of Computer Science and Engineering

Encyclopedia of Consumer Brands

Encyclopedia of Food Technology

Goodheart-Wilcox Automotive Encyclopedia

McGraw-Hill Encyclopedia of Environmental Science and Engineering

McGraw-Hill Encyclopedia of Science and Technology

As valuable as encyclopedias are, do not do all your research using only those reference books. Relying on encyclopedias alone reveals your lack of ability to find and use other sources.

Manuals and Almanacs

Manuals supply explanations of procedures and authoritative overviews of practical and professional issues you will encounter on the job. Consult more than one manual to compare discussions of the same topic.

On-line manuals are plentiful. The National Technical Information Service (*www.ntis.com*) provides a multiplicity of informational manuals on various business and research topics. Another important source for manuals is Online Manuals (*www.pressureisland.com/manual*). Those two sites also have links to other useful sources. Any search engine (see pp. 329–332) also will yield several more listings for manuals and almanacs.

In business, among the most useful references are *Moody's Manuals,* which provide a wealth of information on the history of companies, descriptions of products and services, and basic financial details (such as stocks, earnings, and mergers). Depending on the type of business you're interested in, you can consult one or more of the eight Moody manuals, such as *Moody's Industrial Manual, Moody's Bank and Finance Manual,* or *Moody's Transportation Manual.*

Besides *Moody's Manuals,* you can investigate several company directories that give helpful information on specific companies, including

Million Dollar Directory

Standard and Poor's Registrar of Corporations and Executives

Try Us: National Minority Directory

World Business Directory

And don't forget to check a company's Web site.

Almanacs contain carefully organized statistical information—charts, tables, graphs, price indexes, federal and state budgets—as well as descriptions of events by year or by region. Almanacs are published on a variety of specialized subjects, as the following titles indicate:

Almanac of Science and Technology: What's New and What's Known

Business Week Almanac

Everybody's Business: An Almanac

Information Please Almanac, Atlas and Yearbook

As with encyclopedias and manuals, almanacs are on the Internet. One valuable listing of almanacs can be found at the American University Library (*http://www. newton.library.american.edu/gateway/handbks.html*). That site provides almanacs ranging from the *Almanac of Politics and Government* to the *Old Farmer's Almanac.*

Dictionaries

In addition to giving the meanings of words, dictionaries furnish spelling, pronunciation, etymology (word history), usage, and sometimes biographical information. The following unabridged (comprehensive) dictionaries are excellent references:

The American Heritage Dictionary of the English Language

Funk and Wagnalls New Standard Dictionary of the English Language

Random House Dictionary of the English Language

Webster's Third New International Dictionary of the English Language

Specialized, or field, dictionaries define the words used in the literature of a profession and also characterize the scope and importance of that profession.

Dictionary of Architecture and Construction

Dictionary of Banking and Finance

Dictionary of Computing

Dictionary of Earth Sciences

Stedman's Medical Dictionary

McGraw-Hill Dictionary of Scientific and Technical Terms

The Internet provides some dictionary options as well. The largest is the Web of Online Dictionaries, located at *http://www.facstaff.bucknell.edu/rbeard/diction. html,* which contains more than 1,000 dictionaries in 200 different languages.

Government Documents

The U.S. government is the country's biggest publisher. Through its diverse agencies and departments, the U.S. government engages vigorously in conducting research and publishing its findings. This published material, collectively referred to as **government documents,** includes journal articles, pamphlets, research reports, transcripts of government hearings, speeches, statistical reports, films, maps, and books.

Many government documents are also available on the Internet. Figure 8.10 contains the Government Printing Office (GPO) Access page on the Internet, which gives information about on-line services and databases.

Government documents can have immense practical value for your research. Government reports, for example, discuss virtually every imaginable topic, from care of the aged, computer programs, flood insurance, and farming techniques to fire precautions, housing costs, outdoor recreation, transportation, and urban development.

Three indexes to government publications are especially helpful in guiding you through the vast store of information.

1. *Catalog of U.S. Government Publications.* Published since 1895, this index lists government documents published during that month. The catalog is arranged by agencies that publish or sponsor works (the Departments of Agriculture, Commerce, Interior, State, and so forth). Each entry provides the author's or agency's name, the title, the date, a brief description of the contents of the document (indicating whether it contains a bibliography, maps, or index), when and where the research was conducted and who sponsored it, the price, and how to order a copy. Since 1996, the *Catalog* has been on-line at *www.access.gpo.gov/su_docs.*

TECH NOTE

Using the *Catalog of U.S. Government Publications*
Because the *Catalog* is on-line and updated daily, it offers superior access to timely, authoritative government-published information. In addition, it makes available, free of charge, a partial record of what the various government agencies have put on the Web. To search for government documents before 1996, you have to use the print version of the *Catalog,* known as the *Monthly Catalog,* or *MOCAT.*
This Tech Note supplied by Liam Kennedy.

2. *U.S. Government Periodical Index.* Published quarterly since March 1994 by the commercial Congressional Information Service (CIS), this index covers over 180 federal publications "that have major research, reference, or general interest value" and that appeal "to a broad cross-section of researchers." Each quarter more than

FIGURE 8.10   GPO Access page on the Internet.

Official Federal Government Information at Your Fingertips

What's Available . . .

Legislative
Executive
Judicial
Regulatory
Administrative Decisions
Core Documents of U.S. Democracy

Quick Links . . .

Code of Federal Regulations
Federal Register,Judicial
CBD*Vet*
Congressional Record
U.S. Code
Other Databases

- Site Search
- Site Contents
- Online Bookstore
- Finding Aids
- Library Services
- What's New Archive

What's New on GPO Access . . .

February 11, 2000 -- Economic Report of the President, 2000

February 7, 2000 -- FY 2001 Federal Budget Publications

February 7, 2000 -- President William Jefferson Clinton -- State of the Union Address, January 27, 2000

A service of the Superintendent of Documents, U.S. Government Printing Office.
Questions or comments: gpoaccess@gpo.gov.

Continued

2,500 articles are included. "Topics range from the use of satellites by air traffic controllers, to improving management skills, to testing for lead pollutions." Some sample titles and the U.S. government periodicals in which they appear are found below.

- "Lifetime Risk of Developing Breast Cancer," *Journal of the National Cancer Institute*
- "FDA Reports on Pesticides in Food," *FDA Consumer*
- "How Can We Measure Leadership Performance?" *Program Manager*
- "Pretrial Release and Detention and Pretrial Services," *Federal Probation*
- "When Cultures Meet," *Folklife Center News*
- "GPS: Revolution in Navigation," *Flying Safety*
- "Marine Recreation and Tourism: Dimensions and Opportunities," *Trends*
- "Hazards of Geomagnetic Storms," *Earthquakes & Volcanoes*

The index is available in print and on CD-ROM. For coverage before 1994, consult the *Index to Government Periodicals* (published from 1970 to 1993).

3. *CIS/Index to Publications of the United States Congress.* Published monthly since 1970, this reference work indexes and abstracts House and Senate documents, reports,

FIGURE 8.10   (Continued)

Database List

General search page for all databases.

- Search across multiple databases

Specialized search for detailed search of individual databases.

About the Databases

- Budget of the United States Government
- Catalog of U.S. Government Publications (MOCAT)
- Code of Federal Regulations
- Commerce Business Daily (CBD*Net*)
- Congress

  - Congressional Bills
  - Congressional Committee Prints
  - Congressional Directory
  - Congressional Documents
  - Congressional Hearings
  - Congressional Pictorial Directory, 105th and 106th Congresses
  - Congressional Record

- Federal Register
- GAO Comptroller General Decisions
- GAO Reports
- Government Information Locator Service Records (GILS)
- List of CFR Sections Affected
- Privacy Act Notices
- Public Papers of the Presidents of the United States

Individual federal agency files available for download.

- Federal Bulletin Board

hearings, investigations, and other publications. It is a particularly valuable guide to legislative investigations and decisions. Annual cumulative volumes are published.

States and counties also engage in research and publish their findings. At the county level, practical publications are available on a wide range of topics in agriculture, education, food science, housing, and water resources. Check with your county agent for copies of relevant publications.

The Popular Press

The "popular press" includes reading material written in nontechnical language for the general public. Brochures, consumer documents, and newspapers constitute the popular press. Brochures are readily available from many sources.

This section shows you how to locate and find copies of newspapers. Daily issues of many prominent newspapers worldwide (*New York Times, Boston Globe, Chicago Tribune, Jerusalem Post*) can be found on the Internet, but back issues on the Web usually do not go back more than a few months. To locate articles in back issues, use the reference sources discussed next.

Indexes to Newspapers

A thorough guide to the newspapers published in the United States and Canada is the *Gale Directory of Publications and Broadcast Media.* This work, issued annually, lists the date a paper began publication; its current address, rates, and circulation; and its religious or political preference. The directory also includes a capsule history of the community served by the paper.

Unfortunately, the *Gale Directory* will not refer you to specific stories. For that information you need to consult an index. The *New York Times Index,* which classifies stories by subject and author, helpfully reprints the photographs, maps, and other illustrations that accompanied some of the stories. Still another advantage the *New York Times Index* offers is that once you find the date of an event, you can then use that date to see how other newspapers covered the story. Many libraries have back issues of the *New York Times* on microfilm.

In addition to the *New York Times Index,* look at the indexes for stories published in newspapers representing other areas of the country: the East (*Washington Post*), the Midwest (*Chicago Tribune*), the South (*New Orleans Times-Picayune*), and the West (*Los Angeles Times*). Also consult the indexes to the *Wall Street Journal, Boston Globe,* and *Christian Science Monitor.*

Several databases—for example, EBSCO Newspaper Source—also include information on newspaper articles.

NewsBank

Begun in 1982, NewsBank is an extremely useful newspaper reference service that both collects newspaper stories and indexes topics in them from over 500 newspapers across the United States. Articles before 1995 are available on microfiche (transparent four-by-six inch cards on which newspaper pages are reduced. Since 1996 full text is on the Web at Newsbank infoWeb at *http://infoweb.newsbank.com/.*

NewsBank makes stories from across the country easy to obtain and to read and allows a researcher to see how a story may be reported differently from one section of the country to another. While you will not find stories from the readily available *New York Times, Wall Street Journal,* or *Christian Science Monitor* in NewsBank, you will be able to locate articles that have appeared in major big-city newspapers from Cincinnati, Houston, Kansas City, Las Vegas, and many others.

Searching the NewsBank reference guide, users will find a wide range of subjects, including business, consumer affairs, environmental issues, law and legal issues, performing arts, and science and technology.

Audiovisual Materials

Audiovisual materials include records, cassettes, tape recordings, audio compact disks, photographs, films, and microforms. Digital video disks (DVDs), the newest audiovisual medium, are CD-ROM disks that can store an enormous amount of data in digital format—133 minutes of high-resolution wide-screen video or 4.7 gigabytes of data on each side of the disk. DVDs may replace CD-ROMs as well as VHS videotapes and laser disks.

Audiovisual materials are shelved in a separate part of the library that contains the proper equipment to store and to use them. You will find audiovisual titles listed in the library's on-line catalog. One particular type of audiovisual material, microforms, deserves special attention.

Microforms—microfilm and microfiche—reduce a great deal of information from its original size and store it compactly on film or tape. Microforms save space, increase document durability, and offer libraries a wider range of titles for far less money.

A **microfilm** is a strip of black-and-white film that stores reduced images of book pages, back issues of periodicals and newspapers, directories, government documents, court proceedings, and so forth. The advantages of microfilm are many. Without it, no library could possibly save all the back issues of a local newspaper, let alone a large one like the *New York Times*. Using microfilm, a library can gather a newspaper's daily issues from an entire month on one reel. A special machine called a **microfilm reader** enlarges the images for reading. Your librarian can show you how to operate one.

The Internet: The Virtual Library

What Is the Internet?

The Internet makes the virtual library—the library without walls—possible. The Internet transcends culture, community, and country and provides an informational highway where people can surf and sample at their leisure. Users can connect with people, places, topics, trends, global issues, and local insights. Nothing can equal the Internet as a research tool. It is not just one computer system but a vast interconnection of computers and computer networks, talking to each other and gathering and exchanging information. The Internet is synonymous with *cyberspace,* a word coined to describe the power and control of information.

Some observers call the Internet "a network of networks" interlinked to bring users information. In this largest electronic network, there are an estimated 4 million Web sites and more than 300 million users worldwide. The Internet is classified as a wide-area network (WAN) because the computers on it cover a wide geographical area—the whole world. Internet users are important citizens in a global electronic village. Each day the Net is growing, expanding at more than 1,000 new users every hour.

History of the Internet

The idea for the Internet began during the late 1950s, when the U.S. military connected various researchers via computer to protect Department of Defense information systems in case of a nuclear war. If one computer was knocked out, information would be duplicated by another computer, and communications could travel by an alternative route. The idea of having so many vital, helpful links gave birth to the Internet of today.

The Accessibility of the Internet

Anyone can access the Internet through a computer, a modem, and an Internet connection. Such connections are available through schools, colleges, universities, companies, national Internet service providers (ISPs) such as America Online (AOL), Microsoft Network (MSN), and Mindspring, or local ISPs. All provide local connections directly to the Internet. Monthly fees vary, depending on number of hours, but are usually about $20 a month.

The World Wide Web

One of the main services of the Net is the World Wide Web (WWW). The Web offers an enormous amount of information in the form of text, video, graphics, videoconferencing, e-mail, and newsgroups. With the Net you can search for information in libraries around the globe. And resources are always available, unlike printed books, reports, and journals, which may be checked out of your local library.

Here are some kinds of data on the Web that, in the past, you would have had to look all over a library—or even several libraries—to find:

- hundreds of databases, collections, and other information services worldwide
- tables of contents of technical and trade journals
- copies of articles from popular magazines to technical journals and newsletters
- popular newspapers from around the world
- leading encyclopedias, like the Britannica Web site, with entries updated monthly
- technical manuals, guides, and product descriptions
- video clips and soundbites from today's most popular movies
- statistical data on stocks and bonds, populations, currency exchange rates

Locating Information on the Web

To reap any research benefits from the Web, you need to know something about the way it works.

Hypertext—What Is It?
The Web contains "pages," but they are not like the pages you see in a book or printed magazine. A page on the Web can be a block of text, but it can also include

---

TECH NOTE

Guides to Internet Journals
The *Internet Press* is a guide to on-line journals that deal just with the Internet; also look at *Internet World* (*http://www.mecklerweb.com*). Journal Online News will give you information about accessing journals on the Net, like *Journal of Air Transportation World Wide*. In addition to those general guides, you can also find guides to on-line journals specific to certain areas, for example FindLaw (*http://www.findlaw.com*) and medical journals (*http://www.uib.no/isf/guide/journal.htm*).

TECH NOTE

Newsgroups

The Web is only one feature of the Net from which you can gather information. The Net also provides other research services through e-mail and user groups, for example, listservs. Becoming a part of these special interest discussion groups can greatly enhance the way you obtain information and do research. Some researchers estimate that there are as many as 50,000 newsgroups asking for and providing information on an endless list of specialized subjects. Once you tap into such a network, your possibilities for research expand phenomenally. A helpful, specialized search engine for finding newsgroups is Deja News (*http://www.dejanews.com.*)

graphics, sound, and animation (see pp. 447–454). Web pages are written in **hypertext markup language** (HTML). HTML uses hyperlinks (colored or highlighted words or graphics) as connections—links—to other sites on the Web, as well as other sections within a site. Because hypertext is crucial to the way the Web functions, Web addresses often start with *http://www*, which means *hypertext transmission protocol://world wide web.* Knowing an Internet address, or a uniform resource locator (URL), allows you to go directly to a site. Examples are *http://www.sony.com* for the Sony Corporation Web site, *http://www. econet.apc. org/econet/en.issues.html* for current information from the Environmental Issues Resource Center, and *http://www.indy.radiology.uiowa.edu* to make a visit to a virtual hospital.

How Hypertext Works

When you place your cursor on a hyperlink and click the mouse button, the page connected to that word or graphic is displayed. One page on the Web is thus linked to every other; one page is connected (or placed on top of or next) to another. Think of hypertext as a gigantic company in which every department is linked directly to every other department. Hypertext pages do not have to be read in any specified order, front to back. In your pointing and clicking, you have endless choices about what information you want presented and in what order. You can move easily in any direction from one page of information to another.

An Example from the Library of Congress

Take a look at Figure 8.11, the Web page for the Library of Congress. Clicking on "Using the Library," you would see Figure 8.12, "Collections and Services," which lists the various options, or hypertext layers, you can select. If you clicked on the link Explore the Internet, you would find four other sites (Figure 8.13, p. 326), including Learn About the Internet, which promises guides, tools, and training materials.

FIGURE 8.11   Web page for the Library of Congress.

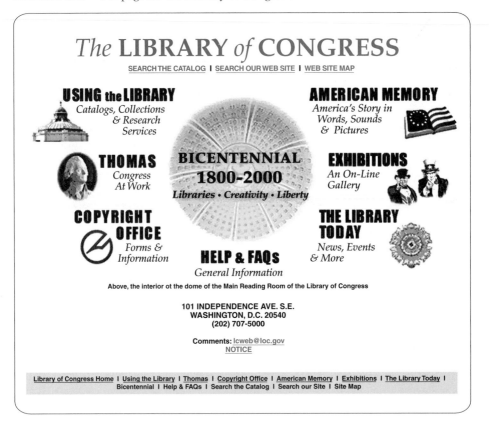

Choosing that hypertext link takes you even further into this specialized subject by displaying sixteen more sites, ranging from Books and Journals about the Internet to Security, Internet Statistics, and Internet Guides and Tutorials.

Let's say you want to learn more about the Internet through the Library of Congress's tutorials. You click on Internet Guides and Tutorials and find more than forty different sites to choose from. You can read a brief description of each of the forty sites. For example, for An Introduction to the Internet and WWW, you find that a "Powerpoint viewer for viewing the slides is available for downloading at this site" and that BCK2SKOL: The Electronic Library Classroom 101 presents "A beginner's course in the Net and its various tools targeted toward librarians and other information professionals." Layers of information unfold before you as you click on one topic after another.

Hyperlinks as Research Tools

Unlike flipping the pages of a book back and forth, hypertext lets researchers connect and retrieve pages from computer networks all around the world. Information flows to you from many different paths—time, countries, companies, individuals—and in what-

FIGURE 8.12   Collections and services accessible from Library of Congress Web site.

USING THE LIBRARY OF CONGRESS
Collections & Services
for Researchers, Libraries, and the Public

Library of Congress Online Catalog - Other Libraries' Online Catalogs
Other LC Research Tools - Explore the Internet - LC Publications

SERVICES
for **Researchers**
for **Publishers**
for **K-12 Educators**
for **Blind & Physically Handicapped**
for **Federal Libraries & Info Centers**
Global Legal Information (GLIN)
Center for the Book
Photoduplication Service
Cataloging Distribution Service

COLLECTIONS
About the Collections
Reading Rooms & Centers
Library Maps & Floor Plans
Digital Collections & Programs
Acquisitions
Cataloging
Interlibrary Loan
Preservation
Standards

*The Main Reading Room of
The Library of Congress*

LC Briefing for ALA Midwinter
Conference 2000

Library of Congress Home I Using the Library I Thomas I Copyright Office I American Memory I Exhibitions I The Library Today I
Bicentennial I Help & FAQs I Search the Catalog I Search our Site I Site Map

 Library of Congress

Comments: lcweb@loc.gov(01/12/2000)

ever sequence you want. For that reason you might enjoyably spend hours pointing and clicking—**surfing**—your way all over the Web. But as a research tool hypertext serves a valuable function because its cross-referencing allows you to link one part of a topic to another, thereby increasing the layers or clusters of information you can search.

Precautions in Using the Web

While the Web offers unprecedented research advantages, it also presents some limitations. The Web's strengths—its accessibility and variety—can also be its weaknesses. One researcher put the main problem of using the Web this way:

> Accessing information on the Web is like going to a bookstore. You have no idea what's very good and what's not. While a library may have a lot of older items and not nearly as many new ones as the Web, the items in a library have at least been edited by a publishing company and have been chosen over less desirable works to be printed. With the Web you are in many cases forced to be your own publisher and editor.

Be realistic. Don't expect to find everything you need on the Web. Keep in mind that it is not only a research tool but also a source of entertainment and an aggressive business.

FIGURE 8.13   Explore the Internet page of the Library of Congress Web site.

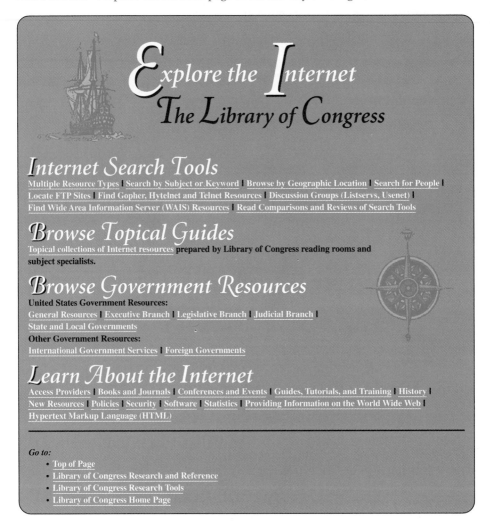

Here are some practical guidelines to follow when you do research on the Web.

- You may not always find the best information. Use the Web along with CD-ROM databases, books, and other reference materials.
- Don't expect to get every article from every professional (or popular) journal on the Web. Not all periodicals are on-line. And many periodicals that are on the Web start with the most recent issues; back issues are not yet available.
- Realize that many periodicals on the Web are either subscription-based or have only selected highlights from the actual magazine (for example, only the table of contents or abstracts).

> ## TECH NOTE
>
> **Punctuation and Structure of a URL**
>
> Just as proper punctuation helps you understand the written language better, so understanding the structure and punctuation of URLs can assist you in navigating the Web.
>
> The URL for the Internet Resources page of the Lyme Disease Information Resource Web site, *http://www.x-l.net/Lyme/internet.html* (see pp. 335–336), is logically divided into separate parts by slashes. Each piece of information between slashes represents different levels of information particular to the information hierarchy. The first portion, *http://,* indicates the **protocol** used. Second, *www.x-l.net,* indicates the server name or **domain** name. It is unique to the http protocol. Third, *Lyme* points to a **directory** of the domain. Lastly, *internet.html* is the name of the **file** being viewed on the Web. Together, the entire string of characters serves as a path the computer follows to get you to certain information.
>
> Knowing the structure can prove useful in at least two ways. First, because natural language is often used to name files and directories, when a source provides an erroneous URL, researchers can often backtrack to the parent directory and search for the relevant file or info. Second, by backing out intentionally, researchers can discover other relevant valuable information.
>
> This Tech Note supplied by Liam Kennedy.

- Because the Web is so vast, you may have to experiment with different search strategies and try a variety of addresses.
- Not everything is free. Accessing some documents on the Web may require passwords that are available only to subscribers.
- Make a hard copy of any material you intend to cite in your paper or report. A Web site can change, be "under construction," or vanish. You need hard evidence.
- Be extremely careful about giving personal information before you are allowed to sample any material at a particular site. The information may be sold to companies or groups that will flood you with unwanted sales pitches or materials.

Evaluating a Web Site

Not everything you find on the Internet will be correct or up-to-date. Just because something is listed on the Web does not make it accurate. Web sites vary tremendously, from giving clear, even authoritative information to expressing unsupported opinions and biases. Use discretion when you surf the Web.

Here are some guidelines to help you evaluate Web sites.

1. **Look for sites maintained by reputable professional organizations,** like the American Chemical Society or the Association for Women in Sales and

Marketing. The information at such sites has been endorsed by a highly respected organization.

2. **Explore Web sites run by federal, state, and local agencies.** These sites are useful for a wide range of information, from searching the job market (for example, the U.S. Bureau of Labor's *www.bls.gov*) to finding out city building codes.

3. **Find out when the information was last posted.** A site that has not been updated for several years or even months may contain incomplete, inaccurate, or even contradictory data and references.

4. **Consider the qualifications or credentials of an individual who maintains and/or expresses viewpoints at a given site.** See if the person has listed credentials—degrees, experiences, memberships in professional societies—all indications of his or her competency.

5. **Do not assume that everything you need is on the Internet.** You may not always find the most relevant and accurate information on the Web. Consult CD-ROMs, databases, print journals, reference books, and resource people.

6. **Do not rely on just one Web site for your information.** Collect data, ideas, confirmations, even conflicting points of view from different Web sites, printed sources (especially reference books), and resource people. Compare the findings of several different sources.

7. **See how often a site is listed through hyperlinks by other sources.** "Netizens"—individuals who construct and use Web sites frequently—are not timid about praising or criticizing a site.

8. **Use only reputable sites when you place orders.** If you think your rights as a consumer have been violated, check the Web site of the National Consumers League at *www.fraud.org,* which describes types of Internet fraud and issues guidelines on safe buying on-line.

The Dynamic Organization of the Web

The Web is constantly changing and expanding. Each day new sites are added and existing ones are modified—supplemented, combined, updated, and replaced. Because the Web is so vast, there could never be one comprehensive index or guide to its resources. Unlike the traditional library, which offers patrons limited, precisely defined information contained in bound volumes, CD-ROMs, or databases, the virtual libraries of the Web are potentially limitless. They can be accessed in a variety of ways and through a variety of searches not possible with the reference works described in the earlier sections of this chapter.

Surfing versus Searching

Surfing the Web describes wandering from one Web site to another without any particular topic or goal in mind. In our example from the Library of Congress in Figures 8.11 through 8.13, a user could easily click on general information, copyrights, or exhibitions, and retrieve a variety of information. When you surf, you "float" through cyberspace just to see what is out there. While enjoyable and entertaining, surfing will not help you to write a restricted report and can be very expensive and time-consuming.

When you *search* the Web, on the other hand, your approach must be more focused, more narrowed, as you labor to find that needle in the haystack. Your search skills have to be careful and precise.

Guidelines for Searching the Web

When you search the Web, keep these points in mind.

- As you encounter a variety of sources, databases, home pages, and virtual libraries, try not to be overwhelmed; you *can* and *will* find something pertinent to your topic.
- Keep your search strategies flexible and open. Information can be indexed and posted in many ways on the Web. Look under different headings and categories. For example, if you have to search for something about computer software, you may start your search with either a "Software" heading or the name of a specific software vendor.
- Familiarize yourself with the scope and strengths of individual search engines (see pp. 331–333).
- Verify information you find at Web sites by consulting, through a keyword search, other independent Web pages and non-Web sources.
- Don't get sidetracked. You will see items that intrigue you and arouse your curiosity. Mark them (with "bookmarks") for later exploration and stay focused on your current goals. Searching the Web requires discipline.

TECH NOTE

Using Bookmarks

Just as you slip a sheet of paper into a book or turn down the page of a magazine to mark your place, you can use a Web browser's bookmark feature to keep track of your favorite sites on the Internet and to return quickly to them later. In Netscape Navigator you choose the command "Add Bookmark"; in America Online's browser you click on a heart-shaped icon in the corner of the Web page. When you want to return to that site later, activate the bookmark, and your Web browser will go online automatically and take you directly to that page.

Search Engines

One of the most productive ways to accomplish research on the Web is to use a search engine. A **search engine** is a guide to the resources on the Web. Basically it is a software program that identifies, describes, and assesses the information on the Net that you need. When you request specific information on the Web, a search engine "looks through" the databases and returns the information that most closely matches your search request based on the keywords you selected. Think of it as a computerized scout, or "spider" that goes through the diverse networks on the Web and brings back a list of relevant documents. A search engine can look through databases such as those on pages 309–312, news wires (Reuters, AP, UPI), periodicals, indexes, abstracts, summaries, articles, Web sites, and user-group lists, and it searches all those resources simultaneously. A search engine goes through an enormous database that includes information found across as many as 40 million Web sites.

Examples of Search Engines

Just as there is no single index to the Web, there is no one best search engine. There are many different types of search engines, as Figure 8.14 shows. Just like Web sites, there are always new engines, and they're getting bigger. If you use the Netscape Web browser and click on "Net Search," you will be presented with one of those engines. They vary in what they cover and what they cost. Some are much faster than others, and some incorporate others. To some extent all of them overlap. No one search engine is comprehensive, though some claim to search 30 billion pages. You may be limited by what is available to you through your library or employer. For information on various search engines, click on Search Engine Watch at *http://www.searchenginewatch.com*.

TECH NOTE

Using Multiple Search Engines

With all its computers, Apple now ships Sherlock, which not only uses as many search engines (and encyclopedias, databases, dictionaries, etc.) as you might want but also searches your own hard drive, any resident CDs in your system, and any of the computers on your local network—all you have to do is type a search term in a single box.

This Tech Note supplied by Michael Salda.

Expect a tradeoff between how fast a search engine works and how good it is. The fastest search engines tend to look only at titles or keywords on a few pages, whereas the slower ones conduct a more detailed look through many more pages.

Follow these guidelines when using a search engine:

- Use a fast, general search engine first and see how much it gives you. Then, as your research progresses, turn to a slower, more exhaustive engine.
- Always take advantage of several search engines. Even though some of the information you receive may be duplicated, you still increase your chances of obtaining precisely the information you need about your topic.

Listed below are some frequently used search engines. Keep in mind that, because Internet technology is rapidly changing, some of these search engines may be replaced by newer, more efficient ones.

FIGURE 8.14   Different types of Internet search engines.

Listserv/Newsgroup Search

E-Mail Discussion Groups
Liszt—Directory of Email
Discussion Groups
CataList, official catalog of LISTSERV(R)
lists
DejaNews Research Service
Tile Net—Listserv, newsgroup, and ftp
directories.
One List—Listserv directory, archive
repository, and host where you can
start your own listserv.
Internet Now—Searches non-Web
sites.

Web Search Engines

Alta Vista	Infoseek/Go
Excite	Google
HotBot	WebCrawler

Multiple Engines

Inference—Removes redundancies and
clusters results by source.
All Search Engines—Search engine
directory listing specialized engines
by category.
ALL-IN-ONE
The Internet Sleuth
ProFusion

Specialized Searches

Webplaces—Clip Art Searcher
ISurf—Search for graphics and images.
Scour.Net—Image and multimedia
searching by keyword.
News Trawler—Search news, magazine,
and journal archives internationally.
World Pages—Search for people and
businesses.
TotalNews—Search engine for online
newspapers.
Filez—Search for files by type, such as
gif, or domain.

Search Directories

Yahoo!
Scout Report
LookSmart
Northern Lights Search
Internet Public Library
Galaxy
Infoseek Guide
eBlast
Britannica Search Helper—Gives out
information on a number of
popular search engines, searching
tips, reviews, etc.

Courtesy of The University of Southern Mississippi Libraries.

   1. AltaVista (*http://www.altavista.com*) has one of the largest databases (40 million Web pages) and may easily give hundreds of thousands of hits for broad keywords. It also offers advanced searching capabilities.

   2. Excite (*http://www.excite.com*) is a general-purpose engine that is a good place to start when you are not sure precisely what you are looking for. It gives percentage values to each of the sites, or **hits,** that are most likely to match the kinds of information you request through your keyword search. Excite also has some ancillary databases such as the City Net, which give information on cities around the world.

   3. Hotbot (*http://www.hotbot.com*) has the ability to search for not only keywords but also phrases, people, and Internet addresses.

   4. Infoseek (*http://www.infoseek.com*) offers a special feature called Infoseek Personal, which allows you to describe information (research topics, news, sports) in which you have an ongoing interest. Infoseek Personal will then retrieve related items for you as they become available.

5. Lycos (*http://www.lycos.com*) has a large database, though smaller than that of Alta Vista. As well as indexing the title, headings, and subheadings in a page, Lycos (Greek for "spider") also searches the first twenty lines of text. It displays a relevancy rating for each hit.

6. WebCrawler (*http://www.webcrawler.com*) actually searches an index of the Web rather than the sites themselves and then categorizes the sites into the Web Site Guide, a compilation of the best sites organized by topics.

7. Yahoo! (http:www.yahoo.com), one of the first Web engines, shines in having a very good directory structure. It is excellent for browsing. If you need to do a directory search, Yahoo! is the place to start.

Guidelines for Restricting Keyword Searches

1. Don't use just one keyword. Choose at least two or three significant keywords to specify your search. For example, if you keyed in just the word *virus,* you might receive vast amounts of information on anything about human and animal illnesses as well as violations of computer systems. Specify *computer virus* to narrow your search.

2. To narrow your search further, identify a precise subject. Don't confuse a broad subject with a more limited heading within it. For example, don't start off with a broad subject such as *computer security.* You might be presented with everything from computer theft at airports to encryptions that protect messages. As in guideline 1 above, start with *computer virus,* which is a much more focused subject under the larger topic of *computer security.*

3. Be prepared to refine your keyword choice(s) as entries come up on the screen. For instance, you might replace *computer virus* with *computer disinfect program.*

4. Link several keywords to pinpoint your search. *Computer virus causes* or *computer virus controls* will net you more precise, pertinent information.

5. Select a synonym if your initial keyword search does not produce results. In the example in guideline 3 above, you might substitute the synonym *software program,* which may retrieve additional, relevant information not generated by the keyword search using just *program.*

6. Consider using delimiters as you search. Here are some examples:

- **Quotation marks** around a term limit your search to just that term. For example, "Wells Fargo" without the quotation marks would pull up sites for Wells Engineering; Fargo, North Dakota; and Fargo Wells.
- The words **and** and **or** restrict what you receive. The word **and** means that *all* the words in your key term joined by **and** must appear in the sites you want the search engine to retrieve. The **or** specifies that the search results **must** contain at least one of the terms.

- A **plus** sign before a term or between terms indicates that you want only sites where both terms are found, for example, *Museums + Chicago.*
- The word **not** as a part of your keyword search excludes unwanted or unnecessary sites. *Telecommuting benefits, not environmental* indicates that you are not concerned with material dealing with how telecommuting saves energy or reduces pollution. Instead you are focusing on other kinds of benefits—to employees and employers. You could also use *telecommuting + benefits + employers.*

Avoiding Long Lists and Duplications

A search engine looks for keywords in titles, abstracts, first pages, and any type of cross-reference. Armed with your keywords or key phrases (note that search engines treat a phrase as a number of distinct words), a search engine sorts through its database and lists what it regards as the most relevant matches for your request.

If you have not refined your search and selected keywords, you could initially be overwhelmed with a list of 3,000 or even 30,000 items. Such a huge list signals that you probably have not done enough homework about your topic. For example, keying in just *women's golf* or *laser surgery* might return thousands of citations. However, don't despair. Follow these suggestions:

1. Look closely at the first ten references (hits) displayed on your screen to see if they are the best matches. If none of them is, do not waste time continuing your investigation. Because hits often are ordered to reflect the probability of a match, chances are slim you will find what you need beyond the first ten hits.
2. Before you eliminate the first ten, though, look at a few to see if you can find any other leads, key subtopics, phrases, patterns, or hyperlinks that might narrow your search.
3. Rephrase your keywords to redefine and focus your search.
4. Consider using a different database and going back to the on-line catalog for further help.

Two Major Types of Web Searches

Topic or Directory Searches

A topic or directory search is the easiest way to get started on the Web if you do not already have a carefully focused topic, or you have only a general topic in mind. Searching through hypertext actually assists your search for a restricted topic. Pointing and clicking through the Web, going back and forth from one Web site to another, you will eventually discover how a subject is restricted and where the most relevant information can be found.

Case Study: Lyme Disease Information on the Internet

Let's say you have to write a report for your class in community health but have no specific topic in mind. Choose one of the search engines provided by your Web browser program. If you use Yahoo! or another widely found search engine, you would first see a screen that brings up a number of general categories and headings, such as *Arts, Entertainment, Health,* and *Sports.* A directory will file hundreds of thousands of documents under those large headings. The most pertinent general category for your purposes is *Health,* so you would click on it. You would then see the Health screen subdivided into numerous categories, including *Diseases and Conditions.*

Going to that screen, you would find a specific reference to *Lyme Disease,* carried by ticks in wooded areas. You may have heard of this disease or recently read a newspaper article about it. Seeing it listed, you decide to learn more about it. By clicking on *Lyme Disease,* you are on your way to a number of helpful sources of information via hyperlinks.

The *Diseases and Conditions: Lyme Disease* page offers four choices; not knowing much about the topic, you decide to click on the first—which takes you to the home page of the American Lyme Disease Foundation. The foundation might be a place to contact via e-mail for some basic information and further leads. Equally important for your search, this home page suggests useful categories that might lead to a focused topic, including *Management, Precautions,* and *Vaccines.* You decide to pursue the idea of *Management* of the disease and want to see what type of (and how much) information is available and pertinent for your class report.

You recall the heading *Lyme Disease Resource* on the *Diseases and Conditions* page, so now you go back to that page by clicking on the *back* button at the top of the screen. You now select *Lyme Disease Information Resource & Tick-borne* displayed in Figure 8.15; there you get a set of further choices, including *General Information, Clinical, Research,* and *Internet.*

Clicking on *Research,* you will be lead to a subsequent page on *Medical Indexes.* You can then select the subset *Medline,* the on-line database of *Index Medicus,* having to do with genetics. This is the most appropriate subset of the large Medline database, since it deals with a specific subdivision here. You decide to restrict your search to just treatment of the disease and so for your query terms you key in *Lyme & Disease & Treatment.*

As a result of your search, you find ninety-one citations from highly specialized medical journals. Taking a look at a few abstracts, available from *Medline Reports,* you realize at once that this information is for geneticists, far too technical for your purposes. At the same time, you conclude that there must be some other options on the Web you need to pursue.

Since you do not want to abandon the idea of writing on the treatment of Lyme disease completely, you decide to restrict your topic by focusing *not* on treatment of the disease in general but on its impact on a specific population—children. Going back to the Lyme Disease Information Resource page (Figure 8.15) you click on *Clinical* and key in *Lyme Disease—Children.* Then you see on your screen an initial list of ten items, sorted by confidence and indicated by percentages, that may be relevant to your topic. Going through these ten hits, you suspect that some are too general but may still be useful for research, especially the first two, including the

FIGURE 8.15   Abbreviated version of Lyme Disease Web pages.

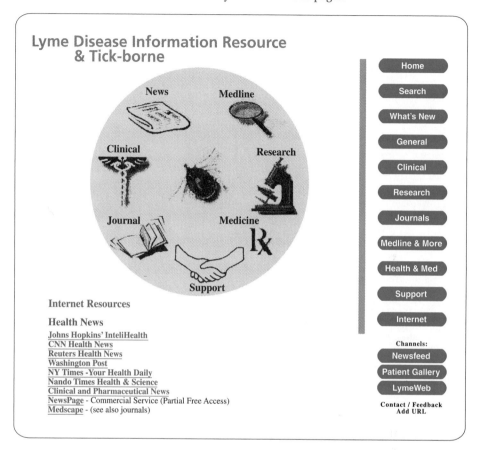

Continued

Lyme Disease Newsletter. You also discover that four items are highly relevant to the disease and children—*Managing the Disease, Neurological Manifestations, Lyme Disease and Preschoolers,* and *Adults and Pregnancy*—and you click to get copies of those articles.

Keyword Searches

A keyword search—as opposed to a directory search—may be the more expedient search strategy if you have a restricted topic in mind. Your success here depends on finding the keywords that will unlock the resources on the Web that you need to write your paper or report. For example, if you needed information on Lyme disease, you would search for "lyme disease." Using quotes narrows the topic and limits the search by weeding. If you did not use quotes, search engines would look for every mention of *lyme* and *disease,* giving you lots of unrelated material.

FIGURE 8.15   (Continued)

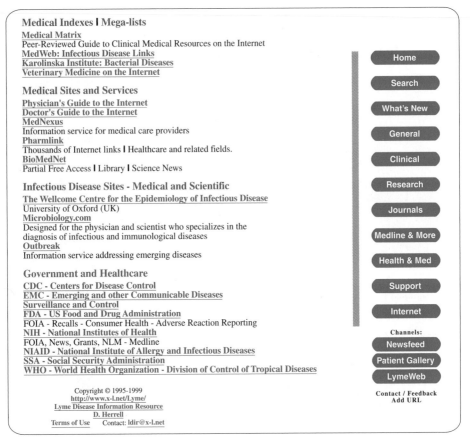

Medical Indexes I Mega-lists

Medical Matrix
Peer-Reviewed Guide to Clinical Medical Resources on the Internet
MedWeb: Infectious Disease Links
Karolinska Institute: Bacterial Diseases
Veterinary Medicine on the Internet

Medical Sites and Services

Physician's Guide to the Internet
Doctor's Guide to the Internet
MedNexus
Information service for medical care providers
Pharmlink
Thousands of Internet links I Healthcare and related fields.
BioMedNet
Partial Free Access I Library I Science News

Infectious Disease Sites - Medical and Scientific

The Wellcome Centre for the Epidemiology of Infectious Disease
University of Oxford (UK)
Microbiology.com
Designed for the physician and scientist who specializes in the
diagnosis of infectious and immunological diseases
Outbreak
Information service addressing emerging diseases

Government and Healthcare

CDC - Centers for Disease Control
EMC - Emerging and other Communicable Diseases
Surveillance and Control
FDA - US Food and Drug Administration
FOIA - Recalls - Consumer Health - Adverse Reaction Reporting
NIH - National Institutes of Health
FOIA, News, Grants, NLM - Medline
NIAID - National Institute of Allergy and Infectious Diseases
SSA - Social Security Administration
WHO - World Health Organization - Division of Control of Tropical Diseases

Home
Search
What's New
General
Clinical
Research
Journals
Medline & More
Health & Med
Support
Internet

Channels:
Newsfeed
Patient Gallery
LymeWeb

Copyright © 1995-1999
http://www.x-l.net/Lyme/
Lyme Disease Information Resource
D. Herrell
Terms of Use   Contact: ldir@x-l.net

Contact / Feedback
Add URL

Copyright © 1995-1999, Lyme Disease Information Resource, D. Herrell.

Note-Taking

Once you have consulted the appropriate library and on-line sources, you need some systematic way to record relevant information from them to use in preparing your paper or report. Before you can begin drafting your work, you must be able to organize and classify data from your research efficiently. (Even after you start to draft your report, you will probably need to continue your research and take additional notes.)

Note-taking is the crucial link between finding sources and writing a report. Never trust your memory to keep all your research facts straight. Taking notes is time well spent. Do not be too quick in getting it done or too eager to begin writing your paper. Careless note-taking could lead you to omit key words in a quotation or even worse, misrepresent or contradict what the author has said. Carelessness could result in crediting one author with another's work.

Basically, you will be preparing two kinds of notes. One type, on the sources you read, will become your working bibliography. The other type will be reserved for the specific information you take from those sources in the form of direct quotations, paraphrases, and summaries.

Traditionally, researchers have used 3" × 5" and 4" × 6" index cards for their note-taking. Some researchers prefer spiral-bound notebooks. A laptop computer or computerized notebook can greatly help you store and retrieve your notes.

How to Prepare Bibliography Notes

Look at the sample bibliography card in Figure 8.16. To record accurate and meaningful information on cards, follow these practical guidelines.

1. Use only 3" × 5" index cards. Do not be tempted to use slips of paper or loose-leaf notebook paper; cards are less likely to get lost, and they will help you to organize, alphabetize, and label material.
2. Write on only one side of the card. It is easier to copy and check information when you list it all on one side.
3. Put only one title (article or book or film) on each card. The cards will later have to be arranged in alphabetical order for your Works Cited page (see pp. 353–359); if you place two titles on one card, you run the risk of omitting one of the titles.

Whether you use cards or a laptop, follow these guidelines:

FIGURE 8.16   Card containing bibliographic information on a source.

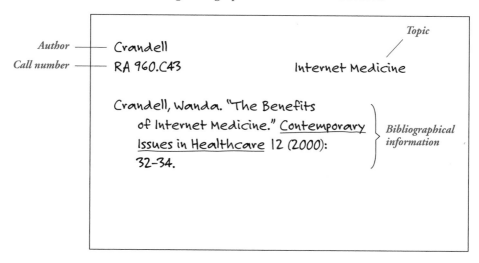

TECH NOTE

Software to Prepare Bibliographic References

You can replace index cards with software that will help you quickly locate, update, cite, format, and integrate footnotes and bibliographic entries into your writing projects. Programs like Microsoft Word, WordPerfect, and Nisus Writer keep track of all citations and let you edit (and renumber) notes in place; they also offer capabilities to ease such tasks as outlining, indexing, cross-referencing, and preparing tables of contents. Their search functions will quickly locate all references to a particular text within a document and will even revise it as you specify.

If you have to manage a large number of bibliographies, consider purchasing a dedicated program like TakeNote, EndNote Plus, or Bookends Pro. Some of those programs work in tandem with the word processors named above and can import and export citations, making it a snap to amass and select from your own up-to-date bibliographies, and EndNote allows you to choose among 300 bibliographic styles.

All these programs can format citations in the styles of particular associations (Council of Biology Editors, Modern Language Association, Chicago Manual of Style, American Psychological Association) or up to hundreds of professional publications. Some bibliography managers also link up with the Internet to locate Web site addresses (URLs) and enter them into bibliographies for later research and citation.

1. Include full bibliographic information for each source. For books, list author, title, chapter title, edition, date, city of publication, publisher, and page numbers; for articles, supply author, title, journal, volume number, date, and page numbers. Keep a record of Internet addresses as well.
2. Decode and spell out any periodical index or journal abbreviations. Record periodical entries with their full and accurate bibliographic information. (See Chapter 9 on documentation.) The abbreviated entries in indexes such as *Applied Science & Technology Index* or in other databases are not in acceptable format for parenthetical documentation or Works Cited page entries in your paper or report.
3. Record the call numbers of any book (in the upper left corner, if you use cards) so you will know where to find the source again if you need it. If you obtained a copy of an article or other source from an on-line search, note from which database it came.

How to Prepare Information Notes

While your bibliographic notes record important facts about authors, titles, and publication data, your information notes contain the specific details from those sources that you need to write your paper. Your notes will contain direct quotations from or paraphrases of your sources. Quotations and paraphrases are discussed below. Here are some guidelines to follow when preparing note cards like those shown in Figures 8.17 and 8.18.

1. Use 4" × 6" cards to keep them separate from the 3" × 5" bibliography cards.
2. Write on only one side of the card. It will be easier for you to arrange the cards in the order that makes sense for your paper.
3. Don't put notes from two different sources on one card.

Whether you use cards or a laptop, follow these guidelines for the notes themselves.

1. Copy names, facts, dates, and statistics accurately from the source. Be sure, too, that you record the author's words correctly; you may want to quote them verbatim in your paper. Always compare what you have written with the original or the copy you may have obtained from an on-line or Internet search.
2. Make sure that you distinguish quotations from paraphrasing by placing quotation marks around any words and sentences you record directly from a source.
3. Write a code word or phrase (in the upper right corner, if you use cards) to identify the topic treated by the source or the information written on the card from that source. Using code words such as "characteristics," "function of," "history of," or "location of" will help you to organize when you write your paper. Figure 8.17 shows how one writer used code words.
4. You might indicate in the note why the material is significant to your argument or where you might include such information in your report or paper. In

FIGURE 8.17   Note card containing a direct quotation.

Crandell 32   Importance of Internet Medicine

"The Internet is a primary source of medical information for consumers. CybMed, an Internet marketing firm, estimates that more than 40 million people in 2000 consulted the Net for a variety of health-related information. Most users searched popular sites such as Medscape to look up the signs and symptoms of their medical problems. Consumers also flocked to the PharmInfo Net, an FDA Web site, to find information on new drugs and their possible side effects. These Web sites are the closest thing to a doctor who makes house calls."

FIGURE 8.18   Note card containing a paraphrase.

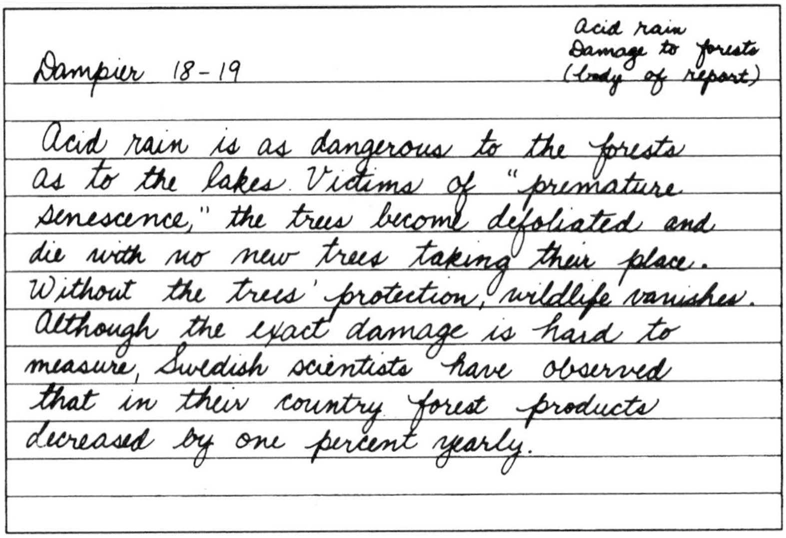

Dampier 18-19   Acid rain
                                  Damage to forests
                                  (body of report)

Acid rain is as dangerous to the forests
as to the lakes. Victims of "premature
senescence," the trees become defoliated and
die with no new trees taking their place.
Without the trees' protection, wildlife vanishes.
Although the exact damage is hard to
measure, Swedish scientists have observed
that in their country forest products
decreased by one percent yearly.

Figure 8.18 the writer identified a possible use for the Dampier paraphrase. You might also write your response to a quotation to help you later organize your paper. But be careful not to include any of your comments within a quotation or paraphrase.

5. Write a short title of the book or journal article, or the author's last name (in the upper left corner, if you use cards) so the information note is coded to your bibliography note. If your notes extend to a second card, make sure you include the source, with appropriate page number(s), on the second card.

TECH NOTE

Electronic Note Taking

QuickNotes™ software "shrinks, snaps, wraps, and organizes input ink" for your PC. Simply enter your notes or handwritten pages with a Jot handwriting recognition system, and QuickNotes dates, stores, and allows you to organize and retrieve them. You can even e-mail and fax your notes. This amazing compression technology can help you to gather and save information without "worrying about losing scraps of paper."

Information taken from "Electronic Note Taking: QuickNotes™" at *http://www.cic.com/ oem/4_ENotes.htm*.

To Quote or Not to Quote

Before recording information from sources, ask yourself three questions:

1. How much should I take down?
2. How often should I copy the author's words verbatim?
3. When should I paraphrase or summarize?

Quote Sparingly

A safe rule to follow is this: Do not be a human photocopying machine. If you write down too many of the author's own words, you will simply be transferring the author's words from the book or article to your paper. That will show that you have read the work but not whether you have evaluated its findings. Do not use direct quotations simply as filler.

Use direct quotations sparingly—save them for when they count most. When an author has summarized a great deal of significant information concisely into a few well-chosen sentences, you may want to quote the summary verbatim. Or if a writer has clarified a difficult concept exceedingly well, you may want to include the clarification exactly as it is listed. And certainly the author's chief statement or thesis may deserve to be quoted directly. Figure 8.17 contains such an important statement. Just be careful that you do not quote verbatim all the evidence leading to that conclusion. The conclusion may be pointedly expressed in two or three sentences; the evidence could cover many pages.

If you are worried about exactly how much to quote verbatim, keep in mind that no more than 10 to 15 percent of your paper should be made up of direct quotations. Remember that when you quote someone directly, you are telling your readers that these words are the most important part of the author's work as far as you are concerned. Be a selective filter, not a large funnel.

Using Ellipses

Sometimes a sentence or passage is particularly useful, but you may not want to quote it fully. You may want to delete some words that are not really necessary for your purpose. These omissions are indicated by using an *ellipsis* (three spaced dots within the sentence to indicate where words have been omitted). Here are some examples.

> Full Quotation: "Diet and nutrition, which researchers have studied extensively, significantly affect oral health."
> Quotation with Ellipsis: "Diet and nutrition . . . significantly affect oral health."

When the omission occurs at the end of the sentence, you must include the end-of-sentence punctuation after the ellipsis. In the following example, note how the shortened sentence ends with four spaced dots: the three dots for the ellipsis and the closing period.

> Full Quotation: "Decisions on how to operate the company should be based on the most accurate and relevant information available from

both within the company and from the specific community that the establishment serves."

Quotation with Ellipsis: "Decisions on how to operate the company should be based on the most accurate and relevant information available. . . ."

At times you may have to insert your own information within a quotation. This addition, known as an *interpolation,* is made by enclosing your clarifying identification or remark in brackets inside the quotation; for example, "It [the new transportation network] has been thoroughly tested and approved." Anything in brackets is not part of the original quotation.

Paraphrasing

Most of your note-taking will be devoted to paraphrasing rather than writing down direct quotations. A *paraphrase* is a restatement in your own words of the author's ideas. Even though you are using your own words to translate or restate, you still must document the paraphrase because you are using the author's facts and interpretations. You do not use quotation marks, though. When you include a paraphrase in your paper, you should be careful to do four things:

1. Be faithful to the author's meaning. Do not alter facts or introduce new ideas.
2. Follow the order in which the author presents the information.
3. Include in your paraphrase only what is relevant for your paper. Delete any details not essential for your work.
4. Use paraphrases in your report selectively. You do not want your work to be merely a restatement of someone else's.

Paraphrased material can be introduced in your paper with an appropriate identifying phrase, such as "According to Dampier's study," "To paraphrase Dampier," or "As Dampier observes." The note card shown in Figure 8.18 paraphrases the following quotation.

> While the effects of acid rain are felt first in lakes, which act as natural collection points, some scientists fear there may be extensive damage to forests as well. In the process described by one researcher as "premature senescence," trees exposed to acid sprays lose their leaves, wilt, and finally die. New trees may not grow to replace them. Deprived of natural cover, wildlife may flee or die. The extent of the damage to forest lands is extremely difficult to determine, but scientists find the trend worrisome. In Sweden, for example, one estimate calculates that the yield in forest products decreased by about one percent each year. . . .[1]

Conclusion

This chapter has introduced you to some very basic yet essential strategies and tools, including the Internet. Clearly, you need to rely on a host of resources—print, databases, various search engines—to conduct effective research. Relying on those

---

[1]Bill Dampier, "Now Even the Rain Is Dangerous," *International Wildlife* 10 (March–April 1980): 18–19.

research tools and strategies, you will have the most correct, most thorough, and most relevant answers to the questions you are asked to investigate and the problems you need to solve on the job. Exploring (and exploiting) all potential resources of the Information Age as described in this chapter will prepare you to write the types of documents—instructions, reports, proposals—discussed in later chapters.

✓ Revision Checklist

Process of Research
- ❑ Identified significant, timely, and limited problem.
- ❑ Selected and evaluated most relevant sources.

Library Search
- ❑ Learned how to use on-line catalogs.
- ❑ Found where appropriate materials are located.

Research Tools
- ❑ Searched library's on-line catalog for major term(s) to start working bibliography.
- ❑ Checked specialized and general indexes.
- ❑ Did preliminary search among relevant databases to check subtopics and scope of material available.
- ❑ Restricted keywords for searches in print and on-line.
- ❑ Determined which CD-ROM and on-line searches library has available and selected most useful ones.
- ❑ Ran an on-line search to compile a list of relevant sources.
- ❑ Read abstracts of relevant items.
- ❑ Obtained copies of full text of relevant articles, conference papers, and the like.
- ❑ Checked relevant reference materials, such as almanacs, abstracts, encyclopedias, in print and on the Net.
- ❑ Used databases and NewsBank InfoWeb to find appropriate newspaper coverage of my topic.
- ❑ Read and scrutinized periodicals, books, government documents.

The Internet
- ❑ Discovered which Internet searches are most helpful.
- ❑ Did a directory search on the Web.
- ❑ Searched for pertinent information using at least two search engines.
- ❑ Located relevant Web page(s) relating to my topic.
- ❑ Continued to refine search when number of hits was too high.

❑ Joined newsgroup relevant to my topic.
❑ Combined library (on-line catalog) search with Internet research when time limits or availability of materials warranted.

Taking Notes
❑ Investigated software options.
❑ Did not quote excessively or out of context, quoted accurately.
❑ Paraphrased fairly, accurately representing original material.
❑ Distinguished my comments and responses clearly from sources.
❑ Used correct punctuation with direct quotations, especially ellipses and brackets for interpolations.

Exercises

1. Find out if your library provides a map or description of its holdings. If it does, bring a copy to class. If it does not, draw one yourself, indicating the location of the circulation desk, the on-line catalog, the reference room, government documents, audiovisuals, and other areas you patronize.

2. Find any book in the library and write a brief description of the steps you took to locate the book—from searching in the on-line catalog to checking the book out at the circulation desk. Refer to the map you used in Exercise 1.

3. Using a subject search on the on-line catalog, find a topic that is subdivided as shown in Figure 8.2. Divide the subdivisions even further until you have a restricted topic and a problem about that topic you can investigate for a report. Bring your topic to class.

4. Using a subject, author, and title search, find four or five books on the topic you selected for Exercise 3. Prepare a bibliographic citation for each book.

5. Prepare a list (providing full bibliographic information) of fifteen articles for the restricted topic you selected for Exercise 3. Use one of the computerized databases discussed in this chapter (pp. 309–312).

6. Write a short memo or e-mail (two or three paragraphs) to your instructor describing the types of on-line searches your library offers and how they assisted you in researching the topic you selected in Exercise 3.

7. Identify three computerized databases that specifically would help you to run an on-line search in your research at school or on the job. List five periodicals/Web sites that you would be able to find indexed on each of the databases. Do not include the same periodical more than once, even though it may appear in more than one database. Be sure to consult a librarian if you need help; he or she may be able to direct you to lists of periodicals indexed on each database.

8. Using the research tools discussed in this chapter, including the Internet, locate the following items related to your major. Select titles that are most closely related to your major and explain how they would be useful to you. Prepare a separate bibliography card for each title.

   a. an index to periodicals
   b. titles of three important journals that are available in print and on-line
   c. an abstract of an article appearing in one of the journals
   d. a term in a specialized dictionary
   e. a description or illustration in a specialized encyclopedia
   f. a film or tape recording
   g. three government documents
   h. a story in the *New York Times* or one of the newspapers covered by News-Bank InfoWeb that, in the last year, discussed a topic of interest to students in your major

9. Assume you have to write a brochure about one of the following topics, introducing it to an audience of consumers. Using the resources of the Internet and those of a few of the databases discussed in this chapter, prepare a working bibliography of relevant materials that contains at least ten sources. After gathering and reading those sources, prepare the text and a visual for the brochure and submit them with your bibliography to your instructor. This assignment may be done as a collaborative writing exercise.

   a. virtual reality
   b. lipoprotein A
   c. fiber optics
   d. CAD/CAM applications
   e. interactive television
   f. avoiding sexist language in the workplace
   g. optical recognition software
   h. voice-activated computer programs
   i. robotics in medicine
   j. the greenhouse effect
   k. computer dating
   l. e-cash
   m. cellular phones
   n. any topic your instructor approves

10. Using appropriate references discussed in this chapter, answer any five of the following questions. After your answer, list the specific works you used. Supply complete bibliographic information. For books, indicate author or editor, title, edition, place of publication and publisher, date, and volume and page numbers. For journals and magazines, include volume and page numbers; for newspapers, precise date and page numbers. For Internet sites, provide complete http://www addresses.

    a. What is biomass?
    b. How many calories are there in an orange?
    c. List three interviews that Bill Clinton granted between 1998 and 2000.
    d. What is the boiling point of coal tar?

e. What was the headline in the *New York Times* the day you were born?

f. List three publications issued by the U.S. Department of the Interior from 1995 to the present on outdoor recreation.

g. What was the population of Spokane, Washington, in 1990?

h. List three articles published between 1997 and 2000 on the advantages of teleconferencing.

i. Who discovered the neutrino?

j. What is the first recorded (printed) use of the word *ozone*?

k. Who edited the second edition of the *Encyclopedia of Psychology,* published in 1994?

l. Give the title, date, page number, and author (if listed) of a story in your local newspaper that focused on child abuse in the last year.

m. List the titles of three articles on the abuse of credit cards that have appeared in professional journals within the past two or three years.

n. What is a high-key photograph?

o. Name five plants that have the word *fly* as part of their common name.

p. What are the names and addresses of all the four-year colleges in the state of South Dakota?

q. Who is the current head of state of Nigeria?

r. What is the current membership of the American Dental Association?

s. What are the names of all the justices who currently serve on the U.S. Supreme Court?

11. Write a paraphrase of two of the following paragraphs.

a. Deep-fat frying is a mainstay of any successful fast-food operation and is one of the most commonly used procedures for the preparation and production of foods in the world. During the deep-frying process, oxidation and hydrolysis take place in the shortening and eventually change its functional, sensory, and nutritional quality. Current fat tests available to food operation managers for determining when used shortening should be discarded typically require identification of a change in some physical attribute of the shortening, such as color, smoke, foam development, etc. However, by the time these changes become evident, a considerable amount of degradation has usually already taken place.[2]

b. Ponds excavated in areas of flat terrain usually require prepared spillways. If surface runoff must enter an excavated pond through a channel or ditch, rather than through a broad shallow drainageway, the overfall from the ditch bottom to the bottom of the pond can create a serious erosion problem unless the ditch is protected. Scouring can take place in the side slope of the pond and for a considerable distance upstream in the ditch. The resulting sediment tends to reduce the depth and capacity of the pond. Protect by

---

[2]Vincent J. Graziano, "Portable Instrument Rapidly Measures Quality of Frying Fat in Food Service Operations," *Food Technology* 33 (Sept. 1979): 50. Copyright © by Institute of Food Technologists. Reprinted by permission.

placing one or more lengths of rigid pipe in the ditch and extend them over the side slope of the excavation. The extended portion of the pipe or pipes may be either cantilevered or supported with timbers. The diameter of the pipe or pipes depends on the peak rate of runoff that can be expected from a 10-year frequency storm. If you need more than one pipe inlet, the combined capacity should equal or exceed the estimated peak rate of runoff.[3]

c. *Using Your ATM Card to Shop*

Matching the Logos: Just as the various logos that appear on ATM cards tell you where they can be used to get cash or make banking transactions at ATMs, they also indicate where your card can be used to make purchases. Simply match the logos on your card with those you see displayed at the entrance to the store or at the cash register. Or just ask whether the store accepts your ATM card.

Depending on which logos you find on your card and whether the store has installed PIN pads, your purchases can be handled in one of two ways: either you will punch in your PIN, just as you would at an ATM, or you will sign for the purchase, as you would with a credit card.

Making a Purchase: Let's say you've planned to buy a desk lamp. You need all your cash for other things and don't have your checkbook with you. At the entrance to the store, you notice an ATM network logo that matches the logo on your card. You decide to use your ATM card to pay.

When you present the lamp to the cashier, you will be asked how you would like to pay for the purchase. You offer your ATM card. The cashier will confirm that your card is accepted by the store, and if it is, the following will occur: 1) You will be asked to slide your card through a slot that reads the information contained in the magnetic strip on the back of your card; 2) the cashier will then enter the amount of the purchase; 3) you will punch in your PIN, or secret code; and 4) the cashier will press a key that initiates an automatic phone call to your bank or credit union. This confirms that the money is available in your account. Once confirmed, your bank or credit union automatically deducts the purchase amount from your account, just like a check. You will receive a receipt of the transaction, if you want one, when the sale is completed. Make sure you record and subtract this amount from your account immediately.

When a Major Credit Card Logo Is on Your ATM Card: If you have an ATM card that also has on it one of two of the major credit card logos mentioned previously, your purchase will be handled as if you were using a credit card, except for three important differences:

- First, the purchase amount will be deducted automatically from your account—like when you write a check—rather than being billed to you at the end of the month.

[3]U.S. Department of Agriculture, Soil Conservation Service. *Ponds for Water Supply and Recreation* (Washington, DC: U.S. Department of Agriculture Handbook No. 387, 1971): 48.

- Second, typically, you'll pay no interest charges, since you're using your own money on deposit, not borrowing it. (However, there may be other fees associated with using this card, an issue addressed later in this brochure.)
- Third, you will usually sign for the purchase instead of punching in your PIN. However, since this is your ATM card, if a store has installed PIN pads to accept your PIN, and it accepts one of the other logos on your card, the store clerk may ask you to use your PIN instead of signing.

Documenting Sources

Documentation is at the heart of all the research you will do at school or on the job. To document means to furnish readers with information about the materials (books, Web sites and other Internet sources, articles, visuals, films, interviews, question- naires) you have used for the factual support of your statements. Without proper documentation, you will not be able to persuade a customer to buy your company's product or service and you will not convince your boss that you are doing your best work.

This chapter will give you practical and precise directions on what to document and how to do it efficiently and consistently. Of the various systems (or formats) of documentation, parenthetical documentation is preferred over documentation through footnotes or endnotes. For that reason, this chapter will emphasize the par- enthetical documentation methods advocated by the Modern Language Association (MLA) and the American Psychological Association (APA). The sample research paper about telecommuting at the end of this chapter uses the MLA style of paren- thetical documentation; the long report on non-native speakers of English in the work force in Chapter 16 (pp. 629–644) follows APA style.

The Whys and Hows of Documentation

Before looking at the specific techniques you need to use when you document, it's necessary to understand why documentation is so important and the major role it plays in your writing strategies.

Why Is Documentation Important?

Documentation is important for at least three reasons.

1. It demonstrates to your readers that you have done your homework by consulting experts on the subject and relying on the most current and authoritative sources to build your case.

2. It gives proper credit to those sources. Citing works by name is not a simple act of courtesy; it is an ethical requirement and, because so much of the material is protected by copyright, a point of law. By documenting your sources, you will avoid being accused of *plagiarism*—stealing someone else's ideas and listing them as your own. Such misrepresentation is unethical and illegal. If you are found guilty of plagiarism, you could be expelled from school or fired from your job.

3. It informs readers about specific books, articles, or Web sites you used so they can find additional information or verify your facts. Incorrect or incomplete documentation means your readers will not be able to locate your sources.

TECH NOTE

The Ethics of Documentation: Some Dos and Don'ts

There are a variety of ways to commit plagiarism. To ensure that your paper or report avoids any type of plagiarism and maintains high ethical standards, follow these guidelines.

- If you use a source and take something from it, document it.
- **Patchworking**—using bits and pieces of information and passing them off as your own—is also an act of plagiarism. Always put quotations marks around anything you take verbatim and document it.
- Even if you do not use an author's exact words but still get an idea, concept, or point of view from that author, document the work in your paper.
- Never alter a source to have it suit your argument. Twisting someone else's ideas to make them agree (or disagree) with yours is unethical. Changing any information—dates, times, test results—is a serious offense.
- Do not misquote or misattribute. Adding a few words—qualifiers, conditions—to a source violates the author's work.
- Do not use just one source or repeatedly cite the same source. You will not have sufficiently researched and documented your work for the reader.
- Never submit the same research paper you wrote for one course for another course without first obtaining permission from the second instructor.
- Be faithful to the rules established by your collaborative writing team. Never submit as your own work that was done through collaboration.

What Must Be Documented?

That question often puzzles writers. If you document the following materials, you will avoid plagiarism as well as assist the reader of your research paper or report:

- any direct quotation(s), even a single phrase or key word
- any paraphrase or summary of another individual's written work or from an oral report or presentation, including lectures
- any opinions, interpretations, and conclusions expressed verbally or in writing that are not your own or any views that you could not have reached without the help of another source
- any statistical data that you have not compiled yourself
- any visuals you did not prepare yourself—photographs, tables, charts, graphs, drawings from the Internet or elsewhere (If you construct a visual based on someone else's data, you must acknowledge that source.)
- any software programs you did not develop yourself

Quotations from the Bible, Shakespeare, or any literary text should be identified according to the specific work (*Exodus, Merchant of Venice*) and the exact place in that work (for example, act 3, scene 4, line 23, which would be listed as 3.4.23).

Of course, do not document obvious facts, such as normal body temperature, well-known dates (the first moon landing in 1969), historical information (Ronald Reagan was the fortieth president of the United States), formulas (H_2O; the quadratic formula), the distance to Jupiter, proverbs from folklore ("The hand is quicker than the eye"), or well-known quotations ("We hold these truths to be self-evident . . .").

Documentation in the Writing Process

Documentation is vital to writing a research paper or report. It begins as soon as you start researching your topic and continues as you organize, draft, revise, and even edit your work. You need to keep a careful record of the sources you use and the exact material you take from them.

Throughout your various drafts be sure to document precisely what you are using and then add every source you refer to in the text of your paper on the Works Cited page. During revision (and editing) be careful to check and double-check the accuracy of your documentation. That means making sure names, Web sites, page numbers, dates, and quotations are correct and that bibliographic information mentioned in the text of your paper matches that on your Works Cited page precisely.

Parenthetical and Footnote Documentation

Numerous formats exist for documenting sources. Two of these formats are *parenthetical documentation* and *footnote documentation.* The following section will introduce you to parenthetical documentation by contrasting it with the footnote method.

TECH NOTE

Recording and Transferring Bibliographic Information

It is relatively easy to transfer bibliographic information—Works Cited pages and other bibliographic citations—from the Net or a CD-ROM into your word processing program. If you are using a Web browser, go to the file menu and click on "Save as." You will see a box in which you can give the information a file name and save the new file in your word processing program. If you want to incorporate bibliographic information into another document—you may be using many of the same sources—open the document into which you want to incorporate the new material. Choose "Insert" from the options at the top of your screen and give the new material a file name. Then a copy of the new bibliographic information will be part of the document you are working on. Keep in mind that you will have to press "Save" after each step in order not to lose the material.

Parenthetical Documentation

One widely used system of parenthetical documentation is found in the *MLA Handbook for Writers of Research Papers,* 5th ed., edited by Joseph Gibaldi (New York: Modern Language Association, 1999). The MLA system is used primarily by individuals in the humanities and other related disciplines; the APA system is used in psychology, nursing and allied health disciplines, the social sciences, and some technological fields. Basically, both MLA and APA

- do *not* recommend footnotes or endnotes to document sources
- do *not* contain a bibliography of works the writer may have consulted but has not actually cited directly in the paper or report

Instead, the MLA and the APA use **parenthetical, or in-text, documentation.** That is, the writer tells readers directly in the text of the paper, at the moment the acknowledgment is necessary, what reference is being cited. MLA style, for example, includes the author's last name in parentheses together with the appropriate page number(s) from which the information is borrowed.

> Creating an effective Web site was among the top three priorities businesses have had over the last two years (Morgan 205).

The citation (Morgan 205) lets the reader know that the writer has borrowed information from a work by Morgan, specifically from page 205 of that work. Such a source (author's last name and page number) obviously does not provide sufficient documentation. Instead, the parenthetical reference refers readers to an alphabetical list of works that appears at the end of the paper. The list—called "Works Cited" in MLA or "References" in APA—contains full bibliographic data—titles, dates, Web sites, publishers, page numbers, and so on—on all the sources cited in the paper.

Footnote/Endnote Documentation

In footnote and endnote documentation, a slightly raised numeral, called a **super-script,** immediately follows the information you wish to document, like this: [1]. Then you provide source information either in a footnote at the bottom (or "foot") of the page, preceded by the same raised numeral [1], or on an endnotes page at the end of the entire paper. The order in which the endnotes are listed must correspond exactly to the order in which the information is cited in the paper.

Comparing the Two Methods

Figure 9.1 shows a section of the endnotes page containing information about the sources that have been cited within a paper. The same sources documented for a paper using the parenthetical documentation format are listed in Figure 9.2, which shows the relevant section of the Works Cited page.

FIGURE 9.1   An example of an endnotes page showing the documentations of sources.

Endnotes

[1] Julie Teunissen, "Opportunities for Technical Writers," Computer Outlook 17 (2001): 43.

[2] George Tullos, "Technical Writers and the Importance of Online Documentation," Journal of Computer Operations 8 (2000): 15.

[3] Mary Bronstein, The New Generation of Technical Writers (San Francisco: FTP Systems, 2002): 107.

FIGURE 9.2   Documentation of sources on a "Works Cited" page.

Works Cited

Bronstein, Mary. The New Generation of Technical Writers. San Francisco: FTP Systems, 2002.

Teunissen, Julie. "Opportunities for Technical Writers." Computer Outlook 17 (2001): 42–45.

Tullos, George. "Technical Writers and the Importance of Online Documentation." Journal of Computer Operations 8 (2000): 15.

To provide accurate parenthetical documentation for your readers, you must first prepare a careful Works Cited page and then include the documentation in the right form and at the right place in your text.

Preparing the Works Cited Page

Before you can document your sources parenthetically, you must first establish what those sources are. Even though the list of references cited comes at the end of your paper, prepare the list *before* you start to document. As we saw, just to give an author's name and a page number in parentheses does not provide readers with adequate publication information. But by preparing the list first, you will know what sources you must cite and what page numbers, when pertinent, you must list. You will also avoid accidentally omitting a source. And you can use your Works Cited page to verify information listed in the text of your paper.

When you prepare your list of references for print sources, include information in the following order in accordance with the MLA style:

Books	Articles
author(s) or editor(s)	author(s)
title (underscored or in italics)	title of article (put in quotation marks)
edition (if second or subsequent)	name of journal (underscored or in italics)
place of publication	volume number (in arabic numerals)
publisher's name	date of publication
date of publication	page number(s)

In Works Cited lists, sources appear in alphabetical order according to authors' last names. Use periods between the elements in the citation and indent the second and subsequent lines five spaces, or half an inch. The examples below show you how to list different types of books and articles according to the MLA style. (Note: Although the following examples are typeset single-spaced to save space, you would double space your Works Cited, as the sample paper shows on pp. 391–393.)

- *Book by one author*

Walker, Juliet Kirkpatrick. <u>The History of Black Business in America: Capitalism, Race, Entrepreneurship</u>. New York: Macmillan, 1999.

Note that no page numbers are listed in this citation; the appropriate page numbers of Walker's book would be included parenthetically in the paper.

- *Two or more books by the same author*

Hordeski, Michael F. <u>Microprocessors in Industry</u>. New York: Van Nostrand, 1984.

---. <u>Personal Computer Interfaces: Macs to Pentiums</u>. New York: McGraw, 1995.

When you cite two or more works by the same author, do not repeat the author's name in subsequent reference(s). Type three hyphens in place of the name and then a period. (List the works in alphabetical order.)

- *Book by two or three authors*

```
Muggins, Carolyn, and Keith Applebauer. Electronic
     Advertising: Principles and Practices. Chicago:
     General Books, 2001.
```

All authors' names are listed in the order they appear on the title page, not in alphabetical order. The first author's name is listed in reverse order, last name first, and the second author's name in normal order.

- *Book by more than three authors*

```
Perez, Jennifer, et al. Holistic Nursing: Practice for
     Body, Mind, and Soul. 3rd ed. Baltimore: Nursing
     Research, 2001.
```

When there are more than three authors, list only the first author's name, in reverse order, and add "et al." ("and others") after a comma following the first author's name. Note that when a book has a subtitle, you must include it. Separate the title and the subtitle by a colon, as in the Perez entry. When a book goes into a second or subsequent edition, list that fact after the title, as in the Perez book, but do not underline the edition.

- *Corporate author*

```
Computer Literacy Foundation. PC's in the Classroom. 2nd
     ed. New York: Technology Press, 2000.
```

A corporate author refers to an organization, society, association, institution, or government agency that publishes a work under its own name—for example, the Federal Aviation Administration. In the example above, the Computer Literacy Foundation is considered the author of the book.

- *Edited collection of essays*

```
Tyson-Jones, Sandra, ed. The Electronic Investor: Building
     Portfolios Online. New York: Merrimack, 2002.
```

The abbreviation "ed." for *editor* follows the editor's name listed in reverse order.

- *Essay included in a collection*

```
Holcomb, Barry T. "No Load Mutuals: A Continuing
     Investment Opportunity." The Electronic Investor:
     Building Portfolios Online. Ed. Sandra Tyson-Jones.
     New York: Merrimack, 2002. 321-29.
```

The name of the author of the article in this collection comes first—in reverse order—and then the title of the article in quotation marks. Next comes the title of the collection underscored or in italics. The editor's name is listed after the title, with "Ed." before her name to indicate that she is the editor. Do not list the editor's name in reverse order. The page numbers on which the essay appears in the collection conclude the entry.

- *Professional journal article*

Garbarino, Ellen, and Mark J. Johnson. "The Different
     Roles of Satisfaction, Trust, and Commitment in
     Customer Relationships." <u>Journal of Marketing</u> 63
     (Apr. 1999): 70-87.

Reese, Shelly. "The New Wave of Gen X Workers." <u>Business &</u>
     <u>Health</u> 17 (June 1999): 19-24.

Note how a reference to a journal article differs from one citing a book in MLA style. The title of the article is in quotation marks, not underscored or italicized; no place of publication is listed. The volume number immediately follows the title of the journal with no intervening punctuation. And the page number(s) on which the article is found follow the colon placed after the publication date in parentheses.

- *Signed magazine article*

Koerner, Brendan. "Can Hackers Be Stopped?" <u>U.S. News &</u>
     <u>World Report</u> 14 June 1999: 46-52

Unlike the more scholarly journal articles, popular and frequently issued magazines (such as *Business Week, Time, U.S. News & World Report*) are listed by date, not volume number.

- *Unsigned magazine article*

"House Buying: Virtual Reality Takes Off." <u>Newsweek</u> 12 May
     1999: 79.

Unsigned works are always listed according to the first word of their title (excluding *a, an,* and *the*).

- *Newspaper article*

Wittington, Delores. "The Dollar Buys More Vacation
     Overseas This Year." <u>Springfield Herald</u> 30 Mar. 2001,
     late ed., sec. 2: 10.

List the article by day, month, and year, *not* according to the cumbersome volume and issue numbers. Identify section, page, and edition information for readers. In the example above, readers know that the story appeared in the late edition on page 10 in section 2. Sometimes the story you cite will not require those details. The next example cites an article found on pages B1 and 4 of a paper that issues only one edition per day.

```
Bounds, Wendy. "Magazines Face Ethics Questions As They
     Push Online Ventures." Wall Street Journal 21 June
     1999: B1,4.
```

- *Encyclopedia article*

```
Strock, O. J. "Telemetering." McGraw-Hill Encyclopedia of
     Science and Technology. 8th ed. 1997.
```

Because it is a multivolume, alphabetical work, only the particular edition and year of an encyclopedia have to be listed on the Works Cited page. When an encyclopedia article is not signed, list it under the first word of the title (excluding *a, an,* or *the*).

- *Pamphlet or brochure*

```
National Institute on Aging. Bound for Good Health: A
     Collection of Age Papers. Bethesda: National
     Institute on Aging, 1999.
```

Document a pamphlet or brochure the same way you would a book. Note here that the corporate author is also the publisher of the book.

- *Film*

```
Understanding AIDS. Video. Philadelphia: Health Care
     Media, 2001. 37 min.
```

Underscore or italicize the title of a film and include the medium, distributor, and date. If you indicate the length of the film, include that information last.

- *Radio or television program*

```
60 Minutes. CBS News. 16 Oct. 2001.
```

```
"The Dilemma." Rich Man, Poor Man. PBS. WTQA, Danville. 13
     Sept. 2000.
```

Underscore or italicize the title of a program episode but put an individual episode in a series in quotation marks, as in the episode title from the series *Rich Man, Poor Man,* above. (In your Works Cited page, *60 Minutes* would be listed under S for "Sixty.")

- *Cartoon or advertisement*

```
Lees, Charlotta. Cartoon. Miami Magazine. Aug. 2002: 36.
```

```
American Resort Council. Advertisement. "Leisure Life Pays
     Off." Vacation Life Feb. 2001: 71.
```

- *Published interview*

```
Zeluto, Thomas. "Interview with Former Budget Director."
     Findlay Magazine Oct. 2002: 2-4.
```

Begin with the name of the individual being interviewed. Then indicate the title of the interview.

- *Unpublished interview*

```
Cilwik, Martin. CEO, Emerson Plastics. Personal interview.
     7 Aug. 2001.
```

```
Chin, Barbara. Professor of Physics, Northwest College.
     Telephone interview. 15 May 2000.
```

Begin with the name of the interviewee—in reverse order—and then indicate how and when the interview was conducted.

- *Questionnaire*

```
Questionnaire for Med Techs. Distributed between 16-20
     Nov. 2001. Southwest Labs.
```

- *Lecture*

```
Melka, Mary. "The Gopher Turtle--An Endangered Species in
     Southeast Pilsen County." Lecture at Franzen State
     University, 21 Mar. 2002.
```

For documenting electronic sources, see pages 366–373.

How to Alphabetize the Works in Your Reference List

Your list of references must be in alphabetical order to enable readers to find an entry quickly. Follow these guidelines when you alphabetize your list.

1. Make sure each author's name is in correct alphabetical sequence, with the author's (or the first of multiple authors') name in reverse order. Thus, you would have Jones, Sally T., not Sally T. Jones.

2. Hyphenated last names should be alphabetized according to the first of the hyphenated names.

   Grundy, Alex H.
   Mendez-Greene, A. Y.
   Mundt, Jill

3. List corporate authors as you would names of individuals, but do not invert the corporate name.

   Marine Fisheries Association
   Nally, Mark
   National Bureau of Standards
   Nuttal, Marion

4. Alphabetize the entries by the author's last name, following the letter-by-letter method. For two or more authors with the same last name, alphabetize by the first name.

Lund, Michael
Lund, William
Lundford, Sarah
Lundforth, Jeffrey

Documenting in the Text

The Works Cited list does not, of course, tell readers what you actually borrowed from your sources or where that information is located in a source. To give readers that information, you must include documentation in the text of your paper or report.

What to Include and Why

As you write and revise your draft(s), make sure that you (1) insert the author's name and appropriate page number(s) for each source that you use; (2) match the information you include parenthetically in the text—names, page numbers, and sometimes short titles—precisely with the information you supply under Works Cited at the end of your paper or report; and (3) begin short titles within parenthetical citations with the first key word used in the title. Remember: If you fail to document in your text, you are guilty of plagiarism. Also, if your documentation is incorrect or incomplete, readers will have trouble finding the source and may doubt the reliability of your work.

How to Document: Some Guidelines

Parenthetical, or in-text, documentation is relatively simple. Keep your documentation brief and to the point so you do not interrupt the reader's train of thought. In most cases, all you will need to include is the author's last name and appropriate page number(s) in parentheses, usually at the end of the sentence. For unsigned articles or radio and television programs, use a shortened title in place of an author's name. Note in the following example that no mark of punctuation appears before the citation and that a period follows it. Also, no "page" or "p." or comma appears between the author's name and the page number.

```
About 5 percent of the world's population has diabetes
mellitus, and 25 percent of the world's population acts
as carriers of the disease (Walton 56).
```

Seeing this parenthetical documentation, the reader will expect to find the title and publication information about Walton's study correctly listed under Walton on your Works Cited page.

```
Walton, J. H. Common Diseases of the World. New York:
    Medical Books, 2002.
```

The number after Walton's name in the parenthetical documentation refers to the page number where the information you cite can be found.

You may refer to the same work more than once in your paper or report. For second or subsequent references use the same method of documentation. For the Walton example, you would place Walton's name and the appropriate page number—even if it is the same as in the previous reference(s)—in parentheses following the borrowed information. Of course, if you included Walton's name in the sentence, there would be no need to repeat it in the parentheses; you would need to give only the page number. (The exact placement of the author's name in the sentence is discussed below.)

If you are using a work that has two authors, list both last names parenthetically.

```
Tourism has increased by 21 percent this last quarter,
thanks to individuals passing through our state on their
way to the World's Fair (Muscovi and Klein 2-3).
```

If one of the works you use has three or more authors, list just the first author's last name in parentheses followed by et al. and the page number(s).

```
The principles of ergonomics have revolutionized the
design of office furniture (Brodsky et al. 345-47).
```

If the work you are borrowing from has a corporate author, use a shortened version of the name in the parentheses. In the following example, "Commission" replaces "Commission on Wage and Price Control."

```
Salaries for local electricians were at or above the
national average (Commission 145).
```

In the preceding examples, the names of the authors have appeared in parentheses. When you mention the author's name in your text, include only the appropriate page number(s) in parentheses. The following examples show three acceptable ways of citing an author's name in the text.

```
Clausen sees the renovation of downtown areas as one of the
most challenging issues facing city governments today (29).
```

```
As Clausen notes, the renovation of downtown areas is one
of the most challenging issues facing city governments
today (29).
```

```
The renovation of downtown areas, according to Clausen, is
one of the most challenging issues facing city governments
today (29).
```

Similarly, if you list the title of a reference or anonymous work in the text of your paper, you need not repeat it for your parenthetical documentation.

```
According to the Encyclopaedia Britannica, Cecil B.
DeMille's King of Kings was seen by nearly 800,000,000
individuals (3:458).
```

The first number in parentheses refers to the volume number of the *Encyclopaedia Britannica;* the second is the page number in that volume. In this case, the writer gives both volume and page numbers to indicate that the information is listed under DeMille and not the title of the film.

If you are citing information from two or more works by the same author, you will have to inform readers clearly from which work a particular fact or opinion comes. Let's say you used information from the following works by the same author:

> Howe, Grace. <u>Networking in the Information Age</u>. New York: Business Publications, 2001.
>
> ---. "Systems Control for Internet Businesses." <u>The Electronic Workplace</u> 15 (2002): 67-81.

You have a number of ways to tell readers from which work by Grace Howe you are borrowing material.

1. Cite the author's name, a short title, and the page number parenthetically.

   > Communication checkpoints are necessary in any business to provide a maximum flow of information (Howe, <u>Networking</u> 132).

   Use a comma after the author's name but not before the page number.

2. Mention the author's name in your sentence and use a short title and page number in parentheses.

   > Howe thinks communication checkpoints in any business are necessary to provide a maximum flow of information (<u>Networking</u> 132).

3. Give the author's name and a shortened title in the text with only the page number included parenthetically.

   > According to Howe's article, "Systems Control," productivity increases by at least 20 percent after each training session involving communication networking techniques (71).

Occasionally you will have to cite two sources at the same time to document a point. Include the names of the authors of both sources (alphabetically) just as if you were listing them individually but insert a semicolon between sources.

> The use of salt domes to store radioactive wastes has come under severe attack (Jelinek 56-57; McPherson and Chin 23-26).

Be careful, though, that you do not overload readers by including a long string of references in your parenthetical documentation.

> Wind energy has been successfully used in both rural and urban settings (Bailey 34; Calderon 78; Henderson 9; Mankowitz 98-99; Olsen 456-58; Vencenti 23; Walker and Smith 43).

Rather than interrupting the reader and crowding references together, consider revising your sentence to make the subject more precise and the references more restricted.

> Wind energy has long benefited the farm community (Calderon 78; Walker and Smith 43). But recent experiments in New York City have shown the effectiveness of this form of energy for apartment dwellers, too (Bailey 34; Henderson 9). Similar experiments in San Francisco also show how wind power helps urban residents (Mankowitz 98-99; Olsen 456-58; Vincenti 23).

If you include a quotation, place the parenthetical documentation at the end of the sentence containing the quotation.

> Pilmer has observed that coffee "is only mildly addictive in the sense that withdrawal will not harm you or produce violent symptoms" (16).

Note that the period follows the parentheses, not the quotation marks. Even if the quotation is short and appears in the middle of the sentence, place the documentation at the end of the sentence.

> Alvin Toffler uses the phrase "third wave" to characterize the scientific and computer revolution (34).

If the material you quote runs to more than four typed lines, set the quotation apart from the text by indenting it *ten spaces or one inch* on the left side and eliminate the quotation marks. Double-space the quotation. Place the parenthetical documentation after the quotation and outside the period, as in the following example.

> L. J. Ronsivalli offers this graphic analogy of how radiation can penetrate solid objects:
>
> > One might wonder how an X-ray, a gamma ray, or a cosmic ray can penetrate something as solid as a brick wall or a piece of wood. We can't see that within the atomic structures of the brick wall and the wood there are spaces for the radiation to enter. If we look at a cloud, we can see its shape, but because distance has made them too small, we can't see the droplets of moisture of which the cloud is made. Much too small for the eyes to see, even with the help of a microscope, the atomic structure of solid materials is made of very small particles with a lot of space between them. In fact, solids are mostly empty spaces. (20-21)

If you omit anything from a quotation, follow the rules governing ellipses on pages 341–342.

If you take a quotation from any place but the original source (if, for example, the quotation you want to use is included in the book you are citing but originally came from another book or article), you should document that fact by including "qtd. in" in your parenthetical documentation.

```
The monthly business meeting serves a number of valuable
functions. In fact, perhaps the most important one is that
"chain-of-command meetings provide the opportunity to pass
information up as well as down the administrative ladder"
(qtd. in Munroe 87).
```

This documentation lets readers know that you found the quotation in Munroe, not in the original work from which these words come.

Documentation in Scientific and Technical Writing

The MLA style is, of course, not the only method for documenting sources. Numerous other formats exist. Many professions publish their own style guide or book, for example, the *Publication Manual of the American Psychological Association,* the *Council of Biology Editors' Style Manual,* and the *American Institute of Physics' Style Manual for Guidance in the Preparation of Papers.* Other professions recommend that writers follow the format used in a specific technical or scholarly journal. Most professional groups, however, advise against using the formats and abbreviations found in databases (see pp. 303–312). The way information is listed in those sources is not offered as a model of documentation. Before you write a paper or report, ask your instructor or employer about the format he or she prefers.

Many professions use the author-date method of documentation or the ordered references method. Both methods rely on parenthetical documentation; that is, rather than using footnotes or endnotes with superscripts, the information about the source is placed in parentheses directly in the text. The MLA method just discussed is one such format. Another is the APA method, which differs slightly from the MLA style.

How APA Differs from MLA Parenthetical Documentation

The APA, like the MLA, uses a simplified form of parenthetical documentation. But in the APA style the publication date is much more prominent than in MLA. Such an emphasis is understandable given the rapidly changing nature and requirements of the world of science and technology. Every parenthetically documented source in APA includes (1) the author's name, and (2) the date of the work. Direct quotations in the text require the page number or numbers in the parentheses preceded by "p." or "pp."

```
The theory that new housing becomes increasingly expensive
as buyers move farther north has been recently advanced
(Jones, 2001).
```

```
Recent theory asserts that "as buyers move farther north,
new housing becomes increasingly more expensive" (Jones,
2001, p. 13).
```

The complete bibliographic information is assembled in a References section, similar to the MLA's Works Cited section. But, unlike MLA, APA requires writers to do the following when they list their references:

```
Jones, T. (2001). The cost of housing on Lincoln's north
     side. Urban Studies, 7, 10-24.
```

1. List just the author's surname and initials rather than spelling out the first name: Jones, T., rather than Jones, Tracy.
2. List all authors, up to six, before using *et al.;* reverse the names of all the authors, not just the first one; use an ampersand, not *and,* before the last author's name.
3. Place the date of publication in parentheses immediately after the author's inverted name: Jones, T. (2001).
4. Capitalize only the first word in an article or book title (except for proper names in the title).
5. Underline or italicize the title of a book, journal, or magazine; write out in full the names of the months; underline or italicize the volume numbers.
6. Do not enclose the title of a journal, magazine, or encyclopedia article in quotation marks.
7. Use a comma to separate the volume number of a journal from the page numbers for that article. (As in MLA style, do not use "p." or "pp." for page numbers.)

▪ *Book with a single author*

```
MLA: Zednick, Dorothea. Optical Properties of Insulators.
         New York: Scientific Publishing, 2000.

APA:    Zednick, D. (2000). Optical properties of
     insulators. New York: Scientific Publishing.
```

▪ *Book with multiple authors*

```
MLA: Smith, Frank S., et al. Global Environmental Change.
         Chicago: The Fermi Institute, 2001.

APA:    Smith, F. S., Pisanto, G., Nicholson, R., & Mel-
     lor, A. (2001). Global environmental change. Chicago:
     The Fermi Institute.
```

▪ *Book with a corporate author*

```
MLA: American Institute of Banking. Electronic Tracking
         Systems. Pittsburgh: Economics P, 2001.

APA:    American Institute of Banking. (2001). Electronic
     tracking systems. Pittsburgh, PA: Economics Press.
```

▪ *Edited book with individual essays*

```
MLA: Katz, Roberta. "Computer-Based Writing Aids." Ed.
         Yvonne Dietrich and Mark Hunt. Social
```

> *Implications of Computing*. Los Angeles:
> Southeastern UP, 1999. 72-79.

APA: Katz, R. (1999). Computer-based writing aids. In
Y. Dietrich & M. Hunt (Eds.), <u>Social implications of
computing</u> (pp. 72-79). Los Angeles: Southeastern University Press.

- *Journal article*

MLA: Perez, Pedro, and Theresa Vali. "The Role of the
Soundtrack in Three Recent Films." <u>Studies in
Film and Culture</u> 14.11 (2001): 54-73.

APA: Perez, P., & Vali, T. (2001). The role of the
soundtrack in three recent films. <u>Studies in Film and
Culture 14</u>(11), 54-73.

Note that APA style italicizes the volume number of a journal.

- *Newspaper article*

MLA: Lai, Neelou. "New Law Affects Internet Providers." <u>The
Springfield Herald</u> 13 July 2002: D2.

APA: Lai, N. (2002, July 13). New law affects Internet
providers. <u>The Springfield Herald,</u> p. D2.

- *Unsigned article*

MLA: "Hottest Internet Sites of the Month." <u>The Net</u> 31 Mar.
2001: 12.

APA: Hottest Internet sites of the month. (2001, March
31). <u>The Net, 13,</u> 12.

- *Encyclopedia article*

MLA: "Topology." <u>The Encyclopedia of Mathematics and
Statistics</u>. 2001 ed. Detroit: Professional Books.

APA: Topology. (2001). <u>The encyclopedia of mathematics
and statistics</u> (Vol. 8, p. 283). Detroit, MI: Professional Books.

Using In-Text Documentation Following the APA Method

Like MLA, APA uses in-text parenthetical documentation. But, as you will see
from the following examples, APA differs from MLA in a number of ways. In APA
style, a direct quotation is followed by, in parentheses, the author, the date, and the
page number(s), abbreviated as "p." or "pp."

> Recent theory asserts that "as buyers move farther north,
> new housing becomes increasingly more expensive" (Jones,
> 2001, p. 13).

The reader sees that Jones developed the theory on page 13 of a work written in
2001. If Jones's name were mentioned in the text, "Jones advances the theory that

new housing . . . ," only "(2001, p. 13)" would be listed. To find Jones's work, readers would turn to an alphabetical References page at the end of the paper, report, or
article, where, under "Jones," they would find a full bibliographic entry for the
work. As in MLA, only works actually cited in a paper are listed in the References.
If two works by Jones were cited, the references for both would be given. If they
were published in the same year, they would be differentiated in the text and in the
list of references by the lowercase letters *a* and *b*.

```
Housing is increasingly more expensive on the north side
than on the south (Jones, 2001a).
```

```
A recent study established a demographic pattern for small
cities in the Midwest (Jones, 2001b).
```

In the accompanying list of references, the two works by Jones might be listed as
follows:

```
Jones, T. (2001a). The cost of housing on Lincoln's north-
side. Urban studies, 72, 10-24.
```

```
Jones, T. (2001b). Demographic density in three Midwestern
small cities. Cincinnati, OH: Western Press.
```

Interviews, e-mail messages, letters, lectures, seminars, and personal communication are cited in the text but are not included in the reference list. Give the initials
as well as the surname of the communicator and provide as exact a date as possible.

```
Dr. Patavi said that this information came from a reputable
source (Dr. W. U. Patavi, interview, April 7, 2000).
```

The sample long report on meeting the needs of non-native speakers in the
workplace in Chapter 16 uses the APA method of documentation.

Documenting Electronic Sources

Up to this point we have been discussing documenting materials that you research in
print. But as part of your research you will also be consulting electronic sources. As
we saw in Chapter 8, you can access electronic sources through a variety of media—
CD-ROM, on-line databases, the Internet. The following discussion is based on the
principles of documentation outlined in the fifth edition of the *MLA Handbook*.

Some General Principles

When you document electronic materials, keep the following general principles in
mind.

1. With electronic sources, as with printed sources, you are obligated to acknowledge
   (a) what you used, (b) where you found it, and (c) how others can obtain a copy.
2. Note that an electronic source is different from a print version and has information that your readers need to be aware of—for example, Internet address, date
   when the material was first posted, and when you actually accessed it.

3. Some of your sources may be available in both printed and electronic versions. If so, you have an additional responsibility to inform your readers of that fact. Give readers as much information as possible.

Documenting Internet Sites

Perhaps the most valuable and frequently used electronic "publication" is the Internet. You will make extensive use of Internet materials both in school and on the job. You can expect to find everything from an e-mail and a corporate Web site to an issue of an electronic journal to an entire book on the Internet. The Internet grows by the hour, with hundreds of new sites being added daily.

How an Internet Source Differs from a Print Source

Citing locations on the Internet poses problems for researchers that print sources do not, for the following reasons.

1. An Internet source is documented with a different set of symbols and punctuation marks than are used with a print source, including angle brackets (< >), dots (. . .), tildes(~), and slashes (/).
2. An Internet source has no page numbers, nor does it always number individual paragraphs.
3. An Internet source can change addresses.
4. An Internet source can have many versions—it can change over months, weeks, or even hours (which is why so many Internet locations are frequently "under construction"). It can be revised and updated any time.
5. An Internet source can be deleted, which is why you should always make a hard copy for your records.
6. A researcher can access an Internet site through many different pathways—different access providers, search engines, and so on.
7. An Internet source can be accessed at any time of the day, week, month, or year. Before or after it is accessed, a site may open, change, or close. The publication date of a site is often different from its access date. You help readers by providing both in your documentation.

Four Types of Internet Sites

You need to know how to document four types of Internet sites:

- World Wide Web (WWW)
- File Transfer Protocol (FTP)
- discussion lists and newsgroups
- e-mail

The following discussion explains how to cite materials from each one.

World Wide Web (WWW)

The World Wide Web is an Internet service that makes browsing, or "surfing the Net," both possible and exciting. The Web uses hypertext markup language (HTML) to link documents to each other and to add graphics to plain text. The result is that you can click your way through colorful links to arrive at the page that interests you most. (And if you click on the bookmark feature when you get there, you can return just as easily.) To provide a bibliographic citation to a WWW site, list the following information in the order given:

Books	Article
author (if given)	author (if given)
title	title
publisher	journal
date of electronic publication	volume number
date accessed	date of electronic publication (if given)
network address (between <angle brackets>)	date accessed
	network address (between <angle brackets>)

Here are some of the Web items you most likely will be asked to document.

- *On-line book available only on-line*

```
Worthington, Tom. Net Traveller: Exploring the Networked
     Nation. Australian Computer Society, 1999. 21 Nov.
     1999 <http://www.tomw.net.au/>.
```

- *On-line book available in print or on-line*

```
Thirlwall, A. P. Growth and Development with Special
     Reference to Developing Economics. Hampshire,
     England: MacMillan Press, 1999. 7 Jan. 2000
     <http://www.macmillan-press.co.uk/economics/index.
     htm#Featured>.
```

Note that a period separates the publication date from the access date but that no publication appears between the access date and the URL (Uniform Resource Locator).

- *On-line scholarly journal article available on-line only*

```
Rowekamp, Thomas, and Liliane Peters. "A Compact Sensor
     for Visual Motion Detection." Videre: Journal of
     Computer Vision Research 1:2 (1998). 10 Mar. 1999
     <http://mitpress.mit.edu/e-journals/Videre/>.

Karg, Christoph, Johannes Köbler, and Rainer Schuler. "The
     Complexity of Generating Test Instances." Chicago
     Journal of Theoretical Computer Science. 4 (1999). 5
     Apr. 2000 <http://mitpress.mit.edu/journal-home.
     tcl?issn=10730486>.
```

- *Newspapers*

Most newspapers are available on-line as well as in print. As with the print version, you have to cite author (if given), title, name of the paper, and date it was published. You also have to indicate the date you accessed the newspaper, even if it is the same day that the story was published. The following examples show the variety of pathways available to you to access newspapers. Note that the date of publication appears in the URL, as well as the word *library* or *archives* when the publication date and the access date differ.

"CAT Scan Process Could Cut Deaths from Lung Cancer." New York Times on the Web 9 July 1999. 22 July 1999 <http://www.nytimes.com/library/nationals/science?7/ 9/99hth-cancer-lung.html>.

Haynes, V. Dion. "Dietary Guidelines Need Cultural Diversity, Group Says." Chicago Tribune Internet Edition 24 June, 1999. 30 June 1999 <http://www.chicagotribune.com/familyhealth/health/ article/06/24/99.html>.

Kelley, Tina. "Behind Closed E-Mail." New York Times on the Web 1 Apr. 1999. 27 May 1999 <http://www.nytimes.com/archives/05/27/99/articles/ html>.

Lewis, Peter H. "Consumer Digital Camera Breaks Pixel Barrier." New York Times on the Web 4 Apr. 1999. 4 Apr. 1999 <http://www.nytimes.com/04/04/99/article/ business/htm>.

- *Magazines*

As with newspapers, the network address of a magazine should include the date of publication.

Haskins, Walaika. "Cyber Counseling." Newsweek.com 9 July 1999. <http://www.newsweek.com/nw-srv/tnw/today/cs/ cs02th_1.html>.

Marcial, Gene. "E spire: A direct Link to the Net." BusinessWeek Online 19 Apr. 1999. 2 May 1999 <http://www.businessweek.com/search kg 041999.htm>.

- *Web sites for companies and individuals*

Include the following information in this order when you cite a Web site.

- person's name (in reverse order) or company's name
- title of the site, underscored or, if there is no title, simply "Web site" (not underlined or italicized)
- date of access
- address

Andersonville Automotive. Driving in Style. 12 May 2000 <http://www.andersonville.com/html>.

Baxter Healthcare. Saving Lives Worldwide. 4 Nov. 1999 <http://www.baxter.com>.

```
Fisk, Janice. Web site. 15 Mar. 2000
     <http://www.speedcorp.ba.200/~jan>.
```

```
Reston Communications. Welcome to Our Company. 2 Aug. 1999
     <http://www.reston.com>.
```

- *On-line dictionary or encyclopedia*

```
"Magnetic Disks." NASA Thesaurus. <http://www.sti.nasa.gov/
     thesaurus/M/word8907.html>.
```

```
"Ergonomics." Grolier Multimedia Encyclopedia. 3rd ed.
     1999. Jan. 1999 <http://www.grolier.com/>.
```

- *Government publication on-line*

```
United States. Dept. of Commerce. Commerce Business Daily.
     May 1999. 30 May 1999
     <http://cbdnet.gpo.gov/papersub.html>.
```

```
United States. Nuclear Regulatory Commission. Weekly
     Information Report for the Week Ending June 25, 1999.
     29 June 1999
     <http://www.nrc.gov/NRC/NEWS/WIR/weekly.html>.
```

- *Radio program and sound clip*

```
Elstein, Aaron. "Dow Hits Record High as Bonds Stall." The
     Wall Street Journal. CNBC. 9 July 1999. Transcript.
     10 July 1999 <http://www.msnbc.com/news/158521.asp?
     cnbc=on>.
```

```
Palca, Joe. "Alzheimers Vaccine." All Things Considered.
     National Public Radio. 8 July 1999.
     <http://programs.npr.org/npr2/PrgDisp.cfm?PrgDate=07/
     08/1999&PrgID=2>.
```

File Transfer Protocol (FTP) Sites

File Transfer Protocol, or FTP, allows you to transfer material over the Internet without having to change disks and download information. To cite FTP sites, include the following information:

- author's name
- full title of the document, in quotation marks
- date the document was posted (if available)
- FTP address and path, enclosed in angle brackets (<>)
- date you accessed the site, in parentheses

```
Exploratorium Science-at-Home Team. "Do You Want to Be
     an Exploratorium Scientist at Home?" <ftp://ftp.
     exploratorium.edu/events/science-fun-at-home> (4 Oct.
     2002).
```

Discussion Lists and Newsgroups

Much valuable information comes via e-mail discussion groups and other on-line postings such as Usenet newsgroups and chat rooms. These sites provide information on a variety of topics—some highly technical, some consumer-oriented—to individuals who participate in or subscribe to them. To cite such on-line postings, provide readers with the following information.

For a *discussion list:*

- author's name (last name first)
- title of the message (taken from the subject line)
- description "Online posting," neither underlined nor italicized
- date it was posted
- name of the forum or discussion group
- date it was accessed
- on-line address in angle brackets

```
Fulmer, Marion. "Improving Campus Lighting for Safety."
     Online posting. 30 Nov. 2000. Campolice. 7 Dec. 2000
     <http://www.univ.secur.edu/ipsa/campolice.htm>.

Suarez-Rios, José. "Recruiting Hispanic Engineers." Online
     posting. 4 Aug. 2001. Southeastern Engineer Discussion
     Group. 8 Feb. 2002
     <http://www.seengin.org/~jobs/recruitment/>.
```

For a *Usenet newsgroup:*

- author's name (last name first)
- title of the message in quotation marks
- the description "Online posting," neither underlined nor italicized
- date material was posted
- date it was accessed
- name of the newsgroup, prefaced with the word *news,* in angle brackets

```
Ahzaz, A. S. "Lipoprotein A—The New Enemy." Online
     posting. 17 Oct. 2000. 6 Dec. 2000
     <news.biochem.res.edu.lipids>.
```

E-Mail

Even though e-mail messages are regarded as unpublished correspondence like memos or letters, you still need to document them by giving the following information.

- writer's name (last name first)
- title of the message (taken from the subject line), if given
- person or organization to whom the e-mail was sent
- date the e-mail was sent

```
Jerach-Gordon, Tina. "Hosco Software Update Problems."
     E-mail to the author. 30 Apr. 2000.
```

```
Wardle, Phillip. "Results of Preliminary Tests." E-mail to
    Parvin Raz, Manager. 7 Aug. 2001.
```

Documenting CD-ROM and On-Line Database Material

The first thing you have to establish is whether the CD-ROM information is also available in print. If a printed version exists, inform readers of that fact first and then cite the CD-ROM source you used. If the information has no print counterpart, you do not have to worry about that.

Basically, for material taken from a CD-ROM, list information in a bibliographic citation in this order:

- author's name (last name first)
- title of the material
- publication date for printed version
- title of the CD-ROM database (underscored)
- publication medium (CD-ROM)
- name of the vendor (if available)
- electronic publication date

- *Work on CD-ROM with a printed source or analogue*

```
Stephenson, Jason. "Sick Kids Find Help in a Cyberspace
    World." JAMA [Journal of the American Medical
    Association] 274 (27 Dec. 1995): 1899-901. MEDLINE
    Express. CD-ROM. 11 Aug. 1996.

Wood, S. H., and V. J. Ransom. "The 1990s: A Decade for
    Change in Women's Health Care Policy. " JOGNN
    [Journal of Obstetric, Gynecological, and Neonatal
    Nursing] 23 (Feb. 1995): 139-43. CINAHL. CD-ROM. 10
    July 1996.
```

- *Work on CD-ROM without a printed source or analogue*

```
"Access Health, Inc.: Annual Cash Flow Statement, 1995-
    96." Compact Disclosure. CD-ROM. 1 June 1996.

Cazzin, Julie. "Kids, Cash, and Capitalism." Maclean's 6
    May 1996. Periodical Abstracts. CD-ROM. UMI Company.
    5 Nov. 1996.
```

- *Article in on-line database with a printed source*

```
Carey, Catherine, and Dawn Langkamp Bolton. "Brand Versus
    Generic Advertising and the Decision to Advertise
    Collectively." Review of Industrial Organization 11
    (Feb. 1996): 93-105. EconLit. On-line. CARL UnCOVER.
    12 Apr. 1996.
```

Hayes, Robert D., and K.W. Hollman. "Managing Diversity:
    Accounting Firms and Female Employees." <u>CPA Journal</u>
    66 (5): 36. 1 May 1996. On-line. CARL UnCOVER. 1 June
    1996.

Smith, S. L. "Is Your Respirator Program Effectively
    Managed?" <u>Occupational Hazards</u> 22 (Mar. 1999): 65-68.
    CD-ROM. UMI-ProQuest. Oct. 1999.

• *Article in on-line database without a printed source*

Chinnock, Chris. "Virtual Reality Goes to Work." Mar.
    1996. <u>Applied Science</u>. On-line. Wilsonline. 12 Apr.
    1997.

Sample Research Paper Using MLA In-Text Documentation

The rest of this chapter consists of a research paper on the advantages of telecommuting. Study the paper to see how the student author has successfully used MLA documentation to cite print, CD-ROM, and Internet sources. Compare the references mentioned in the text with the Works Cited page to see how the writer has handled documentation appropriately. (The sample long report in Chapter 16 on pages 629–644 follows the APA system of documentation. You might want to compare the two papers to become even more familiar with these two methods of parenthetical documentation.)

Henry Holland
Professor Anne McQuin Meyer
Business Writing 301
12 April 2000

The Advantage of Telecommuting
in the Information Age

Today telecommuting is transforming the world
of work. Perhaps the best definition of telecommuting comes from the New York Telecommuting Advisory
Council:

> Telecommuting is using telecommunications
> technology to replace traditional forms of
> commuting. Employees work all or part of the
> time outside the traditional office, at remote
> work locations, which may include home. The
> work goes to the worker rather than the
> worker to the work. People work where they
> are most effective. ("What Is Telecommuting?")

Telecommuters travel to work on the information
superhighway. Any individual whose job depends on
information technology can be a telecommuter, from
skilled professionals such as computer programmers
and analysts, architects, and documentation specialists to telemarketing representatives and travel
agents who process information over the Internet or
telephone (Steve 37). Telecommuters are represented
by national and regional organizations--American
Telecommuters Association, Metro Atlanta
Telecommuting Advisory Council, the International
Telework Association, and others.

Holland 2

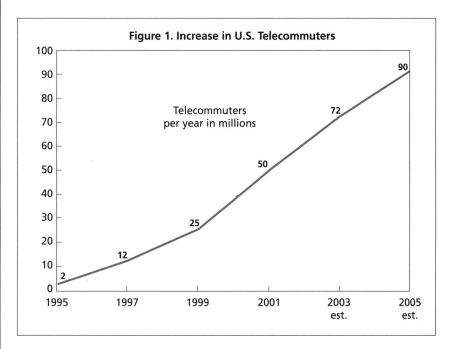

Figure 1. Increase in U.S. Telecommuters

Source: Lewis and Zhang 20.

Telecommuting became a significant part of the American workplace in 1992, when AT&T's telecommuting program began with a handful of employees and grew enormously in the first seven years, as Figure 1 shows (Lewis and Zhang 20). This rapid change reflects a national trend. Telecommuting has grown at a rate of about 20% each year. According to a survey conducted by Hewitt and Associates, an Illinois human resources consulting firm, 57% of all employers now offer their staff telecommuting as "an alternative work arrangement" (qtd. in Koss-Feder 123).

Holland 3

Even more optimistically, Myra Perez-Hoya
believes that by the year 2005 approximately 90 million workers will use telecommuting as an alternative ("Workers" 102). While the United
States "is a world leader in promoting telecommuting" (U.S. Office of Personnel), Canada, Australia,
Japan, and Scandinavian countries also have enthusiastically endorsed the concept.

But telecommuting is much more than the substi-
tution of technology for travel to and from work.
The practice involves important changes in management policies as well as in the way people work and
view their careers. This paper will survey the
growth of telecommuting by discussing (1) the ways
it differs from the traditional office, (2) the
advantages that telecommuting
has for employers, (3) the advantages it offers
employees, and (4) the impact telecommuting will
have on the workplace in the 21st century.

Telecommuting Transforms the Traditional Office

According to Greg Bahue, the publisher of High
Technology Careers Magazine, "Telecommuting can be
likened to the change from telegraph to telephone,
horse and carriage to automobile, black-and-white to
color television" ("The Age of Telecommuting").
Telecommuting is a technology whose time has come.
As society switches from an industrial/manufacturing

Holland 4

economy to one based on information, telecommuting
will become the "new world of work in the electronic
infrastructure" (Perez-Hoya, "Telecommuting" 8).
Advances in communication technology in this
"new world"--fiber optics, modems, broadband cable
services, semiconductors--make telecommuting
practical and profitable. Thanks to those technological advances, telecommuting is radically altering
the traditional idea of work schedules and workplaces.

Traditionally, office operations have functioned
on a fixed schedule. From the days of Scrooge demanding that Bob Cratchit not be late for work to the
child care issues in the film *Nine to Five,* the workday has been run on a "ruthless timeclock" ("Learning
New Work" 12). Employees often had to stay late or
come in early to perform (or keep) their jobs. As one
former 9-to-5er put it, "When a big report had to go
out, we all worked frantically to beat the clock"
(Vint). Communicating electronically, a telecommuter
can conduct business on-line at any time, day or
night, weekends and holidays. No set hours dictate
when something must be done. Offering maximum flexibility, telecommuters can do "time trade offs" to
make up lost "daytime" in the evening hours ("Working
Mother's Guide"). Gone are the days when an employee
had to take work home. As Bahue aptly notes, "home-
based work has become an extension of the workday"
("Age of Telecommuting").

Holland 5

Telecommuting transforms the idea of the work-
place--a centralized office usually in a large downtown building where employees are restricted
to their cubicles. Telecommuters can work at home,
at remote sites, or while traveling at anytime.
Obviously, telecommuting's flexibility of place
is inappropriate for manufacturing, health care,
or other positions that require specialized
equipment or conditions such as person-to-person
interaction for counseling (Bell 10; Minnesota
Office of Technology). But for millions of telecommuters work is accomplished through technologies
that are blind to their surroundings. E-mail sent
from the central office to a customer is identical
to e-mail sent from a sales representative's
home or from her notebook at a remote offsite
location.

Telecommuting does not eliminate the need for a
central office, however. All those modems, phone
lines, computer networks, and the staff
to operate and maintain them have to reside somewhere, and the organization needs a mailing address.
Customarily, some telecommuters work at home three
days a week but must be in an office the other two
days for meetings when emergencies arise (Bredin 27;
Lewis and Zhang 71). Patel stresses that, in his
company, telecommuters are expected to come to the
central workplace to attend seminars, meet clients,
participate in audits, and discuss personnel issues
with management.

Holland 6

Advantages of Telecommuting for Employers

Telecommuting offers many advantages for companies whose overriding corporate concern is "productivity" (Lewis 50; Metro Atlanta). Managers have repeatedly acknowledged that the quality and quantity of an employee's work improve with telecommuting. Many managers report as well that, in Steve's words, "telecommuters have more energy working at home and are more accurate" (37). According to numerous studies (Koss-Feder 122-23; Steve 39), employers further verify that telecommuters have a more positive attitude, which contributes to increased productivity and company loyalty. A telecommuting program "can increase productivity by 30 percent," claims Cory Van Gundy, a senior consultant with the firm of Coopers and Lybrand (qtd. in Blankenhorn).

Many large corporations (AT&T, General Dynamics, Hewlett-Packard) also happily found that telecommuters took less leave time. Allowed to work at home, telecommuters can care for sick children, spouses, or parents too. Moreover, telecommuting helps companies recruit and retain valued, skilled employees who, as Bell notes, might otherwise leave due to a spouse's transfer or other change (11). Faced with less staff turnover, a company will find its production schedules, marketing plans, and customer orders less frequently interrupted or delayed. As one manager of Southwest CyberSystems observed, "Before telecommuting, when

we lost a key person, everything went off center.
Too many times, highly qualified people left not
because of salary or benefits but because of schedules. Switching to telecommuting was one of the
smartest moves the corporation ever made" (qtd. in
Lewis and Zhang 53).

Telecommuting saves a business money, too. By
gaining access to a much larger labor pool, even to
a global labor market, as we'll see below, firms
escape paying relocation expenses (Korzeniowski
47). Companies like AT&T with large numbers of
telecommuters recoup a great deal on facilities
costs. Fewer employees permanently assigned to a
central workplace means smaller facilities can suffice. Based on her own firm's findings, Reynolds
believes that companies can reduce their office
space costs by at least $4,000 to $6,000 per
telecommuter (7). The accounting firm of Ernst &
Young cut its annual real estate budget by $25 mil-
lion when it began telecommuting (Bell 10). And
when reduced costs for power, light, security, and
support staff are factored in, telecommuting is,
according to Alicia Lewis, "a bargain worth the
time and energy that go into implementing and coordinating it" (51). Figure 2 details the amount of
savings an employer can reap.

Telecommuting also helps a company protect the
environment by complying with the 1990 Clean Air
Act. This law, passed to improve air quality in

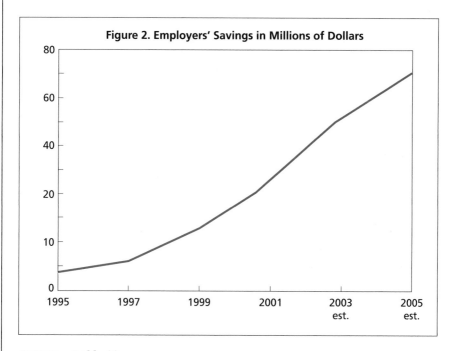

Figure 2. Employers' Savings in Millions of Dollars

Source: Bell 10.

smog-plagued cities, requires companies with more than 100 employees in any one of thirteen specific areas to "curtail work-related vehicle miles traveled by their employees" by at least 25% or risk hefty fines (Bredin 24; Perez-Hoya, "Telecommuting" 8). By encouraging carpooling and permitting telecommuting, a company can adhere to the letter as well as the spirit of the law while enhancing its public image. Predictably, telecommuting saves customers travel and time.

Holland 9

"Taxpayers and veterans in Santa Clara Valley, California, avoid long commutes into downtown Los Angeles by obtaining assistance from IRS and Veterans Affairs benefits coordinators who are telecommuting employees" (U.S. Office of Personnel).

As beneficial as telecommuting can be for the employer, the practice presents some challenges. As Lewis points out, employers have feared losing management or supervisory control (42). But such worries are more potential disadvantages than actual liabilities. By planning telecommuting programs carefully, employers can avert problems before they occur, and by exploring different management styles, companies can improve employee's motivation. The many positive experiences firms see from telecommuting have all but removed the old management fear that telecommuters will "watch Oprah rather than work" (Korzeniowski 46).

Advantages of Telecommuting for Employees

Telecommuting employees benefit by not working fixed hours in a traditional office. Gaining more personal time for self and family was the chief advantage telecommuters cited most often in a recent survey (Metro Atlanta; Sullivan). Telecommuting saves workers enormous commuting time. "The president of the California Chamber of Commerce estimates that

Holland 10

Californians alone spend 300,000 hours each day in traffic delays" (Bahue). A veteran telecommuter, Alice Bredin enthusiastically observes in her widely consulted <u>Virtual Office Survival Handbook</u>:

> Working at least part-time away from a tra-
> ditional work site means you can complete
> your work efficiently and still have some
> time left over. It means you can drop your
> kids off a little later at day care and pick
> them up a little earlier. You can finally find
> time to stay in shape because you aren't
> giving a couple of hours a day to a commute.
> It means you can do the quality of work you
> know you are capable of because you have
> interruption-free time. (3-4)

Reinforcing Bredin's strong sentiments, Bell reported that telecommuters experienced "improved family relationships" and "increased civic involve-ment" (10). Lewis also observed that telecommuters volunteered more (39-40). Overall, telecommuters achieve a better quality of life.

An additional advantage of telecommuting is that it saves employees money. Not having to trav-el back and forth to work each day, five days a week, significantly reduces transportation costs. On the average, an employee travels at least twenty miles a day to work (Lewis and Zhang 42). Taking into account the expense of gasoline, parking, and upkeep of a vehicle (or public transportation fees), a

Holland 11

telecommuter can save $5,000 to $6,000 a year. Other savings result from reduced costs for food (the commuter will eat out less often), clothes, and dry cleaning. Any expenses incurred by telecommuting are small in comparison to the savings a worker receives. As Myra Perez-Hoya maintains, telecommuters should have minimal overhead in establishing a home office, most often set up in a spare bedroom, since employers often pay for additional equipment ("Workers" 106). Specially developed software such as Symantec's pcTelecommute help telecommuters work efficiently and economically.

As a worker, the telecommuter reaps rewards. Flexible schedules allow telecommuters to produce at the time most desirable for them. By starting the workday earlier or later than at a traditional office, telecommuters work when their energy levels are the highest. Being at home also lets the telecommuter take longer, and perhaps more frequent, breaks without worrying that "he or she will have to stay at the office until midnight" to finish the job (Perez-Hoya, "Workers" 103). Bell observes that many telecommuters feel "less affected by a stressful deadline when they can work at home as opposed to a hectic central office" (9).

Another benefit of telecommuting is expansion of the job market to individuals who might otherwise not be able to compete. According to the Minnesota Office of Technology, "Telecommuting offers important

Holland 12

possibilities for some individuals to earn a living
in a rural community independent of the restricted
local economy." For example, when a paper mill
closed in rural Vermont, unemployed workers became
telecommuters for a sports clothing company that
sold most of its products over the telephone and the
Internet.

Telecommuting also offers employment opportunities to disabled and chronically ill persons and the
"mobility impaired" (Metro Atlanta). Sight- and
speech-impaired individuals can, with proper equipment, function superbly as telecommuters. Other types
of workers benefit, too. The Best Western Motel chain
has successfully hired women incarcerated in a correctional facility as reservation takers. Telecommuting
thus offers job training and the possibility of rehabilitation for these individuals (Steve 38).

Although telecommuting is highly productive, it
has some drawbacks. Vint fears it can encourage people to overwork when they are no longer locked into
the 9-to-5 routine. More commonplace, however, is
the sense of isolation that some telecommuters
express (Bell 10; Reynolds 7). As Vint graphically
notes, she sometimes "felt marooned on an island."
Yet many of these potential disadvantages can be
reduced, if not eliminated, if the telecommuter
practices time management. Feeling "out of the loop"
by working alone at home is a normal reaction
telecommuters can overcome by seeing themselves as

Holland 13

part of a global village (Technology Tips). Finally,
since most firms require telecommuters to make regular visits to the office, "separation problems" can
be minimized (Baig 104; Patel).

What the Future Holds for Telecommuting

The future looks even more promising
for telecommuting. As Bahue enthusiastically predicts, "Telecommuting . . . will become as ubiqui-
tous as your VCR, microwave, and bank ATM card"
("Age of Telecommuting"). At the Spring 2000
Festival of Telecommuting, Agnes Reynolds similarly
foresaw many good things: "Imagine our big cities
with no traffic jams, far less pollution, happier and
more productive workers freed from undue stress, and
a better-informed and more cohesive society--all
these are possible through more telecommuting" (8).
Unquestionably, telecommuting has far-reaching implications for workers, especially in terms of teamwork. As Edward Demming points out, "Telecommuting
lends itself to a different model of collaboration.
The analogy to an orchestra is . . . appropriate
because each player needs to practice and be periodically brought together to make sure the music is in
tune . . ." (qtd. in Sullivan).
Future technological advances should make the
telecommuter's job even easier. The technology
telecommuters now use--laptops, modems, cellular

Holland 14

phones--is getting better and faster. As Lewis
and Zhang maintain, "The hardware for effective
telecommuting is in place; all that has to be developed is more efficient software" (74). The production
of faster modems will mean that e-mail and other
electronic networks will rarely be clogged.
Telecommuters will receive e-mail through increasingly efficient networks, cable television, pagers, and
video phones (Lewis 51).

    Videoconferencing will continue to enhance
telecommuting, too. Sprint and Quickdata are now
using technology to link telecommuters to each other
and to their employers with even better clarity and
continuity. Slower to be developed, videophone technology will be the norm and not the exception in
the telecommuter's world of the 21st century
(Reynolds 4). Voice and video transmissions will
benefit from expanded local-area networks (LANs) and
integrated services digital networks (ISDNs). As
Dana Blankenhorn emphasizes, telecommuting will rely
heavily on more "multifunctional devices which combine a printer . . . with a scanner and fax machine.
The good news," he goes on to predict, "is that such
equipment keeps getting cheaper."

    Expansion of the Internet will surely broaden
telecommuting. Telecommuters will become better
informed citizens of the world economy by effort-
lessly gathering critical business data from around
the globe ("Learning New Work" 10). They will not be

limited to reading one stock market quote on a single screen but can compare multiple global market returns on split-screen monitors (Perez-Hoya, "Workers" 102). Beyond that, through increased global collaboration, telecommuters will have colleagues as "intelligent agents," as Perez-Hoya perceptively labels them ("Workers" 105), who research, collaborate, report, and summarize relevant business news along with interpretations over the Internet.

Many distinctions between worker and manager will dissolve because of telecommuting (Lewis and Zhang 80-81). Telecommuters can be much more independent, with the ability to change jobs without changing residences or expertise. "Rather than being part of a company's work force fixed on the payroll, telecommuters can operate more like private contractors responding to the most lucrative proposals" (Perez-Hoya, "Telecommuting" 10). The role of managers, too, is undergoing major changes, according to several experts (Lewis 46; Patel). A manager will become more like a collaborator than a supervisor, working with teams of individuals functioning as complementary, not subordinate, units, thus eliminating the hierarchies of power. "The roles of telecommuter and manager will merge by the year 2005" (Vint).

Conclusion

Telecommuting is transforming the world of work and the way employers and employees think of

Holland 16

their jobs. Presenting a challenging, though profitable, alternative to the traditional office,
telecommuting is proving to be an effective way to
conduct business in the Information Age. As one
telecommuting proponent put it, "Ever since the
introduction of the PC in the early 1980s, the
business world has been moving toward the greater
flexibility and productivity that telecommuting
offers" (Reynolds 3). In 1999, Mortimer Zuckerman,
editor-in-chief of U.S. News & World Report,
asserted that "for the first time ever, information
industries have become the biggest job creators,
accounting for 37%" of the job market (72).
Telecommuters play a major role in this vibrant
economy.

    As we have seen, both employers and employees
profit professionally and personally from telecommuting. Employers gain a more productive and loyal
work force while saving money on office space and
protecting the environment. Similarly, telecommuters
can work at their most productive times during the
day (or night) and still meet family and personal
obligations. Telecommuting also opens the world job
market to individuals who in the past may have been
excluded, one of the most worthwhile effects of
advanced technology.

    Considering that telecommuting has been prac-
ticed for a little more than a decade, telecommuters
and their employers have traveled a long distance
on the information superhighway. As technological

Holland 17

developments make telecommuting even more attractive and feasible, current limitations or problems will surely fade away. The world of business is on the threshold of a new frontier because of telecommuting.

Holland 18

Works Cited

Bahue, Greg. "The Age of Telecommuting." <u>Career Expo</u>
Dec. 1998. 3 Feb. 2000
<http://www.careerexpo.com/pub/docs/telecom.html>.

Baig, Edward C. "Welcome to the Wireless Office."
<u>Business Week</u> 26 June 1995: 104–106.

Bell, Allison. "The Telecommuting Workforce: Advice
for Managing Telecommuters." <u>HR Focus</u> 15 Jan.
2000: 9–10. CD-ROM. UMI-ProQuest. Mar. 2000.

Blankenhorn, Dana. "Dialing into Work." <u>Computer
Currents</u> 6 July 1999. 3 Feb. 2000 <http://
www.currents.net/magazine/atlanta/1007/
atvw1007.html>.

Bredin, Alice. <u>The Virtual Office Survival Handbook:
What Telecommuters and Entrepreneurs Need to
Succeed in Today's Nontraditional Workplace</u>. New
York: Wiley, 1996.

Korzeniowski, Paul. "Telecommuting--A Driving
Concern." <u>Business Communications Review</u> 13 (Feb.
1999): 45–48.

Koss-Feder, Laura. "Perks That Work." <u>Time</u> 9 Nov.
1998: 122–26.

"Learning New Work Technologies." <u>Business Planning</u>
18 (Feb. 2000): 8–15.

Lewis, Alicia. "The Business of Telecommuting."
<u>Journal of Contemporary Business</u> 11 (2000):

Holland 19

39–51. 20 Feb. 2000 <http://www.contempbus.
    jrn.com>.

Lewis, Alicia, and Tim P. Zhang. <u>Telecommuting</u>
    <u>Practices</u>. New York: Technology P, 1999.

Metro Atlanta Telecommuting Advisory Council.
    "How to Set Up a Telecommuting Program."
    5 July 1999. 23 Jan. 2000
    <http://www.matac.org/rocket.htm>.

Minnesota Office of Technology. "Telecommuting."
    <u>Information Resources Management Handbook</u>. 13
    Dec. 1999. 13 Feb. 2000
    <http://www.state.mn.us/ebranch/ot/ot-files/hand-
    book/guideline/guide4-2.html>.

New York Telecommuting Advisory Council. "What Is
    Telecommuting?" 1 April 2000. 3 April 2000
    <http://www.sccsi.com/telecommute/ny/html>.

Patel, Ivor. Personal interview. 26 Feb. 2000.

Perez-Hoya, Myra. "Telecommuting and Tomorrow's
    Workers." <u>Home Office Journal</u> 3 (2000): 7–10.

---. "Workers Become Telecommuters." <u>The Electronic</u>
    <u>Workplace</u> 21.10 (1999): 101–106.

Reynolds, Agnes. "2000: The Festival of
    Telecommuting--The Most Effective Way of Doing
    Business." <u>Business Strategies Today</u>

Holland 20

19(2000): 3-8. InfoTrac. CD-ROM. Information
Access. Apr. 2000.

Steve, Bob. "Telecommuting: Concepts and Resources."
Business Credit 7(Jan. 2000): 36-40.

Sullivan, Sandra. "FAQ's: When Investigating
Telecommuting as a Work Option." Telecommute
Solutions Inc. 27 Jan. 1999. 4 Mar. 2000
<http://www.telecommute.org/faq/htm>.

"Technology Tips." Home Computers, Erie, Mar. 2000.
19 Mar. 2000
<http://www.homecomp./com/homecomp/html>.

United States. Office of Personnel Management. "Reason
for Telecommuting." 1 Feb. 2000. 1 Apr. 2000
<http://www.opm.gov/workfam/
telecom/reasons/html>.

Vint, Barbara. "Re: Telecommuting at Pacific Software
Systems." E-mail to the author. 23 Mar. 2000.

"The Working Mother's Guide to Negotiating Flexible
Work." 15 Sept. 1999. 23 Feb. 2000
<http://www.workoptions.com/teleprop/htm>.

Zuckerman, Mortimer. "The Time of Our Lives:
Technology's Transforming Power . . ." U.S. News &
World Report 17 May 1999: 72. 5 Jan. 2000
<http://www.usnews.com.17599>.

✓ Revision Checklist

❑ Gave full and proper credit to sources consulted and those used for the preparation of my work.

❑ Avoided all forms of plagiarism.

❑ Recorded all direct quotations accurately.

❑ Paraphrased information correctly and acknowledged rightful sources.

❑ Double-checked spelling of authors' and publishers' names and accuracy of all pertinent publication information.

❑ Followed MLA or APA documentation method consistently in preparing Works Cited or References pages.

❑ Included all necessary in-text (parenthetical) references; cited each parenthetical reference in Works Cited list or References pages.

❑ Indicated clearly which work I used when sources included more than one work by same author.

❑ Included only the works referred to in my paper in Works Cited or References pages.

❑ Cited all CD-ROM and on-line database material completely and consistently.

❑ Alphabetized Works Cited and References entries correctly.

❑ Documented all Internet sources properly, giving both posting and access dates.

Exercises

1. Ask a professor in your major what he or she regards as the most widely respected periodical in your field. Find a copy of the periodical and explain its method of documentation (providing examples). How does it differ from the MLA method?

2. Put the following pieces of bibliographic information in proper form according to the MLA method of documentation for Works Cited.

   a. New York, Hawthorn Publishing Company, John Anderson, 2002, pages 95–97, second edition, *A New Way to Process Information.*

   b. Margaret Mannix, Amy Bernstein, Mary Kathleen Flynn; *U.S. News & World Report,* pages 58–60; "The Internet: Best Web Sites for Women"; 1 July 1996; located on InfoTrac or ProQuest on 3 Sept. 1999.

   c. *The Online Journal of Ethics*; publication date 1999; "Imperfect Competition, Price Fairness, and the Pharmaceutical Industry"; <http://www.depaul.edu/ethics/icpfpi.html>; access date August 5, 1999; Ronald F. White and Sean Fraley.

d. *American Journal of Nursing,* Pamela Minarik, Feb. 1999, page 54, "Using Hospital Databases," Vol. 99.

e. *Air Quality Management,* the Environmental Protection Agency, Office of Air and Radiation, the Government Printing Office, available after November 1999, free of charge, page 8.

f. On-line, posted 29 Mar. 2000, home page, Pacific Technologies, Inc., "Buying the Smart Modem This Year," Internet, accessed 18 Apr. 2000, http://pacifictech.com.

g. *HealthWatch: The Online Journal for Health Conscious Internet Users;* published May 2000, "Carpal Tunnel Syndrome: Early Warning Signs," Hattie Grandville and Paul Hall, accessed on May 12, 2000, <http://www.healthwatch.com>.

h. ProQuest, ABI/Inform, Stephanie Stahl, *Informationweek,* Mar. 11, 2001. p. 89, "Groupware for Exchange Server."

i. "Re: Preparation of Computer Graphics"; e-mail to Gayle Lowery, Regional Supervisor; 3 May 2002. Joan Horvath, sender.

j. *Academic American Encyclopedia,* "Computers," Compuserve, 9 Oct. 1995, posted 8 Aug. 1995.

k. *Global Encyclopedia,* posted 8 November 2001, "Olympics," http://www.halcyon.com/jensen/encyclopedia/, written by Enrique Sanchez.

l. An interview with your local police chief that took place in the college auditorium after she delivered a talk on crime prevention on Wednesday, 23 January 2001. Her name is Tina B. Holmes.

m. Today's editorial in a newspaper on-line.

n. Pyramid Films, Inc.; *Pulse of Life;* 2003, Santa Monica, California; order number 342br.

o. *Essays on Food Sanitation;* John Smith (editor); Framingham, Massachusetts; 3rd edition; pages 345–356; Mary Grossart (author); Albion Publishing Company; "Selection of Effective Chemical Agents"; 2002.

p. A business story published 30 days ago in a major newspaper on-line.

q. January to February of 2000, pages 11–13, "Light Sensors and Smoke Detectors," Mathis, Patricia, *Fire Science Quarterly.*

r. 8th ed. of *McGraw-Hill Encyclopedia of Science & Technology,* "Lasers."

s. Women's Business Communication Newsgroup, on-line posting date 3 Feb. 2000, <newsbuscom.edu.>, Cathy Polk, "Eliminating Sexist Language," accessed 10 Apr. 2000.

3. Put the bibliographic references you listed in MLA format in Exercise 2 into APA format.

4. Convert the bibliographic information given for one article in the periodical you chose for Exercise 1 into the MLA parenthetical style.

5. The following passage contains mistakes in the MLA method of documentation. Find the mistakes and explain how to correct them.

More and more companies are allowing employees to "telecommute" (see Smith; Dawson; Brown; Gura and Keith;

and Allen). One expert defines telecommuting as "home-based work" (13). Having terminals in their homes "allows employees to work at a variety of jobs" ("New Employment Opportunities"). It has been estimated that currently 900,000 employees work out of their homes (Pennington, p. 56). That number is sure to increase as computer-based businesses multiply in the late 1990s (Brown). In one of her recent articles on telecommuting, Holcomb (167) found that "in the last year alone 43 companies in the metropolitan Phoenix area made this option available to their employees."

Employees who telecommute cite a variety of benefits for such an arrangement (see in particular articles by Gura, Smith, and Kaplan). One employee of a mail order company whose opinion was quoted observed that "I can save about 15-17 hours a week in driving time" (from Allen). Working at home allows the telecommuting employee to work at his or her optimum times ("The Day Does Not Have to Start at 9:00 A.M."). Also, in articles by Kaplan and Keith the benefits of not having to leave home are emphasized: "A telecommuting parent does not have to worry about child care" (39). Telecommuting may "be here to stay" (quoted in a number of different Web site sources).

6. Submit your preliminary list of references (your tentative Works Cited page) for a research paper or long report to your instructor.

CHAPTER 10

Summarizing Material

A summary is a brief restatement of the main points of a book, report, Web site, article, laboratory test, meeting, or convention. A summary saves readers hours of time because they do not have to study the original work or attend a conference. A summary can reduce a report or article by 85 to 95 percent (or even more) or capture the essential points of a three-day convention in a one-page memo. Moreover, a summary can tell readers whether they should even be concerned about the original; it may be irrelevant for their purposes. Finally, since only the most important points of a work are included in a summary, readers will know they have been given the crucial information they need.

The Importance of Summaries

Summaries can be found all around you. Television and radio stations regularly air two-minute broadcasts called "newsbreaks" to summarize in a few sentences the major stories covered in more detail on the evening news. Popular news magazines such as *Time, Newsweek,* and *U.S. News & World Report* have a large readership because of their ability to condense seven days of news into short, readable articles highlighting key personalities, events, and issues.

Newspapers also employ summaries for their readers' convenience. Daily newspapers such as the *Wall Street Journal* and weekly papers such as *Barron's* and the *National Law Journal* print on the first page brief summaries of news stories that are discussed in detail elsewhere in the paper. Some newspapers simply print a column entitled "News Summary" on the first or second page of an issue to condense major news stories. *Facts On File's News Digest* comprehensively summarizes world news every week. Figure 10.1 is a summary that appeared in *Facts On File* about copyright status for computer-colored films. Note how a few paragraphs capture and emphasize the most significant data that may have taken weeks and numerous reports or stories to record.

FIGURE 10.1   A summary of the copyright status of colorized films.

Copyrights Approved for "Colorization."
Computer-colored films would be granted copy-right status if those tinted versions revealed a certain degree of human creativity and were produced by existing computer-coloring technology, the U.S. Copyright Office of the Library of Congress ruled June 19.

The ruling came after months of debate surrounding the "colorization" process, a debate that had reached all the way to the U.S. Senate.

The copyright office ruled that computer-colored versions of black-and-white films were entitled to copyright protection as "derivative works." Such protection gave a studio the right, generally for 75 years, to distribute a colored version of a movie through broadcast and cable-TV outlets and to sell videotape copies. The studio could also collect damages from companies that copied the colored films.

Films would not be eligible for copyright protection if the tinting "consists of the addition of only a relatively few number of colors to an existing black-and-white motion picture."

The Facts On File Weekly World News Digest. ©1987 by Facts On File News Services, a division of K. III Reference Corporation. Reprinted with permission of Facts On File News Services, New York.

TECH NOTE

Web Site Summaries

Summaries are widely used at Internet Web sites to encourage users to go further into the subject. A home page is in essence a summary of the various links to which it is connected. Summaries are also a vital part of the search strategies on the Net. When search engines retrieve positive "hits," a short summary accompanies each citation to help users determine whether the material is relevant to their needs.

As a student, you probably already know how critical it is to be able to write summaries when you gather and record research. Summaries are crucial in highlighting key ideas from material that students have to include—and frequently evaluate—in research papers.

On the job, writing summaries for employers or co-workers is a regular and important responsibility. Each profession has its own special needs for summaries. Chapter 15 discusses a variety of reports—progress, sales, periodic, trip, test, and incident—whose effectiveness depends on a faithful summary of events. You may be asked to summarize a business trip that lasted a week into one or two pages for your company or agency. A busy manager may ask you to read and condense a ninety-page report so she will have a knowledgeable overview of its contents.

Acute-care nurses must write one- or two-page discharge summaries for patients who are being referred to other agencies (home health, nursing home, rehabilitation center). The nurses must read a patient's record carefully and summarize what has happened to the patient since admission to the hospital—surgeries, treatments, diagnoses, and prognoses—and indicate necessary follow-up treatments (medications, office visits, outpatient care, X-rays).

Figure 10.2 is a summary of a long report evaluating child-care facilities. Note how it concisely identifies the main purpose and conclusions of this report.

Contents of a Summary

The chief problem in writing a summary is deciding what to include and what to omit. As we have just seen, a summary is, after all, a much abbreviated version of

FIGURE 10.2   A summary of a long report on child care.

HIGH MARKS FOR ON-SITE CARE

The best place to find high-quality child care may be your workplace, according to a new study by Burud & Associates, a California-based work/life benefits consulting firm. The study of 205 work-site child care programs found that such centers are eight times more likely than other centers to meet the high standards set by the National Association for the Education of Young Children (NAEYC).

Forty-one percent of work-site centers open at least two years are NAEYC-accredited—compared to only 5 percent of all child care centers. Other key findings:

• Ninety-two percent of work-site centers offer infant care.
• Workplace centers provide "substantially better" employee benefits—which help the centers recruit and retain high-quality caregivers.
• One in four centers is open past seven p.m. and one in seven is open before six a.m. and/or offers weekend care.

Source: Written by In House. Reprinted with permission of MacDonald Communications Corporation. First appeared in *Working Mother* May 1999.

the original; it is a streamlined review of *only* the most significant points. You will not save your readers time if you simply rephrase large sections of the original and call the new version a summary. That will simply supply readers with another report, not a summary.

Make your summary lean and useful by briefly telling readers the main points: purpose, scope, conclusions, and recommendations. A summary should concisely answer the readers' two most important questions.

1. What findings does the report or meeting offer?
2. How do those findings apply to my business, research, or job?

Note how the summary in Figure 10.2 successfully answered those two questions by indicating to working mothers where the best child care is likely to be found—in the workplace.

How long should a summary be? While it is hard to set down precise limits about length, effective summaries are generally 5 to 10 percent of the length of the original. The complexity of the material being summarized and your audience's exact needs can help you to determine an appropriate length. To help you know what is most important for your summary, the following suggestions will guide you on what to include and what to omit.

What to Include in a Summary

1. **Purpose.** A summary should indicate why the article or report was written or why a convention or meeting was held. (Often a report is written or a meeting is called to solve a problem or to explore new areas of interest.) Your summary should give the readers a brief introduction (even one sentence will do) indicating the main purpose of the report or conference.

2. **Essential specifics.** Include only the names, costs, codes, places, or dates essential to understanding the original. To summarize a public law, for example, you need to include the law number, the date it was signed into law, and the name(s) of litigants.

3. **Conclusions or results.** Emphasize what the final vote was, the result of the tests, and the proposed solution to the problem.

4. **Recommendations or implications.** Readers will be concerned especially with important recommendations—what they are, when they can be carried out, and why they are necessary.

What to Omit from a Summary

1. **Opinion.** Avoid injecting opinions—your own, the author's, or a speaker's. You distract readers from grasping main points by saying that the report was too long or missed the main point, that a salesperson from Detroit monopolized the meetings, or that the author digressed to blame the Land Commission for failing to act properly. A later section of this chapter will deal with evaluative summaries.

2. **New data.** Stick to the original article, report, book, or meeting. Avoid introducing comparisons with other works or conferences; readers will expect a digest of only the material being summarized.

3. Irrelevant specifics. Do not include any biographical details about the author of an article. Although many journals contain a section entitled "Notes on Contributors," this information plays no role in the reader's understanding of your summary.

4. Examples. Illustrations, explanations, and descriptions are unnecessary in a summary. Readers must know outcomes, results, and recommendations, not the illustrative details supporting or elaborating on those results.

5. Background. Material in introductions to articles, reports, and conferences can usually be excluded from a summary. Such "lead-ins" prepare the reader for a discussion of the subject by presenting background information, anecdotes, and details that will be of little interest to readers who want a summary to give them the big picture.

6. Reference data. Exclude information found in footnotes, bibliographies, appendixes, tables, or graphs. All such information supports rather than expresses conclusions and recommendations.

7. Jargon. Technical definitions or jargon in the original may confuse rather than clarify the essential information for the general reader.

Preparing a Summary

To write an effective summary, you need to proceed through a series of steps. Basically, you will have to read the material carefully, making sure that you understand it thoroughly. Then you will have to identify the major points and put aside everything else. Finally, you will have to put the essence of the material into your own words. The process of writing a summary demands an organized plan. Follow these steps to prepare your summary effectively.

TECH NOTE

Using Your Computer to Summarize
Your computer's word processing program can help you in a number of ways as you prepare your summary. You can download the material (article, report, technical paper) you need to summarize and then, as you read through it the first time on your screen, cut out extraneous, nonessential material. The first time through, it is easier to cut out what you don't want than it is to select exactly what you do want. To pare down material, simply select what you don't want by running your cursor across the material or, to eliminate an entire paragraph or paragraphs, down the side of the material; then press "Delete."

Another way to use your computer when you have to summarize is to highlight the key points as you read through the material you have downloaded. Highlighting during the first pass through the material will guide you on your second reading as you attempt to include only relevant material for your summary.

1. **Read the material once in its entirety to get an overall impression of what it is about.** Become familiar with large issues, such as the purpose and organization of the work and the audience for whom it was written. Look at visual cues—headings, subheadings, words in italic or boldface type, sidebars—that will help you to classify main ideas and summarize the work. Also see whether the author has included any mini-summaries in the article or report or whether there is a concluding summary.

2. **Reread the material.** Read it a second time or more often if necessary. To locate all and only the main points, underline them. (If the work is a book or in a journal that belongs to your library, work with a photocopy so you can underline.) To spot the main points, pay attention to the key transitional words, which often fall into predictable categories.

- Words that enumerate: *first, second, third, initially, subsequently, finally, next, another*
- Words that express causation: *accordingly, as a result, because, consequently, therefore, thus*
- Words that express contrasts and comparisons: *although, by the same token, despite, different from, furthermore, however, in contrast, in comparison, in addition, less than, likewise, more than, more readily, not only . . . but also, on the other hand, the same is true for, similar, unlike*
- Words that signal essentials: *basically, best, central, crucial, foremost, fundamental, indispensable, in general, important, leading, major, obviously, principal, significant*

Pay special attention to the first and last sentences of each paragraph. Often the first sentence of a paragraph contains the topic sentence, and the last sentence summarizes the paragraph or provides a transition to the next paragraph.

Also be alert for words signaling information you do *not* want to include in your summary, such as the following:

- Words announcing opinion or inconclusive findings: *from my personal experience, I feel, I admit, in my opinion, might possibly show, perhaps, personally, may sometimes result in, has little idea about, questionable, presumably, subject to change, open to interpretation*
- Words pointing out examples or explanations: *as noted in, as shown by, circumstances include, explained by, for example, for instance, illustrated by, in terms of, learned through, represented by, such as, specifically in, stated in*

3. **Collect your underlined material or notes and organize the information into a draft summary.** At this stage do not be concerned about how your sentences read. Use the language of the original, together with any necessary connective words or phrases of your own. Key the draft into your computer. *Expect to have more material here than will appear in the final version.* Do not worry; you are engaged in a process of selection and exclusion. Your purpose at this stage is to extract the principal ideas from the examples, explanations, and opinions surrounding them.

4. Read through and revise your draft(s) and delete whatever information you can. As you revise, see how many of your underlined points can be condensed, combined, or eliminated. You may find that you have repeated a point. Check your draft against the original for accuracy and importance. Make sure you are faithful to the original by preserving its emphases and sequence.

5. Now put the revised version into your own words. Again, make sure that your reworded summary has eliminated nonessential words. Connect your sentences with words that show relationships between ideas in the original (*also, although, because, consequently, however, nevertheless, since*). Compare this version of your summary with the original material to double-check your facts.

6. Do not include remarks that repeatedly call attention to the fact that you are writing a summary. You may want to indicate initially that you are providing a summary, but avoid such remarks as "The author of this article states that water pollution is a major problem in Baytown"; "On page 13 of the article three examples, not discussed here, are found."

7. Edit your summary to make sure it is clear and concise. Check to be certain it is coherent, too. Tell the reader how one point flows into another. Also proofread your summary carefully.

8. Identify the source you have just summarized. Include pertinent bibliographic information in the title of your summary or in a footnote or endnote. That gives proper credit to the original source and informs your readers where they can find the complete text if they want more details.

Figure 10.3, a 2,500-word article entitled "Virtual Reality: The Future of Law Enforcement Training," appeared in the *FBI Law Enforcement Bulletin* and hence would be of primary interest to individuals in law enforcement administration. Assume you are asked to write a summary of the FBI article for your boss, a police chief in a medium-size city who might be interested in incorporating virtual reality into the police academy training program. By following the steps outlined previously, you would first read the article carefully two or three times, underscoring or highlighting the most important points, signaled by key words. Note what has been underscored in the article. Also study the comments in the margins to see why certain information is to be included or excluded from the summary.

After you have identified the main points, extract them from the article and, still using the language of the article, join them into a coherent working draft summary, as in Figure 10.4. Then shorten and rewrite the working draft in your own words to produce the compact final version of your summary, as shown in Figure 10.5. Only 162 words long, the final summary is 12 percent of the length of the original article and records only major conclusions relevant to the audience for the article.

To further understand the effectiveness of the summary in Figure 10.5, review the wordy and misleading summary of the same article in Figure 10.6. The latter summary not only is too long but also dwells on minor details at the expense of major points. It includes unnecessary examples, statistics, and names; it even adds

FIGURE 10.3   An original article with important points underscored for use in a summary.

Virtual Reality
The Future of Law Enforcement Training
By
JEFFREY S. HORMANN

Delete scenario—
example of
background; an opener

A late night police pursuit of a suspected drunk driver winds through abandoned city streets. The short vehicle chase ends in a warehouse district where the suspect abandons his vehicle and continues his flight on foot. Before backup arrives, the rookie patrol officer exits his vehicle and gives chase. A quick run along a loading dock ends at the open door to an apparently unoccupied building. The suspect stops, brandishes a revolver, and fires in the direction of the pursuing officer before disappearing into the building. The officer, shaken but uninjured, radios in his location and follows the suspect into the building.

Did the officer make a good decision? Probably not by most departments' standards. Whether the officer's decision proves right or wrong, the training gained from this experience is immeasurable, that is, provided the officer lives through it. Fortunately for this officer, *the scenario occurred in a realistic, high-tech world called virtual reality*, where <u>training</u> can have <u>a real-life impact without the accompanying risk</u>.

Include important
observation

TRADITIONAL TRAINING LIMITATIONS

Experience may be the best teacher, but in real life, police officers may not get a chance to learn from their mistakes. To survive, they must receive training that prepares them for most situations they might encounter on the street. <u>However</u>, because <u>many training programs</u> emphasize repetition to produce desired behaviors, they <u>may not achieve the intended results</u>, especially after students leave the training environment. Thus, the more realistic the training, the <u>greater the lessons</u> learned.

Important distinction

<u>Additionally</u>, even some in law enforcement may fall prey to the effects of what has come to be termed "The MTV Generation."[1] As products of this generation, today's young officers purportedly have short attention spans requiring new, nontraditional training methods. The <u>key</u> to teaching this new breed is to provide fast-paced, <u>attention-getting instruction</u> that is <u>clear, concise, and relevant</u>.[2]

Delete explanation and
example

Include significant
qualification

Continued

FIGURE 10.3   (Continued)

TRAINING WITH VIRTUAL REALITY

Emphasize author's main point

Virtual reality can provide the type of training that today's law enforcement officers need. By completely immersing the senses in a computer-generated environment, the artificial world becomes reality to users and greatly enhances their training experiences.

Important reason for its neglect by law enforcement

Although considerable research and development have been conducted in this field, only a limited amount has applied directly to law enforcement. The apparent reason simply is that, for the most part, law enforcement has not asked for it.

Restatement of main point above; note parallel items with key words signaling important applications

Because virtual reality technology is relatively new, most law enforcement administrators know little about it. They know even less about what it can do for their agencies. By understanding what virtual reality is, how it works, and how it can benefit them, law enforcement administrators can become significantly involved in the development of this important new technology.

WHAT IS VIRTUAL REALITY?

Include definition

Simply stated, virtual reality is high-tech illusion. It is a computer-generated, three-dimensional environment that engulfs the senses of sight, sound, and touch. Once entered, it becomes reality to the user.

Important explanation

Within this virtual world, users travel among, and interact with, objects that are wholly the products of a computer or representations of other participants in the same environment. Thus the limits of this virtual environment depend on the sophistication and capabilities of the computer and the software that drives the system.

HOW DOES VIRTUAL REALITY WORK?

Significant phrase

Based on data entered by programmers, computers create virtual environments by generating three-dimensional images. Users usually view these images through a head-mounted device, which, for instance, can be a helmet, goggles, or other apparatus that restricts their vision to two small video monitors, one in front of each eye. Each monitor displays a slightly different view of the environment, which gives users a sense of depth.

Delete specific pieces of equipment

Delete example

Another device, called a position tracker, monitors users' physical positions and provides input to the computer. This information instructs the computer to change the environment based upon users' actions. For example, when users look over their shoulders, they see what lies behind them.

Continued

FIGURE 10.3   (Continued)

Because virtual reality users remain stationary, they use a *joy stick* or trackball to move through the virtual environment. Users *also* may wear a special glove or use other devices to manipulate objects within the virtual environment. *Similarly*, they can employ virtual weapons to confront virtual aggressors.

To enhance the sense of reality, some researchers are also experimenting with tactile feedback devices (TFDs). TFDs transmit pressure, force, or vibration, providing users with a simulated sense of touch.[3] *For example*, a user might want to open a door or move an object, which in reality, would require the sense of touch. A TFD would simulate this sensation. At present, *however,* it is important to remember that these devices are *crude* and somewhat *cumbersome to use*.

Delete further examples

Major conclusion

USES FOR VIRTUAL REALITY

In *today's competitive business environment*, organizations continuously strive to accomplish tasks faster, better, and inexpensively. This especially holds true in training.

Major value to audience of administrators

Virtual reality is *emerging rapidly* as a *potentially unlimited* method for providing *realistic, safe,* and *cost-effective training. For example,* a firefighter can battle the flames of a virtual burning building. A police officer can struggle with virtual shoot/don't shoot dilemmas.[4]

Emphasize significant advantages in training situations

Within a virtual environment, *students* can *make decisions* and act upon them *without risk* to themselves or others. By the same token, *instructors* can critique students' actions, enabling students to review and learn from their mistakes. This ability gives virtual reality a great *advantage over most conventional training methods.*

Use only main points relevant to target audience of law enforcement administrators

The Department of Defense *(DOD) leads public and private industry* in *developing virtual reality training. Since* the early 1980s, DOD has actively researched, developed, and implemented virtual reality to *train members* of the *armed forces* to fight effectively in combat.

DOD's current approach to virtual reality training *emphasizes team tactics.* Groups of military personnel from around the world engage in combat safely on a virtual battlefield. Combatants never come together physically; *rather,* simulators located at various sites throughout the world transmit data to a central location, where the virtual battle is controlled. Basically, it costs less to move information than people. Consequently this form of training has proven quite cost-effective.

Continued

FIGURE 10.3   (Continued)

An <u>additional benefit</u> to this <u>type of training</u> is that <u>battles</u> can be <u>fought under varying conditions</u>.

Virtual battlefields <u>re-create real-world locations</u> with <u>interchangeable characteristics</u>. To explore "what if" scenarios, participants can modify enemy capabilities, terrain, weather, and weapon systems.

Note main military advantage

Delete examples

Virtual reality <u>also can re-create actual battles</u>. Based on information from participants, the Institute for Defense Analyses re-created the 2nd Armored Cavalry Regiment Offensive conducted in Iraq during Operation Desert Storm. The success of the virtual re-creation became apparent when, upon viewing the simulations, soldiers who had fought in the actual battle reported the extreme accuracy of the event's depiction and the feeling of reliving the battle.[5] <u>Clearly, virtual reality holds great potential</u> for accurate review and analysis of <u>real-world situations</u>, which would be <u>difficult to accomplish</u> by <u>any other method</u>.

Major conclusion signaled by key word "clearly"

Omit example

Preliminary studies, for instance, show that military units perform better following virtual reality training.[6] <u>Even though</u> virtual environments are only simulations, the complete immersion of the senses literally overwhelms users, totally engrossing them in the action. <u>This realism</u> presumably plays a <u>major role</u> in the <u>program's success</u> and <u>likely</u> will prove positive in future endeavors. <u>In fact</u>, due to its success in training multiple participants in group combat situations, DOD plans to train infantry personnel individually with virtual reality fighting skill simulators.[7]

Note the key word "major"; idea relevant to law enforcement

Omit military application

LAW ENFORCEMENT TRAINING

While virtual reality has proven its value as a training and planning tool for the military, <u>applications for this technology reach far beyond DOD</u>. In varying but key ways, many military uses can <u>transfer to law enforcement</u>, including training in firearms, stealth tactics, and assault skills.

Key point

Major parallel points

Unfortunately, few organizations have dedicated resources to developing virtual reality for law enforcement. <u>According</u> to a recently published resource guide, more than <u>100 companies</u> currently are <u>developing and/or selling virtual reality hardware or software</u>. However, <u>none</u> of these firms <u>mentioned law enforcement uses</u>.[8]

Delete statistics

Subordinate idea

<u>Further</u>, a review of relevant literature revealed numerous articles on virtual reality technology, but only a few addressed law enforcement applications.

Continued

FIGURE 10.3   (Continued)

Restatement of major   <u>Yet</u>, virtual reality <u>clearly offers law enforcement bene-</u>
point   <u>fits</u> in a number of areas, including pursuit driving, firearms training, high-risk incident management, incident re-creation, and crime scene processing.

PURSUIT DRIVING

Include application but   <u>Pursuit driving</u> represents one area in which <u>virtual</u>
omit example   <u>reality application</u> has become <u>reality for law enforce-</u>
<u>ment</u>. Law enforcement personnel identified a need and provided input to a well-known private corporation that developed a driving simulator equipped with realistic controls.

Delete specific   The simulator provides users with realistic steering
mechanism and   wheel feedback, road feel, and other vehicle motions.
explanation of   The screen possesses a 225-degree field of view stan-
operation of screen   dard, with 360-degree coverage optional. <u>As noted in</u>
machanism   <u>demonstrations</u>, simulations can involve one or more drivers, and environments can alternate between city streets, rural back roads, and oval tracks. The vehicle itself can change from a police car to a truck, ambulance, or a number of others.

Virtual reality driving simulators provide police
Note cost efficiency   departments invaluable training at a <u>fraction of the</u>
again   <u>long-term cost of using actual vehicles</u>. In fact, the simulator is being used by a number of police departments around the country.

Include major   During the past year, for example, the Los Angeles
advantage but exclude   County Sheriff's Office Emergency Vehicle Operations
specific example   Center (EVOC) has used a four-station version of the driving simulator to train its officers. The simulators help students develop judgment and decision-making skills, while providing an environment free from risk of injury to students or damage to vehicles. <u>Still</u>, as the
Note major distinction   EVOC supervisor cautions, <u>virtual reality training</u>
for training purpose   should <u>complement, not replace</u>, actual behind-the-wheel instruction.[9]

FIREARMS TRAINING

New subtopic;   In another way, virtual reality could <u>greatly enhance</u>
include advantage but   shoot/don't shoot <u>training simulators</u> currently in use,
delete examples   such as the Firearms Training System, a primarily two-dimensional approach that possesses limited interactive capabilities. A <u>virtual reality system</u> would <u>allow</u> <u>officers</u> to enter any <u>three-dimensional environment</u> alone or as a member of a team and confront computer-generated aggressors or other virtual reality users.

Include significant   Evaluators could specifically observe the <u>training</u>
points on advantages   <u>from any perspective</u>, including that of the officers, or the criminal. The <u>training scenarios</u> could involve actual

Continued

FIGURE 10.3   (Continued)

Next three reasons to use virtual reality signaled by key words in addition, also, and likewise

building floor plans or local city streets, and criteria such as weather, number of participants, or types of weapons could be altered easily.

HIGH-RISK INCIDENT MANAGEMENT

Delete examples

In addition to weapons training, virtual reality could prove invaluable for SWAT team members before high-risk tactical assaults. Floor plans and other known facts about a structure or area could be entered into a computer to create a virtual environment for commanders and team members to analyze prior to action.

INCIDENT RE-CREATION

Law enforcement agencies could also collect data from victims, witnesses, suspects, and crime scenes to re-create traffic accidents, shootings, or other crimes. The virtual environment created from the data could be used to refresh the memories of victims and witnesses, to solve crimes, and ultimately, to prosecute offenders.

CRIME SCENE PROCESSING

Virtual reality crime scenes could likewise be used to train both detectives and patrol officers. First, students could search the site and retrieve and analyze evidence without ever leaving the station. Then, actual crime scenes could be re-created to add realism to training or to evaluate prior police actions.

IS VIRTUAL REALITY VIRTUALLY PERFECT?

Crucial qualification and justification for using virtual reality in law enforcement training

Though virtual reality may appear to be the ideal law enforcement tool, as with any new technology, some drawbacks exist. Currently, areas of concern range from cumbersome equipment to negative physical and psychological effects experienced by some users. Fortunately, however, the field is evolving and improving constantly, and as virtual reality gains widespread use, most major concerns should be dispelled.

PHYSICAL LIMITATIONS AND EFFECTS

Delete examples of limitations/effects

Because computers currently are not fast enough to process large amounts of graphic information in real time, some observers describe virtual environments as "slow-moving."[10] The human eye can process images at a much faster rate than a computer can generate them. In a virtual environment, frames are displayed at a rate of about 7 per second, an extremely slow speed when compared to television, which generates 60 frames per second.[11] Users find the resulting choppy or slow graphics less than appealing.

Adapted from: *FBI Law Enforcement Bulletin* 64, no. 7 (July 1995): 7–12.

FIGURE 10.4   A working draft summary of the "Virtual Reality" article in Figure 10.3.

Law enforcement officers put their lives on the line every day, yet their training does not fully allow them to anticipate what they will find on the streets. Virtual reality will give them realistic, high-tech benefits of encountering criminals without any risks. Traditional training methods, which work through repetition, cannot equal the advantages of virtual reality when it comes to teaching officers the lessons they must learn to survive in the field. This new breed of officers is demanding the attention-getting, highly realistic training that virtual reality affords them. Virtual reality translates the artificial world of the computer into the real world. Yet even though much research has been done on virtual reality, it is new to law enforcement officials. Moreover, manufacturers have not marketed their technology to them. It is essential that these administrators know how virtual reality works and what it can do for them. Virtual reality has been defined as high-tech illusion through the computer user's perceived interaction with the real world. Working through sophisticated software, virtual reality gives users a three-dimensional (hearing, feeling, and seeing) view of the things and people around them. Virtual reality requires specific equipment including goggles/headsets, a tracker, a trackball, and special gloves. But these devices do have problems; at present, they are crude and can be cumbersome. Even so, virtual reality provides cost-effective and life-saving benefits for law enforcement administrators. Thanks to this technology, students will be able to make quicker and better decisions in the field. Virtual reality has already been tried by the Department of Defense; the armed forces have used it to re-create battlefield conditions, helping the troops better understand the enemy and its position. Yet virtual

Continued

FIGURE 10.4   (Continued)

reality holds great appeal for other real-world applications, especially law enforcement. Unfortunately, the 100 companies that manufacture virtual reality equipment have neglected these law enforcement applications. Yet virtual reality easily accommodates law enforcement instruction. Driving simulators help officers prepare for high-speed chases. In Los Angeles County, such simulators complement more traditional training. Virtual reality can help officers in a variety of training missions—firearms, high-risk incidents, re-creating crimes, understanding the crime scene. Using virtual reality, officers never have to leave the station. Admittedly, virtual reality has drawbacks, but as this new technology improves, users should face fewer problems.

new information while ignoring crucial points about the applications of virtual reality to law enforcement officials. But even more serious, the summary in Figure 10.6 distorts the meaning and the intention of the original article. The reader concludes that the article says virtual reality is not very valuable for law enforcement administrators and officers—just the opposite of the point the article makes. You can avoid such mistakes by de-emphasizing minor points, by making sure that all parts of your summary agree with the original, and by not letting your own opinions distort the message of the original article.

Executive Summaries

An executive summary is found at the beginning of a formal proposal (Chapter 14) or a long report (Chapter 16). It is usually one or two pages (four to six concise paragraphs) and condenses the most important points from the proposal or report for a busy manager—the executive. It is written to help the reader reach a major decision based on the report or proposal.

Figure 10.7 is an executive summary of a report on software for a safety training program. The intended readers of the summary, managers at the company, are not interested in the technical details—the formulas, jargon, test protocols, equipment mechanisms. They want to know the big picture, the essential background information to make an informed decision. Managers use executive summaries so they will *not* have to wade through entire reports. An effective executive summary is like a report itself—self-contained and able to stand on its own. For that reason, the executive report is often called an **independent summary.**

FIGURE 10.5   A final, effective summary of the article in Figure 10.3.

Virtual reality offers benefits for law enforcement training that traditional methods cannot provide. This computer-generated technology simulates and recreates real-life crime scenes without placing officers at risk. Thanks to virtual reality's three-dimensional world of sight, sound, and touch, officers enter the criminals' world to gain invaluable experience interacting with them. Because virtual reality is new and has not been marketed for law enforcement use, administrators may not know about it. Yet it provides a cost-effective, realistic way to enhance training programs. The applications of virtual reality far exceed its military use of simulating battlefield conditions. Virtual reality allows administrators to give trainees hands-on experience in pursuit driving, firearms training, SWAT team assaults, incident re-creation, and crime location processing. Officers can investigate a crime without ever leaving the station. Although virtual reality is an emerging technology with limitations, it is quickly improving and rapidly expanding. Administrators need to incorporate it into their curriculum to give officers field-translatable experiences.

What Managers Want to See in an Executive Summary

Executive readers are most concerned with managerial and organizational issues—the areas over which they have supervisory control. These readers will look for information on costs, profits, resources, personnel, timetables, and feasibility. Your summary must supply key information on the executive's **four E's—evaluation, economy, efficiency,** and **expediency.** Executive readers will expect you to reduce large, complex subjects into easy-to-read, easy-to-understand information that they can act on confidently.

Organization of an Executive Summary

An executive summary must be faithful to the report while giving the readers what they need. First read the report carefully, plan what you want to include, then draft and revise using valuable connective words (p. 403). Clearly, you cannot write an executive summary of your report until after you have written the report itself.

Basically, follow this organizational plan when you write an executive summary:

1. **Begin with the purpose and the scope of the report,** for example, to study new marketing strategies, to replace obsolete software, to relocate a branch store.

FIGURE 10.6   A misleading summary of the article in Figure 10.3.

Nonessential introductory material	A rookie police officer makes many mistakes in pursuing subjects. Training can cover many realistic situations, but young officers in the MTV Generation have short attention spans. Given the research so far on virtual reality, it holds little promise for law enforcement use. Virtual reality has too many limitations, but it works interestingly through gloves, helmets, and goggles, and with a position tracker users can see over their shoulders. It even has a joy stick (like those in an amusement park) and a crude device—a TFD—that simulates touch (nice to have in a horror movie). Instructors can gain much from virtual reality because they can better criticize their trainees. In the early 1980s, the DOD used virtual reality to duplicate battlefield conditions. The 2nd Armored Cavalry Regiment Offensive won the Iraqi War because of virtual reality. But companies manufacturing virtual reality technology are not interested in law enforcement applications, another indication of its limitations. The Los Angeles Sheriff's EVOC used a driving simulator—offering a 225-degree field of view but it can be ordered with a 360-degree field—but expressed their caution about it. There have been limited interactions in the use of virtual reality for firearms training, though floor plans might have helped SWAT teams. Witnesses may need to refresh their memories with virtual reality. Again drawbacks exist. Computers are not as fast as the human eye in processing information.
Distorts article, which advocates the benefits of virtual reality for law enforcement	
Dwells on specific virtual reality equipment at the expense of the main advantages	
Overlooks the significance of virtual reality for trainees	
Reverses chronology of events; misrepresents the role of virtual reality	
How relevant to law enforcement? Delete unit's name	
Again, distorts intention of article	
Delete specifications	
One-sided; omits success of simulation	
Focuses on limits rather than usefulness	
Fails to attribute these benefits to virtual reality	
Does not subordinate flaws	

FIGURE 10.7   An executive summary.

A Report on Providing Better Training at Techtron Sites

Management commissioned this report to investigate ways to prepare for the OSHA audits scheduled between February and June 2002, at our seven regional Techtron plants. Most directly, this report focuses on our ability to complete Phase One of ISO 14001 certification.

Currently the Techtron safety training programs are inadequate; they are neither comprehensive nor up-to-date. We lack necessary software to instruct employees about the EPA and OSHA regulations and requirements that apply to hazardous materials or procedures used in our company. Consequently, safety violations have occurred with lockouts, confined spaces, fall protection, and the "Right to Know Law" concerning labeling of chemicals.

Exploring better ways to conduct our training sessions, we purchased a copy of the software program EPA/OSHA Trainer, regarded as the best on the market (available from EDI @ $600 per copy). The Trainer offers effective guidelines on developing safety meetings and giving demonstrations and also includes instructions, written in clear, nontechnical language, on how to identify, collect, and document hazardous materials. Additionally, the Trainer supplies the full text of EPA/OSHA regulations, with updates issued quarterly.

To test the effectiveness of the Trainer software, we scheduled an internal audit at our Hendersonville site last month. After progressing through the Trainer module, a core group of employees interviewed by management successfully completed all required regulatory training. Subsequently, employees who had undergone such training were able to instruct and monitor the performance of other employees.

To ensure the safety of our employees and to compete in a global marketplace, Techtron must pass the OSHA 14001 certification. Purchasing seven additional copies of the EPA/OSHA Trainer software (7 @ $600 = $4200) is a wise and necessary investment.

---

2. **Relate your purpose to a key problem.** Identify the source (history) and seriousness of the problem.
3. **Identify in nontechnical language the criteria used to solve the problem.** Be careful not to include too much information or too many details.
4. **Condense the findings of your report.** Relate what tests or surveys revealed.
5. **Stress conclusions and possible solutions.**
6. **Provide recommendations,** for example, buy, sell, hire more personnel, relocate, or choose among alternative solutions.

The order of information in an executive summary does not have to follow the exact order of the report itself. In fact, some executive summaries start with recommendations. Find out your boss's preference.

Evaluative Summaries

To write an evaluative summary, also called a critique, follow all the guidelines on pages 402–403. As with executive summaries, you will be expected to provide a commentary on the material, that is, give your opinion.

Your instructors and employers may often ask you to summarize and assess what you have read. In school you may have to write a book report or compile a critical, annotated bibliography commenting on the usefulness of the material you found in those sources. On the job your employer may ask you to condense and judge the merits of a report, paying special attention to whether its recommendations should be followed, modified, or ignored. Your company or agency may also ask you to write short evaluative summaries of job applications, sales proposals, or conferences.

Characteristics of a Successful Evaluative Summary

To write an effective evaluative summary, follow these guidelines.

- Keep the summary short—5 to 10 percent of the length of the original.
- Blend your evaluations with your summary; do not save your evaluations for the end of the summary.
- Place each evaluation near the summarized points to which it applies so readers will see your remarks in context
- Include a pertinent quotation from the original to emphasize your recommendation.
- Comment on both the content and the style of the original.

Evaluating the Content

Answer these questions on content for your readers.

1. How carefully is the subject researched? Is the material accurate and up-to-date? Are important details missing? Exactly what has the author left out? Where could the reader find the missing information? If the material is inaccurate, will the whole work be affected or just part of it?

2. Is the writer or speaker objective? Are conclusions supported by evidence? Is the writer or speaker following a particular theory, program, or school of thought? Is that fact made clear in the source? Has the author or speaker emphasized one point at the expense of others? What are the writer's qualifications and background?

3. Does the work achieve its goal? Is the topic too large to be adequately discussed in a single talk, article, or report? Is the work sketchy? Are there digressions, tangents, or irrelevant materials? Do the recommendations make sense?

4. Is the material relevant to your audience? How would the audience use it? Is the entire work relevant or just part of it? Why? Would the work be useful for all employees of your company or only for those working in certain areas? Why? What answers offered by the work would help to solve a specific problem you or others have encountered on the job?

Evaluating the Style

Answer these questions on style for the readers of your evaluative summary.

1. Is the material readable? Is it well written and easy to follow? Does it contain helpful headings, careful summaries, and appropriate examples?

2. What kind of vocabulary does the writer or speaker use? Are there many technical terms or jargon? Is it written for the layperson? Is the language precise or vague? Would readers have to skip certain sections that are too complicated?

3. What visuals are included? Charts? Graphs? Photographs? How are they used? Are they used effectively? Are there too many or too few?

Figures 10.8, 10.9, and 10.10 contain evaluative summaries. Note how the writers' assessments are woven into the condensed versions of the originals. Figure 10.8 is a

FIGURE 10.8   An evaluative summary of an article.

Shelton, Ben. "Building Customer Loyalty on the Web." *EC World* (Mar. 1999): 24–29. www.ecresources.com accessed 6 May 2000.

According to this helpful article, most Web businesses are not developing ways to "convert Web surfers into loyal customers." While pricing and convenience are factors, Shelton maintains that customer assistance is the most important determiner of repeat business. He identifies four significant ways for Web shops to personalize their services. The first is to offer more off-site help; surprisingly, some Web businesses offer none. Second, Shelton advocates better self-assistance through personalized service software. Many Web shoppers need more than an FAQ menu and thus can benefit from layered support options. Third, decision support systems act as a "collaborative filter," making product suggestions and matching a customer's preference with a particular item or service. Finally, for Shelton, customer-care robots, programmed to understand and respond realistically to natural language, answer shoppers' most relevant questions or if there's a problem switch them to a service representative. This readable and informative article offers Web merchants practical advice on how to give customers the convenience and service of a fine retail store.

FIGURE 10.9   A collaboratively written evaluative summary of a seminar.

Sabine County Hospital
Sabine, TX 77231
512-555-6734
http://www.sabine.org

TO: Mohammed Lau, M.S.N.   SUBJECT: Evaluation of Physical
        Director of Nurses   Assessment Seminar

FROM: Judith Kim, R.N.   DATE: September 12, 2002
       Lee Schoppe, R.N.

On September 7, Doris Fujimoto, R.N., and Rick Ponce, R.N., both on the staff of Houston Presbyterian Hospital, conducted a practical and beneficial seminar on physical assessment. The one-day seminar was divided into three units (1) **Techniques of Health Assessment**, (2) **Assessment of Heart and Lungs**, and (3) **Assessment of the Abdomen**.

Techniques of Health Assessment
Four procedures used in physical assessment—inspection, percussion, palpation, auscultation—were defined and demonstrated. Return demonstrations, used throughout the seminar, meant we did not have to wait until we went back to work to practice our skills. The instructors stressed the proper use of the stethoscope and the ways of taking a patient's medical history. We were also asked to take the medical history of the person next to us.

Assessment of the Heart and Lungs
After we inspected the chest externally, we discussed the proper placement of hands for percussion and palpation and the significance of various breath sounds. The instructors helped us find areas of the lung and identify heart sounds. However, the film on examining the heart and lungs was ineffective because it included too lengthy information for many seminar participants.

Continued

FIGURE 10.9 (Continued)

2.

Assessment of the Abdomen
The instructors warned that the order of examination of the abdomen differs from that of the chest cavity. Auscultation, not percussion, follows inspection so that bowel sounds are not activated. The instructors then clearly identified how to detect bowel sounds and how to locate the abdominal and palpate organs.

Recommendations
We strongly recommend a seminar like this for all nurses whose expanding role in the health care system requires more physical assessments. Although the seminar covered a wealth of information, the instructors admitted that they discussed only basics. In the future, however, it would be better to offer follow-up seminars on specific body systems (chest cavity, abdomen, central nervous system) instead of combining topics because of the amount of information involved and the time required for demonstrations.

student's opinion of an article summarized for a class in e-commerce. Figure 10.9 is an evaluative summary in memo format collaboratively written by two employees who have just returned from a seminar. They have divided their labor, one writing the opening paragraph and the summary of "Techniques of Health Assessment" and the other writing the summaries of "Assessment of the Heart and Lungs" and "Assessment of the Abdomen." Together they drafted and revised the "Recommendations" and prepared the final copy of the memo.

Another kind of evaluative summary—a book review—is shown in Figure 10.10. Many journals and Web sites print book reviews to inform their professional audiences about the most recent studies in their fields. Reviews condense and assess books, reports, government studies, tape cassettes, films, and other materials. The short review in Figure 10.10 comments briefly on usefulness to the intended audience and on style, provides clarifying information, and explains how the book is developed. For further examples, look at Amazon.com (*http://www.amazon.com/*), Real Books (*http://www.realbooks.com/*), or Books on Line (*http://www.booksonline.co.uk*).

A book review includes the most important and useful—to a key audience—information about a book or report. Reviews are also important for the kinds of information that they do *not* include—details and irrelevant (for the audience) information that would only clog a summary. For example, the review in Figure 10.10 indicates that the book documents the dangers of computer crime to corpora-

FIGURE 10.10   A book review.

Book Review
By Richard Power

Protection and Security on the Information Superhighway
By Frederick B. Cohen
John Wiley & Sons (New York, NY), softcover, 301 pages, $24.95

The general populace's love affair with the Internet, coupled with increasingly daring escapades on the part of the electronic underground, has propelled the subject of information security into the mass media. The weekly news magazines and major newspapers have begun to cover (albeit rather ineptly) the saga of the cyberspace frontier. Meanwhile, losses from computer crime and telecommunications fraud have been rising for many years. And the most serious dimension of the threat—information warfare waged by rival corporations and governments competing for hegemony in the new global economy—has hardly been addressed at all.

In **Protection and Security on the Information Superhighway**, Cohen has delivered a sober, thorough and detailed study of the grim realities behind the hype of computer crime and information warfare.

Unlike some other books available on information warfare, this tome doesn't indulge in flights of imagination and cries of "Fire!" Instead, Cohen carefully documents the dangers to U.S. corporations, government agencies, financial institutions and other entities with real-world case studies and factual references. He also offers savvy evaluations of information security technologies and practical suggestions for developing comprehensive information security strategies.

To get up to speed on the current and future danger to the entire information infrastructure—from your home PC to the Pentagon War Room—read this book.

Source: Computer Security Journal 11, no. 1 (1995), p. 77.

tions and governments but does not go into detailed descriptions of the security strategies recommended by the author.

Abstracts

Differences Between a Summary and an Abstract

The terms *summary* and *abstract* are often used interchangeably, resulting in some confusion. That problem arises because there are two distinct types of abstracts: *descriptive abstracts* and *informative abstracts.* The informative abstract is another name for a summary; the descriptive abstract is not. Why? An informative abstract (or summary) gives readers conclusions and indicates the results or causes. Look at the summary in Figure 10.5. It explains why virtual reality should be included in law enforcement training: because virtual reality gives officers field-translatable training. Informative abstracts are found at the beginning of long reports. Descriptive abstracts do not give conclusions.

All abstracts share two characteristics: the writer never uses "I" and avoids footnotes.

Writing the Informative Abstract

An informative abstract is not as long as an executive summary, which gives more supporting details. As a part of your course work or your job you will probably have to write informative abstracts for long reports (see Chapter 16).

One way to approach writing the abstract of a report is to think of it as a table of contents in sentence form. The table of contents is, in effect, the final outline; it is easily fleshed out into an abstract, as Figure 10.11 shows. On the left is a table of contents, and on the right is the abstract written from that outline.

This system works only if your table of contents is neither too detailed nor too skimpy. Starting off with a good outline of an article or a report provides the best beginning for your abstract. Make sure your sentences are complete and grammatical. Do not omit verbs, conjunctions, and articles. Proper subordination is essential.

Figure 10.11 Abstract written from a table of contents.

Table of Contents	*Abstract*

Need for Genetic Counseling
  Definition of Genetic Counseling
  Statistics on Genetic Counseling
	Genetic counseling is a service for people with a history of hereditary disease. One in 17 births contains some defect; one-fourth of the patients in hospitals are victims of genetic diseases (including diabetes, mental retardation, and anemia). One of every 200 children born has chromosome abnormalities.

Purpose of Genetic Counseling	Genetic counseling offers advice to parents who may give birth to children with genetic diseases and assistance to those with children already afflicted.

The Counseling Process
  Evaluating the Needs of the
    Counselees
  Taking a Family History
  Estimating the Risks
  Counseling the Family
	The first step in counseling is to evaluate the needs of the parents. A family history is prepared and risks of future children being afflicted are evaluated. The life expectancy and possible methods of treatment of any afflicted child also can be determined. Alternatives are presented.

Determination of a Genetic Disorder
  Amniocentesis
  Karyotyping
  Fluorescent Banding
  Staining
	Four prenatal tests are used to determine if a genetic disorder is present: amniocentesis, karyotpying, fluorescent banding, and staining.

Advantages of Genetic Screening
  Lower Cost
  Increased Availability
	The development of these four relatively simple methods has lowered the cost of genetic counseling and increased its availability.

By permission of Professor Mary Scotto.

FIGURE 10.12   Descriptive abstracts of journal articles.

5464
Community networks: new frontiers, old values. K. G. Schneider. *American Libraries*, 27 (1) Jan 96, p. 96.
Increasingly, librarians in the USA have been using new technologies to develop or collaborate on community networks. These community networks are often created in collaboration with other agencies and advocacy groups, weaving libraries more tightly into the community organism. Gives examples which illustrate some of the roles and relationships libraries are carving out with respect to community networks. EB

5465
Talking to the people: making the most of Internet discussion groups. K. L. Robinson. *Online*, 20 (1) Jan/Feb 96, p. 26-32. refs.
Offers advice on making the best of the knowledge sharing aspects of electronic conferences or discussion groups on the Internet and reducing the stress that sometimes comes with e-conference membership. Explains the different types of e-conferences available, how they are organized, how to locate and select them, how to cope with mailing list overload, and suitable netiquette. SE

5466
Teaching electronic information literacy.
C. Towney and D. A. Barclay. New York,
Neal Schuman, 1996, 150 p. ISBN 1-55570-186-8.
Focuses on ways of teaching and training library users in the environment of electronic information, such as the Internet and electronic classrooms. LT

5473
The Internet and Eastern Europe. T. Konn.
Information World Review, (109) Dec 95, p. 24-5. il.
Presents an overview of information on the countries of Central and Eastern Europe (CEE) accessible through the Internet, both from CEE servers and Western servers. Discusses news services, business information, legal and related information, and academic material. A list of key Web sites is included. JP

5474
Engineers on the Internet. S. Thomas.
Information World Review, (109) Dec 95, p. 25-6.
Presents an overview of engineering resources on the Internet. Includes manufacturing; professional institute activities; commercial companies, industry areas and patents; indexes and search tools; and newsgroups and mailing lists. Provides a list of key engineering information sites. JP

Library & Information Science Abstracts, Volume 5, May 1996, Abstracts 4772-5953.

You should expect to condense a whole paragraph of the original to a sentence, an individual sentence to a phrase, and a phrase to a single word.

Writing the Descriptive Abstract

A descriptive abstract is short, usually only a few sentences. Because it does not go into any detail or give conclusions, it is not actually a summary. A descriptive abstract provides information on what topics a work discusses but not how or why they are discussed. Busy readers rely on a descriptive abstract to decide whether they want or need to consult the work itself. Here is a descriptive abstract of the article summarized in Figure 10.5.

> Virtual reality can be used to teach law enforcement officers firearms training, SWAT team assaults, incident re-creation, and crime location processing. This new training technology will be of interest to law enforcement administrators.

Figure 10.12 reproduces some descriptive abstracts from *Library & Information Science Abstracts,* a reference work devoted exclusively to publishing collections of abstracts of recent and relevant works in this particular field of library science. Letters at the end of each abstract are the initials of the individual who prepared the abstract.

✓ Revision Checklist

- ❏ Read and reread the original thoroughly to gain a clear understanding of the purpose of the work.
- ❏ Used my word processing program to develop a summary.
- ❏ Underlined key transitional words, main points, significant findings, applications, solutions, conclusions, recommendations.
- ❏ Separated main points clearly from (a) minor ones, (b) background information, (c) illustrations, and (d) inconclusive findings.
- ❏ Excluded examples, explanations, and statistics from the summary or abstract.
- ❏ Deleted information not useful to audience—information too technical or irrelevant.
- ❏ Changed language of original to my own words so I am not guilty of plagiarism.
- ❏ Made sure that emphasis of summary matches emphasis in original.
- ❏ Determined that sequence of information in summary follows sequence of original.
- ❏ Added necessary connective words that accurately convey relationships between main points in original.
- ❏ Edited to eliminate wordiness and repetition from summary.
- ❏ Cited source of original correctly and completely.
- ❏ Avoided phrases that draw attention to the fact that I am writing a summary or abstract.
- ❏ Summarized material objectively without adding commentary (for informative summary).
- ❏ Commented on both content and style (in evaluative summary).
- ❏ Interspersed evaluative commentary throughout summary so that assessments appear near relevant points.
- ❏ Included a direct quotation to illustrate or reinforce my recommendation (for evaluative summary).
- ❏ Ensured that descriptive abstract is short and to the point and does not offer a judgment.

Exercises

1. Summarize a chapter of a textbook you are now using for a course in your major field. Provide an accurate bibliographic reference for that chapter (author of the textbook, title of the chapter, title of the book, place of publication, publisher's name, date of publication, and page numbers of the chapter).

2. Summarize a lecture you heard recently. Limit your summary to one page. Identify in a bibliographic citation the speaker's name, date, and place of delivery.

3. Listen to a television network evening newscast and to a later news update on the same station. Select one major story covered on the evening news and indicate which details from it were omitted in the news update.

4. Write a summary of the research paper on telecommuting (pp. 374–393) or on non-native speakers of English in the work force (pp. 629–644).

5. Bring to class an article from the *Reader's Digest* and the original material it condensed, usually an article in a journal or magazine published six months to a year earlier. In a paragraph or two indicate what the *Digest* article omits from the original. Also point out how the condensed version is written so that the omitted material is not missed and how the condensation does not misrepresent the main points of the article.

6. Assume that you are applying for a job and that the personnel manager asks you to summarize your qualifications for the job in two or three paragraphs. Write those paragraphs and indicate how your background and interests make you suited for the specific job. Mention the job by title at the beginning of your first paragraph.

7. Write a summary of one of the following articles.
   a. "Microwaves," in Chapter 1 on pages 35–36.
   b. "Videoconferencing: Ready for Prime Time?" below.

8. Write a descriptive abstract of the article you selected in Exercise 7.

Videoconferencing: Ready for Prime Time?

The goal for videoconferencing hasn't changed in more than a decade: Increase the productivity of scattered individuals and groups by enhancing simultaneous, real-time information sharing through voice, data, and video communication. At last it seems that videoconferencing technology is finally poised to fulfill its promise to users.

Advances in hardware, software, and transmission technologies have combined with market factors to bring a broad spectrum of applications much closer to reality than they've ever been. These applications fall within three broad categories: point-to-point, room-to-room, and interactive corporate broadcasting.

Point-to-Point

When most businesspeople think of videoconferencing they're thinking about point-to-point (desktop-to-desktop) communication. Increasingly common in very large corporations, the hardware normally consists of proprietary cards that plug into a desktop computer, a modem, and tiny video camera. The software that drives this setup is also proprietary. The video, data, and voice transmission usually uses a company's wide area network (WAN) or digital phone lines (ISDN).

Although older systems only permitted two-way communication links, most new systems allow several people at different locations simultaneous access through a central "bridge." This means that a live picture of each person appears in a window on the monitor screen. Data can be displayed, downloaded, or uploaded upon request while conversations take place.

Video quality is a good news/bad news situation. The good news is that the problems of "Max Headroom" jerkiness and seeming delay between the sound and picture have been solved. The bad news is that as a practical matter it may not be available to you.

"The problem isn't hardware, software, or even bandwidth," notes Tony Paradiso, director of marketing for Picture Tel (Danvers, MA), the company that has captured more than half of the point-to-point hardware/software market. "The real problem," Paradiso continues, "is the lack of generally accepted common standards within the videoconferencing industry. Everyone is still producing proprietary support systems."

Paradiso believes that there are two key reasons why this doesn't help users. First, the nature of developing proprietary systems means that some users wind up buying systems that are (or soon will be) obsolete, hurting both the customers and the industry. Second, users are accustomed to total transparency with phones and faxes, and expect as much from videoconferencing.

Room-to-Room

In this form of videoconferencing a small group of people (three to six) gather in a specially equipped room—either inside or outside the company—to communicate with another group of people in a similarly equipped room. This is a way for teams of people to get together without the cost of airfares or hotel rooms for either group.

The real saving, however, is in productivity. Neither group has to spend two or more days away from their primary work location, and they can still share all the needed information. It's important to factor these elements into your calculations, because the cost of setting up a room-to-room facility is at least $13,000 for hardware and software alone. It can be more than worth the cost if you otherwise have to send six or seven people by air away from home for joint team meetings.

Transmission is over ISDN lines, and is often projected onto a screen. The quality of the video, however, is controlled by 384KB bandwidth, which doesn't account for more than 20 percent of the total number of room-to-room and point-to-point systems currently in use.

"There's a natural migration toward higher bandwidths and broadcast-quality video," states Bob Boughton, Eastern regional manager for videoconferencing sales for TIE/communications (Overland Park, KS). The company has focused on providing hardware and software for room-to-room communicating, and to some extent, on large-audience interactive broadcasting. "We still need to resolve the matter of transmission and reception standards with proprietary capabilities," adds Boughton.

Large-Audience Broadcasting

Large-audience corporate interactive broadcasting is the high end of videoconferencing, and in many ways it resembles a commercial television broadcast. All the same capabilities exist for interactivity and data transmission, but the nature of the event and its support systems are such that video transmissions are usually of commercial broadcast quality at 30 frames per second.

"Corporate interactive broadcast is almost exclusively used by Fortune 500 companies," states Steve Holtzman, CEO of Flying Squirrel Production, Inc. (Cherry Hill, NJ), a conferencing company that specializes in technical production of multisite broadcasts. "Audiences at each site are usually large, more than 50 and often more than 200. The meeting itself is more structured than either point-to-point or room-to-room videoconferences. There are frequently large stage sets, props, special lighting and sound requirements, broadcast-quality video cameras, as well as producers, directors, and technicians. In addition to digital land lines, it frequently involves satellite, microwave, and fiber optic transmission."

Boughton comments, "Central capabilities for large-audience videoconferencing put an incredible communications tool in the hands of management. There's no doubt, however, that you'd better know what and how you plan to communicate."

Paradiso sees interactive broadcasting occupying a narrow market niche. "Large-audience videoconferencing doesn't replace the annual sales meeting or stockholders' meeting for big companies, but it may form elements of them. It will replace the 'all hands' meeting when management has to get information out to everyone fast. We still haven't figured out how to exchange information in this setting."

Holtzman is less dubious. "We've seen hot issues being discussed during broadcasts. The questions aren't planted, the responses aren't canned, and the impact isn't faked. That's one of the reasons multiple-city press conferences are often done by interactive broadcasts. Large-audience videoconferencing gives all members of the press access to top executives within a single time frame. This helps build the company's credibility."

Preparing Documents and Visuals

Designing Successful Documents, Including Internet Web Sites

The success of your document—letter, proposal, report, Web site—depends as much on how it looks as what it says. In designing your documents, you need to project a positive, pleasing image of yourself, your company, your product. A report filled with nothing but thick paragraphs of type, with no visual clues to break them up or to make information stand out, is sure to intimidate readers and turn them away. They will conclude that your work is too complex and not worth their effort or time. And if there is one thing that the world of work, especially dislikes it is someone who cannot get to the main point—the bottom line—quickly.

Your documents need to look user-friendly by signaling to readers that your message is

- easy to read
- easy to follow
- easy to recall

Don't bog readers down in unbroken long paragraphs. Break information into smaller units that are visually appealing. You can help readers find key points at a glance through **chunking** (using smaller paragraphs) and using lists, boldface type, and bullets. That way they can find your ideas easily the first time through or on a second reading if they have to double back to check or verify a point.

Organizing Information Visually

Take a quick look at Figures 11.2 (p. 436) and 11.3 (pp. 437–439). The same information is contained in each figure. Which appeals most to you? Which do you think would be easier to read? As the two figures show, the design or layout of your document plays a crucial role in the audience's overall acceptance of your work. Information is organized (and perceived) graphically as well as verbally. A document that looks logical and easy to read and that is clearly organized with the reader in mind will increase your credibility. If you offer readers a densely packed document, with no visual road signs to help them navigate through it, they will conclude that you are poorly organized and that your thinking is not very clear or direct.

Your company, too, will win or lose points because of your document design. A visually appealing document will enhance a company's reputation and improve its sales. A poorly designed one will not. Consumers will think your firm is inflexible, hard to do business with, and uncaring about specific problems customers may have over a policy or a set of instructions. Your company could easily get a reputation for not respecting the individuals it does business with or for being old-fashioned, hard-nosed, or just plain unprofessional.

Chapter 11 explains the tools you need and shows you how to design professional-looking, reader-friendly documents.

Characteristics of Effective Design

As you read this chapter and apply its principles to your own written work, make sure your documents offer readers the following qualities:

- visual appeal
- logical organization
- clarity
- accessibility
- variety
- audience relevance

By incorporating those characteristics into your documents, you guarantee that your work will be well received.

Tools for Designing Your Documents

In the world of work affordable and accessible PC and printer technology makes it easy for you to **design, illustrate, edit, format, store, retrieve, transfer,** and **print** documents. Thanks to this technology, you or your team can design almost any document discussed in *Successful Writing at Work*. In efforts similar to the collaborative writing process discussed in Chapter 3, people in business frequently use the flexibility in automation systems to collaborate on document design.

Three Basic Tools

The three categories of automation tools available for document design include

1. **Computer hardware.** Critical hardware components include the central processing unit (CPU) or microprocessor, the monitor, and the printer. The CPU houses the "brains" of the computer, while the monitor and the printer help you to visualize what is inside the CPU. To design a professional-looking document, you need hardware that consists of the following basic features and components:

- Pentium III 450 MHz–550 MHz or Celeron 333 MHz–466 MHz CPU
- 64–128 MB RAM
- 4.3–13 GB hard drive
- 40X CD-ROM or 6X DVD-ROM disk drive
- 56K fax modem
- two open PCI slots
- floppy disk drive
- keyboard and mouse
- high-resolution monitor
- multimedia system (video, sound, and graphics cards)
- scanner with at least 600 dpi (dots per inch)

2. **Software.** Software tools are operating and program applications. The two primary operating systems are Mac OS and Windows, with Windows by far the more widely used of the two. The basic types of software include word processing, spreadsheet, database, graphics, and communications. Helpful software packages available for page designing include

- word processing programs such as Microsoft Word and Corel's WordPerfect
- desktop publishing programs such as QuarkXPress, Adobe PageMaker, and Microsoft Publisher
- graphics programs such as Adobe Photoshop, Macromedia Flash, and Microsoft PhotoDraw
- scanning software such as Caere OmniPage and Xerox Text Bridge

Word processing programs offer a variety of options that make document design fast and easy to develop and just as easy to change.

TECH NOTE

Desktop Publishing Programs

Word processing programs such as Microsoft Word and Corel WordPerfect have evolved into more and more powerful desktop publishing software programs. Files created in word processing, database, and spreadsheet programs can be imported into specialty desktop publishing programs such as Adobe PageMaker, Microsoft Publisher, and QuarkXPress, as can graphics created or edited in graphic programs such as Adobe Photoshop, Macromedia Flash, Corel DRAW, and Microsoft PhotoDraw.

3. **Printers and scanners.** High-resolution laser printers are graphic-capable, letter-quality, and user-friendly. These high-resolution printers offer quality text and graphic image printing in striking color in a relatively short time. (See Gordon Reynolds's memo on new color laser printers in Chapter 3.)

Once documents (text or graphic pictures) are placed in a scanner, the scanner makes a digital image, and the information is placed in a graphics file. Scanners are discussed in more detail in Chapter 12.

Desktop Publishing

Desktop publishing programs, sometimes referred to as **page layout software,** provide an inexpensive alternative to a professional print shop. Because desktop publishing software permits users to design page layout, include visuals, and produce high-quality final copies, you can professionally create printed documents right in your own home or office.

With desktop publishing you can

- delete, insert, and move entire blocks of text
- take advantage of numerous typefaces
- integrate various changes in typeface—such as bold, italics, and underlining
- vary type sizes
- justify margins
- change line spacing
- center words, titles, or lines of text
- break and number pages
- arrange text in multiple columns
- add headers and footers (printed words that appear at the top and bottom, respectively, of each page of text)
- blow up quotations (pull quotes)
- import graphics, such as drawings, photographs, and logos
- insert sidebars

Type

There are many different styles of type (see pp. 440–442). All computers come equipped with software that contains a large number of typefaces (anywhere from 100 to 1,000). For example, WordPerfect 2000 features more than 1,000 high-quality fonts. Different fonts are also available over the Internet at such sites as Java Boutique (*http://javaboutique.internet.com/appindbut.html*) and Graphic Software Engineering Tools, which offers a library of over 10,000 font styles (*http://www.imaginationengineering.com/html/body_utilities.html*).

Templates

Desktop publishing software is equipped with predesigned **templates.** Templates are patterns and predesigned text columns, like those shown in Figure 11.1, that offer numerous page layout formats for reports, newsletters, brochures, and other marketing and communications documents. A template for a report, for example, would contain all the headings and divisions you need. You can also create and save your own template for an original format you use frequently.

FIGURE 11.1   Examples of templates.

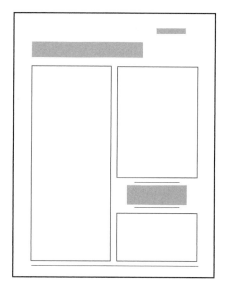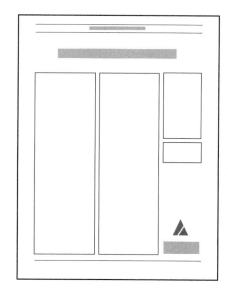

Graphics

A graphics program supplies shapes and lines that can be manipulated (skewed, enlarged) and offers options for sophisticated use of color and shading. With a drawing program you can create diagrams, charts, and illustrations that can be saved as electronic files and imported into word processing or desktop publishing documents.

You can move and place graphics anywhere in a document. Graphic design programs provide customized graphs, charts, tables, and expanded font (design) sizes and shapes.

Here are some types of graphics available to you.

1. Drawing tools. Desktop publishing programs contain tools that allow you to create a variety of shapes, rules, borders, and arrows. Having drawn a box, circle, triangle, or whatever, you can use other tools to fill in or alter the appearance of the shape or to add words to it; then you can rearrange all the elements into a graphic that communicates quickly and effectively.

2. Icons. Icons are symbols or visual representations of concepts or actions. The skull and crossbones on a container of poison is an icon that warns of danger. Many highway signs are icons that tell us quickly what to expect ahead: an S-curve, merging traffic, a railroad crossing. *Graphic icons* are simply pictures that communicate directly. No matter what language we speak—and even if we cannot read—icons tell us at a glance which restroom to use or how to fasten the seat belt in an airplane. (See the discussion of icons for non-native speakers of English in Terri Ruckel's long report in Chapter 16.) A nation's flag is an icon, and so are many religious symbols and most company logos.

Computer software often relies on icons to help us perform common actions without having to remember keyboard commands. Arrows in the scroll bars move us easily around a window; a file folder helps us group related documents; and a trash can holds files to be deleted later. Icons in the menu bar make it easy to print a file, open an address book, search for specific text, cut copy, or dial the phone. Examples of icons are shown below:

3. Clip art. Clip art is a library of simple drawings, often classified by themes, that can be imported (copied) from floppy disk, CD, or the Internet to your document. Some clip art software packages offer as many as 500,000 images, arranged into such diverse categories as animals, holidays, famous people, food, and various technologies. Clip art is widely used to make business documents attractive and appealing. If the graphic is symbolic or represents something unique about the business, it can also be the basis for an icon or a company logo.

4. Stock photos/stock art. Assembled photos and art on CD or the Internet can be imported, sometimes with a permissions fee, sometimes free with the purchase of the CD.

The ABC's of Print Document Design

The basic features of printed document design are

- page layout
- typography, or type design
- graphics

Each page of your document should integrate those three elements. The proper arrangement and balance of type, white space, and graphics involve the same level of preparation that you would spend on your research, drafting, revising, and editing. You need to create a document that cooperates with—not detracts from—your message. Just as you research your information, you have to research and experiment in order to adopt the most effective design for your document.

Page Layout

Each of your pages needs to coordinate space and text pleasingly. Too much or too little of one or the other can jeopardize the reader's acceptance of your message. To make sure you design an effective and attractive page layout, pay attention to the following elements.

1. White space. The proper combination of white space and text is essential to maintain your reader's interest and investment in what you have to say. White space refers to the open areas on the page—areas free of text and visuals. Readers are initially drawn to text on a page because of the pleasant and professional use of white space. White space can entice, comfort, and appeal to the reader's "psychology of space" by

- attracting the reader's attention
- assuring the reader that information is presented logically
- announcing that information is easy to follow
- assisting the reader to organize information visually
- allowing the reader to forecast and highlight important information

Compare Figures 11.2 and 11.3 again. Which document was designed by someone who understands the importance of white space?

2. Margins. Use wide margins, usually 1 to 1½ inches, to "frame" your document with white space surrounding text and visuals. Most documents easily accommodate equal margins on all four sides, a technique that creates balance and prevents the document from looking cluttered or overcrowded. If your document requires binding, you may have to leave a wider left margin (2 inches).

3. Line length. Most readers find a text line of 10 to 14 words, or 50 to 70 characters (depending on the type size you choose), comfortable and enjoyable reading. Line length, or "line measuring," depends, of course, on font type and size, number of columns, width of margins, and space between words. Never exceed your margin settings. In the example below, note how the extra-long lines unsettle your reading and tax your eye movement; they signal rough going.

In order to succeed in the world of business, workers must learn to brush up on their networking skills. The network process has many benefits that you need to be aware of. These benefits range from finding a better job to accomplishing your job more easily and efficiently. Through networking you are able to expand the number of contacts who can help you. Networking means sharing news and opportunities. The Internet is the key to successful networking.

Conversely, do not print a document with too short or extremely uneven lines.

In order to succeed in the world of
business, workers must learn
to brush up on their networking skills. The
network process has many
benefits you need to be
aware of.

Readers will suspect your ideas are incomplete, superficial, or even simpleminded.

FIGURE 11.2   A poorly designed document.

The results for the recent cholesterol screening at our company's Health Fair were distributed to each employee last week. Many employees wanted to know more information about cholesterol in general, the different types of cholesterol, what the results mean, and the foods that are high or low in cholesterol.

We hope the information provided below will help employees better answer their questions concerning cholesterol and our cholesterol screening program.

High cholesterol, along with high blood pressure and obesity, is one of the primary risk factors that may contribute to the development of coronary heart disease and may eventually lead to a heart attack or stroke. Cholesterol is a fatty, sticky substance found in the bloodstream. Excessive amounts of the bad type of cholesterol can deposit on the walls of the heart arteries. This deposit is called plaque and over a long period of time plaque can narrow or even block the blood flow through the arteries.

Total cholesterol is divided into three parts—LDL (low-density lipoprotein), or bad cholesterol; HDL (high-density lipoprotein), or good cholesterol; and VLDL (very low-density lipoprotein), a much smaller component of cholesterol you don't have to worry about. Bad (LDL) cholesterol forms on the walls of your arteries and can cause a lot of damage. Good cholesterol, on the other hand, functions like a sponge, mopping up cholesterol and carrying it out of the bloodstream.

You should have received three cholesterol numbers. One is for your HDL, or good cholesterol, and the other is for your LDL, or bad cholesterol, reading. These two numbers are added to give you the third, or composite, level of your total cholesterol. You are doing fine.

As you can see, a total cholesterol reading of 200 or below is considered safe. Continue what you have been doing. If your reading falls in the moderate risk range of 200–239, you need to modify your diet, get more exercise, and have your cholesterol checked again in six months. If your reading is above 240, see your doctor. You may need to take cholesterol-lowering medication, if your doctor prescribes it. Reducing your total cholesterol by even as little as 25% can decrease your risk of a heart attack by 50%.

The Surgeon General recommends that your LDL, or bad, cholesterol should be below 130. And your HDL, or good, cholesterol needs to be at least above 36. Ideally, the ratio between the two numbers should not be greater than 5 to 1. That is, your HDL should be at least 20% of your LDL. The higher your HDL is, the better, of course. So even if you have a high LDL reading, if your HDL is correspondingly high you will be at less risk.

One of the easiest ways to decrease your cholesterol is to modify your diet. Cholesterol is found in foods that are high in saturated fat. Saturated fat comes from animal sources and also from certain vegetable sources. Foods high in bad cholesterol that you should restrict, or avoid, include whole milk, red meat, eggs, cheese, butter, shrimp, oils such as palm and coconut, and avocados. Generally, food groups low in cholesterol include fruits, vegetables, and whole grains (wheat breads, oatmeal, and certain cereals), lean meats (fish, chicken), and beans.

The goal of our cholesterol screening is to help each employee lower his or her cholesterol level and eventually reduce the risk of heart disease. Besides the advice given above, you can do the following: get regular aerobic exercise—bicycling, brisk walking, swimming, rowing—for at least 30 minutes 3–4 times a week. But get your doctor's approval first. Eat foods low in cholesterol but high in dietary fiber (beans, oatmeal, brown rice). Maintain a healthy weight for your frame to lower your body fat. Minimize stress, which can increase cholesterol. Learn relaxation techniques.

FIGURE 11.3   An effectively designed document with the same text as Figure 11.2.

Cholesterol Screening

The results for the recent cholesterol screening at our company's Health Fair were distributed to each employee last week. Many employees wanted to know more information about cholesterol in general, the different types of cholesterol, what the results mean, and the foods that are high or low in cholesterol. We hope the information provided below will help employees better answer their questions concerning cholesterol and our cholesterol screening program.

Determining Risk Factors

High cholesterol, along with high blood pressure and obesity, is one of the primary risk factors that may contribute to the development of coronary heart disease and may eventually lead to a heart attack or stroke. Cholesterol is a fatty, sticky substance found in the bloodstream. Excessive amounts of the bad type of cholesterol can deposit on the walls of the heart arteries. This deposit is called **plaque** and over a long period of time plaque can narrow or even block the blood flow through the arteries.

Separating Types of Cholesterol

Total cholesterol is divided into three parts: (1) **LDL** (low-density lipoprotein), or bad cholesterol; (2) **HDL** (high-density lipoprotein), or good cholesterol; and (3) **VLDL** (very low-density lipoprotein), a much smaller component of cholesterol you don't have to worry about. Bad (LDL) cholesterol forms on the walls of your arteries and can cause a lot of damage. Good cholesterol, on the other hand, functions like a sponge, mopping up cholesterol and carrying it out of the bloodstream.

Continued

FIGURE 11.3   (Continued)

Understanding Your Cholesterol Results

You should have received three cholesterol numbers. One is for your **HDL** (or good cholesterol) and the other is for your **LDL** (or bad cholesterol) reading. These two numbers are added to give you the third, or composite, level of your total cholesterol.

Cholesterol levels can be classified as follows:

Minimal Risk	Moderate Risk	High Risk
below 200	200–239	above 240

As you can see, a total cholesterol reading of 200 or below is considered safe. You are doing fine. Continue what you have been doing. If your reading falls in the moderate risk range of 200–239, you need to modify your diet, get more exercise, and have your cholesterol checked again in six months. If your reading is above 240, see your doctor. You may need to take cholesterol-lowering medication, if your doctor prescribes it. Reducing your total cholesterol by even as little as 25% can decrease your risk of a heart attack by 50%.

Relationship Between Bad and Good Cholesterol

The Surgeon General recommends that your **LDL**, or bad, cholesterol should be below 130. And your **HDL**, or good, cholesterol needs to be at least above 36. Ideally, the ratio between the two numbers should not be greater than 5 to 1. That is, your **HDL** should be at least 20% of your **LDL**. The higher your **HDL** is, the better, of course. So even if you have a high **LDL** reading, if your **HDL** is correspondingly high you will be at less risk.

Recognizing Food Sources of Cholesterol

One of the easiest ways to decrease your cholesterol is to modify your diet. Cholesterol is found in foods that are high in saturated fat. Saturated fat comes

Continued

FIGURE 11.3   (Continued)

from animal sources and also from certain vegetable sources. Foods high in bad
cholesterol that you should restrict include:

1. whole milk
2. red meat
3. eggs
4. cheese
5. butter
6. shrimp
7. oils such as palm and coconut
8. avocados

Generally, food groups low in cholesterol include fruits, vegetables, and whole
grains (wheat breads, oatmeal, and certain cereals), lean meats (fish, chicken),
and beans.

Realizing It Is Up to You

The goals of our cholesterol screening program are to help each employee
lower his or her cholesterol level and eventually reduce the risk of heart disease.
Besides the advice given above, you can do the following:

- Get regular aerobic exercise—bicycling, brisk walking, swimming,
  rowing—for at least 30 minutes 3–4 times a week. But get your
  doctor's approval first.
- Eat foods low in cholesterol but high in dietary fiber (beans, oatmeal,
  and brown rice).
- Maintain a healthy weight for your frame to lower your body fat.
- Minimize stress, which can increase cholesterol. Learn relaxation
  techniques.

The author is indebted to Sgt. Mannie E. Hall of the U.S. Army for creating this document.

4. Columns. Document text usually is organized in either single-column or multi-column formats. Memos, letters, and reports are usually formatted without columns, whereas documents that intersperse text and visuals (such as newsletters and magazines) work better in multicolumn formats.

Typography

Typeface

Readability of your text is crucial. Select a typeface, therefore, that ensures your text is

- legible
- attractive
- functional
- appropriate for your message
- complementary with accompanying graphics

The most familiar typefaces are Times Roman, Arial, and Helvetica, although other very useful typeface styles are available with WordPerfect, MS Word, and other software packages. Other typefaces include Script, Modern, Old Style, Decorative, and Traditional. Below are some examples.

Times Roman	Frutiger
Helvetica	Palatino
Alexa	**STENCIL**

Type is also classified as having serif or sans serif fonts. **Serif fonts** appear to be the most readable in a body of the text. Serif fonts are distinguished by tail features or crossbars at the ends of the letters. Serifs add flair, arouse the reader's interest, and increase readability. Letter strokes are of varying widths and sometimes tapered.

Stone Serif	Sabon Roman
Courier	Janson Text
Times	Palatino

Sans serif fonts are recommended for headings and subheadings. Having no tails or crossbars, sans serif fonts provide a clear, crisp, legible image ideal for short messages. Avoid sans serif fonts for text copy because they make it harder for readers to process information.

Futura	Stone Sans
Univers Oblique	Geneva
Gill Sans Extra Bold	TradeGothic

Type Size

Type size options are almost unlimited, depending again on your software package and printer capabilities. Type size is measured in units called **points,** 72 points to the inch. The bigger the point size, the larger the type. Most business and educational documents use from 10-point to 12-point type, although the range today varies from 6 to 72 points (and beyond). Newspaper classified ads are in small 6-point to 8-point type, while headlines are set in much larger, 30-point to 36-point type. The text in this book is set in 10-point type.

Times 7 point

Univers 10 point

Palatino 14 point

Frutiger 22 point

Stone Serif 36 point

TECH NOTE

Typeface and Type Style
Be consistent in differentiating between **typeface** and **type style.**

A **typeface** is a specific family of type, such as Times Roman or Helvetica. The word *typeface* is sometimes used synonymously with *font*, a slightly more specific term that refers to the family as well as the size of the type.

Type style, especially as used by software manufacturers, refers to attributes such as boldface, italics, shadowing, and other variations.

Type Styles
Also known as **attributes,** these include boldface, italics, underlining, outline, shadow, small caps, and shading.

Boldface
Italics
Outline
Shadow
Underlining
Small Caps
Shading

Line Spacing
The amount of white space between lines of your text also affects how your document will be perceived. Most word-processing programs refer to line spacing as **leading.** Leading is also measured in points, the same as type size. Standard line spacing should be 2 points more than type size, so 10-point type would use 12-point leading, 12-point type would use 14-point leading, and so on.

Justification
Sometimes referred to as alignment, justification consists of left, right, full, and center options. Left-justified (also called **unjustified** or **ragged right**) is the preferred method because it allows space between words in lines of text to remain constant. In fully justified alignment (both left *and* right) the word spacing varies from line to line. Left justification gives a document a less formal look than full justification.

Narrow columns of text should be set left-justified to avoid awkward gaps between words and excessive hyphenation.

Our new Web site offers consumers a mall on the Internet. It gives shop-pers access to our products and services and makes buying easy and fun. Our new Web site offers con-sumers a mall on the Internet. It gives shoppers access to our

Left-justified text

Our new Web site offers consumers a mall on the Internet. It gives shoppers access to our products and services and makes buying easy and fun. Our new Web site offers consumers a mall on the Internet. It gives shoppers access to our

Right -justified text

Our new Web site offers consumers a mall on the Internet. It gives shoppers access to our products and services and makes buying easy and fun. Our new Web site offers con-sumers a mall on the Internet. It gives shoppers access to our products and

Full-justified text

Our new Web site offers consumers a mall on the Internet. It gives shoppers access to our products and services and makes buying easy and fun. Our new Web site offers con-sumers a mall on the Internet. It gives shoppers access to our

Centered text

Heads and Subheads

Use brief descriptive words or phrases to introduce or summarize a document or a section or subsection within a document. Your headings, called **heads** and **sub-heads,** should be grammatically parallel and not wordy. Note how the headings from a poorly organized proposal from the Acme Company are nonparallel.

- What Is the Problem?
- Describing What Acme Can Do to Solve the Problem
- It's a Matter of Time . . .
- Fees Acme Will Charge
- When You Need to Pay
- Finding Out Who's Who

Revised, the heads are parallel and easier for a reader to understand and follow.

- A Brief History of the Problem
- A Description of What Acme Can Do to Solve the Problem
- A Timetable Acme Will Follow
- A Breakdown of Acme's Fees

- A Payment Plan
- A Listing of Acme's Staff

Heads and subheads immediately attract attention and quickly inform readers about the function, scope, purpose, or contents of the document or section. They help readers prioritize information, too, by emphasizing the main points they need to look for and remember. Additionally, heads and subheads introduce helpful white space to separate text and organize your document. The space around a heading is like an oasis for the reader, signaling both a rest and a new beginning.

Subheads allow the reader to skim or review a document and its content in an outline type of format. Headings and subheadings follow an established order or hierarchy.

In designing a document with heads and subheads, follow these guidelines.

- Use larger type size for heads than for text; major heads should be larger than subheads. If your text is in 10-point type, your heads may be in 16-point type and your subheads in 12- or 14-point type.

Sixteen-Point Head
Subhead in 12 Point
Use larger type for heads than you do for text;
major headings should be larger than subheads.
If your text is in 10-point type, your heads may
be in 16-point type and your subheads in 12 or 14.

- Modify type to differentiate sections. For example, for heads and subheads use uppercase, bold type, underlining, and changes in font style or type.
- Establish a horizontal position for a head, such as centered or aligned left, and keep it consistent throughout the document
- Allow additional space, or leading, above a head to set it off from the preceding section. You may also want to allow additional space below a head.
- If you are using a color printer, consider using a second color for major headings.

Lists
Placing items in a list helps readers by dividing, organizing, and ranking information. Lists emphasize important points and contribute to an easy-to-read page design. Lists can be (a) numbered, (b) lettered, or (c) bulleted. Take a look at the reports, proposals, and memos in other chapters that effectively use lists.

Captions
Used to accompany, explain, highlight, or reference pictures or other graphics (like charts and graphs), captions are titles that help a reader identify a visual and quickly

explain the nature of the picture or other graphic. (Chapter 12 discusses using captions with visuals in a document.)

Graphics

Like other visuals, graphics work in conjunction with your words. A document without visuals or graphics may look boring, confusing, or unattractive. You will have to judge how and when a graphic can improve your message and convince your reader. The list below identifies some common graphics included in DTP software packages.

1. **Clip art.** See page 434 and also Chapter 12.
2. **Boxes.** These lines isolate or highlight text or visuals. Tables 12.1, 12.2, and 12.3 in the next chapter use boxes.
3. **Rules.** These lines are classified as either vertical or horizontal. Vertical rules are used to separate columns of text, while horizontal rules separate sections introduced by subheads.
4. **Letterheads and logos.** A company's corporate image is represented and symbolized by its letterhead, usually consisting of a graphic, or icon, integrated with the company name. Often the company's address, e-mail address, and Web site are included in the letterhead. Company letterhead conveys the firm's message and expresses its character. Typically, logos and sometimes the entire letterhead are imported as graphic files. A letterhead/logo should creatively set one company apart from others.

Poor Document Design: What *Not* to Do

Up to this point we have introduced the various elements of effective document design. Now, in contrast, we'll look at what you need to avoid. By knowing what looks bad from a reader's point of view, you will be much better able to design a document that works well visually for your reader.

Figure 11.2, a poorly designed document, illustrates many of the following common mistakes in document design. But note how Figure 11.3, which contains the same information as Figure 11.2, incorporates many of the effective techniques just described. Avoid the following errors when you design your document.

1. **Insufficient white space.** Narrow margins and limited space between headings and text are classic mistakes. Skimping on white space can frustrate your reader, who is eager to locate key parts of a document to identify and process them easily. A lack of white space between paragraphs or heads or around the borders of a document sends a negative message to your audience. Your work tells a reader, "Roll up your sleeves: this will be tough, unenjoyable reading."

2. **Inappropriate line length.** Excessively long lines are hard to read and signal to your audience that your work is highly complex and unrewarding.

3. **Overuse of visuals.** Too many visuals (boxes, rules, and clip art images) can create barriers and confusion and will crowd your pages. Establish a balance between

TECH NOTE

Using Colors

Color is important in writing for the world of work. Nothing attracts attention and communicates more quickly and more powerfully than color. Color can set moods and create impressions. It may be one of the most important tools to increase sales, gain faster project approval, or provide a major advantage over competitors. Colors help to sell ideas 85 percent more effectively than black-and-white communications.

Color can be used in many ways to organize written information and therefore enhance readability. Color visually breaks up long segments of text and can tie important ideas together. For example, using colored boxes to identify special notes in the text helps readers locate important information quickly. Use colors for borders and graphic accents, headings, titles, keywords, Internet addresses, sidebars, rules, and boxes that link related facts, figures, or information. You can communicate your message far more effectively by using colorful charts and graphs.

Some Guidelines

- Match the most appropriate color with the object you want to display. Keep in mind that an object's perceived size is affected by color. Light colors make objects look larger; dark colors make objects appear smaller.
- Estimate how the color will look on the page—colors look different on the screen than they do on a sheet of paper. Print a sample page.
- Make sure text colors contrast sharply with background colors.
- Use no more than two or three colors on a page unless there are photographs, illustrations, or graphics.
- For graphs and charts, place similar colors close to one another to maximize differences.
- Too many bright colors overwhelm the eye, so use them sparingly to call attention to important elements.
- Select "cool" colors, such as blue, turquoise, purple, and magenta, for backgrounds. However, avoid light blue text, which is hard to read against a dark background.

text and visuals. Also, use visuals for a specific purpose, not just for decorations or to fill space. (For additional discussion of the use of visuals, see Chapter 12.)

4. Mixing typefaces. Select one typeface, usually serif, for text body throughout the document and stick with it. You can then choose a contrasting typeface— say, a sans serif one—for heads. But try not to mix different serif typefaces or different sans serif faces. It's tricky to make them work together, and the result often looks like a printing mistake.

5. Too few or no heads and subheads. Without headings as useful guideposts your document will seem unorganized and illogical. As we saw in Figure 11.3, heads and subheads are typographical markers that signal starting points and major divisions; they thus provide helpful landmarks for readers charting their course through your document.

6. Excessive spacing. Too much space distorts the document and its message. Leaving three or four spaces between consecutive lines of a text signals to readers that your ideas may be lightweight and not very significant. Also, including too much space around a visual or around the borders of your text can call into question the overall professional status of your work.

To avoid such errors, follow these tips:

- Use only one space after a period, not the traditional two spaces.
- Don't indent the first line of text after a head or subhead.
- Avoid full justification on narrow columns.
- Eliminate excessive spacing in lists between the bullets, numbers, or symbols and the actual text entries.

7. Misusing capitals, boldface, or italics. Printing an entire document with capitals (large or small) will make a document hard to read. (But printing heads or subheads in capitals will differentiate them from your text.) Similarly, avoid overusing boldface or italics. Not only will too many special effects make your work harder to read, but you will lose the dramatic impact those attributes have to distinguish and emphasize key points that *do* deserve boldface or italic type.

Designing Web Sites*

The Internet may be the most productive marketing tool ever invented, allowing an individual, a company, or an organization to gain access to a worldwide audience through a Web site. The Net provides a crucial medium from which to present your product or service in words and through graphics, sound, animation, video, and three-dimensional, interactive, immersive virtual-reality applications.

In Chapter 8 we explored the Internet as a research tool, and in Chapter 12 we will examine visuals taken from the Internet. Here we will look at designing and writing a Web site. While there is a great deal of variation and idiosyncrasy in Web designs, principles of good practice still apply. Your Web site should communicate a personality as well as be usable. Its personality should target a range of users and be appropriate for the product or service you want to sell to the user group.

The Web connects sets of information—called pages—at millions of sites around the world. Some pages are quite long, while others take up just one computer screen. Any individual or company can place pages on the Web. The first page

---

*Much of the material in this section comes from Michael Tracey, of Hattiesburg, Mississippi, who designs Web sites and builds and upgrades computer hardware.

TECH NOTE

The Internet: A Growth Opportunity

The convenience the Internet offers consumers and businesses, as well as the potential opportunities for investors, is reflected in its rapid rise. Research compiled by Goldman Sachs from various sources came up with the following information.

- The percentage of U.S. households on-line is expected to grow to 64% by 2002 from over 30% today—a projected growth of nine million households per year.
- On-line advertising surpassed outdoor (billboard) advertising in 1999 for the first time. On-line revenues are projected to rise from $2 billion in 1999 to more than $9 billion in 2002.
- E-commerce is growing rapidly. Forrester Research projects the number of U.S. on-line shoppers will grow to more than 40 million by 2001 from 15 million in 1999, with spending rising from $2.4 billion to $17 billion. Business-to-business commerce is also experiencing strong growth as an increasing variety of companies realize the Internet is integral to competing effectively.
- Internet usage for financial services is also gaining acceptance, especially for on-line brokerage. Goldman projects more than $1.5 trillion in assets will be managed on-line by 2002.
- A recent Cisco Systems/University of Texas study estimates that the entire Internet economy generated $301 billion in revenue and 1.2 million jobs in 1999.

Source: T. Rowe Price's Report Newsletter, Issue 64. Copyright © 1999 by T. Rowe Price Associates, Inc. Used by permission.

of a Web site—the **home page**—is the thread that connects subsequent pages into a seamless presentation. Various programs are available to create a Web site, including Microsoft's FrontPage 2000, Macromedia's Dreamweaver 2, Adobe's Go Live, HomeSite, Trellix, and several shareware programs. The home page is where visitors to a Web site will go first; if it catches their attention, they are likely to click onto your other pages. As you read the rest of this section, look at the sample home pages in Figures 11.4 and 11.5.

Benefits of a Web Site

Web sites can be personal, corporate, informational, or issue oriented. Regardless, a Web site has to arouse reader's interest; show the appeal of a product, service, or topic; demonstrate the application of the product, service, or topic; and include a call to action. For example, thanks to Web-based technologies, a company can

- attract new customers and satisfy repeat customers the world over, because the site is public, international, and available at all times

FIGURE 11.4   Sample home page from FinAid.

- keep track of the number of customers who visit a particular page
- provide additional pages of in-depth technical information (education, troubleshooting) about a product or service
- answer FAQs (frequently asked questions)
- supply sound and graphic support
- accommodate individual customers by tracking purchases (such as size, color, and style of clothing) and orders (shipping status)
- improve research by keeping track of what the competition is doing at their Web sites and exploring their products and services
- allow customers to pay on-line with credit card or e-cash

Planning a Web Site

There are several things you can do to plan a successful Web site.

1. Look at good sites already on the Web. Use your Web browser's links to "Cool Sites" or "Top 100 Sites" to see what works. Pay attention to the various ways a

FIGURE 11.5   A home page from National Maritime Museum.

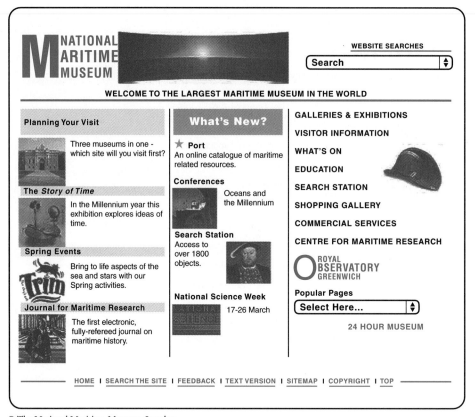

© The National Maritime Museum, London.

Web site can be designed and organized. You will see a lot of variety in the top sites but notice what they have in common and how their information content is organized and presented.

2. Know your competition—print copies of the Web sites of organizations similar to yours.

3. Read magazines dedicated to the Web for in-depth analyses of page designs. For example, check out *Internet World* (*http://www.iw.com*) and *IEEE Internet Computing* (*http://computer.org/internet/*).

4. Study one of the programs mentioned on page 448. Many come with various Web page templates and style sheets to help you develop a site.

5. Join a newsgroup on Web site design. Participants share insights and ideas, offer suggestions, and answer questions. When you purchase a Web design program, such as Microsoft's FrontPage 2000, you will find the names and addresses of several helpful newsgroups and sites.

6. Don't be afraid to ask friends and colleagues who have designed Web pages for advice and input. They can provide practical suggestions and insights from their own experience.

Guidelines on Designing a Web Site

The home page of your Web site has several functions. Its major task is to catch visitors' attention. If it fails to do that, everything else is a waste of time; your visitors will click their mouse and be gone. The next goal is to sell your company's product or service or introduce your organization. That may seem backward, but unless you attract readers to your Web site you cannot promote your product or service. The home pages in Figures 11.4 and 11.5 accomplish both those objectives.

Designing a Web site requires you to follow many of the rules you read about earlier in this chapter for printed pages (see pp. 435–440). In addition, you need to adhere to the following seven guidelines to create an effectively designed and written Web site that will capture and keep a reader's attention.

1. **Make your Web site informative.**

   - Provide all essential information—your company's name, address, e-mail— for readers.
   - Tell a visitor at once what products or services you offer.
   - Indicate the type of information available at your Web site.
   - Constantly update the Web site to keep clients coming back to view new products and services or to find more information.

2. **Make your site easy to find.**

   - Obtain a registered domain name for your site, which may require an initial fee and then a yearly charge. One major benefit of having a registered domain name is that it will remain consistent throughout the life of your site because your company or organization owns it. If your server goes out of business, you can easily transfer your Web site to another server without changing the name and, in the process, losing customers.
   - Submit your Web site to the various search engines, most notably the major ones like Yahoo!, AltaVista, and Lycos to make sure a wide audience knows about your site.
   - If your Web address is long and difficult to remember, take advantage of the free services offered by Goto.Com (*http://www.goto.com*). This company provides an imitation domain name of your choosing that replaces the difficult Web address. For example,

     http://www.lazersites.com/dsi/pc100/personal/Weemco/index.htm

     could become

     Weemco.com.

     The site is fully registered and cannot be used by anyone else.

   - Open your site with keywords that search engines will easily find and list.

3. **Use an inviting layout.**

   - Strike a balance between text and graphics. A Web site with dense text is neither inviting nor eye catching. Similarly, a page with nothing but clever clip art or designs does not provide necessary information.
   - Avoid long pages that ramble and require visitors to keep scrolling. Your audience will give up.
   - Choose text fonts that are easy to read. Helvetica is not as inviting as Courier or Times New Roman. Use one design consistently throughout your site.
   - Make your message look clear; anything hard to distinguish is easy to ignore. Fancy designs may look good on paper, but they don't always enhance the readability of your site.
   - Do not overload your visitors with information; supply enough white space to give readers breathing room.
   - Do not squeeze all the features of your product or organization onto your home page. Leave plenty of unused space—it is easier on the eyes and welcomes the visitor with an unhurried, more relaxed feeling, such as the home page designs in Figures 11.4 and 11.5.

4. **Make your site browser friendly.**

   - Help visitors navigate easily through your site. Lay out a logical and effective method of navigation so all your pages are linked and make sure all links work. See how, in Figure 11.6, the EPA provides such navigational links in its Web site on global warming by using keywords, sidebars, and visuals to aid the user.
   - Link your home page to your other pages by using **hypertext** (highlighted words), **icons** (small stylized images), **thumbnail images** (shrunken versions of larger pictures), full-size images, or a combination of those. The links in Figures 11.4 and 11.5 use a variety of those devices, all with clear descriptors.
   - Choose link indicators that succintly inform visitors about what they will see. Present a list of the options available. A retailer of kitchen appliances, for example, might show a set of pictures that represents various appliance groups; clicking on the picture of a refrigerator moves the visitor directly to the page that provides details about all the refrigerators available.
   - Provide keywords across the bottom or on the side of your home page to let visitors move quickly to the page that interests them, as in Figure 11.6.

5. **Make your site visually attractive.**

   - Choose appropriate icons or pictures for hyperlinks, as in Figure 11.6.
   - Arrange photos so they do not interfere with text, as in Figure 11.5.
   - Be conservative in using animated graphics and anything that might be viewed as a gimmick. Don't let your site become a collection of clutter rather than an invitation to explore further.
   - Don't load your site with graphics that will take a long time to load—visitors may get impatient and click to another site. With Web graphics less can be more.

6. **Use color wisely.**

   - Don't overuse color in variety or extent. Multiple background colors will compete with your text.

FIGURE 11.6   Examples of navigational links.

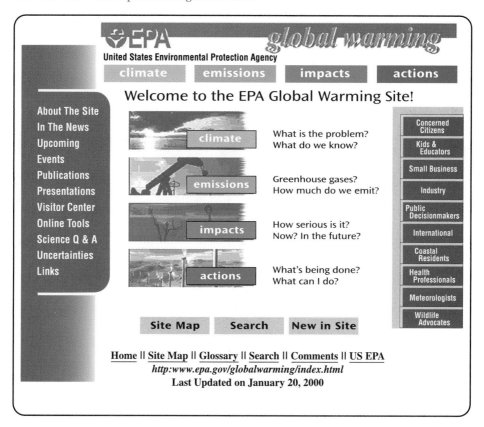

- Choose colors appropriate for your intended audience.
- Use a splash of bright color just to attract attention and only in a limited area of the page.
- Make sure there is a sharp contrast between textual characters and their background. Low contrast makes for poor readability.
- Carefully study the color palettes that come with browsers like Microsoft Internet Explorer and Netscape Navigator. Such palettes offer hundreds of color combinations, patterns, and shades to apply to your text and backgrounds.

7. **Solicit feedback to encourage visitors to return.**

- Always provide an e-mail address or some other way for visitors to provide feedback or to get more information or order your product or service. (Note the hyperlink *Feedback* at the bottom of Figure 11.5, for example.)
- Include a bulletin board where visitors can leave questions to be answered or browse through FAQs.
- Highlight extra enticements. Use sneak previews or other devices to draw visitors back to your site. Note how the Loft in Figure 6.11 invited customers to check its Web site for daily specials.

■ Feature insider news updates specific to your business area or preproduction information on items or services. Provide reviews of new articles, books, journals, or businesses in your area.

Following these guidelines you can create a highly effective Web site. Who knows? Yours may be selected as one of the top 100!

✓ Revision Checklist

Printed Documents

❏ Kept readers' busy schedules and reading time limits in mind when designing a document.
❏ Learned options of desktop publishing program.
❏ Arranged information in the most logical, easy-to-grasp order.
❏ Included only relevant visuals—clip art, icons, stock photos.
❏ Left adequate, eye-pleasing white space in text.
❏ Provided adequate margins to frame document.
❏ Justified margins, right, left, or center, depending on document and reader's needs.
❏ Maintained pleasing, easy-to-read line length.
❏ Kept line spacing consistent and easy on the readers' eyes.
❏ Chose appropriate typeface for message and document.
❏ Selected serif or sans serif font depending on message and readers' needs.
❏ Did not mix typefaces.
❏ Used effective type size, neither too small (under 10 point) nor too large (over 12 point), for body of text.
❏ Incorporated appropriate visual cues (attributes) for readers.
❏ Inserted heads and subheads to organize information for reader.
❏ Made all heads and subheads parallel and grammatically consistent.
❏ Supplied lists, bullets, numbers to divide information.

Web Sites

❏ Used plenty of white space so visitor is not overloaded with text.
❏ Chose colors carefully so pages are easy on the eyes and all text is legible.
❏ Gave essential information about product or service.
❏ Selected and designed appropriate hyperlinks.
❏ Made it easy for visitors to navigate and locate what they need quickly.
❏ Ensured that images and backgrounds would not slow visitor down.
❏ Opened with keywords for search engines to find.
❏ Used appropriate visuals that complement and did not compete with text for visitors' attention.
❏ Provided ways for readers to supply feedback.

Exercises

1. Find an example of an effectively designed document, according to the criteria discussed in this chapter. It could be a memo, a brochure, a newsletter, a report, a set of instructions, a section of a textbook, or a Web site. E-mail or write a short (one-page) memo to your instructor describing the document's design and explaining why it works. Attach a copy of the document or the Web site to your e-mail or memo.

2. Working with a team of three or four students, bring poorly designed documents to class. As a collaborative venture determine which of the documents the group submits is the hardest to follow, the most unappealing, and the least logically arranged. After selecting that document, collaboratively write a memo to your instructor on what is wrong with the design and what you would do to improve its appearance and organization.

3. Redesign (reformat; add headings, spacing, and visual clues; include clip art; and so on) the document your group selected for Exercise 2 and submit it to your instructor.

4. Find an ineffectively designed document—a form, a set of instructions, a brochure, a section of a manual, a story in a newsletter—and assume that you are a document design consultant. Write a sales letter to the company or agency that prepared and distributed the document, offering to redesign it and any other documents they have. Stress your qualifications and include a sample of your work. You will have to be convincing and diplomatic—precisely and professionally persuading your readers that they need your services to improve their corporate image, customer relations, and sales or services.

5. Redesign the document on page 456 to make it conform to the guidelines specified in this chapter.

6. Locate two or three effectively designed Web sites. Write a one-page memo to your instructor describing why you believe they are carefully designed.

7. Locate what you regard as a poorly designed and written Web site. Write a one-page assessment of the site to your instructor pointing out the site's weaknesses and how it could be improved. Attach a hard copy of the site to your assessment.

8. As a collaborative exercise with three other students construct a Web site for one of the following:
   a. a business or technical writing class you are taking this term
   b. a student group to which you belong
   c. a vacation area your group has visited
   d. a college or community association, club, or team

7

TTI's in the loop on effective detector placement

Ever sit in bumper-to-bumper traffic and wish they'd widen the roads so people could get through more quickly? Well, that costs a lot of money. Which is why transportation engineers who deal with traffic congestion and the problems it causes look for more cost-effective alternatives to get you where you're going—and faster.

TTI researchers recently completed a TxDOT/FHWA-sponsored study entitled *Effective Detector Placement for Computerized Traffic Management*. The research sought to expand and improve the use of inductance loop detectors (ILDs) to complement traffic signals, signal systems and other advanced traffic management systems. This is a cheaper congestion solution than building or widening a road.

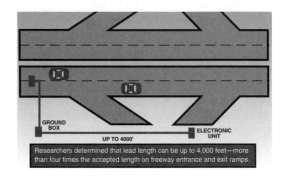

Researchers determined that lead length can be up to 4,000 feet—more than four times the accepted length on freeway entrance and exit ramps.

An ILD is an electrical circuit containing a loop of copper wire embedded in the pavement. As a vehicle passes over the wire loop, it takes energy from the loop. If that change is large enough, a detection is recorded. Thus, we are able to collect data on the movement or presence of vehicles on the roadway. Advanced traffic management systems operate best with accurate information on how many vehicles are present and how fast they are traveling.

The primary goal of the recent project was to use loop detectors as an integral part of the congestion-reduction system. Traditional problems with ILDs were addressed—like crosstalk, or interference between two adjacent loops—and innovative new applications for ILDs in advanced traffic systems—like detecting wrong-way HOV-lane movements.

Other applications include using ILDs to move traffic more

efficiently at diamond interchanges, at high-volume, high-speed approaches and on the freeway entrance ramps. The long-range contribution of the study is a set of guidelines for using ILDs in the situations listed above. As freeway management systems continue to evolve, the guidelines developed through the nine study reports will provide designers with practical information on the most effective placement of ILDs.

A major finding of the research deals with lead length, or the length of wire necessary to connect the loop to the detector electronic unit. The study showed that the loop can be placed more than 4,000 feet from the point of control—four times the currently accepted distance. This information will give traffic designers much more flexibility when integrating ILDs into their traffic system designs.

The researchers also made some important discoveries about using ILDs to measure speed. They found that the best speed trap is nine meters (two loops interconnected

with a timing device and spaced nine meters apart). They also determined that to get reasonably accurate and consistent speeds with an ILD, some things must be the same between a pair of loops: make, type or model of the detector units, sensitivity settings and loop configuration.

The findings from this research facilitate the use of loop detectors in managing traffic. And better management of driver frustration— just as important, even if less measurable than the congestion that causes it—is bound to follow.

Ultimately the three watchwords for this project were optimization, innovation, and implementation. Taking the tried-and-true and finding a better way to use it is, after all, the underlying building block for all engineering endeavors.

To order TTI Research Report 1392-9F, see the back page order form of this issue. For more information on loop detectors, contact Don Woods, 409/845-5792, FAX 409/845-6481 (E-mail: d-woods@tamu.edu).

Source: Texas Transportation Institute's *Researcher;* article author, Chris Pourteau. Reprinted with permission of the Texas Transportation Institute.

Designing Visuals

Experts estimate that as much as 80 percent of our learning comes through our sense of sight. The written word, of course, forms a large part of our visual information. In conjunction with words, though, **visuals** convey a large share of the facts we receive. Visuals are especially useful on the job because they help readers see what you are discussing.

Chapter 12 surveys the kinds of visuals you will encounter most frequently and shows you how to read, construct, and write about them. It also describes the types of visuals and visual configurations you can create and copy with graphics software packages. One software manufacturer advertises that users can select more than 5,000 different visual configurations and make numerous changes in them. The impact and importance of visuals in document design is nowhere better illustrated than on the Internet, a "virtual library" where every successful Web page exploits graphics to capture attention.

Graphic Arts Technology
Computer systems sold today arrive "bundled" with at least basic graphics software (such as Adobe Illustrator, Print Shop DeLux, Print Artist, Microsoft Office, and Arts and Letters) that lets you create simple pictures easily. You also can use graphics software to import clip art and other images from disks or the Internet. Laser printers produce remarkable results—in black and white or full color—easily and economically. Writers who want visual impact but can't afford the services of a designer, an artist, and a print shop are now limited only by their own imaginations and efforts.

Our discussion of visuals is not confined to just this chapter. They are important in preparing successful instructions, proposals, and written and oral reports and are covered in relevant chapters.

The Purpose of Visuals

How can visuals improve your work? Here are several reasons why you should use them. Each point is graphically reinforced in Figure 12.1.

1. *Visuals arouse readers' immediate interest.* Because many readers are visually oriented, visuals unlock doors of meaning. They catch the reader's eye quickly by setting important information apart and by giving relief from sentences and paragraphs. Visuals also help you maintain the reader's interest. Because of their size, shape, color, and arrangement, visuals are dramatic. Note the eye-catching quality of the visual in Figure 12.1.

2. *Visuals increase readers' understanding by simplifying concepts.* A visual *shows* ideas whereas a verbal description only *tells* about them in the abstract. Words without

FIGURE 12.1   A line-and-bar chart depicting the growth of e-commerce compared to traditional businesses.

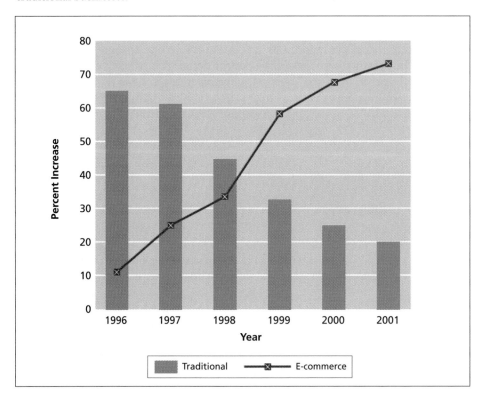

images may be less forceful or more complex. Visuals are especially important and helpful if you have to explain a technical process to a nonspecialist audience. Moreover, visuals can simplify densely packed statistical data, making a complex set of numbers easier to comprehend. Visuals help readers see percentages, trends, comparisons, and contrasts. Figure 12.1, for example, shows at a glance the growth of e-commerce.

3. *Visuals are especially important for non-native speakers of English and multicultural audiences.* Visuals speak a universal language and so can readily be understood by a global audience. Because visuals pose fewer problems in interpretation, they can help reduce ambiguities and misunderstanding. Given the international audience for many business documents, visuals will make your communication with them easier and clearer. See Terri Smith Ruckel's report in Figure 16.3.

4. *Visuals emphasize key relationships.* Through their arrangement and form, visuals quickly show contrasts, similarities, growth rates, and downward and upward movements, as well as fluctuations in time, money, and space. Pie and bar charts (discussed on pp. 473–477), for example, show relationships of parts to the whole; an organizational chart (p. 480) can graphically display the hierarchy and departments of a company or agency.

5. *Visuals condense and summarize a large quantity of information into a relatively small space.* Enormous amounts of statistical or financial data, over many weeks, months, and even years, can be incorporated concisely into one compact visual. A visual also allows you to streamline your message by saving words. It can record data in far less space than it would take to describe those facts in words alone. With a visual a reader can grasp the significance and the relationship of multiple items in a single glance. Note how in Figure 12.1 the growth rates of two different types of businesses are expressed and documented.

6. *Visuals are highly persuasive.* Visuals can convince readers to buy your product or service or to accept your point of view. A visual can graphically display, explain, and reinforce the benefits and opportunities of the plan you are advocating. A visual can also help you introduce a subject or assist you in developing a winning recommendation section of a report. Readers are far more likely to recall the visual than a verbal description or summary of it.

Choosing Effective Visuals

Select your visuals carefully. Special computer software programs allow you to select, create, and introduce visuals. The following suggestions will help you to choose effective visuals.

1. Use visuals only when they are relevant for your purpose and audience. A visual should contribute to your text—not be redundant. Do not use a visual if your text is absolutely clear, and never include a visual simply as a decoration. A short report on fire drills, for example, does not need a picture of a fire station; instructions on how to prepare a company report do not require a picture of an individual seated at a PC.

TECH NOTE

Computer-Made Visuals
The capabilities of a computer to make visuals are almost endless. All you have to do is put the raw numerical data into your computer's database program and then, with a few simple keyboard commands, select the most appropriate visual shape (bar or pie chart, pictogram, graph) to display the statistical data. Following your commands, the computer will analyze and plot the data you keyed in into a proportionately accurate chart or graph. The visual will appear on the screen, and you can then print a hard copy in black and white or in color.

---

2. Consider how a specific visual will help your readers. Ask yourself these questions before you include a visual.

- What do my readers need to know visually?
- What type of visual will best meet my readers' needs?
- How can I create the visual—scan it, import it, or make it myself?

Elaborate graphs and tables are unnecessarily complex for a community group interested only in a clear-cut representation of the rise in food prices over a three-month period. Include detailed, complex visuals only for technical readers. In general, though, keep your visuals simple and direct.

3. Use visuals in conjunction with—not as a substitute for—written work. Visuals do not always take the place of words. In fact, you may need to explain information contained in a visual. A set of illustrations or a group of tables alone may not satisfy readers looking for summaries, evaluations, or conclusions. Note how the visual in conjunction with the description of a magnetic resonance imager (MRI) in Figure 12.2 makes the procedure easier to understand than if the writer had used only words or only a visual. This visual and verbal description is appropriately included in a brochure teaching patients about MRI procedures.

4. Use a visual when it would be more difficult to rely on words alone. A verbal description is sometimes more difficult to follow than a visual presentation. In such cases, a visual gives readers significant information that the text could not easily convey. Use visuals when you have to describe a piece of equipment with many (or concealed) parts, to explain an involved concept, or to account for a process.

5. Experiment with several visuals. Evaluate a variety of options before you select a particular visual. For instance, a graphics software package such as Power-Point (see pp. 494–496) will allow you to represent statistical data in a number of ways. Preview a few different versions of a visual or even different types of visuals to determine which one would be best.

FIGURE 12.2   A visual used in conjunction with written work.

A PICTURE FROM THE INSIDE OUT
At the heart of the magnetic resonance imager is a large magnet that is big enough for you to lie inside. Look at the picture below. The **magnet** directs radio signals to surround sections of your body. When the signals pass through your body, they **resonate** (release a signal). Then your body's response is picked up by a receiver and sent to a computer. The computer analyzes the signal and converts it into a visual **image** of your tissues on a video screen.

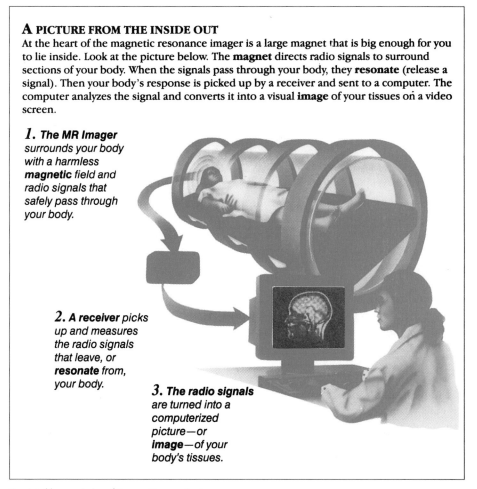

1. **The MR Imager** surrounds your body with a harmless **magnetic** field and radio signals that safely pass through your body.

2. **A receiver** picks up and measures the radio signals that leave, or **resonate** from, your body.

3. **The radio signals** are turned into a computerized picture—or **image**—of your body's tissues.

Reprinted by permission of Krames Communications.

6. Be prepared to revise and edit your visuals. Just as you draft, revise, and edit your written work to meet your audience's needs, create several versions of your visual to get it right. Expect to change shapes or proportions; experiment with different colors, shadings, and labels; and try various sizes before you select the most appropriate visual. Also check each visual against the data you want it to display to make sure it is accurate and ethical, not unclear or distorted. (Review Chapter 1 on the ethics of using visuals.)

7. Always use high-quality visuals. Your visuals should be clear, easy to read, and relevant. If readers have trouble understanding its function and arrangement, your visual probably is not appropriate and you need to change or revise it. Do not assume that readers will have magnifying glasses on their desks or that they will tolerate a crowded drawing or fuzzy resolution. If you photocopy, download, or scan a visual, make sure the copy is clear and readable and does not cut off any part of the original.

8. Consider how your visuals will look on the page. Visuals should add to the overall appearance of your work, not detract from it. Don't cram visuals onto a page or allow them to spill over your text or margins. Many computer programs will let you move your visuals directly into your word processor document so you can insert them properly. See pages 435–440 on effective page layouts.

Writing About Visuals: Some Guidelines

Using a visual requires more of you as a writer than simply inserting it in your written work. You need to *use visuals in conjunction with what you write.* The following guidelines will help you to (1) identify, (2) insert, (3) introduce, and (4) interpret visuals for your readers. By observing these guidelines, you can use visuals more effectively and efficiently.

Reference Visuals
Always mention in the text of your paper or report that you are including a visual. If you don't alert readers to a specific visual, they may skip it or wonder why it is there.

Identify Visuals
Each visual should have a number and a caption (title) that indicates the subject or explains what the visual illustrates. An unidentified visual is meaningless. A caption helps your audience to interpret your visual—to see it with your purpose in mind. Inform your readers about what you want them to look for.

- Use a different typeface and size in your caption than what you use in the visual itself.
- Include key words about the function and the subject of your visual in a caption.
- Make sure any terms you cite in a caption are consistent with the units of measurement and the scope of your visual.

Tables and figures should be numbered separately throughout the text—Table 1 or Figure 3.5, for example. (In the latter case, Figure 3.5 is the fifth figure to appear in Chapter 3.)

- Table 2. Paul Jordan's Work Schedule, January 15–23
- Figure 4.6   The proper way to apply for a small business loan.
- Figure 12. Income Estimation Figures for North Point Technologies.

Cite the Source for Visuals
If you use a visual that is not your own work, give credit to your source (newspaper, magazine, textbook, company, federal agency, individual, or Web site). If your

paper or report is intended for publication, you must obtain permission to reproduce copyrighted visuals from the copyright holder.

Insert Visuals Appropriately

Here are some rules to keep in mind.

- Place visuals as close as possible to the first mention of them in text. By inserting an appropriate visual near the beginning of your discussion, you help readers understand the discussion better than if you placed the visual near the end.
- Never introduce a visual *before* a discussion of it; readers will wonder why it is there. Be sure to tell readers where the visual is found—"below," "on the following page," "to the right," "at the bottom of page 3."
- If the visual is small enough, insert it directly in the text rather than on a separate page. If your visual occupies an entire page, place that page containing your visual immediately after the page on which the first reference to it appears.
- Try not to put a visual more than one page after the discussion to which it pertains.
- Never collect all your visuals and put them in an appendix. Readers need to see them at those points in your discussion where they are most pertinent.

Introduce Your Visuals

Refer to each visual by its number and, if necessary, mention the title as well. In introducing the visual, though, do not just insert a reference to it, such as "See Figure 3.4" or "Look at Table 1." Help readers to understand the relationships in your visual. Here are two ways of writing a lead-in sentence for a visual.

> Poor: Our store saw a dramatic rise in the shipment of electric ranges over the five-year period as opposed to the less impressive increase in washing machines. (See Figure 3.)

This sentence does not tie the visual (Figure 3) into the sentence where it belongs. The visual just trails insignificantly behind.

> Better: As Figure 3 shows, our store saw a dramatic rise in the shipment of electric ranges over the five-year period as opposed to the less impressive increase in washing machines.

Mentioning the visual in Figure 3 alerts readers to its presence and function in your work and helps them to better understand it.

Interpret Your Visuals

Give readers help in understanding your visual and in knowing what to look for. Let them know what is most significant about the visual. In a study on the benefits of vanpooling, one writer supplied the following visual, a table:

**TABLE 1.   Travel Time (in minutes):
Automobile versus Vanpool**

Private Automobile	Vanpool
25	32.5
30	39.0
35	45.5
40	52.0
45	58.5
50	65.0
55	71.5
60	78.0

Source: U.S. Department of Transportation. *Increased Transportation Efficiency Through Ridesharing: The Brokerage Approach* (Washington, D.C., DOT-OS— 40096): 45.

Explaining the table, the writer called attention to it in the context of the report on transportation efficiency.

> Although, as Table 1 above suggests, the travel time in a vanpool may be as much as 30 percent longer than in a private automobile (to allow for pickups), the total trip time for the vanpool user can be about the same as with a private automobile because vanpools eliminate the need to search for parking spaces and to walk to the employment site entrance.[1]

What *Not* to Do with a Visual

- Avoid visuals that include more details than you discuss or than your audience needs.
- Never use a visual that presents information that contradicts your work.
- Never distort a visual for emphasis or decoration.
- Be careful that you don't omit anything when you reproduce an existing visual.
- Never use visuals that discriminate or stereotype (for example, avoid pictures of a work force that excludes female employees).
- Avoid visuals that would be misunderstood or regarded as offensive in another culture.
- Don't offend non-native speakers of English by using a culturally biased color (for example, reconsider using red for warning signals or danger; red in China signals happiness and good fortune and is used at weddings).

See how Figure 12.3 violates many of these rules. It divides the dollar bill into too many slices. Confronted with so many different wedges the reader would have

---

[1]James A. Devine, "Vanpooling: A New Economic Tool," *AIDC Journal* 15 (Oct. 1980): 13.

FIGURE 12.3   An ineffective visual: too much information is crowded into one graphic.

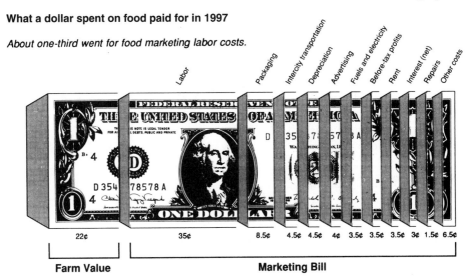

What a dollar spent on food paid for in 1997

About one-third went for food marketing labor costs.

trouble identifying, separating, comparing, and understanding the costs. It would be better to use a different visual to avoid so much clutter.

Two Categories of Visuals

Visuals can be divided into two categories—**tables** and **figures.** A table arranges information—numbers and/or words—in parallel columns or rows for easy comparison of data. Anything that is not a table is considered a figure. Figures include graphs, circle charts, bar charts, organizational charts, flow charts, pictograms, maps, photographs, and drawings.

TECH NOTE

Creating Tables

Most word processing programs include a function to help you create and position a table within your text. Using the "Table" command, specify the number of rows and columns the table will contain, and the word processing software will create an empty table for you to fill in with data or will convert your running text into a table. You can also edit such tables and insert or remove rows (horizontal lines of data) and columns (vertical lines of data), widen columns, and include various spreadsheet templates (such as schedules, investments, and profit margins).

Tables

Tables are parallel columns or rows of information organized and arranged into categories to show changes in time, distance, cost, employment, or some other distinguishable or quantifiable variable. Tables allow readers to compare a great deal of information in a compact space. Electronic spreadsheet programs heavily rely on tables to convey information, as in Table 12.1. Tables also summarize material for easy recall—causes of wars, provisions of a law, or differences among a common cold, flu, and pneumonia, as in Table 12.2. Observe how Table 12.3 easily condenses much information and arranges it in quickly identifiable categories.

Parts of a Table

To use a table properly, you need to know the parts that constitute it. Refer to Table 12.3 as you read the following:

- The main **column** is "Amount Needed to Satisfy Minimum Daily Requirement," and the **subcolumns** are the protein sources for which the table gives data.

TABLE 12.1   A Spreadsheet Table

	A	B	C	D		F	G	H
1	Acct#	Account Description	YTD	April		March	February	Janua
2								
3	**Employee Costs**							
4	110	Payroll	$171,465	$29,750		$28,547	$27,540	
5	120	IRS/FICA/Wk comp/State/SDI	$46,295	$8,032		$7,707	$7,435	
6	130	Commissions	$56,436	$9,520		$8,875	$9,825	
7	140	Retirement Plan	$20,575	$3,570		$3,425	$3,304	
8	150	Insurance	$9,000	$1,500		$1,500	$1,500	
9								
11	**Subcontractors & Services**							
12	201	Telecommunication Services	$2,616	$436		$436	$436	
13	202	Design Consultants	$875	$500		$375	$0	
14	203	Photo/Video Services	$535	$45		$325	$45	
15	250	Graphic Services	$2,957	$765		$95	$375	
16	251	Photo/Stats	$1,612	$568		$755	$0	
17	252	Typesetting	$1,453	$388		$325	$195	
18	253	Printing Services	$6,186	$951		$849	$325	
19	254	Legal & Accounting						
20								
21	**Supplies and Materials**							
22	301	Office Supplies	$875	$500		$732	$433	
23	302	Office Postage	$535	$45		$255	$325	
24	303	Office Equipment & Furniture	$2,957	$765		$78	$21	
25	304	Miscellaneous Supplies	$1,612	$568		$49	$36	
26								
27	**Facilities Overhead**							
28	405	Plant	$1,612	$568		$1,700	$1,700	

Sheet1 / Sheet2 / Sheet3 /

TABLE 12.2   Table Showing Differences Between a Common Cold, Influenza, and Pneumonia

Symptoms	Cold	Influenza	Pneumonia
Fever	Rare	Characteristic high (100.4—104°F) sudden onset, lasts 3 to 4 days	May or may not be high
Headache	Occasional	Prominent	Occasional
General aches and pains	Slight	Usual; often quite severe	Occasionally quite severe
Fatigue and weakness	Quite mild	Extreme; can last up to a month	May occur depending on type
Exhaustion	Never	May occur early and prominent	May occur depending on type
Runny, stuffy nose	Common	Sometimes	Not characteristic
Sneezing	Usual	Sometimes	Not characteristic
Sore throat	Common	Sometimes	Not characteristic
Chest discomfort, cough	Mild to moderate; hacking cough	Can become severe	Frequent and may be severe
Complications	Sinus and ear infections	Bronchitis, pneumonia; can be life-threatening	Widespread infections of other organs; can be life-threatening, especially in elderly and debilitated persons

Source: Jacquelyn G. Black, *Microbiology: Principles and Explorations.* Upper Saddle River, NJ: Prentice-Hall, 1996.

- The **stub** refers to the first vertical column on the left-hand side. The stub column heading is "Source." The stub lists the foods for which information is broken down in the subcolumns.
- A **rule** (or line) across the top of the table separates the headings from the body of the table.

Guidelines for Using Tables

When you include a table in your work, follow these guidelines.

- Number the tables according to the order in which they are discussed (Table 1, Table 2, Table 3).

TABLE 12.3   Parts of a Table

Table number

TABLE 1 Efficiency of Some Protein Sources in Meeting an Adult's Minimum Daily Requirements				
Source	*Percent of Protein*	*Percent of Amino Acids*	*Amount Needed to Satisfy Minimum Daily Requirement*	
			(grams)	*(ounces)*
Cheese[a]	27	70	227	7.2
Corn	10	50	860	30.0
Eggs	11	97	403	14.1
Fish[a]	22	80	244	8.5
Kidney beans	23	40	468	16.4
Meat[a]	25	68	253	8.8
Milk	4	82	1,311	45.9[b]
Soybeans	34	60	210	7.3

← *Title*

← *Column heading*

← *Subheading*

Stub

Source: Adapted from Cecie Starr and Ralph Taggart, *Biology: The Unity and Diversity of Life,* 4th ed. Belmont, CA: Wadsworth, 1987, p. 444. © 1987. Reprinted with permission of Brooks/Cole Publishing, a division of Thomson Learning. ← *Origin of data*

a = Average value
b = Equivalent of 6 cups } *Footnotes*

- Give each table a concise and descriptive title to show exactly what is being represented or compared.
- Label all categories of your table consistently. If some form of measurement is involved, include the unit of measure as part of the column heading, for example, *weight (pounds), distance (miles), times (hours).* But do not jump between miles and kilometers, pounds and kilograms. Be consistent. You do not have to repeat that unit for each entry in a column. Note that *grams* and *ounces* are not repeated for the protein sources in Table 12.3.
- Use words in the **stub** (a list of items about which information is given), but put numbers under column headings. The Source column in Table 12.3 is the stub.
- Supply footnotes (often indicated by small raised letters: [a], [b]) if something in the table needs to be qualified, for example, the number of cups of milk in Table 12.3. Then put that information below the table.
- List items in alphabetical, chronological, or other logical order.
- Never show readers a table before you discuss it.
- Keep your table on one page; it is hard for readers to follow a table spread across different pages.
- Situate your table vertically, not horizontally, on the page; it is easier to read that way.
- Arrange the data you want to compare vertically; it is easier to read down than across a series of rows.
- Place tables at the top (preferable) or bottom of the page and center them.

- Leave at least one inch of white space between text and table.
- Don't use more than five or six columns; tables wider than that are more difficult for readers to use.
- Round off numbers in your columns to the nearest whole number to assist readers in following and retaining information.
- Always give credit to the source (the supplier of the statistical information) on which your table is based.

Figures

As we saw, any visual that is not a table is classified as a **figure.** The types of figures we will examine here are

- line graphs
- circle, or pie, charts
- bar charts
- organizational charts
- flow charts
- pictographs
- maps
- photographs
- drawings

Presentation graphics software (discussed on pp. 493–494) will allow you to produce the visuals shown here very easily.

Line Graphs

Graphs transform numbers into pictures. They take statistical data presented in tables and put them into rising and falling lines, steep or gentle curves.

Functions of Line Graphs
Graphs vividly portray information that changes, such as

- cycles
- fluctuations
- trends
- distributions
- increases and decreases in, e.g., profits
- employment
- energy levels
- temperatures

Graphs are often used in business communications. The ups and downs in graph lines depict changes in sales, profits, production costs, manufacturing output, expenses, staffing, and much more. Such graphs not only describe past and current situations but also forecast trends.

Graphs versus Tables

Because graphs actually show change, they are more dramatic than tables. You will make the reader's job easier by using a graph rather than a table. Many financial Web sites and print publications—the *Wall Street Journal* and *USA Today,* for example—open with a graph for the benefit of busy readers who want a great deal of financial information summarized quickly.

A Simple Graph

Basically, a simple graph consists of two sides—a **vertical axis** and a **horizontal axis**—that intersect to form a right angle, as in Figure 12.4. The space between the two axes contains the picture made by the graph—in Figure 12.4 the amount of snowfall in Springfield between November 2000 and April 2001. The vertical line represents the **dependent variable** (the snowfall in inches), the horizontal line, the **independent variable** (time in months). The dependent variable is influenced most directly by the independent variable, which almost always is expressed in terms of time or distance. The vertical axis is read from bottom to top; the horizontal axis from left to right.

　　When a dependent variable occurs at a particular time on the independent variable (horizontal line), the place where the two points intersect, the **data point,** is marked, or plotted, on the graph. After all the points are plotted, a line is drawn to connect them; the resulting curve gives a picture of the overall pattern—snowfall in Springfield during the winter of 2000–2001.

　　The way in which scales are set up is crucial to the success of a graph. Many graphs may not have ranges indicated by equally spaced lines (**tick marks**). But on

FIGURE 12.4　A simple line graph showing the amount of snowfall in Springfield from November 2000 to April 2001.

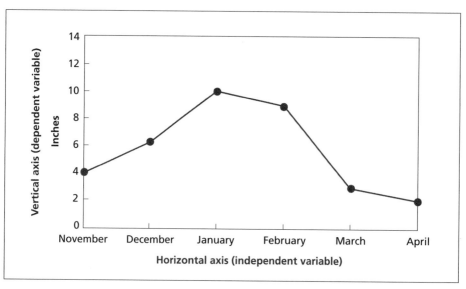

most of the graphs you construct, you should use tick marks as a scale to show values, distances, or time. The topic will dictate the intervals to use. The vertical-axis tick marks in Figure 12.4 indicate inches of snow in increments of 2. The time scale (the independent variable on the horizontal axis) can be calculated in minutes, hours, days, years, or, as in Figure 12.4, months.

Multiple-Line Graphs

The graph in Figure 12.4 contains only one line per category. But a graph can have multiple lines to show how a number of dependent variables (conditions, products) compare with each other.

The six-month sales figures for three salespeople can be seen in the graph in Figure 12.5. The graph contains a separate line for each of the three salespersons. At a glance readers can see how the three compare and how many dollars each salesperson generated per month. Note how the line representing each person is clearly differentiated from the others by symbols and colors. Each line is clearly tied to a **legend** (an explanatory key below the graph) specifying the three salespersons.

Figure 12.6 is another graphic representation of the information in Figure 12.5. The graph in Figure 12.6, known as an **area,** or **multiband graph,** shows relationships

FIGURE 12.5   A multiple-line graph showing sales figures for the first six months of 2001 for three salespeople.

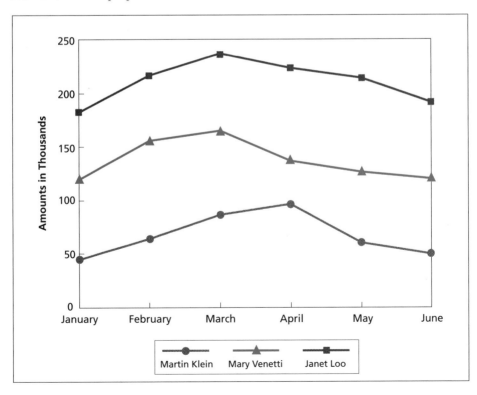

FIGURE 12.6   An area, or multiband, graph of Figure 12.5.

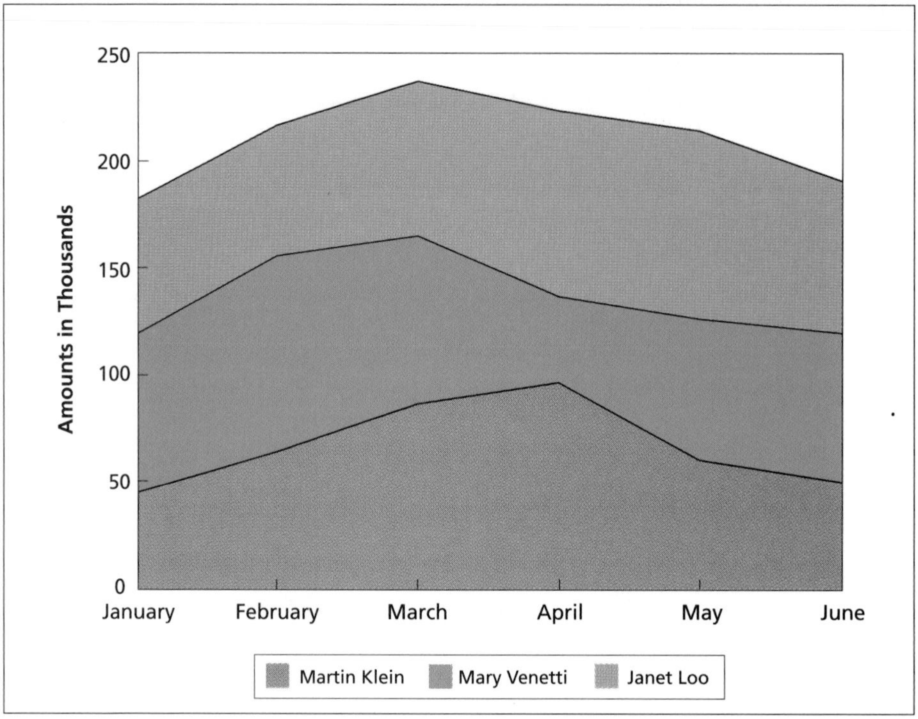

among the three salespeople without providing the exact mathematical documentation of Figure 12.5. In the area graph in Figure 12.6 the spaces between the different curves are filled in, with colors keyed in the legend to identify the three salespersons.

Guidelines on Creating a Graph

1. Make a draft of your graph first to identify the axes, the scale, and how many data points you need to plot.
2. Use no more than three lines in a multiple-line graph, so readers can interpret the graph more easily. If the lines run close together, use a legend to identify individual lines.
3. Label each line to identify what it represents for readers.
4. Keep each line distinct in a multiple-line graph by using different colors, dots or dashes, or symbols. Note the different symbols in Figure 12.5.
5. Make your graph data points large enough to show a reasonable and ethical number of plotted points (using only three or four data points may distort the evidence).
6. Keep the scale consistent and realistic. If you start with hours, do not switch to days or vice versa. If you are recording annual rates or accounts, do not skip a

year or two in the hope that you will save time or be more concise. Do not use, for example, 1992, 1993, 1997, 1999, 2001, 2002. Include all the years you are surveying or equal multiples of them (such as 1996, 1998, 2000, 2002, 2004).

7. For some graphs there is no need to begin with a zero. This is called a sup-pressed zero graph, which automatically begins with a larger number when it would be impossible to start with zero. For others, you may not have to include numbers beyond seven or eight. Your subject and the ranges you are showing will determine what value you give your tick marks.

Charts

Although charts and graphs may seem similar, there is a big difference between them. Because graphs are more complex, charts are preferable when you are com-municating with a consumer audience. A graph is plotted according to specific mathematical coordinates. Charts, on the other hand, do not display exact and com-plex mathematical data. Instead, charts basically give readers the benefit of a signifi-cant visual impact, presenting an overall picture of how individual pieces of data (from a graph or table) fall into place to express relationships. A chart is often con-structed from data contained in spreadsheets and other statistical instruments.

Among the most frequently used charts are (1) circle, or pie, charts, (2) bar charts, (3) organizational charts, and (4) flow charts.

Circle Charts

Circle charts are also known as **pie charts,** a name that descriptively points to their construction and interpretation. The circle chart is one of the most easily under-stood illustrations; Figure 12.7 shows an example of one. Because of its simplicity, the pie chart is popular in government documents (especially the Bureau of the Census), consumer publications, and advertising messages. A table or graph with a

FIGURE 12.7   A three-dimensional circle chart showing the breakdown by department of the proposed Midtown city budget for 2002.

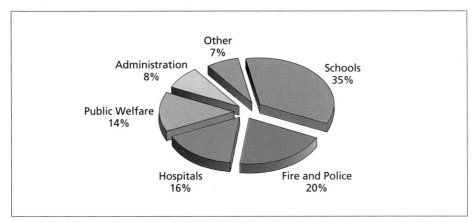

much more detailed breakdown of, say, a city's budget would be more appropriate for a technical audience (auditors, budget planners).

The full circle, or pie, represents the whole amount (100 percent) of something: the entire budget of a company or a family, a population group, an area of land, the resources of an organization or institution. Each slice or wedge represents a percentage or portion of the whole.

A circle chart effectively allows readers to see two things at once: the relationship of the parts to one another and the relationship of the parts to the whole.

Preparing a Circle Chart

Follow these six rules to create and present your circle chart.

1. Keep your circle chart simple. Don't try to illustrate technical statistical data in a pie chart. Pie charts are primarily used for general audiences.

2. Do not divide a circle, or pie, into too few or too many slices. If you have only three wedges, use another visual to display them (a bar chart, for example, which will be discussed later). If you have more than seven or eight wedges, you will divide the pie too narrowly, and overcrowding will destroy the dramatic effect. Instead, combine several slices of small percentages (2 percent, 3 percent, 4 percent) into one slice labeled "Other," "Miscellaneous," or "Related Items."

3. Make sure the individual slices total 100 percent. For example, if you are constructing a circle chart to represent a family's budget, the breakdown percentages might be as follows:

Category	Percentage	Angle of slice
Food	22%	90.0°
Housing	25%	79.2°
Energy	20%	72.0°
Clothes	13%	46.8°
Health Care	12%	43.2°
Miscellaneous	8%	28.8°
Total	100%	360°

If you are preparing the chart by hand, use a protractor to make sure the slices are accurate.

4. Put the largest slice first, at the 12 o'clock position, then move clockwise with proportionately smaller slices. By beginning with the biggest slice, you call attention to its importance.

5. Label each slice of the pie horizontally. Key in the identifying term or quantity inside, but make sure the label is big enough to read. Do not put in a label upside down or slide it in vertically. If the individual slice of the pie is small, do not try to squeeze in a label. Draw a connecting line from the slice to a label positioned outside the pie.

6. Shade, color, or cross-hatch slices of the pie to further separate and distinguish the parts. But be careful not to obscure labels and percentages; also make certain that adjacent slices can be distinguished readily from each other.

Bar Charts

A bar chart consists of a series of vertical or horizontal bars that indicate comparisons of statistical data. For instance, in Figure 12.8 vertical bars depict increases in numbers of working mothers. Figure 12.9 uses horizontal bars to depict the nation's top 20 metropolitan areas, judging by building permits. The length of the bars is determined according to a scale that your computer software can easily compute.

Bar charts make a dramatic visual impression on the reader. They are valuable tools in sales meetings to demonstrate how well (or poorly) a product, a service, or a particular section of the company has done. You often see bar charts recording the financial goals for charitable drives and on home computer screens showing the breakdown of budgets or the relationship of a consumer's income to liabilities.

Advantages of Bar Charts

Bar charts are less exact than tables, as Figures 12.8 and 12.9 show. Note that the percentage of mothers working outside the home and the number of building permits are not expressed in exact figures, as they would be in a table, but are approximated by the length of the bars. Do not assume, however, that the bar chart is inaccurate; many bar charts are based on tables. What you lose in precision with a bar chart, you gain in visual flair. Finally, a bar chart is much more fluid and dynamic than a circle. The circle is static; the bar chart (like the graph) presents a moving view.

FIGURE 12.8   Vertical bar chart with labeled bars.

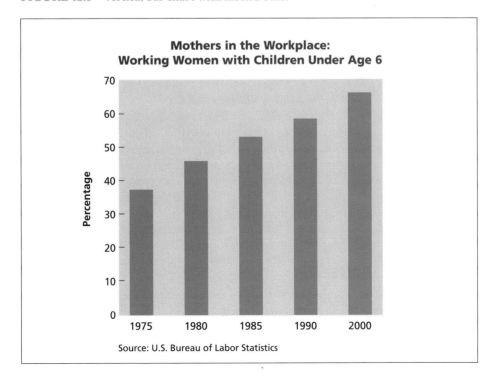

FIGURE 12.9   Horizontal bar chart with labeled bars.

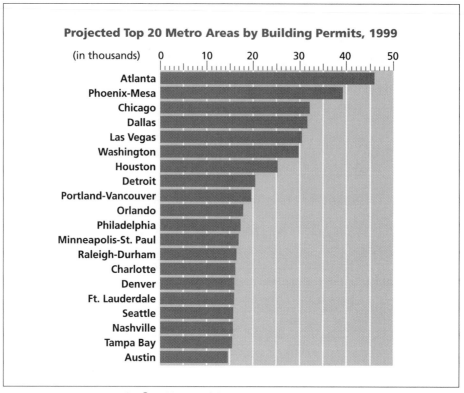

Projected Top 20 Metro Areas by Building Permits, 1999

Source: From *U.S. Housing Markets,*® a publication of the Meyers Group.

Bar Charts, Graphs, and Tables—Which Should You Use?

When should you use a bar chart rather than a table or a line graph? Your audience will help you decide. If you are asked to present statistics on costs for the company accountant, use a table. That reader demands a precise listing. However, if you are presenting the same information to a group of stockholders or to a diverse group of employees, a bar chart may be more relevant because those readers are more interested in seeing the statistics in action—the effects of change—than the underlying causes and precise statistical details. Since it is limited to a few columns, however, a bar chart cannot convey as much information as a table or graph.

Types of Bar Charts

There are three types of bar charts.

1. *Simple bar charts.* Figure 12.8 is the most basic form of bar chart. Each bar represents the percentage of working women with children under the age of 6, and the height of the bar corresponds to the number of percentage points for a given year. To read the chart effectively, note where the top of the bar is in relation to the vertical scale on the left. The chart compares one type of data (the percentage of working mothers) over a period of time (every five years from 1975 to 2000).

2. *Multiple-bar charts.* Figure 12.10 shows a variation of the simple, vertical bar chart. Four different colored bars are used for each year to represent the amount of money spent on different types of advertising in 1998, 1999, 2000, and 2001. A legend at the top of the chart explains what each bar stands for. The multiple-bar chart is useful for showing a variety of comparisons. A word of caution is in order about multiple-bar charts: avoid using more than four bars in a group for any one year. It will make your chart crowded and difficult to read.

3. *Segmented, or cross-hatched (divided), bar charts* To show the different components that constitute a measured whole, use a segmented bar chart like the one in Figure 12.11. A single segmented bar lists the travel expenses of Weemco, a small firm, in October 2001. The entire bar equals the travel total—$137,000—which was spent in four areas: airfare, ground transportation, lodging, and meals. Each of these expenses is represented by a different type of shading on the single column. Combined, the multiple sources account for all travel expenses Weemco had in one month. A group of segmented bars can be used to show multiple comparisons among many categories, as in Figure 12.12, which depicts energy consumption levels and types in five states.

Organizational Charts

Unlike the charts discussed so far, an **organizational chart** does not display statistical data, nor does it record movements in space or time. Rather, it pictures the chain

FIGURE 12.10   A multiple-bar chart showing advertising expenditures by major media, 1998–2001.

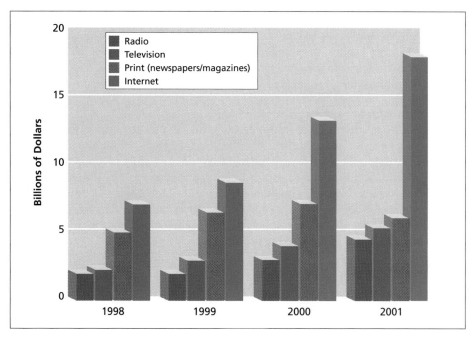

FIGURE 12.11   A segmented bar chart representing total travel expenditures for Weemco Communications for October 2001.

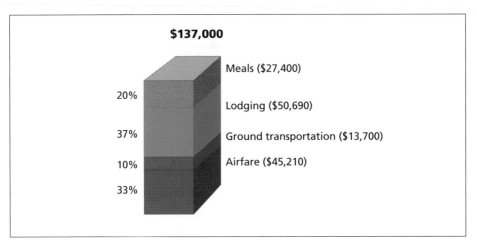

of command in a company or agency, with the lines of authority stretching down from the chief executive, manager, or administrator to assistant manager, department heads, or supervisors to the work force of employees. Figure 12.13 shows a hospital's organizational chart for its nursing services.

Functions of Organizational Charts

Organizational charts have these functions:

- to inform employees and customers about the makeup of a company
- to show the various offices, departments, and units through which orders and information flow in the company or agency
- to coordinate employee efforts in routing information to appropriate departments

Structuring an Organizational Chart

An organizational chart shows relationships by using lines to connect rectangles or circles to each other, starting at the top with the chief executive and moving down to lower-level employees. (Sometimes the name of the individual holding the office is listed in addition to the title of the office.) In the organizational chart in Figure 12.13, positions of equal authority are on parallel lines, and all jobs under the supervision of one individual are joined by bracketing lines. Individuals who serve in advisory capacities or who are indirectly responsible to a higher administrator are listed with broken or dotted lines, as depicted in the unit secretary positions in Figure 12.13.

Flow Charts

Like an organizational chart, a **flow chart** does not present statistical information, but as its name implies, a flow chart does show movement. It displays the stages in

FIGURE 12.12   A multiple-bar, segmented bar chart showing energy consumption by sector in five states that consumed the most energy in a given year.

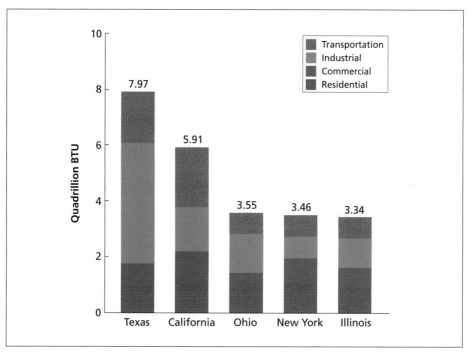

Source: U.S. Energy Information Administration.

which something is manufactured, is accomplished, develops, or operates. Flow charts can also be used to plan the day's or week's activities.

A flow chart tells a story with arrows, boxes, and sometimes pictures. Boxes are connected by arrows to visualize the stages of a process. The presence and direction of the arrows tell the reader the order and movement of events involved in the process. Flow charts often proceed from left to right and back again, as in the flow chart below, showing the steps to be taken before graduation.

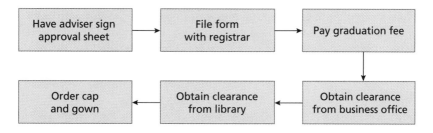

Flow charts can also be constructed to read from top to bottom. Computer programming instructions frequently are written that way. See, for example, Figure

FIGURE 12.13   An organizational chart representing critical care nursing services at Union General Hospital.

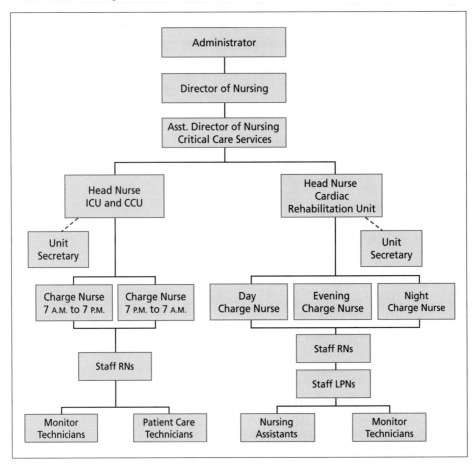

12.14, which uses a computer programming flow chart to show the steps a student must follow in writing a research paper.

A flow chart should clarify, not complicate, a process. Do not omit any important stages, but at the same time do not introduce unnecessary or unduly detailed information. Show at least three or four stages and make sure the various stages appear in the correct sequence.

Pictographs

Similar to a bar chart, a **pictograph** uses picture symbols (called **pictograms**) to represent differences in statistical data, as in Figure 12.15. A pictograph repeats the same symbol or icon to depict the quantity of items being measured. Each symbol stands for a specific number, quantity, or value. Pictographs are visually appealing and dramatic and are far more appropriate for a nontechnical than a technical audience.

FIGURE 12.14   A computer programming flow chart showing steps in writing a research paper.

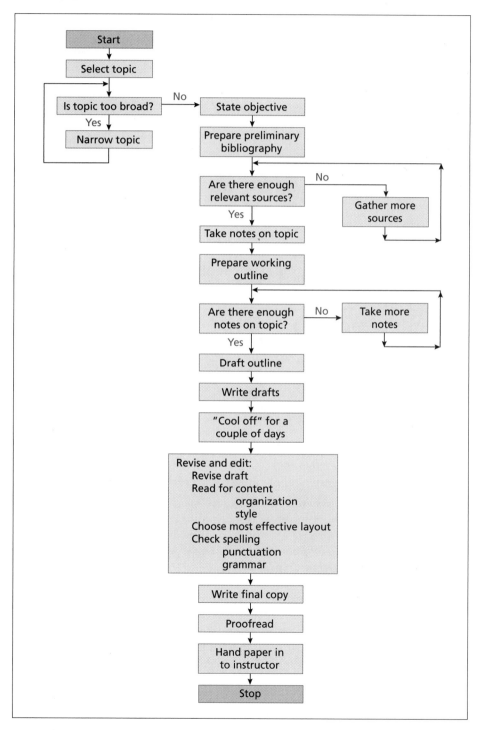

FIGURE 12.15   A pictograph showing the growth of one state's retirement assets.

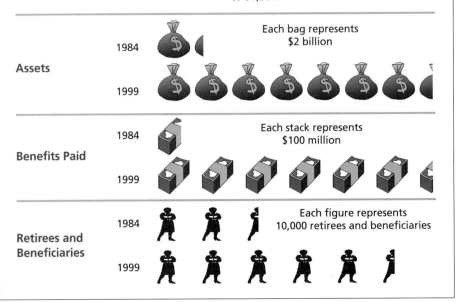

How does the Public Employees' Retirement System (PERS) compare today with 15 years ago?

During that time, PERS experienced spectacular growth, with both assets and benefits paid increasing more than six-fold.

• The market value of assets increased from $2.3 billion to $14.9 billion.
• PERS paid benefits of $94.3 million in FY '84. The total reached $601.1 million during FY '99.
• Retirees and beneficiaries drawing benefits more than doubled, from 24,000 to 51,800.

Assets
1984
1999
Each bag represents $2 billion

Benefits Paid
1984
1999
Each stack represents $100 million

Retirees and Beneficiaries
1984
1999
Each figure represents 10,000 retirees and beneficiaries

Source: PERS Member Newsletter, August 1999. Official Publication of the Public Employees' Retirement System of Mississippi. By permission of Public Employees' Retirement System.

Guidelines on Creating Pictographs

When you create a pictograph, follow these four guidelines:

1. Choose an appropriate symbol for the topic—such as computer screens to represent the increase in the number of fax modems or barns for the number of farms.
2. Always indicate the precise quantities involved by placing numbers after the pictures or at the top of the visual so the reader knows exactly how much the total number of pictograms represents.
3. Increase the number of symbols rather than their sizes because differences in sizes are often difficult to construct accurately (even with a graphics software program) and hard for the reader to interpret.
4. Avoid crowding too much information into a pictograph, such as the one in Figure 12.3, in which a dollar bill is divided into too many sections.

Maps

The maps you use on the job may range from highly sophisticated and detailed geographic tools to simple sketches such as the student-drawn map in Figure 12.16,

TECH NOTE

Using MapQuest

You can easily create detailed road maps, like the one in Figure 12.17, with MapQuest software. First you select a country, say, the United States, then below the map display area, you point and click on "Zoom in." Next point to the area on the map that you are interested in and click again; each time you point and click, a new map will be drawn that is more detailed than the previous one and centered on the place you last pointed to. You just continue to point and click until you have the desired level of detail.

In addition to roads, MapQuest has a number of "Places of Interest" categories you can select to be displayed. As you are zooming in, you can go at any time to the bottom of the screen and select whatever categories of interesting places you want to add to your map. Categories include *Personal* (ones you add yourself), *Dining, Lodging, Entertainment, Education, Recreation, Shopping,* and *Health Care*. Each category has a selection of subcategories from which you can further choose so you will see displayed exactly what you need.

FIGURE 12.16   A map showing the location of Smithville Water Department's filter plants and pumping stations.

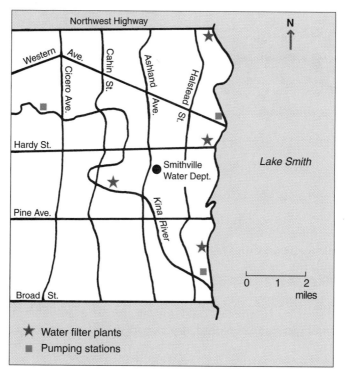

FIGURE 12.17   A large-scale map from MapQuest.

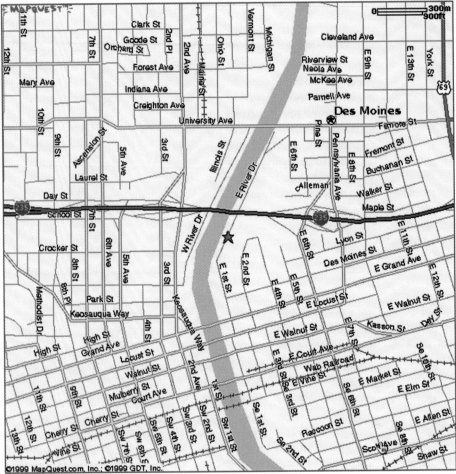

Provided by MapQuest.com.

which shows the location of a town's water filter plants and dumping stations. This is a **large-scale map** that displays a good deal of social, economic, or physical data (such as population density, location of retail businesses, hills, expressways, or rivers) for a small area.

You may have to construct your own map, like the one in Figure 12.16, or scan one in a published source (a government document, an atlas, or an auto club publication) or on the Internet. If you scan a published map, be sure to obtain permission to use it from the copyright holder. Or you may use a map from MapQuest, as in Figure 12.17.

Guidelines for Creating a Map

Follow these steps when you create a map:

1. Always acknowledge your source if you did not construct the map yourself.
2. Use dots, lines, colors, symbols, and shading to indicate features. Markings should be clear and distinct.
3. If necessary, include a legend, or map key, explaining dotted lines, colors, shading, and symbols as in Figure 12.16.
4. Exclude features (rivers, elevations, county seats) that do not directly relate to your topic. For example, a map showing the crops grown in two adjacent counties need not show all the roads and highways in those counties. A map showing the presence of strip mining needs to indicate elevation, but a map depicting population or religious affiliation need not include topographical (physical) detail.
5. Indicate direction. Conventionally, maps show north, often by including an arrow and the letter N: $N\uparrow$.

Photographs

Correctly taken or scanned, photographs are an extremely helpful addition to job-related writing. A photograph's chief virtues are realism and clarity. A photo can

- show what an object looks like (Figure 12.18)
- demonstrate how to perform a certain procedure (Figure 12.19)
- compare relative sizes and shapes of objects (Figure 12.20)
- show comparison and contrast of scenes or procedures (Figure 12.21)

TECH NOTE

Digital Cameras

Digital cameras are revolutionizing photography, allowing you to supply professional-looking, customized photos with your written work. As with other cameras, you point and shoot with a digital camera. But unlike a traditional camera, the digital camera lets you review every photo you take before you print it. Easily fitting inside a coat pocket, the digital camera has sophisticated computer technology built in, and it offers a variety of options. You can shoot a photo, take it in slow motion, and play it back, which allows you to scroll, zoom in, blow it up, adjust darkness or light, even change exposures.

You then download your pictures from the digital camera into your PC and further adjust the colors, sharpen the images, enlarge or crop the picture area, save and print the photos. Digital cameras use smart cards, not film, so you don't have to take film to a photo processing service to be developed. You can also send your photos as e-mail attachments.

If you have a television connector, you can even view photos on your TV set.

FIGURE 12.18   A photo showing what a piece of equipment looks like.

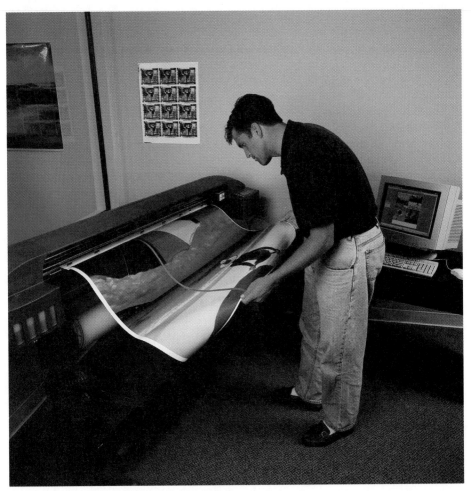

Source: Corbis Royalty Free *(http://www.corbis.com)*

Use special care when you take a photograph. The most important point to remember is that what you see and what the camera records might be two different sights. Before you take a photo, decide how much foreground and background image you need. Include only the details that are *necessary* and *relevant* for your purpose. Each photo you take should have *clarity, definition* (distinct details and outlines), and *appropriateness.* Inexperienced photographers need to remember the following five points.

1. **Focus your camera.** Make sure you have proper lighting.
2. **Select the correct angle.** Choose a vantage point that will enable you to record essential information as graphically as possible.

FIGURE 12.19   A photo showing how to perform a procedure.

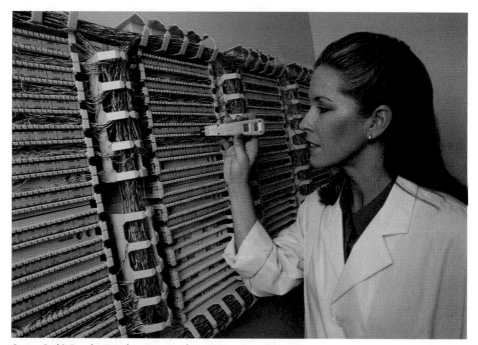

Source: Corbis Royalty Free *(http://www.corbis.com)*

3. **Give the right amount of detail.** Pictures that include clutter compete for the reader's attention and detract from the subject. A real estate agent who wants to show that a house has an attractive front does not need to include sidewalks or streets. At the other extreme, do not cut out a necessary part of an object or landscape. Avoid putting people in a photograph when their presence is not required to show the relative size or operation of an object.
4. **Take the picture from the right distance.** The farther back you stand, the wider your angle will be, and the more the camera will capture with less detail. If you need a shot of a three-story office building, your picture may show only one or two stories if you are standing too close to the building when you photograph it. Standing too far away from an object, however, means that the photograph will reduce the object's importance and record unnecessary details.
5. **Choose the right lens.** A telephoto lens can bring the scene closer; a wide-angle lens will let you include more of the scene.

To get a graphic sense of the effects of taking a photo the right and wrong way, study the photographs in Figures 12.22 and 12.23 on page 490. A clear and useful picture of a hydraulic truck (often called a "cherry picker") used to cut high

FIGURE 12.20   Photo showing the relative size and shape of an object.

Source: Corbis Royalty Free (http://www.corbis.com)

branches can be seen in Figure 12.22. The photographer rightly placed the truck in the foreground, but included enough background information to indicate the truck's function. The worker in the bucket helps to show the truck in operation.

In Figure 12.23 everything merges because the shot was taken from the wrong angle. The reader has no sense of the parts of the truck, their size, or their function.

Drawings

Drawings can show where an object is located, how a tool or machine is put together, or what signals are given or steps taken in a particular situation. By studying your drawing and following your discussion, readers will be better able to operate, adjust, repair, or order parts for equipment. Drawings are especially helpful when you are giving instructions (see Chapter 13).

Advantages of Drawings over Photographs
Drawings generally have two advantages over ordinary photographs:

1. You can include as much or as little detail as necessary in a drawing. The eye of a nondigital camera is not so selective; it records everything in its path, including details that may be irrelevant for your purpose.

FIGURE 12.21   Photos showing comparison/contrast: the top photo shows artwork prepared manually, without use of a computer, while the bottom photo shows artwork prepared and presented electronically using PowerPoint.

Source: © Stephen Frisch, Stock Boston.

Source: © Matthew Borkoski, Stock Boston.

FIGURE 12.22   An effective photograph—truck in foreground, enough background information, and a worker to show the size and function of the truck.

Photograph by David Longmire.

FIGURE 12.23   A poor photograph—taken from the wrong angle so that everything merges and becomes confusing.

Photograph by David Longmire.

2. A drawing can show interior as well as exterior views, a feature that is particularly useful when the reader must understand what is going on under the case, housing, or hood.

Types of Drawings

A drawing can be simple, like the one in Figure 12.24, which shows readers exactly where to place smoke detectors in a house.

A more detailed drawing can reveal the interior of an object. Such sketches are called **cutaway drawings** because they show internal parts normally concealed from view. Figure 12.25 is a cutaway drawing of an antilock brake system.

Another kind of sketch is an **exploded drawing,** which blows the entire object up and apart to show how the individual parts are arranged. An exploded drawing

FIGURE 12.24   A drawing showing where to place smoke detectors in a house.

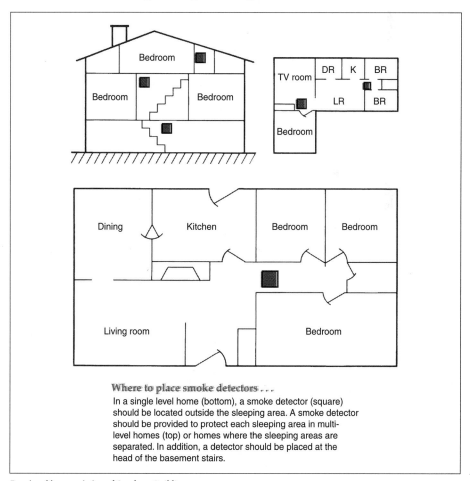

Reprinted by permission of *Southern Building.*

FIGURE 12.25   Cutaway drawing of an antilock brake system.

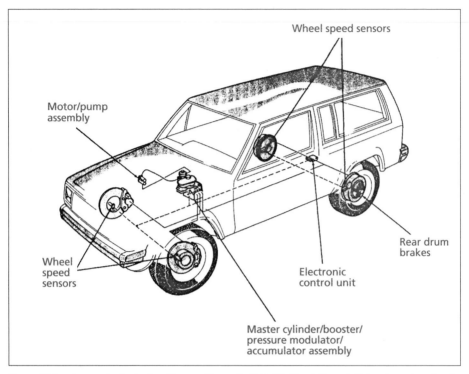

Source: Chilton Automotive Books. *Jeep Wagoneer/Comanche 1984–1996 Repair Manual.* Chilton is a registered trademark of Cahners Business Information, a Division of Reed Elsevier Inc. and has been licensed to W. G. Nichols Inc.

of a laptop computer is seen in Figure 12.26, which also uses **callouts,** or labels, identifying the components. The labels are often attached to the drawing with arrows or lines. As the name suggests, the labels "call out" the parts so readers can identify them quickly.

Guidelines for Using a Drawing

1. Keep your drawing simple. Include only as much detail as your reader needs to understand to assemble or operate the mechanism. Do not include any extra details. Even a line or two might distort the reader's view. Don't add decorations to make your drawing look fancy.
2. Clearly label all parts so your reader can identify and separate them.
3. Decide on the most appropriate view of the object you want to illustrate—aerial, frontal, lateral, reverse, exterior, interior—and indicate in your title which view it is.
4. Keep the parts of the drawing proportionate unless you are purposely enlarging one section. If you change any part(s) of a mechanism in your drawing, indicate where and why.

FIGURE 12.26   Exploded drawing of a laptop computer.

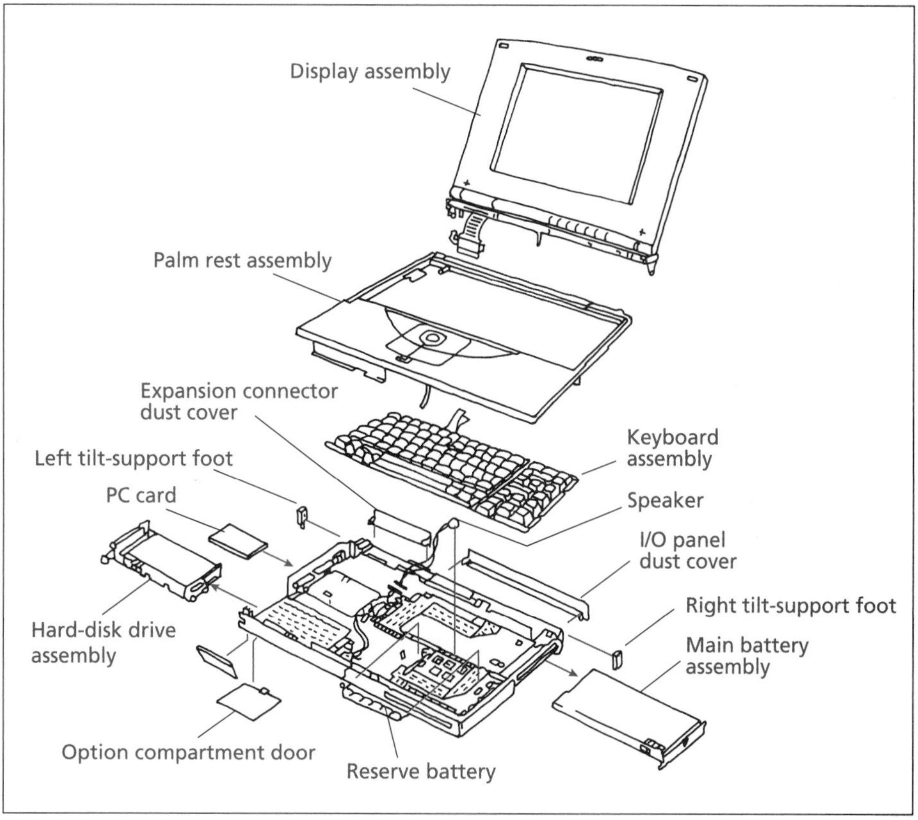

Computer Graphics

With computer graphics software, you can locate, create, edit, and position in your documents virtually all the kinds of visuals discussed in this chapter. Charts and graphs that illustrate, or *present*, data values are sometimes called **presentation graphics.** Other visuals, such as photos, drawings, and preproduced images or icons, are *representational*, as opposed to presentational, in that they are pictures that look like what they are depicting.

Presentation Graphics

A presentation graphics package is designed specifically to produce the kinds of charts and graphs discussed in this chapter. It guides you through the process of inputting your data and selecting the way you want them displayed. You simply plug your raw data into the computer software or use data already stored in a database or from a spreadsheet program. (The presentation graphics software will even store information so you do not have to reenter it when you want to change or update a visual.) Your computer then will plot the data you entered into a proportionately accurate chart, graph, or table. Presentation graphics software also lets you customize every other aspect of your visual—what title to give it, what scale to follow, what annotations to include, and even what colors to use.

Presentation graphics start with a set of data that needs to be represented. The data must first be typed into a spreadsheet program such as Excel. Once you enter the data and data labels through a few clicks of the mouse button, the program then lets you look at a variety of charts and graphs, which you can accept or adapt.

Once you have decided on the graph you want, you can print it or put it into your word processing document. If you put it in your word processing program, you have two options: (1) put a copy of the graph as it is directly into your document, or (2) link the graph to the document.

Graphics Software: PowerPoint

Other graphics software comes with a wide range of capabilities, from the simple to the highly technical. At the simple end of the range, you can use a graphics package such as PowerPoint.

One of the best places to begin your work in computer graphics is Microsoft's PowerPoint, a widely used presentation graphics software package. It contains everything you need to produce effective and professional-looking visuals for proposals, reports, and presentations at a modest cost. You do not need much technical know-how to use PowerPoint. In fact, PowerPoint comes with computer-guided tutorials (PowerPoint Central) that make creating convincing visuals surprisingly easy.

With the graphics capabilities of PowerPoint you can

- create visuals, pictures, tables, drawings, and worksheets
- draw bars, graphs, and charts
- include a wide variety of clip art—signs, people, scenic backgrounds
- insert borders
- incorporate a variety of shapes and symbols—arrows, cylinders, pyramids, cones, flow chart/pictogram icons
- use three-dimensional effects, including shadowing, shading, and other configurations for depth
- label components
- revise and update visuals
- produce slide shows
- develop overhead and on-screen transparencies
- offer animation and voice narration
- create hyperlinks
- import (insert) visuals, photos, and digital art in your text
- include mathematical equations
- design and insert logos and letterheads

With all those capabilities, the possibilities for creating original and highly effective visuals are endless.

PowerPoint is invaluable in presentations at work (see Chapter 17). The electronic slide show it offers can be displayed on any computer running Windows 98 whether or not the computer has PowerPoint installed. In addition, PowerPoint slides can be saved to a disk and developed as 35mm slides by a film processing service. No matter which option you choose, the slides produced by PowerPoint will be in full and clear color.

Editing visuals is simple with PowerPoint, allowing you to customize any visual for a report or presentation. You can copy, move, alter, and delete with PowerPoint. For example, you could edit the number of categories (bars, lines of a graph, items in a table) of an imported visual for a consumer audience that does not need a lot of detail, or you could change the levels and positions of an organizational chart to suit your agency or department. Such editing—including drawing and outlining (for example, changing the color or texture of a background)—will save you time and effort in re-creating a visual. If you do not feel confident about using the program, you can let PowerPoint do the work for you. Simply pull down the File menu, click New, then click the Presentations tab. Double-click AutoContent Wizard, then follow the instructions.

PowerPoint will also save you time and trouble inserting your visuals in the right places. The software will automatically arrange and position the visual(s) in your report or slide show. You can include pictures, tables, charts, graphs, even spreadsheets in the text of your report rather than on separate pages. Figure 12.27 is an example of the type of dynamic visual you can create using PowerPoint.

FIGURE 12.27   Bar graph created using PowerPoint.

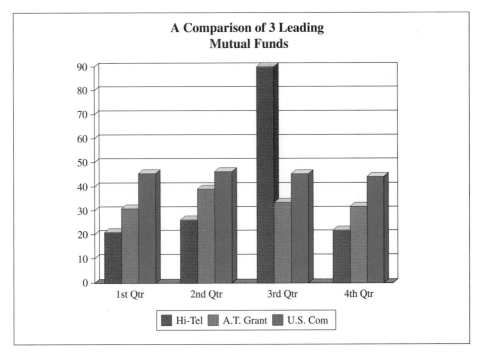

PowerPoint also lets you wrap text around your visuals. With the click of a button you can rearrange the format of you page and the placement and appearance of the visual on the page, giving you greater flexibility when you organize and arrange your informa-tion. Only one step with Pow-erPoint was re-quired to wrap

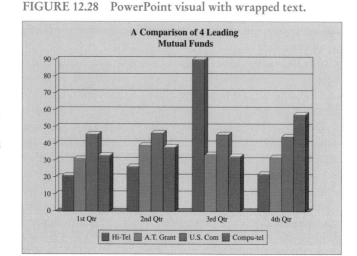

FIGURE 12.28   PowerPoint visual with wrapped text.

this text around Figure 12.28. Note how both the appearance and the placement of Figure 12.28 differ from Figure 12.27. With the drawing and text editing fea-tures available in PowerPoint, another bar was added to the bar chart, the back-ground color was changed, and a new legend was created.

Visuals from the Internet

The Internet has an enormous impact on the types of visuals you can expect to use in the workplace. Companies as well as individuals create their own Web sites, most of which include both text and visual displays. There are several ways to find visuals on the Net.

- Browse the Web for creative new ideas for graphics.
- Use search engines such as Scour.Net, Filez, and Webplaces: Clip art Searcher/ Surf to locate graphics and images.
- Look at some of the "Top Sites" for examples and ideas of the Web's most acclaimed work. A listing of those sites is at *http://scc.ntnu.edu.tw/~cta/ top100/_open.htm.*
- See the portfolios of artists on line (*http://www.starvingartist.com/*) who sell their work for a fee.
- Consult the numerous on-line graphics magazines:
  —*Corel Magazine (http://www.corelmag.com/)*
  —*Design World (http://www.designworld-mag.com/)*
  —*Computer Graphics World (http://www.cgw.com/index2.htm)*
- Take advantage of royalty-free pictures and images available from these services:
  —Corbis (*http://www.corbis.com/*)

—Digital Picture Archive (*http://www.w2s.co.uk/timo/olympus/index.html*)

—Computer Graphics (*http://www.mambo.ucsc.edu/psl/cg.html*)

—Rainbow Collection (*http://www.geocities.com/SiliconValley/Heights/1272/rainbow.html*)

—GraphX Kingdom (*http://www.efni.com/~haven/graphx/index.html*)

If you see a graphic image at a site that you want to use in a report or paper, it is fairly easy to save that image on disk. But remember that because the images you save from the Web were placed there by someone else, you *must* reference your sources. If your work is to be published, or if you intend to put it on the Web yourself, you must obtain written permission from the copyright holders of any images you want to

TECH NOTE

Downloading Images from the Web

Once you have found an image on the Web, put your mouse cursor on the image and press the mouse button. (*Note:* the image may not have a hyperlink so your cursor may not change shape; that does not matter in this case.) A small pop-up menu box will appear:

Back
Forward
View this image
Save this image as . . .
Copy this image location

Use your cursor to select the "Save this image as . . ." option. The normal "Save as" menu box will appear and you can select a name for the file where the image will be saved as well as the disk drive and the directory. This process is exactly the same as choosing "Save as" from the "File" menu at the top of the screen.

Now that the image is on your disk, you can run your word processor and get into your document. Place your cursor at the point in the document where you want the image to appear, then select the "Insert" option at the top of the screen and choose "Picture." The image will then be copied to your word processing file.

Images on computers are saved in a number of different formats; that is, the information the computer will use to produce the picture can be stored in different ways. Sometimes the format of the image you saved from the Web is not a format that your word processor can accommodate. In that case, you need a simple graphics program such as Graphic Workshop (downloadable from the Web) to change the format before you can insert it into your document. Graphics programs will also let you edit an image, such as changing its size so it better fits the space where you want to place it.

FIGURE 12.29   Examples of clip art.

Source: © 1997 The Learning Company and its licensors.

include. Electronic publications require you to follow the same ethical rules you do with print sources.

Incorporating Clip Art

Clip art refers to ready-to-use images stored on disk. These small drawings, such as the ones shown in Figure 12.29, depict almost anything you can think of and pertain to almost every discipline—architecture, computer science, criminal justice, international marketing. Many graphics packages come with comprehensive clip art libraries. To help you select the clip art you need, most packages include a manual with thousands of full-color pictures of all their clip art grouped under such useful headings as energy, government, leisure, health, money, the outdoors, food, technology, transportation. You can use clip art for a variety of projects.

When you use clip art, follow these guidelines:

1. **Use clip art sparingly.** Do not insert clip art as decorations. Using too many will detract from your written work. Each piece of clip art should contribute significantly to, not compete with, your message.
2. **Make sure the clip art is relevant for your audience and your message.** A clip art airplane does not belong in a technical report on fuel capacity or jet engine design.
3. **Make sure your clip art is professional.** Some clip art is humorous, even silly, which may not be appropriate for a professional business report or proposal.

✓ Revision Checklist

❑ Located all places where a visual would help readers better understand my message.
❑ Used Internet as a virtual library of visuals.
❑ Chose most effective visual (table, chart, graph, drawing, photograph) to represent information the audience needs.
❑ Experimented with different software programs.
❑ Drafted and edited visual until it meets readers' needs.
❑ Verified statistical data that visual portrays.
❑ Made sure that visual does not simply repeat information in my written work.
❑ Selected right amount of technical detail to include in visual.
❑ Made sure every visual is attractive, clear, complete, and relevant.
❑ Gave each visual a number, a title, and, where necessary, a legend and a callout.
❑ Numbered tables and figures consecutively.
❑ Inserted visual near the written description or commentary to which it pertains.
❑ Introduced and interpreted each visual in appropriate place in report or paper.
❑ Acknowledged sources for any copyrighted visuals and gave credit to individuals whose statistical data are the basis of a visual.

Glossary

By way of review, the following is a glossary of terms used in this chapter:

band graph   also called an **area graph;** graph in which the spaces between the curves are filled in.

bar chart   a visual using vertical or horizontal bars to measure different data in space and time; bars can also be segmented to show multiple percentages within one bar. Bar charts are used to show a variety of facts for easy comparison.

callouts   labels that identify the parts of an object in a visual.

captions   titles or headings for visuals.

circle chart   a visual shaped in a circle, or pie, whose slices represent the parts of the whole. Circle charts often portray budgets, expenditures, shares, and time allotments.

clip art   ready-made electronic images, symbols, and pictures available in a computer library.

computer graphics a variety of visuals generated by a computer; software (programs) and hardware (computer screens, scanners) create these visuals.

cropping the process of eliminating unnecessary, unwanted details of a photograph by reproducing only the desired portion.

cross-hatching the process of marking parts of a visual with parallel lines that cross each other obliquely; used to differentiate one bar or slice of a circle chart from another.

cutaway drawing a sketch in which the exterior covering of an object has been removed to show an interior view.

data point the intersection of the vertical and horizontal axes on a graph to plot the occurrence of statistical data.

definition the distinctness of a photograph in outline and detail.

dependent variable the element (cost, employment, energy) plotted along the vertical axis of a line graph and most directly influenced by the independent variable.

digital camera camera that uses a smart card instead of film to take photographs; the "processing" takes place in your PC, and the photos are saved in files.

drawing software packages computer graphics software that allows users to create visual representations of data either plotted for accuracy or drawn freehand (charts, graphs, general illustrations).

exploded drawing a sketch of an entire object that has been blown up and apart to show the relationship of parts to one another.

figures any visuals that are not tables—charts, drawings, graphs, pictograms, photographs, maps.

flow chart a sketch with boxes and arrows revealing the stages in an activity or process.

graph a picture that represents the relationship of an independent variable to one or more dependent variables; produces a line or curve to show their movement in time or space. Graphs are used to depict figures that change often—temperatures, rainfall, prices, employment, productions, and so forth.

independent variable the element, plotted along the horizontal axis of a graph, which most directly and importantly affects the dependent variable; most often, the independent variable is time or distance.

large-scale map a map that shows a great deal of detail, whether physical (elevations, rivers), economic (income levels), or social (population, religious affiliation).

legend the explanation, or key, indicating what different colors, shadings, or symbols represent in a visual.

organizational chart a visual showing the structure of an organization from the chief executive to the work force of employees. An organizational chart reveals the chain of command and areas of authority and responsibility.

pictograph a visual showing differences in statistical data by means of pictures varying in size, number, or color.

pie chart see **circle chart.**

presentation graphics software computer graphics software that allows its users to assemble visual images in digital form for presentation purposes (e.g., audio-visual presentation at a sales conference).

spreadsheet   an electronic table generated by a computer graphics package.

stub   the first column on the left side of a table; contains line captions listing those units to be discussed in the columns.

table   a visual in which statistical data or verbal descriptions are arranged in rows or columns.

template   a pattern used as a guide in creating a visual after a standard model, e.g. letterheads, résumé format.

tick marks   equally spaced marks drawn on the vertical or horizontal scale of a graph to show units of measurement.

Exercises

1. Bring to class three or four Web site home pages from the Internet that use especially effective visuals. In a short memo or e-mail (three or four paragraphs) to your instructor, indicate why and how each visual is appropriate for and convincing to a particular audience. What would each home page look like without its visual?

2. Record the highest temperature reached in your town for the next five days. Then collect data on the highest temperature reached in three of the following cities—Boston, Chicago, Dallas, Denver, Los Angeles, Miami, New Orleans, New York, Philadelphia, Phoenix, Salt Lake City, San Francisco, Seattle—over the same five days. (You can get this information from a printed newspaper or on the Internet.) Prepare a table showing the differences for the five-day period.

3. Go to a supermarket and get the prices of four different brands of the same product (hair spray, aspirin, a soft drink, a box of cereal). Present your findings in the form of a table.

4. One government agency supplied the following statistics on the world production of oranges (including tangerines) in thousands of metric tons for the following countries during the years 1998–2001: Brazil, 2,005, 2,132, 2,760, and 2,872; Israel, 909, 1,076, 1,148, 1,221; Italy, 1,669, 1,599, 1,766, 1,604; Japan, 2,424, 2,994, 2,885, 4,070; Mexico, 937, 1,405, 1,114, 1,270; Spain, 2,135, 2,005, 2,179, 2,642; and the United States, 7,658, 7,875, 7,889, 9,245. Prepare a table with that information and then write a paragraph in which you introduce and refer to the table and draw conclusions from it.

5. Keep a record for one week of the number of miles you walk, ride, or drive each day. Then prepare a line graph depicting that information.

6. Prepare a table to show the following statistical data: According to the 1990 census, the town of Ardmore had a population of 34,567. By the 2000 census the town's population had decreased by 4,500. In the 1990 census the town of

Morrison had a population of 23,809, but by the 2000 census the population had increased by 3,689. The 2000 census figure for the town of Berkesville was 25,675, which was an increase of 2,768 from the 1990 census.

7. Prepare a line graph for the information in Exercise 6.

8. Prepare a bar graph for the information in Exercise 6.

9. Write a paragraph introducing and interpreting the following table.

Year	Soft Drink Companies	Bottling Plants	Per Capita Consumption (Gallons)
1940	750	750	10.3
1945	578	611	12.5
1950	457	466	18.6
1955	380	407	17.2
1960	231	292	15.9
1970	171	229	15.4
1975	118	197	16.0
1980	92	154	18.7
1985	54	102	21.1
1990	43	88	23.1
1995	45	82	25.3
2000	37	78	27.6

10. Prepare a circle chart showing the breakdown of your budget for one week or one month.

11. According to a municipal study in 2000 the distribution of all companies classified in each enterprise industry in that city was as follows: minerals, 0.4%; selected services, 33.3%; retail trade, 36.7%; wholesale trade, 6.5%; manufacturing, 5.3%; and construction, 17.8%. Make a circle chart to represent the distribution and write a one- or two-paragraph interpretation to accompany (and explain the significance of) your visual.

12. Construct a segmented bar chart to represent the kinds and numbers of courses you took in a two-semester period or during your last year in high school.

13. Prepare a bar chart for the different brands of one of the products in Exercise 3. Write a paragraph introducing your illustration.

14. Find a pictograph in a math or business textbook, in a magazine (try *Newsweek* or *U.S. News & World Report* in print or on-line), or on the Web. Make a bar graph from the information contained in the pictograph, then write a paragraph introducing the bar graph and drawing conclusions from it.

15. Make an organizational chart for a business or an agency you worked for recently. Include part-time and full-time employees, but indicate their titles or

functions with different kinds of shapes or lines. Then write a brief letter to your employer explaining why this kind of organizational chart should be distributed to all employees. Focus on the types of problems that could be avoided if employees had access to such a chart.

16. Prepare a flow chart for one of the following activities:
    a. jumping a "dead" car battery
    b. giving an injection
    c. sending an e-mail
    d. painting a set of louvered doors
    e. making an arrest
    f. putting out an electrical fire
    g. joining a chat group on the Internet
    h. preparing a visual using a graphics software package
    i. any job you do

17. Draw an interior view of a piece of equipment you use in your major, then identify the relevant parts using callouts.

18. Prepare a drawing of one of the following simple tools and include appropriate callouts with your visual.
    a. golf club
    b. hammer
    c. pliers
    d. stethoscope
    e. swivel chair
    f. stereo speaker
    g. ballpoint pen
    h. soldering iron
    i. table lamp
    j. pair of eyeglasses

19. Prepare appropriate visuals to illustrate the data listed below. In a paragraph immediately after the visual explain why the type of visual you selected is appropriate for this information.
    a. Life expectancy is increasing in America. This growth can be dramatically measured by comparing the number of teenagers with the number of older adults (over age 65) in America during the last few years and then projecting those figures. In 1970 there were approximately 28 million teenagers and 20 million older adults. By 1980 the number of teenagers climbed to 30 million and the number of older adults increased to 25 million. In 1990 there were 27 million teenagers and 31 million older adults. By the year 2000 the number of teenagers should level off to 23 million, but the number of older adults will soar to more than 36 million.
    b. Researchers estimate that for every adult in America 3,985 cigarettes were purchased in 1980; 4,100 in 1985; 3,875 in 1990; 3,490 in 1995; and 2,910 in 2000.

20. Find a photograph that contains some irrelevant clutter. Write a letter to the marketing department of a company for which you presumably work that wants to use the photograph. Tell the department what to delete and why.

21. Following is a visual prepared to accompany a report on problems pilots have encountered with a particular model of jet engine. Redo the visual to make it

easier to read and to organize information. Supply a paragraph to accompany your new visual.

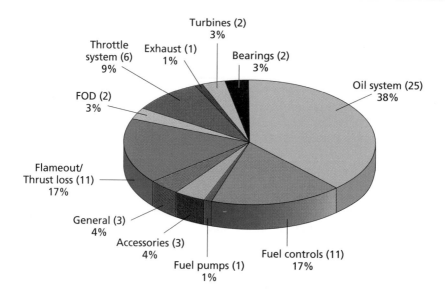

22. Make a simple line drawing of only the relevant portions of the photograph in Exercise 20. Explain in two paragraphs why the drawing works better than the photograph.

23. You work for a large manufacturer of industrial heat pumps and have been asked to help write a section of a report on the increased business your firm has been doing overseas. Based on the sales figures below for the years 1999, 2000, and 2001 (listed in that order) for each of the following countries, prepare two different yet complementary visuals. Also, supply a one-page description and interpretation of the statistics represented in your visuals. You may work collaboratively with one or more students in your class to prepare the visuals as well as to write the section of the report on international sales.

   Argentina, 45, 53, 34; Australia, 78, 90, 115; Bolivia, 23, 43, 52; Brazil, 29, 34, 35; Canada, 116, 234, 256; Denmark, 65, 54, 87; England, 256, 345, 476; France, 198, 167, 345; Germany, 234, 398, 429; Holland, 65, 80, 89; Italy, 49, 52, 97; Japan, 67, 43, 29; New Zealand, 12, 69, 114; Norway, 33, 92, 104; Switzerland, 164, 266, 306; Sweden, 145, 217, 266; People's Republic of China, 7, 100, 296; Korea, 55, 43, 28.

In your written report, take into account trends, shifts in sales, and possible consequences for further marketing and conclude with a specific recommendation to your employer.

Writing Instructions

Clear and accurate instructions are essential to the world of work. Instructions tell—and frequently show—how to do something. They indicate how to perform a procedure (draw blood; change the oil in your car); operate a machine (a pH meter; a digital camera); construct, install, maintain, or repair a piece of equipment (an incubator; a scanner). Everyone from the consumer to the specialist uses and relies on carefully written and designed instructions.

Instructions are found everywhere, from short product inserts to long, complex manuals. Magazines such as *Internet, Popular Mechanics,* and *Popular Photography,* as well as how-to books offer consumers money-saving instructions on topics ranging from repairing their homes to designing a Web site. You might want to read some of those publications and manuals or visit a Web site to see how they identify and meet the needs of the reader trying to perform a certain procedure.

On-line instructions are especially adapted to access from a computer terminal. To assist consumers (and potential buyers) many companies include instructions for their products or services directly on the Internet.

As part of your job, you may be asked to write instructions, alone or with a group, for your co-workers as well as for the customers who use your company's services or products. When writing long, complex instructions, you certainly will be part of a team of engineers, programmers, document design experts, marketing specialists, and even attorneys. But whether the instructions are brief or lengthy, your employer stands to gain or lose much from the quality and the accuracy of the instructions you prepare.

Chapter 13 shows you how to develop, write, illustrate, and design a variety of instructions.

Why Instructions Are Important

Perhaps no other type of occupational writing demands more from the writer than do instructions because so much is at stake—for both you and your reader. The reader has to understand what you write and perform the procedure, as well. You

TECH NOTE

On-Line Instructions

On-line instructions offer added benefits. Most computers have the ability to give you pictures and sounds, but those two features can be limited without additional hardware. With a sound card your computer can provide a much wider range of possibilities, including having someone actually talk you through the various steps of a procedure and alert you to special problem areas. If your computer also has a graphics card, you can speed up the display of images and take advantage of animation that shows the process being done. Such features—visuals and sound—further help instruction writers meet the precise needs of their readers who may need to perform a trial run before attempting a procedure or who may want to double-check a step before going on.

cannot afford to be unclear, inaccurate, or incomplete. Instructions are significant for many reasons, including safety, efficiency, and convenience.

Safety

Carefully written instructions get a job done without damage or injury. Poorly written instructions can be directly responsible for an injury to the person trying to follow them and may result in costly damage claims or even lawsuits. Notice how the product labels in your medicine chest inform users when, how, and why to take a medication safely. Without those instructions, consumers would be endangered by taking too much or too little medicine or by not administering it properly.

Efficiency

Well-written instructions help a business run smoothly and efficiently. No work would be done if employees did not have clear instructions to follow. Imagine how inefficient it would be for a business if employees had to stop their work each time they did not have or could not understand a set of instructions. Or, equally alarming, what if employees made a number of serious mistakes because of confusing directions, costing a business lost sales and increased expenses.

Convenience

Clear, easy-to-follow instructions make a customer's job easier and less frustrating. In the customer's view, instructions reflect a product's quality and a service's quality and convenience. How many times have you heard complaints about a company because the instructions that went with its products were unclear or incomplete? Poorly written and illustrated instructions will cost you business. Instructions are also a vital part of "service after the sale." Owners' manuals, for example, help buyers to avoid a product breakdown (and the headache and expense of starting over) and to keep it in good working order.

The Variety of Instructions: A Brief Overview

Instructions vary in length, complexity, and format. Some instructions are one word long: *stop, lift, rotate, print, erase.* Others are a few sentences long: "Insert blank disk in external disk drive"; "Close tightly after using"; "Store in an upright position." Short instructions are appropriate for the numerous relatively nontechnical chores performed every day as the following procedure illustrates.

How to Replace the Cartridge in a Laser Printer

First, raise the lid of the printer. Press the Off-line button. Move the cartridge tray to the center. Then place your thumb and forefinger on the cartridge and pull it toward you. Lift the empty cartridge out and dispose of it. Insert the new cartridge and push it backward to lock into place. Close the lid.

For more elaborate procedures, detailed instructions may be as long as a page or a book. When your firm purchases a new mainframe computer or a piece of earth-moving equipment, it will receive an instruction pamphlet or book containing many steps, cautionary statements, and diagrams. Many businesses prepare their own training manuals containing instructions for 200 or 300 different procedures.

Instructions can be given in a variety of formats, as Figures 13.1 through 13.4 show. They can be paragraphs (Figure 13.1), employ visuals to illustrate each step

FIGURE 13.1   Instructions on how to repair a halyard.

Easy Temporary Join for Synthetic Ropes

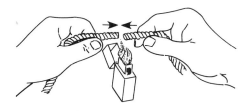

If you are faced with the problem of reeving a new halyard on a flagpole or mast, or through a block or pulley in an inaccessible location, the solution can be easy if both old and new lines are made of nylon or polyester (Dacron, Terylene, etc.). Simply join the ends of the old and new lines temporarily by melting end fibers together in a small flame (a little heat goes a long way). Rotate the two lines slowly as the fibers melt. Withdraw them from the flame before a ball of molten material forms, and if the stuff ignites, blow out the flame at once. Hold the joint together until it is cool and firm.

Source: R. I. Standish, *Parks.*

FIGURE 13.2   Instructions that supply a visual with each step.

Proper Brushing

Proper brushing is essential for cleaning teeth and gums effectively. Use a toothbrush with soft, nylon, round-ended bristles that will not scratch and irritate teeth or damage gums.

1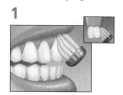

Place bristles along the gumline at a 45-degree angle. Bristles should contact both the tooth surface and the gumline.

2

Gently brush the outer tooth surfaces of 2–3 teeth using a vibrating back and forth rolling motion. Move brush to the next group of 2–3 teeth and repeat.

3

Maintain a 45-degree angle with bristles contacting the tooth surface and gumline. Gently brush, using back, forth, and rolling motion along all of the inner tooth surfaces.

4

Tilt brush vertically behind the front teeth. Make several up and down strokes using the front half of the brush.

5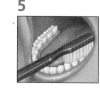

Place the brush against the biting surface of the teeth and use a gentle back and forth scrubbing motion. Brush the tongue from back to front to remove odor-producing bacteria.

Source: Reprinted by permission of American Dental Hygienists' Association. Illustrations adapted and used courtesy of the John O. Butler Company, makers of *GUM* Healthcare products.

FIGURE 13.3   Instructions given in a numbered list describing a sequence of steps.

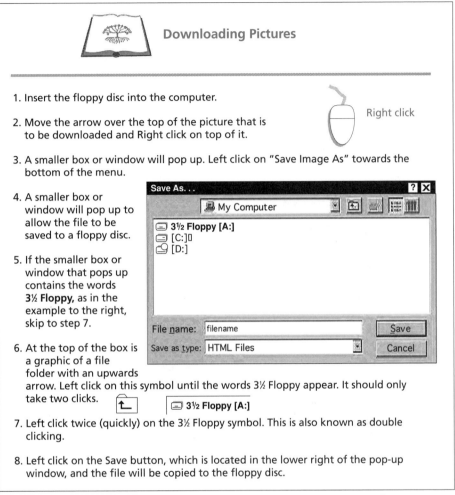

Downloading Pictures

1. Insert the floppy disc into the computer.

2. Move the arrow over the top of the picture that is to be downloaded and Right click on top of it.

    Right click

3. A smaller box or window will pop up. Left click on "Save Image As" towards the bottom of the menu.

4. A smaller box or window will pop up to allow the file to be saved to a floppy disc.

5. If the smaller box or window that pops up contains the words **3½ Floppy,** as in the example to the right, skip to step 7.

6. At the top of the box is a graphic of a file folder with an upwards arrow. Left click on this symbol until the words 3½ Floppy appear. It should only take two clicks.

    🔼   ☐ **3½ Floppy [A:]**

7. Left click twice (quickly) on the 3½ Floppy symbol. This is also known as double clicking.

8. Left click on the Save button, which is located in the lower right of the pop-up window, and the file will be copied to the floppy disc.

Save As. . .   ? ☒

    🖳 My Computer

☐ **3½ Floppy [A:]**
☐ [C:]▯
☐ [D:]

File name: filename   Save

Save as type: HTML Files   Cancel

Source: Elkhart (Indiana) Public Library. Reprinted by permission of Brent Ferguson and Diana Gill.

(Figure 13.2), or use a numbered list (Figures 13.3 and 13.4). You will have to determine which format is most appropriate for the kinds of instructions you write.

Assessing and Meeting Your Audience's Needs

Regardless of the format (paragraphs or lists), instructions must be clear, complete, and easy to follow. Put yourself in the readers' position. In most instances you will not be available for readers to ask you questions when they do not understand something. Consequently, they will have to rely only on your written instructions. Your purpose in writing the instructions is to get the readers to perform the same steps you followed and, more important, to obtain the same results you did.

FIGURE 13.4   Instructions in a numbered list on how to assemble an outdoor grill.

ASSEMBLY INSTRUCTIONS

The instructions shown below are for the basic grill with tubular legs. If you have a pedestal grill, or a grill with accessories, check the separate instruction sheet for details not shown here.

NOTE: Make sure you locate all the parts before discarding any of the packaging material.

TOOLS REQUIRED . . . A standard straight blade screwdriver is the only tool you need to assemble your new Meco grill. If you have a pedestal grill, you will need a 7-16 wrench or a small adjustable wrench.

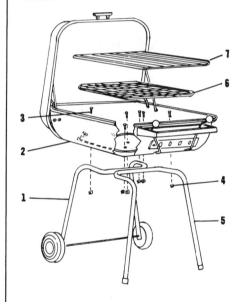

1. Before you start, take time to read through this manual. Inside you will find many helpful hints that will help you get the full potential of enjoyment and service from your new Meco grill.

2. Lay out all the parts.

3. Assemble roller leg (1) to bottom rear of bowl (2) with 1¼″ long bolts (3) and nuts (4).

4. Assemble fixed leg (5) to bottom front of bowl (2) with 1¼″ long bolts (3) and nuts (4).

5. Place fire grate—ash dump (6) in bottom of bowl (2) between adjusting levers.

6. Place cooking grid (7) on top of adjusting levers. Make sure top grid wires run from front to back of grill.

Source: Meco Assembly Instructions and Owners Manual, Metals Engineering Corp., P.O. Box 3005, Greenville, TN 37743. Reprinted by permission.

Do not assume that members of your audience have performed the procedure before or have operated the equipment as many times as you have. (If they had, there would be no need for your instructions.) No writer of instructions ever disappointed readers by making directions too clear or too easy to follow. Keep in mind that your audience will often include non-native speakers of English, a worldwide audience of potential consumers.

Writing instructions is like teaching. Not only must you understand the material yourself, you also must know the best way of presenting it. Set goals for your readers the way a teacher sets goals for students in a course: Establish what you want them to do, how, and why.

Key Questions to Ask About Your Audience

To prepare effective instructions, learn all you can about your audience. Try to anticipate your readers' questions and problems. The best way to establish your audience's needs is to ask yourself the following questions:

- How and why will my readers use my instructions? (Engineers have different expectations than do office personnel and customers.)
- How much do my readers already know about the procedure they have to follow?
- How much essential background or introductory information will I have to supply?
- What steps will most likely cause readers trouble?
- How often will they use my instructions—every day or just as a refresher?
- Where will my audience most likely be following my instructions—in the workplace, outdoors, in a workshop equipped with tools, or alone in their homes?
- What resources—such as special equipment or power sources—will my readers need to perform my instructions successfully?

The Process of Writing Instructions

As we saw in Chapter 2, clear and concise writing evolves when you follow a process. To make sure your instructions are accurate and easy for your audience to perform, follow these steps.

Plan Your Steps

Before writing, do some research to understand completely the job or procedure that you are asking someone else to perform. Make sure you know

- the reason for doing something
- the parts or tools required
- the steps to follow to get the job done
- the results of the job
- the potential risks or dangers

If you are not absolutely sure about the procedure, ask an expert for a demonstration. Do some background reading and talk to or e-mail colleagues who may have written or performed a similar instruction.

If you work collaboratively, everyone in your group needs to understand the procedure, from start to finish. An uneven level of expertise among group members spells trouble; some steps of your instructions will be complete and accurate while others may not be.

Do a Trial Run

Actually perform the procedure (assembling, repairing, maintaining, dissecting) yourself or with all your writing team present. Go through a number of trial runs. Take notes as you go along and be sure to divide the procedure into simple, distinct steps for readers to follow. Don't give readers too much to do in any one step. Each step should be **complete, sequential, reliable, straightforward,** and **easy** for your audience to identify and perform.

Write and Test Your Draft

Transform your notes into a draft (or drafts) of the instructions you want readers to follow. Test your draft(s) by asking someone from the intended audience (consumers, technicians) who may never have performed the procedure to follow your instructions as you have written them. Observe where the individual runs into difficulty—cannot complete or seems to miss a step, gets a result different from yours. Do not coach the reader with verbal cues. Your intended readers won't have you there to coach them. Then note any places in your instructions that are vague, hard to follow, inconsistent (steps bunched up or out of order), or incomplete. Ask your experimenter-user what stumped him or her.

Revise and Edit

Based on your observations and user feedback, revise your draft(s) and edit the final copy of the instructions that you will give to readers. Always consider whether your instructions would be easier to accomplish if you included visuals. (To use and incorporate visuals, see pp. 514–521).

As you revise and edit, pay special attention to the technical language and the amount of detail you include. Analyzing the needs and the background of your audience will help you to determine which words and details are appropriate. A set of instructions accompanying a chemistry set would use different terminology, abbreviations, and level of detail than would a set of instructions a professor gives a class in organic chemistry.

> General audience: Place 8 drops of vinegar in a test tube with a piece of limestone about the size of a pea.
>
> Specialized audience: Place 8 gtts of CH_3COOH in a test tube and add 1 mg of CO_3.

The instructions for the general audience avoid the technical abbreviations and symbols the specialized audience requires. If your readers are puzzled by your directions, you defeat your reasons for writing them.

Using the Right Style

To write instructions that readers can understand and turn into effective action, observe the following guidelines.

1. Use verbs in the present tense and imperative mood. Imperatives are commands that have deleted the pronoun *you*. Note how the instructions in Figures 13.1 through 13.4 contain imperatives—"Move the arrow" instead of "You move the arrow." Deleting the *you* is not discourteous, as it would be in a business letter or report. The command tells readers, "These steps work, so do them exactly as stated." Choose action verbs such as those listed in Table 13.1.

TABLE 13.1   Some Helpful Imperative Verbs Used in Instructions

adjust	determine	insert	pour	save	tilt
apply	dig	inspect	press	saw	transfer
blow	download	lift	prevent	scan	transect
boot up	drag	load in	print	scroll	trim
call up	drain	loosen	pull	send	turn
change	drill	lower	push	shift	twist
check	drop	lubricate	raise	shut off	type
choose	ease	measure	release	slide	unplug
clean	eliminate	mount	remove	slip	use
click	enter	move	reply	spread	ventilate
clip	flip	notify	review	start	verify
close	forward	oil	roll	switch	wash
connect	freeze	open	rotate	tear	wind
cut	hold	paste	rub	tie	wipe
delete	increase	point	run	tighten	wire

2. Write clear, short sentences in the active voice. Keep sentences short and uncomplicated. Sentences under twenty words (preferably under fifteen) are easy to read. Note that the sentences in Figures 13.1 through 13.4 are, for the most part, under fifteen words.

Avoid the passive voice. Instead of "The air blower is to be used last," write "Use the air blower last." Do not write a sentence that sends the reader the opposite message from what you intend. A direction such as "Before using the soldering iron on metal, clean it with Freon" may mislead the inexperienced welder to put Freon on the iron rather than on the metal that is to be cleaned.

3. Use precise terms for measurements, distances, and times. Indefinite, vague directions leave users wondering whether they are doing the right thing. The following vague directions are better expressed through precise revisions.

> Vague: Turn the distributor cap a little. (*How much is a little?*)
> Precise: Turn the distributor cap one quarter of a rotation.
>
> Vague: Let the contents cool for a while. (*How long?*)
> Precise: Let the contents cool for 10 minutes.

Precise measurement and timing are essential to the success of many kinds of instructions, from baking a cake to completing a blood test in a laboratory.

4. Use connective words as signposts. Connective words specify the exact order in which something is to be done (especially when your instructions are written in paragraphs). Words such as *first, then, before,* for example, help readers stay on course, reinforcing the sequence of the procedures.

5. Number each step when you present your instructions in a list. You also can use bullets. Plenty of white space between steps also distinctly separates them for the reader.

Using Visuals Effectively

Readers welcome visuals in almost any set of instructions. Visuals are graphic and direct, helping readers to understand what they must do. A visual can

- simplify a process
- identify the location and size of a part
- show the relationships among components
- reinforce or even save words
- illustrate the "right" way and the "wrong" way
- increase readers' confidence
- help get a job done more quickly

For example, the illustration in Figure 13.1 reinforces the process of joining the two parts of the halyard by fire. Another frequently used visual in instructions is an exploded drawing, like the one in Figure 13.4, which helps consumers see how the various parts of the grill fit together.

The number and kinds of visuals you include will, of course, depend on the procedure or equipment you are explaining and your audience's background and needs. Some instructions may require only one or two visuals. The instructions in Figure 13.3 show users what they can expect to see on a screen as they download a visual. The shot of the screen clarifies the procedure and assists the reader.

Guidelines for Using Visuals in Instructions

Follow these guidelines to use visuals effectively.

1. Whenever possible, place the visual next to the step it illustrates, not on another page or buried at the bottom of the page. To gain the most from visuals, readers must be able to see the illustrations or diagrams immediately before and after reading the accompanying directions.
2. If you are using many visuals, assign each one a number (Figure 1, Figure 2) and refer to the visuals by figure number in your instructions.
3. Make sure the visual looks like the object the user is trying to assemble, maintain, run, or repair. Don't use a photo of an earlier or different model.
4. Always inform readers if a part of an object is missing or reduced in size in your visual.
5. Where necessary, label parts of the visual, as the drawing in Figure 13.4 does.
6. Set each visual off with white space so it is easy to find and examine.

A Portfolio of Instructional Visuals

Figures 13.5 through 13.14 illustrate the variety of visuals you can use to clarify instructions, including photographs, sketches, computer screens, cutaway drawings, exploded drawings, charts, and tables. Study the visuals in these figures to see how they help explain a procedure.

FIGURE 13.5   A photograph showing how a procedure is performed.

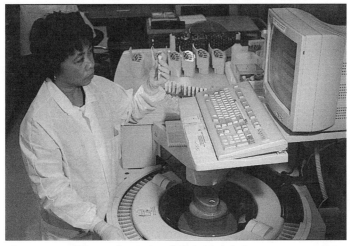

Photo courtesy of The American Society of Clinical Pathologists.

FIGURE 13.6   Exclusive use of visuals to show proper care of a laptop computer.

Source: By permission of 3D Microcomputers.

FIGURE 13.7 A drawing showing how to prune a tree.

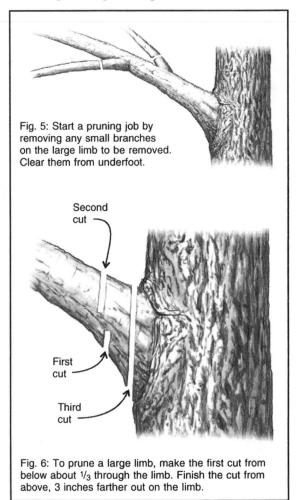

Fig. 5: Start a pruning job by removing any small branches on the large limb to be removed. Clear them from underfoot.

Second cut
First cut
Third cut

Fig. 6: To prune a large limb, make the first cut from below about 1/3 through the limb. Finish the cut from above, 3 inches farther out on the limb.

Source: Lowe's, *Using Chain Saws,* How-To Booklet 151. Reprinted by permission of Creative Homeowner Press.

FIGURE 13.8   A computer screen and an illustration explaining how to use a mouse.

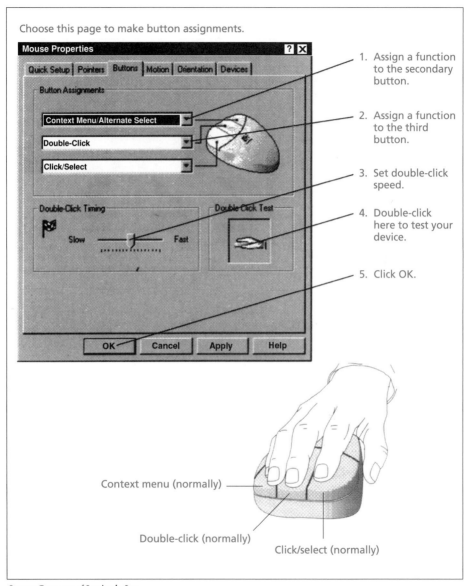

Choose this page to make button assignments.

1. Assign a function to the secondary button.

2. Assign a function to the third button.

3. Set double-click speed.

4. Double-click here to test your device.

5. Click OK.

Context menu (normally)

Double-click (normally)

Click/select (normally)

Source: Courtesy of Logitech, Inc.

FIGURE 13.9   Cutaway drawing illustrating some common modes of infection in a hospital.

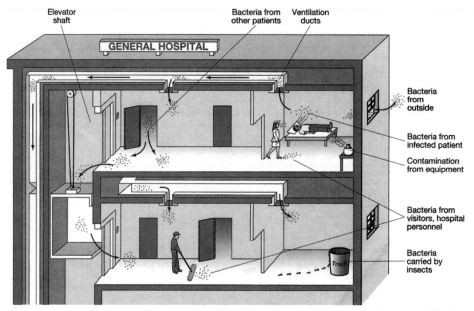

Source: Jacquelyn G. Black, *Microbiology: Principles and Explorations,* 4th ed. (Upper Saddle River, NJ: Prentice Hall, 1999). Copyright © Jacquelyn G. Black.

FIGURE 13.10   Table listing workstation noise levels.

Reaction	dB	Source Comparison
Uncomfortably loud (possible ear pain)	140 120 105	Jackhammer at 2 feet Thunder (near) 12" circular saw at 2 feet
Very loud	90 to 100	Industrial plant, wire mill, boiler factory
Loud	80 to 90	Foundry factory, press room
Moderate	70 to 75	Normal conversation in office at 3 feet
Quiet	40 to 55	Hospital room
Very quiet	30 to 35	Whisper at 2 feet

Source: Robert L. Smith and Stephen L. Herman, *Electrical Wiring: Industrial,* 7th ed. Copyright © 1999 by Delmor Publishers. Reprinted by permission.

FIGURE 13.11   A map and photo illustrating car navigation system and how it works.

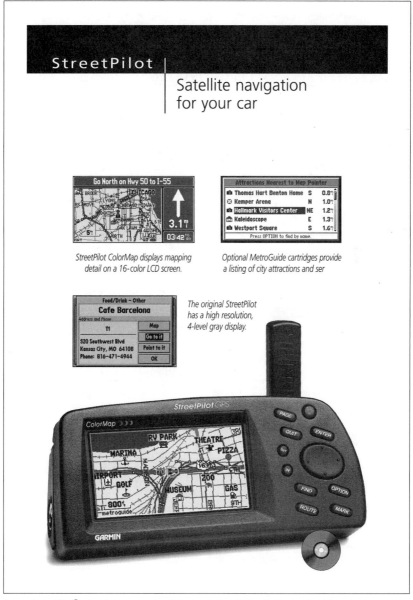

Source: StreetPilot® advertisement reprinted by permission of Garmin International, Inc.

FIGURE 13.12   Picture chart giving instructions on how to prepare materials for curbside recycling.

FIGURE 13.13   Computer screen showing how to use a connection wizard.

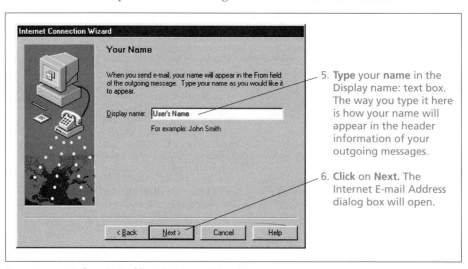

Source: Internet Explorer 4.0 (Rocklin, CA: Prima, 1997), p. 181.

FIGURE 13.14   Exploded drawing and how to assemble an industrial extension cord.

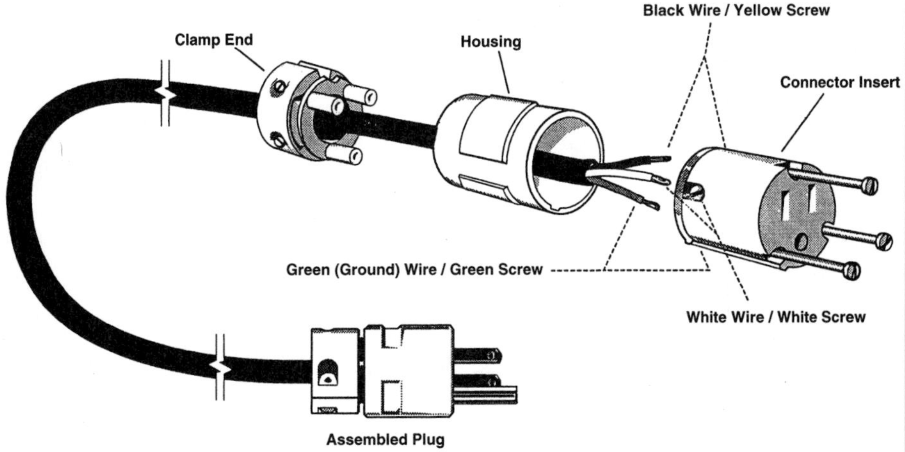

1. Run the end of the cord through the clamp and then through the center hole of the housing.
2. Pull the cord through until it extends 2 inches beyond the housing.
3. Strip about 1¼ inches of outer insulation from the end of the cord.
4. Twist the exposed ends to prevent stray strands.

Source: Drawing courtesy of Sally Eddy and Georgia-Pacific Company.

The Four Parts of Instructions

Except for very short instructions, such as those illustrated in Figures 13.1 through 13.4, a set of instructions generally contains four main parts: (1) an introduction, (2) a list of equipment and materials, (3) the actual steps to perform the process, and (4) a conclusion (when necessary).

The Introduction

The function of an introduction is to provide readers with enough *necessary* background information to understand why and how your instructions work. An introduction must make readers feel comfortable and well prepared before they turn to the actual steps.

Whether you need an introduction depends on the particular process or equipment you are describing. Short instructions require no introduction or only a brief one- or two-sentence introduction. More complex instructions require lengthier introductions. For instance, a ninety-page instruction manual may contain a two- or three-page introduction.

An introduction should be proportional to the kind of instructions that will be given. For example, instructions on how to sand a floor will not need a one-page introduction on how friction works.

What You Include in an Introduction

You can do one or all of the following in your introduction. Not every introduction to a set of instructions will contain facts in all five categories of information listed. Some instructions will require less detail. You will have to judge how much background information to give readers for the specific instructions you write.

Refer to Figure 13.15, which is an introduction to a guide for nurses who have to know how to use an infusion pump.

1. State why the instructions are useful for a specific audience. Many instructions begin with introductions that stress safety, educational, or occupational benefits. Here is an introduction from a safety procedure describing protective lockout of equipment:

> The purpose of this procedure is to provide plant electrical technicians with a uniform method of locking out machinery or equipment. This will prevent the possibility of setting moving parts in motion, energizing electrical lines, or opening valves while repair, set-up, or cleaning work is in progress.

Figure 13.15 highlights the safety and convenience of a piece of equipment for the nursing staff as they meet patients' needs.

2. Indicate how a particular machine, procedure, or process works. An introduction can briefly discuss the "theory of operation," to help readers understand why something works the way your instructions say it should. Such a discussion sometimes describes a scientific law or principle. An introduction to instructions on how to run an autoclave begins by explaining the function of the machine: "These instructions will teach you how to operate an autoclave, which is used to sterilize surgical instruments through the live additive-free stream."

The introduction in Figure 13.15 describes the different modes of the infusion pump and the pump itself.

3. Specify how long it should take to complete all steps of the instructions. If users know how long a procedure should take, they will be better able to judge whether they are doing it correctly—if they are waiting too long or not long enough between steps or if they are going too slowly or too quickly: "It should take about three and one-half hours from the time you start laying the floor tiles until the time they are dry enough to walk on." The introduction in Fig. 13.15 helpfully specifies delivery rates of medicines per hour. You may also have to advise readers when a certain procedure must be monitored or performed. For example, instructions for a premium cartridge for laser printers tell purchasers that they must clean their cartridge corona at the time of installation and after every thousand copies.

4. Stress any advantages or benefits the reader will gain by performing the instructions. Make the reader feel good about buying or using your product by explaining how it will make a job easier to perform, save the reader time and

FIGURE 13.15   Introduction to a guide for using an infusion pump.

1 Overview Orientation

Gives function of equipment

The LifeCare PROVIDER 5500 System is a portable infusion pump, specially designed to deliver analgesic drugs, antibiotics, and chemotherapeutics.

The pump can be programmed in either milligrams or cubic centimeters, and in four different delivery configurations for greater nursing convenience and to tailor precisely the most effective regimen for each patient.

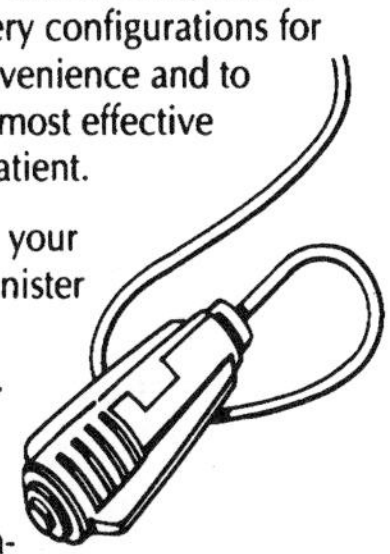

Describes different modes or options

Bolus Mode allows your patient to self-administer analgesia within programmed limits.

This is the traditional PCA delivery, "analgesia-on-demand," based on the patient's need.

Continuous Mode delivers a continuous "background" infusion with no additional PCA doses permitted.

Continuous-plus-Bolus Mode allows the patient to self-administer a Bolus dose in addition to receiving a simultaneous Continuous dose infusion.

Intermittent Mode delivers a specific dose (in cc or mg) at intermittent intervals over 24 hours.

Emphasizes safety features

You can also establish the "lockout" interval, the frequency with which a patient may receive a Bolus dose of analgesic drug.

The PROVIDER 5500 System records all settings in memory and can be quickly re-programmed to save nursing time when repeating established protocols or changing fluid reservoirs.

Saves time

The portable system operates on battery power.

To minimize tampering and discourage theft, there is an optional locking security lockbox that also secures the system to an IV pole.

Offers security

The audible alarm signals in the event of a malfunction, and the digital readout describes the malfunction.

● Compact and lightweight.

Explains convenience features

● Delivery rates between 0.1 cc and 250 cc per hour, in 0.1-cc increments.

Display Panel

● Individual display indicators appear only during programming and operation.

● Only on a *selective* basis.

● Tone sounds when activated.

● Runs on BATTERY POWER ONLY.

● Disposable Primary IV set with integral infusion cartridge.

Reprinted by permission of Abbott Laboratories Hospital Products Division.

money, or allow the reader to accomplish a job with fewer mistakes or false starts. Note how the following introduction to a set of instructions on using an auto dial/auto answer modem encourages the reader to want to learn how to operate this system.

Welcome to high-speed telecommunications and congratulations on choosing the Signalman EXPRESSi. You've made an excellent choice. The EXPRESSi is the ideal link between your computer and the ever-expanding world of information utilities, databases, electronic mail, bulletin boards, computer time sharing, and more.

The EXPRESSi can be used in the IBM Personal Computer. And because the EXPRESSi fits inside your PC, it saves valuable desk space and eliminates expensive, bulky cables.[1]

Nurses learn from the introduction in Figure 13.15 that the infusion pump is quickly reprogrammed.

5. Inform the user about any special circumstances to which the instructions apply. Some instructions precede others or are used only on special occasions. Readers must be informed about those changes or emergency situations. The introduction in Figure 13.15 alerts nursing staff to an audible alarm signal in the event of a malfunction.

Two Short Case Studies on Meeting Audience's Needs

The instructions contained in Figures 13.16 and 13.17 are addressed to two different audiences, each with separate needs. The Hercules memo in Figure 13.16 was sent to a technical audience—firefighters and supervisors—who needed instructions on a special process. Cliff Burgess's memo in Figure 13.17, on the other hand, went to all Burton employees, a more diverse, rather than technical, group of readers. His helpful instructions do not require a list of equipment or materials or a description of steps in a process. Instead, his memo consists of an introduction, three bulleted instructions, a conclusion, and a visual attachment.

List of Equipment and Materials

Immediately after the introduction, inform readers of all equipment or materials they will need. Make your list complete and clear. Do not wait until the readers are actually performing one of the steps to tell them that a certain type of drill or a specific kind of chemical is required. They may have to stop what they are doing to find the equipment or material; moreover, the procedure may fail or present hazards if users do not have the right equipment at the right time.

---

[1]Courtesy of Anchor Automation, Inc., Chatsworth, Calif.

Do not expect your readers to know exactly what size, model, or quantity is necessary for a specific job. Tell them precisely, as Figure 13.18 does. For example, if a Phillips screwdriver is essential to complete one step, specify that type of screwdriver under the heading "Equipment and Materials"; do not list just "screwdriver." Here are some additional examples of unclear references to equipment and materials, with more helpful alternatives given in parentheses: solution (0.7% NaCl solution); pencils (two engineering pencils); electrodes (four short platinum-wire electrodes); file (cheese-grater file); sand (10-lb. bag of sand); needle (butterfly needle); water (2 gallons untreated seawater).

The Procedural Steps

The heart of your instructions will consist of clearly distinguished steps that readers must follow to achieve the desired results. Figure 13.19 contains a model set of steps on how to connect a computer monitor. Note how each step is precisely keyed to

FIGURE 13.16   Instructions alerting a technical audience to special circumstances.

TO: All Shift Supervisors
                All Firefighters
FROM: Robert Ferguson *R.F.*
SUBJECT: Operating Procedures During Energy Shortages
DATE: October 10, 2000

The following policy has been formulated to help in maintaining required pressures during periods of low wood flow and severe natural gas curtailment.

All boilers are equipped with lances to burn residue or no. 6 fuel oil as auxiliary fuels. When wood is short, no. 6 oil should be burned in no. 2 and no. 3 boilers at highest possible rate consistent with smoke standards. To do this, take these steps:

1. Put no. 6 oil on No. 3 boiler lances.
2. Shut down overfire air.
3. Shut down forced draft.
4. Turn off vibrators.
5. Keep grates covered with ashes or wood until ash cover exists.

These steps will result in an output of 25,000 to 35,000 lbs./hr. steam from no. 3 boiler and will force wood on down to no. 4 boiler.

If necessary, the same procedure can be repeated on no. 2 boiler.

Used by permission of Hercules, Inc.

FIGURE 13.17   An instructional memo listing safety precautions for a general audience.

BURTON WORLDWIDE SYSTEMS
www.burton.com

TO: All Burton Employees
FROM: Cliff Burgess, Environmental Safety C.B.
RE: Video Display Terminal (VDT) Safety Precautions
DATE: September 2, 2000

Introduction emphasizes reasons for instructions, gives nontechnical explanation, and offers an analogy

You may experience some possible health risks in using your computer video display terminal (VDT). These risks include sleep disorders, behavioral changes, danger to the reproductive system, and cancer.

The source of any risks comes from the electromagnetic fields (EMFs) that surround anything that carries an electric current—for example, copiers, circuit breakers, and especially VDTs. Your computer monitor is a major source of EMFs. Magnetic fields can go through walls as easily as light goes through glass.

Although EMFs may affect your health, you can considerably reduce your exposure to these fields by following these three simple steps:

Explains how to use equipment; steps stand out through bullets, bold-face, and spacing

- **Stay at least three feet (an arm's length) away from the front of your VDT.** (The magnetic field is significantly reduced with this amount of distance.)

- **Stay at least four feet away from the sides and back of someone else's VDT.** (The fields are weaker in the front of the VDT but much stronger everywhere else.) Refer to the following sketch, which you may want to post in your office.

Uses visual to clarify instructions

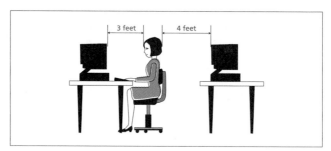

1215 Madison ♦ St. Louis, Missouri 63174
314-555-4300 ♦ FAX 314-555-4311

Continued

FIGURE 13.17   (Continued)

2.

- **Switch your VDT/computer off when you are not using it.** (If the computer has to remain on, be sure to switch off the monitor; screen savers do not affect the exposure to **EMFs**.)

Conclusion reassures readers they are acting safely by following instructions

Our environmental safety team will continue to monitor and investigate any problems. Observing the guidelines above, however, will help you to take all the necessary precautions in order to minimize your exposure to EMFs.

If you have any questions about these procedures or your exposure to EMFs, please e-mail me at burg@burton.com.

Reprinted by permission.

the visual, further helping readers perform the procedure. Refer to Fig. 13.19 as you study this section. To make sure that you help your readers understand your steps, observe the following rules.

1. Put the steps in their correct order. If a step is out of order or is missing, the entire set of instructions can be wrong or, worse yet, dangerous. Double-check every step and number each step to indicate its correct place in the sequence of events you are describing. Never put an asterisk (*) before or after a step to make the reader look somewhere else for information. If the information is important, put it in your instructions; if it is not, delete it.

2. Group closely related activities into one step. Sometimes closely related actions are grouped into one step to help the reader coordinate activities and to emphasize their being done at the same time, in the same place, or with the same equipment. See how step 4 does that in Figure 13.19.

To cite a further example, instructions on how to use a fax machine are clearer when distinct steps are stated separately. The first set of instructions below incorrectly tells users how to transmit a fax by combining steps that must be performed separately. Step 2 asks users to pick up the phone and then dial the number—two separate actions. Step 3 asks users to press the button and return the handset, again two actions that cannot be performed simultaneously.

Incorrect: 1. Load the paper into the outgoing document slot, adjusting the paper guides to the appropriate width.

2. Pick up the telephone handset and listen for a dial tone. When you hear the dial tone, dial the number of the receiving fax machine.

FIGURE 13.18   Illustrated list of jacks and cables needed to connect a DVD player.

Before deciding which method to connect the DVD player, take a moment to familiarize yourself with the different types of jacks and cable.

S-Video Jack and Cable (S-VHS)
The S-Video jack provides excellent picture quality for your DVD player. The jack is available on many TVs. Because the S-Video jack carries only the picture signal, and not the sound, you'll also need to connect the left and right audio cables.

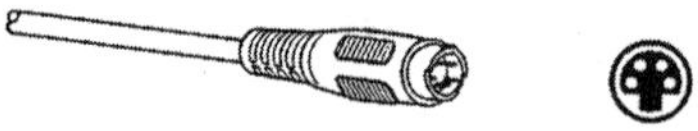

S-Video jack

Audio/Video Jacks and Cables (RCA-type)
The audio/video jacks provide very good picture and stereo sound quality, and should be used if your TV has no S-Video jack. Each jack is color coded (yellow for video, red for right audio, and white for left audio). If your TV has only one input for audio (mono), you may need a Y-adapter (not included) to combine sound from both channels.

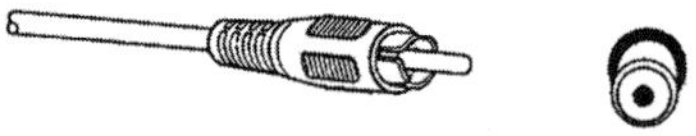

Audio/video jack

Digital Cable
If you own a Dolby Digital receiver with an optical digital input, you can use that cable to connect the DVD player to that receiver to get the best sound quality. All six channels of audio will be transmitted over this cable.

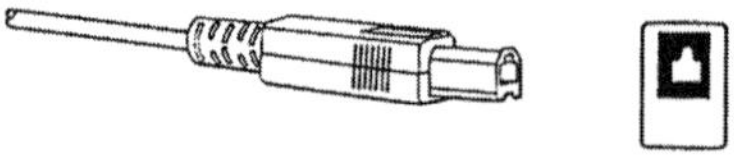

Digital jack

RF Jacks and Coaxial Cables (F-type)
You may not need coaxial cables to connect the DVD player to your TV, but you may need to use coaxial cables to carry the cable, satellite, or off-air signal to your television.

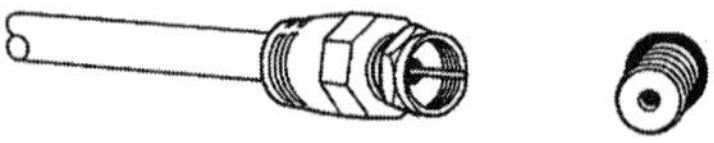

Coaxial jack

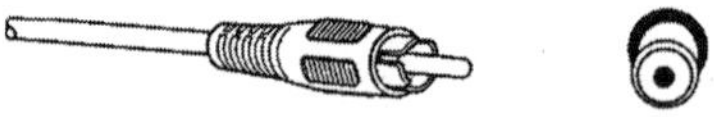

RF jack

RF Modulator
If your television has only an RF input jack, you will need to use an RF modulator (not included) to convert the line output signal to an RF signal.

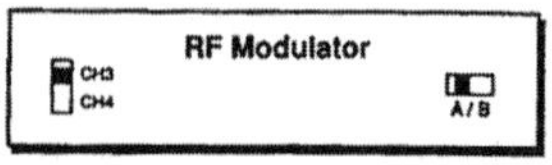

RF Modulator

CH3
CH4

A/B

(front)

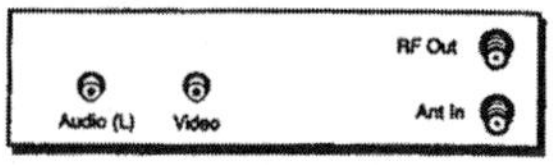

RF Out

Audio (L)   Video   Ant In

(back)

Source: Reprinted by permission of Thomson Consumer Electronics. "Dolby" is a trademark of Dolby Laboratories.

FIGURE 13.19   Instructions (with visual) on how to connect a computer monitor.

Connecting the Monitor to the Computer

1   Make sure the monitor and computer are turned off. (See previous section on safety.)

2   Connect the power cord to the back of the display.

3   Plug the other end of the cable into a grounded outlet.

4   Connect the video cable on the monitor to the 15-pin video graphics connector on the rear panel of the computer, and tighten the fastening screws. (If you have an HP Pavilion computer, this port is marked in orange. For other computers, check your computer manual for the video port location.)

   Note: *Don't force the cable into the connector; line it up carefully so you don't bend the pins.*

5   Connect the microphone cable to the computer's sound input. On HP computers, this port is yellow. The end of the cable is also yellow.

6   Connect the microphone cable to the monitor. The connector and the cable end are both yellow.

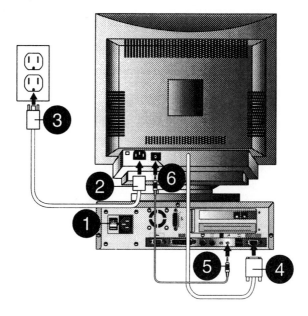

Source: Copyright © 1999 Hewlett-Packard Company. Reproduced with permission.

3. When the receiving fax machine answers the ring, press the start button. After the transmission is completed, return the handset to its cradle.

Correct: 1. Load the paper into the outgoing document slot, adjusting the paper guides to the appropriate width.
2. Pick up the telephone handset and listen for a dial tone.
3. When you hear a dial tone, dial the number of the receiving fax machine.
4. When the receiving fax machine answers the ring, press the start button.
5. After the transmission is completed, return the handset to its cradle.

Don't divide an action into two steps if it has to be done in one. For example, instructions showing how to light a furnace would not list as two steps actions that must be performed simultaneously to avoid a possible explosion.

Incorrect: 1. Depress the lighting valve.
2. Hold a match to the pilot light.

Correct: 1. Depress the lighting valve while holding a match to the pilot light.

Similarly, do not separate two steps of a computer command that must be performed simultaneously.

Incorrect: 1. Press the CONTROL key.
2. Press the ALT key.

Correct: 1. While holding down the CONTROL key, press the ALT key.

3. Give the reader hints on how best to accomplish the procedure. Obviously, you cannot do that for every step, but if there is a chance that the reader might run into difficulties or may not anticipate a certain reaction, by all means provide assistance. Steps 4, 5, and 6 in Figure 13.19 offer readers helpful hints. Particular techniques on how to operate or service equipment also assist readers: "If there is blood on the transducer diaphragm, dip the transducer in a blood solvent, such as hydrogen peroxide, Hemosol, etc." If readers have a choice of materials or procedures in a given step, you might want to list those that would give the best performance: "Several thin coats will give a better finish than one heavy coat."

4. State whether one step directly influences (or jeopardizes) the outcome of another. Because all steps in a set of instructions are interrelated, you could not (and should not have to) tell readers how every step affects another. But stating specific relationships is particularly helpful when dangerous or highly intricate operations are involved. You will save the reader time, and you will stress the need for care. Forewarned is forearmed. Here is an example.

Step 2: Tighten fan belt. Failure to tighten the fan belt will cause it to loosen and come off when the lever is turned in step 5.

Do not wait until step 5 to tell readers that you hope they did a good job in tightening the fan belt in step 2. That information comes after the fact.

Warnings, Cautions, and Notes
At appropriate places in your steps you may have to stop the reader to issue a warning, a caution, or a note.

Warnings. A warning tells readers that a step, if not prepared for or performed properly, can endanger their safety.

WARNING: UNPLUG THE MONITOR BEFORE CLEANING ANY
PART WITH DAMP CLOTH.

DO NOT APPLY PRESSURE UNTIL SAFETY VALVE IS
COMPLETELY SEALED.

Cautions. A caution tells a reader how to avoid a mistake that could damage equipment or to take certain precautions—"Wear protective goggles"; "Do not force the plug."

CAUTION
MAKE SURE BRAKE SHOES WON'T RUB TIRE AND THAT
SHOES MATE WELL WITH RIM WHEN BRAKES ARE APPLIED.

BE SURE TO ENTER CORRECT CODE FOR **WORD SMART.**
KEYBOARDING THE WRONG CODE WILL ERASE DOCUMENT.

Caution: **Formatting erases all data on the disk**

Notes. A note adds a clarification, provides a helpful hint on how to do the step most efficiently, or lists different options.

Drive B disk indicator will glow and the drive will make a few clicking sounds as the disk is formatted.

At 20 degrees F, a battery uses about 68 percent of its power.

You can resize an image during transformation by clicking and dragging the handles in the upper left or lower right corner. You can also move the image in the workspace by dragging it with your mouse curser.

Guidelines on Using Warnings, Cautions, and Notes

1. **Do not regard warnings and cautions as optional.** They are vital for legal and safety reasons to protect lives and property. In fact, you and your company can be sued if you fail to notify the users of your product or service of potentially dangerous conditions.
2. **Put warnings and cautions in the right place.** Place them immediately before the step to which they pertain. If you insert a warning or caution statement too early, readers may forget it by the time they come to the step to which it applies. And if you put the notification too late, you almost certainly expose the reader to danger and the equipment to breakdown.
3. **Put warnings and cautions in a distinctive format.** Warnings and cautions should be graphically set apart from the rest of the instructions. There should be no chance that readers will overlook them. Put such statements in capital letters, boldface type, boxes, different colors (red is especially effective for warnings, yellow for caution). Be careful, though, about using colors for non-native speakers of English. Use one or all of those devices. A symbol, like a skull and crossbones, an exclamation point inside a triangle, or a traffic stoplight is often used to draw the reader's attention to a warning.
4. **Include enough explanation to help readers know what to watch out for and what precautions to take.** Do not just insert the word WARNING or CAUTION. Explain what the dangerous condition is and how to avoid it. Look at the examples of warnings and cautions in Figure 13.20.
5. **Do not include a warning or a caution just to emphasize a point.** Putting too many in your instructions will decrease the dramatic impact they should have on readers. Use them sparingly—only when absolutely necessary—so readers will not be tempted to ignore them.
6. **Use notes only when the procedure calls for them and they will help readers.**

> ### TECH NOTE
>
> **Using Icons**
>
> You can use icons to draw readers' attention to warnings, cautions, notes, even tips. You can find a wide range of icons with any graphics software package you use. Once you select an icon, it is easy to paste it into any word processing document. But choose your icons carefully; use them only when they are functional and unambiguous. An icon of a trash can might ambiguously signal that material is to be thrown away as well as to be saved.

The Conclusion

Not every set of instructions requires a conclusion. For short instructions containing a few simple steps, such as those in Figures 13.1 through 13.4, no conclusion is necessary. These instructions usefully end with the last step the reader must perform. For longer, more involved jobs, a conclusion can help readers finish the job with confidence and accuracy.

When they are necessary, conclusions can help the reader in a variety of ways. They might either provide a succinct wrap-up of what the reader has done or end with a single sentence of congratulations, or they can reassure readers as the conclusion in Cliff Burgess's memo (Figure 13.17) does. A conclusion might also tell readers what to expect once a job is finished, describe the results of a test, or explain how a piece of equipment is supposed to operate. Furthermore, conclusions can give readers practical advice on how to maintain a piece of equipment or how to follow a certain procedure.

Model of Full Set of Instructions

Study Figure 13.20, which is a set of instructions on setting up a new Epson printer that includes the parts discussed in this chapter: an introduction; a list of materials; numbered steps; and warnings, cautions, and notes.

FIGURE 13.20   Complete set of instructions with steps, visuals, cautions, notes, warnings.

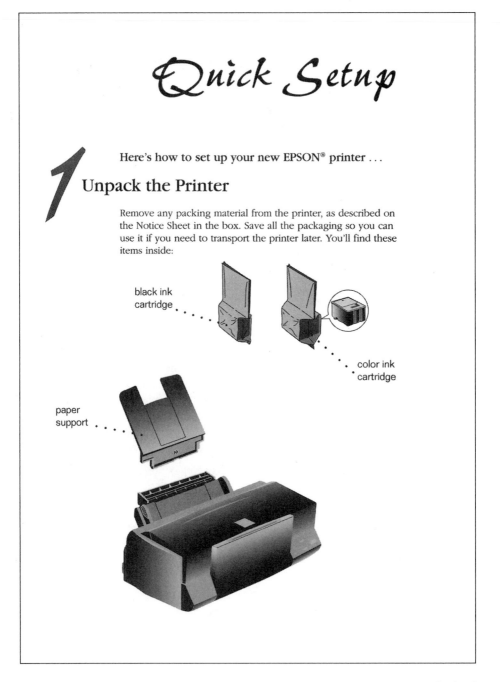

Continued

FIGURE 13.20 (Continued)

Place the printer flat on a stable desk near a grounded outlet. Leave plenty of room in back for the cables and enough room in front for opening the output tray.

Do NOT put the printer:

▶ In an area with high temperature or humidity
▶ In direct sunlight or dusty conditions
▶ Near sources of heat or electromagnetic interference, such as loudspeakers or cordless telephone base units.

Also, be sure to follow the Safety Instructions in the Introduction of your *User's Guide*.

2 Attach the Paper Support

Insert the paper support in the top slot on the back of the printer.

3 Plug In the Printer

First make sure the power is off. Check the ⏻ power button; it's off when its surface is raised above the printer surface.

Caution:
Do not plug the printer into an outlet controlled by a wall switch or timer, or on the same circuit as a large appliance. This may disrupt the power, which can erase memory and damage the power supply.

power

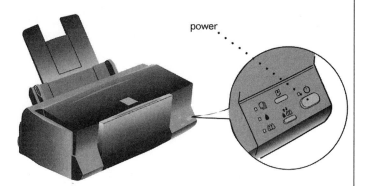

Plug the power cord into a properly grounded outlet.

Continued

FIGURE 13.20   (Continued)

Install the Ink Cartridges

1.   Lower the output tray and raise the printer cover.

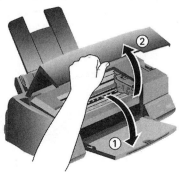

2.   Press the ⏻ power button to turn on the printer. The ⏻ power light flashes, the ● and ⚊ ink out lights come on, and the ink cartridge holders move to the installation position.

3.   Pull up the ink cartridge clamps.

Caution:
You must remove the tape seal from the top of the cartridge or you will permanently damage it. Don't remove the tape seal from the bottom or ink will leak.

Warning:
If ink gets on your hands, wash them thoroughly with soap and water. If ink gets in your eyes, flush them immediately with water.

4.   Open the ink cartridge packages. Remove the disposable yellow portion of the tape seal on top.

black ink cartridge · · · · ·

color ink cartridge

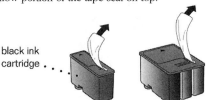

Continued

FIGURE 13.20   (Continued)

5. Lower the ink cartridges into their holders with the labels face up and the arrows pointing toward the back of the printer.

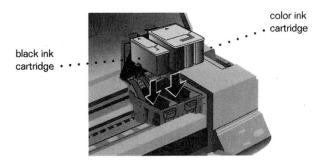

color ink
cartridge

black ink
cartridge

6. Push down the clamps until they lock in place.

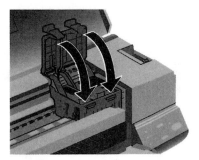

Caution:
Never turn off the printer when the ⏻ power light is flashing.

7. Press the cleaning button to return the print heads to their home position and charge the ink delivery system. Charging can take up to five minutes, with the ⏻ power light flashing until it's finished.

8. Close the printer cover.

Continued

FIGURE 13.20   (Continued)

 Load the Paper

1. Slide the left edge guide all the way left and pull out the output tray extension.

2. Fan a stack of plain paper and then even the edges.

3. Load the stack with the printable surface face up. Push the paper against the right edge guide.

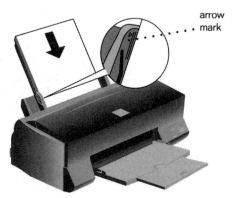

arrow
· mark

Note:
Don't load paper above the arrow mark inside the left edge guide.

4. Slide the left edge guide back against the stack of paper.

Continued

FIGURE 13.20   (Continued)

Check the Printer

1. Turn off the printer.

2. While holding down the load/eject button, turn on the printer. Then release the buttons.

3. A page prints out showing the ROM version and a nozzle check pattern. When it's finished, turn off the printer. If you have any problems with the test, see Chapter 6 in your *User's Guide* for more information.

Connect the Printer to Your Computer

You can connect your EPSON Stylus™ COLOR 600 to either an IBM® compatible PC or an Apple® Macintosh.® You'll need a shielded, twisted-pair parallel cable to connect to a PC or an Apple System Peripheral-8 cable to connect to a Macintosh. For a complete list of system requirements, see the Introduction of your *User's Guide*.

Connecting to a PC

Note:

The printer is assigned to parallel port LPT1; if you want to use a different port, see your Windows documentation for instructions.

1. Turn off the printer and your computer.

2. Connect the cable to the printer's parallel interface; then squeeze the wire clips together until they lock in place. (If your cable has a ground wire, connect it now.)

ground wire

3. Connect the other end of the cable to your computer's parallel port and secure it as necessary.

Continued

FIGURE 13.20   (Continued)

Connecting to a Macintosh

1. Turn off the printer and your Macintosh.

2. Connect one end of the cable to the serial connector on the back of the printer.

Note:
If you're using a PowerBook™, connect your printer to the modem port.

3. Connect the other end of the cable to either the modem port 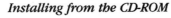 or the printer port 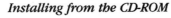 on your Macintosh.

Install the Printer Software

Now you need to install the printer software so you can control printing from your computer.

Installing on a PC

You can install the printer software for Windows 95 or Windows 3.1 from the EPSON printer software CD-ROM. If you don't have a CD-ROM drive, you can install the software using the EPSON printer software diskettes.

Installing from the CD-ROM

In addition to the printer driver and utilities, the CD-ROM contains EPSON Answers, a comprehensive online guide that includes:

EPSON ANSWERS

If you have a CD-ROM drive, you can run EPSON Answers, the on-screen guide to your new printer. It puts you on the right track quickly and easily.

▶ **How To** for step-by-step printer operating instructions
▶ **Color Guide** with practical color printing information
▶ **Problem Solver** to help you fix printer problems
▶ **Test Print** so you can check your print quality

Follow the instructions inside the CD-ROM case to install the software. To run EPSON Answers, click on its icon in the EPSON program group or folder.

Source: Reprinted by permission of Epson America.

Some Final Advice

Perhaps the most important piece of advice to leave you with is this: Do not take *anything* for granted when you have to write a set of instructions. It is wrong and on occasion dangerous to assume that your readers have performed the procedure before, that they will automatically supply missing or "obvious" information, or that they will easily anticipate your next step. No one ever complained that a set of instructions was too clear or too easy to follow.

✓ Revision Checklist

- ❑ Analyzed my intended audience's background, especially why and how they will use my instructions.
- ❑ Took special care with meeting needs of any non-native speaker of English unfamiliar with my culture.
- ❑ Tested my instructions to make sure they include all necessary steps in their proper sequence.
- ❑ Made sure all measurements, distances, times, and relationships are precise and correct.
- ❑ Selected language appropriate for my audience. Avoided technical terms if my audience is not a group of specialists in my field.
- ❑ Used the imperative mood throughout my instructions.
- ❑ Wrote clear, short sentences.
- ❑ Eliminated ambiguity from my instructions.
- ❑ Chose or created effective visuals where necessary and labeled and placed them next to the step(s) to which they apply.
- ❑ Made my introduction proportionate to the length and complexity of my instructions and suited to my readers' needs.
- ❑ Included necessary background, safety, and operational information in the introduction.
- ❑ Included a complete list of tools and materials my audience needs to carry out the instructions.
- ❑ Put instructions in easy-to-follow steps and in the right order.
- ❑ Used numbers or bullets to label the steps and connective words to indicate order.
- ❑ Used warnings, cautions, and notes where necessary and in a form that makes them easily seen and read.
- ❑ Supplied a conclusion that summarizes what readers should have done or reassures them that they have completed the job satisfactorily.

Exercises

1. Bring to class two examples of short directions that require no introduction, list of materials and equipment, or conclusion. Look for these two examples on labels, carton panels, or backs of envelopes. Evaluate the effectiveness of the instructions by commenting on how precise, direct, and useful they are.

2. Find at least one example of long instructions containing an introduction; a list of materials and equipment; procedural steps; warnings, cautions, or notes; and a conclusion. Bring the example to class and be prepared to show how the various steps in this set of instructions follow the principles outlined in this chapter. You can find a set of full instructions in many technical manuals and in some manuals to help consumers assemble or maintain large or complex home appliances.

3. Find a set of instructions that does not contain any visuals, but that you think should have some graphic material to make it clearer. Design those visuals yourself and indicate where they should appear in the instructions.

4. From a technical manual in your field or an owner's manual, locate a set of instructions that you think are poorly written and illustrated. In a memo to your instructor, explain why the instructions are unclear, confusing, or badly formatted. Then revise the instructions to make them easier for the reader to carry out. Submit the original instructions with your revision.

5. Write a set of instructions in numbered steps (or in paragraph format) on one of the following relatively simple activities.
    a. tying a shoe
    b. using an ATM
    c. unlocking a door with a key
    d. making a call from a cellular phone
    e. planting a tree or a shrub
    f. sewing a button on a shirt
    g. removing a stain from clothing
    h. pumping gas into a car
    i. surfing the Internet
    j. checking a book out of the library
    k. parallel parking a car
    l. shifting gears in a car
    m. photocopying a page from a book

6. Write an appropriate introduction and conclusion for the set of instructions you wrote for Exercise 5.

7. Working as part of a collaborative writing team, write a set of full instructions on one of the following more complex topics. Identify your audience. Include an appropriate introduction; a list of equipment and materials; numbered steps with necessary warnings, cautions, and notes; and an effective conclusion. Also include whatever visuals you think will help your audience.

    a. scanning a document

    b. changing a flat tire

    c. designing a computer program

    d. testing chlorine in a swimming pool

    e. shaving a patient for surgery

    f. changing the oil and oil filter in a car

    g. making a blueprint

    h. installing a wind turbine on a roof

    i. filling out an income tax return

    j. surveying a parcel of land

    k. pruning hedges

    l. jumping a dead car battery

    m. using the Heimlich maneuver to help a choking individual

    n. filleting a fish

    o. creating a logo for a letterhead

    p. taking someone's blood pressure

    q. changing a cash register tape

    r. finding and plugging a leak in a tire

    s. downloading a home page from the Web

    t. painting a car

    u. cooking a roast

    v. flossing a patient's teeth after cleaning

    w. creating a computer file

8. The following set of instructions is confusing, vague, and out of order. Rewrite the instructions to make them clear, easy to follow, and correct. Make sure that each step follows the guidelines outlined in this chapter.

Reupholstering a Piece of Furniture

(1) Although it might be difficult to match the worn material with the new material, you might as well try.

(2) If you cannot, remove the old material.

(3) Take out the padding.

(4) Take out all of the tacks before removing the old covering. You might want to save the old covering.

(5) Measure the new material with the old, if you are able to.

(6) Check the frame, springs, webbing, and padding.

(7) Put the new material over the old.

(8) Check to see if it matches.

(9) You must have the same size as before.

(10) Look at the padding inside. If it is lumpy, smooth it out.

(11) You will need to tack all the sides down. Space your tacks a good distance apart.

(12) When you spot wrinkles, remove the tacks.

(13) Caution: in step 11 directly above, do not drive your tacks all the way through. Leave some room.

(14) Work from the center to the edge in step 11 above.

(15) Put the new material over the old furniture.

P.S. Use strong cords whenever there are tacks. Put the cords under the nails so that they hold.

Writing Winning Proposals

A proposal is a detailed plan of action that a writer submits to a reader or group of readers for approval. The readers are usually in a position of authority—supervisors, managers, department heads, company buyers, elected officials, civic leaders—to endorse or reject the writer's plan. Proposals are among the most important types of job-related writing. Their acceptance can lead to improved working conditions, a more efficient and economical business, additional jobs and business for a company, or a safer and more attractive environment.

Writing Successful Proposals

Proposals are written for many purposes and many different audiences; for example,

- to your boss seeking authorization to purchase a new piece of equipment for the office, as Gordon Reynolds did in Figure 2.5 (pp. 50–51) requesting that his firm upgrade their laser printers
- to potential customers offering a product or a service, such as to a fire chief offering to supply special firefighting gear
- to a government agency (like the Department of the Interior) seeking funds to conduct research projects (a study of the mating and feeding habits of a particular species or an investigation to determine the mercury levels in a certain lake)
- to foundations to raise funds for a nonprofit organization

Depending on the job, proposals can vary greatly in size and in scope. A proposal to your employer could easily be conveyed in a page or two. A proposal to do a research project for a class assignment could also be successfully completed in a brief memo. To propose doing a small job for a prospective client—redecorating a waiting room in an accountant's office—a letter with information on costs, materials, and a timetable might suffice. But an extremely large and costly job—constructing a ten-story office building, for example—requires a detailed report hundreds of pages long with appendixes on engineering specifications, detailed budgets, and even résumés of all key personnel working on the project.

A discussion of long, elaborate proposals is beyond the scope of this chapter. But the principles and techniques of audience analysis, organization, and drafting that this chapter does cover apply equally well to any longer project you may be called on to prepare individually or as part of a team.

Proposals Are Persuasive Plans

Proposals, whether large or small, must be highly persuasive to succeed. Without your audience's approval, your plan will never go into effect, however accurate and important you think it is. Your proposal must convince readers that your plan will help them either improve their businesses or generally make their jobs easier.

The tone of your proposal should be **"Here is what I can do for you."** Stress the precise benefits your plan has for the reader. Show readers how approving your plan will save them time and money or will improve employee morale or customer satisfaction.

Competition is fierce in the world of work, and a persuasive proposal frequently determines which company receives a contract. Demonstrate to your reader why your plan is better—more efficient, practical, economical—than a competitor's. In a sense, a proposal combines the persuasiveness of a sales letter (see Chapter 6), the documentation of a report (see Chapters 9 and 16), and the binding power of a contract, because if the reader accepts your proposal, he or she will expect you to live up to its terms to the letter.

Proposals Frequently Are Collaborative Efforts

Like many other types of business and technical writing, proposals often are the product of teamwork and sharing. Even a short in-house proposal is often researched and put together by more than one individual in the company or agency.

Often, individual employees will pull together information from their separate areas (such as finance, marketing, sales, and transportation) and put it into a proposal that each team member then reads and revises until the team agrees that the document is ready to be released.

Types of Proposals

Proposals are classified according to how they originate and where they are sent after they are written. Distinctions are made between *solicited* and *unsolicited* proposals based on how they originate and between *internal* and *external* proposals based on where they are sent. Depending on your audience and your purpose, you may write an internal solicited or unsolicited proposal, or you may write an external solicited or unsolicited proposal.

Requests for Proposals and Solicited Proposals

When a company has a particular problem to be solved or a job to be done, it will solicit, or invite, proposals. The company will notify you and other competitors by preparing a **request for proposals (RFP),** which is a set of instructions that specify the exact type of work to be done along with guidelines on how and when the company wants the work completed.

Some RFPs are long and full of legal requirements and conditions. Others, like the example in Figure 14.1, are more concise. RFPs are sent to firms with track records in the area the company wants the work done. RFPs are also printed in trade publications to attract the highest number of qualified bidders for the job. The U.S. government publishes RFPs in the *Federal Register,* while private companies sometimes send their RFPs to *Business Daily*.

An RFP helps you to know what the customer wants. It is often extremely detailed and even tells you how the company wants the proposal prepared; for example, what information is to be included (on backgrounds, personnel, equipment, budgets), where it needs to appear, and how many copies of the proposal you have to submit.

FIGURE 14.1   A sample RFP.

REQUEST FOR PROPOSALS

Mesa Community College is soliciting proposals to construct and to install fifty individual study carrels in its Holmes Memorial Library. These carrels must be highly serviceable and conform to all specification standards of the ALA. Proposals should include the precise measurements of the carrels to be installed, the specific acoustical and lighting benefits, and the types and amount of storage space offered. Work on constructing and installing the carrels must be completed no later than the start of the Fall Semester, August 29, 2000. Proposals should include a schedule of when different phases of work will be completed and an itemized budget for labor, materials, equipment, and necessary tests to ensure high-quality acoustical performance. Contractors should state their qualifications, including a description of similar recent work and a list of references. Proposals should be submitted in triplicate no later than May 16, 2000, to:

Mrs. Barbara Feldstein-Archer
Director of the Library
Mesa Community College
Mesa, CO 80932-0617

TECH NOTE

On-Line RFPs

RFPs are also posted on the Web. Take a look at a few of them to get an idea of what government agencies and private companies look for when they request proposals. The *Federal Register,* published daily by the U.S. government, issues hundreds of legal regulations as well as requests for proposals from various government agencies. You can browse the *Federal Register* on-line via GPO access—*http://www.access.gpo.gov/su_docs/aces/aces/140.html.* If you have any questions, you can contact the *GPO Access* User Support Team at their e-mail address: *gpoaccess@gpo.gov.*

Following is a summary of a request for proposals from the Department of Transportation on Electronic Payment Systems.

DEPARTMENT OF TRANSPORTATION

Federal Transit Administration

Request for Proposals for an Operational Test of an Electronic Payment System for Transportation and Other Applications

AGENCY: Federal Transit Administration (FTA), DOT.

ACTION: Notice.

SUMMARY: The U.S. Department of Transportation (US DOT) announces a Request for Proposals from eligible applicants for an operational test of an electronic payment system for transit fare collection, parking payment, electronic toll collection and other applications. The US DOT is interested in identifying and evaluating issues associated with the establishment of partnerships between public transit service providers and other entities in the development and use of multiple-application electronic payment systems. The Department is specifically interested in an operational test of a payment system that includes a variety of applications, but must at a minimum include transit fare collection, parking payment and electronic toll collection.

DATES: Proposals shall be submitted by 4 P.M. EST on or before October 25, 1999.

CONTENTS OF PROPOSAL SHOULD FOLLOW THIS PLAN

I.   Background
II. Visions, Goals and Objectives
III. Project Development
     A. General
     B. Management Oversight
IV. Partnerships
V.   National ITS Architecture
VI. Project Evaluation Activities
VII. Funding
VIII. Schedule

Continued

IX.   Proposals
    A. Technical Plan
    B. Management and Staffing Plan
    C. Financial Plan
X.   Proposal Evaluation Criteria

ELIGIBILITY: Only public transit agencies and metropolitan planning organizations (MPOs) in the United States are eligible to submit proposals in response to this RFP.

FOR FURTHER INFORMATION CONTACT: Bert Arrillaga, Chief, Service Innovation Division, (TRI-12), at (202) 366-0231 or Sean Ricketson, Office of Mobility Innovation, (TRI-11), at (202) 366-6678. This notice is posted on the FTA website on the Internet under *http://www.fta.dot.gov/library/legal/fr99toc.htm.*

Another source of RFPs on the Internet is *Commerce Business Daily* (*CBD*), which "lists notices of proposed government procurement actions, contract awards, sales of government property and other procurement information. A new edition of the *CBD* is issued every business day, and each edition contains approximately 500–1000 notices." The *CBD* Web site—*http://www.cos.com*—lists the government's requests for equipment, supplies, and a variety of services from assembling to maintaining equipment to fee-charging dredging.
    Here are a few of the agencies you can search in the *CBD* for RFPs:

- Department of Health and Human Services
- United States Department of Energy
- United States Department of Agriculture
- Defense Support Center and Agencies
- National Aeronautics and Space Administration
- Department of Justice and other law enforcement agencies

The Community of Science Web Server also lets you search the *Federal Register, Federally-Funded Research in the U.S.,* and *Funding Opportunities Database.*

Your own proposal will be judged according to how well you fulfill the terms of the RFP. For that reason, follow the directions in the RFP exactly. Note that the solicited proposal in Figure 14.2 directly refers to the terms of the RFP. You should even use the language (specialized terms, specifically stated needs) of the RFP in your proposal to convince readers that you understand their requirements and to get them to accept your plan.

Unsolicited Proposals

With an unsolicited proposal, you—not the reader—make the first move. Unlike a solicited proposal, in which the company to which you are submitting the proposal

FIGURE 14.2   An external solicited proposal in response to an RFP.

January 21, 2000

Mr. Floyd Tompkins, Manager
General Purpose Appliances
Highway 11 South
Portland, OR 97222

Dear Mr. Tompkins:

Begins with RFP   In response to your RFP 7521 for bids for an appropriate floor covering at your new showroom, Reynolds Interiors is pleased to submit the following proposal. After carefully reviewing your *Identifies best solution* specifications for a floor covering and inspecting your new facility, we believe that **Armstrong Classic Corlon 900** is the most suitable choice. We are enclosing a sample of the Corlon 900 so you can see how carefully it is constructed.

Corlon's Advantages

Describes product's features that benefit reader   Guaranteed against defects for a full three years, **Corlon** is one of the finest and most durable floor coverings manufactured by Armstrong. It is a heavy-duty commercial floor 0.085 inch thick for protection. Twenty-five percent of the material consists of interface backing; the other 75 percent is an inlaid wear layer that offers exceptionally high resistance to everyday traffic. Traffic tests conducted by the Independent Floor Covering Institute repeatedly proved the superiority of Corlon's construction and resistance.

Distinguishes product from competitors'   Another important feature of **Corlon** is the size of its rolls. Unlike other leading brands of similar commercial flooring—Remington or Treadmaster—Corlon comes in 12-foot-wide rather than

Reynolds Interiors • 250 Commerce Avenue S.W. • Portland, OR 97204-2129
http://www.reynolds.com • 503-555-8733 • Fax: 503-555-1629

Continued

FIGURE 14.2   (Continued)

6-foot-wide rolls. This extra width will significantly reduce the number of seams on your floor, thus increasing its attractiveness and reducing the dangers of the seams splitting.

Installation Procedures

Explains how The **Classic Corlon** requires that we use the inlaid seaming
job is done process, a technical procedure requiring the services of a trained
floor mechanic. Herman Goshen, our floor mechanic, has over fifteen years of experience working with the inlaid seam process. His professional work has been consistently praised by our customers.

Installation Schedule

Gives realistic We can install the **Classic Corlon** on your showroom floor during
timetable the first week of March, which fits the timetable specified in your request. The material will take three and one-half
days to install and will be ready to walk on immediately. We recommend, though, that you not move equipment onto the floor for 24 hours after installation.

Costs

The following costs include the **Classic Corlon** tile, labor, and tax:

Lists all	750 sq. yards of **Classic Corlon** at $23.50/sq. yd.	$ 17,625.00
costs	Labor (28 hrs @ $18.00/hr.)	$ 504.00
	Sealing fluid (10 gals. @ $15.00/gal.)	$ 150.00
	Total	$ 18,279.00
	Tax (5 percent)	$ 913.95
	GRAND TOTAL	$ 19,192.95

Our costs are $250.00 under those you specified in your request.

Continued

FIGURE 14.2   (Continued)

---

page 3

Reynolds's Qualifications

Establishes Reynolds Interiors has been in business for more than 28 years.
history of In that time, we have installed many commercial floors in
service Portland and its suburbs. In the last year, we have served more
than 60 customers, including the new multipurpose Tradex plant
in Portland. We would be happy to furnish you with a list of
satisfied customers.

Conclusion

Encourages Thank you for the opportunity to submit this proposal. We
reader to believe you will have a great deal of success with an Armstrong
accept **Corlon** floor. If we can provide you with any further information,
please call us or visit us at our Web site.

Sincerely yours,

Neelow Singh
Neelow Singh
Sales Manager

Jack Rosen
Jack Rosen
Installation Supervisor

---

knows about the problem, your unsolicited proposal has to convince readers that
(1) there is a problem and (2) you and your firm are the ones to solve it.

Doing that is not as difficult as it sounds. See how the writers of the unsolicited
proposal in Figure 14.3 identify a relevant problem for their readers. If your readers
accept your identification of the problem, you have greatly increased the chances of
their accepting your plan to solve it. Just remember that you will have to prove that
solving the problem carries major benefits for your reader.

Internal and External Proposals

An internal proposal is written to a decision maker in your own organization. As
you will see on pages 553–557, an internal proposal can deal with a variety of topics,

including changing a policy or procedure, requesting additional personnel, or purchasing or updating equipment or software.

An external proposal, on the other hand, is sent to a decision maker outside your company. It might go to a potential client you have never worked for or to a previous or current client. An external proposal can also be sent to a government funding agency such as the Department of Agriculture. External proposals tend to be more formal than internal ones.

Guidelines for Writing a Successful Proposal

Regardless of the type of proposal you are called on to write, the following guidelines will help you persuade your audience to approve your plan. Refer to these guidelines both before and while you formulate your plan.

1. Approach writing a proposal as a problem-solving activity. Your goal is to solve a problem that affects the reader. Everything in your proposal should relate to the problem, and the organization of your proposal should reflect your ability as a problem solver. Psychologically, make the reader feel confident that you have the knowledge and the experience to solve the problem.

2. Regard your audience as skeptical readers. Even though you offer a plan that you think will benefit readers, do not be overconfident that they will automatically accept it as the best and only way to proceed. To determine the feasibility of your plan, readers will question everything you say. They will withhold their approval if your proposal contains errors, omissions, or inconsistencies.

3. Research your proposal thoroughly. A winning proposal is *not* based only on a few well-meaning, general suggestions. All your good intentions and enthusiasm will not substitute for the hard facts readers will demand. Spell out your plan or procedure; give the nuts and bolts of how the job will be done. Concrete examples persuade readers; unsupported generalizations do not. You will have to do a lot of homework; for example, researching the problem, doing comparative shopping for the best prices, verifying schedules and timetables, interviewing customers and/or employees, making site visits.

4. Scout out what your competitors are doing. Closely related to guideline 3, assessing your competition is essential when it comes to writing a winning proposal. Become familiar with your competitors' product lines or services, have a fair idea about their market costs, and be able to show how your company's work is better. You can accomplish all that by doing some Web browsing, looking at your competitors' home pages, and seeing what is available. Also look at print and on-line trade publications.

5. Prove that your proposal is workable. The bottom-line question from your reader is "Will this plan work?" Your proposal should be well thought out. It should contain no statements that say, "Let's see what happens if we do X or Y." By analyzing and, when possible, testing each part of your proposal in advance, you can eliminate any quirks and revise the proposal appropriately before readers evaluate it. What you propose should be consistent with the organization and capabilities of the company. It would be foolish to recommend, for example, that a small company with fifty employees triple its work force to accomplish your plan.

6. Be sure your proposal is financially realistic. This point follows from guideline 5. "Is it worth the money?" is another bottom-line question you can expect from readers. Do not submit a proposal that would require an unnecessarily large amount of money to implement. For example, it would be unrealistic to recommend that your company spend $20,000 to solve a $2,000 problem that might not ever recur. Study the economic climate, too—are you in an economic slump or in a boom time?

7. Package your proposal attractively. Make sure your proposal is letter perfect, inviting, and easy to read (use headings, lists, different typefaces, graphics, and other visual devices discussed in Chapter 11). The format as well as the content of your proposal can determine whether it is accepted or rejected. Remember that readers, especially those unfamiliar with your work, will evaluate your proposal as evidence of the type of work you want to do for them. Take advantage of desktop publishing software programs (see pp. 431–434).

Internal Proposals

The primary purpose of an internal proposal, such as the one shown in Figure 14.3, is to offer a realistic and constructive plan to help your company run its business more efficiently and economically.

On your job you may discover a better way of doing something or a more efficient way to correct a problem. You believe that your proposed change will save your employer time, money, or further trouble. (Note how Tina Escobar and Oliver Jabur in Figure 14.3 identified and researched a more effective and less costly way for Community Federal Bank to conduct business and to satisfy its customers.)

Generally speaking, your proposal will be an informal, in-house message, so a brief (usually one- or two-page) memo should be appropriate. You decide to notify your department head, manager, or supervisor, or your employer may ask you for specific suggestions to solve a problem he or she has already identified. Mike Gonzalez's memo in Figure 4.3 responds to such a request from his employer.

Typical Topics for Internal Proposals

An internal proposal can be written about a variety of topics, such as

- purchasing new or more advanced equipment to replace obsolete or inefficient computers, transducers, automobiles, and the like
- hiring new employees or retraining current ones to learn a new technique or process
- eliminating a dangerous condition or reducing an environmental risk to prevent accidents—for employees, customers, or the community at large
- improving communication within or between departments of a company or agency

TECH NOTE

Best Demonstrated Practices

All companies are interested in saving money by streamlining labor, products, and the cost of materials. Some innovative businesses ask employees
to submit ideas for cutting expenses. **"Best demonstrated practices"** refers
to employee-submitted internal proposals. These proposals come from
workers who are most aware of how a job is performed and who can suggest the methods or materials to reduce the time, cost, or energy in getting
it done. Accepted proposals carry a variety of rewards from grateful
employers—gift certificates, paid time off, recognition in the workplace,
credit toward promotions, and raises.

- revising a policy to improve customer service (changing Web servers, speeding
  up deliveries) or employee morale (offering vanpooling, adding more options
  for a schedule, starting a day-care center).

As the list shows, internal proposals cover almost every activity or policy that
affects the day-to-day operation of a company or agency.

Following the Proper Chain of Command

Writing an internal proposal requires you to be aware of and sensitive to office politics. It may be wise first to meet with your boss to see if she or he has already identified the problem or has specific suggestions on how to solve it. Then you might
provide your boss with a draft and ask for revisions or feedback.

You cannot assume that your reader will automatically agree with you that
there is a problem or that your plan is the only way to tackle it. To be successful,
your internal proposal should be written with the needs and likes of your boss in
mind. Remember that your boss will expect you to be very convincing about both
the problem you say exists and the changes you are advocating in the workplace
under his or her supervision. Don't step on corporate toes.

Anticipating and Ethically Resolving Reader Problems

When you prepare an internal proposal, you need to be aware of some difficulties
and some ethical ways of handling them.

1. Realize that your reader may feel threatened by your plan. After all, you are
advocating a change. Some managers regard change as a challenge to their administration of an office or a department. Think about the long-term effect your proposed change will have on your boss's duties, responsibilities, or relationships with
your co-workers or with his or her superiors. Don't step on toes or attempt to
undermine existing authority.

2. Take into account that your reader may have "pet projects" or predetermined ways of doing things. Take those into account and make every attempt to acknowledge them respectfully. You may even find a way to build on or complement such projects or procedures.

3. Keep in mind that your boss may have to take your proposal further up the organizational ladder for commentary and, eventually, approval. Again, refer to Joycelyn Woolfolk's description in Figure 3.5 of the chain of command at her agency.

4. Consider the implications of your plan for other offices or sections in your company. A change you propose for your department or office (transfers, new budgets or schedules, new hires, deploying existing staff) may have sweeping and potentially disruptive implications for another office or division in your company.

5. Accept that even though you draft the proposal, it may not bear your name, or your name may be subordinate to your boss's name. It is not uncommon in the world of work to write a document so another person can sign it. Writing a proposal may mean working as a team with your supervisor, whose name goes on the document, too, for notice and credit.

6. Never submit an internal proposal that offers an idea you think will work but relies on someone else to supply the specific details on *how* it will work. For example, do not write an internal proposal that says the payroll, community relations, maintenance, or advertising department can give the reader the necessary details about your proposal. That unfairly pushes the responsibility onto someone else.

Organization of an Internal Proposal

A short internal proposal follows a relatively straightforward plan of organization, from identifying the problem to solving it. Internal proposals usually contain four parts, as shown in Figure 14.3: **purpose, problem, solution,** and **conclusion.** Refer to Figure 14.3 with these four headings as you read the following discussion.

The Purpose of the Proposal

Begin your proposal with a brief statement of why you are writing to your supervisor: "I propose that. . . ." State why you think a specific change is necessary now. Then succinctly define the problem and emphasize that your plan, if approved by the reader, will solve that problem. Where necessary, stress the urgency to act—within the next week? month?

The Problem

In this section prove that a problem exists. Document its importance for your boss and your company; as a matter of fact, the more you show, with concrete evidence, how the problem affects the boss's work (and area of supervision), the more likely you are to persuade him or her to act.

Here are some guidelines for documenting the problem:

- Avoid vague (and unsupported) generalizations such as, "We're losing money each day with this procedure (piece of equipment)"; "Costs continue to escalate";

"The trouble occurs frequently in a number of places"; "Numerous complaints have come in"; "If something isn't done soon, more problems will result."

- Provide quantifiable details about the implications or consequences of the problem, such as the amount of money a company is actually losing per day, week, or month. Emphasize the financial trouble so that you can show in the next section how your plan offers an efficient and workable solution.
- Indicate how many employees (or work-hours) are involved or how many customers are inconvenienced or endangered by a procedure or condition. Notice how Escobar and Jabur include such information in a table in their proposal in Figure 14.3.
- Verify how widespread a problem is or how frequently it occurs by citing specific occasions. Again, see how Escobar and Jabur cite evidence from the Watson-Perry survey and the interviews they conducted with the manager of the Mayfield branch.

The Solution or Plan

In this section describe the change you propose and want approved. Tie your solution (the change) directly to the problem you have just documented. Each part of your plan should help eliminate the problem or should help increase the productivity, efficiency, or safety you think is possible.

Your reader will again expect to find factual evidence. Do not give merely the outline of a plan or say that details can be worked out later. Supply details that answer the following questions: (1) Is the plan workable—can it be accomplished here in our office or plant? and (2) Is it cost effective—will it really save us money in the long run and not lead to even greater expenses?

To get the reader to say yes to both questions, supply the facts you have gathered as a result of your research. For example, if you propose that your firm buy a new piece of equipment, do the necessary homework to locate the most efficient and cost-effective model available, as Tina Escobar and Oliver Jabur do in Figure 14.3.

- Supply the dealer's name, the costs, major conditions of service and training contracts, and warranties.
- Describe how your firm could use the equipment to obtain better results in the future.
- Cite specific tasks the new equipment can perform more efficiently at a lower cost than the equipment now in use.

A **proposal to change a procedure** must address the following questions.

- How does the new (or revised) procedure work?
- How many employees or customers will be affected by it?
- When will it go into operation?
- How much will it cost the employer to change procedures?
- What delays or losses in business might be expected while the company switches from one procedure to another?
- What employees, equipment, or locations are available to accomplish the change?

As those questions indicate, your reader will be concerned about schedules, working conditions, employees, methods, locations, equipment, and the costs involved in your plan for change. The costs, in fact, will be of utmost importance. Make sure you supply a careful and accurate budget. Moreover, make those costs attractive by emphasizing how inexpensive they are compared to the cost of *not* making the change, as Escobar and Jabur do in the section labeled "Costs." Double-check your math.

It is also wise to raise alternative solutions, before the reader does, and to discuss their disadvantages. Notice how Tina Escobar and Oliver Jabur do that in Figure 14.3 by showing why installing an ATM is more feasible than hiring a fifth teller.

The Conclusion

Your conclusion should be short—a paragraph or two at the most. Remind readers that (a) the problem is serious, (b) the reason for change is justified, and (c) action needs to be taken. Re-emphasize the most important benefits. Escobar and Jabur stress the savings that the bank will see by following their plan as well as the increase in customer satisfaction. Also indicate that you are willing to discuss your plan with the reader.

Sales Proposals

A sales proposal is the most common type of external proposal. Its purpose is to sell your company's products or services for a set fee. Whether short or long, a sales proposal is a marketing tool that includes a sales pitch as well as a detailed description of the work you propose to do. Figures 14.2 and 14.4 are sales proposals.

The Audience and Its Needs

Your audience will usually be one or more executives who have the power to approve or reject a proposal. Unlike readers of an internal proposal, your audience for a sales proposal may be even more skeptical since they may not know you or your work. Your proposal may also be evaluated by experts in other fields employed by your prospective customer.

Make sure your proposal has a competitive edge. Readers will compare your plan with those they receive from other proposal writers. Your proposal has to convince readers that the product and the service your company offers are more reliable, efficient, and timely than those of another company.

The key to success is incorporating the "you attitude" throughout your proposal. Relate your product, service, or personnel to the reader's exact needs as stated in the RFP for a solicited proposal or through your own investigations for an unsolicited proposal. You cannot submit the same proposal for every job you want to win and expect to be awarded a contract. Different firms have different needs.

Typical Questions Readers Will Ask

The most important question the reader will raise about your work is, "How does this proposal meet our company's special requirements?" Some other fairly common questions readers will have as they evaluate your sales proposal include the following.

FIGURE 14.3   An internal unsolicited proposal.

COMMUNITY
FEDERAL BANK

EQUAL HOUSING
LENDER

POWELL
584-5200

MONROE
413-6000

LANGSTON
796-3009

TO: Michael L. Sappington, Executive Vice President
            Dorothy Woo, Langston Regional Manager

FROM: Tina Escobar, Oliver Jabur, ATM Services

DATE: June 12, 2000

RE: A proposal to install an ATM at the Mayfield Park branch

PURPOSE

Clearly states why proposal is being sent

We propose a cost-effective solution to what is a growing problem at the Mayfield Park branch in Langston: inefficient servicing of customer needs and rising personnel costs. We recommend that you approve the purchase and installation, within the next three to four months, of an ATM at Mayfield. Such action is consistent with Community's goals of expanding electronic banking services and promoting our image as a self-serve yet customer-oriented institution.

THE PROBLEM WITH CURRENT SERVICES AT MAYFIELD PARK

Identifies problem by giving reader necessary background information

Currently, we employ four tellers at Mayfield. However, too much is being spent on personnel/salary for routine customer transactions. In fact, as determined by teller activity reports, nearly 25 percent of the four tellers' time each week is devoted to routine activities easily accommodated by ATMs. Outlined in the table below is a breakdown of teller activity for the month of May:

Teller #	Total Transactions	Routine Transactions
1	6,205	1,551
2	5,989	1,383
3	6,345	1,522
4	6,072	1,518
	24,611	5,974

Divides problem into parts— volume, financial, personnel, customer service

Clearly, we are not fully using our tellers' sales abilities when they are kept busy with routine activities. To compound the problem, we expect business to increase by at least 25 percent at Mayfield in the next few

Continued

FIGURE 14.3   (Continued)

months, as projected by this year's market survey. If we do not install an ATM, we will need to hire a fifth teller, at an annual cost of $20,800 ($15,500 base pay plus approximately 30 percent for fringes), for the additional 6,000 transactions we project.

Verifies that problem is widespread

Most important, customer needs are not being met efficiently at Mayfield. Recent surveys done for Community Federal by Watson-Perry demonstrate that our customers are inconvenienced by not having an ATM at Mayfield. They are unhappy about long waits in line to do simple banking business, such as deposits, withdrawals, and loan payments, and about having to drive to other branches to do after-hours banking. Conversations we had with manager Rachael Harris-Ignara at Mayfield confirm customers' complaints.

Ultimately, the lack of an ATM at Mayfield Park hurts Community's image. With ATMs available to Mayfield residents at local stores and other banks, our institution risks having customers and potential customers go elsewhere for their banking needs. We not only miss the opportunity of selling them on our other services but also risk losing their business entirely.

A SOLUTION TO THE PROBLEM

Purchasing and installing an ATM at Mayfield Park will result in significant savings in personnel costs and time. We will

Relates solution to individual parts of the problem

- Save money by not having to hire a fifth teller
- Allocate teller duties more efficiently and productively by assisting customers with questions and transactions not handled through an ATM, such as purchasing savings bonds, traveler's checks, and foreign currency
- Increase time for tellers to cross-sell our services, including our new line of nontraditional banking products—annuities, mutual funds, and global market accounts
- Improve customer satisfaction by giving them the option of meeting their banking needs electronically or through a teller
- Ease the stress on our tellers at Mayfield Park

Shows problem can be solved and stresses how

It is feasible to install an ATM at Mayfield. This location does not pose the difficulties at some older branches. Mayfield offers ample room to install a drive-up ATM in the stubbed-out fourth drive-up lane. It is away from the heavily congested area in front of the bank, yet it is

Continued

FIGURE 14.3   (Continued)

easily accessible from the main driveway and the side drive facing Commonwealth Avenue, as the following photograph shows.

Photo courtesy Taylor Wilson

Judging from the ATM vendor's past work, the ATM could be installed and operational within two to three months. That is the amount of time it took to install ATMs at the first two locations in Powell and for Archer Avenue in Langston. Moreover, by authorizing the expenditure at Mayfield within the next month, you will ensure that ATM service is available long before the Christmas season.

COSTS

The costs of implementing our proposal are as follows:

Itemizes costs

Diebold Drive-up ATM	$28,000.00
Installation fee	2,000.00
Maintenance (1 year)	1,500.00
	$31,500.00

Interprets costs for reader

This $31,500, however, does not truly reflect our annual costs. We would be able to amortize, for tax purposes, the cost of installation of the ATM over five years. Our annual expenses would, therefore, look like this:

$30,000 (28,000 + 2,000) divided by 5 years =
$6,000.00 + 1,500 (maintenance), or <u>$7,500 per year</u>.

Continued

FIGURE 14.3   (Continued)

---

page 4

Compared with the $20,800 a year the bank would have to expend for a fifth teller at Mayfield, the annual depreciated cost for the ATM ($7,500) reduces by nearly two-thirds the amount of money the bank will have to spend for much more efficient customer service.

CONCLUSION

Stresses benefits for reader and bank as a whole

Authorizing an ATM for the Mayfield Park branch is both feasible and cost effective. Adoption of this proposal will save our bank more than $13,000 in teller services annually, reduce customer complaints, and increase customer satisfaction and approval. We will be happy to discuss this proposal with you anytime at your convenience.

- Does the writer's firm understand our problem?
- Can the writer's firm deliver the services it promises?
- Can the job be completed on time?
- What assurances does the writer offer that the job will be done exactly as proposed?

Answer each of those questions by demonstrating how your product or service is tailored to the customer's needs.

Organizing a Sales Proposal

Most sales proposals include the following elements: introduction, description of the proposed product or service, timetable, costs, qualifications of your company, and conclusion.

Introduction

The introduction to your sales proposal can be a single paragraph in a short sales proposal or several pages in a more complex one. Basically, your introduction should prepare readers for everything that follows in your proposal. The introduction itself may contain the following sections, which sometimes may be combined.

1. **Statement of purpose and subject of proposal.** Tell readers why you are writing and identify the specific subject of your work. If you are responding to an RFP, use specific code numbers or cite application dates, as the proposal in Figure 14.2 does. If your proposal is unsolicited, indicate how you learned of the problem, as Figure 14.4 does. Briefly define the solution you propose.

FIGURE 14.4   An unsolicited sales proposal.

 Computer Technologies, Inc.

August 24, 2000

Ms. Alexandra Tyrone-Saunders
Vice President, Operations
Gemini, Inc.
Hartford, CT 06631-7106

Dear Ms. Tyrone-Saunders:

While we were servicing your Webmax PCs last week, I saw several ways in which
Computer Technologies might improve your communications system. Based on our
assessment of Gemini's requirements for the most up-to-date automation available, we
recommend that you purchase 10 Lightstar 686 notebooks, one for each member of
your sales staff. This latest generation of notebooks will provide your staff with a
powerful and affordable system that will meet Gemini's needs well into the 21st
century.

PROBLEM AREAS

Each of your 10 sales staff spends up to 60 minutes at the end of each business day
entering orders he or she has accumulated in the field into the PCs at your office. That
amounts to 50 overtime hours per week. This procedure is costly and inefficient, taking
your staff away from their primary responsibility of serving your clients.

ADVANTAGES OF THE LIGHTSTAR 686 NOTEBOOK

Notebook computers are essential complements to other computer systems. According
to Felicia Gomez, writing at her Web site (http://www.worldtech.org), the Lightstar
686 is "one of the best computer buys of the decade, a powerhouse that will amaze the
most skeptical PC user." The following description of Lightstar's features will show
you how its many advantages can help Gemini.

ADVANCED TECHNOLOGY

The Lightstar 686 is equipped with the following standard features:

* an Intel 333-MHz Pentium III processor
* 1024 × 1200, 14-inch XGA Active matrix display
* 32-MB SDRAM PC 100
* internal 24X CD-ROM (with a 40X optional)
* 4.0-GB hard drive
* built-in touchpad pointing device

Fax 203-555-6714 **Phone** 203-555-1732

techsupport@interserv.com

Continued

FIGURE 14.4   (Continued)

2.

Your Lightstar will allow you to fax, e-mail, and connect to the Web. Please visit our Web site (**http://www.tech.com**) for more detail about Lightstar's technical specifications.

Cost Effective

Your Lightstar 686 will cost you far less than your PCs and offer equal or greater capability. Here are some of the bottom-line savings you will be getting:

* costs $500.00 less than one of your PCs did 2 years ago
* provides software upgrades at no charge
* includes everything integrated into the system—monitor, CPU, software

Assured Security

Lightstar offers a unique protection system to ensure the security of your unit:

* an encryption system requiring a special password to log onto and activate your notebook
* a removable hard drive (weighing only 1.5 pounds)
* a special feature known as "call home" that will alert your other notebooks of unauthorized use
* a log-on procedure to protect against employee misuse

Efficient Accessibility and Customer Service

Because the Lightstar is compatible with your office PCs, your representatives can access all pertinent records at your main office while making sales calls. By having direct access to vital documentation, your staff can more efficiently verify and store information about customer orders. The Lightstar makes the virtual office a reality. And because your sales force would be carrying your office with them, you will enhance their telecommuting capabilities.

Power Supply Capabilities

Equipped with a lithium ion battery, the Lightstar 686 operates up to six hours without recharging. With a car adapter/recharger, the Lightstar can operate without standard electricity almost indefinitely, helping your staff make calls at any location for extended periods of time.

Portability

* weighs only 2.2 pounds (1 kg)
* fits in standard briefcase
* comes with protective case

TRAINING AND SERVICE

Because all software can be preloaded, setup and installation can be brief—10 minutes. Since Lightstar is compatible with your PCs, only minimal training in how to use the

Continued

FIGURE 14.4   (Continued)

3.

Lightstar to upload sales orders or download product availability information will be necessary. Our local sales representative, Darlene Simpson, is available to instruct your staff about the operation and routine maintenance of the Lightstar.

If a problem occurs, we offer customers the latest in remote diagnostics. A modem installed in the Lightstar allows us to diagnose specific problems (and needed replacement parts).

COSTS

Below is an estimated price list for one Lightstar 686 notebook with upgraded features:

* Pentium III, 333 MHz
* 4.0-GB hard drive
* 64-MB SDRAM PC 100
* PCMCIA 56K V-90 fax modem
* Second lithium ion battery

    Total Purchase Price   **$1995.00**

You might also consider purchasing one or all of these options:

Pentium III 450 MHz	345.00
Sound card	75.00
External speakers	45.00
	$465.00 total for options

COMPUTER TECHNOLOGIES' REPUTATION

For the past 16 years Computer Technologies has provided quality products and fast, efficient service after the sale. A list of references is attached.

We appreciate your past confidence in Computer Technologies and look forward to expanding our service to Gemini. Please call me if you have any questions about the Lightstar or Computer Technologies. I would be happy to bring a Lightstar 686 to Gemini for you or your sales staff to use for a few days.

If this proposal is acceptable, please sign and return a copy with this letter.

Sincerely yours,

Marion Copely

Marion Copely

I accept the proposal made by Computer Technologies, Inc.

_____

for Gemini, Inc.

Encl.

2. Background of the problem you propose to solve. Show readers that you are familiar with their problem and why it is important. In a solicited proposal like Figure 14.2, this section is usually unnecessary, because the potential client has already identified the problem and wants to know how you would address it. In that case, just point out how your company would solve the problem, mentioning your superiority over your competitors (see the third paragraph of Figure 14.2).

In an unsolicited proposal, you need to describe the problem in convincing detail, identifying the specific trouble areas. However, if it is an external proposal to a current customer, such as the one in Figure 14.4, it would be unwise to point out past problems your client may have had with your company's service or products. In Figure 14.4 note how the problems of the staff in the field are described mainly as a way to sell the advantages of the Lightstar 686 notebook.

Description of the Proposed Product or Service

This section is the heart of your proposal. Before spending their money, customers will demand hard, factual evidence of what you claim can and should be done. Here are some points that your proposal should cover.

1. Carefully show potential customers that your product or service is right for them. Stress particular benefits of your product or service most relevant to your reader. Blend sales talk with descriptions of hardware.

2. Describe your work in suitable detail. Specify what the product looks like, what it does, and how consistently and well it will perform in the readers' office, plant, hospital, or agency. You might include a brochure, picture, diagram, or, as the writer of the proposal in Figure 14.2 does, a sample of your product for customers to study.

3. Stress any special features, maintenance advantages, warranties, or service benefits. Convince readers that your product is the most up-to-date and efficient one they could select. Highlight features that show the quality, consistency, or security of your work. For a service, emphasize the procedures you use, the terms of the service, even the kinds of tools you use, especially any state-of-the-art equipment.

Timetable

A carefully planned timetable shows readers that you know your job and that you can accomplish it in the right amount of time. Your dates should match any listed in an RFP. Provide specific dates to indicate

- when the work will begin
- how the work will be divided into phases or stages
- when you will be finished
- whether any follow-up visits or services are involved

For proposals offering a service, specify how many times—an hour, a week, a month—customers can expect to receive your help; for example, spraying three times a month for an exterminating service.

Costs

Make your budget accurate, complete, and convincing. Don't underestimate costs in the hope that a low bid will win you the job. You may get the job but lose money doing it, because the customer will rightfully hold you to your unrealistic figures. Accepted by both parties, a proposal is a binding legal agreement. Neither should you inflate prices; competitors will beat you in the bidding.

Give customers more than merely the bottom-line cost. Show exactly what readers are getting for their money so they can determine if everything they need is included. Itemize costs for

- specific services
- equipment/materials
- labor (by the hour or by the job)
- transportation
- travel
- training

If something is not included or is considered optional, say so—additional hours of training, replacement of parts, upgrades, and the like.

If you anticipate a price increase, let the customer know how long current prices will stay in effect. That information may spur them to act favorably now.

Qualifications of Your Company

Emphasize your company's accomplishments and expertise in providing similar services and equipment. Mention the names of a few local firms for whom you have worked that would be able to recommend you. But never misrepresent your qualifications or those of the individuals who work with or for you. Your prospective client may verify if you have in fact worked on similar jobs during the last five to six years.

Conclusion

This is the "call to action" section of your proposal. Encourage your reader to approve your plan by stressing major benefits of your plan. Offer to answer any questions the reader may have. Some proposals end by asking readers to sign and return a copy of the proposal indicating their acceptance, as the proposal in Figure 14.4 does.

Proposals for Research Papers and Reports

You may have to write a proposal when your instructor asks you to submit a report or research paper, a topic for an independent study, or some other major term project.

Writing for Your Instructor

The principles guiding internal and sales proposals also apply to research proposals. As with internal and sales proposals, you will be writing to convince the reader—your instructor—to approve a major piece of work. But otherwise the goals of your instructor/reader will be considerably different from those of other proposal readers. An instructor will read your proposal to help you write the best possible paper or report, and, in examining your proposal, will want to make sure of four things:

- that you have chosen a significant topic
- that you have a sufficiently restricted topic
- that you will investigate important sources of information about that topic
- that you can accomplish your work in the specified time

Your proposal gives your instructor an opportunity to spot omissions or inconsistencies and to provide helpful suggestions.

To prepare an effective proposal for a research project, you must do some preliminary research. You cannot pick any topic that comes to mind or guess about procedures, sources, or conclusions. As other proposal readers do, your instructor will want convincing and specific evidence for your choice of topic and your approach to it. Be prepared to cite key facts to show that you are familiar with the topic and that you can write about it confidently and knowledgeably.

Organization of a Proposal for a Research Paper

Your proposal for a school research project can be a memo or an e-mail divided into five sections, as illustrated in Figure 14.5: *introduction* (or purpose), *scope of the problem* or topic to be investigated, *methods or procedures, timetable,* and *request for approval.* However, be ready to reverse or expand these sections if your instructor wants you to follow a different organizational plan.

The Introduction

Keep your introduction short—a paragraph, maybe two, pinpointing the subject and purpose of your work.

> I propose to research and write a report about the "hot knife" laser used in treating port wine stains and other birthmarks.

> I intend to investigate the relationship that exists between office design and employees' need for "psychological space."

Then briefly indicate why the topic or the problem you propose to study is significant. In other words, be prepared to explain why you have chosen that topic and why research on it is relevant or worthwhile for a specific audience or course objective. Note how Barbara R. Shoemake in Figure 14.5 states how and why her report will be useful to office managers.

Supply your instructor/reader with a few background details about your topic, for example, the importance of using a laser as opposed to conventional ways of treating birthmarks or why psychological space plays a crucial role in employee productivity and morale. Prove that you have thought carefully about selecting a suitable topic.

The Scope of the Problem or Topic to Be Investigated

The second section, which might be entitled "Problems to Be Investigated" or "Areas to Be Studied," shows how you propose to break the topic into meaningful units. Tell your reader what specific issues, points, or areas you hope to investigate. Doing that, you demonstrate how you will limit your topic.

Some instructors ask students to formulate a list of questions their research paper or report intends to answer. The topics included in such questions or in a list

FIGURE 14.5   A proposal for a research paper.

To: Professor Leigh Felton-Parks
From: Barbara R. Shoemake   *B.R.S.*
Date: February 4, 2000
Subject: Proposal for a report on the ethical and security issues involved in
              using e-mail

PURPOSE
For my term project I propose to research and write a report on the ethical and
security issues involved in using e-mail in the workplace.

E-mail is the most frequently used form of business communication. It has been
estimated that 70 million e-mail users receive 15 billion messages a year, most for
internal business communications. E-mail has brought many companies closer to
the paperless office. At West Industries, over 61,000 employees receive their
company publications on-line. Alexis Brown claims that "E-mail gets a higher
reading rate than printed material" *(Public Relations Journal* [Jan. 2000]: 25).

Despite its many advantages, e-mail presents major ethical and legal problems.
Using e-mail technology is not always comfortable and uncomplicated for
employees or their employers. E-mail privacy is at the heart of the controversy.
Major legal battles have been waged over who can and should read an individual's
e-mail at work. An understanding of the ethical considerations and security
drawbacks of e-mail is important for managers evaluating their office's internal
communications. My paper will serve as a background report for those office
managers.

PROBLEMS TO BE INVESTIGATED
At this preliminary stage of my research, I think my report needs to answer the
following questions:

(1) How does e-mail differ from conventional communication methods (telephones,
letters) in terms of confidentiality?

(2) Do employers have the right (or responsibility) to monitor employees'
workplace e-mail or is this a violation of the employees' right to privacy?

(3) What can be done to establish a more secure e-mail system both to protect
confidentiality and to ensure company security?

(4) What types of special training programs—on business communication,
netiquette, and legal issues—are most necessary and effective for e-mail use?

I propose, therefore, to divide the body of my paper according to the four key
issues of confidentiality, monitoring, security, and training.

Continued

FIGURE 14.5   (Continued)

2.

METHODS OF RESEARCH
I will rely heavily on literature dealing with e-mail. Judging from the number of entries found on this general topic through FirstSearch and the search engines Alta Vista and Yahoo!, the subject of e-mail is both popular and significant. I found over 980 entries. Restricting my search to just security and ethical issues, I located 54 items. From a preliminary check of what is available from the holdings at McGovern Library and on-line, I think the following may be most useful.

Baker, Timothy. "E-Mail Security: A Complete How-to Guide." *Nation's Business* 34 (Aug. 1999): 23–28.

Cahlin, Michael. "PC Security." *Smart Computing* 10 (April 1999): 24.

Crinian, Susan. "Company E-Mail Deserves Close Scrutiny for Security." *Business Journal* 19 (April 16, 1999): 54–55.

D'Souza, Patricia. "Keep Those Words to Yourself." *Canadian Business* 12 Feb. 1999: 76.

Electronic Frontier Foundation. "Implementation for Privacy on the Internet." 26 Jan. 1999 <http://www.eff.org/privacy paper>.

Gair, Cristina. "Electronic Services Provide Security for a Price." *Home Office Computing* 16 (Nov. 1998): 22.

Horowitz, Sherry L. "E-Mail's Packet of Problems." *Security Management* 42 (Oct. 1998): 47–49.

"Here's Help for Your Employee E-Mail Problems." 1 Feb. 2000 <http://www.c3c.com/help>.

Hodson, Thomas J., Fred Englander, and Valerie Englander. "Legal and Economic Aspects of Employer Monitoring of Employee Electronic Mail." *Journal of Business Ethics* 19 (Mar. 1999): 99–108.

"Is E-Mail Safe for Your Company's Health?" *Supervisory Management* 42 (Jan. 1997): 17–18.

Lewis, Jamie. "Risky Business: E-Mail Security Gets Serious." *PC Week* 27 July 1998: 88.

Lombardi, Rosie. "Corporate Confidential: Developing an Acceptable Use Policy on Internet E-Mail." *CA Magazine* June/July 1998: 39–40.

Luening, Erich. "Email security flaw discovered." CNET News.com. 28 July 1998. <http://technews.netscape.com/News/Item/0,4,24668,00.html> (30 Jan. 2000).

Continued

FIGURE 14.5   (Continued)

3.

"Media, Information, Society, and Data Protection." 6 Apr. 1999 <http://europa.eu.int/comm/dg15/en/media/dataprot/index.htm> (2 Feb. 2000).

Rainone, Sebastian M., Janice C. Sipior, and Burke T. Ward. "Ethical Management of Employee E-Mail Privacy." *Information Strategy* 14 (Spring 1998): 34–40.

Schneier, Bruce. *E-Mail Security: How to Keep Your Electronic Message Private.* New York: Wilex, 2000.

Sipior, Janice. "Ethics of Employee E-Mail Privacy." *Information Systems Management* 15 (Winter 1998): 41–47.

Van Horn, Royal W. "Personal Privacy." *Phi Delta Kappan* 80 (Sept. 1998): 32.

"What You Don't Know About Your Employees' E-Mail Can Hurt You." Aug 1999. <http://www.miracletechnologies.com/email.htm> (17 Jan. 2000).

Zheng, Ti. *A Beginner's Guide to E-Mail: Protocols and Privacy.* Boston: Amplex, 1999.

I also intend to interview two office managers in Springfield whose companies have offered employee seminars on e-mail security in the last year. My choices right now are Alice Phillips at Dodge & Spenser systems and Keith Wellbridge at General Dynamics. Because of their possible schedule conflicts, I may have to interview two other individuals.

SCHEDULE
I hope to complete my research by April 2 and my interviews by April 8. Then I will spend the following two weeks working on a draft, which I will submit by April 18, the date you specified. After receiving your comments on my draft, I will work on revisions and the final copy of my report and turn it in by May 15, the last day of class. I will submit two progress reports—one when I finish my research and another when I decide on the final organization of my paper.

REQUEST FOR APPROVAL
I ask that you approve my topic and my approach to it. I would appreciate any suggestions on how you think I might best proceed. My e-mail address is bshoemake@bsu.edu, if you prefer to send them to me that way.

Thank you.

of areas or problems to be covered might later become major sections of your paper. Make sure the issues or questions do not overlap and that each relates directly to and supports your restricted topic. Note how the student in Figure 14.5 hopes to divide her study of e-mail into four distinct yet related areas.

Methods or Procedures

In the third section of your proposal inform your instructor how you expect to find the answers to the questions you raised in the previous section or how you intend to locate information about your list of subtopics. It's not enough to write, "I will gather appropriate information and analyze it." Specify what data you hope to include, where they are located, and how you intend to retrieve them.

Most students gather data from the Web and from literature published in print sources about their topics. (In fact, many research papers are based exclusively on literature searches.) The literature can include books, encyclopedias or other reference materials, articles in professional publications, newspapers, bulletins, manuals, or reviews. Inform your instructor what indexes, abstracts, or Internet searches you intend to use (review pp. 299–321) as part of your search. To document your preliminary work, provide your instructor with a list of a few appropriate titles on your topic following the style of documentation used for a Works Cited page (discussed on pp. 353–359).

In addition to on-line and print materials, you might collect information from lab experiments, field tests, interviews with experts, chat rooms and listservs, questionnaires, or a combination of any of those sources.

Timetable/Schedule

Indicate when and in what order you expect to complete the different phases of your project. Your instructor needs that information to keep track of your progress and to make sure you will turn in an assignment on time. Specify tentative dates for completing your research, draft(s), revisions, and final copy.

Some instructors also ask students to turn in progress reports (see pp. 587–593) at regular intervals. If you are asked to do that, indicate when you will submit the progress reports, as Barbara R. Shoemake does in Figure 14.5.

Request for Approval

End your proposal with a request for approval of your topic and a plan of action. You might also invite suggestions from your instructor on how to restrict, research, organize, or write about your topic.

A Final Reminder

This chapter has given you some basic information and specific strategies for writing winning proposals. Keep in mind that a proposal presents a plan to a decision maker for his or her approval. To win that approval, your proposal must be (a) *realistic,* (b) *carefully researched,* and (c) *highly persuasive.* Those essential characteristics apply to internal proposals in memo or e-mail format written to your employer, more formal sales proposals sent to a potential customer, and research proposals submitted to your instructor.

✓ Revision Checklist

❏ Established and distinguished roles of collaborative team members involved in the preparation of the proposal.

❏ Researched appropriate sources for RFPs and followed their instructions.

❏ Identified a realistic problem, one that is restricted and relevant to my topic and my audience's needs.

❏ Tried effectively to convince audience that the problem exists and needs to be solved.

❏ Incorporated quantifiable details demonstrating the scope and importance of the problem.

❏ Persuasively emphasized benefits of solving the problem according to the proposal; incorporated the "you attitude" throughout.

❏ Investigated and overcame competing alternatives or firms.

❏ Offered a solution that can be realistically implemented—that is, it is both appropriate and feasible for audience.

❏ Wrote clearly so audience can understand how and why my proposal would work.

❏ Researched background of problem.

❏ Used specific figures and concrete details to show how proposal saves time, money.

❏ Double-checked proposal to catch errors, omissions, and inconsistencies.

❏ Avoided exaggerations.

❏ Presented information ethically.

❏ Organized proposal with appropriate headings for clarity and ease of reading.

❏ *For internal proposal:* Demonstrated how proposal benefits my company and my supervisor; took into account office politics in describing problem and solution; discussed proposal with co-workers or supervisors who may be affected.

❏ *For sales proposal:* Related my product or service to prospective customer's needs; showed a clear understanding of those needs.

❏ Prepared a comprehensive and realistic budget; accounted for all expenses; itemized costs of products and services in sales proposal.

❏ Provided a timetable with exact dates for implementing proposal.

❏ Cited other successful jobs and satisfied clients to show my company's track record.

❏ Concluded proposal with a summary of main benefits to readers and a call to action.

❏ Proved to my instructor that I researched the problem by supplying a list of possible references and sources for a proposal for a research report/paper.

Exercises

1. In two or three paragraphs identify and document a problem (in services, safety, communication, traffic, scheduling) you see in your office or your community. Make sure you give reader—a civic official (head of a department) or employer (section or department head; manager)—specific evidence that a problem does exist and that it needs to be corrected.

2. Write a short internal proposal, modeled after Figure 14.3, based on the problem you identified in Exercise 1.

3. Write a short internal proposal, similar to Tina Escobar and Oliver Jabur's in Figure 14.3, recommending to a company or a college a specific change in procedure, equipment, training, safety, personnel, or policy. Make sure your team provides an appropriate audience (college administrator, department manager, or section chief) with specific evidence about the existence of the problem and your solution of it. Possible topics include
   a. providing more and safer parking
   b. forming a Usenet or listserv group
   c. purchasing new office or laboratory equipment or software
   d. hiring more faculty, student workers, or office help
   e. reorganizing or redesigning the school yearbook or company annual report or sales catalog or Web site
   f. changing the decor/furniture in a student or company lounge
   g. increasing the number of weekend or night classes in your major
   h. adding more health-conscious offerings to the school or company cafeteria menu
   i. altering the programming on a campus radio station
   j. expanding distance learning offerings

4. Write an unsolicited sales proposal, similar to the one in Figure 14.4, on one of the following services or products you intend to sell or on a topic your instructor approves.
   a. providing exterminating service to a store or restaurant
   b. supplying a hospital with rental television sets for patients' rooms
   c. designing Web sites
   d. offering temporary office help or nursing care
   e. providing landscaping and lawn care work
   f. testing for noise, air, or water pollution in your community or neighborhood
   g. furnishing transportation for students, employees, or members of a community group
   h. providing consulting service to save a company money
   i. digging a septic well for a small apartment complex
   j. supplying insurance coverage to a small firm (five to ten employees)
   k. cleaning the parking lot and outside walkways at a shopping center
   l. selling a piece of equipment to a business

      m. making a work area safer

      n. offering a training program for employees

      o. increasing donations to a community or charitable fund

5. Write a solicited proposal for one of the topics listed in Exercise 4 or for a topic that your instructor approves. You might want to review Figure 14.2. Do this exercise as a collaborative effort.

6. Write an appropriate proposal—internal, solicited sales, or unsolicited sales—based on the information contained in one of the following three articles. Assume that you or your prospective customer's company or community faces a problem similar to one discussed in one of these articles. Use as much of the information in the article as you need and add any details of your own that you think are necessary. This exercise can be done as an individual or collaborative assignment.

Multiuse Campuses: A Plan That Works

Gaylord Community School in Gaylord, Michigan, is a bustling center of activity from the first light of dawn to well after dusk. People of all ages come and go until late into the evening for a multitude of activities that include attending classes and meetings, catching up with friends, getting a flu shot, and seeing a play. That's because in addition to a high school, the campus also includes senior and day-care centers, classrooms for adult education, an auditorium for the performing arts, a community health-care site, and even a space that can be booked for weddings and other special occasions.

In Big Lake, Minnesota, elementary, middle, and high school buildings are all situated on one centrally located campus that makes up the entire Big Lake School District. Also included in this innovative layout are a state-of-the-art theater, a community resource center, and a multipurpose athletic arena, all of which are used extensively by the entire community.

Both the Gaylord and Big Lake schools are models of a growing movement toward multiuse community campuses that serve as "anchor[s] in the civic life of our nation," according to U.S. Secretary of Education Richard W. Riley. I recently had the pleasure of visiting Secretary Riley in his office. Also present were AARP President Joe Perkins and National Retired Teachers Association Director Annette Norsman, both of whom are involved in many facets of education and lifelong learning.

We discussed many things, including our concerns about the current increase in the number of students caused by the Baby Boom echo (children of the Boomers) and how that population is going to further stress the already crumbling infrastructure of American schools. We also talked about the need for resources—to employ more teachers, bring technology into the classroom, strengthen educational curriculum and opportunities for all ages—and the pressing need to build and renovate schools. That led to a discussion about the necessity and benefit of involving the whole community in the design and use of new school facilities.

I always thought that it was a shame that the majority of schools are used only a third of the day, three fourths of the year, by only a fifth of the population. Considering that there will be more school construction over the next decade than at any time since the 1950s, it just makes sense to consider the intergenerational and community benefits of multiuse spaces, benefits that include everything from establishing better learning environments to getting more bang for the tax buck.

There are many additional bonuses for multiuse educational complexes: They create an exciting community hub, bring life and culture to a central area, and revitalize and nourish the neighborhood in which they are located.

It's a win-win situation for everyone involved.

Horace B. Deets, "Multiuse Campuses: A Plan That Works," *Modern Maturity* (July–August 1999): 72. Reprinted with permission from *Modern Maturity*. Copyright © 1999 by American Association of Retired Persons.

Self-illuminating Exit Signs

The Marine Corps Development and Education Center (MCDEC), Quantico, Virginia, submitted a project recently, to replace incandescent illumination exit signs with self-illuminating exit signs for a cost of $97,238. The first-year savings were anticipated to be about $37,171 with an anticipated payback time of 2.6 years—an excellent prospect. The contractor bid much lower, however, and the actual payback will be about 1.5 years.

What are the benefits of these self-illuminating exit signs? The primary benefit is that virtually all operation and maintenance expense is eliminated for the life of the device, normally from 10 to 12 years. Power failures or other disturbances will not cause them to go out.

In new construction, expensive electrical circuits can be totally eliminated. In retrofits, the release of a dedicated circuit for other use may be of considerable benefit. Initial total cost of installing circuits and conventional devices approximately equals the cost of the self-illuminating signs. Installation labor and expense for the self-illuminating signs is about that of hanging a picture.

The amount of electricity saved varies and depends on whether your existing fixtures are fluorescent (13 to 26 watts) or incandescent (50 to 100 watts). Multiply the number of fixtures $\times$ wattage/fixture $\times$ hours operated/day $\times$ days/year = KWH/year savings. For example, assume:

400 incandescent fixtures
$0.08/KWH 0.05 KW/fixture
24 hours/day 365 day/year operation
$400 \times 0.1 \times 365 = 350400$ KWH/year
$350400 \times 0.08 = \$28,032$/year for electricity

Now add in savings achieved from:

- reducing labor to change bulbs
- avoiding bulb material, stocking, and storage costs
- avoiding transportation costs involved in bulb changes
- reusing existing bulbs

The above savings can be significant. For the MCDEC Quantico project, estimates of bulb change interval and savings were 700 hours (29 days) and $13,512/year when all factors were considered.

The cost of a self-illuminating sign depends on whether one or two faces are illuminated primarily and varies between different suppliers. Single-face prices will likely be $100 to $150 while double-face prices may be $250 to $330. The contractor at Quantico found better prices than these ranges indicate. The labor cost should be about $10 per sign.

`If you can use an exit-sign system with high dependability, no maintenance, and zero operations cost in your retrofit on new construction projects, try a self-illuminating exit-sign system in your economic analysis today. "Isolite" signs, by Safety Light Corp., are listed as FSC (Fire Safety Code) Group 99, Part IV, Section A, Class 9905 signs and are available through GSA contract. Contact Gerald Harnett, Safety Light Corp., P.O. Box 266, Greenbelt, MD 20070 for more information.

Lt. James F. McCollum, CEG, USN. "Self-illuminating Exit Signs Equal High Payback." *Navy Civil Engineer* (Summer 1983): 30–31.

Wheelchair-Lift Switch Covers

In order to ensure year-round access to the Springfield Armory National Historic Site (Massachusetts) museum, Michael C. Trebbe designed the cover for switches on wheelchair lifts. During the extreme New England winters, the switch buttons would freeze, thus making the lift inoperable, which in turn required several hours to thaw. The installation of these covers prevented the freezing of the switch buttons and, therefore, allowed maintenance personnel to attend to matters such as snow removal.

The covers were made of materials found on site, which resulted in the covers being almost cost free. The covers can be quickly built, and they are mounted with the same mounting screws as the switch boxes so as to not destroy any original fabric (in the case of Springfield Armory NHS, brownstone). The materials used included:

- 1/8-in. by $4\frac{1}{2}$-in. by 12-in. piece of rubber mat
- $3\frac{1}{2}$-in. by $6\frac{1}{2}$-in. piece of sheet metal
- three aluminum pop rivets
- primer for the sheet metal
- wheelchair symbol
- white paint for the symbol

The sheet metal is bent to a 90-degree angle at the $5\frac{1}{2}$-inch point. The lowest two holes (see diagram) are drilled to mount the screws of the switch box, which also secure the cover. Triangular cutouts and other holes are drilled for the clearance of the housing screws on the rear of the switch box (see diagram).

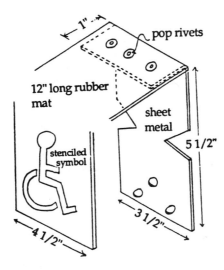

The handicap symbol is stenciled on the front of the piece of rubber mat using white paint.

Michael C. Trebbe, *Grist*, Vol. 36, No. 1 (Winter 1992). U.S. Department of the Interior, National Park Service.

7. Write a suitable research proposal on which the research paper on "The Advantages of Telecommuting in the Information Age" (pp. 374–393) could have been based.

8. Write a research proposal to your instructor seeking approval for a research-based long report. Do the necessary preliminary research to show that you have selected a suitable topic, narrowed it, and identified the sources of information you have to consult. List at least six relevant articles, two books, and two Web sites pertinent to your topic.

Writing Effective Short Reports

This chapter shows you how to write short reports, also called informal or semi-formal reports. A short report can be defined as an organized presentation of relevant data on any topic—money, travel, time, personnel, equipment, management—that a company or agency tracks in its day-to-day operations. You will be asked to write short reports frequently on the job—on your own or in collaboration with co-workers. Short reports are written to co-workers, employers, vendors, and clients.

Because a large part of your annual evaluation for raises and promotions will depend on the caliber of your short reports, it is important to know how to write them effectively.

Why Short Reports Are Important

Business and industry cannot function without short written reports. Reports tell whether

- work is being completed
- schedules are being met
- costs have been contained
- sales projections are being met
- unexpected problems have been solved

You may write an occasional report in response to a specific question, or you may be required to write a daily or weekly report on routine activities. Many organizations—businesses, clinics, mass transportation systems, schools—must submit regularly scheduled reports to maintain their accreditation or funding by state, municipal, or federal agencies.

Types of Short Reports

To give you a sense of some of the topics you may be required to write about, here is a list of various types of short reports common in the business world.

appraisal report	inventory report	production report
audit report	investigative report	progress/activity report
budget reports	justification report	recommendation report
construction report	laboratory report	research report
design report	manager's report	sales report
evaluation report	medicine/treatment	status report
experiment report	error report	test report
feasibility report	operations report	trip/travel report
incident report	periodic report	

This chapter will concentrate on the six most common types of reports you are likely to encounter in your professional work:

1. periodic reports
2. sales reports
3. progress reports
4. trip/travel reports
5. test reports
6. incident reports

The first five reports can be called **routine reports** because they give information about planned, ongoing, or recurring events. The sixth category, **incident reports,** are reports that describe events the writers did not anticipate—accidents, breakdowns, environmental mishaps, delivery delays, or work stoppages. All six, however, can be termed *short* reports because they deal with current happenings rather than long-range forecasts. Short reports focus on the "trees," not the "forest."

Guidelines for Writing Short Reports

Though there are many kinds of short reports, they all are written for readers who need factual information so they can get a job accomplished. Never think of the reports you write as a series of casual notes jotted down for *your* convenience.

The following guidelines will help you write any short report successfully.

Do the Necessary Research

An effective short report needs the same careful planning that goes into other on-the-job writing. Your research may be as simple as telephoning, e-mailing, or leaving a voice mail for a colleague or inspecting a piece of equipment. Some frequent types of research you can expect to do on the job include

- checking data in reference manuals or code books
- exploring the Web, using key search engines
- searching databases for recent discussions of a problem or procedure
- reading background information in professional and trade journals
- reviewing a client's file
- testing equipment
- performing an experiment or procedure

- conferring with colleagues, managers, vendors, or clients
- describing a site
- attending a conference

Anticipate How an Audience Will Use Your Report

Consider how much your audience knows about your project and what types of information they need most. Employers, the largest audience for your reports, may not always know (or be interested in) the technical details of your work. Instead, they want bottom-line information—costs, personnel, organizational structure, problems, or delays. While co-workers may be familiar with your project, colleagues in other departments, consumers, or individuals outside your company (such as site inspectors) may not. Accordingly, those readers may require more background information, definitions, and examples.

To meet your audience's needs, answer the following questions appropriately for your readers:

1. **Why are you writing?** This may be your reader's most significant—and urgent—question. Always explain your reasons for writing. Is your report routine or has it been requested for a special purpose—such as justifying a new position in your department. Tell readers, too, why you think something turned out the way it did.

2. **What happened?** Explain clearly and logically what steps you followed in a lab report, what specific events or circumstances occurred, what conclusions can be made, what prospects are likely for future business.

3. **When did something happen?** Always give dates and specify the exact period the report covers. Just listing "Wednesday" is not enough. Give the date and indicate A.M. or P.M. Some employers may ask you to use a twenty-four-hour clock: 1:00 A.M. is 0100 hours; 1:00 P.M. is 1300 hours. An event occurring on February 19, 2000, at 2:30 P.M. is written 00/2/19/1430—year, month, day, time (hours/minutes).

4. **Where did something happen?** Give precise locations. "Highway 30" is not as helpful as "Highway 30, three miles southeast of the Morton exit."

5. **Who did something or who was involved?** Give readers the names of clients, contact people, technical staff you consulted, members of your collaborative team, or individuals involved in a test or accident.

6. **How did something happen?** Tell readers how a test was conducted. Describe the procedures you used. Inform them about the results you observed or how a delay, problem, or shortage affected your progress. Explain whether a presentation was relevant and effective and how it might affect your business.

Be Objective and Ethical

Your readers will expect you to report the facts objectively and impartially—costs, sales, weather conditions, eyewitness accounts, observations, statistics, test measurements, and descriptions. Your reports should be truthful, accurate, and complete. Your boss's decision will be based on that information.

- Avoid *guesswork.* If you don't know or have not yet found out, say so and indicate how you'll try to find out.
- Do not substitute *impressions* or *unsupported personal opinions* for careful research
- Using *biased, skewed, or incomplete data* is unethical. Provide a straightforward and honest account; don't exaggerate or minimize.

Review pages 24–30 on ethics in business writing.

Choose a Reader-Centered Format and Design

For the most part, reports for readers in your company will be written or e-mailed as memos, while those submitted to clients will be letters. Regardless of the format, help your readers easily find information by including the following:

- *A clear, precise subject line.* Announce your subject and purpose.
- *Headings* that preview and highlight information. Your report needs subdivisions; don't bombard readers with a series of uninterrupted paragraphs.
- *Bullets or numbers* to list and group main points.
- *Underscoring or boldfacing* for emphasis. Make it easier for readers to skim (if necessary) or review.
- *Visuals* to clarify and expedite. Never load readers down with uninterpreted numerical information in the text of your report. Note how much harder it is for readers to wade through Figure 15.1, which does not include a table, than to navigate Figure 15.2, which does. Many of the short reports in this chapter include a clarifying visual—a map (Figure 15.8), a table (Figures 15.2 and 15.11), or an exploded drawing (Figure 15.12).

Write Concisely and Clearly

Say what you need to say without wasting readers' time. Even though a short report is just that—short—allow time for careful revising and editing. Writing concisely—to the point and clearly—requires effort. (You may want to review pp. 57–62). Especially time consuming for your readers are wordy expressions that could be replaced by more serviceable substitutes, such as the following examples.

Wordy	Concise
at this point in time	now
make a concerted attempt to	try
take place in such a manner that	occur

Call machines and other equipment by their precise names. Never use "thing," "gizmo," or "contraption" to refer to parts or tools.

Also, avoid vague and unsupported statements such as the following:

Vague: Sales were brisk this week with many favorable possibilities on the horizon.

Precise: During the first week of June, our sales increased by 12.25 percent over those of the last week in May. Much of the increase can be attributed to our new home page, which makes ordering easier for customers. Many of our new customers specifically mentioned our home page when placing their orders.

FIGURE 15.1   An example of a poorly written, poorly organized, and poorly formatted short report.

GREENFIELD POLICE DEPARTMENT

Emergency 555-1000   **Administration** 555-1001   **Traffic** 555-1002

TO: Capt. Alice Martin
FROM: Sergeants Daniel Huxley, Jennifer Chavez,
                 and Ivor Paz
Vague   SUBJECT: Crime rate
           DATE: July 12, 2000

Introduction doesn't tell reader anything about overall picture

This report will let you know what happened this quarter as opposed to what happened last quarter as far as crimes are concerned in Greenfield. This report is based on statistics the department has given us over the quarter.

Throws facts at reader without any sense of reader's needs

Irrelevant data

Here we'll let the facts speak for themselves. From Jan.-Mar. we saw 126 robberies while from Apr.-June we had 106. Home burglaries for this period: 43; last period: 36. 33 cars were stolen in the period before this one; now we have 40. Interestingly enough, last year at this time we had only 27 thefts. Four of them involved heirlooms.

No analysis or guided commentary—just undigested numbers

Homicides were 9 this time versus 8 last quarter; assault and battery charges were 92 this time, 77 last time. Carrying a concealed weapon 11 (10 last quarter). We had 47 arrests (55 last quarter) for charges of possession of a controlled substance. Rape charges were 8, 1 less than last quarter. 319 citations this time for moving violations: speeding 158/98, and failing to observe the signals 165/102 last quarter. DUIs were good this quarter—only 45, or 23 fewer than last quarter.

Hard-to-follow comparisons and contrasts

Misdemeanors this time: disturbing peace 53; vagrancy/public drunkenness 8; violating leash laws 32; violating city codes 39, including dumping trash. Last quarter the figures were 48, 59, 21, 43.

Conclusion provides no summary or recommendation

We believe this report is complete and up to date. We further hope that this report has given you all the facts you will need.

FIGURE 15.2   A well-prepared quarterly report, revised from Figure 15.1.

GREENFIELD POLICE DEPARTMENT

Emergency 555-1000   **Administration** 555-1001   **Traffic** 555-1002

TO: Captain Alice Martin
FROM: Sergeants Daniel Huxley, Jennifer Chavez, and Ivor Paz
SUBJECT: Crime rate for the second quarter of 2000
DATE: July 12, 2000

From April 1 to June 30, 852 crimes were committed in Greenfield, representing a 5 percent increase over the 815 crimes recorded during the previous quarter.

The following report, based on the table below, discusses the specific types of crimes, organized into four categories: **robberies and theft, felonies, traffic, and misdemeanors**.

Table 1. Comparison of the 1st and 2nd Quarter 2000 Crime Rates in Greenfield

CATEGORY	1st Quarter	2nd Quarter
ROBBERIES and THEFT		
Commercial	63	75
Domestic	36	43
Auto	33	40
FELONIES		
Homicides	16	13
Assault and Battery	77	92
Carrying a concealed weapon	10	11
Poss. of a controlled substance	55	47
Rape	9	8
TRAFFIC		
Speeding	165	158
Failure to observe signals	102	98
DUI	78	45
MISDEMEANORS		
Disturbing the peace	48	53
Vagrancy	40	48
Public drunkenness	19	40
Leash law violations	21	32
Dumping	35	37
Other	8	12

ROBBERIES AND THEFT
The greatest increase in crime was in robberies, 20 percent more than last quarter. Downtown merchants reported 75 burglaries, exceeding $985,000. The biggest theft occurred on May 21 at Weisenfarth's Jewelers when three armed robbers stole more

Continued

FIGURE 15.2   (Continued)

than $97,000 in merchandise. (Suspects were apprehended two days later.) Home burglaries accounted for 43 crimes, though the thefts were not confined to any one residential area. We also had 40 car thefts reported and investigated.

FELONIES
Homicides decreased slightly from last quarter—from 16 to 13. Charges for battery, however, increased—15 more than we had last quarter. Arrests for carrying a concealed weapon were nearly identical this quarter to last quarter's total. But the 47 arrests for possession of a controlled substance were appreciably down from the first quarter. Arrests for rape for this quarter also were less than last quarter's. Three of those rapes happened within one week (May 6–12) and have been attributed to the same suspect, now in custody.

TRAFFIC
Traffic violations for this period were lower than last quarter's figures. This quarter's citations for moving violations (335) represent a 5 percent increase over last quarter's (322). Most of the citations were issued for speeding (158) or for failing to observe signals (98). Officers issued 45 citations to motorists for DUI, an impressive decrease over the 78 DUI's issued last quarter. The new state penalty of withholding a driver's license for six months of anyone convicted of driving while under the influence appears to be an effective deterrent.

MISDEMEANORS
The largest number of arrests in this category were for disturbing the peace—53. Compared to last quarter, this is an increase of 10 percent. There were 88 charges for vagrancy and public drunkenness, an increase from the 59 charges from last quarter. We issued 32 citations for violations of leash laws, which represents a sizable increase over last quarter's 21 citations. Thirty-seven citations were issued for dumping trash at the Mason Reservoir.

CONCLUSION
Overall, while the crime rate has decreased in traffic (especially DUI's) and possession of controlled substances this quarter, we have seen a marked increase in arrests for robberies and battery.

RECOMMENDATIONS
To help deter robberies in the downtown area, we recommend the following:

1. increasing surveillance units in the area
2. offering merchants our workshop on safety and security precautions, as we did during the first quarter

Historically, battery arrests have risen during the second quarter. Our recommendations to counter that trend include:

1. continuing to work closely with the Neighborhood Watch Group
2. including more foot and bicycle patrols in the neighborhoods with the highest incidence of battery reports

Organize Carefully

Organizing a short report effectively means that you include the right amount of information in the most appropriate places for your audience. Many times a simple chronological or sequential organization will be acceptable for your readers. Your employer may have precise instructions on how to organize routine reports, but here is a fairly standard organizational plan to follow.

Purpose

Always begin by telling readers why you are writing and by alerting them to what you will discuss. When you establish the scope (or limits) of your report, you help readers zero in on specific times, places, procedures, or problems. Depending on your purpose and audience, you may have to start with a clear explanation or description of the problem to be studied or solved. You may also need to provide necessary background information (say, a summary of an earlier report or occurrence) to assist readers.

Findings

This is the longest part of your report and contains data you have collected—facts about prices, personnel, equipment, events, locations, incidents, or experiments. Gather the data from your research, personal observations, interviews, or conversations with co-workers, employers, or clients.

Conclusion

Generally, your conclusion tells readers what your data means. A conclusion can summarize what has happened, review what actions were taken, or explain the outcome or results of a test, a visit, or a program.

Recommendations

A recommendation informs readers what specific actions you think your company or client should take. Recommendations must be based on the data you collected and the conclusions you have reached.

The placement of recommendations in a short report can vary. Some employers prefer to see recommendations at the beginning of a report; others want them listed last. Some short reports (including those in Figures 15.4 and 15.7) do not require a recommendation. Be sure to find out if your readers will expect you to make one.

The report in Figure 15.1 fails to follow the six guidelines. The revised version of the report, Figure 15.2, shows how the guidelines work to improve report writing.

Periodic Reports

Periodic reports, as their name signifies, provide readers with information at regularly scheduled intervals—daily, weekly, bimonthly (twice a month), monthly, quarterly. They help a company or agency keep track of the quantity and quality of the services it provides and the amount and types of work done by employees. Information in periodic reports helps managers make schedules, order materials, assign personnel, budget funds, and, generally speaking, determine corporate needs.

You may be responsible for compiling a report based on individual logs or daily or weekly employee activity reports. Figure 15.2, a report submitted to a police captain, summarizes, organizes, and interprets the data collected over a three-month period from individual activity logs. Because of this report, Captain Alice Martin will be better able to plan future protection for the community and to recommend changes in police services.

Sales Reports

Sales reports provide businesses with a necessary and ongoing record of accounts, on-line and mail purchases, losses, and profits over a specified period of time. Sales reports might be considered a special type of periodic report, but because of their importance in the world of business they deserve a separate category here.

Why They Are Important

Sales reports are important at various levels of business. Businesses require a daily sales report in which purchases, classified by bar code scanners, are arranged into major categories. Salespeople often submit weekly reports on the types and costs of products sold in a given district. Branch managers write monthly reports based on the figures given them by their sales force. Higher up the business ladder, the president of a company assesses the financial health of the business for stockholders in an annual report, in which sales reports are a key feature as they relate to profits and dividends.

TECH NOTE

Lateral and Vertical Reports

A report sent to someone at the same level of management as the writer (branch manager to branch manager) is known as a **lateral report.** A report sent to a higher executive level than the level of the writer (branch manager to vice president of marketing) is known as a **vertical report.**

Functions of Sales Reports

Sales reports help businesses assess past performance and plan for the future. In doing that, they fulfill two functions: **financial** and **managerial.** As a financial record, sales reports list costs per unit, discounts or special reductions, and subtotals and totals. Like a spreadsheet, sales reports show gains and losses. They may also provide statistics for comparing two quarters' sales. The method or origin of a sale, if significant, can also be recorded. In selling books, for example, a publisher keeps a careful record of where sales originate—direct orders for single copies from readers, school district adoptions for classroom use, purchases at bookstores and over the Internet, and orders from wholesale distributors handling the book.

Sales reports are also a managerial tool because they help businesses make both short- and long-range plans. By indicating the number of sales, the report alerts buyers and managers about which items or services to increase, modify, or discontinue. The restaurant manager's sales report illustrated in Figure 15.3 guides the owners in menu planning. Knowing which popular entrees to highlight and which unpopular ones to delete, the owners can increase their profits. Note how the recommendations follow logically from the figures Sam Jelinek gives to Gina Smeltzer and Alfonso Zapatta, the owners of the The Grill.

Progress Reports

A progress report informs readers about the status of an ongoing project. It lets them know how much and what type of work has been completed by a particular date, by whom, how well, and how close the entire job is to being completed. A progress report emphasizes whether you are

- maintaining your schedule
- staying within your budget
- using the proper equipment
- making the right assignments
- completing the job efficiently, correctly, and according to codes.

Almost any kind of ongoing work can be described in a progress report—research for a paper, construction of an apartment complex, preparation of a Web site, documentation of a patient's rehabilitation.

Audience for a Progress Report

A progress report is intended for people who generally are not working alongside you but who need a record of your activities to coordinate them with other individuals' efforts and to learn about problems or changes in plans. For example, since supervisors (or non-native speakers of English who manage overseas offices) may not be in the field or branch office or at a construction site, they will rely on your progress report for much of their information. Customers, such as a contractor's clients, often expect reports on how carefully their money is being spent. That way they can adjust schedules or alter specifications if there is a risk of going over budget.

Length of a Progress Report

The length of the progress report will depend on the complexity of the project. A short e-mail about organizing a time management workshop, such as that in Figure 15.4,

FIGURE 15.3   A sales report to a manager.

Thegrill

Dayton, OH 43210 • (813) 555-4000 • (813) 555-4100 fax   grill@aol.com

TO:	Gina Smeltzer	DATE:	June 27, 2001
	Alfonso Zapatta, owners		
FROM:	Sam Jelinek S.J.	SUBJECT:	Analysis of entrée sales,
	Manager		June 12–25

As we agreed at our monthly meeting on June 4, here is my analysis of entrée sales for two weeks to assist us in our menu planning. Below is a record of entrée sales for the weeks of June 12–18 and June 19–25 that I have compiled into a table for easier comparisons.

	Portion size	June 12–18		June 19–25		2 weeks combined	
		Amount	Percentage	Amount	Percentage	Amount	Percentage
Cornish Hen	6 oz.	238	17	307	17	545	17
Stuffed Young Turkey	8 oz.	112	8	182	10	294	12
Broiled Salmon Steak	8 oz.	154	11	217	12	371	13
Brook Trout	12 oz.	182	13	252	14	434	9
Prime Rib	10 oz.	168	12	198	11	366	11
Lobster Tails	2–4 oz.	147	10	161	9	308	10
Delmonico Steak	10 oz.	56	4	70	4	126	4
Moroccan Chicken	6 oz.	343	25	413	23	756	24
		1,400	100	1,800	100	3,200	100

Recommendations
Based on the figures in the table above, I recommend that we do the following:
1. Order at least 100 more pounds of prime rib each two-week period to be eligible for further quantity discounts from the Northern Meat Company
2. Delete the Delmonico steak entrée because of low acceptance
3. Introduce a new chicken or fish entrée to take the place of the Delmonico steak; I would suggest grilled lemon chicken to accommodate our patrons interested in tasty, low-fat, lower-cholesterol entrées.

Please give me your reactions within the next week. It shouldn't take more than a few days to implement these changes.

FIGURE 15.4   A one-time progress report sent as an e-mail.

Subject: Preparations for Time Management Workshop
Date: September 14, 2000 1:23:31 PM Eastern Daylight Time
To: ksands@multiplex.org (Kathy Sands)
From: pjavon@multiplex.org (Paul Javon)

As you requested last week, I e-mailed the managers of all departments in both our Trenton and Frankfurt, Germany, offices on Monday, September 11, to remind them of the time management workshop we will be offering on October 9 by teleconference.

I have confirmed the date and the operation of the technical links and relays with Carmen Suarez in Technical Services and have also e-mailed Jürgen Weiss in Frankfurt to make sure things are in place there.

I have reserved the corporate conference center for October 9 and have ordered DTP copies of all the packets we will need. The packets going to Germany will be Jet-Expressed, overnight delivery, on October 5 so they will be in Frankfurt two days before the teleconference.

By tomorrow, I will complete a list of all those employees scheduled to participate in the workshop and send it to you.

Plans are going according to schedule.

Kathy Sands, Trenton

might be all that is necessary. A report to an instructor about the progress a student is making on a research paper easily could be handled in a one-page memo, such as Barbara Shoemake's progress report in Figure 15.5 or for her research paper described in the proposal in Chapter 14 (pp. 568–570). Similarly, Dale Brandt's assessment of the progress his construction company is making in renovating Dr. Burke's office is given in a two-page letter in Figure 15.6.

Frequency of Progress Reports

Progress reports can be written daily, weekly, monthly, quarterly, or annually. Your specific job and your employer's needs will dictate how often you have to keep others informed of your progress. A single progress report is sufficient for Philip Javon's purpose in Figure 15.4. Barbara Shoemake was asked to submit two progress reports, the first of which is found in Figure 15.5. Contractor Brandt determined that three reports, spaced four to six weeks apart, would be necessary to keep Dr. Burke posted; Figure 15.6 is the second of those reports.

Parts of a Progress Report

Progress reports should contain information on (1) the work you have done, (2) the work you are currently doing, and (3) the work you will do.

How to Begin a Progress Report
In a brief introduction

- indicate why you are writing the report
- provide any necessary project titles or codes and specify dates
- help readers recall the job you are doing for them

If you are writing an initial progress report, supply background information in the opening. Philip Javon's first sentence in Figure 15.4, for example, quickly establishes his purpose by reminding Kathy Sands of their discussion last week. Similarly, Barbara Shoemake in the first paragraph in Figure 15.5 reminds her instructor of the purpose and scope of her work.

If you are submitting a subsequent progress report, your introduction should remind your reader about where your previous report left off and where the current one begins. Make sure you clearly specify the period covered by each report. Note how Dale Brandt's first paragraph in Figure 15.6 calls attention to the continuity of his work.

How to Continue a Progress Report
The body of the report should provide significant details about costs, materials, personnel, and times for the major stages of the project.

- Emphasize completed tasks, not false starts. If you report that the carpentry work or painting is finished, readers do not need an explanation of paint viscosity or geometrical patterns.
- Omit routine or well-known details ("I had to use the library when I wanted to read the back issues of *Safety News*").
- Describe in the body of your report any snags you encountered that may affect the work in progress. See Dale Brandt's section on electrical problems in Figure 15.6. It is better for the reader to know about trouble early in the project, so appropriate changes or corrections can be made.

How to End a Progress Report
The conclusion should give a timetable for the completion of duties or submission of the next progress report. Give the date by which you expect work to be completed. Be realistic; do not promise to have a job done in less time than you know it will take. Readers will not expect miracles, only informed estimates. Even so, any

FIGURE 15.5   A progress report from a student to a teacher.

TO: Professor Leigh Felton-Parks
FROM: Barbara R. Shoemake $\mathcal{B.RS.}$
DATE: April 7, 2000
SUBJECT: First Progress Report on Research Paper

This is the first of two progress reports that you asked me to submit about my research paper on the ethical and security issues of using e-mail.

From March 8 until April 16, I gathered information from print and electronic resources, including library holdings, the Internet, and an interview. Of the twenty references listed in my proposal, I found only twelve. Articles by Cahlin ("PC Security"), Hodson et al. ("Legal and Economic Aspects of Employer Monitoring of Employee Electronic Mail"), and "Is E-Mail Safe?" (*High-Tech Business*) are not available in our library or on the Internet. Two of my Internet sites—"Here's Help" and Sherwood's *A Beginner's Guide*—are under construction. But I e-mailed Sherwood and found that her site will be open in the next few days. In the meantime, I'll try to replace "Here's Help."

On February 23, I had an extended interview (1½ hours) with Keith Wellbridge of General Dynamics, who gave me some seminar handouts as well as a copy of a report on e-mail protocols that he wrote for the Society of Midwest Business Communicators—materials I hope to incorporate in my paper.

Because of an extended trip to Denver, Alice Phillips of Dodge & Spenser could not meet with me. At her suggestion, I am trying to schedule an interview with Gloria Sirkin-Dews, the Office Manager at Mid-Atlantic Power Company. Ms. Sirkin-Dews has given several seminars on e-mail security. Even if she cannot meet with me, Mr. Wellbridge gave me enough information about a business manager's view of systems. However, not currently having the articles and Web sites listed above may slow, but not stop, my work.

Starting tomorrow, I will begin my paper and can submit a draft by April 27. You will receive my second progress report by April 20.

FIGURE 15.6   The second of three progress reports from a contractor to a customer.

Brandt Construction Company

Halsted at Roosevelt, Chicago, Illinois 60608-0999 • 312-555-3700 • Fax: 312-555-1731
http://www.brandt.com

April 27, 2000

Dr. Pamela Burke
1439 Grand Avenue
Mount Prospect, IL 60045-1003

Dear Dr. Burke:

Here is my second progress report about the renovation work at your new clinic at
Hacienda and Donohue. Work proceeded satisfactorily in April according to the plans
you had approved in March.

REVIEW OF WORK COMPLETED IN MARCH
As I informed you in my first progress report on March 31, we tore down the walls,
pulled the old wiring, and removed existing plumbing lines. All the gutting work was
finished in March.

WORK COMPLETED DURING APRIL
By April 8, we had laid the new pipes and connected them to the main sewer line. We
also installed the two commodes, the four standard sinks, and the utility basin. The
heating and air-conditioning ducts were installed by April 13. From April 17–21, we
erected soundproof walls in the four examination rooms, the reception area, your
office, and the laboratory. We had no problems reducing the size of the reception area
by five feet to make the first examination room larger, as you had requested.

PROBLEMS WITH THE ELECTRICAL SYSTEM
We had difficulty with the electrical work, however. The number of outlets and the
generator for the laboratory equipment required extra-duty power lines that had to be
approved by both Con Edison and Cook County inspectors. The approval slowed us
down by three days. Also, the wholesaler, Midtown Electric, failed to deliver the
recessed lighting fixtures by April 25 as promised. Those fixtures and the generator
are now being installed. Moreover, the cost of those fixtures will increase the material
budget by **$2,888.00**. The cost for labor is as we had projected—**$89,450**.

WORK REMAINING
The finishing work is scheduled for May. By May 9, the floors in the examination
rooms, laboratory, washrooms, and hallways should be tiled and the reception area

Continued

FIGURE 15.6   (Continued)

---

page 2

and your office carpeted. By May 12, the reception area and your office should be paneled and the rest of the walls painted. If everything stays on schedule, touch-up work is scheduled for May 15–19. You should be able to move into your new clinic by May 22.

You will receive a third and final progress report by May 11. Thank you again for your business and the confidence you have placed in our company.

Sincerely yours,

Dale Brandt

Dale Brandt

---

conclusion must be tentative. Note that the good news Dale Brandt gives Dr. Burke about moving into her new clinic is qualified by the words "If everything stays on schedule." He is also well aware of the "you attitude" by thanking Dr. Burke again for her business.

You may have to add a recommendation as part of your conclusion. A recommendation might advise readers of a less costly, equally durable siding than the one originally planned, suggest that a new software program would considerably improve the design of your document or your company's schedules, or show that hiring an additional telecommuter would help ease the workload over a particularly busy sales period.

Trip/Travel Reports

Reporting on the trips you take is an important professional responsibility. Trips can range from a brief afternoon car ride across town to a month-long globe-hopping journey. In documenting what you did and saw, trip reports keep readers informed about your efforts and how they affect ongoing or future business. Trip reports are also written after you attend a convention or sales meeting or call on customers.

Questions Trip Reports Answer

Specifically, a trip report should answer the following questions for your readers.

- Where did you go?
- When did you go?

- Why did you go?
- Whom did you see?
- What did they tell you?
- What did you do about it?

For a business trip you are also likely to have to inform readers how much the trip cost and to supply them with receipts for all your expenses.

Common Types of Trip/Travel Reports

Trip reports can cover a wide range of activities and are called by different names to characterize those activities. Most likely, you will encounter the following three types of trip/travel reports.

1. **Field trip reports.** These reports, often assigned in a course, are written after a visit to a plant, military installation, office complex, hospital, detention center, or other facility to show what you have learned about the operation of those places. You will be expected to describe how an institution is organized, the technical procedures and/or equipment it uses, pertinent ecological conditions, or the ratio of one group to another. The emphasis in these reports is on the educational value of the trip, as Mark Tourneur's report in Figure 15.7 demonstrates.

2. **Site inspection reports.** These reports inform managers about conditions at a branch office or plant, a customer's business, or on the advisability of relocating an office or other facility. After visiting the site, you will determine whether it meets your employer's (or customer's) needs.

Site inspection reports tell how machinery or production procedures are working or provide information about the physical plant, the environment (air, soil, water, vegetation), or computer or financial operations.

Figure 15.8, which begins with a recommendation, is a report written to a district manager interested in acquiring a new site for a fast-food restaurant.

TECH NOTE

Benchmarking

You may have to write a trip report as a result of **benchmarking,** the collaborative effort of two companies with similar products or services to exchange noncopyrighted information through coordinated site visits to each other's facility. Employees from one company tour the other firm's location, ask questions about equipment, procedures, and policies, and are given demonstrations of appropriate operations. Returning to their home office, the employees then submit a trip report outlining what they learned and suggesting what might be implemented or improved in their own company. **Benchmarking** provides an excellent opportunity for you to network.

FIGURE 15.7   A student's field trip report.

TO: Katherine Holmes, RN, MSN
            Director, RN Program
FROM: Mark Tourneur M.T.
            RN Student
DATE: November 13, 2000
SUBJECT: Field Trip to Water Valley Extended Care Center

On Friday, November 10, I visited the Water Valley Extended Care
Center, 1400 Medford Boulevard, in preparation for my internship in
an extended care facility next semester.

Philosophy and Organization
Before my tour started, the director, Sue LaFrance, explained the
holistic philosophy of health care at Water Valley and emphasized the
diverse kinds of nursing practiced there. She stressed that the agency
is not restricted to geriatric clients but admits anyone requiring
extended care. She pointed out that Water Valley is a medium-sized
facility (150 beds) and contains three wings: (1) the Infirmary, (2) the
General Nursing Unit, and (3) the Ambulatory Unit.

Primary Client Services
My tour began with the Infirmary, staffed by one RN and two LPNs,
where I observed a number of life-support systems in operation:

  • IVs
  • oxygen setups
  • feeding tubes
  • cardiac monitors

Then I was shown the General Nursing Unit (40 beds), staffed by
three LPNs and four aides. Clients can have private or semiprivate
rooms; bathrooms have wide doors and lowered sinks for patients
using wheelchairs or walkers. The Ambulatory unit serves 90 clients
who can provide their own daily care.

Continued

FIGURE 15.7   (Continued)

Additional Client Services

Dietetics

Before lunch in the main dining room, I was introduced to Doris Betz, the dietitian, who explained the different menus she coordinates. The most common are low-sodium and ADA (American Diabetic Association) restricted-calorie. Staff members eat with the clients, reinforcing the holistic focus of the agency.

Pharmacy

After lunch, Jack Tishner, the pharmacist, discussed the agency's procedures for ordering and delivering medications. He also described the client teaching he does and the in-service workshops he conducts.

Physical/Spiritual Therapy

I then observed clients in both recreational and physical therapy. Water Valley's full-time physical therapist, Tracy Cook, works with stroke and arthritic clients and helps those with broken bones regain the use of their limbs. In addition to a weight room, Water Valley has a small sauna that most of the clients use at least twice a week.

The clients' spiritual needs are not neglected, either. A small chapel is located just south of the Ambulatory Unit.

Benefits for My Internship

From my visit to Water Valley, I learned a great deal about the health care delivery system at an extended care facility. I was especially pleased to have been given so much information on emergency procedures, medication orders, and physical therapy programs. My forthcoming internship will be even more useful, since I now have first-hand knowledge about these various services.

-2-

FIGURE 15.8   A site inspection report using a map.

VAIL's

TO: Dale Gandy   DATE: July 3, 2000
FROM: Beth Armando   *B.A*   SUBJECT: New Site for Vail's #8
         Development Department

RECOMMENDATION
The best location for the new Vail's Chicken House is the vacant Dairy
World shop at the northeast corner of Smith and Fairfax Avenues—1701
Fairfax. I inspected this property on June 21 and 22 and also talked to
Marge Bloom, the broker at Crescent Realty representing the Dairy World
Company.

THE LOCATION
Please refer to the map below. Located at the intersection of the two
busiest streets on the southeast side, the property allows us to take
advantage of the traffic flow to attract customers. Being only one block
west of the Cloverleaf Mall should also help business.

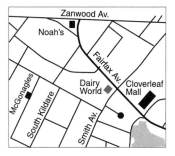

Customers will have easy access to our location. They can enter or exit
the Dairy World from either Smith or Fairfax. Left turns on Smith are
prohibited from 7 A.M. to 9 A.M., but since most of our business is done
after 11 A.M., the restriction poses few problems.

Denver, CO 87123   (303) 555-7200   http://www.vails.com

Continued

FIGURE 15.8 (Continued)

AREA COMPETITION

Only two other fast-food establishments are in a one-mile vicinity. McGonagles, 1534 South Kildare, specializes in hamburgers; Noah's, 703 Zanwood, serves primarily seafood entrées. Their offerings will not directly compete with ours. The closest fast-food restaurant serving chicken is Johnson's, 1.8 miles away.

PARKING FACILITIES

The parking lot has space for 45 cars, and the area at the south end of the property (38 feet x 37 feet) can accommodate 14–15 cars. The driveways and parking lot were paved with asphalt last March and appear to be in excellent condition. We will be able to make use of the drive-up window on the north side of the building.

THE BUILDING

The building has 3,993 square feet of heated and cooled space. The air-conditioning and heating units were installed within the last fifteen months and seem to be in good working order; nine more months of transferable warranty remain on these units.

The only major changes we must make are in the kitchen. To prepare items on the Vail's menu, we would need to add three more exhaust fans (there is only one now) and expand the grill and cooking areas. The kitchen also has three relatively new sinks and ample storage space in the sixteen cabinets.

The restaurant has a seating capacity of up to 54 persons; 10 booths are covered with red vinyl and are comfortably padded. A color-coordinated serving counter could seat 8 to 10 patrons. The floor does not need to be retiled, but the walls still have to be painted to match Vail's color decor.

3. Home health or social work visits. Nurses, social workers, and probation officers report daily on their visits to patients and clients. Their reports describe clients' lifestyles, assess needs, and make recommendations. Figure 15.9 is a report from a social worker to a county family services agency. The report begins with the information the writer acquired from a family and concludes not with a recommendation but rather a list of the actions the social worker has taken.

How to Gather Information for a Trip/Travel Report
Regardless of the kind of trip report you have to write, your assignment will be easier and your report better organized if you follow these suggestions.

1. Before you leave on the field trip, site inspection, or visit, be sure you are prepared as follows.
   a. Obtain all necessary names; street, e-mail, and Web site addresses; and telephone and fax numbers.
   b. Check the files for previous correspondence, case studies, or terms of contracts or agreements.
   c. Locate a map of the area (use the Internet research tool described on p. 483) or a blueprint of the building.
   d. Download work orders, instructions, or other documents pertinent to your visit, for example, Web sites and ads.
   e. Bring a laptop computer with you.
   f. Depending on your job, you may also need to bring a camcorder, tape recorder, camera, or calculator to record important data.

2. When you return from your trip, keep the following hints in mind as you compile your report.
   a. Write your report promptly. If you put it off, you may forget important items.
   b. When a trip takes you to two or more widely separated places, note in your report when you arrived at each place and how long you stayed.
   c. Do not include everything you saw or did on the trip. Exclude irrelevant details, such as whether the trip was enjoyable, what you ate, or how delighted you were to meet people.
   d. As you edit the final copy of your report, check to make sure you have listed names and calculated figures correctly.

Test Reports

Much physical research (the discovery and documentation of facts) is communicated through short reports variously called **experiment, investigation, laboratory, operations,** or **research reports.** They all record the results of tests, whether the tests were conducted in a forest, computer center, laboratory, shopping center, or soybean field. No doubt you have already written a **test report** (or **lab report**) after performing an experiment in a science class.

FIGURE 15.9   A social worker's visit report.

**GREEN COUNTY
FAMILY SERVICES**

Randall, VA 21032
703-555-4000
greenfam@msn.net

TO: Margaret S. Walker, Director
          Green County Family Services
FROM: Jeff Bowman, Social Worker
SUBJECT: Visit to Mr. Lee Scanlon
DATE: October 10, 2001

PURPOSE OF VISIT
At the request of the Green County Home Health Office, I visited Mr. Lee
Scanlon at his home at 113 West Diversy Drive on Monday, October 8. Mr.
Scanlon and his three children (ages six, eight, and eleven) live in a two-
bedroom apartment above a garage. Last week, Mr. Scanlon was discharged
from Lutheran General Hospital after leg surgery and has asked for financial
assistance.

DESCRIPTION OF VISIT
Mr. Scanlon is a widower with no means of support except unemployment
compensation of $1,084 a month. He lost his job at Beaumont Industries when
the company went out of business four weeks ago and wants to go back to
work, but Dr. Marilyn Canning-Smith advised against it for six to seven
weeks. His oldest child is diabetic and the six-year-old daughter must have a
tonsillectomy. Mr. Scanlon also told me the problems he is having with his
refrigerator; it "is off more than it is on," he said.

Mrs. Alice Gordon, the owner of the garage, informed me that Mr. Scanlon
had paid last month's rent but not this month's. She also stressed how much
the Scanlons need a new refrigerator and that she had often let them use hers
to store their food.

Continued

FIGURE 15.9   (Continued)

Margaret S. Walker
October 10, 2001
Page 2

Here is a breakdown of Mr. Scanlon's monthly bills:

Expenses	Income
$ 550 rent	$1,084 unemployment compensation
150 utilities	
450 food	
120 drugs	
80 transportation	
$ 1,350	

ACTION TAKEN
To assist Mr. Scanlon, I have done the following:

1. Set up an appointment (10/19/01) for him to apply for food stamps.
2. Talked with Blanche Derringo regarding Medicaid assistance.
3. Asked the State Employment Commission to aid him in finding a job as soon as he is well enough to work. My contact person is Wesley Sahara; his e-mail address is wsahara@empcom.gov.
4. Visited Robert Hong at the office of the Council of Churches to obtain food and money for utilities until federal aid is available; he also will try to find the Scanlons another refrigerator.
5. Telephoned Sharon Muñoz at the Green County Health Department (555-1400) to have Mr. Scanlon's diabetic daughter receive insulin and syringes gratis.

Writing an effective test report, of course, involves specific training in a scientific or technical field. But remember that the ability to write clearly and concisely about a procedure (and the results) is as significant as the technical skills required to perform the test itself.

Style

Objectivity and accuracy are essential ingredients in a test report. Readers want to know about your empirical research (the facts), not about your feelings (the "I"). Record your observations without bias or guesswork in a laboratory journal or log book and always include precise measurements. Follow the accepted practices of your profession in documenting your findings. Use standard symbols and abbreviations.

Questions Your Report Needs to Answer

Readers will expect your test report to supply the following information.

- why you performed the test: an explanation of the reasons, your goals, and who may have authorized you to perform the test
- how you performed the test: under what circumstances or controls you conducted the test; what procedures and equipment you used
- what the outcomes were: your conclusions
- what implications or recommendations follow from your test: what you learned, discovered, confirmed, or even disproved or rejected

When you sign the final copy of your report, you are certifying to your readers that things happened exactly when, how, and why you say they did.

Two Sample Test Reports

Figure 15.10 is a relatively simple and short test report in memo format regarding sanitary conditions at a hospital psychiatric unit. The report follows a direct and useful pattern of organization:

- statement of purpose—*why?*
- findings—*what happened?*
- recommendations—*what next?*

Submitted by an infection control officer, the report does not provide elaborate details about the particular laboratory procedures used to determine whether bacteria were present; nor does it describe the pathogenic (disease-causing) properties of the bacteria. Such descriptions are unnecessary for the audience (the housekeeping department) to do its job.

A more complex example of a short test report is found in Figure 15.11, which studies the effects of four light periods on the growth of paulownia seedlings (a flowering tree cultivated in China). The report, published in a scientific journal, is addressed to specialists in forestry. Such a test report follows a different, more detailed pattern of organization than the report in Figure 15.10 and includes an **informative abstract,** an **introduction,** a **materials and methods section,** a **results and discussion section,** and a **list of references cited in the study.**

To meet the needs of an expert audience, the writers of the report in Figure 5.11 had to include much more information than did Janeen Cufaude, the infection control officer who wrote Figure 15.10, about the way the test was conducted and the types of scientific data the audience needs. The researchers did not have to define technical terms for their audience, and they could confidently use scientific symbols and formulas as well.

As the two reports show, you should always determine how much technical knowledge an audience has about your field and how they will use your report to accomplish *their* specific jobs.

FIGURE 15.10   A test report with recommendations.

Charleston Central
HOSPITAL

TO: James Dill, Supervisor
           Housekeeping
FROM: Janeen Cufaude *J.C.*
           Infection Control Officer
DATE: December 7, 2000
SUBJECT: Routine sanitation inspection

As part of the monthly check of the psychiatric unit (11A), the following areas were swabbed and tested for bacterial growth. The results of the lab tests of these samples are as follows:

AREA	FINDINGS
1. cabinet in patient's kitchen	1. positive for 2 colonies of strep germs
2. rug in eating area	2. positive for food particles and yeasts and molds
3. baseboard in dayroom	3. positive for particles of dust
4. medicine counter in nurses' station	4. negative for bacteria— no growth after 48 hours
5. corridor by south elevator	5. positive for 4 colonies of staph germs isolated

ACTIONS TO BE TAKEN AT ONCE
1. Clean the kitchen cabinet with K-504 liquid daily, 3:1 dilution.
2. Shampoo rug areas bimonthly with heavy-duty shampoo and clean visibly soiled areas with Guard-Pruf as often as needed.
3. Wipe all baseboards weekly with K-12 spray cleanser.
4. Mop heavily traveled corridors and access areas with K-504 cleanser daily, 1:1 dilution.

Charleston, WV 25324-0114 ✳ (304) 555-1800 ✳ www.cch.org

FIGURE 15.11   A short test report published in a scientific journal.

Paulownia Seedlings Respond to Increased Daylength

M. J. Immel, E. M. Tackett, and S. B. Carpenter

Abstract

Paulownia seedlings grown under four photoperiods were evaluated after a growing period of 97 days. Height growth and total dry weight production were both significantly increased in the 16- and 24-hour photoperiods.

Introduction

Paulownia (*Paulownia tomentosa* [Thunb.] Steud.), a native of China, is a little known species in the United States. Recently, however, there has been increased interest in this species for surface mine reclamation (*1*).* Paulownia seems to be especially well adapted to harsh micro-climates of surface mines; it grows very rapidly and appears to be drought-resistant. In Kentucky and surrounding states, paulownia wood is actively sought by Japanese buyers and has brought prices comparable to black walnut (*2*).

This increased interest in paulownia has resulted in several attempts to direct seed it on surface mines, but little success has been achieved. The high light requirements and the extremely small size of paulownia seed (approximately 6,000 per gram) may be the limiting factors. Planting paulownia seedlings is preferred; but, because of their succulent nature, seedlings are usually produced and outplanted as container stock rather than bareroot seedlings. Daylength is an important factor in the production of vigorous container plants (*5*).

Our study compares the effects that four photoperiods—8, 12, 16, and 24 hours—had on the early growth of container-grown paulownia seedlings over a period of 97 days.

Materials and Methods

Seeds used in this study were stratified in a 1:1 mixture of peat moss and sand at 4°C for 2 years. Following cold storage, seeds were placed on a 1:1 potting soil-sand mix and mulched with cheesecloth. They were then placed under continuous light until germination occurred. Germination percentages were high, indicating paulownia seeds can survive long periods of storage with little loss of viability (*3*).

Thirty days after germination, 3- to 4-centimeter seedlings were transplanted into 8-quart plastic pots filled with an equal mixture of potting soil, sand, and peat moss.

* To save space, the Works Cited section has been omitted.

Continued

FIGURE 15.11 (Continued)

Seventy-five seedlings were randomly assigned to each of the four treatments. Treatments were for 4 photoperiods—8, 12, 16, and 24 hours—and were replicated three times in 12 light chambers. Each chamber was 1.2- by 1.2-meters with an artificial light source 71 centimeters above the chamber floor.

The light source consisted of eight fluorescent lights: four 40-watt plant growth lamps alternated with four 40-watt cool white lamps. Light intensity averaged 550 foot-candles (1340μ einsteins/m^2/s) at the top of each pot and the temperature averaged 23°C (±2°C).

Seedlings were watered and fertilized after transplanting with a 6-gram 14-4-6 agriform container tablet. Beginning 1 month after transplanting, two seedlings were randomly selected and harvested from each chamber for a total of 24 trees. Height, root collar diameter, length of longest root, and oven-dry weight (at 65°C) were determined for each seedling. Harvests continued every week for 5 additional weeks.

Results and Discussion

Results indicate that early growth of paulownia is influenced by photoperiod, as shown in Table 1.

TABLE 1. Height Diameter, Root Length, Total Dry Weight, and R/S Ratio for Paulownia Seedlings Grown Under Four Photoperiods After 97 Days.

Photo period (hrs.)	Height (cm)	Diameter (cm)	Root length (cm)	Total dry weight (gm)	R/S ratio
8	13.1b	0.48	16.0	1.65c	0.18
12	17.8b	0.67	34.7	7.27b	0.32
16	27.3a	0.93	31.1	15.92a	0.39
24	29.2a	0.90	43.9	18.56a	0.33

Expanding the photoperiod from 8 to either 16 or 24 hours increased height growth by 100 percent. Height growth in the 12-hour treatment also increased, but did not differ significantly from the 8-hour treatment. Heights under photoperiods of 8, 12, 16, and 24 hours were 13.1, 17.8, 27.3, and 29.2 centimeters, respectively.

Previous studies have also shown that photoperiod affects the growth of paulownia seedlings (4, 6). Sanderson (6), for example, found that paulownia seedlings grown under continuous light averaged 27.2 centimeters in height after 101 days compared with 29.2 centimeters for our 24-hour seedlings. Other corresponding photoperiods were equally comparable. Downs and Borthwick (4) also concluded that height growth of paulownia was affected by extending the photoperiod.

Continued

FIGURE 15.11   (Continued)

The greatest treatment differences were shown in total dry weight production. Refer again to Table 1. The mean weight of 1.65 grams for seedlings in the 8-hour treatment was significantly less than that of any of the other photoperiods. The 16- and 24-hour treatments did not differ significantly. In fact, they more than doubled the average weight for seedlings in the 12-hour treatment.

Root-to-shoot ration (R/S) indicates the relative proportion of growth allocated to roots versus shoots for the seedlings in each photoperiod. In this study, shoots were developing at nearly three times the rate of the roots for seedlings in the 12-, 16-, and 24-hour photoperiods.

The 0.18 R/S ratio for seedlings in the 8-hour treatment was much lower, indicating that relative growth of the shoot is approximately five times that of the root. The shorter photoperiod therefore decreased root development relative to shoot development as well as significantly reduced total dry weight production.

Although root collar diameter and root length did not significantly differ under the different photoperiods after 97 days, there was a trend for greater diameter and root growth with longer photoperiods.

Conclusions

Results indicate that the growth of paulownia seedlings is affected by changes in the photoperiod. Increasing the photoperiod significantly increased height growth and total dry matter production. The distribution of dry matter (R/S ratio) was altered by increasing the photoperiod; the ratio was larger in the longer photoperiods. In contrast to earlier studies (4), we found paulownia seedlings subjected to extended photoperiods were still growing after 97 days.

Incident Reports

The reports discussed thus far in this chapter have dealt with routine work. They have described events that were anticipated or supervised. But every business or agency runs into unexpected trouble that delays routine work. Employers, and on some occasions government inspectors, insurance agents, and attorneys, must be informed about those events that interfere with or threaten normal, safe operations.

When to Submit an Incident Report

An incident report is submitted when there is, for example,

- an accident
- a law enforcement offense
- an environmental danger, including a computer virus
- a machine breakdown
- a delivery delay

- a cost overrun
- a production slowdown

Figure 15.12 is an incident report about a train accident submitted by the engineer on duty.

Protecting Yourself Legally

An incident report can be used as legal evidence. It frequently concerns the two topics over which powerful legal battles are waged—health and property. The report can sway the outcome of insurance claims, civil suits, or criminal cases and therefore requires careful planning and revision.

To ensure that what you write is legally proper, follow these guidelines.

1. Be accurate, objective, and complete. Recount clearly what happened in the order it took place. Never omit or distort facts; the information may surface later, and you could be accused of a cover-up. Do not just write "I do not know" for an answer. If you are not sure, state why. Also be careful that there are no discrepancies in your report.

2. Give facts, not opinions. Provide a factual account of what actually happened, not a biased interpretation of events. Indirect words such as "I guess," "I wonder," "apparently," "perhaps," or "possibly" weaken your objectivity. Stick to details you witnessed or that were seen by eyewitnesses. Identify witnesses or victims by giving names, addresses, places of employment, and so on. Indicate who saw what. Keep in mind that stating what someone else saw is regarded as hearsay and therefore is not admissible in a court of law. State only what *you* saw or heard. When you describe what happened, avoid drawing uncalled-for conclusions. Consider the following statements of opinion and fact:

> Opinion: The patient seemed confused and caught himself in his IV tubing.
>   Fact: The patient caught himself in his IV tubing.
>
> Opinion: The equipment was defective.
>   Fact: The bolt was loose.

Be careful, too, about blaming someone. Statements such as "Baxter was incompetent" or "The company knew of the problem but did nothing about it" are libelous remarks.

In law enforcement work, further identify suspects by their aliases and by any distinctive characteristics—for example, "jagged 4-inch scar on left forearm."

3. Do not exceed your professional responsibilities. Answer only those questions you are qualified to answer. Do not presume to speak as a detective, inspector, physician, or supervisor. Do not represent yourself as an attorney or claims adjuster in writing the report.

Parts of an Incident Report

You will use either a memo or a specially prepared form with spaces for detailed comments. Note how Figure 15.12 includes the following details.

FIGURE 15.12   An incident report in memo format.

THE GREAT HARVESTER RAILROAD
Des Moines, IA 50306-4005
http://www.ghrr.com

TO: Angela O'Brien, District Manager
            James Day, Safety Instructor
FROM: Ned Roane, Engineer *N.R.*
DATE: March 3, 2000
SUBJECT: Derailment of Train 28 on March 3, 2000

DESCRIPTION OF INCIDENT
At 7:20 A.M. on March 3, 2000, I was driving Engine 457 traveling north at a speed of fifty-two miles an hour on the single main-line track four miles east of Ridgeville, Illinois. Weather conditions and visibility were excellent. Suddenly the last two grain cars, 3022 and 3053, jumped the track. The train automatically went into emergency braking and stopped immediately. There were no injuries to the crew. But the train did not stop before both grain cars turned at a 45° angle. After checking the cars, I found that half the contents of their loads had spilled. The train was not carrying any hazardous chemical shipments.

I notified Supervisor Bill Purvis at 7:40 A.M., and within forty-five minutes he and a section crew arrived at the scene with rerailing equipment. The section crew removed the two grain cars from the track, put in new ties, and made the main-line track passable by 9:25 A.M. At 9:45 A.M. a vacuum car arrived with Engine 372 from Hazlehurst, Illinois, and its crew proceeded with the cleanup operation. By 10:25 A.M. all the spilled grain was loaded onto the cars brought by the Hazlehurst train. Bill Purvis notified Barnwell Granary that their shipment would be at least three hours late.

CAUSES OF INCIDENT
Supervisor Purvis and I checked the stretch of train track where the cars derailed and found it to be heavily worn. We believe that a fisher joint slipped when the grain cars hit it, and the track broke. You can see the location of the cracked fisher joint in the drawing below.

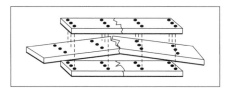

RECOMMENDATIONS
We made the following recommendations to the switch yard in the Hazlehurst to be carried out immediately.
1. Check the section of track for ten miles on either side of Ridgeville for any signs of defective fisher joints.
2. Repair any defective joints at once.
3. Instruct all engineers to slow down to five to ten mph over this section of the road until the rail check is completed.

1. Personal details. Record titles, department, and employment identification numbers. Indicate if you or your fellow employees were working alone. For customers or victims, record home addresses, phone numbers, and places of employment. Insurance companies will also require policy numbers.

2. Type of incident. Briefly identify the incident—personal injury, fire, burglary, delivery delay, equipment failure. In the case of injury, identify the part(s) of the body precisely. "Eye injury" is not enough; "injury to the right eye, causing bleeding" is better. "Dislocated right shoulder," or "punctured left forearm" is descriptive and exact. A report on damaged equipment should list model numbers. Note how Ned Roane's report specifies the grain car numbers. For thefts, supply colors, brand names and/or manufacturer, model names, serial numbers, and quantities. "A stolen laptop" will not help detectives locate the right object; "a Newtech Model 5000" will.

3. Time and location of the incident. Follow the advice given at the beginning of this chapter, page 580.

4. Description of what happened. This section is the longest part of the report. Some forms ask you to write on the back, to attach another sheet, or to add a photograph or diagram. Put yourself in the reader's position. If you were not present or did not speak directly to witnesses, would you know by reading the report exactly what happened and why, how it occurred, who and what were involved, and what led up to the incident?

5. What was done after the incident. After describing the incident, describe the action you took to correct conditions, to get things back to normal. Readers will want to know what was done to treat the injured, to make the environment safer, to speed delivery of goods, to repair damaged equipment, or to satisfy a customer's demands.

6. What caused the incident. Make sure your explanation is consistent with your description of what happened. Pinpoint the trouble. In Figure 15.12, for example, the defective fisher joint is discussed under the heading "Causes of Incident." In the following example, the two causes cited in a report of an accident involving a pipe falling from a crane are exact and helpful.

1. The crane's safety latch had been broken off and was never replaced.
2. A tag line was not used to guide the pipe onto the truckbed.

7. Recommendations. Readers will be looking for specific suggestions for solving the problem and for preventing the incident from happening again. Recommendations may involve discussing the problem at a safety meeting, asking for further training from a manufacturer, adapting existing equipment to meet customers' needs, doing emergency planning for the next storm damage, or modifying schedules. The following two appropriate recommendations appeared in the report dealing with the fallen pipe.

1. Order safety latches to replace the broken latch and have additional spare latches on hand.
2. Have a pipeshop supervisor conduct a safety meeting for employees and use a computer-enhanced drawing of the incident as an aid.

✓ Revision Checklist

- ❏ Had a clear sense of how my readers will use my report.
- ❏ Consulted appropriate sources to give my audience enough information to help them make informed decisions.
- ❏ Provided significant information about costs, materials, personnel, and times so readers will know that my work consists of facts, not impressions.
- ❏ Double-checked all data—costs, figures, dates, places, and equipment numbers.
- ❏ Verified necessary statistics and trends so that my periodic and sales reports are thorough and accurate.
- ❏ Made sure all my comments and recommendations were ethical.
- ❏ Followed all agency or organization guidelines.
- ❏ Adhered to all legal requirements.
- ❏ Eliminated unnecessary details or those too technical for my audience.
- ❏ Made report concise and to the point.
- ❏ Used headings whenever feasible to organize and categorize information.
- ❏ Supplied relevant visuals to help readers understand my message and crunch any numbers.
- ❏ Employed underlining, boldface, or italics to set headings apart or to emphasize key ideas.
- ❏ Began report with statement of purpose that clearly described the scope and significance of my work.
- ❏ Incorporated tables and other pertinent visuals to display data whenever appropriate.
- ❏ Explained clearly what the data means.
- ❏ Determined that recommendations logically follow from the data and that recommendations are realistic.

Exercises

1. Bring to class an example of a periodic report from your present or previous job or from any community, religious, or social organization to which you belong. In an accompanying memo to your instructor, indicate who the audience is and why such a report is necessary, stressing how it is organized, what kinds of factual data it contains, what visuals were used, and how it might be improved in content, organization, style, and design.

2. Assume that you are a manager of a large apartment complex (200 units). Write a periodic report based on the following information—26 units are vacant, 38 soon will be vacant, and 27 soon will be leased (by June 1). Also add a section of

recommendations to your supervisor (the head of the real estate management company for which you work) on how vacant apartments might be leased more quickly and perhaps at increased rents. Consider such important information as decorating, advertising, and installing a new security system.

3. Assume you work for a household appliance store. Prepare a sales report based on the information contained in the following table. Include a recommendation section for your manager.

	Number Sold	
Product	October	November
Kitchen Appliances		
Refrigerators	72	103
Dishwashers	27	14
Freezers	10	36
Electric Ranges	26	26
Gas Ranges	10	3
Microwave Ovens	31	46
Laundry Appliances		
Washers	50	75
Dryers	24	36
Air Treatment		
Room Air Conditioners	41	69
Dehumidifiers	7	2

4. Write a progress report on the wins, losses, and ties of your favorite sports team for last season. Address the report to the director of publicity for the team and stress how the director might use those facts for future publicity. As part of your report, indicate what might be an effective lead for a press release about the team's efforts.

5. Submit a progress report to your writing teacher on what you have learned in his or her course so far this term, which writing skills you want to develop in greater detail, and how you propose doing so. Mention specific memos, e-mail, letters, instructions, reports, or proposals you have written or will soon write.

6. Compose a site inspection report on any part of the college campus or plant, office, or store in which you work that might need remodeling, expansion, rewiring for computer use, or new or additional air-conditioning or heating work.

7. You and your collaborative team have been asked to write a short preliminary inspection report on the condition of a historic building for your state historical society. Inspecting the building, the home of a famous late nineteenth-century governor, you discover the problem listed on page 612. Include all these details in your report. Also supply recommendations for your readers—a director of the

state historical society, a state architect, and four representatives of the subcommittee on finance from your state legislature. Design two appropriate visuals to include in your report.

- The eight front columns are all in need of repair; two of them may have to be replaced.
- The area below each bottom window casement needs to be excavated for waterproofing.
- The slate tile on the roof has deteriorated and needs immediate replacement.
- The front stairs show signs of mortar leaching and require attention at once.
- Sections of gutter on the northwest and northeast sides of the house must be changed; other gutters are in fair shape.
- Wood shutters need to be repainted; four of the twelve may even need to be replaced.
- All trees around the house need pruning; an old elm in the backyard shows signs of decay.
- The siding is in desperate need of preparation and painting.
- The brick near the front entrance is dirty and moss-covered.

8. Write a report to an instructor in your major about a field trip you have taken recently—to a museum, laboratory, health care agency, correctional facility, radio or television station, agricultural station, or office. Indicate why you took the trip, name the individuals you met on the trip, and stress what you learned and how that information will help you in course work or on your job.

9. Submit a test report on the purpose, procedures, results, conclusions, and recommendations of an experiment you conducted on one of the following subjects:

   a. soil
   b. Internet access
   c. water
   d. automobiles
   e. textiles/clothing
   f. animals
   g. recreational facilities
   h. computer hardware or software
   i. forests
   j. food
   k. air quality
   l. transportation
   m. blood
   n. noise levels

10. Write an incident report about a problem you encountered in your work or at home in the last year. Document the problem and provide a solution. Use the memo format in Figure 15.12.

11. Write an incident report about one of the following problems. Assume that it has happened to you. Supply relevant details and visuals in your report. Identify the audience for whom you are writing and the agency you are representing or trying to reach.

    a. After hydroplaning, your company car hits a tree and has a damaged front fender.
    b. You have been the victim of an electrical shock because an electrical tool was not grounded.
    c. You twist your back lifting a bulky package in the office or plant.

    d. Your boat capsizes while you are patrolling the lake.

    e. The crane you are operating breaks down and you lose a half-day's work.

    f. The vendor shipped the wrong replacement part for your computer, and you cannot complete a job without buying a more expensive software package.

    g. An electrical storm knocked out your computer; you lost 1,000 mailing labels and will have to hire additional help to complete a mandatory mailing by the end of the week.

12. Choose one of the following descriptions of an incident and write a report based on it. The descriptions contain unnecessary details, vague words, insufficient information, unclear cause-and-effect relationships, or a combination of those errors. In writing your report, correct the errors by adding or deleting whatever information you believe is necessary. You may also want to rearrange the order in which information is listed. Use a memo format, like that in Figure 15.12, to write the report.

    a. After sliding across the slippery road late at night, my car ran into another vehicle, one of those fancy imported cars. The driver of that car must have been asleep at the wheel. The paint and glass chips were all over. I was driving back from our regional meeting and wanted to report to the home office the next day. The accident will slow me down.

    b. Whoever packed the glass mugs did not know what he or she was doing. The string was not the right type, nor was it tied correctly. The carton was too flimsy as well. It could have been better packed to hold all those mugs. Moreover, since the bus had to travel across some pretty rough country, the package would have broken anyhow. The best way to ship these kinds of goods is in specially marked and packed boxes. The value of the box contents was listed at $575.

CHAPTER

16

Writing Careful Long Reports

This chapter will introduce you to long reports—how they differ from short reports, how they are written, and how they are organized. It is appropriate to discuss long reports in one of the last chapters of *Successful Writing at Work*. The long report is often assigned last in class because writing one gives you an opportunity to use and combine many of the writing skills and research strategies you have already learned. In business, a long report is the culmination of many weeks or months of hard work on an important company project.

The following skills will be most helpful to you as you prepare to study long reports; appropriate page numbers appear for those topics that have already been discussed.

- assessing and meeting your audience's multiple needs (pp. 6–11)
- gathering and summarizing information, especially from print and on-line sources (pp. 299–321; 397–421)
- generating, drafting, revising, and editing your ideas (pp. 38–69)
- reporting the results of your research accurately and concisely (pp. 57–65; 581)
- creating and introducing visuals (pp. 457–501)
- using an appropriate method of documentation (pp. 349–394)
- preparing an informative abstract (pp. 419–421)

Having improved those skills, you should be ready to write a successful long report.

How a Long Report Differs from a Short Report

Both long and short reports are invaluable tools in the world of work. Basic differences exist, though, between the two types of reports. A short report is not a watered-down version of a long report; nor is a long report simply an expanded version of a short one. The two types of reports differ in scope, research, format, timetable, audience, and collaborative effort.

614

The following section explains some of the key differences between these two reports. By understanding these differences, you will be better able to follow the rest of Chapter 16 as it covers the process of writing a long report and the organization and parts of such a report. A model long report (Figure 16.3) appears at the end of the chapter.

Scope

A long report is a major study that provides an in-depth view of the problem or idea. For example, a long report written for a course assignment may be eight to twenty pages long; a report for a business or industry may be that long or, more likely, much longer, depending on the scope of the subject. The implications of a long report are wide-ranging for a business or industry—relocating a plant, adding a new line of equipment, changing a computer programming operation.

The long report examines a problem in detail, while the short report covers just one part of the problem. Unlike a short report, a long report may discuss not just one or two current events, but rather a continuing history of a problem or idea (and the background information necessary to understand it in perspective). For example, the short test report on paulownia in Figure 15.11 would be used with many other test reports in a long report for a group of environmentalists or a government agency on the value of planting those trees to prevent soil erosion.

The titles of some typical long reports further suggest their extensive (and in some cases exhaustive) coverage:

- *A Master Plan for the Recreation Needs of Dover Plains, New York*
- *The Transportation Problems in Kingford, Oregon, and the Use of Monorails*
- *Building and Technology Requirements for Rivera Plastics over the Next Five Years*
- *The Use of Virtual Reality Attractions in Theme Parks*
- *Public Policy Implications of Expanding Health Care Delivery Systems in Tate County*
- *The Contributions of the Internet in Providing Health Care in Rural Areas*

Research

A long, comprehensive report requires much more extensive research than a short report does. Such research can be gathered over time from the Internet and other sources—books, articles, laboratory experiments, on-site visits and tests, interviews, and the writer's own observations. For a course report, you will have to do a great deal of research and possibly interviewing to identify a major problem or topic, to track down the relevant background information, and to discover what experts have said about the subject and what they propose should be done.

Information gathered for many short reports can also help you prepare a long report. In fact, as the example of paulownia shows, a long report can use the experimental data from a short report to arrive at a conclusion. Also for a long report writers often supply one or more progress reports (one type of short report).

TECH NOTE

The Internet as "Virtual Library"

The Internet offers access both to primary research and to long reports published by scientists and mathematicians (.sci), university researchers (.edu), government agencies (.gov), the military (.mil), and every kind of organization (.org) and business (.com). Below is a short—very short—list of government Web sites.

- *http://www.epa.gov* will lead you to press releases, test guidelines, and information about grants, contracts, and job opportunities at the Environmental Protection Agency.
- *http://www.osha.gov* and *http://www.osha-slc.gov/osha.html* are Web sites of the Occupational Safety and Health Agency, where you'll find information about OSHA standards, news releases and fact sheets, publications, technical information, and safety links.
- *http://www.astd.org* is the home page of the American Society for Training and Development, which oversees research and maintains databases of information about employee training in business, industry, education, and government.
- *http://www.aaas.org* is the site of the largest general scientific organization, the American Association for the Advancement of Science, which publishes *Science* magazine and many research reports.
- *http://english.ttu.edu/acw/* leads you to the Alliance for Computers and Writing; its members include educators and researchers who collaborate on the methods and technology of electronic communication.

Other U.S. government agencies and departments that maintain Web sites include the following:

Advanced Research Projects Agency, Bureau of Labor Statistics, Central Intelligence Agency, Department of Agriculture, Department of Education, Department of Energy, Department of Interior, Federal Bureau of Investigation, Federal Communications Commission, General Services Administration, Library of Congress, National Performance Review, Small Business Administration, Social Security Administration, U.S. Business Advisor, U.S. Census Bureau, U.S. House of Representatives, U.S. Patent and Trademark Office, U.S. Senate Gopher Site, and the White House.

Finally, preparing a proposal can lead to writing a long report. You might suggest a change to an employer, who then would ask you to write a long report containing the research necessary to implement that change. Your instructor may ask you to write a proposal on doing a long report for a class project, as Barbara Shoemake did in Figure 14.5.

Format

A long report is too detailed and complex to be adequately organized in a memo or letter format. The product of thorough research and analysis, the long report gives readers detailed discussions and interpretations of large quantities of data. To present the information in a logical and orderly fashion, the long report contains more parts, sections, headings, subheadings, documentation, and supplements (appendixes) than would ever be included in a short report. A long report often includes many graphs, spreadsheets, charts, and tables to give readers extensive background information.

Timetable

The two types of reports differ in the time it takes to prepare them. Writers of these two reports work under different expectations from their readers and under different deadlines. A long report is generally commissioned by a company or an agency to explore with extensive documentation a subject involving personnel, locations, costs, safety, or equipment. Many times a long report is required by law, for example, investigating the feasibility of a project that will affect the ecosystem. A short report is often written as a matter of routine duty, with the writer sometimes given little or no advance notice. The long report may take weeks or even months to write. When you prepare a long report for a class project, select a topic that really interests you, because you will spend a good portion of the term working on it.

Audience

The audience for a long report is generally broader—and goes higher in an organization's hierarchy—than that for a short report. Your short report may be read by co-workers, a first-level supervisor, and possibly that person's immediate boss, but a long report is always intended for people in the top levels of management—presidents, vice presidents, superintendents, directors—who make executive, financial, and organizational decisions. These individuals are responsible for long-range planning, seeing the big picture, so to speak. Copies of long reports may also be sent to appropriate department heads for their information and commentary. A long report written about a campus issue or problem may at first be read by your instructor and then sent to an appropriate decision maker, such as a dean of students, a business manager, a director of athletics, or the head of campus security.

Collaborative Effort

Unlike many short reports, the long report in the world of business may not be the work of one employee. Rather, it may be a collaborative effort, the product of a committee or group whose work is reviewed by a main editor to make sure that the final copy is consistently and accurately written. Individuals in many departments within a company—art, computer programming, engineering, legal affairs, public relations, safety—may cooperate in planning, researching, drafting, revising, and editing a long report. Your instructor may ask you to work in a group (or alone) in preparing your long report (review Chapter 3 on collaborative writing).

The Process of Writing a Long Report

As we just saw, writing a long report requires much time and effort. Since your work will be spread over many weeks, you need to see your report not as a series of static or isolated tasks but as an evolving project. Before you embark on that project, review the information on the writing process found in Chapter 2. You may also want to study the flow chart in Figure 12.14, which illustrates the different stages in writing a research paper. Follow these guidelines:

1. Identify a broad yet significant topic. You'll have to do some preliminary research—general reading, on-line searching, conferring with and interviewing experts—to get an overview of main problems, key ideas and individuals involved, and implications for your company and/or community. Many times in business you will likely be assigned a given subject area and will be expected to arrive at a focused topic only after doing some preliminary research. Note the kinds of research Terri Smith Ruckel did for her long report in Figure 16.3.

2. Expect to confer regularly with your supervisor. In these meetings, plan to ask a lot of questions to pin down exactly what your boss wants. Focus your questions on the company's use of your report, how the company wants you to express certain ideas, and the amount of information it wants. Your supervisor may want you to submit an outline before you draft the report and may expect several more drafts for his or her approval before you write the final version.

3. Revise your work often. Your revisions may sometimes be extensive, depending on what your boss, instructor, or collaborative team recommends. You may have to consult new sources and arrive at a new interpretation of those sources. Be sure to share major changes in your thinking with coauthors or the supervisor who assigned the project. As you narrow your purpose and scope, you may find yourself deleting information or modifying its place in your work. At the earlier stages of outlining and preparing drafts, you may move material around a great deal to avoid unnecessary duplications and to ensure adequate coverage. At the later stages, you will be revising and editing your words, sentences, and paragraphs.

4. Keep the order flexible at first. Even as you work on your drafts and revisions, keep in mind that a long report is not written in the order in which the parts will finally be assembled. You cannot write in "final" order—abstract to appendix. Instead, expect to write in "loose" order to reflect the process in which you gathered information and organized it for the final copy of the report. Usually, the body is written first, the introduction later so the authors can make sure they have not left anything out. The abstract, which appears very early in the report, is always written after all the facts have been recorded and the recommendations made or the conclusions drawn. The title page and the table of contents are always prepared last.

5. Prepare both a work calendar and a checklist. Keep both posted where you do your work—above your desk or computer—so you can track your progress. Make sure your collaborative team is following the same calendar and using the same checklist. The calendar should mark **milestones,** that is, dates by which each stage of your work must be completed. Match the dates on your calendar with the dates your instructor or employer may have given you to submit an outline, progress report(s), and the final copy. Your checklist should list the major parts of your report. As you complete each section, check it off. Before assembling the final copy of your report, use the checklist to make sure you have not omitted something.

Parts of a Long Report

A long report may include some or all of the following twelve parts, which form three categories: *front matter* (letter of transmittal, title page, table of contents, list of illustrations, abstract); *report text* (introduction, body, conclusion, recommendations); and *back matter* (glossary, references cited, appendixes). The entire report may be placed in a clear plastic folder or other suitable cover.

Front Matter

As the name implies, the front matter of a long report consists of everything that precedes the actual text of the report. Such elements introduce, explain, and summarize to help the reader locate various parts of the report. Use lowercase roman numerals for front matter page numbers, not Arabic numbers.

Letter of Transmittal
This three- or four-paragraph letter states the purpose, scope, and major recommendation of the report. If written to an instructor, the letter should additionally note that the report was done as a course assignment. Sometimes a letter of transmittal is bound with the report as part of it; most often it comes before the report, serving as a cover letter. Figure 16.1 is a sample letter of transmittal for a business report.

Title Page
The title, which often is printed in all capital letters or in boldface, tells the reader what your topic is and how you have restricted it in time, space, or method of research. The title page also gives the name of the company or agency preparing the report, the name(s) of the report writer(s), the date, any agency or order numbers, and the name of the firm for which the report was prepared. For a report for a class, give your instructor's name and the specific course for which you prepared the report.

It is important that your title page look professional. Center your title and logically and graphically subordinate any subtitles. Experiment with different type sizes and fonts.

Table of Contents
The table of contents tells readers on which pages they can find different parts of your report and shows how you organized your report. In Figure 16.2, for example, the reader can see how the report "A Study to Determine New Directions in Women's Athletics at Coastal College" is divided into four chief parts (Introduction, Discussion, Conclusion, and Recommendations). A table of contents emerges from many

FIGURE 16.1 A letter of transmittal for a long report.

ALPHA CONSULTANTS
1400 Ridge
Evanston, California 97214-1005
805-555-9200   FAX 805-555-0221
alpha@org   www.alpha.com

August 3, 2001

Dr. K. G. Lowry, President
Coastal College
San Diego, CA 93219-2619

Dear Dr. Lowry:

We are happy to offer you the enclosed report, "A Study to Determine New Directions in Women's Athletics at Coastal College," which you commissioned us to prepare. The report contains our recommendations about strengthening existing sports programs and creating new ones at Coastal College.

Our recommendation is that Coastal should engage in more active recruitment to establish a more competitive women's baseball team, to offer additional athletic activities in women's track and field by August 2002, and to create a new interdisciplinary program between the Athletic Department and the Women's Studies Program.

We hope that you find our report useful in meeting students' needs at Coastal College. If you have any questions or if you would like to discuss any of our recommendations, please call us.

Sincerely yours,

Barbara Gilchrist

Lee T. Sidell

Encl. Report

FIGURE 16.2   A table of contents for a long report.

CONTENTS

outlines and drafts. The items on those outlines frequently expand, shrink, and move around until you decide on the formal divisions and subdivisions of your report.

Include front matter components in your table of contents, but never list the contents page itself, the letter of transmittal, or the title page in your table of contents. Never have just one subheading under a heading. You cannot divide a single topic by one.

Incorrect: EXPANDING THE SPORTS PROGRAM
      Basketball
   BUILDING A NEW ARENA
      The West Side Location

Correct: EXPANDING THE SPORTS PROGRAM
      Basketball
      Track and Field
   BUILDING A NEW ARENA
      The West Side Location
      Costs

List of Illustrations

This list of all the visuals indicates where they can be found in your report.

Abstract

As discussed in Chapter 10, an abstract presents a brief overview of the problem and conclusions; it summarizes the report. An informative abstract is far more helpful to readers of a report than is a descriptive one, which gives no conclusions or results.

Not every member of your audience will read your entire report, but almost everyone will read the abstract. For example, the president of the corporation or the director of an agency may use the abstract as the basis for approving the report and passing it on for distribution. Thus, the abstract may be the most important part of your report.

Abstracts may be placed at various points in long reports—on the title page, on a separate page, or as the first page of the report text.

Text of the Report

The text of a long report consists of an introduction, the body, conclusions, and sometimes recommendations.

Introduction

The introduction may constitute as much as 10 or 15 percent of your report, but it should not be any longer. If it were, the introduction would be disproportionate to the rest of your work, especially the body section. The introduction is essential because it tells readers why your report was written and thus helps them to understand and interpret everything that follows. Do not regard the introduction as one undivided block of information. It includes the following related parts, which should be labeled with subheadings. Keep in mind, though, that your instructor or employer may ask you to list these parts in a different order.

1. Background. To understand why your topic is significant and hence worthy of study, readers need to know about its history. This history may include information on such topics as who was originally involved, when, and where; how someone was affected by the issue; what opinions have been expressed on the issue; what the implications of your study are. See how the long report on non-native speakers in the work force (Figure 16.3) provides useful background information on when, where, how, and why these employees entered the U.S. work force.

2. Problem. Identify the problem or issue that led you to write the report. Because the problem or topic you investigated will determine everything you write about in the report, your statement of it must be clear and precise. That statement may be restricted to a few sentences. Here is a problem statement from a report on how construction designs have not taken into account the requirements of a growing number of older and disabled Americans.

> The construction industry has not satisfactorily met the needs for accessible workplaces and homes for all age and physical ability groups. The industry has relied on expensive and specialized plans to modify existing structures rather than creating universally designed spaces that are accessible to everyone.

3. Purpose statement. The purpose statement, crucial to the success of the report, tells readers why you wrote the report and what you hope to accomplish or prove. In explaining why you gathered information about a particular problem or topic, indicate how such information might be useful to a specific audience, company, or group. Like the problem statement, the purpose statement does not have to be long or complex. A sentence or two will suffice. You might begin simply by saying, "The purpose of this report is. . . ."

4. Scope. This section informs readers about the specific limits—number and type of issues, times, money, locations, personnel, and so forth—you have placed on your investigation. The long report in Figure 16.3 concentrates on adapting the U.S. workplace to meet the communication and cultural needs of a work force of non-native speakers of English, not trends in the international market—two completely different topics. To cite another example, a report on waste disposal might include a scope statement, such as

> This report examines the recent techniques involved in the disposal of liquid and solid wastes; gaseous wastes are not discussed in this report.

In your report, you may not have studied individuals in an adjacent town or county because of time or may not have reviewed certain types of electronic equipment because of their costs or nonavailability. If so, indicate that in your scope section. You also might limit your report by directing it to a particular audience or by writing at a particular technical level for that audience.

> This report is intended for nonengineering managers to acquaint them with recent investigations in unit mechanization design.

A careful statement of the scope should tie in with the purpose of your report.

The Body

Also called the *discussion,* this section is the longest, possibly making up as much as 70 percent of your report. Everything in this and all the other sections of your report grows out of your purpose and how you have limited your scope. The body of your report should supply readers with statistical information, details about the environment, and physical descriptions, as well as the various interpretations and comments of the authorities whose work you consulted as part of your library research. (Follow one of the methods of documentation discussed in Chapter 9.)

The body of your report should be carefully organized to reveal a coherent and well-defined plan. Separate the material in the body into meaningful parts to make sure that you identify the major issues as well as subissues in your report; they must be clearly related to each other. Headings help your reader identify major sections more quickly.

Your organization should reflect the different headings (and even subheadings) included in your report. Use them throughout your report to make it easy to follow. Organizational headings will also enable someone skimming the report to find specific information quickly. The headings, of course, will be included in the table of contents. (Note how Figure 16.3 is carefully organized into sections.)

In addition to headings, use transitions to reveal the organization of the body of your report. At the beginning of each major section of the body, tell readers what they will find in that section and why. Summary sentences at the end of a section will tell readers where they have been and prepare them for any subsequent discussions. The report in Figure 16.3 does an effective job of providing internal summaries.

Conclusion(s)

The conclusion should tie everything together for readers by presenting the findings of your report. Findings, of course, will vary depending on the type of research you do. For a research report based on a study of sources located through various reference searches, the conclusion should summarize the main viewpoints of the authorities whose works you have cited. Perhaps your instructor will ask you to assess in your conclusion which resource materials were most thorough and helpful and why. For a marketing report done for a business, you must spell out the implications for your readers in terms of costs, personnel, products, location, and so forth.

Regardless of the type of research you do, your conclusions should be based on the information and documentation in the body of the report. Be careful that your conclusions do not contradict the evidence/information you gave in the body of your report.

Also, your conclusions should not stray into areas that your report did not cover. In essence, to write an effective conclusion, you will have to summarize carefully a great deal of information accurately and concisely. Notice how the following conclusion of a long report on well casing materials concisely summarizes the findings of the report by reviewing the literature at this crucial stage in the document.

Conclusion

Many materials are used to coat monitoring wells. These casing materials, when they interact with ground water, are affected by pH levels, composition of the ground water, and the casing–ground water contact time. The complex and varied nature of ground water makes it difficult to predict the sorption and leaching potential of these various casings. Consequently, selecting the proper casing material for a particular monitoring application is difficult. Researchers disagree about which is the best material.

The two main classes of casing materials are metals and synthetics. SS304 and SS316 are the preferred metals, whereas PTFE and PVC are the two preferred synthetic polymer casing materials.

Research offers no clear choice as to which material is best for sampling organic or inorganic material. However, we can draw the following conclusions from our review of the literature:

1. If metals are to be tested, metallic casing of any type should not be used.

2. If organic materials in high concentrations are to be tested, SS metals are preferred, since PVC and PTFE are questionable.

3. If metals and low levels of organic materials or compounds are to be tested, PVC and PTFE are the acceptable choices.[1]

---

[1]Adapted from *Ground-Water Issue: The Effects of Well Casing Material on Ground-Water Quality.* U.S. Environmental Protection Agency, Office of Solid Waste and Emergency Response.

Let's look at another effective example of a conclusion. The following conclusion to a long report on the Japanese tuna market clearly summarizes the market opportunities explained in the report.

Conclusion

The U.S. tuna industry has great potential to expand its role in the Japanese market. This market, currently 400,000 tons a year and growing rapidly, is already being supplied by imports that account for 35 percent of all sales. Our report indicates that not only will this market expand but its share of imports will continue to grow. The trend is alarming to Japanese tuna industry leaders, because this important market, close to a billion dollars a year, is increasingly subject to the influence of foreign imports. Decreasing catches by Japan's own tuna fleet as well as an increased preference for tuna by affluent Japanese consumers have contributed significantly to this trend.[2]

---

[2]Adapted from Sunee C. Sonu, *Japan's Tuna Market.* U.S. Department of Commerce, NOAA Technical Memorandum NMFS.

Recommendations

A research report for a course may not require a recommendation section. But for a business or scientific report, the most important part of the report, after the abstract, is the recommendation(s) section, which tells readers what should be done about the findings recorded in the conclusion. Your recommendation section shows readers how you want them to solve the problem your report has focused on.

The report on the Japanese tuna market mentioned above, uses a numbered list to make its recommendations.

Recommendations

Based on our analysis of the Japanese tuna market, we recommend five marketing strategies for the U.S. tuna industry:

1. Farm greater supplies of bluefin tuna to export.

2. Market our own value-added products.

3. Sell fresh tuna directly to the Tokyo Central Wholesale Market.

4. Sell wholesale to other Japanese markets.

5. Advertise and supply to Japanese supermarket chains.[3]

---

[3] Adapted from Sonu, *Japan's Tuna Market*.

Back Matter

Included in the back matter of the report are all the supporting data that, if included in the text of the report, would bog the reader down in details and cloud the main points the report makes.

Glossary

The glossary is an alphabetical list of the specialized vocabulary used in the report and the definitions. A glossary might be unnecessary if your report does not use a highly technical vocabulary or if *all* members of your audience are familiar with the specialized terms you do use.

References Cited

Any sources cited in your report—Web sites, books, articles, television programs, interviews, reviews, audiovisuals—are usually listed in this section (see Chapter 9 on preparing a Works Cited or References page). Also, ask your instructor or employer how he or she wants information to be documented. Sometimes, in the world of work, employers prefer all information to be documented in footnotes or cited parenthetically in the text. Note that the long report in Figure 16.3 uses the American Psychological Association (APA) system of documentation.

Appendix

An appendix contains supporting materials for the report—tables and charts too long to include in the discussion, sample questionnaires, budgets and cost estimates, correspondence about the preparation of the report, case histories, transcripts of telephone conversations. Group like items in an appendix, as the examples under "Appendixes" in Figure 16.2 show. (Note that the plural of *Appendix* is *Appendixes,* not *Appendices.*)

A Model Long Report

The following long report in Figure 16.3 was written by a senior training specialist, Terri Smith Ruckel, for her boss, the human resources director who commissioned it. Ruckel's main task was to demonstrate what U.S. businesses should do to meet the needs of multinational workers and thus promote diversity in the workplace. She gathered relevant data primarily through reading print and electronic sources and interviewing experts. Figure 16.3 contains all the parts of a long report discussed in this chapter except a glossary and an appendix. (Intended for general readers interested in learning more about the problems multinational workers face, Ruckel's report does not contain the technical terms and data that would require a glossary and an appendix.)

FIGURE 16.3   A long report.

RPM *Technologies*

4500 Florissant Drive
St. Louis, MO 63174

(314) 555-2121
www.rpmtech.com
truckel@britestar.com

July 15, 2000

Jesse Butler
Human Resources Director
RPM Technologies
St. Louis, MO 63174

Dear Director Butler:

With this letter I am enclosing my report on effective ways to recruit and
retain a multinational workforce for RPM Technologies, which you
requested six weeks ago. My report argues for the necessity of adapting
the workplace to meet the needs of multinational employees, including
promoting cultural sensitivity and making business communications
more understandable.

Multinational workers will undoubtedly play a major role in U.S.
business. With their technical skills and homeland contacts, they can help
RPM Technologies compete in the global marketplace. Businesses like
RPM need to recruit qualified multinational workers aggressively and
then provide equal opportunities in
the workplace. But U.S. firms must also be sensitive to cultural diversity
and communication demands. By including cross-cultural training—for
native and non-native English speaking employees alike—businesses
promote cultural sensitivity. In-house language programs and plain-
English or translated versions of corporate documents will further
improve the workplace environment for multinational employees.

I hope you will find this report useful and relevant in your efforts to
attract more multinational employees to RPM Technologies. If you would
like to discuss it with me, I can be reached at extension 5406 or write me
at the e-mail address above.

Sincerely yours,

Terri Smith Ruckel

Terri Smith Ruckel
Senior Training Specialist

Enclosure

Adapting the U.S. Workplace for Multinational Employees in the New Millennium

Terri Smith Ruckel

July 14, 2000

Prepared for

Jesse Butler
Human Resources Director
RPM Technologies

Table of Contents

List of Illustrations

Abstract

U.S. businesses can gain a competitive advantage in today's global marketplace by attracting and retaining a multinational work force. Arriving from all over the world, this new wave of immigrants is in great demand for their technical skills and economic ties to their homelands. U.S. firms must recruit qualified multinational employees and then provide them with opportunities to succeed in the workplace. Yet many companies still adhere to work policies designed for native speakers. Businesses should provide cultural sensitivity training to employees who are native speakers of English while still encouraging communication among multinational workers. To promote sensitivity, businesses should adapt their vacation schedules and workplace environment to meet the cultural, religious, and social needs of their multicultural work force. Finally, businesses need to ensure, either through translations or plain-English versions, that all documents are understandable to multinational workers. Businesses also could offer non-native speakers of English in-house language instruction while providing foreign language training for their employees who are native speakers of English.

Introduction

Background

The U.S. work force is undergoing a remarkable revolution. The Bureau of Labor Statistics predicts that major demographic changes will take place in the next decade (1997). The future U.S. work force will comprise older employees (with an average age of 45) as well as a greater number of women at all corporate levels. But the most dramatic change in the U.S. work force will be in the growing numbers of multinational employees. The new wave of immigrants — Indians, Pakistanis, Hispanics, Asians, Caribbeans, East Europeans — will increase to an unprecedented 17% of the labor force by 2002 and soar thereafter. The Office of Employment Projections calculates that by 2010, the number of multinational workers will increase by more than 32% (2000). The Office of the Census Bureau places immigration at 820,000 persons per year, confirming that the United States is becoming the most multiculturally diverse country in the global village (2000).

New York City: Setting the Trend

Immigration figures for New York City exemplify this trend in the national work force. The city today has the largest, most ethnically varied immigrant population in its 400-year history (Martin, 1999). New York has attracted immigrants from more than 200 countries, and the city trades with nearly all those countries. Ali Sabbah, an Arab community leader in New York City, reports that the number of Arabs in New York surpassed the number of Arabs working in Riyadh, the capital of Saudi Arabia, by 11.5% (qtd. in Parker, 2000). Looking a little further into the future, Carlos Harrison, editor of *Latinos,* the largest Hispanic publication in the United States, believes that by 2025 Hispanics will comprise one-quarter of the U.S. population, with most of them residing in New York and the Southwest (qtd. in LaJoya, 1999).

Immigration: Then and Now

Although the United States has long been called a nation of immigrants, the experiences of the current influx of new arrivals differ radically from those of their predecessors (Sontag & Dugger, 1998). The first great surge of immigration occurred in the late nineteenth and early twentieth centuries. At the peak of the immigration wave, from 1901 to 1910, nearly nine million individuals entered the United States, mostly from west and central European countries, as shown in Figure 1(a). Many of those new citizens never went back to their homeland (Brown, 1999). Today's immigrants, however, arrive from India, Pakistan, China, Mexico, Indonesia, the Philippines, and almost every other place across the globe, as Figure 1(b) reveals. Actively maintaining ties with their native countries, today's new immigrants travel back and forth so regularly they have become what could

2

be called global citizens. In many cases, they use their contacts back in their homeland to start new businesses. For example, as more immigrants from Latin America and the Caribbean have settled in New York, the city's exports to those regions have increased (Levanthall, 2000).

Undeniably, modern-day immigrants possess high levels of technical training. *Fortune* magazine reports that 31% of the highly technical jobs in

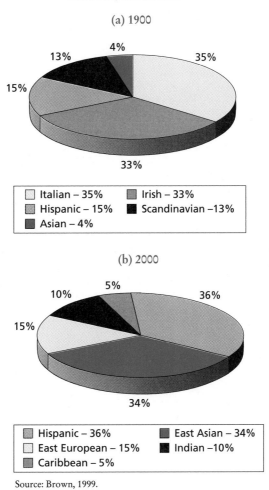

Figure 1
**Major Ethnic Groups Immigrating to New York City
in (a) 1900 and (b) 2000**

(a) 1900

4%
13%
35%
15%
33%

☐ Italian – 35%	☐ Irish – 33%
☐ Hispanic – 15%	☐ Scandinavian –13%
☐ Asian – 4%	

(b) 2000

5%
10%
36%
15%
34%

☐ Hispanic – 36%	☐ East Asian – 34%
☐ East European – 15%	☐ Indian –10%
☐ Caribbean – 5%	

Source: Brown, 1999.

3

Silicon Valley are held by Asians (Colvin, 1999). "We're in a war for talent," says Rich McGinn, CEO of Lucent Technologies, "and the only way to meet business imperatives is to attract all people to be a part of your talent pool" (qtd. in Jones, 1998, p. 35). In fact, the shortage of qualified talent for high-tech positions is being met and solved by the growing numbers of skilled workers who readily receive temporary visas to work in the United States.

Furthermore, those multinational workers who do not arrive with technical skills already in hand quickly enroll in training and education programs. Higher-education officials in New York estimate that by the 2001–2002 school year, non-native speakers of English will account for more than 50% of full-time, first-year students in the City University of New York system, which has been called a "microcosm of the United States as a whole" (Kasper, 1998, p. 58).

The Challenge to U.S. Businesses

As the nation's population — and consequently its work force — becomes more culturally diverse, U.S. firms are being challenged to organize and conduct business in new ways. Companies are striving to adapt their corporate policies and training to fit the communication needs of a growing group of multinational consumers and employees (Adamson, 1999). Enterprising U.S. firms have already begun to adapt to this new multilingual climate. Annuncio Software in Los Altos, California, may set the pace for the rest of the U.S. corporate world. CEO Didier Moretti boasts about the high level of cultural diversity of his employees: "The last time we counted, we had 18 languages, ranging from French to Italian to German, several Indian languages, a few Chinese dialects, and Arabic. I think having a diversity of background is a big help. Both small and large businesses . . . need to think about hiring employees who can relate to customers in foreign markets" (qtd. in Jones, 1998, p. 37). It is a win-win situation for employees and U.S. businesses. Multinational employees excel in the U.S. business culture, and employers profit from their expertise and contacts.

Problem

While Annuncio and other companies celebrate a multicultural work force, too many other corporations lag behind. U.S. businesses need to consider seriously how they will meet the cultural and communication demands of this important work force. Unfortunately, many corporate policies and programs were created for native-born, English speaking employees (Adamson, 1999; Loysk, 1997). Rather than rewarding multinational workers, such companies unintentionally punish them. Moreover, there seems little agreement about how best to address the communication challenges of a new multilingual, highly technical work force.

U.S. businesses must provide effective training strategies and work opportunities to accommodate this new wave of workers effectively. The

4

traditional workplace has to be transformed to understand and to honor the ways in which multinational employees communicate about business and even home-related activities. To do that, firms first have to recognize and incorporate the cultural heritage underlying all communication and then aggressively promote cross-cultural literacy (Parker, 2000). Native English-speaking employees as well as their international co-workers will then be better prepared to understand and appreciate each other as well as their international customers.

Purpose

The purpose of this report is to argue that because of increasing numbers of multicultural employees in the workplace, U.S. businesses must recognize and provide for the needs of a diverse work force.

Scope

This report explores cultural diversity in the U.S. workplace in the new millennium and suggests ways for the United States to compete successfully in the global village by providing equal employment opportunities for multinational workers, fostering cross-cultural literacy, and improving training in intercultural communication.

Discussion

Providing Equal Workplace Opportunities for Multinational Employees

Aggressive Recruitment of People from Diverse Cultures

A multilingual work force makes good business sense for the new millennium. Organizations can hire people who are able to assist them with the day-to-day business of providing services and products for a culturally diverse global market. To do that, firms need to establish or modify hiring policies and procedures to attract the best-qualified multinational workers for the job. To begin with, companies could establish specific goals concerning multinational recruitment and adopt policies such as linking managerial bonuses to fulfilling those goals (Martin, 1999). Routine visits to U.S. campuses provide excellent opportunities to identify the best-qualified multinational job candidates. Some companies even visit foreign universities that have distinguished technical programs to attract qualified multinational employees. All firms should use the Internet to conduct global searches for the best potential multinational employees and advertise their eagerness to attract a culturally diverse workforce.

5

Capitalizing on the power of diversity is necessary in a growing global market because, logically, customers buy from people they can relate to. Union Bank of California, for instance, effectively serves the diverse West Coast population, especially its Asian and Hispanic customers. Accordingly, the bank has a successful recruitment history of hiring employees with language skills in Japanese, Vietnamese, Korean, and Spanish. In fact, Union Bank is listed as one of the top five companies for Asian employees (Robinson & Hickman, 1999). Making up 25.6% of the bank's work force, Asians lead in the representation of ethnic employees. Seven of the bank's seventeen-member board of directors are also Asian Americans. Figure 2 shows Union Bank's track record in hiring multinational employees. Certainly, Union Bank has benefited from a diverse spectrum of employees who can better solve problems for its increasingly multicultural customer base.

Another successful business, Darden Restaurants of Orlando, Florida, selected Richard Rivera, a Hispanic, to serve as president of Red Lobster, the nation's largest full-service seafood chain. Overseeing 680 restaurants nationwide, Rivera is the "most powerful minority in the restaurant industry" (Royster Jackson, personal interview, May 3, 2000). Under Rivera's leadership, Red Lobster has built an impressive record for adding more ethnic employees, totaling more than 35% of its work force, than it had in previous years. Rivera believes that management cannot properly respond to customers from different ethnic backgrounds if the majority of its employees are limited to native speakers of English. Closer to home, Whitney Abernathy, manager of Netshop, Inc., a consulting firm, found that contracts from the Middle East increased by 12% after she hired Rashid Asan, a Syrian national who recently graduated from an English program for non-native speakers in Fort Worth (Adamson, 1999).

Commitment to Ethnic Representation

Many companies already have mission statements on diversity in the workplace that formally acknowledge the importance of multinational employees. The most progressive of those companies, such as Toyota Motor Sales, SBC Communications, and Wal-Mart, promote multinational employees to serve as mentors and interpreters within the company. A proactive mentoring program recognizes the leadership abilities of multinational employees in the company. "Glass ceilings," which in the past have prevented women and ethnic workers from moving up the corporate ladder, are being shattered. More and more CEOs are emphasizing recruitment and promotion of non-native speakers of English based on their actual job performance (Jones, 1998). Jay Harris, publisher of the *San Jose Mercury News*, affirms, "Diversifying our staff is not some side project. It's a core part of our business strategy" (Harris, 1999).

Fannie Mae, the nation's largest source of home mortgages, has established a "Diversity Department" headed by a vice president who reports directly to the

6

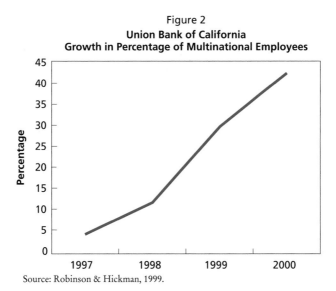

Figure 2
Union Bank of California
Growth in Percentage of Multinational Employees

Source: Robinson & Hickman, 1999.

agency's chief executive officer (Katz-Stone, 1998). Spearheaded by this "Vice President of Diversity," Fannie Mae's commitment to ethnic representation is praiseworthy; 40% of the company's 3,700 employees and 19% of its officers have international backgrounds. Fannie Mae was recently selected by *Fortune* magazine as having one of the best track records in hiring highly qualified multicultural workers (Robinson & Hickman, 1999).

Promoting and Incorporating Cultural Awareness Within the Company

Cross-Cultural Training

Some companies are creating cultural awareness programs for international employees to learn about other cultures. Both employees and employers profit: employees find it easier to work with someone whose values and beliefs they understand, while employers benefit from effective on-the-job collaboration. One of the best cultural sharing programs is at American Express, whose work force represents more than twenty different nations. According to Moira Valdez, "culturally diverse employees have an opportunity to reach their maximum potential while still maintaining their cultural identities" (2000). Extel Communications, with its large percentage of Hispanic and Vietnamese employees, offers several workshops on those two cultures each year. Similarly, United Parcel Service (UPS) has developed a program whereby employees volunteer to work on a project with someone from another cultural group, with both parties gaining invaluable insights in problem solving and communicating. Celine Galvez, a UPS employee since

7

1988, claims that her multicultural experience with Loo Tuan was one of the most rewarding experiences of her job (Crowe, 1998).

Along with encouraging cultural sharing, U.S. firms need to be cautious about severing international workers' cultural ties — a delicate balance. Multinational workers do not like to be singled out because of their differences, yet successful U.S. businesses still must express sincere respect of their workers' cultures. When management actively promotes bonds among employees with similar identities, workers are less fearful about losing their cultural identity and becoming "token" employees (Prasad, Mills, Elmes, & Prasad, 1997). The Amoco Corporation offers networking to its employees, and Chase Manhattan Bank mobilizes culturally similar groups by introducing workers of homogeneous backgrounds to one another (Gabriel & Bentzman, 1999). For instance, employees from Chase Manhattan's New York City office who are of Turkish background lunch twice a month with fellow Turkish-born employees from the Newark branches. Chase Manhattan hosts the business luncheons as well as provides the transportation and in return receives from those workers a bi-monthly written evaluation of its Turkish and Middle Eastern policies.

Cultural education must go both ways, though. Both sides have things to learn about doing business in a global environment and working with each other. The United States, too, has social conventions in the business world, and few international employees want to ignore them, if only someone would tell them what those conventions are (Adamson, 1999). Perhaps one problem with U.S. businesses is that we assume everyone knows how we do things and how we think — it never occurs to us to explain ourselves. Problems often stem from simple misunderstanding. For example, in West Africa it is very important for the work day to begin with lots of hand-shaking. Such behavior, however, may be regarded as a waste of time by a supervisor at a U.S. firm. But the West African employee may interpret a lack of personal acknowledgement as a sure sign he or she is about to be fired (Crowe, 1998).

Promotion of Cultural Sensitivity

Company efforts to validate different cultures might include the recognition, and even celebration, of a non-Western ethnic group's holidays or memorable historical events. Techsure, Inc., an Illinois software firm, allows Muslim employees to change their work schedules to accommodate Ramadan, Islam's holy month of fasting (Michael Saradayan, personal interview, April 12, 2000). During Ramadan believers must abstain from eating and drinking from sunrise to sunset. Creating a culturally sensitive workplace, Techsure reschedules company dinners, picnics, and other events that would disrupt this time of religious reflection. Corporations with a Hispanic work force might honor National Hispanic Heritage Month, which coincides with the independence celebrations of five Latin American countries (U.S. Department

8

of Equal Employment Opportunity [USEEO], 1999). GRT Electronics sends New Year's greetings at Waisak to its Chinese employees and to Indian workers at Rama Dipawli. Bert Pestilozzi, GRT's General Manager, wisely pointed out: "We send native-born employees Christmas cards; why shouldn't we honor our international work force, too?" (Personal interview, May 10, 2000). Finally, Techsure and GRT have rethought vacation schedules so their multinational employees can visit relatives during times most appropriate according to their cultural calendars.

In recent years, U.S. firms have been sensitive to the special needs of its changing work force. Flexible scheduling, telecommuting options, day care, and preventative health programs have become part of corporate plans to take care of employees. An international work force presents additional opportunities for management to respond with sensitivity to its employees. For example, company cafeterias could easily accommodate the particular dietary restrictions of workers who are vegetarian or who abstain from certain meats, such as beef or pork. At Ameritech, Inc., soybean and fish entrees are always available (Stone, 2000). Moreover, adding new ethnic items sends a powerful message of cultural awareness as well as contributes to networking and cultural sensitivity. Serving special foods in honor of different cultural events, holidays, and feast days is another advantageous possibility.

Day care raises critical issues for all working parents, non-native as well as native speakers of English. Often children of multinational workers are accustomed to different menus, customs, and personal affinities. By providing child care that is informed about such culturally diverse needs, companies give their multinational work force greater peace of mind and better equip them for their jobs. DEJ Computers, which offers one of the best on-site day care programs in the Northwest, insists that at least two or three of its day care workers must be fluent in Korean or Hindi (Parker, 2000). Another culturally sensitive employer, Angelica Nurseries in Kennedyville, Maryland, assists its Hispanic work force by hiring bilingual day care workers and also by serving foods the children eat at home. Angelica also helps Hispanic children enroll in school and arranges with local churches for free instruction in English (Morgan, 1999).

Making Business Communication More Understandable for Multinational Employees

Translation of Written Communications

All employees must be able to read and respond to business communications that directly affect them and their jobs. Among the most essential business documents that may cause trouble for multicultural readers are company handbooks, insurance and health care documents, OSHA and EPA safety regulations, and retirement fund policies (Morgan,

9

1999). To ensure maximum understanding by a multinational work force, companies might provide a translation or at least a plain-English version of those and other crucial business documents. U.S. firms can solicit the help of employees who speak the non-native English speaker's language as well as contract with professional translators to prepare documents that are readily understandable to a multinational work force.

Workplace signs, especially safety messages, should take into account the needs of international workers. It is in a company's best interest to translate signs to the languages represented in the workplace and/or to post signs that use global symbols, as shown in Figure 3. Unquestionably, companies must avoid signs that workers would find hard or impossible to decipher (Stone, 2000). For example, a large Ⓟ for "parking" might be unfamiliar to non-native speakers of English.

Exchange of Language Learning

Providing English language instruction for employees who need it also has obvious advantages for the workplace of the new millennium. Unskilled workers may even need instruction in their native language, including tutoring in literacy or basic mathematics (Adamson, 1999). Companies that cannot provide in-house language training should reimburse employees for appropriate courses, language books, tapes, and software, thus encouraging workers to communicate better. At the very least, every business could make available an audio library of specific vocabulary and phrases commonly used on the job and multilingual dictionaries or phrase books with relevant technical terms. Furthermore, businesses could invite religious and civic groups to participate in conversation groups and other language programs.

Hiromi Naguchi, a senior analyst at PowerUsers Networking, testified to the value of the English language training she received on the job. Although Naguchi had twelve years' training in English in the Japanese school system and graduated from a language institute in the United States, she needed regular practice in conversation to develop her listening and speaking skills. As a result of her diligence and the initiative of PowerUsers, Naguchi was recognized as her company's "Most Valuable Employee for 1999" (Hiromi Naguchi, personal interview, June 9, 2000).

Language training has to be reciprocal — for native as well as non-native speakers of English — if international communication is to succeed in the global marketplace. Sadly, "only four percent of high school graduates in the United States have had at least two years of foreign language training, while one hundred percent of limited English speaking students have capabilities in other languages" (Ortiz, 2000, p. 72). Many international workers are trilingual, and several world cultures have two or more national languages. In Canada, for instance, people who speak both English and French have the

10

Figure 3
**Safety Messages with Translations
for Multinational Employees**

Danger: Radioactive

Peligro! Radiactivo
(Spanish)

Dhamki! Jauhari
tawaanaa'i! (Urdu)

Caution: Wet floor

Precaución!
Mojado Suelo (Spanish)

Khabar darrkarna!
Aabi farsh (Urdu)

For your protection
wear safety glasses

Pour votre protection,
verres de sûreté d'usure
(French)

Paheñna âasim chashmah
(Urdu)

Source: Stone.

advantage over those who speak only one of those languages; in India and South Africa the average person uses three or more languages every day, all essential to conduct business (Demruajian, 1999). A quick Internet search turns up dozens of companies that specialize in foreign language instruction for U.S. businesspeople (e.g., Atkins International, Lingua Service Worldwide). Such instruction can include ways to engage in friendly business conversation and provide phrases to build trust and to make task assignments or simple introductions. Instruction can be industry specific as well.

Conclusions

Because of a competitive world market, U.S. businesses must incorporate cultural diversity into the workplace. Companies should design policies and programs that provide new opportunities for the growing and essential multicultural work force. Technologically educated and experienced multinational workers will be in greater demand in the new millennium. In fact, U.S. embassies in Indonesia, Nigeria, and Turkey encourage highly trained workers in those countries to apply for U.S. visas. U.S. organizations that do not recruit and recognize this vital group of employees will surely suffer in the international marketplace. As Joseph Stegner, President of the University of Cincinnati, put it, "Without change in our emotional commitment to diversity of languages and cultures worldwide, we will fail as a worldwide leader in the next century" (1999, p. 52). Equal opportunities, diversity training, and attention to communication issues will keep U.S.

11

business globally competitive. Ultimately, businesses in the United States, the most multicultural country in the world, can expand only by making a commitment to learn about other cultures and their ways of life.

Recommendations

To be competitive in the global economy, RPM Technologies must attract and retain highly skilled international employees. As this report has shown, both hiring and training policies need to be adjusted to accommodate the cultural — linguistic, social, and religious — needs of a new wave of immigrants. By implementing the following recommendations, RPM Technologies can succeed in its recuitment and training efforts.

1. Recruit multinational students more effectively at campuses both in the United States and in other countries.
2. Establish a mentoring program to identify leadership abilities in multinational employees.
3. Form cultural sensitivities and networking groups to ensure the dissemination of cultural information.
4. Provide relevant translations and plain-English versions of company handbooks, manuals, and codes.
5. Reassess our day care facilities to take into consideration the needs of the children of multinational employees.
6. Develop educational materials for employees who are native speakers of English about the cultures of their multinational co-workers.

12

References

Adamson, R. (1999, February). Challenges ahead for American business. National Economics Review, 11, 45-46.

Brown, P. (1999, December). History of U.S. immigration. [WWW document]. URL: http://immigration.ucn.edu.

Bureau of Labor Statistics. (1997). Labor force 2006: Slowing down and changing composition (BLS Report No. 80-3562). Washington, DC: U.S. Government Printing Office.

Colvin, G. (1999, July). The 50 best companies for Asians, Blacks, and Hispanics. Fortune, 18, 53-58.

Crowe, M. (1998, September). UPS managers trained in the real world to deliver results. Business Journal Serving San Jose & Silicon Valley, 15(21), 26-28.

Demruajian, P. (1999). Linguistic diversity in business. Hillsdale, NJ: Lawrence Erlbaum Associates.

Gabriel, B., & Bentzman, J. (1999, July). The 50 best companies for Latinas to work for in the U.S. Latina Style, 50, 1.

Harris, J. (1999, August 5). Business strategies for a successful paper. San Jose Mercury News, p. B1.

Jones, M. L. (1998, May 15). Diverse work force = competitive advantage; Why multiple perspectives can help companies relate more closely to their markets. Dallas Business Journal, 21(38), 35-37.

Kasper, L. F. (1998, February). ESL writing and the principle of nonjudgmental awareness: Rationale and implementation. Teaching English in the Two-Year College, 10(12), 58-60.

Katz-Stone, A. (1998, October 2). Promoting diversity is Fannie Mae's usual policy. Washington Business Journal, 17, 42-44.

LaJoya, R. (Director). (1999). Noticias por la gente [Television program]. Extra TV. (Transcript available from Merganser Communications, 61 Woodlawn Street, Miami, FL 33166).

Levanthall, M. (2000). New York! New York! Most popular spot to immigrate. All Around New York, 10(13), 14-17.

Loysk, B. (1997). Managing a changing work force: Achieving outstanding service with today's employees. Davie, FL: Workplace Trends.

Martin, P. (1999). Migration news. [WWW document]. URL: http://www.migration.ucdavis.edu.

Morgan, D. (1999, July). We say talk the talk. N Pro [On-line magazine]. URL: http://bsipublishing.com.

13

Office of the Census Bureau. (2000). <u>Immigration figures</u> (OCB Publication No. A 82-[995]). Washington, DC: U.S. Government Printing Office.

Office of Employment Projections. (2000). <u>Employment outlook: 2000–2010</u> (OEP Report No. 12-632). Washington, DC: U.S. Government Printing Office.

Ortiz, M. (2000, January). <u>Linguistic abilities of ESL students</u> (Report No. NCRTL-zz-99-1). East Lansing, MI: National Center for Research on Teacher Learning. (ERIC Document Reproduction Service No. ED 888 097).

Parker, M. (2000, May). Immigration facts. [WWW document]. URL: http://immigration.org.

Prasad, R., Mills, A. J., Elmes, M., & Prasad, A. (1997). <u>Managing the organizational melting pot: Dilemmas of workplace diversity.</u> Thousand Oaks, CA: Sage.

Robinson, E., & Hickman, J. (1999, July). The diversity elite. <u>Fortune 18,</u> 62- 63.

Sontag, D., & Dugger, C. (1998, July 19). The new immigrant tide: A shuttle between worlds. [<u>New York Times Online</u>]. URL: http://www.nytimes.com/library/natl/reg/071998.immigration.html.

Stegner, J. (1999, August). "Competing in the world market." <u>Business World, 34,</u> 51-52.

Stone, E. (2000, March). Serving up culture. [WWW document]. URL: http://www.culture.org.

U.S. Department of Equal Employment Opportunity. (1999). <u>Hispanic employment program report for 1999</u> (EEO Publication No. B 56.2245). Washington, DC: U.S. Government Printing Office.

Valdez, M. (2000, Spring). Cultural diversity in the workplace. (From <Business 2000>[SIRS Researcher CD-ROM Spring 2000], Art. No. 35, Boca Raton, FL: SIRS, Inc. [Producer and Distributor]).

Final Words of Advice About Long Reports

Perhaps no piece of writing you do on the job—or as a course assignment for your instructor—carries more weight than your work on a long report. Your readers will inevitably place a great deal of emphasis on your work. As we have seen, these reports deal with major issues affecting long-range planning and decision making. The long report requires you to use all the researching, organizing, drafting, revising, and editing skills you have learned.

The preparation of a long report may appear at first to be a formidable task. But you can simplify your job and increase your chances for success by following the guidelines offered in this chapter. Among those guidelines, these four points are especially helpful:

1. Plan and work early—do not postpone work on identifying, researching, and drafting until a deadline draws near.
2. Divide your workload into meaningful units—reassure yourself that you do not have to write the report or even an entire section of a report in a day or two.
3. Set up mini-deadlines for each phase of your work and then meet them.
4. If you are preparing the report as part of a team, confer often and carefully with others on your team.

✓ Revision Checklist

- ❑ Concentrated on a major problem—one with significant implications for my major, neighborhood, city, or employer.
- ❑ Identified, justified, and described the significance of the main problem as opposed to focusing on a minor side issue.
- ❑ Did sufficient research—in the library, on the Internet, through interviewing, from personal observation and/or testing—to convince my readers that I am knowledgeable about this problem, its scope and effects, and likely solution.
- ❑ Became familiar with key terms, major researchers in the field, major changes, trends, and accomplishments.
- ❑ Anticipated how various readers will use and profit from my report for their long-range planning.
- ❑ Made sure I understand what employer/teacher/reader is looking for.
- ❑ Followed company's/instructor's guidelines for the format and documentation of work.
- ❑ Followed company's/instructor's schedule for completing various stages of long report.
- ❑ Divided and labeled the parts of long report to make it easy for readers to follow and to show careful plan of organization.

❑ Supplied an abstract that leaves no doubt in readers' minds about what report deals with and why.

❑ Designed attractive title page that contains all the basic information—title, date, for whom the report is written, my name—readers require.

❑ Gave readers all the necessary introductory information about background, problem, purpose of report, and scope. Made sure that introduction is neither too long nor too short.

❑ Included in body of report the weight of all my research—the facts, statistics, and descriptions—that my readers need in order to know that I have done my homework on the topic well.

❑ Included subheadings to reflect the major divisions into which I have organized the research that forms the nucleus of the text.

❑ Wrapped up report in succinct conclusion. Told readers what the findings of my research are and accurately interpreted all data.

❑ Supplied a recommendations section (if required) that tells readers concretely how they can respond to the problem using the data. Recommendations make sense—are realistic and practical and related directly to the research and topic. Ensured that recommendations are persuasive.

❑ Included in the final copy of report all the parts listed in table of contents.

❑ Supplied a one-page letter of transmittal or cover letter informing readers why the report was written and describing its scope and findings.

Exercises

1. Send an e-mail to your instructor on how one of the short reports in Chapter 15 could be useful to someone who has to write a long report.

2. Using the information contained in Figures 16.1 and 16.2, draft an introduction for the report "A Study to Determine New Directions in Women's Athletics at Coastal College." Add any details you think will be relevant.

3. What kinds of research did the student do to write the long report in Figure 16.3? As part of your answer, include the titles of any specific reference works you think the writer may have consulted. (You may want to review Chapter 9.)

4. Study Figure 16.3 and answer the following questions based on it.
   a. Why can the abstract be termed informative rather than descriptive?
   b. How has the writer successfully limited the scope of the report?
   c. Where does the writer use internal summaries especially well?
   d. Where and how has the writer adapted her technical information for her audience of general readers?
   e. What visual devices does the writer use to separate parts of the report and divisions within each part?

     f. How does the writer introduce, summarize, and draw conclusions from the expert opinions she cites in order to substantiate the main points?

     g. What are the ways in which the writer documents information she has gathered?

     h. What functions does the conclusion serve for readers? Cite specific examples from the report.

5. Come to class prepared to discuss at least two major problems that would be suitable topics for a long report. Consider an important community problem—traffic, crime, air and water pollution—or a problem at your college. Then write a letter to a consulting firm or other appropriate agency or business, requesting a study of the problem and a report.

6. Write a report outline for one of the problems you decided on in Exercise 5. Use major headings and include the kinds of information discussed in the Front Matter section of this chapter (pp. 619–622).

7. Have your instructor look at and approve the outline you prepared for Exercise 6. Then write a long report based on the outline, either individually or as part of a collaborative writing team.

Making Successful Presentations at Work

Almost every job requires employees to have and to use carefully developed speaking skills. Your oral presentations can be just as important to your career as your written ones are. In fact, to get hired, you have to be a persuasive speaker at your job interview. And to advance up the corporate ladder you will have to continue to be a confident, well-prepared, and persuasive speaker.

New Communication Technologies
Being an effective speaker in the business world means more than simply standing in front of a group. More and more, the tools of business communication are integrating digital, audio, and visual information through the Internet, picture phones, and videoconferencing. Each of these widely used technologies will require you to be a clear and effective speaker who also projects a professional image to your boss, co-workers, and customers around the globe.

Types of Presentations at Work

On the job you will have numerous presentation responsibilities that will vary in the amount of preparation they require, the time they last, and the audience and the occasion for which they are intended. Here are some frequent types of presentations you may have to make as part of your job:

- sales pitches to prospective clients
- evaluations of products or policies
- progress reports to your collaborative team and your boss
- reports to superiors about your job accomplishments
- justifications of your position or even your department
- appeals and/or explanations before elected officials

Whatever type of oral presentation you are called on to deliver, this chapter gives you practical advice on how to become a better, more assured communicator in both informal briefings and formal speeches.

Informal Briefings

If you have ever given a book report or explained laboratory results in front of a class, you have given an informal briefing. Such semiformal reports are a routine part of many jobs. Here is a list of some of the typical informal briefings you may need to deliver at work:

- a status report on your current project
- an update or end-of-shift report, like those nurses and police officers give
- an explanation of a policy to co-workers
- a report on a conference you attended, as Judith Kim and Lee Schoppe do in Figure 10.9.
- a demonstration of new equipment or software
- an introduction of a speaker, co-worker, supervisor, or inspector
- a summary of a meeting you attended

Such informal presentations are usually short (one to seven minutes, perhaps), and you won't always be given advance notice. When the boss tells you to "say a few words about the new Web site (or the new programming procedure)," you will not be expected to give a lengthy formal speech. For example, the human resources officer informing employees about recently extended insurance coverage does not read them the fine print in the policy but rather covers the key points, saving detailed questions for private conferences.

Guidelines for Preparing Informal Briefings

Follow these guidelines when you have to make an informal briefing:

- Make your comments brief and to the point.
- Keyboard a few bulleted items you plan to cover.
- Highlight key phrases and terms you need to stress.
- Include in your notes only the major points you want to mention.
- Arrange your points in chronological order or from cause to effect.

Figure 17.1 is an informal outline with key facts used by an employee who is introducing Diana Rizzo, a visiting speaker, to a monthly meeting of safety directors.

FIGURE 17.1   Some notes for an informal briefing to introduce an engineer to a group of safety directors.

- Diana J. Rizzo, Chief Engineer of the Rhode Island State Highway Department for twelve years.

- Experience as both a civil engineer and safety expert.

- Consultant to Secretary Habib, Department of Transportation.

- Member of the National Safety Council and author of "Field Test Procedures in Highway Safety Construction."

- Designed specially constructed aluminum posts used on Rhode Island highway system.

- Received "Award for Excellence" from the Northeastern Association of Traffic Engineers in May 2000

Formal Presentations

Whereas an informal briefing is likely to be short, generally conversational, and intended for a limited number of people, a formal presentation is much longer, far less conversational, and intended for a wider audience. Therefore, it involves more preparation and more sustained interaction between speaker and audience; it is, in other words, more "formal."

Many of us are uncomfortable in front of an audience because we feel frightened or embarrassed. Much of that anxiety can be eased if you know what to expect. The two areas you should investigate thoroughly before you begin to prepare your presentation are (1) who will be in your audience and (2) why they are there.

Analyzing Your Audience

The more you learn about your audience, the better prepared you will be to give them what they need. Just as you do for your written work, for your oral presentation you will have to do some research about the audience, emphasizing the "you attitude" and establishing your own credibility.

Consider Your Audience as a Group of Listeners, Not Readers

While many elements of audience analysis pertain both to readers of your work and to listeners of your presentation, keep in mind that there are several fundamental differences between these two groups. Unlike a reader of your report, the audience for your presentation

- is a captive audience
- has only one chance to get your message
- has less time to digest what you say
- has a shorter attention span
- can't go back to review what you said or jump ahead to get a preview
- is more easily distracted—by interruptions, chairs being moved, people coughing, and so on
- cannot absorb as many of the technical details as you would include in a written report

Take all those differences into account as you plan your presentation and assess your audience.

Remember that everything in your presentation is being delivered for the benefit of that audience. Relate everything in your talk to them. Do that by selecting only details that are relevant to your audience and your purpose. Choose concrete (not abstract or general) examples; look for memorable stories, analogies, or events that an audience can easily recall after you have completed your presentation.

Analyzing Your Listening Audience

Here are four key rules you need to follow when analyzing the audience for your presentation.

1. **Find out what unites them as a group.** Are they

   - members of the same profession?
   - customers using the same products?
   - employees of the company you work for?
   - supporters of the same club or organization?
   - members of the same ethnic, religious, or political group?
   - united in their emotional response to a topic, such as a campaign to curb property taxes?

2. **Determine how much they know about your topic.** Are they

   - all consumers who have little or no technical knowledge of your subject?
   - all technical individuals who understand the terms, jargon, and background of your subject?
   - a mixed audience?

3. **Establish their interest in your topic.** Will they be

   - a highly motivated, willing audience eager to hear what you have to say and happy to endorse your conclusions?
   - mildly interested but not totally convinced of your point of view?

- neutral—waiting to be informed, entertained, or persuaded?
- uninterested in your topic, listening indifferently or reluctantly, there only because their attendance is mandatory?
- hostile—opposed to your opinion?

4. **Anticipate their most likely response to you.** Will they be

- positive and clearly interested?
- open-minded and uncommitted?
- mildly skeptical?
- uncooperative and antagonistic, likely to challenge you?

Special Considerations for a Multinational Audience

Given the international make-up of audiences at many business presentations, it is not unlikely that you will have to address a group of listeners whose native language is not English or even make a presentation before individuals in a country other than your own. While it is difficult to generalize about specific communication guidelines, consider your audience's particular cultural taboos and protocols. Do they accept your looking at them directly, or do they frown on eye contact? Will they expect you to stand in one place, or will they be comfortable if you move about the room while you speak?

As you prepare a talk before an audience that includes people of other cultures, keep the following points in mind.

1. Brush up on your audience's culture, especially accepted ways they communicate with each other (see pp. 172–176).
2. Find out what constitutes an appropriate length for a talk before your audience. (German listeners might be accustomed to hearing someone read a thirty- to forty-page paper, while members from another culture would regard that practice as improper.)
3. Be especially careful about introducing humor—avoid anything that is based on nationality, dialect, religion, or race.
4. Think twice about injecting anything autobiographical into your speech. Some cultures regard such intimacy as an invasion of privacy.
5. Steer clear of politics; you risk losing your audience's confidence.
6. Choose visuals with universally understood icons and logos.

Speaking for the Occasion

Understanding why your audience has gathered will help you deliver a successful presentation. An audience may be present for a variety of reasons—for a social gathering, a business meeting, or an educational forum. Shape your remarks to fit the occasion.

Your Allotted Time

Consider also how much time is allotted for your presentation and never exceed it. In fact, your audience may be even more likely to respond enthusiastically if you finish a little early.

Also factor in whether you are the only speaker scheduled. It makes a big difference in your preparation if you are the first or only speaker at a breakfast meeting or the last of four speakers at an evening meeting.

Take into account your audience's interest level and attention span at various times of the day or week. Are you speaking on early Monday morning or late Friday afternoon?

Also find out whether someone will introduce you or whether you will begin on your own. If someone introduces you, it would be embarrassing if you repeated (or contradicted!) the information from the introduction.

Number of People in Your Audience

The number of people in your audience is also significant. A formal presentation to a small group—five or six supervisors or buyers—seated around a conference table can be made more personal; you can walk around the table or interrupt your talk a few times to answer questions. You obviously will have much less flexibility when addressing a large group—seventy or eighty people—in an auditorium.

Ways to Make a Formal Presentation

Your effectiveness depends directly on the extent of your preparation. Of the four approaches that follow, the extemporaneous is best suited to most individuals and occasions. But first we will examine three other possibilities and their advantages and disadvantages.

1. Speaking "off the cuff." The professional speechmaker may be comfortable with an off-the-cuff approach, but for most of us, the worst way to make a presentation is to speak without any preparation whatsoever. You may know a subject very well and think that your experience qualifies you for an on-the-spot performance. But you only fool yourself if you think you have all the necessary details and explanations in the back of your head. It is equally dangerous to believe that once you start talking, everything will fall into place smoothly. The "everything works out for the best" philosophy, unaided by a lot of hard work, does not operate in public speaking. Without preparation, you are likely to confuse important points or forget them entirely. Mark Twain's advice is apt here: "It takes three weeks to prepare a good impromptu speech."

2. Memorizing a speech. The exact opposite of the off-the-cuff approach, a memorized speech has advantages for certain individuals—safety trainers, guides, and salespeople—who must deliver the same speech verbatim many times over. But for the individual who has to deliver an original speech just once, a memorized one has pitfalls.

- The hours spent memorizing exact words and sentences would be better devoted to organizing your speech or gathering information for it.
- If you forget a word or a sentence, you may lose track of your speech.
- A memorized delivery can make you appear stiff and mechanical; it ties you to your exact words, not your audience's reaction to them.

3. Reading a speech. Reading a speech may be appropriate if you are presenting information on company policy or legal issues on which there can be no deviation from the printed word. Most presentations, however, will not require rigid adherence to a text; they will be more acceptable, socially and professionally, when you interact with the audience. In reading, you set up a barrier between yourself and the audience by not establishing eye contact for fear of losing your place.

4. Delivering a presentation extemporaneously. An extemporaneous delivery is the most widely used method for a variety of occasions. Unlike relying on a memorized or written speech, you do not come before your audience with the entire presentation in hand. *By no means, though, is an extemporaneous delivery an off-the-cuff performance.* It requires a great deal of preparation, but what you prepare is an outline of the major points. You will have rehearsed using the outline, but the actual words you will use in your presentation will not necessarily be those you have rehearsed. In that way you are free to establish contact with your audience.

The rest of this chapter discusses various effective ways of preparing and delivering an extemporaneous presentation.

TECH NOTE

Toastmasters

To get helpful experience delivering both impromptu briefings and formal speeches, consider joining Toastmasters International, an educational organization that has transformed many frightened speakers into accomplished speechmakers. Members of Toastmasters meet at least once a month (sometimes as often as every week) to listen to and evaluate one another's speeches. From feedback and strategic training, you will grow to be a more confident public speaker. The Toastmasters Web site is *http://www. toastmasters.org.*

The Parts of a Presentation

As you read this section, refer to Marilyn Claire Ford's outline in Figure 17.2.

The Introduction

The most important part of a presentation, your introduction should capture the audience's attention by answering these questions: (1) Who are you? (2) What are your qualifications? (3) What specific topic are you speaking about? and (4) How is the topic relevant to us?

As you answer those four questions, your first and most immediate goal is to establish rapport with your audience, win their confidence, and elicit their cooperation. Since

FIGURE 17.2   Formal outline of a formal presentation.

Outline for a Presentation Promoting
Desktop Videoconferencing to a Potential Customer

Audience: Executives of GTP Systems
Purpose: To convince management to invest in videoconferencing technology
Speaker: Marilyn Claire Ford, World Tech Telecommunications

Introduction

I. World Tech Desktop Videoconferencing can increase the efficiency of GTP's communications by 50 to 100 percent—and dramatically cut costs. **[PowerPoint Slide 1: Map of GTP's sites with airplanes connecting them.]**

    A. GTP spent over $350,000 for business travel last year (much more than necessary). **[PowerPoint Slide 2: Graph of travel expenditures, 1999–2000]**

    B. Conducting staff meetings among branch offices poses several problems: extensive preparations, scheduling conflicts, travel delays.

    C. Desktop Videoconferencing solves those problems; employees at different sites interact as though all in the same room (a competitive advantage).

    D. Desktop Videoconferencing transforms existing computers into interactive, multimedia conference rooms.

Body

II. World Tech's technology for Desktop Videoconferencing is easy to use and cost effective. **[PowerPoint Slide 3: Photo of employees connecting with distant sites by dialing the Microlink.]**

    A. Desktop Videoconferencing is as simple as a telephone call.

        1. Arrange a meeting time with colleagues at other sites.

        2. Use your computer to access World Tech's Microlink.

        3. Dial in to the conference (see and hear all participants access the Microlink).

        4. Talk directly with all participants by telephone.

    B. Reap great benefits with an inexpensive or existing computer system.

        1. Technology is based on a Pentium class computer with 32 MB of memory; if new, cost ranges from $900 to $1,500.

        2. Existing computer system can be upgraded quickly for less than the cost of a new computer.

        3. Cost of additional equipment (software, camera, modem, video and sound card) is under $1,400.

Continued

FIGURE 17.2   (Continued)

2

C. Integrated service data network (ISDN)—a dedicated phone line that transfers digital data—costs only $900/year to rent.

D. Desktop Videoconferencing can cut data processing costs by 60 percent or more.

III. Desktop Videoconferencing is a strategic weapon in the international marketplace.

  A. Competitive businesses are information driven, not product driven.

    1. GTP can accelerate global sales via the Internet.

    2. Desktop Videoconferencing provides flexible, low-cost networking.

  B. Telecommunications is transforming the traditional office.

    1. Desktop Videoconferencing consolidates your communications network into a single point of contact for all types of information—data, image, voice, and video.

    2. For less than the cost of a personal computer, GTP can create an interactive, multimedia conference room.

IV. World Tech Telecommunications offers three communication benefits.

  A. Desktop Videoconferencing enhances employees' collaboration and interaction.

    1. Communication improves when employees can see each other's facial expressions and body language.

    2. World Tech's "whiteboard" allows employees to work simultaneously on a document (they see each other's revisions while sharing ideas on the telephone). **[PowerPoint Slide 4: Scanned video of employees using the whiteboard at different sites to edit a document simultaneously.]**

  B. Desktop Videoconferencing will increase GTP's productivity.

    1. Employees transmit both audio and video information, sharing more data with more people—from 50 to 100 percent more effectively.

    2. Employees interact directly, streamlining collaborative projects by 35 to 45 percent.

    3. Employees work more efficiently in their own workspaces.

  C. Desktop Videoconferencing makes better use of time and saves money.

    1. Schedules meetings quickly and avoids conflicts.

    2. Brings the right people together, no matter where they are.

      a. Important discussions will no longer depend on one person's travel schedule.

      b. Schedule emergency meetings quickly when problems arise.

Continued

FIGURE 17.2   (Continued)

3

Conclusion

V. World Tech Telecommunications can bring the communication benefits of Desktop Videoconferencing to GTP Industries. **[PowerPoint Slide 5: Map of GTP's sites with Microlink web connecting them.]**

    A. Desktop Videoconferencing will save GTP both time and money. **[PowerPoint Slide 6: Graph of projected cost savings.]**

    B. Desktop Videoconferencing will enhance the professional development of GTP's employees.

    C. World Tech Telecommunications will tailor Desktop Videoconferencing to GTP's needs, ensuring a competitive advantage in today's complex business world.

---

your audience is probably at their most attentive during the first few minutes of your presentation, they will pay close attention to everything about you and what you say. Seize the moment and build momentum.

An effective introduction is proportional to the length of your presentation. A ten-minute speech requires no more than a sixty-second introduction; a twenty-minute speech needs no more than a two- or three-minute introduction.

How to Begin

You can begin by introducing yourself, emphasizing your professional qualifications and interests. (This self-introduction is unnecessary if someone else has introduced you or if you know everyone in the room.)

TECH NOTE

Using Effective Body Language

In business presentations, it is crucial to make a good first impression. Research shows that people decide what they think of you in the first three or four minutes of your presentation. Seventy-five percent of your audience's impressions are influenced by your body language rather than what you actually say. The nonverbal signals you send affect how your audience will regard your leadership abilities, your sales performance, even your truthfulness and sincerity. No matter how many hours you have worked to get your message across, if your nonverbal presentation is misleading or inappropriate, the impact of what you say will be lost.

Never begin by apologizing for taking up the audience's time; by pointing out your limitations as a professional speaker; by criticizing the room, the lighting, the furniture, or the time and date of your speech; or by finding fault with the audience for any past decisions or actions.

Instead, be positive and thank the audience for the opportunity to address them.

Give Listeners a Road Map

Give listeners a "road map" at the beginning of your presentation so they will know where you are, when you are there, and what they have to look forward to or to recall. Indicate what your topic is and how you have organized what you have to say about it.

> My presentation today on Digital Business software will last about 30 minutes and is divided into three parts. First, I will outline briefly recent software changes. Second, I will give a detailed review of how those changes directly affect our company. Third, I will show how our company can profitably implement those changes. At the end of my presentation there will be time for your questions and comments.

The most informative presentations are the easiest to follow. Restrict your topic to ensure that you will be able to organize it carefully and sensibly—for example, a tasty diet under 1,000 calories a day or a course in learning JAVA or another software package.

Capture the Audience's Attention

Moving from your announcement of the topic to your actual presentation requires skill at inducing an audience to listen. Use any of the following strategies to get your audience to "bite the hook."

- Ask a question. "Do you know how much actual meat there is in a hot dog?"
- Start with a quotation. Winston Churchill said, "We get things to make a living but we give things to have a life."
- Give an interesting statistic. "In 2001, 2 million heart attack victims will live to tell about it."
- Relate an anecdote. Be sure it is relevant and in good taste; make your audience feel at ease and friendly toward you by establishing a bond with them.
- Provide background information. Supply information about some local history, event, or tradition to show knowledge of your audience's past.
- Compliment the audience. Find some way to praise or recognize your audience (or someone prominent in the audience) for an accomplishment related to your talk.

The Body of Your Presentation

The body is the longest part of your presentation, just as it is in a long report. It supplies the substance of your speech by (1) explaining a process, (2) describing a condition, (3) telling a story, (4) arguing a case, or (5) doing all of the above. See how the body of Marilyn Claire Ford's speech outlined in Figure 17.2 is organized around the customer benefits of GTP's desktop videoconferencing.

To get the right perspective, recall your own experiences as a member of an audience. How often did you feel bored or angry because a speaker tried to overload you with details or could not stick to the point?

Ways to Organize the Body of Your Presentation

Here are a few helpful ways you can present and organize information in the body of your presentation. In writing a report, you assist readers by designing your document to help them visually, supplying headings, underscorings, bullets, necessary white space, and headers and footers. In a speech, switch from those purely visual devices to aural ones, such as the following.

1. Give signals (directions) to show where you are going or where you have been. These signals will convince an audience that your speech does not ramble. Enumerate your points: *first, second, third.* Emphasize cause-and-effect relationships with *subsequently, therefore, furthermore.* When you tell a story, follow a chronological sequence and fill your speech with signposts: *before, following, next, then.*

2. Comment on your own material. Tell the audience if some point is especially significant, memorable, or relevant. "This next fact is the most important thing I'll say today." "The best determiner of pressure is the volume of liquid present in the chamber."

3. Repeat key ideas. Concisely restate your main idea or topic. You can repeat a sentence or a word to emphasize its importance and to help the audience remember it. But do that sparingly; repeating the same point over and over bores an audience.

4. Provide internal summaries. Spending a few seconds to recap what you have just covered will reassure your audience and you as well.

> We have already discussed the difficulties in establishing a menu repertory, or the list of items that the food service manager wants to appear on the menu. Now we will turn to ways of determining which items should appear on a menu and why.

The Conclusion

Plan your conclusion as carefully as you do your introduction. Stopping with a screeching halt is as bad as trailing off in a fading monotone. An effective conclusion leaves the audience feeling that you have come full circle and accomplished what you promised. See how Marilyn Claire Ford ends her speech emphasizing how GTP Systems can ensure having a competitive edge, a point with which she began.

What to Put in Your Conclusion

A conclusion should contain something lively and memorable. Never introduce a new subject in your conclusion or simply repeat your introduction. A conclusion can contain the following:

- a fresh restatement of your three or four main points
- a call to action, just as in a sales letter—to buy, to note, to agree, to volunteer
- a final emphasis on a key statistic (for example, "The installation of the stainless steel heating tanks has, as we have seen, saved our firm 32 percent in utility costs, since we no longer have to run the heating system all day.")

Note how Marilyn Claire Ford ends her speech (Figure 17.2) with a concise summary of her main points and urges her listeners to invest company money in her product, World Tech Telecommunications Desktop Videoconferencing system.

Mean It When You Say, "Finally"

When you tell your audience you are concluding your talk, make sure you mean it. An audience will resent a speaker who gives them a false ending. Saying, "In conclusion," and then talking for another ten minutes only frustrates your listeners and makes them less receptive to your message.

The Outline for a Formal Presentation

Using information from the discussion of the parts of a speech, you will need to construct an outline to represent the introduction, the body, and the conclusion. In an extemporaneous presentation, remember, you do not write out what you are going to say in manuscript form. Instead you will put together an outline similar to Marilyn Claire Ford's in Figure 17.2.

Your outline has to be far more substantial than the notes shown in Figure 17.1 for an informal briefing. To construct an effective outline, you will have to do research, analyze your audience's needs, and collect suitable data (and visuals) for them. Your outline has to be detailed enough to give your readers the three Ds:

- direction you will follow
- development of your topic
- documentation of your topic

Your outline not only will assist your readers but it also will have great psychological value for you. The outline gives you enough facts to handle your speaking engagement confidently, yet it is not so detailed that it places you in a straitjacket.

The presentation outline illustrated in Figure 17.2 contains an appropriate amount of detail to represent the introduction, body, and conclusion. A roman numeral designates each major point; capital letters indicate appropriate supporting facts. Be careful about crowding too much into a speech outline. You do not need an outline as highly developed as the one below; an audience would get lost trying to follow five levels of subordination.

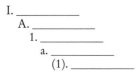

Make sure each point, whether indicated by a roman numeral or a capital letter, is written as a complete sentence. Your outline must be easy to read and follow, so leave wide margins and double-space the entire outline. Mark, perhaps with color or in capital or boldfaced letters, where visuals appear in your speech. That way you won't overlook or omit them.

Using Visuals

The more successful a presentation, the greater the chances that the speaker has effectively incorporated visuals into it. Many listeners judge a presentation by the quality of the visuals the speaker presents. Visuals have numerous benefits for speakers and their audiences. Visuals can

- arouse an audience's interest
- add variety
- explain information quickly
- summarize a great deal of information
- reinforce and enhance the main points of your talk

Keep in mind that visuals in any presentation must be constructed even more carefully than for a written report. Unlike a reading audience, a listening audience may not be able to refer to a visual again or have time to study the visual in detail. Keep your visuals clear, simple, and memorable.

Types of Presentation Visuals

You may use a variety of visuals during your presentation: photographs, maps, dry-erase boards, foamboards, diagrams, transparencies, slides, and computer displays that take advantage of text, sound, animation, and even virtual reality, especially PowerPoint (see pp. 494–496).

TECH NOTE

Creating Computer-Generated Visuals
You can create and display electronic visuals for your audience directly from your desktop software program such as PowerPoint. On your computer screen you can design an appropriate visual and then transfer it from your computer file to a specially equipped overhead projector. That way you will be spared the difficulty of having to make transparencies. Furthermore, you will not have to worry about adapting or enlarging existing graphics and photocopying them for your audience.

Guidelines for Using Visuals in Your Presentations

1. Make Sure Visuals Are Readable
Make sure your visuals are large and easy to read, even from the back row or from the far corner of a long conference table. If they cannot be seen clearly from a distance and understood at once, they are not very useful. If possible, before using any

visual, place it in the front of the room and sit in the last row of chairs to see whether your audience will be able to decipher it. You might decide to enlarge your visual or create a handout.

2. Make Your Visuals Easy to Understand

Each visual should be clear and simple, easy to understand the first time an audience sees it. If you suspect that your audience may have trouble, even momentarily, understanding what your visual is or why and how it works, redesign it or delete it. For example, using technical (or excessively complex) computer flow charts may detract from rather than add to your presentation if the audience does not recognize what the flow charts show.

3. Make Your Visuals Self-Explanatory

Don't make the mistake of taking five minutes to explain the content of one visual; the visual itself should explain the content of your talk. Use that time more profitably to deliver your presentation.

4. Make Sure Your Visuals Are Relevant

Be careful that each visual relates directly to your topic and that it does not interfere with your message. Will it lead an audience off on a tangent? Will it contradict the message you are attempting to deliver? If so, delete or revise it.

5. Determine How Many Visuals to Use

Use visuals only when your audience needs them. Even a very long presentation may need only two or three visuals. Their purpose is to clarify (or supplement)—not compete with—what you say. Nor are they a substitute for your speech. (Note Marilyn Claire Ford's effective use of visuals in the outline for her presentation in Figure 17.2.) As a general rule, too many visuals will distract your audience.

Getting the Most from Your Noncomputerized Visuals

The following practical suggestions will help you get the most from your visuals when time and space may prohibit using computer set-ups.

1. **Do not set up your visuals before you begin speaking.** The audience will be wondering how you are going to use them and so will not give you their full attention. When you are finished with a visual, put it away. Your audience will not be distracted by it or tempted to study it instead of listening to you.

2. **Firmly anchor any maps or illustrations.** Having a map roll up or a picture fall off an easel during a presentation is embarrassing.

3. **Never obstruct the audience's view by standing in front of your visuals.** Use a pointer or a laser pointer (a pen-sized tool that projects a bright red spot up to 150 feet) to direct audience attention to your visual.

4. **Avoid crowding too many images onto one visual that you transfer to a projector or onto one pasteboard.** Use different screens or pasteboards instead.

5. Do not put a lot of writing on a visual. Elaborate labels or wordy descriptions defeat your reason for using the visual. Your audience will spend more time trying to decipher the writing than attempting to understand the visual itself. If any writing must appear on one of your visuals, enlarge it so your audience can read it quickly and easily.

6. Be especially cautious with a slide projector. Check beforehand to make sure all your slides are in the order in which you are going to discuss them and that they are right side up. Most important, make sure the projector is in good working order. Practice changing from one transparency to another. And test your tape recorder if you are using one as part of your presentation.

Using Videos in Your Presentation

Many business presentations rely on video players and large-screen televisions to sell a product, service, or idea. Animation, sound, color—all can engage an audience's interest. There is no doubt that a film (or video) can show things that could never be duplicated in a conference room or described in such vivid detail. If you intend to show a film or video to your audience, follow these guidelines.

1. Prepare your audience for viewing the video. Don't just walk into the room and turn on the VCR or DVD (digital video display). Also, don't stop your presentation and say, "Now let's view this." Help your audience by telling them why you are going to show them the video, what they should look for, and how long the video will last.

2. Never substitute a video for a talk. Don't show a film or video and think it alone will sell your product or make all your points. Preview the video or film and show only those sections that are essential to your presentation. The film or video should become a selected part of your presentation, not the presentation itself.

3. Always identify the source of the video. Tell your audience where the video comes from, even if from your own company, and indicate whether your audience can obtain a copy of the edited or full video.

Rehearsing Your Presentation

Efficient writers never submit a rough draft of a paper as final copy to an instructor or employer. Rather, they revise, edit, and carefully check the draft before printing and sending a final copy. Similarly, careful speakers do not write a speech and march off to deliver it. Between the time you write your presentation and deliver it, rehearse it several times. Going over your ideas aloud may help you to spot poor organization and insufficient or inaccurate content.

Effective Rehearsal Strategies

Rehearsing will help you become more familiar with your topic and overall message, building your confidence. It will also help you to acquire more natural speech rhythms—pitch, pauses, and pacing. Here are some strategies to use as you rehearse your speech.

- Speak in front of a full-length mirror for at least one rehearsal to see how an audience might view you.
- Talk into a tape recorder to determine whether you sound friendly or frantic, poised or pressured. You can also catch and correct yourself if you are speaking too quickly or too slowly. A rate of about 120 to 140 words a minute is easy for an audience to follow.
- Time yourself so you will not exceed your allotted time or fall far short of your audience's expectations.
- Practice with the visuals or equipment you intend to use in your speech for valuable hands-on experience.
- Videotape your final rehearsal and show it to a colleague or instructor for feedback.

Delivering Your Presentation

A poor delivery can ruin a good presentation. You will be evaluated by your style of presentation just as you are in your written work. When you speak before an audience, you will be evaluated on the image you project: how you look, how you talk, and how you move (your body language). Do you mumble into your notes, never looking at the audience? Do you clutch the lectern as if to keep it in place? Do you shift nervously from one foot to the other? All those actions betray your nervousness and detract from your presentation.

The following suggestions on how to deliver a presentation will help you to be a well-prepared, poised speaker.

Before You Speak

Your name is called, and within a minute or two you will have to begin addressing the audience. You will be nervous. Accept that fact and even allow a few seconds for "panic time." Then put your nervous energy to work for you. Chances are, your audience will have no idea how anxious you are; they cannot see the butterflies in your stomach. See your audience as friends, not enemies.

Always have a wristwatch with you. Before you speak, lay it on the table or lectern so you can occasionally glance down to see how much time you have left.

During the Presentation

Begin your presentation slowly. Give listeners a chance to sit back in their chairs and establish a mental connection with your topic. Rushing into your talk may be startling, causing you to lose the audience from the start. To speak effectively, pay attention to the following points.

1. Establish eye contact with your listeners. Look at your audience to establish a relationship with them. Never bury your head in notes; you will signal your lack of interest in the audience or your fear of public speaking. Some timid speakers think that if they look only at some fixed place or object in the back of the room, the audience will regard this as eye contact. But that kind of cover-up does not work.

Another tactic poor (or frightened) speakers use is to look at only one member of the audience or to focus, with frequent sidewise glances, on the individual next to them on the stage, perhaps the person who has introduced the speakers.

Establish a pattern of glancing at your notes and then looking up at various individuals in the audience. If the group you are addressing is small (five to ten people), look at each person in the course of your talk. When you speak to a large audience (fifty or more individuals), visually divide the group into four or five sections and look at each section a number of times as you speak.

2. Adjust to audience feedback. Watch your listeners' reactions and respond appropriately—nodding to agree, pausing a moment, paraphrasing to clarify a confusing point.

3. Use a friendly, confident tone. Speak in a natural, conversational voice, but avoid verbal tics ("you know," "I mean") and fillers ("um," "ah," "er") repeated several times each minute. Such nervous habits will make your audience nervous and your speech less effective. Use pauses instead.

4. Vary the rate of your delivery. Talking in a monotone, never raising or lowering your voice, will lull your audience to sleep or at least inattention! Use your rate to help you emphasize key points and make transitions in your speech. Talk slowly enough for your audience to understand you, yet quickly enough so you don't sound as if you are belaboring or emphasizing each word.

5. Adjust your volume appropriately. Talk loudly enough for everyone to hear, but be careful if you are using a microphone. Your voice will be amplified, so if you speak loudly, you will boom rather than project. Watch out for the other extreme—speaking so softly that only the first two rows can hear you.

TECH NOTE

Using the Correct Pronunciation

As you rehearse your speech, look up in a dictionary the pronunciation of any words you are unsure about. Pay special attention to the pronunciation of individuals' names and company and city names. Consult a dictionary (*Webster's Collegiate Dictionary,* 10th Edition, or *The American Heritage Dictionary of the English Language,* 3rd Edition). Whenever you are in doubt, ask ahead of time. It's far less embarrassing than having someone in the audience stop you in the middle of your speech to correct you or tell you *after* your speech that you pronounced the CEO's name wrong ten times!

6. Watch your posture. Do not slouch or look wooden. If you stand motionless, looking as if rigor mortis has set in, your speech will be judged cold and lifeless, no matter how lively your words are. Don't stand in one spot as if your legs were set in concrete. Be natural yet dynamic; move, and let your body react to what you are saying. Smile, nod your head, move your arms, point at an object, stand back a little from the lectern. That is not to say you should be a moving target. Never sit on a desk or lean on a lectern in front of your audience. Listeners will be waiting to see if you fall off your perch.

7. Use appropriate body language. Be natural and consistent. Do not startle an audience by suddenly pounding on the lectern for emphasis. Be careful you don't distract an audience with your gesturing. Let your material suggest appropriate movements. If you are itemizing two or three points, hold up the appropriate number of fingers to indicate which point you are discussing. Use your hands and arms to indicate direction, size, or relationships.

Avoid gestures that will distract or alienate your audience. For example, don't fold your arms as you talk, a gesture that signals you are unreceptive (closed) to your audience's reactions. Also, avoid the nervous habits that can divert the audience's attention: scratching your head, rubbing your nose, twirling your hair, pushing up your glasses, fumbling with your notes, tapping your foot.

8. Dress professionally. Do not wear clothes or jewelry that call attention to themselves. Be conservative and dress formally. Wear clothes that are the business norm. Know your company's dress code. Women should wear a businesslike dress or suit. Men should wear a dark business suit, white shirt, and a tasteful tie.

When You Have Finished

Don't just sit down, walk back to your place on the platform or in the audience, or, worse yet, march out of the room. Thank your listeners for their attention and stay at the lectern for audience applause or questions. If appropriate, give the person who introduced you a chance to thank you while you are still in front of the group.

If a question-and-answer session is to follow your speech try to anticipate questions your audience is likely to ask. But give your audience a time limit for questions. For example, you might say, "I'll be happy to answer your questions now before we break for lunch in ten minutes." By setting limits, you reduce the chances of engaging in a lengthy debate with members of the audience, and you also can politely leave after your time elapses.

Evaluating Your Presentation

A large portion of Chapter 17 has given you information on how to construct and deliver a formal speech. As a way of reviewing that advice, study Figure 17.3, an evaluation form similar to those used by instructors in communication classes. Note that the form gives equal emphasis to the speaker's performance or delivery and to the organization and content of the presentation.

FIGURE 17.3   An evaluation form for a presentation.

Name of speaker_____ Date of presentation _____

Title of presentation _____ Length of presentation _____

PART I: THE SPEAKER (circle the appropriate number)

1. Appearance:	1 sloppy	2	3	4	5 well groomed
2. Eye contact:	1 poor	2	3	4	5 effective
3. Voice:	1 monotonous	2	3	4	5 varied
4. Posture:	1 poor	2	3	4	5 natural
5. Gestures:	1 disturbing	2	3	4	5 appropriate
6. Self-confidence:	1 nervous	2	3	4	5 poised

PART II: THE PRESENTATION (circle the appropriate number: 1 = poor; 5 = superior)

1. Speaker's knowledge of the subject—carefully researched; factual errors; missing details:

     1   2   3   4   5

2. Relevance of the topic for audience—suitable for this group:

     1   2   3   4   5

3. The speaker's language—too technical; filled with clichés or slang expressions; or crisp and descriptive:

     1   2   3   4   5

4. Presentation easy to follow—speaker gave signs where he/she had been and where he/she was going:

     1   2   3   4   5

5. Speaker's conclusion—clearly identified major points:

     1   2   3   4   5

✓ Revision Checklist

- ❏ Anticipated audience's background, interest, or even potential resistance to message.
- ❏ Prepared introduction to provide "road map" of presentation and to arouse audience interest.
- ❏ Started with interesting and relevant statistics, a question, an anecdote, or similar "hook" to capture audience attention.
- ❏ Limited body of presentation to main points.
- ❏ Arranged main points logically and made connections among them.
- ❏ Used supporting examples and illustrations appropriate to audience.
- ❏ Made sure conclusion contains summary of main points of my presentation and/or specific call for action.
- ❏ Prepared outline and identified and corrected any weak or redundant areas.
- ❏ Double-spaced outline with wide margins to make it easy to read.
- ❏ Designed visuals that are clear and easy to read.
- ❏ Rehearsed presentation thoroughly so I am familiar with its organization and am comfortable using visuals.
- ❏ Monitored volume, tone, and rate to vary delivery and emphasize major points.
- ❏ Double-checked gestures to make them relevant and nonintrusive.
- ❏ Timed presentation, complete with visuals, so as to run close to allotted time.

Exercises

1. Prepare a three- to five-minute presentation explaining how a piece of equipment that you use on your job works. If the equipment is small enough, bring it with you to class. If it is too large, prepare an appropriate visual or two for use in your talk.

2. Find an article on a technical subject from a professional journal in your field. Prepare a five- to seven-minute briefing on the topic of the article but adapt your remarks for a general audience of consumers.

3. You have just been asked to talk about the students at your school. Narrow the topic and submit an outline to your instructor, showing how you have limited the topic and gathered and organized evidence. Use two or three appropriate visuals (tables, photographs, charts, or even videos). Follow the format of the outline in Figure 17.2.

4. Prepare a ten-minute presentation on a controversial topic that you would present before a civic group—the PTA, the local chapter of an organization, a post of the Veterans of Foreign Wars, a synagogue or church club. Submit an outline similar to that in Figure 17.2 to your instructor, together with a one-page statement of your specific call to action and its relevance for your audience.

5. Using the information contained in the research paper on telecommuting in Chapter 9 (pp. 374–393) or the long report on multinational workers in Chapter 16 (pp. 628–644), prepare a short presentation (five to seven minutes) for your class.

6. Using the evaluation form in Figure 17.3, evaluate a speaker—a speech class student, a local politician, or a co-worker delivering a report at work. Specify the time, place, and occasion of the speech.

7. Deliver a formal presentation (fifteen to twenty minutes) on the various uses and advantages of the Internet for individuals in your chosen career field. Use at least three visuals with your talk. Submit an outline to your instructor.

A Writer's Brief Guide to Paragraphs, Sentences, and Words

To write successfully, you must know how to create effective paragraphs, write and punctuate clear sentences, and use words correctly. This guide succinctly explains some of the basic elements of clear and accurate writing.

Paragraphs

Writing a Well-Developed Paragraph

A paragraph is the basic building block for any piece of writing. It is (1) a group of related sentences (2) arranged in a logical order (3) supplying readers with detailed, appropriate information (4) on a single important topic.

A paragraph expresses one central idea, with each sentence contributing to the overall meaning of that idea. The paragraph does that by means of a *topic sentence,* which states the central idea, and *supporting information,* which explains the topic sentence.

Supply a Topic Sentence

The topic sentence is the most important sentence in your paragraph. Carefully worded and restricted, it helps you to generate and control your information. An effective topic sentence also helps readers grasp your main idea quickly. As you draft your paragraphs, pay close attention to the following three guidelines.

1. Make sure you provide a topic sentence. In their rush to supply readers with facts, some writers forget or neglect to include a topic sentence. The following paragraph, with no topic sentences, shows how fragmented such writing can be.

No topic sentence Sensors found on each machine detect wind speed and direction and other important details such as ice loading and potential metal fatigue. The information is fed into a small computer (microprocessor) in the nacelle (or engine housing). The microprocessor automatically keeps the blades turned into the wind, starts and stops the machine, and changes the pitch of the tips of the blades to increase power under varying wind conditions. Should any part of the wind turbine suffer damage or malfunction, the microprocessor will immediately shut the machine down.

Only when a suitable topic sentence is added—"The MOD-2 wind turbine is designed to be operated completely by computer"—can readers understand what the technical details have in common.

2. Put your topic sentence first. Place your topic sentence at the beginning—not the middle or end—of your paragraph because the first sentence occupies an emphatic position. Burying the key idea in the middle or near the end of the paragraph makes it harder for readers to comprehend your purpose or act on your information.

3. Be sure your topic sentence is focused. If restricted, a topic sentence discusses only one central idea. A broad or unrestricted topic sentence leads to a shaky, incomplete paragraph for two reasons.

- The paragraph will not contain enough information to support the topic sentence.
- A broad topic sentence will not summarize or forecast specific information in the paragraph.

The following example of a carefully constructed paragraph, contains a clear topic sentence in an appropriate position (highlighted in color) and adequate supporting details.

> Fat is an important part of everyone's diet. It is nutritionally present in the basic food groups we eat—meat and poultry, dairy products, and oils—to aid growth or development. The fats and fatty acids present in those foods ensure proper metabolism, thus helping to turn what we eat into the energy we need. Those same fats and fatty acids also act as carriers for important vitamins like A, D, E, and K. Another important role of fat is that it keeps us from feeling hungry by delaying digestion. Fat also enhances the flavor of the food we eat, making it more enjoyable.

Three Characteristics of an Effective Paragraph

Effective paragraphs have **unity, coherence,** and **completeness.**

Unity
A unified paragraph sticks to one topic without wandering. Every sentence, every detail, **supports, explains,** or **proves** the central idea. A unified paragraph includes only relevant information and excludes unnecessary or irrelevant comments.

Coherence
In a coherent paragraph all sentences flow smoothly and logically to and from each other like the links of a chain. Use the following three techniques to achieve coherence.

1. Use transitional words and phrases. Some useful connective words, along with the relationships they express, are listed in Table A.1.

> *Paragraph with connective words* — Advertising a product on the radio has many advantages over using television. *For one thing,* radio rates are much cheaper. *For example,* a one-time 60-second spot on television can cost $750. *For that money,* advertisers can purchase nine 30-second spots on the radio. *Equally attractive* are the low production costs for radio advertising. *In contrast,* television advertising often includes extra costs for models and voice-overs. *Another* advantage radio offers advertisers is immediate scheduling. *Often* the ad appears during the same week a contract is signed. *On the other hand,* television stations are *frequently* booked up months in advance, so it may be a long time

TABLE A.1 Transitional, or Connective, Words and Phrases

Addition	again also and as well as besides	first, second, third furthermore in addtion many moreover	next too what's more
Cause/effect	accordingly and so as a result because of	consequently due to hence if	on account of since therefore thus
Comparison/ contrast	but conversely equally however	in contrast in the same way likewise on the contrary	on the other hand similarly still yet
Conclusion	all in all at last finally in brief	in conclusion in short in summary on the whole	to conclude to put into perspective to summarize
Condition	although even though granted that	if of course provided that	to be sure unless
Emphasis	above all after all again as a matter of fact as I said	for emphasis indeed in fact in other words of course	obviously surely to repeat unquestionably
Illustration	for example for instance in effect	in other words in particular specifically	that is to illustrate
Place	across from adjacent to alongside of at this point behind	below beyond here in front of next to	over there under where wherever
Time	afterward at length at the same time at times beforehand currently during	earlier later meanwhile next now once	presently soon then until when while

before an ad appears. *Furthermore,* radio gives advertisers a greater opportunity to reach potential buyers. *After all,* radio follows listeners everywhere—in their homes, at work, and in their cars. *Although* television is very popular, it cannot do that.

2. Use pronouns and demonstrative adjectives. Words like *he, she, him, her, they,* and so on, contribute to paragraph coherence and increase the flow of sentences.

Paragraph with pronouns   Traffic studies are an important tool for store owners looking for a new location. These studies are relatively inexpensive and highly accurate. They can tell owners how much traffic passes by a particular location at a particular time and why. Moreover, they can help owners to determine what particular characteristics the individuals have in common. Because of their helpfulness, these studies can save owners time and money and possibly prevent financial ruin.

3. Use parallel (coordinated) grammatical structures. Parallelism means using the same *kind of* word, phrase, clause, or sentence to express related concepts.

Orientation sessions accomplish four useful goals for trainees. First, they introduce trainees to key personnel in accounting, data processing, maintenance, and security. Second, they give trainees experience logging into the database system, selecting appropriate menus, editing core documents, and getting off the system. Third, they explain to trainees the company policies affecting the way supplies are ordered, used, and stored. Fourth, they help trainees understand their responsibilities in such sensitive areas as computer security and use.

Parallelism is at work on a number of levels in that paragraph, among them,

- the four sentences about the four goals start in the same way grammatically ("... they introduce/give/explain/help ...") to help readers categorize the information.
- Within individual sentences, the repetition of *present participles* (logg*ing*, select*ing*, edit*ing*, gett*ing*) and of *past participles* (order*ed*, us*ed*, stor*ed*) helps the writer to coordinate information.
- Transitional words—*first, second, third, fourth*—provide a clear-cut sequence.

Completeness

A complete paragraph provides readers with sufficient information to **clarify, analyze, support, defend,** or **prove** the central idea expressed in the topic sentence. The reader feels satisfied that the writer has given necessary details.

Skimpy paragraph   Farmers can turn their crops and farm wastes into useful, cost-effective fuels. Much grown on the farm can be converted to energy. This energy can have many uses and save farmers a lot of money in operating expenses.

Fully developed paragraph   Farm crops and wastes can be turned into fuels to save farmers on their operating costs. Alcohol can be distilled from grain, sugar beets, potatoes, even blighted crops. Converted to gasohol (90 percent gasoline, 10 percent alcohol), this fuel can run such farm equipment as irrigation pumps, feed grinders, and tractors. Similarly, through a biomass digestion system, farmers can produce methane from animal or crop wastes as a natural gas for heating and cooking. Finally, cellulose pellets, derived from plant materials, become solid fuel that can save farmers money in heating barns.

Sentences

Constructing and Punctuating Sentences

The way you construct and punctuate your sentences can determine whether you succeed or fail in the world of work. Your sentences reveal a lot about you. They tell readers how clearly or how poorly you can convey a message. And any message is only as effective and as thoughtful as the sentences of which it is made.

What Makes a Sentence

A sentence is a complete thought, expressed by a subject and a verb that can make sense standing alone.

> *subject*   *verb*
>
> Web sites   sell   products.

The Difference Between Phrases and Clauses

The first step toward success in writing sentences is learning to recognize the difference between phrases and clauses. A **phrase** is a group of words that does not contain a subject and a verb; phrases cannot make sense standing alone. Phrases cannot be sentences.

in the park	No subject: Who is in the park?
	No verb: What was done in the park?
for every patient in intensive care	No subject: Who did something for every patient?
	No verb: What was done for the patients?

A **clause** does contain a subject and a verb, but *not every clause is a sentence.* Only **independent** (or **main**) **clauses** can stand alone as sentences. Here is an example of an independent clause that is a complete sentence.

> subject   verb   object
>
> The president closed the college.

A **dependent** (or **subordinate**) **clause** also contains a subject and a verb, but it does not make complete sense and cannot stand alone. Why? A dependent clause contains a subordinating conjunction—*after, although, as, because, before, even though, if, since, unless, when, where, whereas, while*—at the beginning of the clause. Such conjunctions subordinate the clause in which they appear and make the clause dependent for meaning and completion on an independent clause.

After
Before
Because   }   the president closed the college
Even though
Unless

"After the president closed the college" is not a complete thought but a dependent clause that leaves us in suspense. It needs to be completed with an independent clause telling us what happened "after."

dependent clause	*independent clause*		
	subject	*verb*	*phrase*
After the president closed the college,	we	played	in the snow.

Avoiding Sentence Fragments

An incomplete sentence is called a **fragment.** Fragments can be phrases or dependent clauses. They either lack a verb or a subject or have broken away from an independent clause. A fragment is isolated: it needs an overhaul to supply missing parts to turn it into an independent clause or to glue it back to an independent clause to have it make sense.

To avoid writing fragments, follow these rules. *Note that incorrect examples are preceded by a minus sign, corrected revisions by a plus sign.*

1. Do not use a subordinate clause as a sentence. Even though it contains a subject and a verb, a subordinate clause standing alone is still a fragment. To avoid this kind of sentence fragment, simply join the two clauses (the independent clause and the dependent clause containing a subordinating conjunction) with a comma—*not* a period or semicolon.

- Unless we agreed to the plan. (What would happen?)
- Unless we agreed to the plan; the project manager would discontinue the operation. (A semicolon cannot set off the subordinate clause.)
+ Unless we agreed to the plan, the project manager would discontinue the operation.
- Because safety precautions were taken. (What happened?)
+ Because safety precautions were taken, ten construction workers escaped injury.

Sometimes subordinate clauses appear at the end of a sentence. They may be introduced by a subordinate conjunction, an adverb, or a relative pronoun (*that, which, who*). Do not separate these clauses from the preceding independent clause with a period, thus turning them into fragments.

- An all-volunteer fire department posed some problem<u>s. E</u>specially for residents in the western part of town.
+ An all-volunteer fire department posed some problem<u>s, e</u>specially for residents in the western part of town. (The word *especially* qualifies <u>posed,</u> referred to in the independent clause.)

2. Every sentence must have a subject telling the reader who does the action.

- Being extra careful not to spill the water. (Who?)
+ The technician was being extra careful not to spill the water.

3. Every sentence must have a complete verb. Watch especially for verbs ending in *-ing*. They need another verb (some form of *to be*) to make them complete.

- The machine running in the computer department. (Did what?)

You can change that fragment into a sentence by supplying the correct form of the verb.

+ The machine *is running* in the computer department.
+ The machine *runs* in the computer department.

Or you can revise the entire sentence, adding a new thought.

+ The machine running in the computer department processes all new accounts.

4. Do not detach prepositional phrases (beginning with *at, by, for, from, in, to, with,* and so forth) **from independent clauses.** Such phrases are not complete thoughts and cannot stand alone. Correct the error by leaving the phrases attached to the sentence to which they belong.

- By three o'clock the next day. (What was to happen?)
+ The supervisor wanted our reports by three o'clock the next day.

Avoiding Comma Splices

Fragments occur when you use only bits and pieces of complete sentences. Another common error that some writers commit involves just the reverse kind of action. They weakly and wrongly join two complete sentences (independent clauses) with a comma as if those two sentences were really only one sentence. Such an error is called a **comma splice.** Here is an example.

- Gasoline prices have risen by 10 percent in the last month, we will drive the car less often.

Two independent clauses (complete sentences) exist:

+ Gasoline prices have risen by 10 percent in the last month.
+ We will drive the car less often.

A comma alone lacks the power to separate independent clauses.

As the preceding example shows, many pronouns—*I, he, she, it, we, they*—are used as the subjects of independent clauses. A comma splice will result if you place a comma instead of a semicolon between two independent clauses where the second clause opens with a pronoun.

- Rosa approved the plan, she liked its cost-effective approach.
+ Rosa approved the plan; she liked its cost-effective approach.

However, relative pronouns (*who, whom, which, that*) are preceded by a comma, not a period or a semicolon, when they introduce subordinate clauses.

- She approved the plan. Which had the cost-effective approach.
+ She approved the plan, which had the cost-effective approach.

Ways to Correct Comma Splices

1. Remove the comma separating two independent clauses and replace it with a period. Then capitalize the first letter of the first word of the new sentence.

+ Gasoline prices have risen by 10 percent in the last month. We will drive the car less often.

2. Insert a coordinating conjunction (*and, but, or, nor, for, yet*) **after the comma.** Together, the conjunction and the comma properly separate the two independent clauses.

+ Gasoline prices have risen by 10 percent in the last month, and we will drive the car less often.

3. Rewrite the sentence (if it makes sense to do so). Turn the first independent clause into a dependent clause by adding a subordinate conjunction; then insert a comma and add the second independent clause.

+ Because gasoline prices have risen by 10 percent in the last month, we will drive the car less often.

4. Delete the comma and insert a semicolon.

+ Gasoline prices have risen by 10 percent in the last month; we will drive the car less often.

Of the four ways to correct the comma splice, sentences 3 and 4 are equally suitable, but sentence 3 reads more smoothly and so is the better choice.

The semicolon is an effective and forceful punctuation mark when two independent clauses are closely related, that is, when they announce contrasting or parallel views, as the two following examples reveal.

+ The union favored the new legislation; the company opposed it. (contrasting views)
+ Night classes help the college and the community; students can take more credit hours to advance their careers. (parallel views)

How Not to Correct Comma Splices
Some writers mistakenly try to correct comma splices by inserting a conjunctive adverb (*also, consequently, furthermore, however, moreover, nevertheless, then, therefore*) after the comma.

– Gasoline prices have risen by 10 percent in the last month, consequently we will drive the car less often.

Because the conjunctive adverb (*consequently*) is not as powerful as the coordinating conjunction (*and, but, for*), the error is not eliminated. If you use a conjunctive adverb—*consequently, however, nevertheless*—you still must insert a semicolon or a period before it, as the following examples show.

+ Gasoline prices have risen by 10 percent in the last month; consequently, we will drive the car less often.
+ Gasoline prices have risen by 10 percent in the last month. Consequently, we will drive the car less often.

Avoiding Run-on Sentences

A **run-on sentence** is the opposite of a sentence fragment. The fragment gives the reader too little information, the run-on too much. A run-on sentence forces readers to digest two or more grammatically complete sentences without the proper punctuation to separate them.

Run-on   The Internet is unquestionably a major source of information and students and other researchers are right to call it a virtual library this library is not like the collections of books and magazines that are carefully shelved always waiting for students to check and recheck them too often a Web site disappears or changes considerably and without a back-up file or a hard copy the researcher has no document to quote from and no exact citation to prove that he or she consulted an authentic source.

Revised   The Internet is unquestionably a major source of information. Students and other researchers are right to call it a virtual library, although this library is not like the collections of books and magazines that are carefully shelved, always waiting for students to check and recheck them out. But too often a Web site disappears or changes considerably. Without a back-up file or a hard copy the researcher has no document to quote from and no exact citation to prove that he or she consulted an authentic source.

As the revision above shows, you can repair a run-on by (1) dividing it into separate, correctly punctuated sentences and (2) by adding coordinating conjunctions (*and, but, yet, so, or, nor*) between clauses.

Making Subjects and Verbs Agree in Your Sentences

A subject and a verb must agree in number. A singular subject takes a singular verb, whereas a plural subject requires a plural verb.

Singular Subject	Plural Subjects
the engineer calculates	engineers calculate
a report analyzes	reports analyze
a policy changes	policies change

You can avoid subject-verb agreement errors by following several simple rules.

1. Disregard any words that come between the subject and its verb.

Faulty: The customer who ordered three parts want them shipped this afternoon.
Correct: The customer who ordered three parts wants them shipped this afternoon.

2. A compound subject (two parts connected by *and*) **takes a plural verb.**

Faulty: The engineering department and the safety committee prefers to develop new guidelines.
Correct: The engineering department and the safety committee prefer to develop new guidelines.

3. When a compound subject contains *neither . . . nor* or *either . . . or*, the verb agrees with the subject closest to it.

Faulty: Either the residents or the manager are going to file the complaint.
Correct: Either the residents or the manager is going to file the complaint.
Correct: Either the manager or the residents are going to file the complaint.

4. Use a singular verb after collective nouns (like *committee, crew, department, group, organization, staff, team*) **when the group functions as a single unit.**

> Correct: The crew was available to repair the machine.
> Correct: The committee asks that all recommendations be submitted by Friday.

BUT

> Correct: The staff were unable to agree on the best model.
>   (The staff acted as individuals, not a unit, so a plural verb is required.)

5. Use a singular verb with indefinite pronouns (such as *anyone, anybody, each, everyone, everything, no one, somebody, something*).

> Each of the programmers has completed the seminar.
> Somebody usually volunteers for that duty.

Similarly, when *all, most, more,* or *part* is the subject, it requires a singular verb.

> Most of the money is allocated.
> Part of the equipment was salvageable.

6. Words like *scissors* and *pants* are plural when they are the true subject.

> Correct: The trousers were on sale.
> Faulty: A pair of trousers was available in his size. (*Pair* is the subject.)

7. Some foreign plurals (*curricula, data, media, phenomena, strata, syllabi*) **always take a plural verb.**

> The data conclusively prove my point.
> The media are usually the first to point out a politician's weak points.

8. Use a singular verb with fractions.

> Three-fourths of her research proposal was finished.

Writing Sentences That Say What You Mean

Your sentences should say exactly what you mean, without doubletalk, misplaced humor, or nonsense. Sentences are composed of words and word groups that influence each other.

Writing Logical Sentences

Sentences should not contradict themselves or make outlandish claims. The following examples contain errors in logic; note how easily the suggested revision handles the problem.

> Illogical: Steel roll-away shutters make it possible for the sun to be shaded in the summer and to have it shine in the winter. (The sun is far too large to shade; the writer meant that a room or a house, much smaller than the sun, could be shaded with the shutters.)
> Revision: Steel roll-away shutters make it possible for owners to shade their living rooms in the summer and to admit sunshine during the winter.

Using Contextually Appropriate Words

Sentences should use the combination of words most appropriate for the subject.

> Inappropriate: The members of the Nuclear Regulatory Commission saw fear radiated on the faces of the residents. (The word *radiated* is obviously ill advised in this context; use a neutral term.)
>
> Revision: The members of the Nuclear Regulatory Commission saw fear reflected on the faces of the residents.

Writing Sentences with Well-Placed Modifiers

A **modifier** is a word, phrase, or clause that describes, limits, or qualifies the meaning of another word or word group. A modifier can consist of one word (a *green* car), a prepositional phrase (the man *in the telephone booth*), a relative clause (the woman *who won the marathon*), or an *-ing* or *-ed* phrase (*walking three miles a day*, the student was in good shape; *seated in the first row*, we saw everything on stage).

A **dangling modifier** is one that cannot logically modify any word in the sentence.

– When answering the question, his calculator fell off the table.

One way to correct the error is to insert the right subject after the *-ing* phrase.

+ When answering the question, he knocked his calculator off the table.

You can also turn the phrase into a subordinate clause.

+ When he answered the question, his calculator fell off the table.
+ His calculator fell off the table as he answered the question.

A **misplaced modifier** illogically modifies the wrong word or words in the sentence. The result is often comical.

– Hiding in the corner, growling and snarling, our guide spotted the frightened cub. (Is our guide growling and snarling in the corner?)

– All travel requests must be submitted by employees in green ink. (Are the employees covered in green ink?)

The problem with both of those examples is word order. The modifiers are misplaced because they are attached to the wrong words in the sentence. Correct the error by moving the modifier to where it belongs.

+ Hiding in the corner, growling and snarling, the frightened cub was spotted by our guide.
+ All travel requests by employees must be submitted in green ink.

Misplacing a relative clause (introduced by relative pronouns like *who, whom, that, which*) can also lead to problems with modification.

– The salesperson recorded the merchandise for the customer that the store had discounted. (The merchandise was discounted, not the customer.)
– The salesperson recorded the merchandise that the store had discounted for the customer. (The salesperson recorded for the customer; the store did not discount for the customer.)
+ The salesperson recorded for the customer the merchandise that the store had discounted.

Always place the relative clause immediately after the word it modifies.

Correct Use of Pronoun References in Sentences

Sentences will be vague if they contain a faulty use of pronouns. When you use a pronoun whose **antecedent** (the person, place, or object the pronoun refers to) is unclear, you risk confusing your reader.

Unclear: After the plants are clean, we separate the stems from the roots and place them in the sun to dry. (Is it the stems or the roots that lie in the sun?)

Revision: After the plants are clean, we separate the stems from the roots and place the stems in the sun to dry.

Unclear: The park ranger was pleased to see the workers planting new trees and installing new benches. This will attract more tourists. (The trees or the benches or both?)

Revision: The park ranger was pleased to see the workers planting new trees and installing new benches, because the new trees and benches will attract more tourists.

Words

Spelling Words Correctly

Your written work will be judged in part on how well you spell. A misspelled word may seem like a small matter, but on an employment application, e-mail, incident report, or letter it stands out to your discredit. You will look careless or, even worse, uneducated to a client or a supervisor. Readers will inevitably question your other skills if your spelling is incorrect.

The Benefits and Pitfalls of Spell-checkers

Computer **spell-checkers** can be handy for flagging potential problem words. But beware! Spell-checkers recognize only those words that have been listed in them. A proper name or infrequently used word may be flagged as an error even though the word is spelled correctly. Moreover, it will not differentiate between such homonyms as *too* and *two* or *there* and *their*. A spell-checker identifies only misspelled words, not misused words. In short, do not rely exclusively on spell-checkers to solve all your spelling and word-choice problems.

Using Apostrophes Correctly

Apostrophes cause some writers special problems. Basically, apostrophes are used for four reasons: (1) contractions, (2) possessives, (3) plurals, and (4) abbreviations. The guidelines below will help you to sort out those uses.

1. In a **contraction,** the apostrophe takes the place of the missing letter or letters: *I've = I have; doesn't = does not; he's = he is; it's = it is.* (*Its* is a possessive pronoun (the dog and its bone), not a contraction. There is no such form as *its'.*)

2. To form a **possessive,** follow these rules.

a. If a singular or plural noun does not end in an -*s,* add *'s* to show possession.

Mary's locker   the woman's jacket
children's books   the women's jackets
the staff's dedication   the company's policy

b. If a singular noun ends in -s, add 's to show possession.

The class's project   the boss's schedule

c. If a plural noun ends in -s, add just the ' to indicate possession.

employees' benefits   computers' speed
lawyers' fees

d. If a proper name ends in -s, add 's to form the possessive.

Jones's account   Keats's poetry
the Williams's house   James's contract

e. If it is a compound noun, add an ' or 's to the end of the word.

brother-in-law's business   Ms. Allison Jones-Wyatt's order

f. To indicate shared possession, add just 's to the last name.

Warner and Kline's Computer Shop   Sue and Anne's major

g. To indicate separate possession, add 's to each name.

John's and Mary's transcripts   Shakespeare's and Byron's poetry

3. To form the plural of numbers and capital letters used as nouns, including abbreviations without periods, just add s. To avoid misreading some capital letters, however, you may need to add the apostrophe.

during the 1980s   all perfect 10s
his SATs   several local YMCAs
the 3 Rs   straight A's

4. For abbreviations with periods and for lowercase letters used as nouns, form the plural by adding 's.

his *p*'s and *q*'s   Ph.D.'s

Using Hyphens Properly

Use a hyphen (- as opposed to a dash —) for

- **compound words**
  four-part lecture   heavy-duty machine   hand-held PC

- **most words beginning with self**
  self-starting   self-defense   self-regulating   self-governing

- **fractions used as adjectives**
  at the three-quarter level   two-thirds majority   three-dimensional drawing

Using Ellipsis

See pages 341–342.

Using Numerals versus Words

Write out numbers as words rather than numerals

- **to begin a sentence**

Nineteen ninety-nine was the first year of our recruitment drive.

- **to list the first number when two numbers are used together**

The company needed eleven 9-foot slabs.

Use numerals, not words,

- **with abbreviations, percentages, symbols, units of measurement, dates**

17%	11:30 A.M.	70 ml
Dec. 3, 1997	$250.00	50K

- **for page references**

pp. 56–59

- **for large numbers**

3,000,000

Use both numerals and words when you want to be as precise as possible in a contract or a proposal.

> We agreed to pay the vendor an extra twenty-five dollars ($25.00) per hour to finish the job by the 18th of May.

Matching the Right Word with the Right Meaning

The words in the following list frequently are mistaken for one another. Some are true homonyms; others are just similar in spelling, pronunciation, or usage.

accept (v) to receive, to acknowledge: *We accept your proposal.*
except (prep) excluding, but: *Everyone attended the meeting except Neelou.*

advice (n) a recommendation: *I should have taken Leroy's advice.*
advise (v) to counsel: *Our lawyers advised us not to sign the contract.*

affect (v) to change, to influence: *Does the detour on Route 22 affect your travel plans?*
effect (n) a result: *What was the effect of the new procedure?*
effect (v) to bring about: *We will try to effect a change in company policy.*

all ready (adj) two-word phrase *all + ready;* to be finished; to be prepared: *We are all ready for the inspector's visit.*
already (adv) previously, before a given time: *Our Webmaster had already constructed the sites.*

attain (v) to achieve, to reach: *We attained our sales goal this month.*
obtain (v) to get, to receive: *You can obtain a job application via their Web site.*

cite (v) to document: *Please cite several examples to support your claim.*
site (n) place, location: *They want to build a parking lot on the site of the old theater.*
sight (n) vision: *His sight improved with bifocals.*

complement (v) to add to, enhance: *Her graphs and charts complemented my proposal.*
compliment (v) to praise: *The customer complimented us on our courteous staff.*

continually (adv) frequently and regularly: *This answering machine continually disconnects the caller in the middle of the message.*
continuously (adv) constantly: *The air conditioning is on continuously during the summer.*

council (n) government body: *The council voted to increase salaries for all city employees.*
counsel (n) advice: *She gave the trainee pertinent counsel.*

discreet (adj) showing respect, being tactful: *The manager was discreet in answering the complaint letter.*
discrete (adj) separate, distinct: *Put those figures into discrete categories for processing.*

dual (adj) double: *A clock-radio serves a dual purpose.*
duel (n) a fight, a battle: *The argument almost turned into a real duel.*

eminent (adj) prominent, highly esteemed: *Dr. Felicia Rollins is the most eminent neurologist in our community.*
imminent (adj) about to happen: *A hostile takeover of that company is imminent.*

foreword (n) preface, introduction to a book: *The foreword outlined the author's goals and objectives in her research study.*
forward (adv) toward a time or place; in advance: *We moved the time of the visit forward on the calendar so we could meet the overseas manager.*
forward (v) to send ahead: *We forwarded her e-mail to her new server.*

imply (v) to suggest: *Mr. Chin implied that the mechanics had taken too long for their lunch break.*
infer (v) to draw a conclusion: *We can infer from these sales figures that the new advertising campaign is working.*

it's (noun + verb) contraction of *it* and *is*: *Do you think it's too early to tell?*
its (adj) possessive form of *it*: *That old printer is on its last legs.*

lay/laid/laid (v) to put down: *Lay aside that project for now. He laid aside the project. He had already laid aside the project twice before.*
lie/lay/lain (v) to recline: *I think I'll lie down for a while. He lay there for only two minutes before the firefighter rescued him. She has lain out in the sun too often.*

lose (v) to misplace, to fail to win: *Be careful not to lose my calculator. I hope I don't lose my seat on the planning board.*
loose (adj) not tight: *The printer ribbon was too loose.*

passed (v) went by (past tense of *pass*): *He passed me in the hall without recognizing me.*

past (n) time gone by: *We've never used their services in the past.*

personal (adj) private: *The manager closes the door when she discusses personal matters with one of her staff.*

personnel (n) staff of employees: *All personnel must participate in the 401(k) retirement program.*

perspective (n) view: *From the customer's perspective, we are an honest and courteous company.*

prospective (adj) expected, likely to happen or become: *E-mail the prospective budget to district managers.*

precede (v) to go before: *A slide show will precede the open discussion.*

proceed (v) to carry on, to go ahead: *Proceed as if we had never received that letter.*

principal (adj) main, chief: *Sales of new software constitute their principal source of revenue.*

principal (n) the head of a school: *She was a high school principal before she entered the business world.*

principal (n) money owed: *The principal on that loan totaled $32,800.*

principle (n) a policy, a belief: *Sales reps should operate on the principle that the customer is always right.*

quiet (adj) silent, not loud: *He liked to spend a quiet afternoon surfing the Net.*

quite (adv) to a degree: *The officer was quite encouraged by the recruit's performance.*

stationary (adj) not moving: *Miguel rides a stationary bicycle for an hour every morning.*

stationery (n) writing supplies, such as paper and envelopes: *Please stop off at the stationery store and buy some more address labels.*

than (conj) as opposed to (used in comparisons): *He is a faster keyboarder than his predecessor.*

then (adv) at that time: *First she called the vendor; then she summarized their conversation in an e-mail to her boss.*

their (adj) possessive form of *they*: *All the lab technicians took their vacations during June and July.*

there (adv) in that place: *Please put the printer in there.*

they're (noun + verb) contraction of *they* and *are*: *They're our two best customer service representatives.*

who's (noun + verb) contraction of *who* and *is*: *Who's up next for a promotion?*

whose (adj) possessive form of *who*: *Whose idea was that in the first place?*

you're (noun + verb) contraction of *you* and *are*: *You're going to like their decision.*

your (adj) possessive form of *you*: *They agree with your ideas.*

Proofreading Marks

Mark	Example	Result
⌢o	Correct a typo.	Correct a typo.
r⌢/m⌢/⌢o	Correct more than one typo.	Correct more than one typo.
t	Insert a letter.	Insert a letter.
or words	Insert a word.	Insert a word or words.
ℒ	Make a deletion.	Make a deletion.
ℒ	Delete and close up space.	Delete and close up space.
⌒	Close up extra space.	Close up extra space.
#	Insert proper spacing.	Insert proper spacing.
#/⌒	Close up and insert space.	Close up and insert space.
eq #	Regularize proper ⌄ spacing.	Regularize proper spacing.
tr	Transpose letters indicated.	Transpose letters indicated.
tr	Transpose as words indicated.	Transpose words as indicated.
tr	Reorder shown as words several.	Reorder several words as shown.
[	[Move text to left.	Move text to left.
]	] Move text to right.	Move text to right.
¶	Indent for paragraph.	Indent for paragraph.
no ¶	[No paragraph indent.	No paragraph indent.
//	// Align type vertically.	Align type vertically.
run in	Run back turnover lines.	Run back turnover lines.
	Break line when it runs far too long.	Break line when it runs far too long.
⊙	Insert period here.	Insert period here.
⋀	Commas commas everywhere.	Commas, commas everywhere.
⋁	Its in need of an apostrophe.	It's in need of an apostrophe.
⋁/⋁	Add quotation marks, he begged.	"Add quotation marks," he begged.
;	Add a semicolon don't hesitate.	Add a semicolon; don't hesitate.
:	She advised "You need a colon."	She advised: "You need a colon."
?	How about a question mark.	How about a question mark?
(/)	Add parentheses as they say.	Add parentheses (as they say).
lc	Sometimes you want Lower case.	Sometimes you want lower case.
caps	Sometimes you want upper CASE.	Sometimes you want UPPER CASE.
ital	Add italics instantly.	Add italics *instantly.*
bf	Add boldface if necessary.	Add **boldface** if necessary.
wf	Fix a wrong font letter.	Fix a wrong font letter.
sp	Spell out all 3 terms.	Spell out all three terms.
⌄	Change y to a subscript.	Change $_x$ to a subscript.
⌄	Change y to a superscript.	Change ^{y} to a superscript.
stet	Let stand as is.	Let stand as is. (To retract a change already marked.)

Index